WHY RELIGION?

About one of the strongest and
most productive motifs in human life

BY

Yehuda Cohen

PRIESTS PUBLISHING

JERUSALEM

2003

Graphics: Ayelet Segal

ISBN 965-90615-0-1

Printed in Israel
Flower Press, Mishor Adumim

PRIESTS PUBLISHING
Jerusalem Israel

Distribution: WWW.Whyreligion.com
Email: relig@whyreligion.com
or
Yehuda Cohen, Advocate, 3 Ben-Yehuda St. Jerusalem, Israel

To my wife and closest friend Esthi
To my daughter Orit, her husband Avraham and their children
Zvi, Aharon, Mordehai, Shoshanah, Rahel, Emunah, David,
Izhaak, Yedidia, Sarah, Hadasah
To my son Gideon, his wife Orit, and their children
Morya, Neriya, Shir
To my daughter Hagit, her husband Reuven, and their children
Ben, Or, Zuf

To all children of God
With unlimited belief and love

Why Religion?

About one of the strongest and most productive motifs in human life

Introduction

This book speaks about a most powerful phenomenon in social life, religion, regarding it as one of the strongest and most productive motifs in human life. This book deals with religion from its sociological point of view. It shows in part 1 that myth and rituals are tools that assist in the reception, and strengthening of religion, which together create a morality that enables people to live in society. They, together, form the wellspring of society. Since society, as will be elucidated later, has existed from the beginning of human life; religion, myth and ritual - together with speech – have also existed, as will be seen in parts 1 and 9, since the beginning of mankind. It will be concluded that all these exist today and willcontinue to exist till the end of humanity. Ethnic groups may be crystallized, within the context of certain religions, myths, rituals, language, arts, and sentiments- into a religion and its byproducts - and nations follow the same course, with the additional help of ethnicity, and lately, with the help of the state. Modern states are involved in creating new nations in order to survive. It will be shown how the endeavors of modern states are problematic, aswill be described in parts 3,4,6,8 of the book. There is a difference in strength between civil religions, ideological religions, and theistic religions; and concerning the last-mentioned, differences in strength between polytheistic religions and monotheism. No discussion of ethics, which is described in part 5 of the book, and nationalism, can take place without relating to religion.

A person reading this book may well imagine that it was written in the aftermath of the September 11, 2001 World Trade Center explosion in New York. The fact is that though this book opens a window into answers not yet proposed to many of the questions that that tragedy has raised; it was mostly written before that.

This book deals with the main anthropological and religious researchers (I'm not sure if you are referring to the studies or the people researching, if to the studies replace "researches" with studies- D. F) in the West who investigate the source of religions as well asthe social and individual phenomena of the religious creed, its outgrowths, especially in the fields of morality and nationality, as well as the variant and particular characteristics of different religions. Comparing the different routes of several religions, it appears that nobody in the West has put enough emphasis on the huge power and the complete spectrum of social byproducts hidden within the phenomenon of religion. It appears also that nobody in the West has understood, until now, that without religion there is no humanity. Only few imagined how that phenomenon became part of human life; not one of them has understood the basic truth, viz. that that phenomenon was a "must" for humanity andit is going to last for as long as humanity lasts.

Not many have understood that it is difficult to form a nation with no common religion (in the broadest meaning of that word, including religions with no God, like civil religion) as its basis. It appears, too, that what many imagine is a nation, is in fact a group at the beginning stages of its nationhood that is trying to create a nation out of its state's civil society.

It appears that no single thinker in the west has understood the common ground of all secular moral thinkers of the West and the common ground of all monotheistic religious (of Israelite origin) morals. Within that discussion this book reveals some special measure of morality that is unique to Jewish morality.

This book is made up of 9 parts, 4 volumes. The central message is that religion is a force that is indispensable to the formation, existence, and true source of any human group. The 4 volumes and 9 parts are as follows:

Volume I: The origins of Society - Religion and Myth
- Part 1: Religion and Society
- Part 2: Myth and Religion

Volume II: Products of religion - morality, ethnic Groups, nations
- Part 3: Nation
- Part 4: Ethnic Groups
- Part 5: Morality and Religion

Volume III: Specific Social Products
- Part 6: Black Africa
- Part 7: Imperial China
- Part 8: Latin America

Volume IV: Religion and the Believer
- Part 9: Religion itself

Part 1 starts with an anthropological review of why divine religions came into being among humans, and incorporates a long-range historical review and a forecast based on a realistic look at the present, at modern life.

Part 2 deals with myths and their religious tasks. It speaks about their inherent power to form societies, whether religious, national (ethnic or state based), or cultural; the way it (together with rituals) delineates the human borders of societies; and how they make the members of society feel as if they have known each other closely,inducing them to feel sympathy and solidarity for one another

Part 3 speaks about the nationhood and the term "Nation" and the influence of religion upon it.

Part 4 speaks about ethnic groups and their relations with religion.

Part 5 speaks about morality and its relationship with religion.

Part 6 deals with primitive religions, spirits and witchcraft.

Part 7 deals with Imperial China and the West as a comparative case study from which one can understand the great influence of different attitudes to religion andto God.

Part 8 deals with Latin America in comparison with the United States onthe one hand and with Canada on the other, as well as a comparison between the United States and Canada. The discussion is about the influence of religions, for example, the different attitudes to native Indians. It appears that the motif of introverted hierarchical relations amongst the people of Catholic tradition enabled the settlers in South and Central America to occupy their part of America without a policy of genocide. They mostly arrived in America without female partners, taking Indian females to be their wives. In contradistinction the idea of equality inherited by the English settlers did not extend to the natives and they would not marry Indian women and in fact practiced a form of genocide. They could not, mentally, place the Indian lifestyle on par with their own.

Part 9 deals with religion itself.

This book considers and searches for answers to basic questions about the social life, many of which have not yet been dealt with or elucidated upon in the Secular Western Thought; questions that relate to religion from a social perspective.

The most salient of these questions, that inverts Religion, viewing it as the focus of social life, even in our Modern Society, are as follows:

1. 'Why religion?' – What interests, pressures, or needs impelled man to seek a connection with other worlds? Why couldn't man exist, in general, and as a social being specifically - before he formed a spiritual connection with God or with an entity that was beyond his realm of existence? Why did man desire and need to heed the voice of his God and the moral obligations imposed upon him, according to his beliefs, by his God? Why does human society – **every** human society – need to believe in and indeed follow something that is not from the world where man lives and that cannot be proven? (This book refers to something as "religion", even if it is a belief in liberalism, communism, or Zionism). Why does Biblical-Christian religious morality exist even among secular people in the

West? Why has modern Western man failed to design a moral code that would replace the Judeo-Christian tradition that shapes the life of his contemporary society?

2. Among all the components of nationalism, what degree of salience does religion, ethnicity, language, and economic interests each bear? How do these different factors interact? How does a religion create a nation, expand its sphere of influence, or change its essence?

3. What happens to a country that has no nation? How does it create one for itself?

4. What characteristics are shared by all Western systems of morality and how do they differ from divinely inspired systems of morality?

5. The struggle between secular and divine religions. The United States of America emasculates the divine religions, and bars them from any possibility of involvement in or connection to, the government of the country, trampling upon the rights of the Catholic and Jewish educational systems as part of the religious war it wages.

6. Western materialism and utilitarianism in contrast to Judaism's moral educational system.

7. Modernity versus tradition. The spiritual advantages of tradition and the scientific and technological advantages of modernity. Western world's inability to comprehend the traditional world of native Africans.

8. A comparison between African nepotism and Israeli-American nepotism (protective policy).

9. Understanding the difference between a tribe with roots in a primitive religion and a group whose religion strives to embrace the whole world.

10. The difference between ethnicity and nationalism.

11. The position of primitive tribes in a world of advancing nationalities

12. Ethnic and religious roots of aggression

13. Aggressive and non-aggressive religions

14. More resilient and less resilient religions.

Clearly it is unrealistic to attempt to extricate divine religion from nationalism or even from civil religion. Hence any comprehensive discussion of these matters must includea discussion of the essence of divine religion, civil religion, nationalism, and ethics.

The approach to the contents, like the book itself, was not made up according to an ordered plan. This is because I did not imagine at the very outset that I would eventually write a systematic book of research that would contend with the huge and most ambitious task as it emerged at the end of the day. The whole thing came about like the calf that sprang out in front of Aaron, the brother of Moses. In the course of the last six years of research fora PHD decree in constitutional Law at the Hebrew University of Jerusalem I was free to learn whatever I liked. Being interested in the motif of religion because of my own personal motives, I have, in every Seminar of most of the 23 Seminars in which I participated, found a religious angle. It was a remote connection as remote as a plane is from the ground below. Maybe it was hidden inside my bones; maybe it was within my human essence. I strive to understand, yet, the same happened to the contents of my writing. It was neither planned nor plotted. Also, I cannot explain why I chose, for example, Imperial China or Latin America in order to prove, with their assistance, how strong religion is. It could be the same with any other part of the world or of history that could or could not prove the motif of power emanating from the motif of religion. Yet, maybe, and there is no proof for this at all, that in anything I search for, the motif of religion is aroused, with huge force, a possibility that religion is a phenomenon that exists all through human life, and is mostly predominant. I suggest that the lack of a pre-organized plan for that search is not an essential factor, without which conclusions in this book cannot be accepted. In a retrospective look, one may learn from the case of Aaron and his calf. There, the wide range of gifts given by many different people who had the same intention or motivation caused their common intention to be fulfilled. Likewise, in this book, the composition of time and place, worldwide, speaks in favor of the conclusions reached in this book, namely, that the picture from so many different examples teaches us about same common motifs inherent in different societies, and points to the common characteristics of religion. These common characteristics, mainly, look unchanged and unchangeable, at **any time, any place,** and under **any circumstances.**

Table of Contents

Volume II: Products of Religion - Morality, Ethnic Groups, Nations

(Pages 135-304)

Part 3: What is a nation? What is a civil religion? The case of Israel

(Pages 135-202)

Part 4: Ethnic Groups as co-builders (together with Religion) - of Nations (Pages 203-256)

Part 5: Morals and religion

Western and Jewish, secular and religious morals (Pages 267-304)

Part 8: Latino America and North America.
The main different roles explained by religious differences
(Pages 377-450)

Volume IV: Religion and the Believer (Pages 451-546)

Part 9: The Religion Himself
How he is revealed in one's mind? The attitude unto Him
(Pages 451-546)

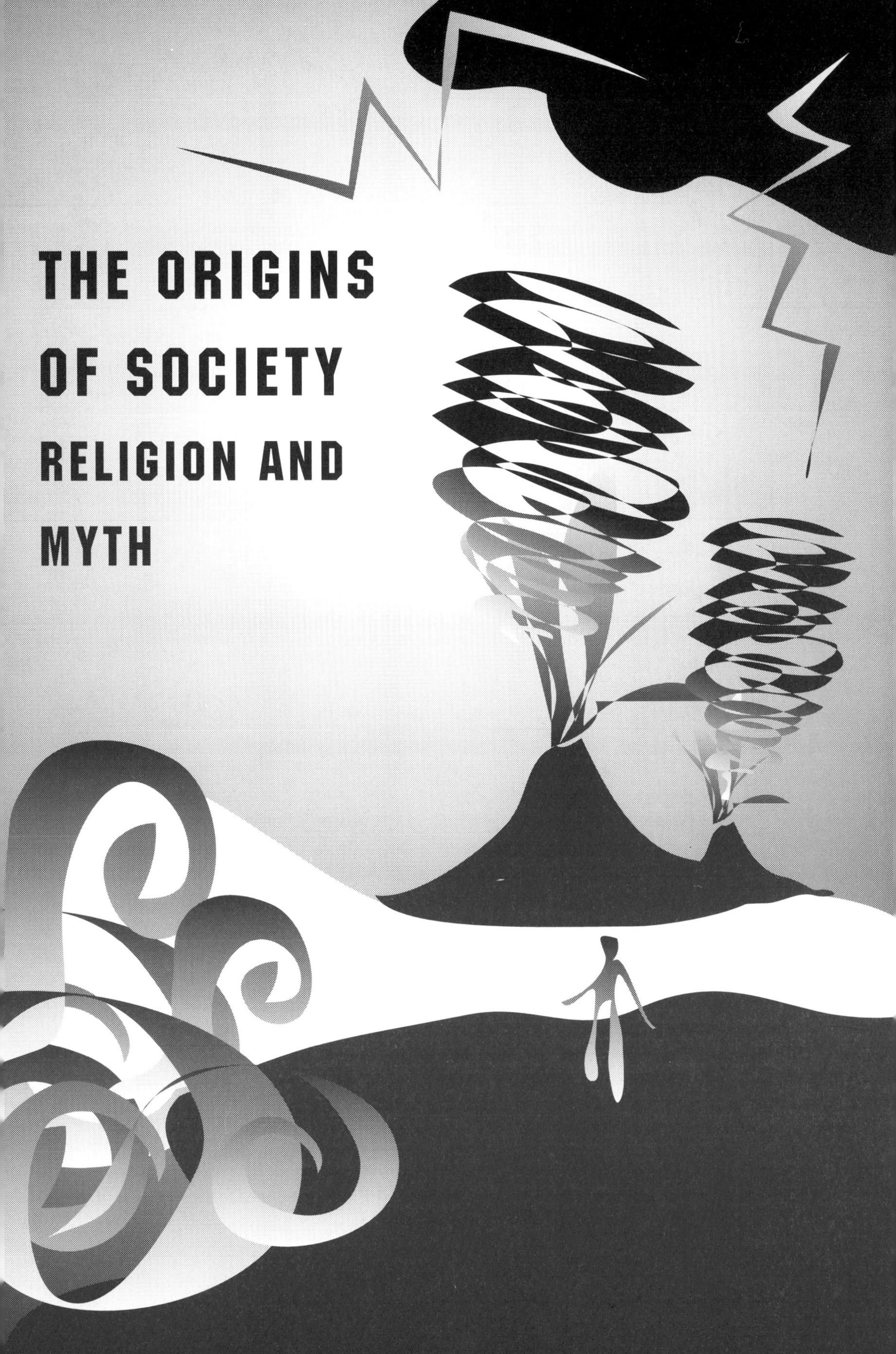
THE ORIGINS
OF SOCIETY
RELIGION AND
MYTH

Why Religion?

About one of the strongest, most fruitful, motifs in human life

Volume I:

Religion - Origin and Perpetual Creator of Society

Part 1:

Religion and Society

Structure of the Discussion in this part of the book:
This Part deals with a central issue – expressed in its title "Why religion?" It will discuss this subject on the basis of four sub-definitions and surveys. Following upon an examination of each of these, it will extrapolate an answer to the pivotal question "Why religion?" The four sub-topics are:

a) Of what kind of religion does this Part speak?
b) Primitive man and what he gains from religion.
c) Religion's influence on the modern state and its impact, through history, upon nationality and morality.
d) Can wo/man live without religion?

The first sub-category – which will be discussed in Chapter 1 – constitutes an initiatory determination of boundaries. The definitions used are relevant only to the scope of this particular chapter and do not in any way constitute general meanings. The definition of religion given here is socially determined. The second sub-category – discussed in Chapter 2 – examines the mutual relations between religion and the rest of human social features and components. It includes a critical review of extant publications that proffer original solutions to the issues.

The third sub-category discussed in Chapter 3 looks at the connection between ethics and the modern state, the reciprocal influence of religion and nation throughout history, and religion's impact on morality. The common denominator of Chapter 3 is the quality of human social life and the extent to which it is influenced by religion. While Chapter 3 focuses on our current condition, the fourth sub-category – discussed in Chapter 4 – looks at and towards the future, via an exploration of the past and present. The final chapter – Chapter 5 – draws conclusions from the four previous chapters and presents a comprehensive answer to the question:

e) "Why religion?"

Whereas the definition applied to the title is very broad, the sub-categories are designed to focus the discussion and to prevent the study wandering beyond its proper bounds. Despite the fact that the title is delimited according to sub-categories, the subject retains its width in relation to the intended structure of this Part. Consequently, and given that the parameters of the subject have not yet been determined, or only partially so, it is reasonable to expect that the answer or answers which arise here will be provisional in nature, requiring further investigation and elaboration.

Chapter 1: About what Religion Does This Part Speak?

Whenever religion is discussed it refers to something spiritual (outside the real world but connected to it) – a divine presence, symbol, principle, or idea which influences, or endeavours to influence, human social life and people's inner strength and emotions, whether through their behaviour or through their relations with other societies. Such religion impacts the strength of the human society in which its adherents live.

It devolves from such a definition that any religion which does not express itself institutionally – does not demand action or a certain conduct, or restraint from a certain conduct or behaviour, and exerts no influence on the world or on the quality of societal life – cannot be recognised as a religion. In the same way, any organised human activity designed to advance some principle or idea which does not extend beyond a limited intellectual circle devoid of influence on the world of action and values, or the worldview of a specific thinker in raw or published form, is excluded from the definition of religion. On the other hand, any faith which includes belief in some deity, spirit, totem, or image and expresses itself through rites and rituals and/or requires conformity to a certain code of behaviour is considered a religion. Communism, for example, which constitutes itself as a political movement in opposition to and/or infiltration of the ruling power, or establishes itself as a ruling government in its own right, falls into the category of religion. Likewise, to the extent that such ideals as democracy, conservatism, liberalism, anarchism, atheism,[1] natural living, modesty, family purity, and

[1] W. James, *The Variety of Religious Experience* (NY: Modern Library, 1929). In the second of a series of lectures given at Edinburgh University, James addressed the subject of defining religion for the purposes of the lectures, including atheism within the definition: "'He believes in No-God and worships him' said a colleague of mine of a student who was manifesting a fine atheistic ardor; and the more fervent opponents of Christian doctrine have often enough shown a temper which, psychologically considered, is indistinguishable from religious zeal. But so very broad a use of the word of 'religion' would be inconvenient, however defensible it might remain on logical grounds". For the including of democracy, conservatism, liberalism, anarchism, atheism and so on I may add, according to Emile Durkheim, **Pragmatism and Sociology**, (Cambridge: Cambridge University Press, 1983 - English translation, originally published in French in 1955) p. 91,

abortion rights lead people to a communal activity or to the prevention of such, these are also to be considered religions. Although such activity may be ritual or moral, it will always come to expression on a societal level and impact the quality of human life. Nationalism and civil religion also influence social and/or political life – or seek to do so – and are thence included under the definition of religion for the purposes of this Part as well. The institutionalised zionist movement of the twentieth century – up to and following the establishment of the State of Israel – is consequently defined as a religion, as is the Palestinian nationalist movement and all other nationalist movements.

In consequence of this broad definition and the purpose of this Part – to examine any and all religions which impact societal life and guide human beings in a certain social direction – no distinction will be made here between religions on the basis of their "truth" content. The question asked by anthropologists researching primitive African religions and cultures regarding which criteria they should apply to their study is well known: Should they evaluate the primitive religion or culture according to the subjects' own norms or should they employ the modern scientific standards in which they themselves have been educated?[2] This issue is irrelevant for the present purposes, since determining which religion is true or whether religions in general are true/contain truth is not under discussion here. For the purposes of this Part, messianic faith is no better or profounder than idol worship – or the contrary. Only one valid criterion exists: The exertion and extent of a particular religion's influence. Our focus is moreover upon religion in general rather than upon specific religions. The question "Why religion?" is an eternal question, unconnected to any particular time or phenomenon and immaterial to competition or rivalry between individual religions. The only criterion by which an entity may be included in or excluded from the definition of "religion" is whether or not that particular framework exerts an impact on societal life. If it does, it is considered to be a religion, equal among equals. When Marx defines theistic religion as "the opium of the people" our reply to him is: "Stand in line with the rest of the religions. For the purposes of our present discussion, you rank as one of them."

..."That is why there are formulae in our societies which we imagine are not religious, but which nevertheless do have the character of dogma, and are not questioned. Of this kind are ideas such as 'democracy', 'progress', 'the class struggle' and so on. Thus, we can see that scientific thought cannotrule alone. Thered is, and there always will be, room in social life for a form of truth which will perhaps be expressed in a very secular way, but will nevertheless have a mythological and religious basis."

[2] See E. Gellner, "Concepts and Society" in B. Wilson (ed.), *Rationality* (Oxford: Basil Blackwell, 1979), 30.

Chapter 2: Primitive Man and His Benefit from Religion

The primitive and the modern:

What kind of primitive wo/man does this Part deal with and what expression does his/her relation to religion take? The primary subject here is those tribes discovered and studied by anthropologists in the twentieth century in Australia, Africa, the Pacific islands, and America who are totem worshippers. They also include African tribes in central west Africa – on the Sudanese border and southwards to Morocco – studied at the end of the nineteenth and beginning of the twentieth century whose religion centres around witchdoctors, magicians, spirit healing, and spiritism. A man like this is known to have lived in pre-historic France.[3]

The primitive wo/man addressed here lives in a social setting. In contrast to Part 2, which deals with ethics, this section does not deal with homo sapiens throughout his/her existence. For the purposes of the present discussion no need exists to conduct such a comprehensive survey. At this point the pre-historic period is not under discussion. Part 2 will look at this period, in its focus on ethics, through an examination of Geertz's theory, according to which a change occurred in wo/man's forebears before s/he became homo sapiens, over millions of years. The logical framework and conclusions of this Part make discussion of this phenomenon superfluous here.

Perusal of ancient anthologies, literature, legends, and fables demonstrates that along side the great technological advances and changes which have occurred in the way human beings live their lives no appreciable parallel change has taken place in relation to human emotions, including such basic motifs[4] as the seeking after power, fear of death, the perpetuation of human life, love between men and women, the sexual drive, the aesthetic sense, the emotional familial relationship, compassion towards human beings, cruelty towards one another, the positive

---

[3] R.R. Marett, *The Threshold of Religion* (London: Methuen & Co. Ltd.: 1979[2]), 203, 219.

[4] See E. Kübler-Ross, *On Death and Dying* (London: Macmillan, 1969). Kübler-Ross claims on the basis of the examples she brings regarding the fear of death, that people have not changed in any general way – only in the way in which they deal with their problems. She speaks thus of the difference in dealing with death between the modern and ancient periods: "We would think that our great emancipation, our knowledge of science and of man, has given us better ways and means to prepare ourselves and our families for this inevitable happening. Instead the days are gone when a man was allowed to die in peace and dignity in his own home. The more we are making advancements in science, the more we seem to fear and deny the reality of death" (p. 6-7).

evaluation of justice and morality, the sense of curiosity, human intelligence, the esteem of wisdom, the honouring of one parents – and this is merely a partial list of human inclinations, emotions, feelings, weaknesses, and qualities, in no particular order of significance. On this basis it can be said that the primitive tribal Australian who performs totem rituals and the owner of a chain of steel-mills in America are both alike afraid of death, concerned that they will have descendants to continue their line, seek intimate-sexual relations, and may be happy in a familial framework or miserable without one, aware that their reach of information is limited, may sense of believe in the existence of supernatural forces or powers which influence or have the potential to influence the concrete reality in which they live.

The question which must be asked at this point, before going any further, is whether two such people may seek a relationship with such forces out of faith or hope that it will aid them in their difficulties[5] – will search for a refuge from or cure for their troubles in religious beliefs and rituals and in the acceptance of ethical obligations according to one religion or another: the one within the framework of the Catholic Church in prayer to Jesus, the other through totem worship. The modern, non-religious person is strengthened through what s/he believes, whether it be the communist ideal or a liberal society or civil religion. All of the latter are religions according to the definition adopted for the purposes of the present discussion, as we have already noted, even if they are not theistic religions. Kt can be said henceforth: People will fortify themselves in the face of their fears and frustrations through taking hold of religion.

Whether the answer to the last question is affirmative or negative, some benefit from religion is apparently anticipated by both parties in the example, in that in turning to religion that person finds an answer to his/her fear of death[6] or the

---

[5] James suggests that religion bestows spiritual support and security and in this way alleviates the fear of death and adds that it also supplies something which no logic or intellect can provide (*Varieties*, 47f).

[6] The plethora of books and articles written about the subject witness to the preoccupation with death which prevails in contemporary society. See Kübler-Ross, *Death*, who quotes Rabindranath Tagore's views on death. She continues: "When we look back in time and study cultures and people, we are impressed that death has always been distasteful to man and will probably always be. From a psychiatrist's point of view this is very understandable and can perhaps best be explained by our basic knowledge that, in our unconscious, death is never possible in regard to ourselves. It is inconceivable for our unconscious to imagine an actual ending of our own life here on earth, and if this life of ours has to end, the ending is always attributed to a malicious intervention from the outside by someone else. In simple terms, in our unconscious, we can only be killed; it is inconceivable to die of a natural cause or of old age. Therefore death in itself is associated with a bad act, a frightening happening, something that in itself calls for

loneliness which s/he experiences. The following description of a person about to die illustrates the breakdown which occurs in the life of the modern wo/man who abandons theistic religion and sometimes even refuses to allow a non-theistic religion to assist him/her in his/her emotional troubles:

> I think there are many reasons for this flight away from facing death calmly. One of the most important facts is that dying nowadays is more gruesome in many ways, namely, more lonely, mechanical, and de-humanized; at times it is even difficult to determine technically when the time of death has occurred. Whoever has been very sick and has required rest and comfort especially may recall his experience of being put on a stretcher and enduring the noise of the ambulance siren and hectic rush until the hospital gates open. Only those who have lived through this may appreciate the discomfort and cold necessity of such transportation which is only the beginning of a long ordeal – hard to endure when you are well, difficult to express in words when noise, light, pumps, 'and voices are all too much to put up... When a patient is severely ill, he is often treated like a with no right to an opinion. It is often someone else who makes the decision if and when and where a patient should be hospitalized. It would take so little to remember that the sick person too has feelings, has wishes and opinions ... He may cry for rest, peace, and dignity, but he will get infusions, transfusions, a heart machine, or tracheostomy ... Is this approach our own way to cope with and repress the anxieties which a terminally or critically ill patient evokes in us? Is our concentration on equipment, on blood pressure our desperate attempt to deny the impending death which is so frightening and discomforting to us that we displace all our knowledge onto machines, since they are less close to us than the suffering of another human being which would remind us once more of our lack of omnipotence, our own limits and failures, and last but not least perhaps our own mortality? Maybe the question has to be raised: Are we becoming less human or more human?[7]

Evans-Pritchard, Horton, Turner, Douglas, and Appiah:

The attitude of primitive wo/man is completely the opposite to modern sensibilities regarding the person about to die. Primitive wo/man does not have a sophisticated medical system at his/her disposal as does modern wo/man. S/he dealt with death with the tools s/he possessed, which were emotional support

---

retribution and punishment". As for other emotions and the general idea here see last part of this book, about Bergson and Durkheim.

[7] Kübler-Ross, in remark 4, *Death*, 7-9.

rather than the material means of modern medicine. Not only did primitive wo/man face the fear of death but s/he also faced many other things which troubled him/her and in the face of these adopted magical practices which didn't necessarily provide a physical solution to the problem but essentially encouraged primitive wo/man and gave him/her the sense that s/he possessed the tools with which to deal with his/her problems. A partial list of the things which disturbed primitive wo/man can be found in the research of such anthropologists as Evans-Pritchard, Robin Horton, Victor Turner, Mary Douglas, and Kwame Anthony Appiah.[8] These studies review a variety of the disturbances and problems of primitive wo/man and the ways which primitive tribes found to deal with them with the means at their disposal, together with the measure of social completion and order which these means brought about in the lives of these primitive peoples. The list of problems includes lack of success in hunting, the case of a man whose foot was pierced by a thorn while walking barefoot in the forest, different illnesses – dangerous and less serious – and even old age, in the threat of dying from it. From the perspective of primitive wo/man, old age, when a person is about to die, is considered to be unnatural condition, something brought about by magic in order to combat him. If its confrontation – in the form of measures against magic – is unsuccessful and the person dies (in effect from old age), this is regarded as a failure on the part of the measures rather than as the outcome of a natural and inevitable aging process. The person who is old and likely to die lives according to the belief that s/he does not stop when s/he dies, and does not experience the possibility of a death which cannot be arrested. When an adolescent male reaches puberty and an adolescent girl leaves her mother's authority – events which are accompanied by a mental crisis on both the pubescents' and parents' side not only amongst primitive peoples but also in contemporary society – this necessary passage is eased by ritual ceremonies. If puberty is not the issue, primitive wo/man's traditional means of dealing with things may be through finding a magician who will effect a defect or illness, and cautions to the magician to cease his dangerous magic. They may also take the form of a ritual in which symbolic actions are performed which actualise through simulation the pubescent's separation and detachment from his/her parents. Status as magician is accorded by the person considered to be the expert in magic, who determines that the magician has performed magic and effected an imbalance

[8] E.E. Evans-Pritchard, *Witchcraft, Oracles, and Magic Among the Azande* (Oxford: Clarendon Press, 1976); V. Turner, "Witchcraft and Sorcery: Taxonomy versus Dynamics" in *The Forest of Symbols* (NY: Cornell University Press, 1967), 111-127; M. Douglas, *Purity and Danger: An Analysis of Concepts of Pollution and Taboo* (London: Routledge and Kegan Paul, 1966); R. Horton, *Patterns of Thought in Africa and the West* (Cambridge: Cambridge University Press, 1993); K.A. Appiah, *In My Father's House: Africa in the Philosophy of Culture* (Oxford: Oxford University Press, 1992).

expressed in an illness or any other disturbance which he has been requested to deal with and find a remedy for. However, the identification of an accident-causing magician will be made on the basis of people whom the requester considers suitable according to their actions – the person who suffers the mishap, retains a grudge against its invoker, and desires his/her death or misfortune. Such a magician is cautioned and if, according to the experts' identification as a magician, he brings about someone's death, is executed by determination of the experts who confirm his guilt. The "guilty" party, whose magical culpability is posited by the magic experts – who constitute a kind of jury in terms of the Anglo-American judicial system or a judge in other modern judicial systems – may simply be someone who lives in the same village rather than someone who lives at some distance from the victim of the magic. All of this actually occurs – if the sickness in question leads to the person's death. Under these primitive conditions, people endeavour to avoid acting wrongfully towards their neighbours in order to avert suspicion as magicians who have brought about the death of one of their neighbours. The better a person behaves towards his neighbours and his surroundings the less chances exist of him/her being accused of witchcraft and a neighbour's death by magic. This situation encourages good and courteous neighbourly relations. Something else which encourages good relations amongst primitive tribes is the obligation imposed on those participating in various rites, such as those of initiation, to share the refreshments provided with their neighbours. A person who is sick and who receives traditional treatment is a person is at relative peace, since s/he believes and can actually see that s/he has been given means to deal with what is disturbing him/her – including sickness. In this way the level of the sick person's fear and the anxiety of anyone suffering from various hardships and difficulties recedes. S/he knows that s/he has in his/her hand a means to treat the illness or disturbance which s/he faces.

It was precisely the poverty of concrete measures in terms of primitive wo/man's technological and scientific progress and his/her relative fragility in relation to his/her surroundings which opened up wide possibilities through the aid of his/her imagination when searching for primitive remedies in the symbolic and spiritual world. In his/her search for cures in such circumstances, modern wo/man developed technological and scientific tools which produced more effective remedies than his/her primitive forebears. This is not a full picture in terms of comparison since modern wo/man in the contemporary world also deals with alternative medicine, whose correspondence to primitive tribal cures may be noted – although it will not receive here the attention which it deserves. The question remains: What effect did imaginary remedies possess in primitive tribal society – cures which, in modern scientific terms, lack any empirical impact on the reality in which wo/man lives? To what extent did his/her remedies aid primitive wo/man? The answer to this question cannot be confined exclusively to material elements

from medical science. One of the factors in this potential examination – which shall not be investigated here – is wo/man's spiritual dimension.
The virtual and magical remedies which primitive wo/man developed certainly induced greater spiritual well-being in him/her, as well as a softening social impact in result of intentions to act in a relatively pleasant and soft manner towards one's fellows in one's social setting. This produced a less conflictive social life – out of which arose, routinely and naturally, a social framework of mutual assistance. The aid which the primitive tribal wo/man received was accompanied by an assistance which s/he could – and in fact did – receive from forces external to his/her physical reality, forces such as spirits, gods, totems, and other imaginary forces produced with the help of two innate human qualities – imagination and emotion. In primitive society, these two qualities helped grant wo/man things which, in the later modern period, s/he sought to obtain through an third innate quality – the human intellect. This development occurred through the enlightened psychological treatment which modern wo/man developed. In this sense, the modern psychologist and psychoanalyst have replaced the primitive witchdoctor and expert at locating magicians.

The Taboo:
The suggestion that primitive wo/man was not merely a remedy-supplying imagination but also an emotional life brings this discussion to the contribution of one of the greatest modern researchers, Sigmund Freud. Freud spoke of the dominance of the father figure in the memory of sons who rebelled against their parent and killed him in order to release his hold on the women in the family.[9] In the well-known continuation of Freud's story, when the son overcomes his father and kills him, his siblings place a collective prohibition on themselves against conducting sexual relations with the women who have been freed from the father's possess in order to prevent the eruption of a familial blood feud. This is the origin of two elements of the taboo: The prohibition against patricide on the one hand and against sexual relations with one's mother and sisters on the other. This taboo, which is cross-generational according to Freud, is not the result of logic as much as its source is emotive – the trauma which the sons experienced and passed down to the following generations and cultures.
Although I do not wish to contend with Freud at this stage,[10] I want to recall here something which is found in many religious heritages, including Judaism, and which Freud should have known as a Jew. In many prayers, especially those

[9] See S. Freud, *The Future of An Illusion* (The Kibbutz HaArtzi HaShomer HaTza'ir: 1943; trans. into Hebrew from the original title *Culture and Religion*), 144; ibid, *Totem and Taboo* (Tel Aviv: Dvir, 1988), 129.
[10] This will be done later.

recited during the Days of Awe, the expression "Our Father, our God" occurs as an invocation for protection. This does not present the Father as someone who should be killed, whom people are seeking to kill, or are afraid of, but a merciful God who, even if we are unworthy of His lovingkindness, promises to come and save us, the only condition being that we seek Him with a full heart and complete repentance as a sinful soul and out of a sincere desire to do what is right and proper – a foundation which constitutes a fundamental moral component in all theistic religions. Spirits exist in primitive religion and it is obvious that the human motivation out of which arises the ghost of the dead wo/man to whom one turns originates – as at least one possibility – from the fact that the person who is dead and hides his spirit is missing and longed for on the part of the living person who calls up his/her spirit. The person who calls up a spirit wishes to establish connection with him/her. This desire arises from the fact that the person who imagines senses that the dead person – had s/he been alive at that moment – would undoubtedly have given him his/her support, as if s/he had been standing by his/her side right then. To whom is it more natural that a person should turn for assistance and comfort than one's mother – and after her, to one's father? When talking about physical obstacles and threats, what figure calls up the idea of support and aid more than the strong father known from a person's childhood? This is the memory which the small child retains when s/he grows up and becomes an adult and which appears in the face of difficult and troubling problems. In such a situation, the adult once again experiences him/herself as the small child whose father protected and defended him/her against dangerous events and wild beasts. "If only my father was here" – cries the grown-up wo/man in face of his/her impotence. The father figure arises out of this distress and summons by means of the imaginative power innate in wo/man. At this moment, this figure is the similitude of the father's spirit, a figure which arises out of the reality of periodicity and the new growth of nature in which nothing vanishes from the world but always springs up afresh. This may be the origin of the institution of spiritism in general. It may be that this is the spirit of a hero (warrior?) from the past which the child received from his/her father in his/her childhood, whom his/her father believed protected him, as he himself received such a figure from his father, and so on and so forth. Or it may be a spirit defined according to the function which it plays, without a name.[11] The Jewish expression "the Lord God of spirits" represents a development of this idea. Even Moses, when he came to the enslaved Israelites in Egypt, declared that he came as an agent of the God of their fathers, without mentioning His name. There is no contradiction between the figure of the father as protector, the spirit of the father out of whom other spirits

[11] The spirit may be that of a great mythological figure. See M. Weber, *The Sociology of Religion* (Boston: Beach Press, 1963), 4.

also arose and became gods, and Freud's taboo theory. Ambivalence is a natural quality in human beings and it includes both spirits and gods which concretise and institutionalise the idea of spiritism. This is part of the inner wealth with which people have been blessed. What is important at this stage, however, is to present the benefits which primitive wo/man gains from religion. This has been illustrated above.

Emile Durkheim:

Following the initial stages of its evolution in the totemic period,[12] religion developed in the direction of ritual, being linked to both the imagination and the emotions. This is an assumption made by many anthropologists, including Durkheim.[13] Durkheim argues that religion is important for social order and is largely connected with rituals which link the individual to the community of his blood ties and bestow on him/her spiritual power. He further claims that religion does not exist in order to save a person's soul but to preserve the quality of human social life, and that when modern religion entered into an era of searching after logic, this function of religion was enervated.

Durkheim states the following about the cause and significance of perennial rituals: "If the sacred beings lways manifested their powers in a perfectly equal manner, it would appear inconceivable that men should dream of offering them services, for we cannot see what need they could have of them. But in the first place, in so far as they are confused with things, and in so far as they are regarded as principles of the cosmic life, they are themselves submitted to the rhythm of life. Now this goes in oscillations in contrary direction, which succeed one another according to a determined law. Sometimes it is affirmed in all its glory; sometimes it weakens to such an extent that one may ask himself whether it is not going to fade away. Vegetation dies every year; will it be reborn? Animal species tend to become extinguished by the effect of natural and violent death; will they be renewed in such a time and in such a way as is proper? Above all, nature is capricious; there are long periods during which it seems to have disappeared forever. These periodical variations of nature bear witness to the fact that at the corresponding periods the sacred beings upon whom the plants, animals, rain etc. depend are themselves passing through grave crises; so they, too, have their periods of giving way. But men could not regard these spectacles as indifferent spectators. If he is to live, the universe life must continue, and consequently the gods must not die. So he seeks to sustain and aid them; for this, he puts at their

---

[12] During which the figure of the father played a central role, not necessarily with respect to the subject of the taboo.

[13] See E. Durkheim, *The Elementary Forms of the Religious Life* (London: George Allen and Unwin, 1976), in the Introduction by Robert Nisbet.

service whatever force he has at his disposition, and mobilizes them for this purpose."[14]

General reflections:
Both the reasons and the consequences of ceremonial rituals linked to forces greater than wo/man, forces which are abstract and cannot be manipulated except through the ways people's fruitful and creative imagination lead them repetitively, as in nature, are visible. The propulsion of natural phenomena is attributed to these forces. Similar power and influence are attributed to the spirit of the father and to other spirits connected to figures who live in the same social group, figures of those who have died to whom, had they still been alive, the person would have turned for aid. Since beings outside the world are under discussion, wo/man found a spiritual way to turn to them. Such turning is accomplished by way of the raising of memories and myths, stories which reoccur and are repeated over the generations. These stories are developed in wo/man's close social group, especially group linked by blood ties, a wo/man's ethnic group. This makes it clear why these myths are developed: Not only do they possess a ritual function but they themselves also strengthen wo/man's spirit. They constitute repetitive and recurrent proof of the way in which the early ancestors overcame problems similar to those people face today. Through association with them primitive wo/man obtains spiritual power, encouragement, and confidence that through their assistance s/he could overcome the dangers and obstacles which s/he faced. This is the very source of social life, since each group has a common ancestor and this fact encourages the individual to remain with the communal framework. In this way, alongside the answer to the question "Why society?" the answer to the question "Why religion?" – as also to the questions "Why myth?" and "Why ritual?" – can all be understood. All these are fundamental entities which strengthen one another and are strengthened by one another and strengthen wo/man's spirit.

Sigmund Freud:
At this point the discussion returns to Freud's theory of the totem and taboo in connection with the story of the father's murder, a theory according to which every distant tribe, from those in Australia, Africa, America, the Pacific Islands, who all worshipped totems made in the father's image and imposed a grave taboo against patricide and sexual relations within the family. They all preserved one primal memory of brothers who banded together and killed their father who had forbidden them to conduct sexual relations with the family women, a privilege he reserved exclusively for himself. They also remember the agreement which the

---

[14] Durkheim, ibid, *Elementary*, 344 (385-86).

brothers made following their father's murder in order to avoid engaging in a familial blood feud – that they would refrain from conducting sexual relations with the same women over whom they had killed their father. This raises the question: "Can this be true?" Does this story and explanation relate to Adam or to Noah, in reference to the murder of one single primal ancestor from whom the whole human race arose? Has this theory been preserved with so much devotion in every culture? Freud's theory seems too farfetched. Freud himself raised the possibility of an alternative explanation. He describes human beings as a result of their spiritual state as experiencing guilt over their desire to commit a certain act, as if they had actually committed it, even though they had not. He therefore says that if a wo/man wishes to perform a deed about which s/he will afterwards feel guilty for committing, and if this aspiration/lust is very strong, that person will undergo the spiritual/mental experience of having actually performed the act. It is true that Freud continues and says that he dismisses this idea in relation to the totem, patricide, and taboo, but this dismissal is not made in decisive language. This is what he says about the above assumption: "This is a powerful argument, but not a conclusive one. The alteration might have been effected in a less violent fashion and nonetheless been capable of determining the appearance of the moral reaction ... If wishes and impulses have the full value of facts for primitive men, it is our business to give their attitude understanding attention instead of correcting it in our accordance with our own standards ... It is not accurate that obsessional neurotics, weighed down under the burden of excessive morality, are defending themselves only against *psychical* reality and are punishing themselves for impulses which were merely felt. *Historical reality* has a share in the matter as well. In their childhood they had these evil impulses pure and simple, and turned them into acts so far as the impotence of childhood allowed. Each of these excessively virtuous individuals passes through an evil period in his infancy – a phase of perversion which was the forerunner and pre-condition of the later period of excessive morality. The analogy between primitive men and neurotics will therefore be far more fully established if we suppose that in the former instance, too, psychical reality – as to the form taken by which we are in no doubt – coincided at the beginning with factual reality: that primitive men actually *did* what all the evidence shows that they intended to do."[15]

I cannot find in these words of Freud any defence against the criticism which I have raised regarding the unfeasibility of the theory that the primal father's murder and the siblings' contract has become the heritage of all human beings, common to all human societies and cultures. Freud's alternative rationale, which is the only theory which can explain the unitary and universal nature of the phenomenon under discussion, must therefore be accepted. The theory suggested here is based

---

[15] Freud, in remark 9, *Totem*, 142 (160-61).

on the assumption that human nature is the same, however distributed it may be, and that this homogenous nature produces the same feelings of guilt everywhere. There is no need to speak of an early ancestor, only of human nature, which is homogenous and unitary and found over widely-scattered areas. It is not a question of a sophisticated tribal communication network but of a homogenous nature shared by all. Out of this universal human nature arise similar figures, myths, and guilt feelings.

At any rate, the existence of the spirits of the dead and the narratives and myths related to them assisted primitive wo/man in overcoming the fear of annihilation which accompanies death. Out of the desire to reinforce this (comforting) belief that death is not the end of human life developed the custom of respecting the dead by burying them in their clothes and refraining from distribution of their possessions immediately after their burial.[16]

Rudolf Otto:

Rudolf Otto's work raises a particular issue in the present discussion.[17] Otto's theory of the "numinous" is anchored in an existential understanding of something "Other" which is holy, irrational, and based on a feeling of insignificance in the face of a perfect God. He speaks of the experience of the "mysterium tremendum" – a feeling of great mysteriousness, full of awe and threat, inexplicable, appalling.[18] In Luther's words as Otto quotes them, "To the extent that that which is holy arouses the awe of glory in us, yet we do not flee from it but on the contrary are drawn towards it."[19] Otto speaks of the mixture of emotions in the wo/man who undergoes a religious experience, who suffers a confusion of feelings. He argues that the close link between religion and emotion is known both from experiential knowledge and from observation of the fervour of religious wars

---

[16] See M. Weber, in remark 11, *Sociology*, 6.

[17] See. R. Otto, *The Holy: On the Irrationality of the Idea of God and its Relation to Rationality*, trans. by Miriam Ron (Jerusalem: Carmel, 1999).

[18] Even though Otto does not say so explicitly, his words may be understood to mean that the more that a wo/man promotes him/herself, s/he creates in his/her experience – outside him/herself – a greater, more majestic, more persuasive deity. It is as though the deity is filled with content, substance, and persuasive power in correspondence to the extent to which the wo/man standing opposite him/her reduces his/herself-image. Wo/man invites the deity's presence by making him/herself nothing. This resembles the shroud (kittel) with which an Ashkenazi Jew envelops him/herself during the Days of Awe and declares "Here I am ready and willing every minute to become nothing and to return to a place of dust, worm, and maggot, according to Your decision and instruction" – thereby connecting him/herself with his/her Creator, in that the more s/he becomes nothing, the more Creator's presence is given to him/her.

[19] Otto, remark 17, *Holy*, 40.

and the fanaticism of the religious zealot on those around him/her, to the point of sacrificing his/her life.

Reflections:
From what the present discussion it would appear that wo/man is attracted to religion and gains some benefit from it, being strengthened by it. This is also evident from human experience, as well as from observation. This raises an apparent contradiction: The benefit attached to religion radiates logic, calculation, and rationality which are connected to religion. Horton's work also demonstrates how the African who is attached to his/her traditional religion only turns to witchdoctors and magicians when s/he cannot find a cure for his/her problem elsewhere.[20] According to Horton's theory, this African resembles a modern wo/man in need of conventional treatment – as long as it can cure him/her – and a psychologist when s/he must learn to come to terms with his/her illness. The psychologist corresponds in modern terms to the traditional witchdoctor in African terms. The question is therefore: "Is religion (all religion, in every culture, across all times) not that irrational thing to which a person turns when logic fails him?" Is there any logic in the argument that a person turns to the irrational when s/he cannot find a rational cure? Is not Otto's description[21] of experiential religion more rational, demonstrating that a person seeks to connect with that which is beyond rationality, the channel to the irrational necessarily being through the irrational which, in wo/man, is human emotion? experience? wo/man's sense of nullity in opposition to which s/he must, through human rationality, stand facing something else, some great and awesome deity? Does there not stand behind this lack of rational planning nothing other than a really cunning rationality, a craftiness which wo/man reaches intuitively? Wo/man is cunning – be s/he modern or primitive, both are made of the same cloth – and let us remember the dervish who goes into a trance and does not feel the needles with which he pierces himself, in an "irrational" but well planned manner! This represents a combination of planning and experience. This is precisely what happens in the technique of prayers and hymns which help a person enter into a religious experience. However the religious experience is described, the proper
question is: "What benefit did primitive wo/man gain from religion?" receives the answer: Religion supplies primitive wo/man with a sense of protection against those things which rationality cannot protect. Moreover, it gets rid of the worst of all – the lack of knowledge, the lack of knowledge why one is sick, why one has to die, when, and under what circumstances, why a person has recently experienced a lack of success in hunting, why the rains have stopped, why s/he received a thorn

[20] Horton, in remark 8, *Patterns.*
[21] James' theory is similar in this respect.

in his/her leg, why a dreadful storm occurred, and other such things. This explanation holds true even in our day in relation to theistic religion. Things weren't only this way in the primitive period. In our own day, if you ask an observant Jew whether s/he believes in luck, s/he will say yes, but if you ask whether s/he believes in accidents, s/he will say absolutely not. Judaism does not allow for accidents because everything is under God's providence, and it is the latter which is responsible for miracles, a miracle merely being God's specific intervention. Luck has to do with human actions and errors which devolve from the free-will which the Creator bestows on His/Her creatures to choose between good and evil. Luck is the indirect divine intervention which guides the outcome of wo/man's actions, people still being able to overcome their bad luck in the framework of the free-will to choose between good and evil which has been bestowed upon them. In this way, the human order becomes the divine order and all questions have an answer, even if – as in the end of the book of Job – it is not always revealed to wo/man. This constitutes the common factor shared by all religions, from the primitive wo/man who deals with his/her problems through witchcraft to the Jew. Religion orders everything and endows the life of the believer with order and security.

In another sphere of life, religion guides and directs wo/man – including primitive wo/man – towards a social behaviour which integrates him/her with his/her surroundings.[22] The studies reviewed so far with respect to primitive African tribes, particularly the work of Evans-Pritchard, indicate that the rules of witchcraft obligate and direct wo/man to live rightly with his/her neighbours so that s/he him/herself will not be accused of witchcraft. The rituals, rites, and spirits and myths of tribal figures strengthen the social-tribal bond and aid the primitive wo/man in experiencing him/herself as part of the continuing tribal existence. This belonging destroys the fear of extinction to a large degree and personal death and grants a dimension of continuity, rootedness, and eternity to the lives of the members of the community by way of the tribalism generated through religious rites. This tribalism also helps the individual know that s/he is not alone in the world, that there is someone to stand by him/her in difficulties and troubles and times of danger, against the forces of nature and wild beasts.

Nina Ramon:

Partial proof of this thesis can be found in the work of Nina Ramon, which concentrates on the important but circumscribed subject of death and the fear of

[22] Studies conducted in the United States have demonstrated that the crime rate among churchgoers is considerably lower than amongst the general populace.

death.[23] Ramon concludes that "The birth of the belief in God originates in man's incapacity of recognising death as nothing, whereas the death of belief in God is based on human recognition of death as extinction." In other words, the appearance of religion is directly tied to the fear of the extinction which is death, and the apperception of death as extinction abolished religious belief (or perhaps the reverse: the dissolution of the belief in God brought about the recognition that death is extinction). With all death's central importance in human life, to focus exclusively on the life of the person and his/her life after death is an erroneous path. Human life is incomparably richer than the single, sole question of the fear of death and extinction. So while Ramon's research is well built and structured in its analysis of various thinkers such as Kierkegaard[24], who sees the punishment for man's eating from the tree of knowledge in the Garden of Eden as death, it neither corresponds to the biblical text nor can it stand on any other grounds. The biblical story specifically deals with other punishments given to Adam and Eve, even though the tree of life does hint at the fact that wo/man is prevented from learning that s/he can change his/her condition as a mortal being by eating of the fruit of the tree of life. Still, the expulsion from the Garden of Eden did not make wo/man immortal, but only prevented an alteration of his/her mortal status. The story of the Garden of Eden cannot hold a proper place in a scientific inquiry into the centrality of death in human life. Not that the subject of death is not central, but it is merely one among other important issues in life. The alteration in seasons in nature demonstrate to wo/man that *continuity* exists, not extinction. Ramon's reference to Otto's argument that the religious sense is related to threat is not an accurate reading of Otto. The latter does not speak of the fear of God but of an attraction to God through awe. Ramon's claim that fear in the face of divine revelation threatens the guarantee of continued human existence displays her misunderstanding of Otto.[25] Ramon states in regard to divine revelation and the fear which it induces: "The only way which man possesses to overcome death is to attempt to deny it and to get round it in every way possible. Thus the transcendent power is 'revealed' to man, a mysterious force which first of all and above all arouses threat and fear. This is the 'point of time', if so it can be put, in the human spirit on which a finger can be placed and said: This is the moment at which God was 'born.' At this irrational moment when consciousness is salvaged, man, out of an inner drive, seeks aid and assistance from this same force and endeavours to appease and implore it so that it will not harm him. In other words, this power,

[23] N. Ramon, "The Birth and Death of God: Man and Death in Primitive Religion and Existentialism." Thesis presented to the Department of Comparative Religion at the Hebrew University in fulfilment of the requirements for the MA, 1983.

[24] Ramon, ibid. *Birth*, 5.

[25] Ibid, 14.

when it has the capacity to hurt man or to leave him be, is the power of life and death."

In the continuation of her discussion, Ramon addresses the issue of the transcendent God, the fear of whom, as the researchers whom she mentions indicate, "birthed." In reference to this argument it should be noted that it is precisely the renewal of nature which provided primitive wo/man with an excellent "cover story" in defence against the idea of extinction. In order to "invent" the concept of spirits which perpetuate the life of wo/man after his/her death it was not necessary to "invent" the notion of a deity (or a totem or god). Neither of the ideas of totem and deity which accompany wo/man are necessarily linked to the anticipation of death but are rather primarily connected with the daily, concrete problems of crops or success in hunting (problems of self-support, in modern terms) and the rest of mundane matters of the course of life. It is not the one, single, unique moment of death which stands at the centre of religious rites but multiple moments in the conduct of one's life. Primitive, as also modern, religion has many and varied tasks. However important it is, death is only one of these. Consequently, God was not necessarily "born" in connection with death but more importantly with respect to, for, and in relation to life. So while Ramon's research is right in its fundaments it is only partially accurate and correct overall.[26]

Ezekiel Kaufman:

Towards the conclusion of this discussion, the work of Kaufman is relevant. Kaufman writes: "The failure of the attempt to explain cultural creativity by these conditions and circumstances which are likely to be revealed to our eyes particularly when we come to the creative personality, to the individual genius ... Is it possible to 'explain' Homer, Plato, Shakespeare, Goethe, Rembrandt, Beethoven, and so forth by circumstances and conditions? The 'conditions' indeed worked in vain in all their fellow countrymen, members of society, standing, times, and before which they united ... Not only this but we discern in the cultural creativity of the ethnic group a certain organic phenomenon in that it constitutes a natural and uniform creative source ... A primary example of this is language ... The theory of the 'national spirit' or the 'spirit of the nation' which has been prevalent since Montesquieu and up to Hegel and his disciples was born precisely out of study of the phenomenon of the uniformity of cultural styles and an exaggerated generalisation of this uniformity ... Montesquieu demonstrated that a 'spirit' exists in the rules of every people ... An historical-empirical view of the

[26] The rest of Ramon's study looks at Nietzsche's "death of God," Kierkegaard's "religious escapism," Heidegger's philosophical escapism, Camus' "absurd," and existential nihilism as modern ways of coping with human problems, and is consequently not relevant to the present discussion.

history of culture cannot ignore the fact that the true creative force of every original culture which is primary is the ethnic grouping ... there are religions, styles of faith, statutes, legends, etc. which arise out of their national source and spread out ... Therefore it makes no difference when the unique religion evolved – it cannot be explained by any circumstances or conditions. The religion of the individual is a new cultural creation, and like every cultural creation its final source can be tentatively defined as the creative spirit of man, and because this was born and developed only in Israel we must add: it was born out of the creative spirit of the people of Israel."[27]

General insight from the work of Otto, Kaufman, and Roth:
Neither the appearance of religion, being a universal human phenomenon nor the taboo linked to the father's murder and the sexual relations with the women of the immediate family are national creations, produced by one group or people. It is not feasible that these things spread from one primal father-family (Adam or Noah, according to the biblical text). It is more likely that there human culture developed in nearly identical ways in widely-separated places without any means of transmission. Without any sophisticated communication in the early days no recourse exists but to look for the source in the nature which is innate in wo/man, together with similar conditions of life, and to say that wo/man blessed with insight, emotions, and imagination, a sense of curiousity, the ability to make abstractions, and intuition, whose feelings include fear, arrived at the conclusion, through his/her insight, that there are (and it can be added, from the perspective of one looking backwards, that there will always be) forces which wo/man's physical senses, intellect, and other faculties will never grasp and understand in full. These supernatural forces present threats and difficulties to wo/man. Being dispersed and separated, primitive wo/man came to the conclusion, due to the universal qualities innate in his/her nature, that s/he must seek allies in his/her struggle against these supernatural forces. S/he must search for something else outside the world in which s/he lives. This power which aids wo/man may be the same entity which causes wo/man all his/her problems, or it may be another force – but even in the latter case it will be something outside normal experience, that being what constitutes its power. That which is above and beyond the human world is what wields influence, the world being influenced by it. The anthropological studies mentioned explain well how the sacrifices which primitive wo/man was accustomed to offering to the gods and spirits did not constitute things which the god or spirit could not find from someone else but proved the intention in wo/man's heart to submit to the god or spirit. A poor person who need to sacrifice

[27] E. Kaufman, *The History of the Israelite Religion – From its Beginning until the End of the Second Temple Period* (Jerusalem: Mossad Bialik,), xxiiif.

an ox and did not have the means to obtain one, for example, could offer a cucumber instead. So in truth, wo/man cannot influence the gods but is influenced by them and the god's help is not the fruit of some cunning action on the part of wo/man who "manipulates" the god but an expression of his/her submission to the will of the god or spirit. According to this will, and not according to wo/man's will, the god or spirit agrees to help wo/man. This is the central motif, even if there are some divergences from it. Observation of nature which renews itself led wo/man by means of his/her creative imagination to the obvious concept of the spirit in wo/man and in every animate object, a spirit which continues to exists after the person's death, as well as to the concept of "supernatural" forces outside reality which influence it and drive nature and its laws – forces which certainly at one stage "created" the reality in which wo/man lives and guide his/his destiny. When faced with difficulties, wo/man (every primitive wo/man to the extent that all primitive peoples experienced similar problems, realities, conditions and shared a similar nature) turned to these forces and religious belief was thus formed, out of which religious rites then developed. Otto speaks thus, among other things, of this development: "It is a well-known and fundamental psychological law that ideas 'attract' one another and that one will excite another and call it into consciousness it if resembles it. An entirely similar law holds with regard to feelings. A feeling, no less than an idea, can arouse its likeness in the mind; and the presence of the one in my consciousness may be the occasion for my entertaining the other at the same time … the idea of transmutation … [explains how] the feeling, for example, of moral obligation 'evolves' or develops … the feeling of the numinous[28] …is not to be derived from any other feeling, and is in this sense 'unevolvable' … Yet at the same time, [it] has numerous analogies with others [other feelings], and therefore it and they may reciprocally excite or stimulate one another and cause on another to appear in the mind … [these] 'stimuli' or 'excitations' … cause the numinous feeling to appear in the consciousness, to intimate by virtue of what analogies they came to be able to do so and so to discover the series or chain of these stimuli by whose operation the numinous feeling was awakened in us … But this is indubitably a stimulus that only makes it appearance late in the excitation series and it is probable that the feeling of the sublime is itself first aroused and disengaged by the precedent religious feeling – not from itself but from the rational spirit of man and its *a priori* capacity which arouses the sense of the numinous was undoubtedly an exalted sense in many cases, which even today is likely to be aroused … However, this stimulation only appeared by itself at a

---

[28] As we have already noted in our discussion of this term, wo/man's sense of extinction in the face of God's greatness approaches the point of threat and terror, yet without the element of goodness and morality, a feeling which rather than causing one to flee from the numinous in fear strongly attracts wo/man to God.

relatively late stagė in the chain of stimulations and developments. It is therefore almost certain that the religious sense appeared on the scene before wo/man developed a sense of the exalted and it was this religious sense which aroused it and helped give it birth – not out of itself, of course, but of the spirit and its a priori capacities And it is for some reason inherently probable that there is more, too, in the combination of 'the holy' with 'the sublime' than a mere association of feelings; and perhaps we may say that, while as a matter of historical genesis such an association was the means whereby this combination was awakened in the mind and the occasion for it, yet the inward and lasting character of the connexion in all the higher religions does prove that the sublime, too, is an authentic schematic of 'the holy'. The intimate interpenetration of the non-rational with the rational elements of religious consciousness, like the interweaving of warp and woof in a fabric, may be elucidated by taking another familiar case, in which a universal human feeling, that of personal affectation, is similarly interpenetrated by a likewise thoroughly non-rational and separate element, namely, the sex instinct. It goes without saying that his latter lies just on the opposite side of 'reason' to the numinous consciousness; for while this is 'above all reason', the sex impulse is below it, an element in our instinctive life. 'The numinous' infuses the rational from above, 'the sexual' presses up from beneath, quite wholesomely and normally out of the nature which the human being shares with the general animal world, into the higher realm of the specifically 'humane'. But though the two things being compared are manifestly opposite extremes, they exhibit a closely corresponding relation to that which lies between them, viz the reason. For the quite specific domain of the 'erotic' is only brought into existence as the reproductive instinct passes up out the merely instinctive life, and penetrates the higher humane life of mind and feeling, and infuses wishes, cravings, and longings in personal liking, friendship, and love, in song and poetry and imaginative creation in general. Whatever falls within the sphere of the *erotic* is therefore always a composite product, made up of two factors ... Another point in which the 'erotic' is analogous to the 'holy' is in having in the main no linguistic expression but terms drawn from other fields of mental life, which only cease to be 'innocuous' (i.e., only became genuinely 'erotic' terms) when it is realized that the lover, like the orator, bard, or singer, expresses himself not so much by the actual words he uses as by the accent, tone, and imitative gestures which reinforce them."[29]

Together with Kaufman's work, this explains somewhat the creative mode of spirit of wo/man and the significance of the imagination at the foundation of religion and the cultus amongst primitive tribes lacking means of inter-tribal communication. The picture has been diversified with the discussion of Roth, who

[29] Otto, *Holy*, 53-58 (43-48).

speaks of the contribution made by the human intellect to the creation of the belief in God, distinguishing between the emotion which leads to deity – as a concept – and the intellect, which brings a wo/man to recognition of his/her God as a specific being – rather than a conceptual, principled, experiential idea.[30] It is easy to reply to Roth by saying that, contrary to his argument, it is difficult to speak about religious wo/man without also speaking of the religious sense, even though the religious person's religiosity derives from feelings of the heart and his/her connection to religion is an emotional one based on the "childhood knowledge" which s/he received with his/her mother's milk. S/he is linked to his/her religion through his/her umbilical cord. In reference to wo/man in the first example – whose religion is emotionally based – it can be said that although his/her religion is not perfect it is deep-rooted and strong. In contrast, the second example shows that an intellectually-based religion lacks roots and existence. It appears that perfect religion requires a synthesis between emotion and intellect. Such a synthesis is demanded not only for the perfect existence of religious belief but also in order for religion and religious rites to enter human experience. Even though it should not be claimed that primitive wo/man was as philosophically sophisticated as modern wo/man, it can be argued – as attempted above – that primitive wo/man instinctively understood that things exist which s/he could not reach on his/her own, things which put the first wheels in motion and influenced his/her life, fears, and destiny. By a similar instinct, s/he also grasped that in order to deal with things outside the world s/he had to find "allies" outside the world on a level similar to that of the forces which drive the concrete world. Such an ally may be his/her deceased father who has passed from this world and in the wake of the phenomenon of renewal and continuity in nature obviously possesses a continuation -- even if this spirit, which reaches beyond reality, may not be his/her father's spirit but the spirit of natural, concrete forces, or a spirit which rests over them and governs them. Primitive wo/man did not necessarily need to make use of spiritual concepts in this respect. The Nuer tribe[31] believe that, in addition to being a beast of prey, a crocodile is a spirit in its own right. It is a spirit in the sense of a kind of god, of a force greater than reality. It can be seen here that the actual crocodile symbolises the deity for the Nuer. Although it is a symbol, in the language of the Nuer it is called "crocodile." This symbolism operates in another area amongst the Nuer in their use of words taken from the world in substitution for the philosophical analysis employed in the modern West. Take the following case, for example: The Nuer are obligated on certain occasions to sacrifice an ox. If the person so obligated is poor and does not posses an ox, s/he will offer a

[30] See Ch.Y. Roth, *Religion and Man's Values: A Selection of Essays* (Jerusalem: Magnes Press,).

[31] See E.E. Evans-Pritchard, *Nuer Religion* (Oxford: Clarendon Press, 1956), 127-28.

cucumber. Because of the person's intention to offer an ox, the cucumber will be considered an ox. It will be called an ox and treated as one. Hundreds of similar examples can be found in the anthropological literature in which a word is taken from the concrete world in order to express what a modern person would require special abstract words to articulate. In summary, despite primitive wo/man's lower scientific, philosophic, and technological standard, as well as the lower material-economic level of his/her standard of living, his/her religious life made a great leap forward. Primitive wo/man discovered and found the deity. S/he did so not out of spiritual longing but because of pressing circumstances, out of a need, and in correspondence with his/her natural inclinations, inclinations which – apparently from the beginning – made him/her a social being.[32] Religion was the source of the rules of social conduct, and in this respect primitive wo/man's religiosity and his/her being a social animal merged together. Religion was forged as a necessary outcome of wo/man's social substance and his/her need as members of a society to obey social rules, rules necessary for the running of society, but which as wo/man-made lacked significant, absolute, and eternal persuasive force.[33] It was necessary to derive these rules of behaviour from the highest source, that which influences and not that which is itself influenced, from an extra-terrestrial force, a force defined as transcendent, whose word must be obeyed. In this way, at

---

[32] See. H. Bergson, *The Two Sources of Morality and Religion* (Garden City, NY: Doubleday & Co., 1935), 13.

[33] See M. Fortes, *Rules and the Emergence of Society* (Royal Anthropological Institute of Great Britain and Ireland, Occasional Paper no. 39), 2. In summarising the views of well-known anthropologists to the end of the twentieth century Fortes argues that society existed from the beginning of humanity and that from the beginning of society a culture existed which distinguished wo/man from the rest of creation, despite the similarity in his/her behaviour such as suckling and procreation. Apart from beliefs, values, and standards of conduct (about which I do not intend to argue), this culture includes knowledge and expertise, as well as the taboo against incest. I must contend the expansive approach which speaks of culture in all its elements, including a culture of technological progress and knowledge which advances the standard of living. It is not necessary to claim that these things existed from the beginning, from the origin of human life. What determined wo/man's human essence and made him/her a human being, beyond the question of the shape of his/her brain, the length of his/her hands, and his/her hunting capabilities, is his/her rules of social conduct, rules which establish the very possibility of human existence, including mutual assistance as a part of social life, society lying at the heart of human existence. Human existence is not defined by the standard of living but by mutual assistance within society. Fortes makes the same point more accurately later in the book (pp. 3-6), in the sense that society does not exist without rules of conduct, that these rules are passed down from generation to generation, primarily through language, which is a necessary component in this process, and that it must be possible to impose these rules on society.

one and the same time, both human culture and (theistic) morality were formed and mutually support one another. Religion will be elaborated as the source of social conduct and ethical codes of behaviour in the following chapter. It should be noted here, however – something which will not be discussed in the next chapter – that religions which do not involve commandments regarding social behaviour, such as the hellenistic Greek pagan religions which, in contrast to Roman religion which contains obligations such as the prohibition imposed on a army general against going out to battle if the sacrifice's innards demonstrate a bad omen (even if this is an obligation on the low side, since the sacrifice's innards only predict the outcome of the battle and caution against going out to war, they do not forbid doing so, even though the consequence resembles a prohibition, for what Roman general will go out to battle if he knows that his defeat is predicted? In order to go out to battle in the sure knowledge of defeat, an extreme religious conviction must operate, like that displayed by those who barricaded themselves on Masada in their lost battle against the Roman forces. The Greeks believed in the existence of gods possessed of supernatural powers, even if their image was very primitive in the sense that they behaved as mortal beings with human attributes. At the same time, the fact that they possessed superior powers, above those of human beings, explained the events which occur amongst mortal wo/men (the gods being immortal) and the Greeks therefore had an explanation for events over which they had no control. In any event, they could understand things and thereby a find partial remedy for their fears. It is true that some things are predestined, as in the story of Oedipus, but wo/man at least understands and thus reduces his/her spiritual anguish. This acts as a sort of spiritual cure. The Greeks also offered sacrifices to appease the gods and in this way endeavoured to minimise the dangers which they faced, dangers whose existence and activities s/he could not prevent in any other way, apart from offering sacrifices to appease the gods. They also possessed a system of foretelling the future, even if one which was very vague, through the Oracle at Delphi. Here too they found a way to strengthen their spiritual life. But, as has been seen, in the sense that primitive African tribes adapted inner-social codes of behaviour for themselves out of their "primitive" religion they were superior to the hellenistic Greeks. It must be assumed that the earliest social crystallization enabled wo/man to hew or to "take" social codes of behaviour from the gods and thus to create a social fabric, since without codes of conduct society cannot exist. It may be that the early Greeks, before the appearance of hellenistic religio-culture, came together in cities and ordered, organised societies on the strength of early religions, before the appearance of hellenistic religio-culture, and on the basis of these behavioural customs hellenistic religio-culture developed, the hellenists already possessing established and crystallized codes of conduct and on the basis of these established behavioural customs, and this religion could depict a world of gods who were not governed by this or that conduct.[34]

Chapter C:
The Impact of Religion on the Modern State throughout History, and on Nationality and Morality

Sigmund Freud:
The description given concerning the benefit which wo/man gains from religion is not a description accepted by everyone. Freud expressed another opinion when he wrote in 1927: "Every civilisation rests on a compulsion to work and a renunciation of instinct ... with the prohibitions that established them, civilisation – who knows how many thousands of years ago – began to detach man from his primordial animal condition culture established on compulsion and on the surrender of the impulse ... We have found to our surprise that these privations are still operative and still form the kernel of hostility to civilisation. The instinctual wishes that suffer under them are born afresh with every child ... Cannibalism alone seems to be universally proscribed. Under certain conditions killing is still practised and indeed commanded by our civilisation ... It is not true that the human mind has undergone no development since the earliest times ... Every child presents this process of transformation to us; only by that means does it become a moral and social being ... Those in whom it has taken place are turning from being opponents of culture into being its vehicles ... Now the degree of this internalization differs greatly between the various instinctual prohibitions ... There are countless civilised people ... who would shrink from murder or incest but who do not deny themselves the satisfaction of their avarice, their aggressive urges or their sexual lusts, and who do not hesitate to injure other people by lies, fraud, and calumny. In such conditions an internalization of the cultural prohibitions among the suppressed people is not to be expected. The extent which a civilisation's precepts have been internalized ... is not the only form of mental wealth that comes into consideration in estimating a civilisation's values. There are in addition its assets in the shape of ideal and artistic creations – that is, the satisfactions that can be derived from those sources ... These satisfactions which the ideal offers to the participants in the culture is thus of a narcissistic nature; it rests on their pride

---

[34] On the "flight" of western secular thinkers from finding an explanation for the need for religion – from completely understandable reasons in terms of the reader who finishes this book – even if these reasons obviously remain in the subconscious and do not find their way to the consciousness of these researchers, the foundation of whose culture world would collapse if they acknowledged the need for religion, see G.S. Kirk, *Myth, Its Meaning and Functions in Ancient and Other Cultures* (Berkeley: University of California Press, 1970), 7-8.

... To make this satisfaction complete calls for a comparison with other cultures which have aimed at different achievements and have developed other ideals. On the strength of these differences every culture claims the right to look down on the rest. In this way the cultural ideals become a source of discord and enmity between different cultural units, as can be seem most clearly in the case of nations ... The right to despise the people outside it compensates them for the wrongs they suffer within their own unit ... Art ... offers substitutive satisfactions ... it serves as nothing else does to reconcile a man to the sacrifices he has made on behalf of civilisation ... When those creations picture the achievement of his particular culture and bring to his mind its ideals in an impressive manner, they also minister to his narcissistic satisfaction. No mention had yet been made of what is perhaps the most important item in the psychical inventory of a civilisation. This consists in its religious ideas in the widest sense – in other words (which will justified later), in its illusions ... Nature ... destroys – coldly, cruelly, relentlessly ... It was precisely because of these dangers with which nature threatens us that we came together and created a civilisation, which is also, among other things, intended to make our communal life possible. For the principle task of civilisation, its actual reason d'etre, is to defend us against nature ... Few people dare hope that she [nature] will ever be entirely subjected to man ... There are the elements ... the earth, which quakes ... water ... diseases... and finally there is the painful riddle of death ...[35]

Freud's writings contain very harsh words regarding the relationship between religion and "culture" – a relationship of opposites, as if (theistic) religion is by definition a-cultural. To Freud, culture means an enlightened and advanced social banding together which makes wo/man[36] higher than the animals in the sense that s/he possesses an ordered and structured social life. Freud defines religion as an organisational principle at the inceptual stage of social life, a stage which is still unenlightened. The roots of this organisation are embedded "in a prolonged lack of salvation and in the child's need for shelter. Over time, when the human being recognises his concrete loneliness and his weakness in the face of the determined forces of life and experiences his situation as similar to his childhood, he seeks to deny his lack of comfort through regressive renewal of the protective forces of his childhood." Freud perceived religion as a veil and an illusion for a wo/man in

---

[35] Freud, *Culture*, 98-106 (10-16).

[36] Ibid, 92. According to Freud, "By human culture I mean everything which raises man's life above the animal state, everything which has some remnant from the animals ... This culture reveals, as we know, two faces to its observer. On the one hand it contains all the knowledge and salvation which a man can acquire in order to subdue the forces of nature and to draw from them the properties for the gratification of human needs, and on the other, all the institutions which he requires for the ordering of human relations, and primarily the ordering of the accessible properties."

flight from adversity who crosses over to the reality of religion. This evaluation serves as the basis of Freud's criticism of religion. According to Freud, religion fetters wo/man's faculties of judgment and stands as an obstacle in the way of insight and knowledge. Religion is the enemy of science. It poses a danger in that it knows how to control wo/man's spirit. It is a "powerful force which governs man's greatest emotions. It once encompassed everything which wo/man considered spiritual, took the place of science when science did not yet exist, and created a conclusive and complete world-view which, while shaken, continued to exist."[37] In light of the date at which this piece was written, before World War II and the concentration camps which the secular Nazi enlightenment produced, it should be noted that the concentration camps gave harsh, if not overwhelming, reply to Freud's belief in modern enlightenment liberated from religion. Moreover, the very essence of Freud's theory which sees human development from the religious period – which in his eyes constitutes human "childhood" – up until the modern period, when humanity matures, wo/man being conceived as an individual who develops and matures, is absurd and untenable. Humanity has no "personality" like that of an individual human being. Freud's negative attitude towards religion blinded his eyes.[38]

---

[37] Ibid, 33-34, in a chapter entitled "Freud and the Criticism of Culture."

[38] In order to persuade his readers to abandon the ethical commandments which various religions impose Freud supplies his readers with a fanciful and untenable explanation of religion as the cause and source of all human morals, an explanation so untenable that we merely need to mention it in a footnote, without devoting any length to its discussion. Freud argues that as a public or society wo/men behave (in their conduct, emotions, and spiritual lives) as though they were neurotic individuals. He fails to explain how he arrives at the conclusion that "We know that the child cannot successfully complete its development to the civilised stage without passing through a phase of neurosis, sometimes of great and sometimes of small distinctness. This is because so many instinctual demands which will later be unserviceable cannot be suppressed by the rational operation of the child's intellect but have to be tamed by acts of repression, behind which, as a rule, lies the motive of anxiety. Most of these infantile neuroses are overcome spontaneously in the course of growing up, and this is true of the obsessional neuroses of childhood. The remainder can be cleared up later still by psychoanalysis treatment. In just the same way, one might assume humanity as a whole, in its development through the ages, falling into states analogous to the neuroses, and for the same reasons – namely because in the times of its ignorance and intellectual weakness the instinctual renunciations indispensable for man's communal existence had only been achieved by it by means of purely affective forces. The precipitates of these processes resembling repression which took place in prehistoric times still remained attached to civilisation for long periods. Religion would thus be the obsessional neurosis of humanity; like the obsession of childhood, it arose out of the Oedipus complex, out of the relation to the father. If this view is right it is to be supposed that a turning-away from religion is bound to occur with the fatal inevitability of

Freud severely criticises religion. He claims[39] against theistic religion that many people are miserable in their religion, that they obey its laws out of lip-service and pressure and that through the help of the priests they use religion as a crutch for immorality no less than for morality. He also argues that in the framework of European Christian culture human belief in religion's promises has dwindled, together with the fact that natural science has exposed the errors which are found in religious literature. He goes on to contend that in such circumstances "No prohibition exists against killing one's fellow except for God's commandment and because the murderer obtains severe punishment either in this world or in the next, for when he confesses to him [to wo/man – Y.C.] that there no gracious and compassionate God and that there is no need to fear His punishment, he will rise up against his fellow and kill him without apprehension, and no human authority can prevent him from doing so."

Kaufman:

Kaufman[40] provides another approach which describes religion as the offspring of nation to whose culture it contributes and fashions: "The cultures of peoples

---

a process of a growth, and that we find ourselves at this very juncture in the middle of that phase of development." In other words, Freud perceives humanity as a child who undergoes periods of development. Ostensibly we are currently experiencing the stage of maturation and the resolution of our (humanity's) childhood neuroses. Freud does not relate to every human culture but to humanity as a universal culture. In this respect, the various primitive tribes which lived independently 300, 3000, or 10,000 years ago in Australia, Africa, and the Pacific Islands constituted one entity which passed down from generation to generation the concrete memory of one primal father (the first man?) who was killed – literally – by his sons and as a result of their spiritual trauma these primal sons experienced – before they dispersed to the various continents – all human beings took it upon themselves to obey the commandments of a god who took the place of the early murdered father in their consciousness – or, in Freud's words (pp. 144-45; 42), "As was shown by the argument which needs no repeating here, the primal father was the original image of God, the model on which later generations have shaped the figure of God. Hence the religious explanation is right: God actually played a part in the genesis of that prohibition; it was His influence, not any insight into social necessity, which created it. The displacement of man's will on to God is fully justified. For men knew that they had disposed of the father by violence and in their reaction to that impious deed, they determined to respect his will henceforward. Thus religious doctrine tells us the historical truth – though subject, it is true, to some modifications and disguise – whereas our rational account disavows it." Freud would like us to accept this fairy tale as "scientific" truth – while he himself denies the other testimony of the revelation on Mount Sinai.

[39] Ibid, 137-40.

[40] Kaufman, *History*, xxx-xxi.

cannot therefore be considered as the fruit of a universal spiritual 'essence.' The culture of a people is not created from a specific 'national spirit' in the sense of a permanent spiritual-ideal being which produces symbols in every cultural sphere. However, the symbolical ideonismus is not produced out of thin air, as has been said. The phenomena upon which it rests are empirical, although as a system it hangs in the air. These phenomena require explanation. It is a fact that there exists a universal coinage and style in human cultures, even if this isn't inclusive and absolute. Ethnic culture isn't a multitude of variable forms but inclines towards the permanent, towards the continuation of 'tradition' and where no foreign influence is wielded people are likely to follow a tradition of culture-style over many generations. Not only does ethnic culture include spherical universality but it also contains a certain measure of inter-spheral universalism, of the sort which Montesquieu advocates, which possesses a 'spiritual' harmony in the people's life and culture. Tyrannical regimes do not go together with spiritual development (education), ascetic religion does not go together with cheerful and sensual artistry, a military character does not go together well with a commercial spirit. No free development of society is possible in the climate and 'spirit' of the Indian caste system. This and more: There are certain phenomena in culture whose essence the symbolic ideonismus expresses well. Not all cultural values are carriers of the 'idea' and are certainly not the expression of one idea. But some cultural values do interweave in this foundation. Religion and everything which it produces is a conceptual entity. Legends, cultus, song, and so forth all serve as an expression and symbol. And because in ancient times almost all the foundations of culture were deeply linked to religion, they too inherited a conceptual foundation from religion. Religion created symbols for itself in construction, sculpture, painting, dance, song and so forth. There is a symbolic foundation behind the attire, decoration, and customs of culture. The judiciary, ethics, the state, the family, and verbal expression are all conceptual entities, and not in the sense that there an idea exists in these spheres – a universal idea, whatever its source likely to serve as the source of image-forming and symbol-making ... On the basis of the empirical observation of the history of culture we have to say that the universalism of culture derives from the influence-wielding force inherent in creativity. When it arose from the spiritual creative force and took form in values, in an 'objective spirit' ... the collective retains values and hands them down from generation to generation."

Kaufman explains here why monotheism, the belief in one God, is the creation of the Israelite nation rather than a natural continuation of the pagan culture of the peoples amongst and within whom the people of Israel dwelt. He also argues that there is no place for the view that belief in one God was the inheritance exclusively of the priests and levites in Israel – of an educated elite alone and not one given to the whole people – and asserts that the claim that this belief was disseminated among the people only after their exile is erroneous. At the same time, and in accord with Kaufman's view, different peoples – even in periods during which religion did not play a central role in their culture – exhibited a particular and characteristic cultural style and special abilities, each in its own way. Being a cultural component, the creation of religion is also a cultural phenomenon. Each example of a unique national culture reinforces the idea that religion may be a national product. A discussion of unique cultures is relevant to this subject, including the modern period, when religion is no longer determinative, generally speaking. The development of seafaring amongst the English and the Spanish, the development of music, and in contrast, in a different epoch, the Nazi regime of fanatical blind obedience which led to the creation of the concentration camps as a German cultural expression, if a horrible and distorted one, or in contrast again, the different style of courtship and love characteristic of the French, Spanish, and English – can therefore be adduced in reinforcement of Kaufman's argument. At the same time, as a degree of disagreement with Kaufman, the Japanese and the English exhibit a measure of correspondence, as do the Jews in Israel and the South Koreans with regard to passivity or activism in judgmental faculties as well as in the general style of inner conversation. This correspondence is created against the background of similar conditions which various peoples shared and which produced similar national experiences.[41] This fact strengthens the possibility that different nations produce similar cultures under similar conditions or when they experience similar traumas, even when they do not share a geographical proximity or have not experienced cross-fertilization.

Insight from comparison:

The differences between Freud and Kaufman with regard to the religious creation can be elaborated and enlarged on thus: Freud favours secular western culture and sees in religion something dark and obscure from whose clutches people should free themselves. Kaufman, on the other hand, perceives religion as a human, national possession which bestows and receives values and experiences and advances wo/mankind and his/her culture – at least in relation to earlier times. In this opposition, and in light of Kaufman's discussion of the divine unity in comparison with ancient paganism, the religious history of wo/mankind can be seen as beginning at a low level in a motif which develops from the primal father, an idea associated with ethnicity.[42] From this initial state of theistic religion as a

---

[41] See Y. Cohen, *Who is Afraid of a Jewish State? A Constitutional and Ideological Examination* (Tel Aviv: The Association of Lawyers Press, 2001), 266, note 19.

[42] One of its marks, which is found until today in the Jewish Prayer Book, can be seen in the prayer recited on taking the Torah Scroll out of the Ark: "Father of compassion, do

national god related to a specific ethnic group religion developed into a higher sphere encompassing the whole world and produced the concept of a God who symbolises unity – the Creator of the world. This transition resembles the experience of Abraham when, according to the midrash, he shattered his father's man-made idols to reach a more spiritual stage which was not "man-made." And now comes modern wo/man and returns humanity to the pagan period by declaring the "death of God."[43] Modern wo/man has substituted the transcendent God who governs wo/man's fate with wo/man him/herself, suggesting that s/he can take control through his/her intellect[44] or through other devices of the human spirit, such as Hobbes' social contract, utilitarianism, the fairness in the agreement which wo/man's makes beyond the "mask of ignorance" according to Rawls, Nietzsche's übermensch, or the postmodern idea that every group of human beings follows its own inclinations and ways. All these concepts resemble a return to paganism, the work of wo/man's hands. Is not modern wo/man's greatest disappointment[45] a mark of wo/man's loss of direction, his/her loss of God? It is not clear whether modern wo/man who "controls" his/her own fate, discerns that his/her decision that s/he must prove God's existence as sh/e must prove other things in the world is an absurd claim for several reasons. Not only is the difference between what exists in reality and what is beyond reality a difference between what is created and influenced and what creates and influences. No one in the created, influenced world can judge or influence the forces of creation which operate in this world. What is created is vulnerable to change and influences; what creates is not vulnerable to change or influences. The created can exist one moment and disappear the next; what creates is not dependent upon anything which is spoken. Consequently, if the forces of the non-influenced creative power exist our "scientific" findings will not influence its transcendence and supernaturalism since it is not something which can be proved by someone whose diagnostic powers – the tool whereby a person proves or disproves a thing, including its limitations – are by definition determined by what creates, which this same tool seeks to discern

---

good with Zion according to Your will; rebuild the walls of Jerusalem. For we trust in You alone, O King, God, exalted and uplifted, Master of worlds." This passage follows another which portrays God in a general, universal context and says: "To you it was shown that you might know that the Lord, He is God; there is no other besides Him. There is none like You among the gods, and there is nothing like Your works. Your kingdom is a kingdom spanning all eternities and Your dominion is throughout every generation" (Art Scroll: 433).

[43] See. R. Aviram "Secularisation as an Introduction to the Growth of the Last Man: Modern Criticism of Friedrich Nietzsche." In D. Stetman and A. Sagi (eds.), *Between Religion and Morality* (Ramat Gan: Bar-Ilan University Press, 1996), 75-94.

[44] According to Kant.

[45] See Abiram, together with the disappointment of contemporary postmodernism.

in order to negate or to verify its existence (of what creates). This issue recalls the ending of the book of Job, which speaks of wo/man's lack of capabilities in the face of divine logic. The only transitional tool which makes human creativity regarding the supernatural world possible is faith. But faith is not a legitimate scientific tool. Faith from the heart does not go together with scientific proof – just as a painting is not linked to science. A painting is the fruit of a person's spirit, even if it belongs to the world of reality. Its material can be tested scientifically and can even be destroyed, but the image which it contains can never be annihilated, nor can it be evaluated scientifically. The same is true of the human spirit which, immediately following its creation by wo/man, lives its own existence. Books can be burnt, but their content cannot be destroyed. The deity may be a product of wo/man's spirit, but once it is created it lies beyond proof. Some of the anthropologists who studied primitive African religions understood when they realized they do not possess the right to determine the truth of primitive religion.[46] The substantial interest which western thinkers have displayed in the field of ethics[47] regarding the truth which morals contain, or the fact that morality must be measured by scientific means and meet scientific standards (according to Dewey), or the difficulty of determining whether morality is a matter of absolute, objective or relative or subjective truth (as though it is clear that morality is a question of truth) – resembles the person who seeks to measure Beethoven's creativity according to scientific standards or to find out whether it contains truth ... The very interest in the philosophy of religion in the sense of the truth of the religious message, or the interest in Jewish thought with respect to the truth of the God of Israel's existence seem displaced. How much better it would be if these thinkers were of the stature of Maimonides or Spinoza.

---

[46] See Gelner, *Concepts*.

[47] Apart from a few who have not taken the western approach. See V. Frankel, *The Unknown God: Psychotherapy and Religion*, trans. by S. Levi (Jerusalem-Tel Aviv: Dvir, 1984), 30-32. The original German edition was published in 1948, the third edition in 1979. Frankel argues that wo/man's conscience is not logical but intuitive and deals with decisions in specific cases and conditions without relating to any "categorical imperative" along the lines of Kant – certainly the opposite of the idea of logical truth. An example of the logical approach can be found in the recent article by J.J. Gross, "Why Do We have an Obligation to Obey God's Commandments" in *Between Religion and Morality* (Ramat Gan: Bar-Ilan University Press, 1994), 43. In a discussion of western and Jewish ethical systems Gross examines obedience to the Jewish religio-ethical commandments on the basis of logical reasoning. The logical tools of analysis do not stop serving the writer even when he gets to the rationale of "the fear of God," when he cites Saadia Gaon's justification of obedience on the basis of logic. It would appear that even he is not immune to the influence of hellenistic logic.

General review:
Alwyn Smith[48] has demonstrated just how much religion in the United States has contributed to the state in describing how all faiths contribute to the consolidation of the American nation in the face of the state's attitude of neutralism/alienation to religion based on the separation of state and religion. This recalls the problematic status of the sabbath and Jewish tradition in the State of Israel. The Israeli High Court, which possess the highest power in the State,[49] has placed these values in a dark corner and acts as if the State were "a state of all its citizens" rather than a "Jewish State" as defined in the Declaration of Independence and ordered Basic Law of 1980. It does so despite the fact that had Jews not observed the sabbath or the Jewish tradition had not existed the State of Israel would not have been established and the Jewish people in general would not have existed up until today, so that there would have been no basis for its own existence.

Religion and state in the modern period:
The advice of the French minister in the wake of the Revolution is well known: For the sake of stability, French citizens should be encouraged to study religion since it evident that the same faithfulness and obedience religious people display to God they are also inclined to exhibit towards the State, of whatever kind it may be. One may impose taxes on them without arousing opposition. Thus to the extent that the religious groupings do not seek to take power, they constitute a faithful and quiet foundation of the State. Obviously this principle does not hold good when the ruling power oppresses the religious simply because of their religion. The unrest in Algeria comes against the background of the attempt by fundamental religious groups to take power, as well as the infringement of their religious, civil, and democratic rights to vote for their preferred candidates for government. Although they won in the free elections which began to be conducted in Algeria, the secular government intervened and stopped the electoral process when it perceived that the religious parties were going to win by democratic vote. The Chechin rebellion against the Russians is an ethnic revolt mixed together with the Chechin religious tradition. The military guerilla movement against the Muslims in Kashmir arose against the background of the inter-religious rivalry for power between Hindus and Muslims. Many central national elements are involved in the Palestinian intifada, together with the strengthening of the Muslim religious faction. The fanatic religious Muslims amongst the Palestinians, who believe that they support national Palestinian interests, strengthen the national foundation within the Palestinian people. The Copts in Egypt endeavour to protect their rights

---

48 See A. Smith, "The Voluntary Establishment of Religion." In E. Smith (ed.), *The Religion of the Republic* (Philadelphia: Fortress Press, 1971), 154.

49 See Cohen, *Afraid.*

in the face of a Muslim majority and even though the Egyptian regime is secular the Copts feel oppressed by the Muslim majority. This is the background of the unrest in Egypt: the Egyptian Muslims are seeking to take power from the secularists, while the latter take care through their constitutional power to preserve the State's fundamentally secular nature and prevent the penetration of fanatic Muslim elements into the governmental system. In Canada – which was founded as an alliance between the Protestant majority and Catholic minority, two communities divided by their religious and cultural allegiance, and whose educational system was dominated by religious interests from both sides right from the beginning – the secular trend towards division of state and religion is growing, together with a call for secularisation of the educational system and an end to the dominance of the English-speaking over the French-speaking populations. The religious groupings are losing their hold on the educational system and are coming to terms with the weakening of their power. In Israel, despite the percentage of religious people and those who support the religious nature of the State – their power and status having grown – the religious way of life is on the wane. The religious in Israel feel that the religious status is being undermined. The religious orthodox population in Israel is in involved in an attempt to defend itself against the secular population, displaying a greater support for Jewish nationalism which expresses itself in greater interest on the part of the non-zionist orthodox in the State's problems and in their willingness to entertain the possibility of a compromise involving concessions regarding the military conscription of yeshiva students such as the well-known Tal law. Growing numbers of religious zionists are serving in elite military combat units. From the perspective of state-religion and religious-national relations, the general picture in Israel is therefore one of a process of greater support on the part of the religious population as a whole for the interests of the State and the Jewish nation.

In the wars between various European nations – al of them Christian – the priests and bishops served as pawns for those in power and the soldiers on both sides frequently found themselves fighting in the name of the same God. They worshipped the same God – just as His priests did – and laboured so mightily on behalf of their country that they brought their nations to the point of war in defence of His honour and name. In the Thirty Years war a catholic cardinal in the French government fought against another Catholic state – Austria – by making an alliance with Protestant forces. Only cynical interpretations can explain the absurdity of religion being used as a pawn – and not for the advancement of religion but for the interests of one king or another. Religion served masters who only worked on behalf of their own power. And during all this time, religion filled important functions in society, the religious ability to enlist people being important to those who held the reins of power.

The above review clearly demonstrates the existence of a widespread phenomenon of religious support for the state and nationalism. Less widespread – in modern days – is the state's support of religion and nationality. There are very few states in which religious institutions aspire to take power, and equally few states in which they even seek a place in the government as a religious institution.

Religion and nation in the modern period:
In discussing the influence of religion on nationality it is important to mention the work of Liah Greenfeld[50], whose doctoral dissertation looks at how Protestantism, the force which established the English in their habit of reading Scripture, also created in them a sense of superiority over their French and Spanish catholic counterparts, the latter being the last to remain dependent upon the priest when seeking to know what is written in the Book of Books. This sense of superiority instilled in the English a pride and sense of uniqueness which, together with their literacy, enabled them to develop a level of commerce and travel which further gained for them a higher standard of living. While the English suffered from famine infrequently and only over short periods of time, the French regularly endured hunger. The literate English were accustomed to reading newspapers, showed a great regard for what happened in parliament and actively participated in the electoral process, and developed an interest in politics. The development of the printing industry was faster in Britain than in any other European country and the literary catalogue flourished. As a result of the sale of ecclesiastical land under Henry VIII, who rebelled against the Pope, the middle class acquired estates, thus creating a new and vibrant class of nobles. Their reading of Scripture also led the English to develop an awareness of constituting the "New Israel" – the chosen people, possessed of a commission on the basis of which they proceeded to create a worldwide empire. They further developed a willingness to serve in the army greater than that evident among the French. English nationalism was founded on the waves of enlightenment which spread and their sense of uniqueness, together with the translation of the Bible into English and their anger at the catholic expulsion of the protestant Huguenots. The persecution of Protestants during the short reign of the catholic Queen Mary also helped to further internal English political processes. The basic element in these processes was the reading of Scripture, a phenomenon which snowballed, created, and supported a special English form of nationalism. In the wake of these developments, falling in battle against the Spanish was considered to be a death more on behalf of the English nation than on behalf of the Crown. The latter thus turned into a tool of the English nation, the "chosen people." Following the "praised" revolution, nationalism gradually established itself in Britain and religion – which had until then played

[50] See L. Greenfeld, *Five Roads to Modernity* (London: Harvard University Press, 1992).

an active part in politics – began to lose its influence, as is evident in the well-known saying (not as a quote from Greenfeld), "The black has done his work, the black can go home." This statement holds also true for the United States, Canada, Israel, and generally speaking with respect to almost all nations in the world, some less and some more. Religion is destined to play the motherly role of nourishing nationalism, and when the daughter grew up on her mother's knees she – nationalism – abandoned the source of her birth – religion – without sustenance, in the spirit of the slogan "separation of state and religion." Linda Colley's book[51] constitutes a continuation in the same spirit as Liah Greenfeld's work, the difference between them lying in the fact that Colley surveys a later period. Here the subject is Britain and the British nation, which combines three separate nations, and not of English nationalism. A further difference can be seen in the fact that the war against the French, which Colley examines in her book, had already taken on a more nationalistic than religious hue, against the background of the earlier aid which the French had extended to the Americans in the latters' revolt against the British and in consequence of the resulting depressions created in Britain. Despite this, religion still had a part to play, and indeed continued to strengthen British nationalist feelings. Greenfeld reviews the crystallisation of Russian nationalism during the days of Catherine the Great and Peter the Great – a period and process in which the pravoslavic religion played a central role on behalf of the Czars. The role of national crystallisation before the American nation had yet been established – a role played by the English-style puritan stream of Protestantism in the United States – is described by Avihu Zakkai.[52] Zakkai depicts how the Americans believe that they are the "chosen people" and as a result how America is also the "promised land". Americans believe up until today, on the basis of their puritan religious background, that God has given them a mission in the world. This belief leads them to disseminate American ideals and the American form of government throughout the whole world. On the other hand, even though Zakkai does not include this in his purview, which focuses on the period up until the American War of Independence, it is known that American excels today in her "castration" of the theistic religions within her boundaries through her adoption of their main festivals as national holidays. She has stolen the unique theistic-religious content from these holidays – first and foremost in their protestant religious form. Thus "Christmas" has become a national holiday in the American civil religious calendar, a holiday which not a few Jews also

---

[51] L. Colley, *Britons – Forging the Nation 1707-1837* (London: Yale University Press, 1992).

[52] See A. Zakkai, "Religion and Revolution: The Contribution of Puritan Rhetoric to American Democracy." In Democracy in America (Tel Aviv: Zemora-Beitan Modan, 2001).

celebrate, the same have happened earlier to Thanksgiving, whose original purpose was to give thanks to Jesus, within the protestant religious framework, for the good which he gave to the protestant immigrants to America. The United States is the only enlightened country in the world in which catholic parents who send their children to a catholic school bear the costs of this education, while protestant parents – who do not need a protestant school but are quite happy sending their children to public schools in consequence of the different educational ideals held by catholics and protestants – are not required to pay for their children's education. In this sense it is not protestant religion which is favoured but Protestants, as adherents of the American civil religion, since the public school system in America is the cradle of American civil religion. Since the end of the nineteenth century, even reading of the Bible in public schools has been prohibited, such reading being a protestant custom and the separation of church and state being stricter than in any other western nation. No representative of any theistic religion is allowed in the United States – as a public religious official – to stand for election to government. In this way American civil religion has become the sole recognised legal religion of America. This demonstrates the truth of the axiom "free religion supports nationalism" – but once nationalism has strengthened itself on the back of religion it kicks religion down the steps leading to power (in the States, to the Capitol).

Summary of the relations between religion and the state and nationalism:
The removal of religion from politics did not do any good to nations and peoples with respect to their internal crystallisation. American is one example of this, where national identity has been weakened due to Americans' dual loyalty – to the State on the one hand and to one's country of birth on the other.[53]
As has been seen, religion possess great power, and the force of nationalism is even greater, as shall become clear in Part 3, due to be published soon.[54] When religion and nationalism join forces, they become particularly powerful, as can be seen from the different responses of Israeli Arabs to the rumour that Haram al-Sharif – the El Aksa mosque – was under threat. Israeli Arabs did not participate in the first intifada with their Palestinian brethren. In the second, however, the rumour concerning the mosque was sufficient to drive them to join. This demonstrates the combination of two foundational elements, the national and the religious. The struggle in Kashmir is also a combination of these two elements. Likewise, the troubles in Northern Ireland bear the stamp-marks of the

---

[53] See M. Walzer, *What it Means to be an American* (New Delhi: Affiliated East-West Press, 1994).

[54] The anticipated publisher is HaUma, the tentative title being: "Jewish and Arab Nationalism in Israel."

catholic-protestant conflict which arose on the heels of the British-Irish, or English-Irish, conflict. The war between Iran and Iraq demonstrates similar characteristics, apart from its national element, in its Sunni-Shi`ite rivalry. In general, the Israeli-Palestinian conflict is also a combination of the two elements of religion and nationalism. Religion's power expresses itself both for good and for bad. Side by side with the vicious fighting conducted in the name of religion – religion's negative face – the influence of theistic religion on morality began from the dawn of history and continues up until this day.[55]

Religion and Ethics:

The power of theistic religion can be clearly seen in its strong influence on morality, an influence which continues to exist even when people have stopped believing in religion or adhering to it. It may be said that a wo/man without God in his/her heart lacks the spiritual weight which might give him/her and his/her race the rules of conduct to which the heart is drawn. The concept of "God" here goes back to the definition given at the beginning: God is any idea or heart-faith which directs the actions of the person who adheres to the particular idea or faith. In order to exist, morality must constitute a special inner quality. It must be able to convince a person to behave according to its dictates, as well as persuade his/her human environment to exert public ("moral") pressure on him/her to make sure that s/he will behave thus. The concepts that governmental laws are insufficient to guarantee conformity – in the sense of compliance to an ordinance in order that the law will prevail and that human beings must get to a state in which the majority of human beings in society are convinced that it is right to comply with the law – and the need for moral laws to be a more powerful persuasive force than the force of law have been addressed by Hart, who differs in this respect from Austin's views.[56] Immanuel Kant's theory may be understood against this particular background of theistic religion's influence derived from its supernatural nature, together with its objectivity, derived from the same source and in contrast to human subjectivity derived from wo/man's mortality and dependence on the world. Kant sought the source of morality in a place unconstrained by concrete reality. He claimed that moral laws must be created out of pure practical reason. This view may be interpreted and understood in light of the central problematic of

---

[55] On the influence of religion in the modern period, see the Introduction in the last edition of Dewey's *Reconstruction in Philosophy* (London: University of London Press, 1921); Y. Ezrahi, "Modes of Reasoning and the Politics of Authority in the Modern State," in O. Torrance and N. Torrance (eds.), *Modes of Thought: Explorations in Culture and Cognition* (Cambridge University Press, 1996), 72-89); L. Devlin, "The Enforcement of Morals," in D.R. Devlin (ed). The primitive period has been examined in the authors cited in notes 8, 23, 28, 32.

[56] See H. Hart, *The Concept of Law* (Oxford: Clarendon Press, 1991-97), 6-7, 193, 201ff.

the period, the problem of alienation from an immutable source of moral laws in the past – the divine source – and from the non-discovery of a substitute source whose validity cannot be questioned – just as in the religious period the religious source of moral laws could not be doubted. What will a person seeking for such a source, who believes in human reason, do? S/he will consider it possible for human reason which is not embedded in personal interests and inclinations to be accepted as an impeachable source of moral laws – and that this "invention" has the power to save the human society (white, European, Christian society) in which s/he lives from the anticipated chaos due to the loss of the theistic source. And indeed this was a successful invention in Kant's time for the wo/man who had removed the fetters of theistic morality and divine authority from over him/herself and seated him/herself on the seat of authority in his/her world. In this way a person is delivered from the undermining of his/her control. According to Kant's thesis, this person could be strengthened and find a way through his/her own resources (and with the aid of his/her own pure practical reason as a rational being) and to impose a moral imperative on him/herself and on his/her fellows to replace the divine imperative. In this way it was possible to come to terms with the secular revolution of the great rebellion against God. This constitutes a purely analytic way to rebel against Him, even though Kant, contrary to his own ethical system, remained a believer in God. Indeed, this is one of the tragic aspects of Kant's personal experience.[57]

Regarding the educated discussion of morality and religion and the power of both, the source of which lies in theistic religion, one must stop and ask: Is morality a matter of emotion or intellect? Is religion a matter of emotion or intellect? Does the power of theistic religious morality derive from emotion or from intellectual persuasion? And consider: the religious and ethically-motivated person is a being of dual inwardness – i.e., a being given to both intellect and emotion. He serves both attributes, even though the second part of this book will demonstrate that a hierarchy obtains between them and that emotion has the upper hand.

This raises a lengthy discussion, all of whose issues not be able to resolve here. It has been seen that the different positions of Kaufman, Otto, and Roth[58] represent three ways of approaching God or recognising His/Her existence. This subject cannot be exhausted in this part of the book. As will become clear later, wo/man always follows the inclination of his/her heart and only when his/her heart (or emotions) do not explicitly guide him/her in a specific direction does s/he turn to

---

[57] See I. Kant, ** (Jerusalem: Magnes Press, 1998), 10. On Kant's argument that morality does not derive from human beings but from pure practical reason, see pp. 63, 68, where Kant speaks of the complete objectivity of the imperatives which derive from pure practical reason.

[58] See notes 28, 29, and 31.

his/her intellect and enlist its help in reaching a decision. The power of religion is primarily the power of emotion, and no philosophical analysis of deity can change this fundamental fact. Morality is also, in its essence, a matter of emotion, neither Kant's theory of pure practical reason, nor Hobbes' insight into the social contract, nor even the logical American commercial system of Rawls regarding the public consensus based on the veil of ignorance and – a proper (commercial-like) consensus being able to deal with the biblical morality of the senses which continues to influence the conduct of the western individual, as will be demonstrated in chapter 5 of this book, which reviews the work of Rawls, Nozick, and American injustice.

Secular western culture, known for its science, among other ways also through mechanistic means according to Darwinian evolutionary theory which is devoid of emotion, has attributed the concept of morality, which has been considered to be a matter of emotion here, to evolution. Sober and Wilson[59], who contend that, in contrast to the prevalent view in the 1960's that the natural human tendency which corresponds to human genes is not necessarily selfishness and that what directs wo/man is not wo/man him/herself (whether by means of his/her intellect or in the framework of emotions) but human genes. While genes are actually "selfish," concerned with self-perpetuation, to the extent that they are implanted in a social being – wo/man – they are "preoccupied in an egoistic-selfish manner" with their self-propagation in the framework of society or a given group – in other words, they are concerned with the self-preservation of the group. Sober and Wilson argue that the guarantee of the existence of a given human society requires the presence of altruistic individuals who place the good of their fellow-citizens over their own personal good. Genes consequently "direct" the conduct of individuals in society towards altruism rather than towards individual egoistic tendencies.

This is a phenomenon examined by Rudolph M Nesse[60], who asserts that according to this principle the mother who cares for her children tenderly and with love does not do so out of maternal feelings but in order to satisfy the selfish needs of the genes of the group to which she belongs. Her behaviour is not due to altruistic motives but a result of her feminine genes. Nesse consequently asks whether it is not reasonable to think that these same genes will make sure that more males will be born than females, since that will produce more genes of the

---

[59] See E. Sober and D. Wilson, "Summary of: 'Unto Others, the Evolution and Psychology of Unselfish Behavior'," *Journal of Consciousness Studies* 7 (2000), 185-206. This article discusses the authors' book, published by Harvard University Press under the same title in 1998. See also the continuation of the discussion there by a list of respected critics, and the authors' responses, 207-268.

[60] Ibid, 228-229.

same type. The fact that males are able to produce many females avoids the need for an equal distribution (50/50) between males and females. Nesse also contends that the social perspective demands the preference (in terms of the male group, which is the dominant one) of sexism and that in the framework of the ethnic group, members of the same ethnic community will be preferred, that in a national group the national motive will be preferred, and in a racial group race will be preferred. He asks whether this is the way in which morality develops in practice, the natural answer being that if this does not constitute the sole permanent stream in human beings Sober and Wilson's argument is defective.

It is a pity that despite such a forceful argument, with its fundamentally correct basis, Nesse is trapped in the web of the western society in which he flourishes and rather than destroying the theory which he criticises so harshly he contents himself with adding additional motives to those of Sober and Wilson, numbering four in all:

a) Social classification. The person who deviates from the path which society values and removes it from his/herself. Here Nesse repeats Sober and Wilson's theory, acknowledging his debt to the latter but also arguing that they do not make their claims explicit. This point applies both to Nesse and to Sober and Wilson, who also addressed the topic. Social esteem and social sanctions, even state sanctions (in a state), are merely tools and means and do not provide a remedy for defects in the system, of which Nesse speaks.

b) Altruism derived from commitment. According to Nesse, commitment is expressed by the person who possesses the quality of decency, or derives from love. Nesse argues that the person who does not possess a sense of decency does not live up to his/her commitments in a time of crisis and that the decent person carries greater weight in his/her society. This a form of social selection according to which decent people are preferred. Regarding love, Nesse asserts that it gives a person inner power to stand behind his/her commitments. Human genes will consequently prefer decent people and those with the capacity to give and to receive love. Nesse adds that only the person who is capable of loving gains the ability to be loved. In this way he turns the delicate emotion of love into a genetic game or, more accurately, into a pawn under the rules of the genes which play with these tools and prefer this utilitarian attribute, called love. Nesse thereby falls into the field into which he himself is shooting arrows and turns love into something to be ridiculed, something which exists only for the utilitarian value which can be drawn from it. Wo/man him/herself turns his/her emotions into a game of human genes. Wo/man does not possess the capacity of decision or choice but is a pawn in his/her very essence. In place of the Jewish principle that "everything is foreseen, yet the freedom of choice is given" – in which wo/man stands opposite God – human genes have become God. Genes, however, are a much crueler God, heartless and very, very cold.

c) Sexual relations. Nesse recalls that wo/man's structure necessitates that s/he conduct protracted sexual relations and carries an inherent tendency towards relationships. He remarks that in choosing a partner, intellect, wisdom, pleasantness, and other qualities, including goodness of heart, are considered very important. Here too Nesse follows, unsuccessfully, the cold path of western reason and does not even attempt to loose himself from its grip. Once love has turned into a beating stick in the framework of the "section" on commitment and utilitarianism, goodness of heart becomes an appendix to rationality and human intellect. Its value is due merely to the benefit which people who favour it gain from it. It is through goodness of heart that wo/man merits protracted sexual relations according to his/her natural aspiration, and human genes, which oversee from above (or perhaps from below), produce happy and good hearted genetic types from the same business-utilitarian good-heartedness.

d) The possibility of transition to another group. Here Nesse adopts the western openness which cuts itself off from its own roots. In this he deviates from Darwinian evolutionary principles. Do human genes receive information through some sophisticated means of communication regarding a person's decision to move to another group? Do they transfer the original gene type of this person, the essence of the self, to the care of genes from another family in response to some such "message,"? How do two gene types communicate? The whole theory becomes confused, even though it is stamped with the seal of western rationality and openness, which is itself tied to confusion, as shall be seen in the framework of the criticism levied against the West in Parts 2, 5, 7.

In general, the work of Sober and Wilson and Nesse is based on Darwinism, the theory which promised that it would explain in the future how all beings developed through evolution. With the emergence of this doctrine Darwin claimed that the fact that anthropological research did not contain a continuity of findings regarding the transition from single-cell beings to superior beings – derived from the short period during which, correct to Darwin's time, excavations and the collection of biological findings were collected. Today, another fifty years have passed and this continuity has not been fulfilled. Despite this, the secular West still clings to Darwin's theory. The question is: Is this clinging due to the fact that western secularism has not found a substitute concept? The framework of the existing concept has erected a barrier which hides from our eyes the relationship between emotion and morality and directs our thoughts away from theistic religion and emotion to civil religion and logic, as will be examined in detail in Parts 2-4.

The last word about religion with regard to the question "Is religion a matter of morality or intellect?" has not yet been said. The answer received from the wo/man in the street, generally speaking, when s/he is an uneducated secular person, clearly indicates that religion is a matter of emotion – that wo/man "senses" whether or not a certain action is moral. The educated secular western person, in contrast, usually replies that religion is a matter of logic. The religious person will respond that a divine morality stands above secular morality, a morality based on God's commandments rather than feelings or logic. These three answers reflect different periods of development in human history, as well as different approaches to one's relationship with God. As noted above, the secular person sought substitutes for God's commandments, the only plausible replacement found being something s/he him/herself created, whether through pure practical reason, the social contract, or in other ways which this chapter has examined. In this way modern wo/man reached a general crisis. The two other answers unite, religious morality being tied to emotion – just as religion itself is tied to emotion. To this is joined the insight proffered above regarding the preference of emotion over intellect in wo/man's decision-making. Emotion is something deep rooted and clear which give direction; the intellect hovers and possess no orientation. This chapter suggests that the roots are vital to wo/man, morality not being a matter of truth and logic as much as a matter of emotion. Emotion joins together the family cell and the ethnic weave, two of the strongest fabrics which have proved themselves from the beginning of human existence and are appropriate to wo/man in light of his/her natural tendencies.

Beyond the general discussion conducted here regarding religion and morality much debate has been expended amongst western thinkers regarding the source of morality in human society, debates which, while mentioning religion, have recalled it alongside other causes. Such thinkers include the psychoanalyst Sigmund Freud, the sociologists Emile Durkheim, Black, and Christopher Boehm, and biologists like Matt Ridley.[61] Freud and Durkheim referred to field studies on the totem amongst Australian, African, and American tribes, an almost unified phenomenon despite clear evidence that no communication existed between them. The central features of this phenomenon were a) a prohibition against sexual relations between mother and son and brother and sister, but not between father and daughter; b) the prohibition against patricide; c) tribal allegiance obligating mutual aid and assistance between a man and his wife's family members, an obligation which did not apply to the members of the father's side of the family.

As already described in this chapter, Freud spoke in of his field of inquiry and specialty of one primal father common to all the tribes who reserved all the women in the group for his personal sexual needs and satisfaction and forbade his sons sexual relations with them – until the sons rebelled and killed him. In order to

---

[61] See Durkehim, *Elementary*; ibid, *On the Division of Power in Society* (London: Macmillan, 1933); A. Brill, *The Basic Writings of Sigmund Freud* (NY: Modern Library, 1938); C. Boehm, "Conflict and the Evolution of Social Conflict," *Journal of Consciousness Studies* 7:1/2 (2000), 79-102; Black, *Human Instincts and the Evolution of Cooperation* (NY: Penguin, 1996).

prevent further conflict between them they imposed on themselves a prohibition against conducting sexual relations with their mother and sisters. The guilt feeling they experienced at having murdered their father and the prohibition against sexual relations with female family members of the first degree passed down as an inheritance and thence arose the prohibition against murder and incest. This theory is hard to accept. It is difficult to think that a guilt feeling is passed down through the generations and it is hard to imagine that a single son not in conflict with his brothers would be prevented from engaging in sexual relations with his sister on the basis of an event which occurred in the distant past,. It is difficult to ascribe general rules of morality which remain permanent over generations to a single event. It is more logical to assign similar moral codes to human nature which does not change in its fundamentals over generations, a nature which produces similar motifs across different cultures.

Durkheim speaks of values which differ from society to society and guide community opinion, the latter imposing rules of conduct in correspondence to these values. While his work is undoubtedly correct on the field level, his conclusions do not go sufficiently deep to uncover the source of the values – the source of morality. Although values are moral principles determined as particular rules according to Durkheim, the question of how these principles were created and the foundation of morality still remains unanswered.
Black refers to social forces which influence controversies and social supervision. But interested social forces change, whereas the foundations of morality are fixed and permanent. It may be that a certain temporary force may dictate rules of behaviour acceptable to group A (let us assume men, or people from a certain ethnic group, for example), but when the society's social structure changes the play of forces also changes, causing a change in rules of conduct as well. Moral codes are fundamentally immutable.
Ridley holds to Darwinian theory and places morality within the same sphere as biological evolution. Morality does seem to have become purer over the generations, however, and if once women and slaves were oppressed, today the situation has changed for the better. While biological evolution – if this theory still stands in the face of the many negative proofs against it – is a necessary process tied to the substance and rules of nature, as well as to the use and even the very essence of existence, morality is an existential phenomenon, even though it does possess utilitarian value. And despite being realized in practical living, it possesses a spiritual element and relation to what is above and beyond the concrete world. Just as love between the sexes is not confined to sexual relations, even though it is connected to them, so also morality cannot be reduced to the biological, even though a link can be made between them, and not necessarily in an analogical sense. The initial source of morality is certainly not assisted by Darwinian theory.

For this reason the similarity of behaviour displayed by other mammals is nto instructive. Human morality is spiritual and tied to emotion and must consequently be dissociated from biology.
Boehm speaks of socio-political forces which hold the power to oppress groups or the person who deviates from the path, forces which are intended to prove the point which politic power groups aspire to make. This approach also seems too shallow to reach the depths of the anthropological perspective which will lead to understanding the origin of morality.

Chapter D:
Is the Existence of a Non-religious Person Possible?

Geertz[62] suggests that "The drive to find meaning in trials, to give it form and order, is no less concrete or urgent than the more familiar biological drives. As argued here, no need exists to interpret human symbolic activities – religion, art, ideology – as if they were nothing else but some veiled expressions of something else. They should be taken at face value: Attempts to develop an orientation for an organism which cannot live in a world it does not understand."[63] In the light of Geertz' more detailed earlier explanations it appears that human symbolic actions – which include religion and ideology in general (the latter has been included within the definition of religion for the purposes of this discussion) – are necessary for wo/man since they provide mortal human beings with the only way of obtaining "objective" answers (in Geertz's terms) to questions to which they can find answers nowhere else – such questions being eternally present in human life. In other words, wo/man will always need religion.
Geertz argues that wo/man's possession of an absolute will to understand constitutes a direct source of theistic religion and an indirect source of morality as derivative of religion. He also asserts that the construction of ethics by such philosophers as Aristotle, Spinoza, and Moore is irrelevant since it is not founded on an empirical basis. Earlier, he links Taylor's statement that human beings need religion in order to be convinced that "God is not crazy" with Carver's claim that "man can somehow adapt to everything with which his imagination can grasp; but he cannot endure chaos."[64]
From this it appears that Geertz proposes that wo/man's fundamental need is to make order in his/her world and that this necessarily brings him/her to theistic

[62] See C. Geertz, *The Interpretation of Cultures*, trans. By Yoash Meisler (Jerusalem: Keter, 1973), chs. 4-5.
[63] Geertz, ibid, *Interpretation*, 136.
[64] Geertz, ibid, *Interpretation*, 99.

religion. The ethical system which religion imposes further plays a central role in human life. However, Geertz's theory adds a further dimension to the basic emotional factor which leads human beings to seek transcendental connection with God as the sole way of overcome their fears and impotence in the face of forces which they find to be governed by powers outside the world, as already explained. It is difficult to see the need to make order and natural curiosity to discover explanations for everything as a necessary source of the motivation to obey what God commands, to restrain oneself from one's lusts and appetites, and to agree to the infringement of one's basic interests, as the religious person does. The fear of death is far stronger than curiosity. Extinction due to sickness, floods, drought, beasts of prey, and enemies is far more powerful a force than the difficulty which a person experiences in the face of a lack of order in his/her world.

At this point, Geertz's theory intersects with Weber's work on charisma.[65] In this selection of essays, Eisenstadt explains Weber to say that "The charismatic trait in man ... in his connection to ... God ... a holy or transcendental power ... rules which govern the universe ... most human beings ... do not come into contact whatsoever with such an awesome power. But most of those who are incapable of reaching Him by themselves, respond – at least from time to time – to His revelations through the words, actions, and creations of others who do succeed in finding Him ... the response to charismatic traits and actions ..." A little later Geertz elaborates on Weber's argument that the obedience to transcendent messages which charisma conveys exists "under conditions which are liable to be ambiguous, undefined and contradictory, situations in which his identity is threatened by some danger, with respect to a likeness to his status or his ability to sustain a consistent view on the world in general and social order in particular." Weber's opinion and method is interwoven with and linked to the main arguments made above in regard to primitive wo/man's relationship to the transcendental source in times of crisis and danger and the continued need for a religious dimension as long as wo/man faces difficulties and fears and lack of confidence – in other words, as long as s/he lives and is alive.

The present contention is that above explanations concerning wo/man's fears, combined with Geertz's ideas, should be adopted. Together with other anthropologists, Geertz concurs that wo/man is a social creature and that s/he cannot conduct a social life without rules of behaviour and morality which, when they receive the backing of governmental institutions in the state, become legal regulations. Although rules of law are backed up by governmental institutions and state enforcement, the power of the latter is limited, so that the main source of authority behind the laws rests on public consensus. This consensus rests on a

---

[65] See M. Weber, *On Charisma and the Construction of Institutions* (Jerusalem: Magnes Press, **), Intro. pp. 17-19.

conviction that the sources of the laws are legitimate and that this legitimacy possesses validity the more legitimate its source. When speaking of moral laws, the legitimacy of their source is particularly important. In the eyes of its adherents, the commandments of theistic religion possess the value of things which are "objectively" right to do – in contrast to everything else whose source is wo/man, a subjective being.[66]

As has been seen, the dominance of theistic religion over the hearts of human beings is firm and strong, even amongst people who do not believe the claims of theistic religion to be true, and even amongst states which have removed the right of participating in the governing process from theistic religion.

It may be right to attribute the strength of theistic religions – apart from the proven value of the ethical systems which they have produced – to the fact that modern society, which is undergoing frequent and successive changes because of the modern element inherent in it, is finding a growing need for spiritual support in order to cope with such challenging changes to a spirit which feels its foundations being threatened and its picture of the world being changed. Support for transitions was created in primitive societies from the period of the dominance of primitive religions – as will be seen in the discussion of the work of Mircea Eliade in Chapter 1 of Part 8 and at the beginning of Chapter 2 in this Part – whether rituals linked to changes in the season of the year or those associated with puberty/maturity and other rites of passage. The modern world faces many more changes than the primitive world did, on the one hand, and the ritual and other support systems which societies have created since the religious and primitive period have been destroyed. The challenge to modern wo/man's spiritual life is one of the greatest problems of the modern world. Being a nation of immigrants, modern American society has received a double share of these problems. An immigrant who enters into the modern experience undergoes many more changes than the individual in a society constituted by an ethnic group rooted in its location for many years which makes the transition into the modern world as a group and not as a mass of individuals.[67]

At any rate, when the concept of "religion" is expanded to include the belief in any ideal, including civil religion[68], and when it is considered that no society can exist

---

[66] See Geertz, *Interpretation*, 91, 131.

[67] On the particular problems of American spiritual life, see J. Pfister and N. Schnog, *Inventing the Psychological: Towards a Cultural History of Emotional Life* (New Haven: Yale University Press, 1997).

[68] Regarding African civil religion, see T. Dunbar Moodie, *The Rise of Afrikanerdom: Power, Apartheid, and the Afrikaner Civil Religion* (Los Angeles: University of California Press, 1975); C. Liebman and E. Don-Iyechiya, *Civil Religion in Israel: Traditional Judaism and Political Culture in the Jewish State* (Los Angeles: University of California Press, 1983). For American civil religion, see footnote 47.

without faith on the part of all its citizens in some central idea out of which or on the basis of which moral codes or the law (such as the idea of "democracy" – itself a form of religion), it is clear that there is no society without religion at its centre.

Chapter E: Why Religion?

It must be remarked straightaway that the question "Why religion" can be understood in at least two ways. This Part intends to deal with both aspects. The first meaning is causal, while the second is teleological. "Why religion" may be a question of the chain of events – how and by what causes the sudden appearance of religion in human society was produced. The second meaning relates to wo/man's destiny, to the question which wo/man asks him/herself: "Why do I need religion?"(in the sense of its future benefit) or "Why religion" (in the sense of something which will direct his/her path to a purpose on whose behalf it is good and right for him/her to exist, something which will turn wo/man from an "animal" to a human being, superior to the beasts. The question of religion's value for the future is linked to the causal version – how religion appeared in human life. The question of spiritual purpose is that which gives meaning to human life, a question which elevates us to the heights, a question whose answer is worth seeking, aspiring to, as a purpose for our human life, both as individuals and as societies.

It has been seen, in terms of the cause and the motivater, that religion appeared in human life as a vital social need, as a way of enabling human beings to organise their lives in a social framework and to conduct a society, as well as to strengthen the human spirit in the face of difficulties and dangers with which material forces were insufficient to deal. This was the need, first and foremost an existential-organisational need, together with a spiritual need.

With respect to its future value, the historical need is affirmed and is sufficient to prove that people need religion, both for human existence and organised social life and as a support for human souls, in addition to the rationalistic mental health treatment which modern practioners endeavour to give people. But religion possesses a greater and deeper task than this, a task which it indeed fulfils, and one must merely locate this and say confidently: People need religion in order to be human beings. A person who believes in nothing, who is solely preoccupied with his/her standard of living, with his/her "quality of life," in the modern sense of the word – even if s/he has a private plane and island or beach, even if s/he own a chain of stores and plays the stock market – is not necessarily by that fact a human being. S/he is merely an animal, in the guise of a human being.

Part 2: Myth and Religion

The discussion will focus on the detailed narratives that are found in Ancient Christianity, Nazi Race Laws, Imperial China, Ancient India and Ancient Japan.

Chapter A:
Social Definitions of the Concept "Myth"

>From a social science perspective it would seem correct to deal with the concept "myth" by looking at the limits of its influence upon the crystallization of society or upon other social processes while at the same time putting the emphasis on the cultural aspect, as the concept "culture" is broadly defined. For this purpose this last mentioned concept will, at one and the same time, include religious culture and national culture as well as any other uniquely cultural element. This approach appears to be the correct one, especially since myths are a socio- cultural phenomenon. Myths do not relate to the individual per se but rather to his capacity to act within his social environment. Myths are only promulgated within a social class. There exists no human society which does not possess some type of myth in its traditions. It is not possible to unify society into one bloc without the assistance of a grand myth, and in the same vein it is not possible to have a society that does not believe in a religion, as this concept is very broadly defined. The term "religion" includes those non- theistic religions which are adhered to by their followers, although they have not been nor cannot be scientifically proven, and yet those people who believe in them conduct their lives according to the norms that they think these religions demand of them or according to norms that can be either inferred or linked to those very specific religions. In a later discussion the spotlight will turn its attention to those pagan societies that are not bound by any ordinances emanating from a transcendental source, viz. the pagan sphere, and yet there are also among them ethical rules that relate to their way of life and which, as a consequence of their belief in the deities, become binding, not because they are precepts that emanate from the Above, but because they are vital in weaving the social tapestry that is necessary for sustaining the belief in these pagan gods. Later on the differences between individual morality and horizontal morality will be raised for discussion. It is patently obvious that within modern secular society, the rules and principles of behavior are determined by making reference to a basic belief system, a system that is responsible for forming the foundation stone, which is at the core of, and which sustains that society's faith in its specific organizational structure.

Myths are responsible for the phenomenon of social integration; they act as the unique identity card for every type of culture. There is no society (religious or national) that does not have at least one unique cultural nuance and therefore a unique myth of its own. In a situation where there are no recognizable differences between various cultural groupings from the cultural, religious, mythological, and ritual perspectives, that is a sign that that these different cultural groupings are only at the beginning stages of unifying into a separate entity and breaking off from a wider cultural environment. Things may also be moving in the opposite direction and it may then also be a sign that the various, and previously separate, cultural societies are crystallizing into one cultural bloc where they weave together their various experiences to form a new enlarged social tapestry representative of a mega cultural grouping.

What is ritual? Ritual may be defined as an activity in which cultural groupings or sections thereof perform certain ceremonies or enact a pseudo- drama. It is an activity which brings to life a fundamental idea that the community firmly supports. This idea is used as a building block for the construction of shared social values. Whereas a myth informs the reader of an event that occurred, a ritual is the physical reenactment of that historical event.

Not every story can be classified a myth, neither is every show that is performed deemed a ritual. The staging of a Shakespearean drama can obviously not be called a ritual; neither can the script of such a play be classified as a myth. This is because this kind of play will find a comfortable audience amongst groups of various cultural backgrounds; it having ceased to act as a unifying factor in the formation of an English cultural and national identity. If it could be said, for the sake of honing in on this analogy, that the performance of such a play in England looks and sounds very different to any other country or society that is not English, and that the audience watching the play, be they in Liverpool or in London, understand things from a totally different angle than the tourists who are part of that same audience and who are watching the drama unfold at the same time, it would be appropriate to term this play an English ritual and to define its script as an English myth. These types of plays could theoretically be classified as uniquely English depending on their extent of solidifying an English identity as opposed to a universal one.

One of the trademarks of a **nation** is the fact that it is constructed on the lap of myths and rituals that are able to relate specifically to the heart of that community of men who view themselves as a distinct nation. With rituals and myths acting as the backdrop for their uniqueness, the English are endowed with the feeling of a mutual internal closeness that differentiates them, at least in their own eyes, from all other national groups.

What is **the secret of social construction** that is buried in myths and in rituals? Outside of the nuclear family and those modest sized social groups where each member is vested with the authority to voice his own personal opinion and whose membership is small in number, it is not possible to maintain internal social adhesion without using methods that adequately substitute intimate personal recognition. This type of personal recognition is the basis for the sense of belonging and of feeling closely bound up, a sense that develops within man at a very tender age and which continues to play a role into adulthood and especially among his own group of peers towards whom this particular man feels a sense of intimacy. Familiarity is the "mother" of all human relationships. Human social life is built on familiarity; familiarity with those things that are close to us, at its very core, is something that accompanies memories of childhood or other intimate memories. Familiarity is also the basis for strengthening human solidarity. For example, when many women of various cultural backgrounds have a common familiarity with what it means to experience a menstrual cycle and where each has bitter and shared memories of being cast off into the margins of society by the more dominant men folk, it is possible that a certain feminist solidarity may even tie two women who hail from cultural milieus where the lingua franca is different, where the national interest and professions of each are at variance with the other, and whose fields of interest are totally unconnected. This is a case of solidarity that arises out of shared memories. A similar theme was employed by the playwright who penned the Greek drama *Lysistrata* where women from enemy camps cooperate with one another since their matter of cooperation fulfils a task that reflects the common feminine point of view on war, a point of view that despises war which for them acts as a bitter reminder of the maternal pain that is suffered when these women lose a son or husband on the battlefield.

When it comes to the formation of a society, as opposed to the examples of solidarity and sympathetic understanding between women who hail from different societies and which very societies are oftentimes at conflict with one another, there must be a varied and multilayered relationship between the parties in which each shares the finest and most personal chartraits and which relationship in turn creates a network of feelings of solidarity and a desire to assist in the forming of a group to the extent that the said group feels a sense of alienation towards anyone who is not part of the same network. A strong closeness within the group, when its foundations are embroidered together by feelings of mutuality, strengthens the sense of alienation and difference that is felt towards others who are not part of that group's network. Closeness and alienation are two sides of the same coin; an intimate collective feeling of closeness is the cause of a feeling of alienation towards anyone who does not belong to that group. In order that these feelings of alienation towards this outsider are annulled, the latter must first and foremost be accepted as a member of that group.

The value of the myth and ritual rests on the above mentioned foundations. Year in, year out Jewish children coming from different backgrounds all enjoy the same Passover *Seder* experience, even if these selfsame children never meet each other and even if the ceremonies are not all alike. Each participant asks the same "four questions", each, in a pseudo- ritual way, "steals" the *afikoman* that the father or other central male figure in the family has hidden, and each receives gifts for their agreement "to return safely the stolen *afikoman*". Each *Seder* experience places the ceremonial at centre stage and thus raises the importance of each member of the family who are thrown into the centre by virtue of the fact that without their active participation the ceremony will not be properly performed. The story of the Israelites' exodus from Egypt which is retold during that ceremonial occasion is a grand myth that is shared by Jews the world over; and this myth still attaches itself to those Jews who are no longer children and who are unable to still be "stealing the *afikoman*" . This is just a minor but telling example that goes to demonstrate the "Jewish bond" that ties together Jews who speak different languages, who in the normal course of events would have trouble understanding one another, and yet because they are of the same religion and of the same unique nationality, grouped together they may be set apart from all other nations and religions.

A mutual relationship is thus formed by means of the story of the exodus from Egypt, which takes its tangible form on the *Seder* night that takes place at the very beginning of Passover, and which Festival continues for seven days. All of us Jews went out of Egypt. We did this together. This is our common experience. We look upon anyone who is not Jewish as if he were in the same category as an (ancient) Egyptian, an alien and cruel pursuer. We regard ourselves as the pursued, who, by joining forces, managed to escape servitude and experience liberation. Together we were all there at the time of the departure from Egypt, and it is really unimportant that in reality the event took place 3,300 years ago. **We were** there. All of us **together** experienced the going out of Egypt, we all crossed the sea while walking on dry land, and the Egyptians who chased us and who tried to return us to slavery drowned and perished at sea. After going through a shared experience such as this what importance can be attached to the fact that the Jew placed in front of me appears alien in my eyes, dressed in strange clothes and speaking a language that I am not able to understand? Bearing in mind such a history it becomes perfectly clear why and how it is that Jews who had never set foot in Europe felt that they were being pursued during the time that the Nazis under Hitler were placing European Jews into gas chambers until they suffocated to death, everyone, men, women, and children. We all suffocated. These feelings of being pursued were experienced by the Jews alone, not the Turks, not the Christian Americans, not the Spanish, not the Argentineans, and not even the Chinese, Japanese, Indians, or Arabs. Bearing this in mind it becomes obvious why so many Jews were prepared to fight for the establishment of the State of Israel, including those Jews who personally had no desire to live in a Jewish State or to be that state's citizens. It explains why these Jews viewed the Arabs as their enemies, and why in turn the Arabs who came from different countries to join in the war felt such a strong sense of solidarity with their Palestinian brothers who were fighting the Jews. This solidarity on the hand, and desire to fend off others on the other, in this instance, like in all similar instances in history, form two sides of the same coin. All the Jews who fought in that war felt as if they had grown up in the same home and had suckled from the same mother's breast. The closeness between with them was wholly and tangibly felt, in the same way as their feeling of enmity was expressed towards the opposing side, a side peopled by those they had never seen and against whom, on the face of it, they had no good reason to fight. This fact also needs no further elucidation.

Obviously similar myths exist among various societies and nationalities, but the interpretation accorded these similar figments of the imagination take on very different and unique meanings among the various cultures and societies. Identical motifs in myths that vary with one another, with each myth being attributed to a separate society, proves nonetheless that there is a mutual influence and that there is in reality one root cause for the developments of a myth within a culture and amongst various cultures. The various interpretations that each culture places upon the same motif, as in the case of the various societies, is a sign however that the society in question has distinguished itself and has created for itself a sense of uniqueness that is felt by each of the separate group's members.

Myths play a socio- cultural role. Mythology facilitates the construction or preservation of a cultural grouping which in turn fosters a unique cultural society. This is not to say that it is solely due to myths that cultural societies are formed.

One of the characteristics, signs, and symbols of a specific cultural society is the fact that it makes no difference whether the myth in question is that of a story that in actuality took place, whether it is the product of the imagination, or whether it was merely a work of literature or the lyrics of a poem.

Amongst the various types of myths, those myths that are especially powerful and whose impact is greatly felt are those which retell the story of the founders of the religion or nation that it deals with. The strength of this myth is especially felt, since, expressed within it, is a unique worldview or special values that are attributed to the founding fathers and which are related also to the group since their founders bequeathed these qualities to those who follow in their path. A myth such as this, constructs, deepens, and promotes, in a very significant way, both the group identity, and the power of the messages or values entailed therein. A myth may take the form of a narrative, it may also take the form of a poem, and it may even be encompassed within a dramatic presentation, or anything else that effectively conveys moral tidings to the members of a certain group for a period of generations. The more emotional the mythological story, the more captivating and influential it is.

Philosophical doctrines that have no storyline cannot be classified as myths (in the sense of their relationship towards their society) even if they quite possibly act towards the formation of a society. This may occur when the philosophical teachings are transmitted within the framework of a learning experience or when it imparts a special value to the group that meditates upon these philosophical ideas. Jews, who from their childhood sat and learnt religious laws and discussed intricate discussions from the Talmud, a book that contains ideas and laws that have to do with the correct behavior that a Jew is obliged to stringently follow, certainly managed to acquire thereby a uniquely Jewish collective heritage that strengthens thefeelings of Jewish solidarity. Since this type of study is closely connected with the Jewish religion it intensifies the sense of specialness amongst the Jewish groups, and may even be responsible for bestowing a unique sense of self esteem. There is then a certain element of socio- religious formation; and it is even possible that this type of study contributes towards national feelings; however it has nothing to do with mythology and certainly cannot be classified as a ritual.

A storyline without any spiritual, ideological or normative message and one which has no unique cultural atmospheric element also fails to qualify as a myth, even if from a literary perspective it is possible to refer to it by such description. This qualifies as a story and nothing further. That said, a storyline that deals with the plotting of the gods and which strengthens a certain religious belief does qualify as a myth for that group of believers that believe in that specific religion, since it plays a role in strengthening their religious collectivity.

This perspective of viewing myths does not necessarily conform to the definition put forward by the various philosophers who over the ages have tried to come to grips with mythology, and the reason for this can be found in the fact that not everyone related to this topic from its social standpoint. A literary standpoint may very well include very different definitions of this concept, but insofar as this book is concerned this literary definition will not determine what is or what is not mythological.

In the next chapter a number of philosophers and their philosophical teachings that have a bearing on the mythological discourse, and which grapple with its essential features, will be surveyed.

Chapter B:
Various Opinions on the Sources Responsible for Spawning Religious Myths

In chapter one of the last Part of this book (Part 10- D.F) the opinions of the various writers will be surveyed in detail. Here only the final conclusions of four out of a total of twenty four philosophers, whose philosophical approaches are given full scope in that chapter, will be discussed.

Ezekiel Kaufman[1] developed the idea that cultural creativity, which includes religious creativity (which apparently also includes mythology), cannot be understood nor explained by referring to the milieu in which it is created, as had similarly been contended by Durkheim. He argues rather[2] that monotheism, the belief in one God, is the creative product of Israelite nationalism. In relating to the identity of the creator of these myths it appears correct to construe his writings as saying that myths are the result of a collective creativity, without necessarily being the product of one individual.

William James[3] advocated relying exclusively upon the physical senses; in addition to this he still harbored a deep belief in a reality that existed beyond that which was felt by one's ordinary and personal senses. The underlying root causes for man's belief, according to James, are desire and self interest; according to his opinion, then, the myth is an individual creation, the product of man's desire.

---

[1] See Ezekiel Kaufman, *History of Israelite Belief from Ancient Days Until the End of the Second Temple* (Jerusalem, Tel Aviv: Bialik Institute, Dvir, 1948), p. 22

[2] See *ibid.*, at pp. 7- 8, and see also at p. 23 ffd.

[3] See William James, *Religious and Other Experiences – A Study of the Nature of Man* (Jerusalem: Bialik Institute, 1968).

Sigmund Freud[4]__views religion as a negative phenomenon. Freud's pronouncements on this subject, especially when related to the field of mythology, may be construed as claiming that myths are in fact the product of a collective effort and are thus intimately linked with the guilt feelings of the elite class. Myths are created and preserved within human society precisely because they refer to traumatic events that actually took place in the past. He sees in mythology a reflection of social processes that are not static.

Henri Bergson[5] divides the religions into two, the earlier religions he calls static, and the later he calls dynamic. He speaks about human feelings and human needs as the source for the static religions. Religion at that time was created to satisfy a personal and very human need and to deal with the specific social needs of the primitive societies. Its emergence was influenced by human emotions, as is evinced by the idea of the spirit of a dead man, which spirit continues to exist for perpetuity. This idea came about as a natural response to the yearnings of those individuals who survived the deceased and who still harbored strong feelings towards him. He sees religions and myths as the product of human effort. Mythology came about, in his opinion, because of a strong inner conviction, which conviction simultaneously led man into exploring mysticism, an experience which only a select few have the privilege of enjoying.

For the purposes of this discussion alone, the differences between Kaufman who sees Judaism as a religion whose very essence and whose collective national endeavor created the myth of belief in one God, and Henri Bergson who speaks of mythology and religion as if they were the product of the will and effort of a select few, must be noted.

In the sphere of national myths as opposed to the sphere of religious myths- there exist writers who speak about myths that were specifically spawned by the hegemonic states for the aim of – artificially-constructing nationalities- so that the resultant myth is in fact a falsification of historical events. These myths were fashioned and are continually being fashioned for the purpose of creating internal

---

[4] See Sigmund Freud, Culture and Religion (Merchavia, Doar Afula: Kibbutz Haartzi Publication, HaShomer Hatzair 1943) and see also Sigmund Freud, *Totem and Taboo – and Other Essays*, translated by Haim Isaac, appears in the original – *Writings of Sigmund Freud* – part 3, (Tel Aviv: Dvir, 1988), and also Sigmund Freud, *Culture Without Satisfaction – and Other Essays* (Tel Aviv: Dvir, 1988).

[5] See Henri Bergson, *The Two Sources of Morality and Religion*, translated by R. Ashley Audra and Claudesley Brereton with assistance of W. Horsfall Carter (Garden City, N.Y.: Doubleday & Company 1935).

adhesion and consolidation of the civil society in order to turn it into an imagined nationality.[6]

In the next chapter the early Christian myths will be analyzed as well as the changes that occurred to this religion which contributed to its dissemination worldwide. For present purposes the point will be raised that the early shepherds of Christianity and those who established it notably avoided quoting too much from the words and language of Jesus, confining themselves only to those teachings that were absolutely necessary.

Chapter C:
Early Christianity and the Amendments that were made to its Basic Myths.

Aviad Kleinburger[7] describes Jesus as a Jew who viewed himself as the mortal son of two natural parents, but who also believed that he was the messiah. He was closely connected to the Jewish belief system, as it was interpreted by that religion's Essene sect.[8] He was apparently born in Nazareth; the ascription of his birthplace to the city of Bethlehem, an ascription made by two of the authors of the New Testament, was for the purposes of tailoring their belief in Jesus being the Messiah so that it would suit the writings of the Prophet Micah who prophesied that the Messiah will originate from Bethlehem.[9] Although this false ascription was indeed premeditated, it was, no doubt, based on the premise that the main contention, that relating to Jesus' messianic claim, was undeniably true; fabricating the place of birth was a marginal matter but one that was necessary in order for the people to believe in the truth, which is, as has been said, the fact that Jesus was indeed the Messiah. If in order to disseminate this kernel of truth it is necessary to include some or other marginal technical detail to reinforce the

[6] See Benedict Anderson, *Imagined Communities* [Hebrew edition] (Tel Aviv: Leor Publication House of the [Israel] Open University) Translated from English by Dan Daor, from the original English version of Benedict Anderson, *Imagined Communities* (1983, 1991).

[7] Aviad Kleinburger, *Christianity from its Genesis until the Reformation* [in Hebrew] (Tel Aviv: A publication of the Israel Foreign Ministry, 5755- 1995)

[8] *Ibid.*, at p. 24.

[9] *Ibid.*, at p. 18.

credibility of the tidings relating to the messiah, that marginal detail relating to his birthplace cannot become a stumbling block.

Jesus saw himself as God's messenger, exclusively for the Jewish People; decidedly not an emissary of any other nations. This is testified to in Jesus' own words when he says: "Do not go the way of the gentile, and to the City of the Samaritans do not come close. Go instead to the lost flock, which are from the House of Israel". This approach is given radical expression in the episode where Jesus encounters the "Canaanite Woman" who met him in the Valley of Tzur and Sidon and who asked Jesus to save her ailing daughter; Jesus refused saying that he was sent only to mission to the "lost flock who are from the House of Israel". The woman went back to Jesus and pleaded in front of him, to which Jesus responded "it is not good to take away the bread of the children and throw it to the waiting puppy dogs." In this way Jesus gave vent to his feelings and attitude towards those who were not of the Jewish race, viewing them as no better thdogs. Eventually however he did indeed give in to the woman's request, but this he did only after she made a declaration saying that "let the puppy dogs eat from the crumbs that fall from their master's table", and only after she thereby acknowledged Jesus' declared qualitative distinction between Jew and gentile.[10]When Jesus was dying, after being crucified, he felt lonely and forsaken, and he even said this much during the last moments of his life.[11]All the aforementioned go to show that Jesus viewed himself as Jewish, as mortal, and as a messiah whose messianic mission was confined exclusively to his People.

Peter, the disciple of Jesus who was personally acquainted with him, was interested in widening the small circle of his master's admirers. He was confronted with the problem of how to relate to those who were not Jewish but were desirous of joining this Jesuit community without at the same time willing to be bound by the Jewish commandments. Of these commandments circumcision was thought to be the biggest obstacle to attracting would- be adherents especially since the Greeks at that time viewed it almost as badly as they did castration.[12] Therefore, Peter independently came to the decision, that because the number of Jewish adherents to the Christian sect was so severely limited, and because he was desirous of overcoming the problem of being such a small minority, he had to actively attract non- Jews to his community. Going against the express wishes of Jesus, who saw in Christianity an offspring of Judaism and whose followers were therefore bound, as was Jesus himself by the laws relating to permitted and

[10] *Ibid.* at pp. 23-24.
[11] *Ibid.*, at p. 27.
[12] *Ibid.*, at p. 32.

forbidden foods (*kashruth).* Peter directed his flock to eat and drink freely with the non- Jewish candidates for Christian conversion, without paying strict attention to the intricacies of *kashruth* observance. Consistent with this decision, Peter laid down the rule that any gentile who had joined his new religion was not bound by the laws of *kashruth,* even if Jews at that time and even if Jesus` own following did regard themselves as bound by these laws. Only those members of the Christian community who were originally Jewish were duty- bound by the laws relating to *kashruth.*[13]

Jesus was crucified at the age of 33. A very short time after the crucifixion, Paul, who had never met Jesus but who had studied his teachings under the tutelage of Jesus` close disciples, joined the Christian movement. Paul was executed in the city of Rome in 64 C. E., 31 years after Jesus' crucifixion. During the decades preceding his death, Paul led his Christian flock down the path of nullification of the observance of a great number of commandments and even applied this nullification to those adherents who were practitioners of the Jewish faith before joining his community. This latter move was a deviation from the path set by Peter. While attempting to appeal to the non- Jewish community, Paul had, at the same time, to acknowledge the obvious fact that Jesus did not come to contradict the words of the prophets; those same prophets, [certainly according to the interpretation of the Essene sect whose views Jesus had accepted and had adopted- Y. C], who had prophesied that God's salvation would come to one People, the Jewish People, and not to the gentiles of the world. Paul [according to his own understanding- Y. C] then concluded that because the Jews refused to listen to Jesus` teachings, they had transgressed the covenant that was entered into between God, the forefathers and their physical offspring – causing the prophecy relating to the redemption to be transferred from the "Jew by flesh" to the "Jew by spirit"- the latter of whom was defined as someone who accepted Jesus` doctrinal beliefs. Following this logic Paul could have easily nullified all of the Holy Scriptures, but such a radical step was at this stage unnecessary for attracting a wide following to his community, and Paul instead stuck to the Scriptures as did, quite obviously, Jesus himself.

In this way Paul avoided the creation of a religion that was completely severed from that envisaged by Jesus, and he contented himself with those amendments that were absolutely necessary for the expansion of the community of followers of the Jesus the Messiah . (Savior= Christus, since the word "Savior" in Greek is literally translated as "Christus")

---

[13] *Ibid.*, at p. 30.

By adopting this new line of thought Paul was able to exert pressure on those who had already become adherents to this faith to work tirelessly to enlist other followers to the cause; and in fact Paul directed his Christian following to preach salvation to all the nations of the world.[14]

Just as the basic laws adhered to by Jesus and his early Christian following had undergone changes, so too the myth relating to Jesus' resurrection was also added in an effort to make Christian doctrine palatable to those tribes who dwelled within the borders of Judea, and amongst whom the myth of a god who had died and who had subsequently been resurrected was widespread at that time. Adding another myth in terms of which Jesus was proclaimed the son of God conformed well to the myth of resurrection which was so widespread amongst the masses making it easier to attract people who were not Jewish to this new Christian sect.[15] It is possible to link the myth about Jesus having been resurrected, which myth was believed by his earliest group of followers, with the myth of his being the actual son of God- a myth that Jesus himself never officially ascribed to- by seeing this innovation as effectively accommodating the powerful desire of the early Christians to enlarge their community. They could then pick their followers not just from amongst the Jews- who had never displayed much enthusiasm in the first place- but more importantly from those gentiles who believed in the myth specifically of a god who had died and who had subsequently been resurrected.

Historically the time was ripe for intellectuals and middle class individuals who belonged to a pagan culture to join any type of community that preached belief in one God instead of a multitude of deities; these pagan believers could no longer continue to truly and wholeheartedly believe in idols.[16]In order to entice this population, which indeed joined the ranks of Christianity during the course of the second century C. E., it was necessary to prove that Christianity was the "*genuine* continuation" of Judaism- known by all to be an ancient longstanding religion. This was done through the orchestration of changes to the original message of Judaism as it was accepted by Jesus, and by rendering Jesus' and his world, whose roots were deeply entrenched in the provincial experiences of a Jew living in the Land of Israel into philosophical and cosmopolitan constructs that were commonplace in the Hellenic- Roman world.[17] These changes were put in place in order to successfully transmit Jesus' gospel. Doubtless those people responsible for these reforms believed that they were conveying the essence of the doctrinal

---

[14] *Ibid.*, at pp. 32- 33.
[15] *Ibid.*, at pp. 36- 37.
[16] *Ibid.*, at p. 40.
[17] *Ibid.*, at p. 40.

beliefs, while considering the finer points of the religion to be less important. They therefore altered those myths that related to Jesus and his preaching.

Both the intellectuals and others were seeking, during the course of the second century, an additional element of religiosity that would provide them with the feeling of being personally connected to the Divine, and which would offer more spiritual explanations for their religious experiences than had been offered in the pagan world. Members of the Christian community were able to satisfy these seekers who were at the time part of the pagan community. The job was made easy after the demand to observe the commandments was dropped, and after the Jewish religion which was always geared towards the performance of specific acts, something which is hard to carry out, was changed into a religion where the only thing required was pure intention, which is much easier to acquire and to carry out than intricate Jewish commandments. The early Christians even changed Plato's teachings arguing that Plato himself had recognized the truth of Christianity.[18]There are two possibexplanations for this perversion; either it did not bother them that during Plato's time Christianity had not yet come into existence, or they did not take pains to clarify this point to themselves, since they were so awestruck by Christianity that they needed to prove its worth over and above that of Hellenistic culture.

Nonetheless Christianity like Judaism, believed, and built myths upon this basic belief, that there is only one truth and that there is only one God[19]. This declaration prepared the groundwork for Christianity becoming the religion of the Roman Empire which owed its allegiance to one individual Caesar. Within a setting where various nations were forced to coexist, the regime demanded loyalty to one Caesar who ruled over the (most important and discovered parts of the) world, rather than to a multitude of rulers as was reflected in the case of paganism which posited a belief in the existence of a multitude of deities. Christianity took precedence over Judaism for the simple reason that Judaism was a national religion, belonging exclusively to the Jewish People. Early Christianity tailored its content and mythology to enable itself to deal with the possibility of expansion so that it would suit all the various nations that made up Imperial Rome. On the hand then, it rallied behind the idea of one God, but on the other hand it eschewed the nationalism that was an inherent part of the materialistic Jewish People who had established themselves on narrow ethnic grounds. Christianity became the religion that was accessible to all nations, without at the same time making any demands on its newfound adherents to abandon their nationality or ethnic background that

[18] *Ibid.*, at p. 41.
[19] *Ibid.*, at p. 42.

made them different to their co-religionist. The Roman Caesar who intended in the future to convert to Christianity did not need to become Jewish in the national sense of the word in order to fully accept upon himself the yoke of Christianity. He could hold on to his Roman identity. The path of Christianity diverged from that of Judaism in the sense that it no longer cleaved onto the "corporeal Jewish People", but rather spread itself among the nations who, after evincing a belief in Jesus turned into the "spiritual Jewish People'; a "spiritual nation" included- and could even include today – any member of any nation, without the necessity of those nations relinquishing their nationality. A change in the content of Christian mythology already occurred during Paul's lifetime. The whole reform process was brought to fruition within a few decades relatively shortly after Jesus' crucifixion.

By the year 312 C. E the time was ripe for the Christians to exploit an historic opportunity for which they had prepared themselves by deliberately instituting bendable changes into their mythology. That year Constantine stood alongside the walls of the City of Rome in order to conquer it and to proclaim himself Caesar. At the same time, inside the city, Magentas, Constantine's enemy, arose, also claiming entitlement to the Emperor's throne. The pagan fortune tellers were predicting that Constantine would have a difficult battle ahead of him and therefore Magentas, discarding the option of secluding himself within the city walls and inflicting a battle of attrition upon Constantine's camp, chose rather to leave his safe abode, and to enter into open battle. Constantine, for his part chose to detach himself from the Roman deities who, as mentioned, were predicting his downfall and rather to cling to a different belief, one that was totally independent of these fortune tellers. He went out to battle, then under the protection of the cross. After emerging victorious he adopted Christianity, a religion, about which he knew very little. In this way Christianity became the religion of the Caesar and, by definition, of his empire. This expansion was unprecedented, and would never have occurred had changes to the mythology, that originated with the Early Christians, not been effected. From this point in time and onwards Christianity was disseminated throughout the empire.

In this day and age there is no great importance to the fact that these myths underwent change. Nowadays Christianity has become so rooted in many countries of the world, that the changes that were effected to the mythology have no bearing whatsoever and were only important in making Christianity attractive to the early fourth century inhabitants of Imperial Rome. Relating to Christianity in the Modern Period, Bultmann[20]claims that one needs to view those myths that

[20] Rudolf Bultmann, *Jesus Christ and Mythology*,(Englewood Cliffs, New Jersey: Prentice Hall, A Simon and Shuster Company, 1958)

are associated with Christianity through the lens of the modern world, a world that is governed by science and the scientific approach. The modern world requires proof of anything before it can be accepted. Under these required conditions, he opines, Christian mythology can be viewed only in terms of allegory and symbolism. Bultmann documents those elements that are common to both Christianity and Hellenistic culture and discovers that these two ideologies share many basic features.

In this way Bultmann demonstrates- even if he had no intention of doing so- to what extent Christianity bent itself backwards in order that its myths and its ideology articulated through its mythology suit the outlook of the Hellenist world, and to what extent Christianity adapted itself in order that it gain widespread acceptance in a world that during the era of Early Christianity was dominated by Hellenist culture-this filled the gap caused by Judaism's refusal to similarly institute such modifications.

Bultmann maintains that both Christianity and Greek philosophy look forward to a happiness that comes about only after death, a contentment that is the result of a feeling of liberation[21]. In both Christian and Greek mythology, only after entering the next world is it possible for man to uncover his best and truest qualities. Both ideologies view the world of the living as imperfect, and advocate a quest, a craving, and a longing (for something better). The difference between these two ideologies, in his opinion, lies in their opposing conceptions of human nature. According to Plato, human nature is a fixed attribute, invulnerable to change, so that the passing of time has no effect upon it. Contrarily, in Christian thought, man is a creature of his times in the sense that it is his past that has shaped him, and it is his future that will cause him to confront new challenges where buried beneath them are the recipes for an internal makeover to his whole nature; the future, for every man is quite different from the past in that it is able to recreate the personality of every single individual. This aspect of the Christian dogma provides its believers with encouraging expectations as to the future that will be meted out to them. Viewed from this standpoint, a Hellenist man who converts to Christianity is provided, during the transition period, and because of the transition itself, with the hope of a future that is different, especially when it comes to how his personality will eventually develop, from the future that Hellenist culture, to which that convert had previously belonged, had in store for him.[22]

[21] *Ibid.*, at p. 28.
[22] *Ibid.*, at p. 33.

In addition to what has been said by Bultmann, mention must also be made of the fact that since Christianity includes in its basic tenets the idea of Divine loving kindness, and teaches that Jesus' suffering came to atone for the sins of his believers, the Christian adherent is filled with the expectation that God's loving kindness will better his lot. This expectation was an incentive created by Early Christianity- an incentive for the Greco-Roman population to join the ranks of Christianity. Moreover one who believed in Jesus, even if he died a mortal death was promised that in the future he would live once again. The true Christian believer never really dies. This type of belief did not only bode well for the prospects of attracting new Christians to the cause but also secured the chances for ancient Christianity to expand. It is possible to link the appendages and modifications that were described above and which were applied to Christian mythology with the conscious treof the early Christians to seek expansion, a trend that these pioneering Christians bequeathed to the generations that followed them, and which has lasted until the present-day.

It is possible, then, that a switch has taken place between the real story of Jesus' life and the mission he set himself, on the one hand, and the stories that have emerged from Christian mythology that was created a short time after his crucifixion, on the other. On one end of the spectrum stands Jesus, a man who had no desire whatsoever to gather round him a following that consisted of any nation that was not Jewish, and who had never sought to establish a religion that was separate from his own Judaism. Occupying the other end is Peter, Paul and the other apostles and leaders of Christianity who had created a cultural religion that had separated itself from Judaism. This switch in thinking had as its aims the widespread distribution of Christian ideology, and it more than succeeded. The changes made to the original myths played a key role in this success story.

Chapter D:
The Nazi Race Theory

Lincoln[23] explains how it was that up until 1783 there was no such thing as an "Aryan" race, neither was there the concept of the Indo- European. He further explains how it was that this race group became the brainchild of the fertile imaginations of race theorists and researchers beginning with Herder (Johann Gottfried Herder, 1744- 1803) -a German priest and one affiliated with the

[23] See Bruce. Lincoln, *Theorising Myth: Narative, Ideol;ogy and Scholarship,, 1999*

Romantic movement, who began to publish his works in 1785 where he posited that there is one human source for all of humanity and that differences only crept in as a result of outside factors such as climate, language and the different constructs used in the formation of a collective and individual culture- and carrying on with Jones (Sir William Jones, 1746- 1794) an English Orientalist and legal scholar who began publishing his theories on the similarities between Sanskrit, an ancient Indian language, and those languages belonging to the Gothic and Celtic groups, a theory which many have interpreted as positing a unity between, and tracing the common origins of the Indo-European nations which theory then gave way to the idea of an Aryan race. Although Herder viewed myths as no more than popular folktales[24]his writings landed on ground, firmly rooted in the desire arising in Germany and in other countries in Central and Northern Europe to find a super collective identity with which they could be affiliated, a tradition that they sorely lacked. This need arose because internally there was mounting pressure exerted by the local communities to consolidate for themselves independent national group identities.[25]

The roots of the problem of trying to balance self esteem with feelings of self-deprecation began in Germany centuries before Jones entered the scene. The seeds of the conflict were planted as a result of a dispute over who was considered superior, a dispute that was manifest in the power struggle between the German Imperial Government on the one hand and the Papal clerical and political leadership, on the other, and which took place in the first half of the fifteenth century. Arguments were raised by the closed circle of the papal court in Rome against the German Kaiser over the issue of which of the two bodies was superior- the pope in Rome and his spiritual leadership, or the German Kaiser and his corporeal government.[26] The dispute over the question of the supremacy of the Pope was prompted by the controversy surrounding the Tacitian text, when, following his own initiative, Picoloni (soon after to be appointed pope) tried to prove, using this document, that the Germans were barbarians. Based on this finding Picoloni claimed that the Germans needed to show their appreciation to the Church for endowing them with the gift of enlightenment; and therefore, and in accordance with the logic of this argument, the German Kaiser was duty- bound to obey the pope. In response it was alleged, relying on the same document, (that, according to Lincoln, was a forged document) that Noah had had a fourth son whose name was Tuyscon, who was the patriarch of the tribes that dwelt between the Rhein and the Danube. >From this it emerges that the Germans could trace

---

[24] *Ibid.*, at the end of page 72.
[25] *Ibid.*
[26] *Ibid.*, at pp. 47- 48.

themselves back to an ancient noble, who had no connection with Noah's other three sons, Shem, Ham and Japheth. This imaginative allegation was enough to satisfy the burning desire of a great many of Germany's and her surrounding neighbors' populace who were desperate to ascribe to themselves such honorable pedigree.[27] This discovery left the populations of Central and Southern Europe hungrily seeking a vague definition of their past, that would at least partially satiate them. Their desires were answered in the form of a translated New Testament dated 1640. Lincoln shows how the past history of the Peoples of Central European continued to be retold in the writings of Mallet (Paul Henri Mallet), who in 1755- 6 translated the Eddas myths into French, and who then ascribed these stories to the European "Golden Age", as he would term it. He claimed that these myths reflect an old European cultural tradition of honor, love and freedom. Following on the heels of this French publication, these myths were swiftly translated into Danish, German and English, becoming feverishly popular reading material.

A few years later James McPherson (1736- 96) was to take the lead from Mallet and published during the years 1760- 3 three volumes of poetry that were attributed to a blind third century poet, and which were presented as if they were translations of an original Gallic manuscript that could be traced back to an ancient Scottish highlands tradition. These poems quickly became the sensation that everyone was talking about. Only after he had died in 1796, was it discovered that the manuscript was indeed nothing more than a sham.[28]

The thirst for unknown roots was also quenched by Hamaan (Johann George Hamaan- 1730- 88) a priest who was fluent in many languages (Greek, Latin, Hebrew, French, English, Italian, Portuguese, Lithuanian and a sprinkling of Arabic).Basing himself on his wide and varied knowledge of languages he founded a theory about the uniqueness of each of the various languages, positing that it was not possible that at any time in history there was only one language medium that was used by all humanity to communicate with one another; according to his *weltaunshaung* each and every language was a direct gift from God. Out of this theory the idea emerged that each European language group was endowed with a value unique to it; moreover this theory posited that each of these aforesaid language groups had the independent merit of being linked with the Divine, without being dependent on any intermediate authority, but rather under the direct authority of God Himself. Hamaan's primary motive was faith based, and arose out of the desire to strengthen the link between Christendom and the

---

[27] *Ibid.*, at p. 48.
[28] *Ibid.*, at p. 50.

Divine. However he also had an ulterior motive that had to do with his local German background, and that arose out of his feelings for his German flock; he therefore sought to provide an answer to the heartfelt wishes of the German people. Included among those who had read his writings were German luminaries such as Goethe, Kant, Moses Mendelssohn, and Frederick Jacoby, as well as Johann Herder who is mentioned above. Confident about the veracity of these writings, which grabbed the attention of a fairly large readership, the Germans viewed themselves as derived from independent, primary and exemplary origins, which were much more powerful than all other nations. Basing themselves on these writings they felt well- equipped to compete with the ancient Greeks and Romans.

In 1835, Jacob Grimm (1785- 1863) published a four volume encyclopedia of German myths and claimed that Christianity, that was an offshoot of the Semitic Peoples, destroyed and thus deprived the Germans of both their three pronged identity that was comprised of land- myth-nation and the original German culture. He wrote very emotional accounts relating to this topic and expressed the hop, with his writings forming a humble attempt at rectifying the situation, that the injuries caused by Christianity and inflicted upon German culture once again be healed.

The one most naturally endowed with the ability to continue Jacob Grimm's ideology was Richard Wagner (1813- 83) who took part in the 1848 "Spring of the Nations" revolution in Germany, and who was consequently forced to spend a number of years in political exile in Paris. As a German nationalist and as a musician he developed a theory that was based upon the antisemitic utterances of Feurwach; Feurwach had made the claim that Jews had never had their own language or homeland, since the Yiddish that they spoke was merely a perverted and distorted form of German, and for this reason the Jews were incapable of setting up a separate nationality and were unsuited for developing their own kind of music. Sticking to this basic hypothesis, Wagner independently added his own theory, positing that language is the essential ingredient necessary for developing poetry and music and that every nationality creates for itself its own myths, language, and art. In terms of Feurwach's theory, Jews are egoists and pleasure seekers; their egoism stems from the fact that they harbor monotheistic beliefs, which posits the existence of one transcendental entity, while the Greeks in contradistinction developed their art because of their belief that the world of the deities and of nature are all constituents of one unified bloc; this then allowed the latter to adopt the aesthetic approach and to promote scientific development. The Jews, on the other hand who were incapable of composing their own music, who were egoistic hedonists, who owned property, and who lived off the interest of other people's loans, enjoyed music only in their capacity of being its patrons, and not its innovators; and yet they threatened to the control the world and culture of music, because of their ill gotten wealth. Feurwach's hypothesis left Wagner with the distinct impression that the modern world was experiencing a cultural atrophy and was fast approaching its twilight. This degenerative situation could only be remedied through the recreation of a cultural milieu, which would be aided by manufacturing additional popular myths, which in turn would bear testimony to the national ingenuity. It was in the circle to which Wagner was affiliated, which included within its ranks his son-in- law, that Nazi theory germinated, a theory that was fed on racist myths that spoke about the Aryan race, as the concept had gradually developed, as mentioned above in the beginning of this chapter.

That the desire of the German's and the other Northern and Central European language groups was so fervently entrenched can be seen from the fact that later on Jones' himself after reanalyzing his theory rejects any racial relationship to the Aryan race as many (particularly those in Germany and Northern and Central Europe) had too hastily concluded. Jones, when first embarking upon his career, was still wrestling with the facts, unable to immediately recognize what he had discovered. This changed soon after he had completed a series of lectures on the topic, when the final racial and national portrait to emerge depicted the world's nations as classified according to their lineage with the three basic progenitors being Shem, Ham and Japheth. Although it is true that included among the offspring of Ham were indeed the Indians they did not share their heritage exclusively with the Persians, the Romans, the Greeks, and the Goths. Rather the ancient Egyptians, the Ethiopians, the Phoenicians, the Scandinavians, the Chinese, the Japanese, and even the American Indians, could all make the exact same claim. Under the heading, *descendants of Shem*, were included the Jews, the Arabs, and the Syrians, while Japheth's offspring included the Tartars, the Slavs and the Northern European natives.

Not only did the inclusion of the Chinese, the Japanese, and the American Indians in the category of Aryan elite races put a question mark over the theory that postulated German superiority (After all who is left out of the Aryan definition over whom they may prove their superiority, especially since this whole bundle of nations includes most of the world), but Jones' theory itself, as Lincoln explains, would appear even at a superficial glance to be "pretty lame". Not only is the above problematic, but even more worrisome is the fact that his theory is not based on any great storehouse of knowledge. This can be seen in the way in which the material is presented, where, in order to compensate for his severe lack of knowledge in many crucial areas he inappropriately lays great stress on those areas where he does possess some expertise. Moreover it should be noted that the whole explanation relating to a common ancestor is primarily based upon a linguistic analysis, as Jones himself admits, and must be regarded, then, as most unreliable, not only because prima facie it appears to be dubious, but because the experience of history proves that relying upon linguistic analyses yields incredible results. Researchers who have followed this path have, then, come up with a multitude of answers to the question concerning the most ancient language from which all others are mere offshoots. The answers vary between Dutch, Swedish, Phoenician, Greek, Latin, and Persian.

Another independent question that may be raised is how was it that this Jones, who was an intellectual, very familiar with Darwin's Theory, and who without doubt, acknowledged the truthfulness of its scientific axioms, as was fashionable at that time, permitted himself to seriously consider, and even rely, for his theory on the development of the races and of human language, on the Bible and on the story of Noah's sons, which story had been completely refuted by Darwin and his theory.

Myths have not only been responsible for founding religions and for creating nationalities; they have also assisted, and continue to assist, rulers in managing their regime, and they have stood alongside other forms of governance which every regime relies upon, such as an enforceable legal system. Imperial China serves as a good example of this kind of model, as will be will be demonstrated in detail in the following chapter.

Chapter E:
Myth and the Law
in the Service of the Imperial Chinese Regime

All of China's imperial dynasties worked towards setting up a uniform legal system within the boundaries of their regimes, and within this framework they sought to produce a detailed statutory code. The first known statutory code came about even before Imperialism; it comprised an anthology drafted by Shang Yang in the Chin province in 338 B. C. E.[29] Similar codes were to spring up during the course of the various empires, yet these specific statutory codes, although they continued to influence one dynasty after another, were not wholly preserved. The

[29] See *The T'ang Code*, Volume 1, General Principles, translated with an introduction by Wallace Johnson (Princeton, New Jersey: Princeton University Press, 1979) p. 7.

Code that survived, that held sway, and that continued to apply, at least partially, right until the end of the Imperial era (in 1911 C. E) was that of the T'ang dynasty. This Code was the most detailed of all, and there is a reason for its thoroughness. The reason stems from the Code's reliance on the philosophy of Dong Zhongshu (who lived during the second century B. C. E.) which philosophy had already been expounded upon in China during the Han Dynastic regime. This philosophy assumes that nature and man make up one holistic unity and are so interconnected to the extent that man's deeds have a direct bearing upon the course of nature. Completing this holistic chain is the emperor whose every action has a profound impact on the order of things both in regards to man and in regards to nature. This philosophy, then, lends weight to His Imperial Highness's elevated stature, and at the same time immeasurably strengthens his grasp on power. This is especially so since any harm attaching to him would be considered as dangerously threatening the world order, which would consequently bring about terrible disasters that ordinary man would find impossible to withstand.

According to theory, there are five forces within the abovementioned holistic system that all represent the same side of the equation (i.e. the sun, man, Imperial kindness, spring, and summer), and for each the theory provides an opposing force that operates against it (Operating against the sun, then, is the moon, against man- woman, against Imperial kindness- the death penalty, against spring- autumn, and against summer- winter) The core of this holistic system is based on the number five. There are five different colors, and five different paths (the middle one is in fact the fifth). Any transgression committed by man negatively alters the universal holistic balance, and therefore punishment must immediately follow in order to repair the damage and to restore the equilibrium. An overly harsh punishment has the same detrimental effect as does a laxly dealt with or, unpunished crime. The emperor's task is to see to it that everyone is appropriately punished so that the universe remains evenly balanced. It is therefore vital that the judge administers the punishment in exact accordance with the provisions of the Code that has been determined, and drafted, by the lawmaking emperor. In this way, the whole empire will have exactly the same punitive systems. In order to achieve the abovementioned balance, anyone falsely accusing another on trumped up charges, receives the exact same punishment that would have been meted out to the wrongly accused. Admitting theft and subsequently returning the stolen goods is enough to restore a breach in the equilibrium that was caused as a result of the theft, to the extent that the necessity to punish is rendered redundant. This is especially the case since the only aim of punishment is to correct an imbalance.

According to this system, the emperor's status is elevated above all else when it comes to acting as the final link that joins man to the other natural worlds. It follows, then, that a transgression committed against the Emperor and his household is considered to be the severest of all, binding the law enforcer to impose punishment upon the whole family of the accused. It follows too that procedural defenses that are, in the ordinary course of events, open to all accused, are inadmissible in this situation.

Looked at from this context the Emperor's regime is safely ensconced because of the vital need to have a government that correctly and accurately balances all the workings of nature. To further this goal it was decided to set up an institution of watchdogs who would supervise those connected with balance achievement, including, amongst others, the judiciary. A judge, then, who did not perform these prescribed duties in a meticulous manner, was duly punished. The distance between this outlook and one which considers China to be positioned in the centre of the universe is indeed very small. China is at the centre because it balances the whole world, including nature and humankind. China is then entrusted with a great responsibility towards the world, most of it being borne by its leader, the emperor. Therefore the legal system in China carries crucial weight as does the system of law enforcement. Someone who refuses to accept upon himself the authority of the legal system and by extension the authority of the responsible Imperial government shows himself to be willfully boorish, lacking any semblance of culture. The Chinese statutory Code later acted as a model for the legal systems that were to arise in Japan, Korea, and even Vietnam. This type of statutory system borrowed principles from Confucian philosophy. One may speculate that one of the reasons for the heavy Chinese influence on its surroundings, has to with the fact, as has already been stated, that there was an acknowledgement that Chinese enlightenment arose out of the fact that one of its key components was Confucian philosophy, and that the prevailing and successful system of law and order that had been achieved was made possible through assimilating principles of this philosophical doctrine.

In light of the stability that ensued as the result of the rule of law, which every Chinese person quickly learned to respect, the emperors inserted extra principles into the criminal and civil code that were to strengthen the Imperial regime, and that were based chiefly upon Confucian philosophy, a philosophy that was already proclaimed to be legally binding at the time of the Han Dynasty. The latter applied both the criminal code and the Confucian system to all extra territories that fell under the jurisdiction of members of its dynasty, but it was the Confucian system that on its own acted as an effective and important toll of government. The Confucian system obligates its adherents to show respect to one's father or master on the part of the son and the servant; it contains a set of obligations more than a set of rights, a disciplinary system, and other basic principles that enshrine social stability and that prevent the subversion of the dividing lines of authority and, of the distinctions within the economic and ruling classes. These principles were absolutely vital for the Chinese emperors and for prolonging their regime. It is therefore no wonder that the Code of Laws drafted during the period of the T'ang Code managed to survive, virtually unchanged, for a period close on 1300 years. If these meticulously set- out laws were responsible for maintaining the world's equilibrium, no one could easily go and change them. Rather they needed to be preserved in order to ward off any harm affecting the world's balance, which could only lead to catastrophic results. It is possible to view this whole scheme, including the belief that the emperor played the role of balancing the forces of nature, as a religion, and from this perspective it is the emperor who assumes the highest authority within this religion. This is a type of religion that tolerates and accepts those other religions that do not oppose nor undermine it, including the Chinese folk religion with its gods and its rituals that celebrate its forefathers, namely: Daoism, Confucianism, and Buddhism.

The path to the judiciary was paved with academic scholarship and examination. While it may have been the case that other administrative jobs did not require admission tests, in order to be a judge one did have to undergo a series of tests. The very fact that judges had to pass tests in order to be accepted leads one to conclude that it was one of the few government positions that was open to those who came from classes that were ranked on a lower peg than the upper classes, and it was therefore one of the few ways in which a lowly ranked individual could gain promotion to a higher class. The local judge was also the government administrator, and the collector of taxes; in effect the judge performed all duties of government. In order to be accepted into the judiciary one had to be equipped with a thorough knowledge of the law. At the same time a judge was answerable to the government supervisors and was not immune to their punishment if it was discovered that he was not exacting in his judgment. This, because of the view pertaining then that considered meticulousness in sentencing critical for the continued existence of nature. Against this backdrop, and in an environment where Chinese culture was on the rise, an increasing number of people within Imperial China began studying and delving into literature, poetry, art, and trade, and during the period of the T'ang dynasty, few even began to study law.[30] The emperor was legislator, Chief Justice and head of the executive, and was therefore bestowed with the untrammeled authority to lighten or to increase the punishment that had already been imposed- and from this perspective he was the only individual who was unrestricted by the statutory laws. The belief in Chinese philosophy was so powerful that the overseers, whose duty it was to supervise the administration and

[30] *Ibid.*, at pp. 4- 5.

the judiciary and to thus order to restore balance to the world, in furtherance of their emperor's commandment, were on more than one occasion during their work so absorbed in their worand so determined to recognize and to fulfill their ideal that they denounced the policies of the emperor, even though they were well aware that such a course of action could lead to their decapitation, and in fact it often did. It is possible to infer from this, that the philosophy that led to the establishment of the regime in China succeeded in implanting itself into the ordinary Chinese in a very strong way. The great Chinese empire required that their ruling class remain large but in order to check abuses of the system, there were those in the royal courtyard whose job it was to alert the emperor to those cases that required that the penalty meted out be lightened. Nonetheless in some aspects the regime was concentrated among the very few making it impossible to carry out any death sentence without express permission from His Majesty.

The Imperial Chinese statutory laws entrenched the advantageous position of functionaries of the state, including those who had worked for the state in the past, and including others who held titles of nobility that they had inherited from their ancestors (hereafter these three categories will be collectively referred to as "officers" and will also include judges)[31]

Transgressions against the emperor and his government, against the state or against the religion as it was practiced within the family (for example- transgressing mourning rites after the death of a father or mother) were considered the most severe of all crimes, and when such a crime included rebelling against the emperor or even planning such a rebellion, a collective punishment was imposed upon all family members of the offender (and for these purposes any accomplice was considered on par with the actual offender). Within this framework- the more severe transgressions carried with them the death penalty for all male relatives of the offender even if they had no knowledge of the plan to commit a crime, while the more distant relatives would be exiled and their property forcibly removed. In these matters a wide variety of punishments could be imposed, but the general trend was as described immediately above.[32]

Owing to the fact that the judges were public servants who were subordinates of the state's interests and of Imperial edicts, they concentrated all their efforts on adjudicating matters that had to do with rules pertaining to the criminal statutory

[31] *Ibid.*, at p. 22. The accepted trend at that time was that women were not deemed fit to stand trial, but where they had interfered with the male authority as in the case of witchcraft, exceptions to this rule were accommodated.

[32] *Ibid.*, at pp. 17 -20.

code and to the stability of the regime, trying as much as possible to avoid dealing with commercial, or private disputes[33] that had nothing to do with structure of the family hierarchy or with the discipline expected of a servant towards his master. Consequently laws pertaining to the commercial/ private sphere were shoved into a corner. By now the results of such an attitude are well known as may be witnessed in contemporary Japan, which imported wholesale this type of attitude from China together with the latter's criminal code and general legal system. In Japan, the result has been that people have learnt that when it comes to their own affairs they must be willing to solve their problems through the art of compromise[34]. They very rarely, then, deal with private and commercial matters in the courtroom; to the extent that even in this day and age the number of lawyers remains very small. As regards to China during the T'ang dynasty, and as it would appear, during the whole Imperial period, though commerce was very advanced and though there were courts specifically authorized to adjudicate commercial disputes, the prevailing trend was to solve these disputes without having resort to court trials; in fact it was considered beyond the pale to pressure judges into arbitrating commercial matters that they never had an interest in dealing with in the first place.

As regards to personal legal status, those seven years of age and younger, and those who have reached their ninetieth year and over were not considered fit to be punished. However for the purposes of carrying out collective punishment their age was no bar to being included with the rest of those condemned. Within a framework where the trend was to strengthen the control exerted by the fathers and by the oldest in the family, and against the backdrop of encouraging discipline within the nuclear family, it made sense that while a son who struck his father

---

[33] *Ibid.*, at p. 6.

[34] See T'ang Leang-Li, China in Revolt – How a Civilization Became a Nation (London: Noel Douglas, reprint edition published in 1976 by University Publications of America Inc., Arlington, Virginia)The Tang Code, Volume I, General Principles, translated with an Introduction by Wallace Johnson (Princeton, New Jersey: Princeton University Press, 1979) In Japan in addition to what has been said there was a trend during the period of the centralised government of the Magi regime to adopt an aggressive authoritative approach any time a disturbance took place that affected the public order or in order to put an end to a violent private dispute, but to avoid getting involved so long as the village's disputes could feasibly be solved internally and without undue formality. In these circumstances, the Japanese villagers became accustomed to exerting domestic pressure upon these private litigants so that they would solve the problems between them through reaching a compromise solution. This trend was implanted into the Japanese and became an extra reason, quite apart from what I have already mentioned, for entrenching the trend of mediation and compromise that is so common amongst the Japanese.

would be guilty of a serious offence, the father who struck his son, or the man who beat his wife or his concubine was not guilty of anything; in fact there were detailed rules surrounding this matter, which basically laid forth that the more distant the blood relative(in accordance with the five levels of mourning rites, which determined the proximity in blood relationship) the less the disparity in punishments for reciprocal acts committed by each party. To determine when discrepancies in punishment were applicable a special table was annexed to the code so that a network of gross inequality was de facto created when it came to the laws of domestic injuries. This was commensurate with the basic principles enunciated by Confucius in respect of the respect family members need to show towards their parents and older relatives. These principles were interpreted so that they came to include the relationship between supervisor and underling, and falling within this broad definition, within the confines of a monastery, was the relationship between teacher and disciple. In a similar vein respect had to be displayed by those on the lower rung of the regime's bureaucratic ladder towards those positioned a few steps higher. These rules, as they applied to the various scenarios outlined above, were not exclusively confined to crimes of assault but also covered other offences, such as theft and robbery.[35]

The trend of the regime to place the emperor's honour above the ideal of preserving the nuclear family, may be illustrated by the fact that so long as the emperor's honour is not impeached, a family member may hide the fact that another family member has committed an offence, and is even allowed to warn the said transgressor that the state has opened an enquiry based on suspicions that he is involved in criminal wrongdoing. In this way family unity is encouraged and family loyalty is strengthened; it follows then that if family members conspire jointly to commit a crime, only the eldest male member, never female, will be brought to trial.[36] Stealing within the family was dealt with very leniently especially if there was a very close relationship between the thief and the person who had his goods stolen. Accordingly, a son who stole from his father would not be punished unless the amount exceeded a certain minimum, and even in that event the punishment would be very light.[37]

What in fact did happen to the universe's equilibrium, when a person was found to be guilty by law, and so paid his fine, and only afterwards it was discovered that his conviction was not legally justified? How then would the universe adjust its equilibrium? How would it return to the situation where everything was weighted

[35] See the book referred to in note 1 supra, at pp. 29 -32.
[36] *Ibid.* at p. 32.
[37] *Ibid.*, at p. 33.

equally? One thing was clear from the very beginning: if an execution did wrongly take place, the universe was forced to absorb the shock inflicted to its system, and this was not only because of the impossibility of the Chinese legal system restoring life into the wrongly condemned man, but also because the emperor was never mistaken, and the death penalty was never carried out without express permission of the emperor; so since the emperor was not wrong, a shock had not really taken place, and there was no need for him to repair anything. In all other cases, there would be an acknowledgement that an injustice had occurred and the so called offender would then be compensated since he had not, in fact, committed the offence he was accused of.[38]

How was the culpability of an accused proven? The prosaic answer is quite simple: The accused would be tortured until he would either confess his guilt or until it would become obvious that he was not going to admit anything. Accompanying this physical torture was a verbal interrogation, both of which were conducted in exact accordance with what was writtand decreed in the law books in relation to the type of felony with which the accused was charged. For every type of crime there was a specific kind and amount of torture that could be legally administered. If an accused was tortured but refused to confess, the torturers would turn their attention to the plaintiff and would start investigating and torturing him, and if, as a result, this plaintiff would admit that he made a false accusation against the accused, the law decrees that he receives the same punishment that would have been in store for the accused, had the charges been proven correct. Nonetheless, if the plaintiff in the case held an important position in the regime or if he was a man of the cloth, and it turned out that he had charged the accused with a false allegation, his punishment, as mentioned earlier, would not be the same as that that would have been in store for the accused; instead through a certain calculation system the punishment would either take the form of a demotion in rank or alternatively a redemption fee would be paid in place of the physical punishment.[39] This favorable treatment would also apply to the investigative stage where the office holder or clergyman would not be tortured during questioning, but rather witnesses would have to be sought, and their guilt would only be considered a proven fact after at least three witnesses were found that would testify against them.[40] In this way the principle of equilibrium integral to Chinese philosophy finds its practical application. One cannot confuse the situation where one admits guilt as a result of being tortured, and so has punishment imposed upon him, with the situation where one admits guilt freely

[38] *Ibid.*, at p. 16.
[39] *Ibid.*, at p. 15.
[40] *Ibid.*, at p. 25.

and at one's own initiative, and where one returns that which was taken illegally, in which case the guilt is rescinded, on condition- obviously- that the offence is not one of accepting bribes, or any other similar felony where there can be no absolution for simply confessing the crime and returning the goods.[41]

How was it that the Chinese accepted such gross disparities being incorporated into the Code that was drafted by their emperor? How did they tolerate discrimination based on one's position and on one's status? Buried in the answer to these questions is the great secret of the Chinese system. Since the emperor assumed the pseudo- Divine role of achieving equilibrium between nature and humanity, and since it was he alone who knew how to manage this dangerous and finely tuned business of maintaining balance, a balance that has been achieved through the cumulative effort of generations, proving that it was exclusively the imperial system that worked, and which therefore rendered any other person powerless to prevent any great disaster that may occur should the emperor for one moment cease his holy work of achieving balance, the Chinese accepted his judicial decisions and methods. The alternative would have been to rebel against His Imperial Majesty with the attendant risks of changing the course of heaven and earth. The Chinese were always very fearful of this risk materializing. The price for such fear: complete acceptance of imperial justice and its methods of implementation. Certainly one may say- and with full justification- that Confucian values, both in relation to the myth surrounding the emperor's role in achieving balance in nature and in relation to the statutory books, had laid so much stress on order and hierarchy within the family and within society s that they had became integral elements within the prevailing philosophy so that they were accepted as part of the natural order. The Confucian system, like the law books which incorporated it, became an integral part of the whole set of principles that sustained the imperial order, and which in turn ensured social order. This system then managed to serve two distinct interests; society's for which Confucius originally labored, and, as is noted above, the imperial interest of maintaining law and order.[42]

---

[41] *Ibid.*, at pp. 35- 36.

[42] A good example of this may be found in Edward L. Farmer, *Zhu Yuanzhang and Early Ming Legislation, the reordering of Chinese society following the era of Mongolo rule*, (Leiden, New York, Cologne: Brill 1995) where it describes at length how and why the founders of the Ming Dynasty chose Neo- Confucianism to model their policies of executive rule.

In order to elevate the authority of the nuclear family it was laid down in the T'ang[43] statutory books that a son who had struck his father or grandfather, or had planned to kill either one of them would be decapitated. In any event even if harm was done to the property of the father or grandfather for the express purpose of inheriting their property during their lifetime, the offender would be punished with three years hard labor.

Included among those offences for which not only the offender in question would be penalized, but also his family, in line with the idea of collective punishment, was that of rebelling against the emperor. In the criminal code it is explained that since the emperor is on par with heaven and earth and since he is the father of all his subjects- rebelling against him is the same as causing a natural disaster, and the only way to counter such activity is to completely destroy the source of the rebellion from its very roots, which necessarily includes all family members of the offender. Obviously this type of mandated punishment had an especially wide deterrent value since the loss of family continuity was the harshest punishment one could inflict on someone trained in Chinese culture.[44] The reason the code refers to the emperor as the father of all his subjects is to show that the penal system compares the elevated position and authority of the father figure with that of the emperor's.

In regard to the position of the family as it related to the regime and to the legal system in place during China's imperial period, so long as the families were relatively small and politically impotent, they were considered the focal point of loyalty and authority for the regime, so that the support given by the government towards family institutions squared off a positive relationship of reciprocal bonds between the family, at the one end, and the institutions of law and order, at the other. Since government positions were decided by the royal courtyard, in accordance with recommendations made by the local population and its dignitaries, and since the social criteria that were to influence such a recommendation were measured in terms of the loyalty and honour a man demonstrated towards his parents, and the amount of obedience he showed specifically towards his father, as well as the academic level, of the candidate, and also, owing to the fact that the positions that were connected to the judiciary were conditional on passing examinations on topics of law, philosophy, and religion, it became the accepted practice that the families would finance the academic studies of one of the children who seemed to them to be the most gifted, in order that he may be promoted by receiving a government career, and thus

[43] See note 1 *supra,* at p. 21.
[44] *Ibid,* at p. 20.

elevate the reputation of the forefathers of that family.[45] Studies were also partially funded by a tax exemption on part of the family's income so that in effect the government was partially subsidizing education.
The traditional Chinese education that nurtured the family included motifs of belief in man and in his good nature, in contradistinction to the western Christian institutions which had continued to teach the idea that the nature of man's heart was evil from his youth.[46]

Chapter F:
Japan and India- Myths and nationalism

Introduction

Japan and India were greatly influenced by the West, yet the uniqueness in each one of them remained with them; their cultural uniqueness was not wiped out, despite the powerful forces of the West that has exerted itself upon Japan for close on two hundred years and upon India for a somewhat longer period. Prior to being under the spell of the West, India was influenced by cultures and religions ranging from Hellenists to the Persians and through to the Islamists; the Muslim influence however was the result of a conquest led by Muslim invaders. As a result of this Islamic conquest a significant part of the Indian subcontinent was turned over to the Muslims, whereas those living in the unconquered sections created for themselves a new religion going by the name Sikhism. Buddhism, on the other hand, came into being as a reactionary movement that rebelled against the Hindu religion. The Muslim conquest, however, eradicated Buddhism from India, yet at the same time it became a primary cause for the rise of Sikhism. Buddhism, in the mean time split into two separate denominations; the first one spreading into South East Asia was identified as the Southern denomination, whereas the Northern denomination had its base in Central Asia and gradually moved onto China, then Korea, and finally Japan. Japan, for its part, long before the arrival of Buddhism to its shores, had already developed rituals celebrating their ancestors, rituals that were practiced by the Shinto religion, and which were similarly practiced in China, the country from which Japan had taken the Confucian system. Japan had accepted Confucianism into its country- via China- before Buddhism arrived there. A striking feature common of both India and of Japan was their burgeoning

[45] *Ibid.*
[46] *Ibid.*, at p. 21.

independent belief systems and religious rituals: In India, Hinduism and in Japan, Shinto. Buddhism however, which had been completely obliterated from India, actually reached Japan, via China. -.

During the ancient period myths were independently nurtured and thus those in India and Japan were very different from one another, and this resulted in the histories of these countries being so different and opposed to one another from the perspective of military invasions that were unleashed upon and from these countries. The geographic locations of Japan and of India served vastly different purposes. Japan is not a transit country, as is the case in India. Japan has only one dominant neighbour- China- India, on the other hand, is surrounded by number of different and mutually hostile powerful neighbours. Japan dwells (or at least dwelled) at "at the furthest corner of the East" in so far as it being untouched by Hellenism, Islam, Christianity and the fire religion (Zoroastrianism). India, in contradistinction is situated within the range of possible physical conquest for all the above named religions, each of which had its own built- in culture. Japan lay outside the range of possible conquest even for the Mongolians and the Chinese; "conquest" as such is relevant in the case of Japan could only take the form of cultural or economic takeover; from this standpoint Japan was indeed "conquered" (without any opposition and at times with the enthusiastic participation of the Japanese themselves) not only by the Chinese but also by the Indians and by those practicing Western culture.[47]

This study's premise will be that myths that were formed during an early era of cultural and national evolution, and that were actively preserved throughout the generations, and which were unique to a specific group of people, and which moreover took the form of serving as a unique monument to that very group- such myths have an incalculable influence in shaping the unique character traits of the said group. The question that will be raised at a later occasion, in relation to Japan

---

[47] The literature that serves as a background and even as a source for what has been written up until now as well as for later on, apart from the other sources that are specifically noted, are the following

(a) Chaim Spielberg, *India-Beliefs and Opinions*, [Hebrew], (Israel: Hadar, 1990)

(b) Jacob Raz, *Japanese Mythology* [Hebrew], (Tel Aviv, Sifri, 2000)

(c) Ben- Ami Shiloni, *Modern Japan-Culture and History* (Schocken, 1997)

(d) Carol Gluck, *Japan's Modern Myths - Ideology in the Late Meiji Period* (Princeton, New Jersey: Princeton University Press, 1985)

(e) Robert King Hall, *Shushin: The Ethics of a Defeated Nation* (New York: Bureau of Publications, Teachers College, Columbia University, 1949)

(f) Masao Maruyama, ed. By Ivan Morris, *Thought and Behviour in Modern Japanese Politics* (London: Oxford University Press, 1963)

and India will be: Is this influence one that forges general collective cooperation, and can therefore be said to instigate national unification, or is this influence of the kind that waves the banner of separatism in that very group, in which case what we have before us is a culture that is not at the same time a national grouping.
Surely when speaking of myths that were created during the pre-scientific period, it was easy and simple for those myths to be absorbed by the imagination, especially since there was no scientific and knowledge induced barrier that would put a stop to any imaginative story. Despite the correctness of this supposition, even nowadays during the modern era, the era of television, there are stories that rely upon the imaginative faculties, such as fantasy films that are geared for children, and decades before then literature that was classified as science fiction, and as there was at an even earlier stage children's literature that relied very much on the imagination, for example, *Snowwhite and the Seven Dwarfs*. War films as well as those of the Wild West genre rely heavily on the imaginative faculties, and their influence from this perspective is indeed powerful. Yet even Wild West features do not classify as the exclusive ironclad inheritance of the American people, rather they try to appeal to a much wider audience. Are we approaching, then, a single universal culture, as a result of all of the above? This question will remain outside the confines of the discussion that will take place within this framework.
The present framework will deal with the type of ancient myths that were unique to a specific delineated territory, and which coloured the nature of that territory's inhabitants; this phenomenon will be tested in the individual cases of Japan and India.

A supplementary premise of this study will be that myths that came about generations ago, amongst a group that before then did not have a clearly defined culture or common history, myths that in their wake were nonetheless successful in forging a collective framework, so that these became the founding myths of the collective, possess a power that is indeed one to be uniquely reckoned with. If for each individual they form the memories of his infancy and early childhood which in turn assisted in forming his personality, for the group they may be considered the prime factors behind its basic and typical impulses, as well as its characteristic behaviour patterns. In the case where the group evolves into a nationality these same myths will accompany this nationality for as long as the latter exists.
A methodological question that begs to be asked - against the backdrop of the completely different historical developments of Japan and of India, and against the backdrop of the primary national or social unification processes of each one of these national of social entities- and one which will eventually be dealt with - is whether fingerprints or other signs can be detected that point to the influence of these various ancient myths upon the historical developments that were unique to

India and to Japan; is perhaps the opposite (also or exclusively) true, viz. that myths are just a mirror of superficial events, including invasions and conquests or an absence of raids and conquests (hereafter: invasions), or of geopolitical circumstances that give rise to the prevalence or absence of these raids. The term invasion is used to describe both those invasions into Japan or India and those that took the form of military assignments outside the said countries` borders, for the purposes of military conquests. These conquests then may be viewed through the lens of either the conqueror or the conquered. The question that remains is to what extent these created myths assisted in forging a feeling of being a national collective, and in turn to what extent did this nationalist feeling take the form of a belligerent nationalism, whether for pre-emptive –conquering warfare, or for defensive warfare, against an external conqueror. Likewise the differences between the formation of a culture othe one hand and the unifying of a nation, on the other, will be examined.
The discussion will therefore have to deal, later on, with the mutual influences exerted by each of the following factors:The geopolitical circumstances:

i. The invasions or absence of invasions, and the conduct of the group or society in relation to these invasions
ii. The myths that were created
iii. The nationalism that was formed, if and when this came about.

As to the order of setting things out, the questions that have been formulated thus far, will not be dealt with separately and in any ordered structure. Rather by providing an overall description of events that will take note of specific things and that will draw certain conclusions, an answer will be given to all the questions that have been raised in this introduction.

Section 1: Ancient Japan

Human life has existed in Japan, as far as is known, for 100,000 years. For most of these years it was part of the Asian continent. Japan became an archipelago about 20,000 years ago. As will be shown later, in the course of a vast period of time, waves of immigrants reached the shores of Japan. Japan never suffered conquest as a result thereof, but rather underwent an assimilative process that was to contribute to its progressive features.

The *Jo'mon* Period:
During the period extending from 7,500 B.C.E. to 5,000 B.C.E Japan`s inhabitable areas were populated by groups consisting of 10- 15 persons. Life expectancy in Japan, at that point in time, averaged, according to anthropologists, not more than

30 years. Human life was sustained during that period by searching and gathering. Coming straight after this period was the Early Jo`mon Period (5,000 B. C. E-3,500 B. C. E) where, according to anthropologists, fishing, and hunting villages offering cooked food, proliferated. The Middle Jo`mon Period (3,500 B. C. E-2,400 B. C. E) which started off with a population increase, witnessed the introduction of socially oriented ritual; cooking became a household activity and specially decorated utensils were thus in vogue. There developed a mystical aura surrounding snakes, and people began to understand something about the human soul, marking the gradual formation of a religious consciousness. Graven images were carved out for the purposes of religious ceremonies and certain symbols were identified with giving birth, or with the rejuvenation of the soul. From the way in which the dead were treated it is possible to deduce that there was a belief in life after death. The dead were buried on the ground floor of purpose built homes where they were interred in large pitchers. Towards the end of this period the weather conditions worsened bringing in their wake heavy rains accompanied by ferocious storms. This, in turn, caused many people to flee from the mountainous regions making their way towards the beaches and valleys. During the Third Jo`mon Period (2,400 B. C. E- 1,000 B. C. E) rituals were even more advanced, in line with the increasingly various ways of earning a livelihood, most of which were dependent upon seasonal changes, that were more readily available to the populace. The most important occupations included fishing, hunting, collecting oysters and assembling them, and, at this stage, a primitive form of bartering merchandise was also introduced. During the fourth and Last Jo`mon Period (1000 B. C. E. - 300 B. C. E) the weather in the south western parts of Japan was especially bad, and the local population decreased sharply. Yet, contemporaneously, agriculture was making its mark on the people. Though the continually worsening weather conditions towards the end of this period led to a sharp decrease in Japan's south western population, it also produced in its wake a parallel increase in those preoccupied with religious ceremony and ritual. Apparently this was an attempt at seeking refuge from the very difficult times that had so damaged the population's livelihoods that they had found it nigh impossible just to manage to survive. This may explain, as will be noted later, the dominant theme of preoccupation with magic and with communicating with the gods, which was a leading motif adopted by the ruling class. It also explains the trend by the ruling elites of the small political entities to bind together and to form various federations. It even sheds light on the later and more radical move, viz. the formation of the grand monarchies which had come about as the result of the unification of the disparate federations under a single and all- powerful centralized government.

Yayoi Period

As a result of the aforesaid a new period in Japanese history was inaugurated. It would later be referred to as the Yayoi (300 B. C. E- 300 C. E). It is speculated that the population that flourished during this period was quite different from that of the Jo`mon Period. This was a migrant population who had arrived in Japan as the result of regime change in China, as well as the attendant reorganization of political life by the centralised Chinese Imperial Regime, which had also conquered parts of Korea. Japan now witnessed new developments in agriculture, and with the importation of bronze implements, advances were made in the quality of weaponry on the one hand and of household necessities (e.g. bronze mirrors) on the other. Sustainable villages that were equipped with defensive tunnels sprung up, and concomitantly separate cemeteries were set up where the decisive factor for burial was the well-connectedness of the deceased's blood relatives. The industry for developing bronze tools gradually expanded so that iron weapons made their appearance. [48] The development of trade in merchandise required that suitable political organizations be set up, and so there emerged communities, headed by a shaman, or religious priest, where this priest would confer binding authority on those who took it upon themselves to organize and restructure political institutions within their communities. This later evolved, as was hinted to above, into federations that consisted of smaller political entities, where each of these entities were in fact individual villages, groups of villages, or a larger tribe that lived together within a specific geographic location. For a long period of time there were specific cultural differences between two competing regimes: On the one hand there was the Western Japanese Federation/ Kingdom, which was a kingdom that was based in the Nara Valley, and which fell under the influence of, and established strong links with Korea and China. On the other hand, there was the ruling federation that had established itself in the south eastern parts of Japan. The Nara Valley Kingdom was especially advanced having had a very sophisticated irrigation system. Its fortified cities with its strongly defended trenches and watchtowers were equipped with the finest armoury thanks to Korean suppliers arming this kingdom with bronze and iron weapons.

According to the Chinese narrative, this period witnessed wars that raged on for a number of decades and that were fought amongst the multitude of mini- states that then existed. A truce was reached after each state renounced its premier and recognized as the Supreme Sovereign over their combined states, an unmarried woman by the name of *Fimiko*. Her main source of authority lay in her ability to

---

[48] All that has been said until now is culled from The Cambridge History of Japan, vol. 1, ed. Delmer M. Brown (Cambridge: Cambridge University Press, 1993).

perform magic, and she managed the affairs of the state with the assistance of her younger brother. *Fimiko* sent a delegation armed with gifts for the Chinese emperor who returned the favour by sending his peappointed ambassador to her federation. After *Fimiko* passed away, war resumed. It continued until, eventually, the various factions accepted the sovereignty of a girl, 13 years old. Like her predecessor, she accepted recognition from the ambassador of the Chinese Emperor as governess of the federation, especially after she displayed similar care in taking care to send the Chinese emperor a delegation that bore with them her gifts.[49]

The motif of governance that had gained popularity at the time of the *Yayoi* regime, a regime peopled by refugees who had originated from the Asian continent and who had therefore absorbed the Chinese culture, was an adaptation of a specifically Chinese fundamental principle. This fundamental principle that was essentially predominant in the whole of the inhabited world was not unique to Eastern Asia. In terms of this principle, the ruling class had to establish a direct link with the gods. If in China, a philosophy developed endowing the Chinese Imperial Ruler with supernatural powers that had emanated from celestial bodies, and which supernatural powers provided this emperor with the ability to prevent disasters, and because being acknowledged as one possessed of supernatural abilities, any hint of a rebellion would be regarded as a mega disaster - then - Japan too would follow this general route. Therefore those wishing to acquire the reins of leadership, whether their ambitions were confined to being a premier of one of the many mini- states or whether their ambition extended further to being the Supreme Sovereign under whose jurisdiction the many states are united to form one centralized country, they had to navigate the paths that would lead them to a direct link with the Upper Worlds. In order to locate this path religious ceremonies and rituals would have to be performed, and the prospective leader would have to be fortunate enough to be included in the mythology that ascribes to him a special relationship with the gods. The reins of power could not be acquired by military prowess alone, but to a great extent there had to be the popular belief that the future leader possessed supernatural abilities. Those who had attained the status of premier-whether over a small kingdom, or whether over a monarchy that had exercised its jurisdiction over the smaller kingdoms- were only recognized as de jure leaders if it was confirmed that they indeed were possessed of supernatural powers. To prove the above, rituals, ceremonies and witchcraft were performed under the auspices of the leadership. The heads of government were scrupulous not to personally undertake the daily running of affairs of state, but preferred to

---

[49] See above, and see also Sources of Japanese Tradition ,ed. Theodore de Bary, (New York: Columbia University Press, 1958)

appoint subordinates who, working on behalf of their superiors, would independently implement the decisions reached by them as regards to government. The position of the ruling elites was also enhanced by the personal recognition granted by the chief Imperial Ruler of that time, the Chinese Emperor, whose acknowledgement aided in forming the unassailable impression that the declared leader was indeed in charge, and therefore such recognition was cherished by all of Japan's leaders.

What marked out this period most was Japan's unashamed imitation of the standard required of Chinese rulers - a standard, as was described above. That standard had had universal application during the primeval period (associating the leader with supernatural abilities) - but was reconstructed to conform to the Japanese reality and to the Japanese nature. Certain features of Japan's administration were always at variance with that of China's. In its final crystallized incarnation Japan allocated separate roles for those claiming to have acquired supernatural powers, who were then appointed its nominal leaders, and those who did not claim such power but were nevertheless part of Japan's de facto leadership. The rituals, albeit based loosely on Chinese general principles, were uniquely Japanese, the independent product of Japanese ingenuity, and thus when describing the creation of the world these rituals depicted the Japanese islands as the first land masses that were created. Befitting its status of being a far- flung country that was not located at the centre of the world like in the case of China, Japan did not seize onto any pretentious myths of their rulers being blessed with the ability of balancing the forces of the universe. It was precisely this centrality that was wittingly not woven into the fabric of Japanese mythology. While there was a definite allusion to the Chinese system of government, in practice there were marked differences to it. In China, for instance, the "Emperor of the Sun" was assisted by others in his regime's administration who formed the bureaucracy, and who acted under direct orders of their emperor, being totally subordinate to him. In Japan, contrarily, both the local shamans and the king or Supreme Emperor were not directly assisted in the running of affairs by those personally subordinate to them. Rather, they contractually conferred limited and lay authority onto an individual who in terms of the contract became the de facto local leader which in turn provided the latter with a free hand at running local affairs. From this perspective it is apparent that the Japanese regime was a lot less centralized than was its Sino counterpart.

Yamato Kingdom

Unable to survive the radical changes imposed upon its government, the (Chinese) Han dynasty came to an abrupt halt causing the, albeit temporary, crumbling of centralized government in China which in turn ensured that the governments of China and Korea were unable to function properly. As a result thereof a new wave of refugees fled to Japan's shores, this time, the majority, hailing from neighbouring Korea. These refugees after encroaching upon the south western parts of Japan, which according to various estimations, was, at that time, sparsely populated, established a government which in the course of time expanded its presence to the rest of Japan. Thus the Yamato period enters the annals of Japanese history. This kingdom established, as would be expected, strong ties with Korea and managed to procure from that country iron lodes, enabling them to attain superior might by manufacturing iron weapons (swords and spears) from this imported material. In addition this kingdom experienced growth and development in other areas by virtue of them setting up irrigation systems that improved the soil and enlarged the tracts that were available for agricultural exploitation so that the rice yield was markedly enhanced. In light of these feats and in light of the fact that religious ceremonies emphasized that it was the Yamato followers who were instrumental in helping their king establish such a powerful empire, the Yamato kingdom managed to gain superiority over all the other competing Japanese powers, and their territorial jurisdiction just grew. This emboldened kingdom spread itself out [50] so that it now reigned over parts of Korea and became an ally of one of the Korean kingdoms, assisting the latter in waging war against another kingdom. Indeed, it was these types of war adventures in Korea that were responsible for the Yamato kingdom sustaining irremediable losses, so that, after deliberating amongst themselves, the decision was taken to cease getting mired further into Korea's battles, and instead to concentrate on investing in Japan's booming agriculture.

This kingdom owed its success, according to some researchers in this field, to the national origin of the ruling classes of the Yamato kingdom, (as well as other ruling classes who were then in Japan), which was Korean. The effect of welcoming to its shores immigrants who had originated in China and who had passed through Korea before arriving in Japan indeed made a cultural mark on the Japanese lifestyle but not to the same extent as did the new population influx. It was, however the indigenous inhabitants who, running their internal affairs to such a remarkable degree, ensured that any immigrant coming from the Asian continent

[50] This, according to Japanese Chronicles mentioned in notes 64- 65 supra; however, Korean annals omit this episode. It would appear; in any event that the direct Korean influences and the more indirect Chinese influence that was filtered through by traversing Korea was indeed very powerful in Japan of that time. Burial customs, as in the shrouds that were worn and other related customs, that were preserved until this day in Japan, and which date back to the Yamato period, do more than merely hint at the Korean and Chinese influences that infiltrated into Japan.

and disembarking in Japan was immediately woven into the Japatapestry; and even though during the internecine wars with their attendant conquests and inevitable captive taking, prisoners of war were effectively treated like slaves, on the whole, Japan never treated its ordinary newcomers as slaves, and neither was there ever any attempt at expelling populations wholesale, rather the prevailing policy was to encourage assimilation of the races where everyone benefited from an infusion of culture and technology. This assimilative process was responsible for transforming a heterogeneous population into a uniform cultural bloc where each shared a similar lifestyle under one sovereign. The expansion of the territorial jurisdiction of the sovereign was attributable to religious ceremonies that relied upon religious motifs, more so than it was on the use of force, which was of secondary importance. The leader who expanded his territory was also the one who initiated the more advanced economic systems, especially in the area of agricultural watering systems and promoting overall agricultural prosperity as well as improving methods of government. Despite the odd occurrence of internal warfare, the most common way of gaining control over any of the Japanese provinces was through assassinating its premier. In this scenario the subjects of the previous leader change their allegiances, and without any resistance they pledge their loyalties to the assassin of their previous leader- this because leadership was based its association with the power of the magi- which guaranteed a direct link to the deities- more so than it was based on coercion. This can be explained by realising that the people had undergone a cultural and religious transition and had been conditioned to believe that it made no difference which person occupied the seat of power, so long as that person was thought to have the power of communicating with the gods. The gods were those forces that had had supernatural powers or, at the very least, had powers equal to the forces of nature. Woven out of this reality was a cultural tapestry whose material belief was the notion that their leadership had to be religious, and that their leaders or kings had an intimate link with the gods. The Yamato kingdom governed according to the belief system and culture that were imported from China, while preserving their ties not only with Korea but also with China and the Sino imperial court. This manifested itself when during the period of the *Yamato* kingdom the Japanese king, *Ahakomi* who reigned from 581- 600 C. E, sent a gift bearing delegation, to His Chinese Imperial Majesty, with a message. The message read "the boy child of the sun that rises in the east sends his greetings to the boy child of the sun that sets in the west." This gesture proved that the Japanese king, being the Chinese* emperor's equally-ranked ruler, viewed himself as joined with the Divine, as that concept was religiously interpreted in China. It would be superfluous to add that this last message failed to find favour in the eyes of the Chinese emperor [51] who

[51] See Sources of Japanese Tradition, at note 65 above, at p. 11.

was of the opinion that all of the neighbouring governed states were subject to his imperial governance. And indeed in the ordinary course of events the Yamato king, like the kings who reigned in Korea, understood that the highest and most central authority was that of the Chinese Imperial Highness. However there were flashes in that period, when, within the framework of one uniform culture prevailing in China and its environs, the Japanese head of state perceived himself as on par with his Chinese counterpart.

Thoughts on the Uniqueness of Japan

The Japanese are a nation of immigrants that arrived at "the edge of the world". This is especially true as viewed through the lens of Chinese culture; which culture held that Japan was by its very nature a place of last resort from which one could travel or emigrate no further. There was therefore no alternative for those who reached Japan's shores from nearby, bearing in mind their feelings and orientations during those ancient times, but to integrate into the existing society and to continue to accept the arrival of newer and fresher immigrants. So, eventually, all the population and their various cultures would be assimilated into one bloc for the mutual benefit of all. For those immigrants arriving on this archipelago there was no place where they could expel the native inhabitants. At a time when fragile continental bridges joined Japan to the Asian continent, and at a time when the ocean straits containing relatively shallow waters covered over those bridges at every occasion when the ocean level exceeded its limits, it was quite obvious that there was no place where the exiting population in Japan could be deported. This is especially true since sailing to far off southern islands such as Taiwan and the Philippines was made difficult by the inadequate sea vessels of the time, which would have found it impossible to convey a whole host of refuges in one go. These abovementioned facts were responsible for people viewing Japan as indeed placed at "the edge of the world"; neither a place from which one could travel any further nor a place from which one could expel others. Without doubt this perception was to wield its influence upon the evolving religious motifs, cultural ideas and systems of government that had spurted forth from the "centre of the universe", China. The geographic location of Japan was to influence the uniqueness of that country, which never had pretensions of being original but which openly craved approval in the following areas: culture, religion, technology as well as systems of government which included burial customs and general attitudes towards the ruling class. Nonetheless by virtue of the Japanese receiving their institutions second- hand from others, and at the same time being physically positioned at a "dead end" so that they were handicapped from extending their influence any further, and given that Japan's fa⊓ade underwent constant facelifts with the ever increasing waves of immigrants arriving at the Japanese "cul-de-sac," forcing the different waves of immigrants to submit their cultures to the melting pot of assimilation, the Japanese melded their received traditions so that they were commensurate with their unique circumstances, character, and lifestyles. Concomitantly, not only did the Japanese not recoil from setting up innovations, but they regarded any introduction of change as inherently sanctified. From the Japanese perspective this last- mentioned fact was the prime reason why they were totally unafraid of foreign influences. Reinforcing this trend of the Japanese to dispose of suspicious thoughts regarding foreigners and foreign influence was the fact that they were based on an island that was naturally fortified from any outside invaders. [52]

In order to appreciate the Japanese uniqueness especially in relation to China as well as seeing the similarity between the two perspectives that will be outlined in subparagraph (a) and (b) below, it would be appropriate to relate both to the differences and similarities when comparing China with Japan,
so that:

(i) When viewing the unique differences between these two nations the different sources for moral authority in each country should be investigated, and

(ii) When viewing the common moral ground that exists in both China and Japan, it may be recorded that in both these countries the religion that prevails is one where social and familial behaviour are determined by the

---

[52] Skipping to the perspective of the 20th and 21st centuries and looking back at history from the heights of this century, a similarity is raised but also a distinction may be made between the British Isles' attitude to the European Continent and Japan's attitude to the Asian Continent. Invaders from France and Northern Europe came to the British Isles for the express purpose of taking control of it since their culture was somewhat different from the conquered native British Isles population, and although a process of cultural assimilation did eventually take place this was not at the same "smooth" pace and unruffled way as that that occurred in Japan. Nevertheless, the non- aggressive internal dialogue that took place in Britain, which had very few bloody revolutions, is somewhat reminiscent of the situation that prevailed in Japan. The tendency that prevails nowadays where the judiciary is reluctant to call into question a decision by the executive who implement the law nor by the legislature who draft it, reminds one of the restraint and non-judicial activism of the English judges particularly, and the British ones in general. All this alludes to the fact that both cultural tapestries were woven in situations where no traumas of external invasion were suffered. Traumatic experiences caused by invasions would have left their mark on the political and judicial dialogues that each country fosters. It is in this scenario, then that the similarities come into view as well as the differences, between Japan and Britain.

horizontal relationship between man and his fellow(this, in contradistinction to Christianity where the religious- behavioural stress was laid on the obligations that further the fulfilment of the Divine precepts), which ties into the functions ascribed to the Chinese and Japanese deities ,a function that is epitomized by and which primarily focuses upon the motif of aid and comfort that the Deity tenders or is meant to tender towards humanity . This is sharply differentiated from God's punitive function where He punishes or is bound to punish the sinner, or to the related idea of confession which provides man with Divine fand pardon. It is even at variance with the idea of Godly kindness that absolves humanity of its sinfulness. Having nothing to say about sin it is far removed from the idea of the fires of hell. All of these ascriptions are commonplace in Christianity, but are completely absent from the Chinese and Japanese religions.

The above requires elucidation, and I shall therefore begin with the second subparagraph, subparagraph (b), which looks at the characteristics shared by China and Japan as well as those features that distinguish both of these from Christian culture:

Japan like China was raised on the lap of religion, or more correctly, polytheistic religion, where the gods are undemanding in their relationship to the individual and to his social behaviour. They do not punish the individual for this or that type of behaviour in his responses towards his social environment. Christianity, like Judaism before it, belongs to the monotheistic family of religion, which speaks of one solitary God Who created the earth and all that is in it. This God is differentiated from his creations, and he therefore requires that man fulfil the commandments and duties that are imposed upon him. Accordingly, monotheistic religions mandate that man be punished and held accountable for acting in a disgraceful manner towards his society. Therefore, as analyzed in Dale's book on Japan [53], it can be claimed in regards to Japan that they do not have the concept of guilt feelings (the internalisation of the idea that one is destined to be Divinely punished, an idea that exists in the Western- Christian world, even after this same world became composed of states where the regimes there have separated religion and politics); the Japanese, according to this claim developed the idea of feeling terribly ashamed, and these feelings are primarily instigated by the social environment. According to this understanding, guilt feelings are the internalisation of Divine punishment and feelings of shame are an internalisation of social belittlement. Social ridicule rears its head as a result of the ethical mores that are

[53] Peter N. Dale The Myth of Japanese Uniqueness, (Beckenham, Australia: Croom Helm Ltd., 1986).

contained in the Laws of Confucius. Therefore the internalization of these ethical mores, mores that have been submerged into the national myths that determine what is and what is not proper behaviour has no relationship to the wrath of the gods or even to God Himself. This is what is meant by the horizontal relationship that was referred to above, a relationship that is sharply at variance with that depicting an angry and punishing God reacting to man. That latter scenario is an apt description of a vertical relationship.

Religion governs behaviour according to a set of rules; the question that arises however is how compliance is judged. If when discussing the punitive measures that are meted out, the concept of punishment and reward that emanates from the Divinity (or from the idol) is spoken of then one knows that this discussion is directly shaped by the religious morality as it relates to social behaviour and conduct. If, contrarily, the religion talks about myths and stories filled with plots that allude to or internalize certain behaviour, then, this type of religion, immersed as it into this kind of mythology, contains fundamental principles. These principles guide man in how he should conduct his social affairs, without, however, basing it on a Divine imperative, or any imperative for that matter. Even those portions in mythology that are devoted to the conduct of the deities and how they related to each other is only recorded in order to teach man how to act within a social framework and how to stick by the rules. However since this is a polytheistic religion (like the Japanese and *Sino* model, and even the Hindu religion as well as other pagan religions) there is no mention of punishment and at the very most there is only an allusion to the consequences of one's actions. A god does not actually punish, and he too may suffer as a result of some misunderstanding (as is often the case in Japanese examples[54]), and from this episode people are taught that suffering is something that at times is impossible to avoid. Yet what is also implicit is the fact that errors in behaviour may be the result of both positive and negative influences that inspire the person committing the error. From here it is evident that human behaviour is very important, one has therefore to study its principles and to be meticulous in fulfilling its dictates. This then is the Rule of Behaviour which gives rise to the Rules of Morality.

After comprehending what is said above it is becomes apparent that the horizontal relationship that prevails between the gods in the course of their social and mutual conduct teaches one how he should approach human interpersonal relationships. Just as the gods commit mistakes when acting within their reciprocal relationships, whereas it would be preferable were they to conduct themselves without committing the unfortunate error, so too human beings, when dealing with their

---

[54] See Sources of Japanese Tradition, note 65 supra, at pp. 17- 18 that speaks of the romance that took place between the god of the storms and the goddess of the sun.

fellow man, need to find a mode of behaviour that is correct for them. Therefore, the Japanese, as was maintained above, were traditionally preoccupied with developing the whole notion of (social) embarrassment and viewing it as a core belief of their moral laws. In contrast, the modern-Christian, world, at the same time, were developing the concept of sin and of punishment, of a good inclination and of a bad inclination, of man being evil from his infancy, and from here one did not have to make a great leap to arrive at guilt feelings.
This above description enlightens us as to the common attributes shared by the Chinese and Japanese heritages, and as was, also, in all likelihood developed further by the wider circle of Far eastern countries that were spread across South East Asia. It is these attributes that fundamentally distinguish the Eastern and Southern parts of Asia from the Western world. [55] However even within the framework of features that are shared by the Chinese and the Japanese, it is noticeable that the Japanese heritage has some unique and exclusive characteristics. To understand why Japan was so exclusive, it has to be queried how and who produced Japan's Shinto mythology, and whether this mythology was responsible for Japan standing out, and for being so unique in this field. It needs to be reiterated: what is discussed is its uniqueness in the field of mythology, and therefore it has to do with subparagraph (a) above.
In order to understand things from a broader perspective, it would be proper to refer to Chapter 2 above, where our discussion led us to talk about the various opinions as to the sources for the creation of religious myths, and where, to this end, the views of Ezekiel Kaufman and Henri Bergson were canvassed. Kaufman speaks of the idea of monotheism being the product of a collective, not the brainchild of one individual, but rather of a nationality. Bergson relates it, contrarily to the personal product of single individuals who reached their conclusions through exercising their powerful wills and exerting their supreme human effort, until they reached an elevated level. He speaks about the very strong inner desire that led man to mystical encounters, encounters that only an elite few were given the opportunity to experience.
Kaufman's view, in so far as it speaks of a collective spiritual creativity, concurs with the findings of the German historical school of thought, as expressed by Gierke, Savingy, and Fuchta, especially when these three gentlemen discuss those

[55] See Dale's book mentioned in note 69, supra, where he lists all the differences between the Japanese and the Western nations, where he takes pride in the fact that his research details the differences between the behaviour of Japanese bees and the behaviour of bees reared in the West.

customs that are endowed with the same validity as a statute since they are reflective of the "spirit of the nation." [56]
The Chinese theory of morality is built on layers upon layers but at its centre stands one theory, the heritage of one great- spirited individual, Confucius, who although not credited with the powers of creation *ex nihilo*, accurately mirrored all the ethical principles that had shaped China, even before his time. Consequently the Chinese regard Confucius as their Great Teacher.
The Japanese also adopted the moral teachings of Confucius, as they adopted othersocial and religious features that originated in China. In any event the Japanese* modified anything that was received by them from external sources, so that it suits their unique independence, the Japanese "People's spirit". The heritage of the Japanese, although built with imported materials, was the product of collective Japanese national "masticating". The Chinese had raised on a pedestal the art of exact copying whether it related to drawing ancient pictures or copying ancient poems after they had been destroyed not just once, but a recurring number of times, whenever a Chinese regime takeover occurred. [57]
Though the Chinese introduced a number of creative innovations when perfecting their art of replication, so that creativity, indeed, was something that beat within their chests no less than it did within the Japanese', the very fact that they channelled so much of their personal artistic energies into mastering the art of copying is indicative of the veneration the Chinese had for their cultural motif of "honouring elders", [58] which is an offshoot of the wider principles of "going backwards (honouring past events)." Therefore the Chinese institution of copying did not find any parallel in, nor was it incorporated into, Japanese artwork that refused to adopt this copying system. The Japanese, then, did not view things of the past as inherently sanctified so that they require to be wholly replicated rather they viewed past artwork as a good basis from which they could build on to their creativity. This is related to the Japanese creative process which was a process of collective artistry, rather than following after one "outstanding Master", and teacher, to a whole mass of intellectuals, as was the case in China. [59] The

[56] See Sir Carleton Kemp Allen, Law in the Making, (Oxford: At the Clarendon Press, 1958), pp. 91- 92.

[57] See Rykmans, " The Chinese Attitude Towards The Past," Papers on Far Eastern History (1989), 39: 1

[58] It was this very principle that Mao Tse Tung tried so hard to uproot when he embarked upon his "cultural revolution". That he so obviously failed in his mission to annul this motif can be seen in the very old age of his successors to the premiership of China.

[59] Therefore the Japanese, like the Jews- as Kaufman interprets it in note 1 supra- are creative as a collective and are group oriented rather than being comprised of a few

Japanese, as has been previously stated, made creative use of the raw materials that were handed over to them, so that they shaped them, improved them and adapted them into the Japanese heritage.

The Chinese up until the 15th century had advanced at a much faster pace than had Europe. While Chinese inventions, like paper and gunpowder, were readily imported into Europe, the Chinese found it much more difficult to return the compliment and to adopt and adapt Western innovations. This situation was to last until 1911, at which time imperial rule came to an abrupt end. The Japanese in contradistinction, already during the Meiji period, perhaps before, but for certain afterwards, studied and researched the culture, inventions, and work habits of the Europeans. Just as they had studied and adopted things from China so too they would diligently study and adopt elements of the West. The Chinese during the Imperial period tried very hard to preserve their status of being a country that was at the centre of the planet; a country where others would visit its shores in order to learn from it, not a country that would learn from others. This is not to say that the Chinese did not receive anything from others, and Buddhism is probably the best

---

individual creative people after whom the masses flock. Collective creativity, as Kaufman understands it, allowed the Jews to penetrate into the idea of monotheism and to further develop it over the course of generations. The wealth of discussions in the Talmud (Mishna and Gemorrah), the medieval commentators, and those of the Modern Period of Jewry (dating back to the 17th century) which has run its course over thousands of years has all in all produced a multilayered and collective effort which has its distinct advantages. So too has been the case with Japanese creativity. It is possible to find an Egyptian myth where it speaks of only one deity, but this does not mean that it in any way resembles the monotheism of the Children of Israel that developed within Judaism as a collective and rich cultural product. So too, the motifs that the Japanese imported from China and from the West were passed through a fiery furnace so that they were completely altered by Japanese collective creativity in such a way that surpassed the individual artistry of "geniuses of that generation" or even of the grand masters. The circumstances that led to Japan developing a culture of collective creativity, like that found in Judaism, has been briefly hinted at here, without completely clarifying the reasons, a more complete elucidation may be put on hold until a later opportunity arises. For the time being it may be speculated, without actually vouching for its veracity, that this collective nature is attributable to the short height of the Japanese especially in relation to those from whom they were learning, so that so long as they were in their presence individually they felt short. Likewise the Jews who received the Pentateuch felt dwarfed by the Presence of the Creator of the Universe. The Chinese, during the Imperial reign, felt as if they were at the centre of the world, and this feeling of superiority was then receptive to the idea that those on an even more elevated level like the Grand Master and other specially gifted individuals are the only ones who are supremely endowed with creativity. They therefore by definition could only recognize the creativity of the individual and not of the group.

example of the fact that they did adopt ideas that were imported. However the Chinese, like the Japanese adapted Buddhism and created strains of it that were appropriate for them. In theory this does contradict the motif of imitation and of honouring those from whom one is studying, however in this case the Chinese regime were vested with an interest to hitch Buddhism to its wagon. Therefore when the regime realized that Buddhism may be undermining the status of government they had no misgivings when harming the Buddhist priests and dispersing them across the country as came to pass in the 9th century C.E. This approach of the Chinese regime ties in with another Chinese motif, viz. distinguishing ancient objects and ideas that are of Chinese origin, which must be meticulously studied and observed, without allowing for any alterations, from those things that have reached China from the outside. The latter, if adopted in its entirety would invalidate the Chinese belief that they are central to everything, and therefore by definition these objects cannot be considered hallowed (i.e. worthy of imitation). Against this backdrop, a backdrop that is somewhat different from the Japanese one, the Chinese, in line with the interests of their centralized regime, tailored the Buddhist religion so that it could be synchronized with the Chinese lifestyle and with its ancient religions. The Japanese, on the other hand, always acted with awe and respect towards those whom, in their estimation, were worthy of learning from, and so regarded it as completely natural to receive knowledge from outside their boundaries. The Japanese never had pretensions of being placed at the centre of the world. Not only did the Japanese not possess any of the Chinese arrogance that was an inevitable consequence of that country's belief in its prime importance, but the former were also a lot less concerned about outside infiltrators and therefore did not feel threatened by theories and knowledge that had originated beyond their borders. Ultimately, the phenomenon of tailoring Buddhism so that it suits local conditions was shared in equal measure by both China and Japan, yet the underlying motifs in each of these countries were poles apart.

The question arises: does all that has been stated above have anything to do with the developments Japan underwent until it was forced to witness the end of the Yamato reign? And did these developments create a solid and fundamental cultural principle that was to leave its mark upon the Japanese heritage and upon the deep-seated inclinations of the Japanese, even after these developments were put on hold? Though the evidentiary material that has thus far been presented is far from complete and it would appear that it contains insufficient information to construct any reasonably stable theories so that an impenetrable barrier has been set up, it may be cracked open, by relying, not on unassailable proof, but upon conjecture. This guesswork might at some later stage be refined, refuted, and then rehabilitated, as will, in fact, be the case, yet there is a basis even at this juncture for vague definitions and speculative remarks.

There is a possibility, ·then, that the Japanese adoption of grand pagan culture at that time, and now, allowed it to relate to changing events and to new possibilities without feeling a drop of guilt; they managed to quite easily view things from their utilitarian perspective without pausing to think, for any significant amount of time, about the moral ramifications, as did people in the West. Because they are so adept at focusing on the pragmatic, the Japanese are unhindered by any fears concerning philosophies, *weltaunshaung*, and systems that are innovative but that are imported from the outside. Rather they gracefully honour anyone who is able to teach them. The honour of the Japanese is not harmed when they confront others who know more than them, neither are they held back by feelings of inferiority from initiating links with those endowed with more constructive knowledge. The foothold for these character traits was constructed steadily over a period of one millennium that stretched roughly from the 3rd century B. C. E. until the 7th century C. E.

Returning back to the Yamato Kingdom

The idea that religion and government should be unified, an idea that was an important element of Chinese governance, was altered by Japan already during the Yayoi regime, which separated the religious authorities who were nominally in charge, from the secular de facto authorities even if they had to recognize and submit to the superior religious power. However during the Yamato reign the absolute ruler was still the one who was closely connected to the gods or whose lineage could be traced back to some deity. The myths surrounding the gods were used to inaugurate the Shinto religion, a religion that was exclusive to Japan, and whose mythology elevated the centrality of Japan alongside its raising of the Japanese premier's stature.

In Japan, instead of adopting the Chinese bureaucratic system, the central authorities were less formal and more familial. One of the innovative idemployed by the government was to invent the familial lineage of the provincial governors, so that fictitious blood ties to the king, to one of his ministers, or to members of the central government that was located in the royal court were created. There were other kinds of links between the provincial governor and the royal palace, for instance, religious, economic, military, and sundry other ties. Since Japan accommodated a variety of groups each of which bonded together because of the kinship shared between each group member, it was ties of blood that were to act as the glue holding together the ruling elites' grasp on power. There was a hierarchy, then, that divided the various groups within the kingdom, so that the group that could show a relationship to those who lived in the area upon which the palace was built were placed at the highest rung, especially since it was their particular land that was allocated for royal burials. Since each of these classes vied amongst themselves for prime position and since within the classes themselves competing claims on the delicate question of ancestry was threshed out, the king, at least according to one of the few stories that have survived, worked towards putting an end to this unhealthy competition that without doubt hampered the exercise of his authority. He accomplished this goal by resolving that one who claims that his lineage makes him eligible for a leadership role, must state his version of events before the king who then tests his credibility by placing the claimant's hands into a utensil of boiled water in which are placed scalding stones. If the aspiring leader is successful in removing one of these stones, without burning his hands in the process, then his story is believed. As would be expected, most of those invited to offer their version did not pitch up, and those who did escaped for their lives, and so in this way, at least according to fable, competition over lineage was stalled. [60] This story demonstrates the struggle that took place firstly between the central government and other centres of authority that claimed supremacy on the basis of their blood ties, and secondly between the central government and those personas who also owing to their kinship represented a competing claim. The situation was altered when those holding the position of regional governor were blood relatives of the royal family. The position of these regional governors and the regional government's other key employees, which was continually being upgraded in the course of the Japanese kingdom's expansion into heretofore unoccupied territories, was further augmented by very unique means. Long before expansion the class of people who were closely related to one another and whose task it was maintain the royal palace, and for which purpose they dwelled within the vicinity of the palace, sent their own people out to the far off provinces where they would exercise their powers of authority. In this way this closely knit family secured the loyalty of the key officeholders in the peripheral regions and was thus able to ward off the possibility that these regional government officials would unite behind the local region's leaders. Another way the central government strengthened its hold was by training their relatives, even those distantly related, for professional work that required special qualifications. This guaranteed that these professionals were at the forefront of the construction of the sophisticated canal and irrigation systems and were also responsible for building large burial sites. In addition they carried out the professional work that was associated with iron lodes, viz. sword manufacture, as well as horse breeding and similar occupations that played a key role in the management and control of government. As the number of these experts increased,

[60] See The Cambridge History of Japan, in note 64 supra at pp. 137- 138, where this story is associated with King Ingyo who lived at the beginning of the 5th century C. E. and which is verified in two early written sources: Nihon Shoki and Kojiki.

the prestige of the king grew manifold; after all the abovementioned jobs were highly regarded and were thus in great demand.
In any event there were rebellions that had to be suppressed, and the greatest of these rebellions managed to leave a traumatic scar on the Royal household. Likewise the defeat at the hands of the Korean army left severe wounds in its wake. In answer to these calamities the central government decided to concentrate its efforts on advancing the economy and on raising the standard of living as well as upgrading the organizational abilities of the government. This was all predicated on the premise that a wise ruler is one who is able to better the lot of his subjects. Another way of strengthening the will of the populace was through establishing regal estates in the far flung regions of the kingdom. [61]
The state's punitive system was very harsh and as a result thereof the number of criminal felonies like theft was indeed very low. The boiled water and scalding stone method was employed a number of times during criminal trials, and the mere hint of it was enough to ward off individuals not get entangled in criminal activity. [62]

From the standpoint of criminal proceedings, therefore, the Japanese had the upper hand against the Chinese, who even though, had used torture during criminal proceedings, the methods of torture employed by the Chinese were graduated, well established, and subject to various, and strict rules so that it was possible at times that an accused underwent torture while still managing to avoid confessing his guilt.

The disintegration of the Chinese Imperial government, right at the beginning of the Yamato period and immediately thereafter, caused waves of intellectuals, who had previously been connected with the Imperial regime, to emigrate from China and Korea and enter Japanese territory. These immigrants bore with them knowledge about Buddhism, the Confucian dogma and the skill of being able to write. All of these things were helpful in the later egging on of reform in Japan.
The writing system that arrived in Japan, either directly from China or intermediately through Korea was helpful in organizing the government and in flexing its muscles in relation to a number of different aspects:
One of these aspects had to do with civilian government, and this was quite manifest at the beginning of the 6th century C. E. when the king set up a bureaucratic network whose task it was to list all the citizenry, noting whether they were privately housed or whether they lived on estates that were under the

[61] All this recalls the motto employed by the Meiji Regime which was popular in the 19th and beginning of the 20th century C. E., whose motto was "Rich Country, Strong Army".
[62] See note 48 supra The Cambridge History of Japan at p. 12.

jurisdiction of Korea, and at a later date a census was taken of those remoter regions over which the king was eager to extend his hold.
Another aspect related also to the renewed prominence attached to the government as a result of exploiting its recently acquired skill of writing was the takeover by the religious government of the civilian government infrastructure. This aspect manifested itself when there was a drive to put into writing those myths that had been part of the oral tradition and which validated the assertion that indeed the king was descended from the gods. Two books which, in reality, were an anthology of myths were published. One of them, completed in 712 C. E, was written in Japanese, and was distributed under the title *Kojiki.*[63] The second, completed almost a decade later in 720 C. E., was written in Chinese and was called *Nihongi*. [64] The first of these publications (*Kojiki*) did not pretend to chronicle history, and it omits any reference to dates even while it reviews the period that stretches until the 5th century C. E. The second publication, which was double the length of the first, does have pretensions of accurately portraying Japanese history and its respective royal dynasties, even while failing to provide a strictly accurate picture. This publication traces historical events up until the end of the 7th century which was two more centuries than its predecessor.
Apart from the fact that the two above- named anthologies reasserted the king's mythical connection to the gods, they also contained educational ethical lesson that were delivered through emotional and lyrical motifs. In addition they accurately reflected the Japanese thinking in regard to the gods, each of whose powers were to a specific geographic locale, and of the need then, to align oneself with these local gods in order to successfully annex territory within the said god's jurisdiction. This outlook was responsible for synthesizing religion with government. Hidden between the lines of these mythical legends there was a warning directed to those planning an uprising against the king, and therefore their central motifs concentrated on the prime importance of a unified and a united Japan. The fact that these stories were merely reflective of a collective creative consciousness that had expressed itself for some time before it was transmitted into writing meant that the actual publication did not bring to the fore any new insights; they were rather a written record of myths that had been woven into the Japanese fabric during the course of hundreds of years. These myths, way before they appeared in book form, reinforced the feelings of Japanese unity, a shared

---

[63] See Masao Yaku, The Kojiki in the Life of Japan, (Tokyo: The Centre for East Asian Cultural Studies, 1969, reprinted 1972).

[64] See W. G. Aston, Nihongi, (Translated by him from the original Chinese and Japanese)-Chronicles of Japan from the Earliest Times to A. D. 697, (Tokyo: Charles E. Tuttle Co., 1972)

cultural memory, a unique Japanese collective spirit, and the belief in the Divine ordainment of the Japanese kings which in turn enhanced these kings' respective powers. It must be admitted, however that there was something innovative about writing down these myths: the power of the written word which was carefully transcribed and spread throughout the breadths and depths of Japan endowed these books with a force that was above and beyond those other motifs which had had a hand in promoting the Japanese people and their reigning monarchs, and which had previously played a role in consolidating Japan's unique belief system.

Section 2: Ancient India until the beginning of British Rule:

Hinduism developed in India as a means of securing the superior status of the, internally classified, upper classes, whose superiority emanated from their belonging to the class of foreign invaders who were called "Aryans,"[65] who had reigned over the Indian subcontinent from about the year 1500 B. C .E. It seems that in the beginning the Aryans' control was confined to the northern parts of India. After their victory they turned the indigenous inhabitants of the land into water drawers, so that the latter became regarded, in the eyes of their conquerors, as an "inferior race."[66] Sanskrit Aryan literature supports this analysis. The great epic *Ramayana* speaks about the "monkey tribe" whose first commander was Hanuman. Since this tribe extended aid to Ramah and Seta, the royal couple, Hanuman is included among the gods in Hindi mythology. The idol of him that remains preserved bears the appearance of a monkey. The Tama sect, which was considered an underclass, similarly supports our analysis. The system of dividing Indian society into four classes (Brahman, Coushatta, man and Sutra) conforms to the religious system of the Aryans, which system was in use even before their invasion of India. After their takeover of India the Aryans added a fifth class the "inferiors", who were comprised of the local inhabitants of India who were conquered by the invading Aryans. Though the Aryans imposed their religious system on their subjects they were also influenced by their captives, in the sense that additional gods and goddesses were added to their religious framework- that is, to the framework that had comprised a pantheon of Aryan gods- that had not existed prior to the conquest. Joined then to the two chief gods within this framework (Brahma and Yeshno) was a third, the Shewa Deity, an ancient deity who was worshipped by the original Indian dwellers, the Drawids. In the main, however, the Aryan system, with its amendments and its addenda, prevailed, in that equality was only achieved specifically between the gods of the Aryans and

---

[65] Dissociated from any negative connotations of this concept by the Germans, these Indians will be referred to – as is the common practice- as "Aryans"

[66] See Spielberg's book, note 47, *supra* n 1 at p. 14.

the gods of the indigenous Peoples, but not between the people themselves. Amongst the humans the Aryans established themselves as members of the upper class. This is true as it applies to the majority of the conquered masses. There was however a minority among the conquered, those whose skin color was paler than the rest, and whose skin therefore resembled that of the Aryans, who managed to assimilate among the Aryans, so that after a short passage of time they too were regarded as Aryans. The fact that the religion is referred to as Hinduism and not Aryanism is, it is speculated, a result of a linguistic error. The word Hindu is derived from the word *Sindhu*; the northern part of what today is referred to as the Punjab was called by the Aryans "the region of the seven rivers", which in Sanskrit, the language spoken by the Aryans, translates into *Sapato Sindhu.* In those days the Aryan tribes who had originated from Persia were unable to pronounce the letter "s", and therefore their pronunciation of that place became *Hapato Hindu.* It is for this reason that the inhabitants of that area came to be referred to as Hindu.

In the beginning the Aryans enlarged their creative capacities through publicizing tracts on wisdom (*wads*) which were studied by Brahman families off by heart, and which would then act as proof to their spiritual superiority. This all took place until around 1000 B. C. E., at which time the Aryans turned their skills to writing. Knowledge of the *wads* was unique to the Brahmans, and became a symbol of their superiority. In this way the idea of the Brahmans inherent superiority that could only be transmitted genetically took root in the minds of the other classes. Apparently in an attempt to cement the status of the Brahman class the latter regarded those wads that had been committed to memory as more important than those wads that had already been committed into writing. This, because those wads that had taken written form were readily available to anyone who was not Brahman, and this, apparently, reflected negatively upon the superior status and uniqueness of the Brahmans.

The Brahmans were unable to convincingly frame their philosophy, a philosophy, which spoke in terms of reincarnation of thsoul, in such a way that would cement the submission of others towards them. The belief in the reincarnation of the soul deepened the sense of complacency amongst the working classes ensuring that they would remain disciplined and would not rebel against the caste system. If one did rebel, his soul was destined to be reincarnated into something even more inferior, like an insect's body. Though in a very superficial way the Brahmans-like the classes positioned lower down the rungs- were in favor of the idea of reincarnation, in so far as classifying the people according to their social class, reincarnation of the souls was an unhelpful yardstick. Someone who was Brahman would give birth to offspring who were Brahman, and it was not possible to explain to that Brahman person that because of reincarnation of the soul, a soul of inferior value may have entered into the body of their offspring which may have then caused a downgrading in the class of that child.

As has been said, a member of the lower class would know that though in his present life cycle he was doomed to be lowly ranked, if he was to behave in the proper manner, complying with a set agenda that was insusceptible to change, his soul, which was the essence of his being, would rise and would be re-embodied, in the next cycle of reincarnations, in the physical body of someone of higher ranking. In this way a lowly ranked Hindi, even one who was a member of the Tama sect, would receive compensation for his humiliating situation and for his self imposed discipline within the context of his present life cycle.

How, though, was this system able to instill fear into someone who was member of the Brahman class to the point where the latter would feel compelled to behave in a proper manner? Apparently, as far as his soul was concerned, it was destined that it would be re-implanted in a member of the Tama sect, or even in the body of a disgusting animal or creepy crawly. In any event his descendants would suffer no harm and they were always guaranteed to remain part of the Brahman class. On the other hand, he himself was not immune from having his rank stripped away from him, especially in the event that he married someone not of the same class.

Yet, the Brahman member who married within his class could not expect any punishment for incorrect behavior at least not in his current life cycle, only in some future incarnation. It is therefore hard to believe that that the system of reincarnation of the souls was indeed useful in ensuring the correct modes of behavior amongst members of the upper class, and its usefulness was probably confined to preventing the lower classes from rebelling against the ruling system. Indeed a member of the lower classes would be fully cognizant of the fact that his son or daughter would never become Brahmans, however he believed that his own soul, which was the core symbol of his being, would merit the honor of being re-embodied, in the next life cycle, in the physical body of someone of higher status; in this way a member of the lower classes would receive his reward for his obedience. Generally, it is difficult to understand the logic that lay beneath the Hindi system, other to interpret it as preserving the status of the invading Aryans who had grasped the reins of power in India.

If this speculation is correct it would have to be expected that the affected lower classes in India would have grasped the fact that the system was covering up its vicious thorns, and that they would have, as a result thereof, risen up in revolt against the prevailing system.

And indeed this is exactly what happened, but only to a degree. The reason this attempt was only half heartedly carried out has to do with the elaborate myths and rituals which were part of a mythology bequeathed by the Hindi- Aryan system. These myths left their imprint upon the minds of members of all the classes in India; their influence having to do with the fact that the concept of reincarnation of the souls had become entrenched, and because members of the lower classes were dependent upon the Brahmans for organizing their marriages and for determining their personal status, as well as many other functions that were regarded as exclusively religious.

The first of the two well known personalities famed for having challenged the principal beliefs of the Brahmans went by the name *Charwaks*, and he questioned the existence of souls. He claimed that until it can be demonstrated to him that there are such things as souls he refuses willy-nilly to accept their existence. He also claimed that since man was provided with physical senses, he must satisfy them by obeying the demands of his physical body.[67]

The second personality known for his heresy was *Brihaspati* who composed satirical lyrics and was unequivocal in his condemnation of the caste system.

A third personality to emerge was the prince of Guatama, known to all as **Buddha**, who had abandoned all belief in the deities; even though after his death his believers turned him into a deity, he himself, during his lifetime, did not harbor any pagan beliefs. His life goal, rather, was to introduce to man the notion that he teaches himself not to be fearful of fear. He promised the masses that had been filled with various fears, (fears that were prompted by Hinduism for its own purposes, as has been recorded above), a new path; he spoke, then, of the path to spiritual wholeness and calm, a path that leaves no room for notions of Brahman class superiority. The aim was to attain Nirvana, which is the dousing of covetousness, of evil, and of mockery, which eventually leads to the snuffing out of the spirit. He did not believe in the independence of the soul, as that concept was interpreted by the Hindi idea of reincarnation of the souls. Buddha preached that one must attempt attaining Nirvana; Nirvana appeared to him to be the reward for man choosing the middle road, a road paved with: generosity, renouncing lust, repealing a physical connection to this world, and repudiating evil and deception. This also meant liberation from boorishness, jealousy, and lust; an escape from a poisoned atmosphere; freedom from the constant fear of annihilation; a feeling of indifference as to one's fate caring not whether one will die now, or whether one will escape death for the time being. According to his theory if a person is critically wounded and there is a possibility of receiving medical attention and thus being saved, that person should receive the medical treatment while at the same time feeling indifferent as to which of the two possible outcomes he is facing, death or recovery. He did not accept the idea of an abstract world, though he was cautious in avoiding an explicit denial of the existence of the Divinity or of the existence of a collective of deities; he simply avoided any discussion dealing with topic of gods. Man must rely upon himself and not on any other entity; man alone is responsible for his own salvation. In one of his depictions, Buddha

---

[67] *Ibid.*, at pp. 48- 49.

searches for the redemption from the suffering of man and from his troubles, finding it in humanity's soul. He avoided, and possibly abandoned the idea of, seeking redemption in the Divine.
As far as the Hindi caste system was concerned, Buddha did not mince his words. It is he who is quoted as having said: "No man is class- less by birth, no man is Brahman by birth, it is only deeds that make man class-less, and it is only through his actions that a man becomes a Brahman"
Buddha, when starting out his life journey, expressed doubts as to the usefulness of women, seeing in them a stumbling block to men achieving the middle path; however at the end of his life, he accepted the idea that they too may receive salvation to the same degree as men. He established tough rules for those who had chosen an ascetic lifestyle, and viewed flora and fauna as being possessed of a living soul, and he thus prohibited the offering of sacrifices of animals. Nonetheless he did not stretch his theory to the same extremes as did those following the teachings of Zen, who only allowed their members to breathe air through wovenmaterial, in order to minimize the killing of air bacteria. In any event Buddhism allowed their priests to tread on the grass after it had been rained upon because at that very moment there was an increased amount of bacteria in the atmosphere.
Buddha would frequently relocate so that he managed to gain a large following throughout the length and breadth of India. During his life time, and immediately afterwards Buddhist monasteries witnessed a rapid increase.
As Buddhism expanded, some time after Buddha himself, who had lived around the fifth or sixth century B. C. E., had died, it changed directions and turned Buddha into an idol. There are some who say that the Far Eastern societies were unable to set their minds upon an unmodified belief system without grasping on to some tangible idol. Buddha's philosophy, standing on its own, was too lofty, then, for those living under the same cultural conditions as Buddha himself. The aforesaid concurs with the opinion of Ezekiel Kaufman[68], who wrote the following:

The failure of the attempt to explain cultural creativity by reference to the underlying conditions and circumstances especially when it comes to explaining the creative personality, the individual genius...is it possible to "explain" by reference to their conditions and circumstances, (personalities) such as Homer, Plato, Shakespeare, Goethe, Rembrandt, Beethoven, etc.? The "conditions" existed equally for all the people of that country, nation, class, and time, so for what reason were these specific people special... and not only is this problematic,

---

[68] Ezekiel Kaufman, *History of Israelite Belief from Ancient Days Until the End of the Second Temple* (Jerusalem, Tel Aviv: Bialik Institute& Dvir, 1948), pp. 23 ff., in the Introduction)

but we also notice in the cultural creativity of an ethnic group certain original phenomena that are designated to be the natural and uniform building block for the creativity.. an example of this is first of all language...however the theory of the "national spirit" or the "spirit of the People" which had made its appearance during Montesquieu's days and continued until Hegel and Hegel's disciples was drafted from an understanding of the phenomena that were responsible for a uniformity in cultural style, and from an exaggerated generalization with regards to that uniformity... Montesquieu showed that there is a "spirit" lurking behind the laws of each and every nation.... An empirical-historical outlook on the history of culture cannot ignore the fact that the true innovator of any original culture, in the sense that it is unprecedented, is the ethnic group... there are religions, styles of belief, laws, and legends that originate from the parameters of the national breeding grounds and expanded outwards...therefore, the first question is: at which time may one determine the beginning of belief in the Unity?- it is impossible to explain it by reference to any conditions or circumstances. Belief in the Unity is a completely novel cultural innovation, and like all other cultural innovations the last source that may be empirically observed is the creative spirit of man, and because this spirit was born and bred exclusively amongst the Israelites, we have to amend our findings and we have to state unequivocally: "it was born from the creative spirit of the People of Israel"

Either way, it remains a fact that from India to Japan, including China, the belief in one God never penetrated the consciousness of the masses, and it would appear unlikely that the idea of a spiritual God who had no tangible form would gain currency there. One exception to this is militant Islam, which forced its belief in one God upon others by means of the sword. Another exception is the Sikh religion which arose and developed in India as a reaction to the cruelty of practiced Islam, as a means of obliging those impressed with the force of argument inherent in the Muslim's belief which for them appeared more logical than the belief in a multitude of deities, what has been termed polytheism.[69]

Amidst the Buddhist circles, after Buddha had already died, those forces that wanted to turn Buddha into a god had gained the upper hand and they even begun the practice of offering sacrifices to Buddha's graven image. In Buddhist literature many writings have been preserved that show the contradiction between Buddha's actual teachings and the Buddhism of idols and sacrifices. Below is

[69] In this respect, even Christianity that regarded Jesus to be Divine, and especially its Catholic branch, which put up graven images of Jesus and Mary in their churches, was unsuccessful in elevating the Divinity without depicting an image thereof and without extricating the Divinity from a tangible existence. Therefore, one cannot attach this difficulty in comprehension exclusively to those who inhabited the Far East.

reprinted a conversation on this topic taken from a dialogue between King Melinda and Harish Nagasana discussing these matters:

> King Melinda: If indeed Buddha turns towards the sacrifices, is that not a sign that he has not yet attained Nirvana, and that he is still clinging to the worldly life...
>
> Nagasana: No, great king, you are wrong, without doubt Buddha did attain a state of Nirvana, and he is not connected to any shape or form on this physical world. He himself does not gaze upon the sacrifices...
>
> King Melinda: If that is so, what is the real reason for offering sacrifices?
>
> Nagasana: ...Buddha does not want the sacrifices, and it is not he who has any need for them. However, the bringer of the sacrifices is likely to awaken the "resonant sounds" of Buddha's righteousness and holiness through bringing his offerings. This is the reason for offering sacrifices to Buddha. The Holy Buddha, himself spoke thus to Ananda, his favorite disciple: Do not think that after I have died there will no longer be any Buddha. "The statutes and various ideas will make their appearance and they will replace me..."

A hundred and fifty years after the death of Buddha, at the end of the fourth century B. C. E., a division took place in the Buddhist camp over the argument of whether Buddha's doctrine should be tailored to suit the needs of the masses.[70] The southern school of thought that had set up fort in Ceylon and Burma adopted a hard line in their demands, whereas the northern school which had relocated to Tibet, China, Korea, and Japan, relented somewhat. As a result of this approach the northern school was able to develop the Mahayana (or Great Chariot) system, which allowed individual man, relying exclusively upon his internal powers, to attain Nirvana. This system envisions a slow and gradual process that is open to anyone, and which does not rely, whatsoever, on the monastery brokering one's individual development. Even so, this system adopted polytheism, the belief in a multitude of deities, turning Buddhism into a typical religious denomination. According to this system man is dependent upon a deity. His dependence on a deity, though, does not mean that he requires the monastery to act as his intermediary.

According to the Northern system, man is dependent exclusively upon himself, not upon a deity. Man has the power within himself to find his own salvation, but this requires the regime of asceticism which can only be followed in a monastery specifically built for the purpose of facilitating this difficult process. The Southern

---

[70] On this matter see Kaufman *supra* and his opinion with regard to the background to human society in general, and with regard to the power that society and culture exercise in overcoming the power of the individual, as has emerged in the case of the development of monotheism in Judaism.

system, nonetheless, held that the path to Nirvana could only be attained through enduring an infinite amount of rebirths. In contradistinction, the Northern system, which held that one could attain Nirvana, only with the help of a deity, believed that one could attain Nirvana in one's present lifetime.

With regard to India, home of the original Buddhism, there was no necessity whatsoever for a monastery, since man, in accordance with the original Buddhist philosophy did not require the assistance of priests, nor was it necessary to attend a monastery. The Buddhist individual who was not affiliated to the Buddhist institution relied upon the Brahmans for matters relating to the marriage ceremony, to births, and to funerals. The Buddhists, then, in India did not form separate communities, neither did they attempt creating frameworks that would harm the Brahman control over the community. To the extent that there were monasteries in India, these were destroyed by the Muslim invasion in the tenth century C. E. Buddhist monasteries and temples were destroyed, and many Buddhists were forced to convert to the Islamic religion. Buddhist colleges were also destroyed, and the Buddhist students were slain. Even before the Muslims wrought havoc on the Buddhists the Brahmans had already inflicted their own kind of harm on the Buddhists, but in a conniving fashion, viz. by proclaiming Buddha to be one of the deities of the Hindu religion. The overall result of all these calamities was the almost complete eradication of Buddhism from the Indian subcontinent. Nonetheless, the appearance and influence of Buddhism in, and upon, India bore testimony to the widespread and deeply felt societal need to rebel against the caste system and against the superior class status of the Brahmans. What became clear during the Muslim invasion of India was that Buddhism, like Hinduism, did not produce in its wake a spirit of opposition towards a foreign conqueror. Both of these philosophies dealt with questions relating to the salvation of the spirit and of the soul, and working to repair the soul of man; at the same time they did not concern themselves with weaving together a network of mutual communal assistance (apart from encouraging personal generosity), nor did they worry about fashioning a supportive vibrant community, which would in turn strengthen social bonds. The Muslim conquest proved that a society that does not have a collective consciousness but which cares only for individualistic needs is incapable of withstanding an occupying force.[71]

At this point in our analysis, let us return to those Hindi myths that put an emphasis on the importance of highlighting the individual and his salvation without really caring about social cohesion, and those myths that explain the lack of Hindi decisiveness when faced with a task that requires a war effort. This lack of decisiveness is taken for granted by those who are able to see in Hindu

[71] The ramifications this episode has upon the individualist system prevalent in modern day America is beyond the parameters of this study.

mythology a mere tapestry of images that are woven together for the sole purpose of depriving the lower classes of their rightful portion and for ensuring the superior status of the Brahman caste members, but at the same time a mythology that has no subliminal values of crystallizing and consolidating society. The crystallization and consolidation of society, on the one hand, alongside the preservation of internal social gaps, on the other, can only be referred to as "a contradiction in terms." All this considered, the ambivalent attitude towards war becomes much clearer, as will be demonstrated later.[72]

Conspicuous among Sanskrit literary stories and parables that still remain intact are two book compilations *Pancha Tantra* and *Hitopadisa*. Though this body of literature was produced primarily with the masses in mind, it was also read by the *Sadhusists*, by the *Pandists*, and by the *Rishists*, all of whom were scholar- priests: learned men and original thinkers.

The **Pancha Tantra** speaks about a father of three sons who was concerned that his children were being raised without proper manners and were not acquiring sufficient knowledge. He therefore hired a tutor by the name of Vishnu- Sarma whose teaching methods included shortening the time spent on the sciences by converting the subject matter into simple everyday stories. It took this tutor only half a year to teach all three boys what they needed to know. The stories that he invented appear in the book compilation under the title *Pancha Tantra*. Within the covers of this book stories that remind one of Biblical story of the binding of Isaac can be found, only in this instance it is flavored by polytheistic imagery. On the other hand there are stories that sound like they were later retold by De Cameron. One story speaks about a bee that wanted to suck nectar from a flower, but the latter stipulated that his consent was conditional upon the bee providing him with something that he really desires but has not yet been able to acquire. After a long period of searches, the bird came across a holy man who was able to understand the language of the fowl of the field, of the animals, and of the plants, and following his advice the bee bombarded the flower with an avalanche of kisses; the flower consequently opened up allowing the bee to suck from its nectar. Another story deals with women's insufferable attitude, from the perspective that it is impossible to survive without them. Yet another story is told of an insect that escaped danger, and it soon became known that he was in fact the reincarnation of a great Hindu Rishi, the philosopher Narada. To the question asked of the Rishi-insect, why it was that his soul was trapped in the body of an insect, and why then did he bother escaping in order to save his present body form, the soul of the Rish

[72] The connection between social consolidation on the one hand and equality and nullification of class differences, on the other, will be raised later on, when discussing the Magi regime in Japan. That discussion will underscore the differences between the national Japanese philosophy and the philosophy underlying traditional Indian society

answered and explained that even insects view themselves as important creatures, and the insect also thinks that all of creation was produced for the sole purpose of serving him. Other fables bear with them ethical lessons in terms of which a person should not try to alter the status that he was born with, someone who attempts doing so- can look forward to a bad and bitter life experience. Another moral lesson dressed in a fable is one that directs man not to listen to the advice of someone with a vested interest in the subject at hand. There is yet another parable from which we may learn that it is both correct and appropriate to try and beat our inclination for covetousness. Other stories speak of the Deity's mercy towards those who truly and fully believe in him. Another anecdote demonstrates the foolishness of those wanting to revoke a decree imposed upon them, teaching that one cannot flee from that which has been ordained. In a similar vein another tale tries to inculcate the idea that someone of a lowly position should not pretend that he will be able to improve upon his present standing, and should he even attempt doing so he will meet up with an ill and bitter fate.

Appended to this compilation are many folk sayings that instill the messages that: education successfully negates feelings of anger; one must learn to appreciate wisdom; one must oppose showiness, gluttony, and covetousness; one must not be swayed by what feels natural; and one should combat miserliness and love of money. Instead one should prefer to recognize reality, to strive for unity, modesty, and for humility of the spirit, recognizing one's ignorance while all the time remaining a loyal servant.

The corpus of Sanskrit literature includes two great epics that were written in the early period: *Ramayana* and *Mahabharata*. These epics present the reader with the lifestyles and customs of their principal heroes, who were kings and princes who started their life's journey leading a licentious and pleasure seeking existence, but who were gradually educated to embrace elevated ideals and character traits. These epics do not shy away from describing those who remained corrupt, and thus they are checkered with vivid depictions of war. The main heroes are always irreproachable while the others have an assortment of character traits, both laudable and condemnable. These two epics took root in the minds of the many different Hindu social ranks. The explicit line adopted by these epics put forward the notion that wars and the reasons for waging them, was exclusively the result of a high ranking decision, made by someone at the top, even if these wars were, at times, fought for the completely personal reasons of those in charge, as a way of showing off their might and prestige, and even if in practice the individual fighters had absolutely no say in the matter, the reason for going to battle was completely beside the point, war was not fought to advance their interest, the only factor motivating them to do battle was their education that had instilled in them loyalty towards those whom they were serving. Sometimes, loyalty drives people to battle against, and to even kill, those who they love and who are near and dear to them, all because they are "pawns of the system". All that need interest these fighting men is a willingness to overcome their personal feelings and to perform that that is imposed upon them in accordance with their duty of loyalty which in turn binds them to obey officers of higher rank. While supplying vivid depictions, in very strong and colorful language, of the dead, of blood, of cruelty, and of killings, there are very ambivalent feelings towards those very shocking scenes that occur ifront of them, which as a collective whole may only be referred to as war.

An overview of the ancient epics, parables and fables reveals that each was composed for the sake of preserving class distinctions by assigning each class its own rank, and for the sake of granting legitimacy to the notion that that those of superior rank are entitled to do whatever they please. After all, for the lower classes, there is no escaping the fact that fate has determined that they are not permitted to raise themselves an inch higher than that that has been allotted them, and that they will never be able to independently make their own decisions. Society consists of those who, on the hand, are freely able to decide things for themselves, and who work in fulfillment of their own interests and for their own good, and on the other, of those who work because they have been constrained to show loyalty to others.

Nanak, the founder of **Sikhism** was one of the disciples of Kabir, who was active during the end of the 15th century C. E. and who preached the existence of one God, even if at the same time he accepted the idea of reincarnation of the souls. While Kabir was unsuccessful in setting up any significant type of movement, his sidekick, Nanak, who had rebelled against the rituals of his forefathers, but who did believe in reincarnation of the souls, and who never had any intentions of setting up a new type of religion, but rather saw his life's mission as one devoted to introducing reforms to Hinduism in conformance with monotheistic principles, was in practice the progenitor of a whole new nation that practiced its own and unique religion. This made him the only person capable of putting the brakes on the progressive Islamic takeover of India. Nanak accepted the idea of pilgrimage to Mecca. He however wanted to preserve a form of Hinduism that was devoid of polytheistic Brahmanism, a Hinduism that did not believe in re-embodiments of the Deity or deities, that did not divide Hindu society into upper and lower classes, and that did not carry out various ceremonies; he rather preferred prayer without ceremonies. For him (the exclusive) God was "indescribable, abstract, but in any event a very real entity". Owing to the fact that the Sikhs were egalitarian they managed to establish communities and a communal lifestyle that was able to rely upon the might of their army and the protection of their fortresses.

After Nanak's death he was succeeded by ten leaders (calling themselves "guru"), each peacefully inheriting the reins from his respective predecessor, and some actively waging a military struggle against Muslim rule in India. The tenth guru declared that each Sikh was required to grow a beard and let his hair grow wild (so as not to hide the fact that he was in fact a Sikh, and not to be embarrassed about it), to wear short trousers (in order to preserve his freedom to exercise so that he is able to protect himself from any attackers), to wear an iron ring on his right hand (again, out of a need not to hide the fact that he was Sikh), and to be constantly bearing a dagger, (for self defence purposes). Sikhs quickly gained recognition within their castes, especially because of the popularly backed military struggles waged by them, so that they were consequently granted partial independence in the provinces.

The Sikhs developed a well organized economic infrastructure and a Sikh armed force, while at the same time ensuring that their members be educated in the values of modesty, austerity, compassion and sanctification of God`s name. They developed institutions to govern their domestic lifestyle that were democratic to the core: equality, the abolition of the caste system, and unity. The God, to whom Nanak, the founder of the Sikhs referred, became the national Deity of the Sikhs so that over the course of time the Sikhs began conducting religious ceremonies, even enacting a strict regimen of daily laws and customs; all this in opposition to the guiding principles laid down by Nanak. The Muslims viewed the Sikhs as their sworn enemies, since the former had little regard for their other competitor, the Hindus.

The Sikh state disintegrated soon after the English decisively defeated the Muslim regime. The Sikhs surrendered to the English while at the same time preserving partial autonomy including the right to bear daggers, which in any event had to be pared down in terms of the treaty with the British. For their part the British enlisted Sikhs in their army since they understood that they provided the most important fighting force in all of India, and it was therefore worthwhile for the British to regard their relationship with the Sikhs as almost on a par with that of allies.

The Sikhs authored a book of exhortations and prayers that for them became their Bible; when going on parade with it they would ensure that it was locked it in a box (a religious element that is reminiscent of the Jews or of the Israelites, like many of their other elements mentioned thus far). The Sikhs even tailored a language/dialect that was unique to them.

Section 3: Japan during the 19th and 20th centuries

from a perspective that links mythology to policy

As may be deduced from the detailed account in section 1, Japan functioned as one unitary state from the 7th century C. E. Though the emperor and his government stood at the helm of the state's core institutions, the real political power lay with a few noble families who de facto ran the state. Over the course of time, army officers, or Samurais, had successfully taken control of the reins of power, but owing to internal power struggles they gradually became responsible for the state's disintegration. Still, no one had dared remove the imperial dynasty from its seat of power, for it remained a symbol of the state and it was the focal point for religious functions. The government was in the main feudal, which in conformity with the values of the Samurais waved the banner of: loyalty to one's master, courage, respect, self sacrifice, and a Spartan way of life. It also followed the principles outlined in Confucian philosophy viz. fulfilling one's duties, and bearing responsibility for one's deeds. Towards the end of the 16th century, all provinces of the state were compulsorily united under one powerful administration headed by an exclusive premier (or in Japanese, a Shogun) named Tokogawa, who bequeathed his powerful position and authority to his descendants, which family, in practice, ruled under the imaginative tile of emissary of the emperor, while at the same time preserving the feudalistic framework until the restoration of 1868. The restoration took place as a result of Japan being forced by United States military pressure, which took the form of lining up naval boats and heavy shelling, to sign a treaty opening up a number of Japanese ports for the use of American naval boats. The Japanese also agreed to grant humanitarian assistance to American sailors who were encountering difficulties along their shores, so that the latter could be provided with United States diplomatic representation. Indeed Americans would be provided with the same concessions that were granted any other state, by the Japanese. This whole incident was interpreted by the Japanese as a blow to their honour triggering, in response, internal maneuverings which culminated in the fall of the Shogun regime, in turn benefiting the 16 year old Japanese emperor, Magi. In line with the emperors who had preceded him over the centuries, Magi did not, in practice, rule over his subjects, but rather gave his stamp of approval to the collective leadership acting within the framework of his responsible government, a government that included in its ranks the instigators of the 1868 Restoration.

In 1871, renewed pressure from the royal courtyard working under advice of the Restoration instigators, brought into being a gradual process resulting in: the abolition of the feudal administration, the rescinding of class differences, and the introduction of freedom of movement and of economic activity for all. This whole process began voluntarily, outof feudal loyalty to the emperor, so that when the royal edict was sent out announcing this new policy abolishing feudal estates (the hans) almost all of the hans had ceased to operate as part of an agreement with, and a sign of loyalty to the emperor, so that the latter would be enabled to lead Japan into the modern period and thus advance the state's economic standing.

In the beginning, as compensation for having their feudal status rescinded the property owners and samurais received a stipend, and at the same time were given administrative positions under the auspices of the central government, yet later on, already in 1876, the samurais stopped receiving their stipends, even if they continued to benefit from plum roles in the government institutions. The separate Han army was dismantled right from the very beginning of the process, so that the army that took over was composed not merely of samurai warriors but also of peasant farmers. In 1873 a Conscription Act was passed proclaiming that all those who had reached the age of 20 could be called up to serve three years compulsory military service, and would later be expected to perform reserve duty. This army was under the direct command of the emperor.

In 1890 the emperor granted his People a Constitution. This was done amidst great ceremony in which the emperor appeared in his palace together with the first elected members of the new Japanese parliament, the Diet. Shinto was established as the State religion, and the emperor was appointed the official head of the Shinto religion. Buddhism was relegated from its prime position and many of its temples were forcibly shut down. Buddhist priests were forced to work for a living. A department was set up for the supervision of ideologies within the framework of the Government's Ministry of Education, which had also published pedagogical books exhorting loyalty to the emperor and equality for all citizens, subjects of the emperor. Within the educational system precedence was given to inculcating good character traits as these were interpreted by Confucian philosophy, over and above scientific studies and general knowledge. In contradistinction to what had become accepted practice during the reign of Tokogawa and his predecessors, a weekly rest day was instituted, and for this purpose the designated day was a Sunday. National festivals were also instituted; again something that had not existed previously. The idea that the empire had remained unchanged from the year 660 B. C. E. became anchored into the consciousness of the People, an idea, that, as has been recorded in section one, was very far from the truth, but which ultimately succeeded in glorifying the myth of the emperor insofar as it left him with a dynasty approximately a thousand years older than that which was historically verifiable.

Owing to its successful military victories and conquests, Japan steadily gained international recognition from the end of the 19th century right until World War II's eruption. International treaties acknowledging its powerful position permeated the Japanese atmosphere, to the extent that it became dizzy with its unlikely successes during that period. There was the feeling, and even belief, amongst the 70 million Japanese inhabitants spread across the five Japanese islands, and also amongst those tens of millions of Japanese that lived outside its borders, that the emperor of Japan had secured the goodwill of the gods owing to his descent from the god of the sun and thus all his orders and all his decisions were correct and wise and thus bound for success. This national mood was just another result of the basic education of loyalty to the emperor, as such loyalty had became manifest during the Restoration of 1868 and the years immediately thereafter; words fail to adequately describe a situation where so many of the nation's finest, who had occupied key positions, ceded their rights to benefits to which they had become traditionally entitled for periods extending tens if not hundreds of years, without even putting up a significant fight, a situation that indeed prevailed as a consequence of the Restoration of the Magi regime in Japan.

Accordingly the theory, developed by Western scholars, researching these matters, which suggested that indoctrination, which was the policy pursued by the education system and promoted through Japanese (print) media, was responsible for the uniformity of spirit, self sacrifice and submission of the Japanese during World War II[73], cannot be accepted. Obviously Japanese successes on the eve of World War II caused an even greater adhering of the Japanese to their emperor and to his orders and increased their readiness to sacrifice themselves on the battlefield. Nonetheless it was the weight of Japanese mythology that had been operational since ancient times and that had never disappeared from the Japanese folkloric education in all its generations that had left its mark; this was much stronger than the indoctrination of a short "moment in history," lasting only a few decades.

The problem of indoctrination in education: In line with arguments put forward by Hall and by Maruyama[74] it was indoctrination in the Japanese education system towards the end of the Magi period that was the cause, so to speak, of the Japanese decision to bomb Pearl Harbor and it was this same indoctrination that explains the Japanese fanaticism on display during the Second World War. This argument is identical to the claims raised by the Americans, who had found fighting the

[73] See especially Hall in his book, note 1, *supra*.
[74] See their book titles in note 1, *supra*.

Japanese a very difficult task and who had tried to exploit this argument in order to overcome, thereby, the difficult feelings that had accompanied them during World War II with regard to the atom bomb attack which they (the Americans) had viewed themselves as forced to execute in the face of such obstinate Japanese fighting. Against this backdrop the Japanese had accepted upon themselves the task of redrafting legislation on the subject of education, legislation that had sought to compel the Japanese education system to construct an opposite blueprint for the new generation, a blueprint that had encompassed the qualities of the young Japanese generation. This then became a kind of counter- indoctrination, that reversed direction and became liberal democratic; this, a deliberate attempt to finally remove the national indoctrination that had prevailed pre World War II.

Typical of this line of thinking is the survey conducted by Teruhisa Horio on the supervision over educational content and over government school syllabi in Japan during the 1950s and 1960s.

Horio wrote a book on the topic of educational thought and ideology in Modern Japan, with specific reference to the State Authority's and freedom of thought.[75] He writes concerning himself that he remembers how as a six year old child he handled the news of the death of his father, who, while on active military service in the Imperial Japanese Armed Forces during the Second World War, died from a disease. The predominant feeling going through the child's mind was one of intense shame, especially since his friends' fathers had died honorably in battle, whereas his father had succumbed to mere illness.[76] This personal history led him to research what happens from an educational perspective when tender children are taught a single and narrow doctrine and are not exposed to the idea that there are other possible truths apart from this one, as was the practice during the imperial period.

Horio was not alone in dealing with this question; the drafters of Japan's democratic constitution of 1947 and the drafters of the Basic Law- Education were also of the opinion that openness was a central democratic principle, and it was appropriate then that the younger generation deal with this issue. Therefore the text of sec. 10 of the Education Act reads as follows:

---

[75]Teruhisa Horio, *Educational Thought and Ideology in Modern Japan, State Authority's and Intellectual Freedom,* edited and translated by Steven Platzer, (Tokyo: University of Tokyo Press), 1988.

[76] *Ibid.*, at p. 17 of the Introduction of the translator and editor.

School Administration: Education shall not be subject to improper control, but it shall be directly responsible to the whole people. School Administration shall, on the basis of this realization, aim at the adjustment and establishment of the various conditions required for thpursuit of the aim of education.

Section one of the same act defines the aims of education as the complete development of the personality, aiming at raising the nation to be healthy of body and of mind, to love truth and pursue justice, to appreciate everyone's' individual characteristics, to respect the work ethic and to be possessed of a deep sense of responsibility, and to be infused with the independent spirit common to founders of a peace loving state and society.[77]

During the 1960s government spokesmen and political leaders began to speak of *academisation* and of competition and of a selection process, as necessary for creating the desired Japanese image , so that they began to tailor the education system to suit the aforesaid. [78] Section 10 of the Education Act was considered a sort of "mini stumbling block" which had to be moved out of the way. In 1961 amidst strong opposition a national academic examination measuring scholastic aptitude was introduced and steps were taken to destroy the power of the nationwide teachers union, which opposed the above moves or any similar moves. Included in these new measures was one that targeted the independent continuing education programs that exited at that time. Various kinds of external "guidance" were increasingly being offered to the teachers. In 1964 a manuscript was published portraying the ideal image that a teacher had to produce. A year later supplemental instructions were published giving more specificity than that that had appeared in the original manuscript with the declared intention that the new manuscript comes to amend the inferiorities of the Education Act and to instill in the students the unique Japanese spirit so that a new generation of Japanese be firmly embedded to the venerable Japanese traditions and be infused with a love for their homeland. These explanations were accompanied by expression reminiscent of Imperial Japan including the notion of the centrality of the emperor.[79] Thus, at the same time as citing the 1882 oath of loyalty taken by the Japanese soldiers and naval officers, it explicitly made reference to the need of overhauling the reforms that were carried out at the end of World War II as well as the necessity of educating the young generation to defend their homeland[80]. All

[77] *Ibid.*, at pp. 400 -401.
[78] *Ibid.*, at p. 152
[79] *Ibid.*, at pp. 153- 156.
[80] *Ibid.*, at p. 157.

this took place while grudgingly acknowledging a very unusual Japanese constitutional amendment of 1947, in terms of which Japan declared (section 9 of the Constitution) that she will never go to war again. Consequently Japan became only the second country in the world to constitutionally determine that the state was barred, now and forever, from entering into war against another state.

This new governmental- political trend was strengthened and augmented by the Japanese economic elite's demand, which, against the backdrop of stiff competition with other industrial countries of the world, proposed that Japan make advances in the technological and scientific fields. Accordingly, the educational reforms of the 1960s were backed by two of the most well-established sectors of society, the national- political- traditional clique, on the one hand, and the economic- scientific- technological elite, on the other. The efforts of both these sectors were responsible for the events of 1970s which were witness to what has since been termed the third educational reforms.

In 1970, an organization that named itself *The Society for the Study of Educational Law*, and that united parents, teachers, and academics under one umbrella, was established. It initiated legal debates on the system used to classify teachers, on the process of authorizing text books, and on testing academic aptitude. In the course of the ensuing debates, Japan's democratic constitution was broadly analyzed as was the nature of the impact of education. Consequently a widespread national movement for the Protection of the Education Act, incorporating teachers' and academic unions, was formed.

The government and Education Ministry personnel had tried, as far back as 1957, to present the Diet with a Bill amending sections of the Education Act that related to the contents of the text books. Owing, however, to stark opposition on the part of the community in general and the Diet in particular, this attempted legislation failed; however certain amendments were successfully passed through administrative measures. Twenty years later, in 1976 a new act was finally legislated that followed exactly the same proposals that had failed to take off in 1956, on the basis that de facto these proposals were already being carried out. This tactic employed by the Japanese government had successfully been implemented in yet another area of the law- the function of the teachers' superintendent, who had been appointed by administrative fiat and who had been selected by staff of the Education Ministry in 1957. In 1973, this appointment became entrenched in the new Act based upon the same above reasoning viz. that it had, long ago, for all practical purposes, become incorporated into the law. The tactic then was to institute an amendment via administrative means, especially at a time when the political circumstances did not favor legislative intervention, and then, later on, to obtain retrospective legislative ratification when political circumstances turned more favorable.

In a similar vein Education Ministry apparatchiks attempted in 1976 to strengthen supervision over the nature of education by exploiting its administrative powers, powers that were meant for overseeing the smooth running of the extant Act, not for introducing changes to its supervisory role. The Ministry of Education overstepped its limits of authority by extending its supervisory powers into areas that did not fall within the jurisdiction allotted to the central government's Ministry of Education, but were rather under the autonomous control of the local Education Council; and for these purposes the whole subject of aptitude testing fell within the exclusive jurisdiction of this or that autonomous body, specifically barring any say on the part of the Education Ministry. The aforesaid was, in theory, recognized by the Supreme Court, yet the same Supreme Court, in practice, refused to draw the necessary conclusions viz. to openly declare that in exercising extraterritorial supervisory powers the Ministry was acting illegally. Instead the court meekly determined that since testing was in any event taking place under the auspices of local autonomous councils the fact that the ministry in exercising its own supervision was overstepping its territorial jurisdiction did not ipso facto invalidate it. [81]

Beginning from 1947 and continuing right until 1958, teachers in Japan were referred to optional text books and other learning materials without in any way being compelled to teach from them. The material, then, was considered as comprising a possible rather than a mandatory teaching syllabus. The teachers were given the full right to choose the books, the contents, and the sources of study, according to the personal understanding of each and every one of them, and the material that would then be used was chosen in order to ease the burden of having to independently find materials necessary to relay information to the students.

In 1958 a dramatic change occurred with the introduction of government directives and their attendant instructions charging teachers to compulsorily follow a set curriculum which paid very scant lip service to the principles behind the

---

[81] *Ibid.*, at pp. 164- 165. According to the writer, the Supreme Court's actions proved how correct and serious the criticism of the Ministry of education's staff was and how far the Supreme Court was willing to stand by the Ministry of education's staff and to support their activities. Later on the writer adds a few more examples of the illegality of the activities of Education ministry personnel and the extent to which there was joint cooperation with the Supreme Court, but at this stage I shall be brief and I shall not dwell on any further detail.

Education Act including clauses such as "educating for peace, truth and justice". Additionally, the number of supervisors was enlarged, and a political campaign against those textbooks recommended by the Peace Education Movement was waged. This intensive supervision by the many inspectors who had recently been appointed to their jobs created a situation in which a number of teaching subjects were not taught, unless specifically endorsed by the Ministry of Education, or directly by the supervisor in charge.[82]This new state of affairs resulted in the disqualification of *The Stream*, a nursery rhyme taught to the lower grades and basedon onomatopoeic sounds (where the structure is composed of sounds that are similar to, at least according to the imagination of the author, the sound of the thing the author sought to describe) since it did not match the sounds with which the inspector was familiar from his childhood. Similarly various other inspectors banned the book of Nobel Prize laureate Tomonaga Shini'ichiro on the basis that it did not at all qualify as a text book, since its literary structure did not match that of an ordinary text book. In yet another incident a book was disqualified because it contained the word "altercation", and the inspectors had requested that the word's meaning be changed to instead refer to a certain game.[83] Similarly, books that made reference to the various houses belonging to the imperial family, that described the reforms that took place straight after the war, that provided details of the Defence Treaty signed with the United States, that told the story of the Japanese Defence Forces, and even those that reported the presence of Russian troops on an island which the Yan government had argued was occupied by these Russians illegally were all banned. The Education Ministry's inspectors began to simply dictate to the writers how they should correct the versions of the text books that they authored.

This prompted the historian Lenaga Sabuto[84] to initiate legal proceedings against the Ministry of Education for withholding its endorsement from certain text books he had authored, and for corrections he was forced to insert against his will that ensured that all approved Japanese text books would be one- sided when it came to reporting the truth. Lenaga was successful at all levels of the lower courts forcing the Education ministry to register appeal after appeal until the case reached the Supreme Court, where through diplomacy and stealth the court managed to conceal the matters at hand. Legal wrangling continued for 20 years, and because of the Supreme Court's siding with the Education Ministry, Lenaga, for all his efforts, failed to make his mark.

---

[82] *Ibid.*, at pp. 172- 173.
[83] *Ibid.*, at p. 174.
[84] See *ibid.*, at pp. 177- 180 and also at pp. 189- 212.

In 1961 the staff at the Ministry of Education sent out a directive to the teachers to hand out a questionnaire wherein the students would reveal to the inspectors whether the teachers were sticking to the text books recommended by the inspectors and whether the contents of those recommended text books were being assimilated into the consciousness of the students and, if so, to what degree this assimilation process was taking place. The teachers saw this initiative as an affront, and in a carefully orchestrated fashion they refused to cooperate. They were then charged with contempt of the law. At some of the legal trials that followed the teachers were convicted, yet in the majority of them they were let off the hook, in light of the fact that the Education Ministry's directive was found to be illegal and unconstitutional. The court hearings were transferred from lower to higher courts until they reached the Supreme Court which invariably accepted the position of the Education ministry.[85]

The conclusion that must be drawn with regards to the war against indoctrination[86] in the period following World War II is that when the Japanese Justices were given the option of choosing either the traditional path which accorded with Confucian philosophy and with ancient Japanese mythology, on the one hand, or the path of cleaving to democratic values as these were adumbrated in the Constitution, on the other, they overwhelmingly chose the first path, that opposed both the current law and the democratic Constitution. The influence of the Japanese myths and their cleaving to them as well as the desire to remain united as one Japanese People is as strong today as it has always been.

Section 4: Indian Partition

The revolution within India's regime illustrates the changing fortunes of a religion that started off as being relatively weak, and only changed when it presented its believers with a mission of war against the believers of another religion, a mission which its followers could hardly afford to ignore. As recorded in the writings of Ashutosh Varshney,[87] Mahatma Gandhi[88] marshaled his forces to establish the Congress Party that would be based not on any national ethnicity but rather on

[85] *Ibid.*, at pp. 181- 189.

[86] Or perhaps: The indoctrination in democratic values which replaced indoctrination in hierarchical values that were ingrained in the ancient Japanese myths and in the Confucian philosophy that was woven into these myths

[87] Ashutosh Varshney, "Contested Meanings: India's national Identity, Hindu nationalism and the Politics of Anxiety", in *Daedalus* (Summer 1993), pp. 227- 261

[88] See *ibid.*, at pp. 240- 241.

civil religion as that concept was interpreted in the West, viz. the unification of all the citizens. The rise of the National Hindu Party that has at last succeeded at the polls and that has thus been steering the government in place of the old Congress Party, is a sign of the growing strength of nationalism amongst the Hindi population. It is only because of the fierce religious enmity between Hinduism and Islam which resulted in a bloody war against the Muslims that an independent and united (Hindu) entity emerged which consolidated its forces for the sake of pursuing a common goal. Prior to this, Hindu nationalism was considered the identifying mark of a minority in India, only those who belonged to the group that spoke Hindi. Otherwise those who spoke other languages, even if by religion they identified themselves as Hindi, were not considered as belonging to the national-ethnic Hindi group. However as a result of this war even those who spoke languages other than Hindi, but whose religion was Hindu, considered themselves as Hindu nationalists. Gradually, then Hindu nationalism changed from being the province of a minority into that of a majority, finally crowning itself with a victory in the Indian general elections. All this occurred at the same time, and as a result of, the abolition of the caste system, as well as the de facto abandonment of the Indian mythology whose whole thrust was directed at emphasizing class differences.

>From the moment the Hindu religion relieved itself of its burden of a past that had remained for a long time in a stagnant position, it accumulated power and formed a Hindu nationality that was very broadly defined and that did not exist prior to then. Yet it managed to overcome the Muslim enemy during its war effort, an effort that in the past the Hindis would have been incapable of managing, since, as it has been recalled, it was only because of the Sikhs that they were saved from a general Muslim conquest in the first place.

Section 5: Epilogue

This chapter has chartered the three and a half thousand year history of two nationality groups in Asia, the Japanese whose general origins may be traced to its Chinese immigrant community who merged together with an earlier population whose identity is unknown, and the Hindi, who comprise a mixture of Aryan conquerors who arrived from Persia and an ancient population whose identity for the purposes of this manuscript was not made clear. The flow of Chinese into Japan took on the nature of immigration rather than of conquest, whereas in India, the Aryans arrived there specifically for the purpose of conquest. There was never any real possibility for the ancient indigenous Japanese tribes to escape from Japan to another place, in India that option was always open, practically speaking however the emigrations that did take place were not on a large scale, at least insofar as this topic has been looked at in this manuscript. Both in Japan and in India a distinct and common culture was cultivated using the resources of those who had recently arrived from near as well as from those who had always been part of the landscape. One of the conspicuous differences between these two cultures was the institution of the caste system, a system that hierarchically graded the various classes and one which was prominently followed in India immediately after the Aryan invasion of that country, but which did not exist in any form in Japan. The ancient myths in both Japan and in India ascribed different statuses amongst various categories of people. In Japan the imperial family was accorded a different status to the general Japanese population. In India the population was divided along class lines so that every individual in society was classified according to his class. In both these countries rituals were conducted in honour of the ancestors (as was the case iChina). Originally Japan exclusively adopted Confucianism, and it was only much later on that they welcomed Northern Buddhism to their shores. This was deemed acceptable because this form of the religion did not essentially have to rely upon monasteries for its functioning, and therefore did not threaten to create a focal point of power that competed with the regime. From this point of view Japan is similar to China. In contradistinction, in India, there never was a Confucian tradition, even if the idea of a duty of loyalty towards one's superiors, an idea that is an important component of Confucian ideology, was meticulously followed in India. Buddhism as it took shape in the North had its origins in India, and yet it was completely eradicated in the subcontinent, since its mere mode of operation was viewed as a threat to Hinduism, especially since Buddhism was opposed to the caste system. This Buddhist opposition to class distinctions obviously did not affect its chances of integration in China, in Japan, or in any other Asian country; the reason for this was that the caste system that prevailed in India was not imitated in any other territory.

The whole subject of class differences and of the superiority of the upper class in India is intimately connected with the mythology that upheld this motif. In Japan the myths were used as an adhesive substance unifying the nation by spreading the message of the uniqueness of the Japanese as well as the inherent superiority of their emperor especially with respect to his religious preeminence. In India myths did not come to unify the Indians rather they came to split them; from this perspective what is evident is the diametrically opposed scenarios when comparing the effects of myths in Japan to those in India. In India there is no talk of myths being used to glorify the land called India. Myths, there, do not even instill an obligation of loyalty towards this or that ruler or emperor. The difference between Japanese mythology and Hindu mythology lies in the fact that the Japanese myths were active in bringing together a nation under one centralized regime, which regime was recognized as holy from a religious perspective. Contrarily, in India the Hindu myths (as distinct from the Buddhist and Sikh myths) were invented for the express purpose of ensuring that members of the inferior classes do not rebel against the superior status accorded members of the upper classes. In India myths were used specifically for preserving the status quo ante of the societal composition. In Japan they came to strengthen the people, the state, and the sole, unique, and legitimate government of Japan.

Obviously the myths of the Buddhists and those of the Sikhs were quite different from one another, as different as each was to the Islamic myths, but all of this is not relevant; the Buddhists were in any event wiped out, and the Sikhs and Muslims were segregated from the general Indian population.

Another aspect has also been illuminated: **Myths are never co-incidental. Despite the fact that they are, apparently, simple narratives of events, there is nothing at all simple about them. Mythical fables comprise the fundamental Constitutions of social co-existence in (perhaps) all human frameworks, and this is true at least of India and of Japan.**

If, nowadays, in the modern Western world, the most essential clauses providing for the smooth running of society and of their institutions are drafted in a document called a *Constitution*; at other times in history and in other countries this document would variously be referred to as a myth, a folk tale, a parable, an epic, the Jewish Bible, the New Testament, or the Koran. Therefore the Hindu story which contains images styled on the Biblical binding of Isaac is a Constitutional-Judicial proclamation cautioning each man in Hindi society to believe that which is attributed to their deities and to obey those precepts that have to do with the status of the Brahmans, and for example, the given fact of the superiority of the Aryan race within the framework of Indian society.

As Hall quotes in his book, [89]it was Baron Kikuchi Dairoku who, in a series of lectures that he delivered in London in 1909, argued the case for Japan's uniqueness and superiority, over and above all other nations in the universe, when he said:

---

[89] See Hall's book, note 47, at p. 58.

>From the first Emperor, Jinmu, there has been an unbroken line of descent to the present Emperor. This unique character of our Imperial dynasty, together with the fact that all Japanese ... are regarded as either descended from the Imperial family or from those who came over with it from the ... Plain of High Heaven, may be said to constitute the fundamental character of our nationality as distinguished from other nations

The support for this contention is contained in an unimpeachable source- Japanese mythology. This is reminiscent of the primary Jewish claim, which is based upon that which is written in the Hebrew Bible, viz. that the Pentateuch was given to the Israelites at Mount Sinai.

In light of the aforesaid is it correct to say that for the Japanese the devastating surrender suffered by them at the end of World War II was equivalent to the shattering experience of the heavens falling down on earth? If so, it would appear that the power of myths, especially that of the Japanese, was able to withstand such a calamity. The myths continued to fill the hearts of the Japanese, ensuring that they remain fiercely attached to Japanese nationalism; after all this nationalism continued to thrive despite being fractured by surrendering the war. Thus the myths have never changed. Reality will always be incapable of inflicting damage to them. It is the latter that will triumph over reality. And indeed that is exactly what happened. The democratic Constitution inspired by American values was overcome by a reality that pushed it in the direction of the Ancient Mythological Constitution, which is the hushed but deeply entrenched Japanese Constitution.[90] This Constitution was not drafted during the Magi period, as Marayuma[91]has proposed. After all he did not even try to search out the roots for displaying loyalty specifically to the Japanese emperor, and which explain the reason behind the local pride the Japanese people take in themselves, which both go to the core of nationalism, or the thing which Marayuma calls fascism; roots which facilitated the rise of the Magi regime. Nationalism was always around even if such a nomenclature was unknown and unfamiliar.

When it came to the Indian reality the exact opposite happened. The myths, which were not at all linked to nationalism but were rather the mainstay behind the caste system, were forced into submission. The power of the Indian myths ceased the

---

[90] As has emerged from various rulings of the Japanese Supreme Court, as can be seen from the activities of the executive arm of the government, and as has been demonstrated by the whole episode of study curricula in the classroom, the above is invariably true. In this limited framework I will not analyze this any deeper, and I will leave the ramifications of this insight to a separate and more thorough study of the matter.

[91] See Maruyama's book at note 47 *supra*.

moment. an end was decreed to the caste system. These myths did not try and shape society or create a nationality. Instead these myths were an historic anachronism since they preserved class distinction. When the idea of splitting society along class lines was thrown out into the dust heap of history, the myths that encouraged this divisive approach, an approach that was no longer in vogue, also became a thing of the past. It is even possible to say that today's Indian nationalism is possessed of a deep historic past which over the course of time has been filled with nostalgia for class distinctions that once exited but have since ceased to be the norm. >From this perspective, Hindi myths even nowadays make up a great part of the national Indian historic memory. Memory- yes, reality- no.

A separate question relates to the extent to which myths- independently in India and independently in Japan- played a part in the willingness and execution of a foreign invasion. India never initiated an invasion outside its borders. External wars were only fought in the context of Kashmir and only in order to ward off Pakistani intentions to annex Indian Kashmir to its borders. This does not classify as an Indian incursion but rather as an instance of Indian self defence. Since ancient mythology revolved around class difference rather than national unification or the formation of a nationality,it becomes completely evident why India has never been able to provoke a war in which it would invade areas outside of its borders. The main reason then is because national integration did not exist at the time when India had just gained its independence. Such integration was difficult to achieve without myths specifically geared towards such an eventuality. Integration did come about, as it did in the United States, only after wars had been fought and blood had been spilt, which in turn facilitated the creation of new myths.

It goes without saying that as far as Japan is concerned national myths do present one with the option of executing an invasion, even if it does not render invasions such as these inevitable. National Japanese pride had obviously contributed to the Japanese war mood especially when a situation had arisen where the Japanese had felt that Japan had not been accorded proper respect or had not been treated as an equal; these situations did come about, for example, when international treaties had been signed which had treated the parties unequally, including the time when the amount of boats allowed to patrol the seas had been unequally distributed giving Japan a significantly lower volume than that that had been accorded the United States and the United Kingdom, and also counting the time when the "yellow" Japanese had had to deal with a very different treatment towards them than that that had been received by the "white" Western Powers in relation to the possibility of imperial conquests; Western countries had viewed it their right to hold on to property situated in the Imperial colonies but when Japan had occupied colonies which had in the past belonged to the European countries but which had been subsequently conquered by Japan's ally, Germany, as in the case of the French or Dutch colonies, or when Japan had occupied territories formerly under German control, or even when Japan had considered herself at liberty to be active in China no less than the other Europeans, in all these and in similar cases Japan had had to withstand a hostile attitude from the world's leading states. Against the backdrop of such an attitude Japanese national pride made its way to the forefront and demanded from the Japanese government a tough approach in its contacts with the West. >From this perspective the ancient Japanese myths contributed to the international whirlpool in which Japan had found herself. It is abundantly clear that the more wars Japan fought, wars that were nourished by national pride nurtured by ancient mythology, the more new myths were created as a result of these very wars.

New myths are continuously being created. Myths are not the sole province of the ancient historic past, as was already mentioned in the introduction above. There is also the myth of civil religion in every modern state; whether it takes the form of national holidays or whether it comprises heroic stories of the recent past, myths are intimately connected with the rituals that are themselves connected to the establishment of a state and the attendant struggles and sufferings of its inhabitants during its wars. In the Magi's Japan, for example, a national holiday was proclaimed to celebrate the day of the commencement of the reign of the first emperor; nonetheless, as has been mentioned in the introduction, just like there is no replacement for the memories of infanthood and of childhood , and just like one cannot compare the memories of infanthood and childhood to the events that occur to a person in his mature years, from the point of view of shaping one's behavior and one's feelings, so too with the life of a nation; but this question goes beyond the confines of this present discussion.

Chapter G:
Myths as the creator of a common identity and history and as setting of boundaries

Emerging from what has been said thus far is that, just as the existence of society is a fundamental element of the human lifestyle, so too myths, like language and religion, are the basic things upon which human society is founded.

Myths are the essential building blocks used in the construction and preservation of social frameworks and also of theistic religions, as opposed to the non- theistic religions. Mythology is used by human society, regardless of the latter's make up, and regardless of the latter's various incarnations. Mythology is thus exploited, in equal measure, by a nationalistic society, a political society, a religious society made up of believers in some or other type of deity, and a cultural society. All these types of societies are defined by actual and potential ranges, so that in the case where there is a difference between its actual range, and its potential one, the myths deal with the potential ranges, which are always wider than, or identical to the actual range. In the case of early Christianity its potential range spread to all of humanity who was not at that time affiliated with another theistic religion, and even then only if that religion explicitly contradicted the precepts of Christianity. No reservation was made as to the nationality, race, language, and culture of the potential convert. It was possible for a Jew to affiliate himself with Christianity so long as he believed that Jesus being the messiah, the son of God and one of the three entities that made up the Holy Trinity did not contradict his view of Judaism. So too one who had practiced Hellenic culture, or any other pagan believer, for that matter could join Christianity, on the condition that he had abandoned his faith in idols to the extent that that idolatrous belief had contradicted a belief in One God, expressed by the belief in the trinity, and who now also believed that Jesus was the messiah. Thus, the Greek Hellenists, the Romans, and any other pagan worshippers were able to preserve those traditions that were influenced by the pagan cultures from which they originated so long as those traditions were merely superficially adhered to without forming the core beliefs of the Christian convert, and so long as monotheism, as expressed through the trinity, was regarded as supreme. From this perspective it makes sense why there was nothing holding back those from the eastern cultures, and ethnic groups, from preserving certain pagan characteristics within the framework of the Christianity that they accepted upon themselves. This, to the extent that the Eastern Orthodox (Christian) religion that emerged was quick to integrate and incorporate these types of indigenous characteristics into the religion without such a practice being considered non-Christian. Christianity was able to include within its ranks and contemporaneously, Egyptians, Romans, and even Germanic tribes without cutting away at each individual's ethnic background or separate national affiliation. All these nations became integrated into Christian society where the myths relating to the *last supper* and the crucifixion of Jesus, and Judas Iscariot became the common heritage of all believers, and left them with the feeling that each was acquainted with his fellow and that each was attached to the other through emotional and intimate ties. Therefore when the Ottomans reached the gates of Vienna, the battle that ensued was not merely part of a war in which Austria tried to fend off the attacking Turks, but rather it became a war that pitted Christianity against Islam. It became a war between religions or a "war between cultures", as those imbued with 21st century notions would like to refer to it.

Myths are responsible for creating a familiar setting (through the sharing of a common mythological heritage), which is enough to rouse powerful sentimental feelings, intimacy and even solidarity in the hearts of all of those who share the same mythology. Contrariwise a myth can turn enemy on anyone who wages a war of destruction, or who tries to inflict serious damage, or who acts in a tyrannical manner towards others who have affiliated themselves with the same mythological school. Collective solidarity, in its negative construction, determines the level of rivalry and even animosity that should be applied to all those who are not in the same mythological circle. A natural covenant between individuals on the one hand and a common feeling of enmity towards a specified "other" on the other hand both creates and defines a social framework.

The definition of a social framework is also a delineation of the limits of that group as they have been confined by the framework. From this perspective myths are also responsible for marking out the boundaries. For example, a myth may relate to all Japanese inhabitants, yet, so long as not all the Japanese fully and intimately come to terms with that specific myth a gap is created between the actual domain of the group that positively relates to the myth (the actual boundary), and the boundaries to which the myth purports to delineate, or to sketch out, or to which its actual contents relate to and to whom it is designated for (the etched out boundary). The etched out boundary is the optional boundary that is fixed by the myth, and if we relate to a myth as having a "pseudo- intention", it is also a designated boundary.

The actual boundary is never meant to exceed the limits of the designated boundaries. If, then, people who live outside the area of the designated boundary approach the people who do live there with the request to join their group, an internal problem is bound to flare up amongst the latter group. Therefore in order to enable this designated merger, it is vital that a way be discovered to alter the mythology. An example of this dilemma may be found in the problem surrounding "who is a Jew?" that sprung up amongst an Israeli sub- group that was part of a larger Jewish societal group, when within the framework of the Jewish State's institutions, the State of Israel, a man by the name of Benjamin Shalit[92] who had a married a non- Jew sued to get his son Tomer to be recognized, within the legal framework of the Jewish State, as a Jew, and, moreover, to have him registered within the framework of the Populations Registry of that state (the State of Israel) as a Jew. Jewish mythology, as it has been expounded upon and as traditional

---

[92] See *Ex Parte Benjamin Shalit and as representative of his minor son Tomer Shalit v. Minister of the Interior et al*, H. C. J. P"D 26 (1) 335. See also H. C. J. 58/68 P"D 23(2) p. 477.

commentary has interpreted it, has establthat its myths apply exclusively to Jews who have been born to a Jewish mother. Since in this case the wife of the Jew was not Jewish, his request was refused and was dismissed in the final instance by the Supreme Court. This was all done after it became clear that the laws of the State of Israel in force at that time and as they were interpreted and understood, laid down the rule that the only person who may be registered as a Jew is one who the Jewish religion (in this case it is actually Jewish mythology which includes the religious discussions of the members of the group to which Jewish mythology refers) has determined belongs to the Jewish race, and the Jewish religion, as it was acknowledged there, rejects the son of that Jew, who was born from a non- Jewish mother and holds that that son (Tomer Shalit) does not belong to the circle of Jews. This then is an example of an attempted break-in by someone who finds himself locked outside the framework designated for the Jews, a break-in that in the final analysis was thwarted and was halted by those to whom the matter was brought. Obviously the way of getting this same child (Tomer Shalit) into the national- religious framework[93] would have been possible if, and only after, a condition had been stipulated allowing the religious mythology of the Jews, which are at one and the same time also national myths, to amend itself in a way that the designated boundaries of the Jewish group were to additionally include all sons of Jewish fathers, whether or not the mother is Jewish.

On precisely this point there emerges an additional dimension to mythology, the context dimension, and what is meant by this term is not the storyline per se of the myth, but rather the context, ultimate destination, value system, and rules of behavior, to which the myth refers and to which it aspires. The myths of the Japanese Shinto speak about loyalty to the emperor, which extends to the value of loyalty in general; about honoring one's father in particular, and honoring one's parents in general; about showing respect to elders and to sages; and about the importance and the centrality of the Japanese isles, as well as other additional values. Someone who accepts Shinto upon himself in the sense that he feels emotionally intertwined to this religion, and who views Shinto as especially meant for him, will try his utmost to faithfully fulfill those behavioral precepts. On the basis of this value system multitudes upon multitudes of Japanese soldiers sacrificed their lives in the Second World War and in many other wars. There is, then, hidden behind Japanese mythology a very potent force, just as there are significantly powerful forces in nearly all other mythologies. From here it emerges that myths play a very forceful role in determining the personal behavior of the constituents of a society that functions within a framework of a particular mythology (i.e. a religious group or a national one, and to certain extent even a

[93] Judaism is at one and the same time both a religious group and a national group.

culturally defined society). This conscious role is given expression in the form of a moral code that directs constituent members to subscribe to a particular ethical mode of behavior that has been prescribed by that society's collective heritage. There are three types of heritages each suiting a particular society:

(1) An ethical religious heritage- found in a society bounded by and infused with religious themes.
(2) A national ethical heritage- found in a society bounded by and infused with national themes
(3) A culturally ethical heritage- found in a society bounded by and infused with cultural themes

Thus far the **functional aspects** of mythology have been analyzed which encompass:
(i) Familiarity
(ii) Intimacy
(iii) Solidarity
(iv) Internal and mutual aid against external factors
(v) Opposition and enmity to those who are hostile to, or opponents of, allies who have been grouped in the same mythological circle
(vi) Practical delineation as it interrelates to the designated delineation of that group
(vii) A collective ethical pedagogic heritage and the drafting of hereditary ethical codes

Additionally three types of social groupings that myths delineate have also been surveyed:

i. The social religious grouping
ii. The social cultural grouping
iii. The traditional/ nationalist which, as will be explained below, is divided into :
   (1) Civil- political nationalism which is an outgrowth of the heritage formed by the civil and political society
   (2) Ethnic nationalism, constructed within the framework of an ethnic group which has expanded itself and has formed a national lifestyle unique to it.

This last mentioned division of nationalism into two separate types was a division which came about as a result of policies that were put into place by modern states, during the end of the nineteenth and at the beginning of the twentieth century, when the states, in an attempt to deal with the allure that mythology held for ethnic societies, and trying also to compete with the magnetism, gravitational pull, and inner cohesion that bonded these ethnic societies together, and furthermore in light of the fact that there was usually more than one ethnic group exiting within the political framework of one state, concluded that without creating nationalized myths they were doomed to witness total dismemberment. Under these circumstances, these modern states, and more especially those which made up western society, toiled hard, in order to cultivate their own mythology.[94] In the United States this process begun straight after the Constitution was ratified and was given more impetus especially after the American Civil War. This was done through the construction of myths that centered on the Founding Fathers, the Framers of the Constitution, and on events that led to the War of Independence. It included the creation of national American festivals such as Thanksgiving Day in celebration of the first tilling of the land by the pioneer settlers of the North American colonies and the adventurous tales surrounding this event. It continued with days of remembrance for the leaders of the United States (which are rituals) commemorated through studying their historical achievements (which qualify as myths). It also includes adapting theistically- religious festivals such as Christmas and turning it into a national American holiday- at least from the ritualistic aspect. Even the genocide of the American Indians (Native Americans), with the help of the private movie industry- ostensibly a private sector, but effectively working for the public interest-was turned into a myth. At the same time the phenomenon of repeatedly watching these types of films became a tradition- effectively turning into a ritual.

Myths surrounding Nazi Race theory were ostensibly based upon "studies", whose credibility is very much in doubt, and which were in any adopted by the Germans without great discernment. These studies merely filled their feverish desires of finding a source to the superior heritage of the German nation.[95]

Without implying, in any way, Heaven Forefend, that it was invalid aspirations and warped tendencies that were responsible for the alterations and the add-ons that were inserted into the myths of Early Christianity, and stressing, rather, that doubt cannot be cast upon the pure intentions of Peter and Paul, it must nonetheless be admitted that those myths that came about during Christianity's early period were ignited with the burning desire of the then Christian spiritual

---

[94] See Benedict Anderson Imagined Communities [Hebrew Edition] (Tel Aviv: Haifa University Publishing House, 5760- 2000)

[95] This does not mean to say that the fabricators of the Nazi Race theories did not themselves believe in the truth of their theory.

leadership to increase the numbers of Christians. Against this backdrop Christianity tailored itself to fulfill it goal- which was considered sacrosanct to the heads of Christianity- of spreading Jesus' gospel to as many followers as possible. This same goal was foremost in the minds of the Spanish and Portuguese during their expeditions of conquest and expansion in Latin America, only by this time there was no longer a need in augmenting Christian mythology. As has emerged from part 1 of this book, it was specifically because of this very goal that there never was a policy of genocide carried out upon the "Indians" in Latin America- as, contrarily, there was on the North American continent within the context of tProtestant's mission of expansion[96]- since the aim was always to enlist them as members of the Christian religious society and to endow them with the legacy of Christian mythology.

In part 8 of this book the differences between the West and Imperial China will be discussed. In that Part it is concluded that the basic difference between the two is that in the West man rebelled against the political regime of the Deity and his human earthly messengers as was witnessed in the separation of religion and politics, whereas in China there was no necessity to rebel against Divine political authority because there the Divine was never involved in the political regime. In light of the insights gained in this Part the aforesaid may be refined especially as it relates to Imperial China and it may be acknowledged that both in regards to Imperial China and in regards to Early Japan the only type of regime (whether under emperor or king) that could succeed was one that relied upon the grace of religious mythology, not the grace of religious people. The regime itself was inundated with religious beliefs, but because the ruler himself was held to be part of the divinity, or the "son of a deity", there was no conflict of interests between him and the religious clergy; and the latter considered themselves subordinate to the ruler whom they worshipped. In China, as was recounted, the emperor himself was would appoint the deities. The emperor was regarded to be on the same level as a Supreme Deity, and there was therefore a delicate but institutionalized balance between the emperor, on the one hand, and forces that emanated from a supernatural source, on the other. The emperor's divinity acted as a buffer that prevented any insurrections. If however war was waged against the empire, the eventual victor would also be endowed with the status of demigod. There is then no reason to speak of a rebellion, whether it be in China, at least not until 1911 C. E., or whether it be modern day democratic Japan, where no rebellions seem to be emerging on the horizon. Therefore man's great revolt against the Divine that took

[96] Requiring further investigation is whether the treaty signed between the French Catholic settlers and the Indians was not influenced by the different approaches that were adopted by the Catholics and the Protestants with regard to the native Indians.

place in the West could never have happened and indeed did not happen, until at least 1911, when China's imperial period finally ended. Mythology in Japan, and to a great extent, in China as well, played both a national and religious role. Myths were responsible for uniting the both the Japanese and the Chinese, each one having built its nation upon the founding principles of these super narratives. This is true both in the sense of establishing a distinct and singular ethnic/national collective (in practice the ethnic differences between the subgroups were wiped out from the national consciousness, thanks to a common mythology), and in the sense of establishing a distinct religious collective. Shinto is not merely a religion. It is also one of the basic elements responsible for a unified national identity in Japan. Therefore, as a result of various mythologies, the Japanese, the Chinese, and the Jews regard themselves as comprising a distinct nation, and - at their very core and generally speaking- a distinct religious collective. Here is manifest another of mythology's capabilities- creating a collective that is nationally-religiously defined, so that these two disparate but fundamental elements are welded together to form an internally lethal combination. It is possible to claim, with regard to the Jews, that the aforesaid has been proven true by the very fact that the Jewish dispersion across foreign and often hostile lands in every corner of the globe for a period approximating 2000 years failed to prevail over their national- religious mythology. This in itself is an indication of the strength of the three- fold combination of myth, religion, and nation.

PRODUCTS OF RELIGION

MORALITY, ETHNIC GROUPS, NATIONS

Volume II:
Products of Religion - Morality, Ethnic Groups, Nations

Part 3:
What is a Nation? What is a Civil Religion? The case of Israel

Part Outline

In this part of the book, the general notion of the nation and nationality will be studied and discussed taking the example of Israel as a starting point. Speaking about the special case of Israel it will be shown how the structural maladies and wide ranging activism of the Israeli Supreme Court has turned it into a submissive tool by those elements who seek to create a new nation in Israel, neither Arab nor Jewish, but Israeli. This nation is in the process of consolidating itself, a process of severing itself from both the Jewish and Arab Diaspora, a nation that merges Jew and Arab together to form one homogenous whole. This nation establishes a new religion, calling itself "Israeli Civil Religion". The State of Israel undergoes this process while in the opposite direction a process of disengagement takes place between Jews and Arabs in Israel, as was demonstrated in the previous part of this book. The ambivalence of these trends is not only a phenomenon characterising the life of the individual and wrenching his soul, but also has the ability to wrench human society, causing inner schisms and internal struggle. This book will not directly deal with this inner schism. This schism is not an easy subject; it can be dealt with at the fringes of another discussion. It is worthy of special consideration, separate and in-depth, which in my opinion should be done within a different framework; here it may be noted that the trend of creating a new nation by eliminating ethnic and national attributions and by living within the framework of a shared state is a widespread phenomenon that has occurred in other countries.[1] The success of this process bodes an end to the vision of a Jewish State.

In this chapter this process as a general phenomenon will be reviewed, and the process in Israel will be viewed as a special phenomenon within the framework of the more general phenomenon. This, together with a deeper understanding of human nature, the deep and compulsive reasons for the formation of religions, the processes of the formation of ethics, the essential difference between religious mores and between behaviour enacted for the sake of self interest alone, and the advantages of religious mores over a self interested lifestyle will be reviewed, as well as the built-in weaknesses of Western mores in the last one hundred years ranging from Kant to postmodernism, and the division of Contemporary religions into three types (Monotheistic religion from the Jewish school of thought, the Far Eastern religions form the Hindu school of thought, and Civil Religion).[2] While analysing these things, civic society will be diagnosed according to the educational structure that is in place and it will be studied from the perspective "tell me how the education is organised in the state and I will tell you which elements are dominant in the regime and which are barred from entering the halls of power in it." Through analysing the school structure in the USA, it will be discovered how civil religion has reigned in the USA and how Theistic religion has been banned from the Halls of Justice there. Similarly, the review will include how Canada moved from the Covenant of the Protestant and Catholic Religions whose adherents shared power between them to a state in which the process of Americanisation whose connotations are the spreading of Canadian civil religion by the power holders, as a result of the changes in the Canadian educational system. It will be seen that the situation in Israel is exactly the same because of the

---

[1] On 'The Civil Religion of the Afrikaner People,' that the Nation created between the beginning of the nineteenth century and the beginning of the twentieth century, the *Boer* nation in South Africa, which was a mixture of nations from different origins that amalgamated to form one people in the new territories, to which they arrived, immigrants who came from Holland and France, see T. Dunbar Moodie, *The Rise of Afrikanerdom, Power, Apartheid and the Afrikaner Civil Religion*(University of California, Berkley, Los Angeles, London 1975).

[2] In regard to the general secular ideology, that does not confine itself to any specific nationality, and that sways and continues to hold sway over Western culture within their each national civil religions separately see Jacob Talmon *The Beginning of Totalitarian Democracy* (Tel Aviv, Dvir, 1956), *Ibid.*, on *p.* 11 it is defined as a religion.

parallels between the different school networks of 'governmental', 'religious governmental', 'Independent', '*El-Hamayan*' 'Arab-governmental' on the one hand and the Zionist parties, the NRP, Agudath-Israel, '*Shas*' and the Arab parties on the other.

These are just a number of the topics that will be raised in the course of analysing and proving these things, but the full picture will only be seen in the later on in the main section of this part, where the discussion unfolds, in all its length and breadth, as will be done now.

The importance of this subject

In 1999 half a million religious and ultra-Orthodox Jews demonstrated against the decisions of the Supreme Court. No speeches were made during the demonstration, rather chapters of psalms were chanted after which the crowd dispersed peacefully. This was a quiet but very powerful protest in which a tenth of Israel's Jewish population participated, including children, the ailing and the aged. From the perspective of the percentage of Israel's Jews participating in this demonstration, the numbers were impressive, generally speaking for any demonstration, but especially taking into account the fact that only one other demonstration in Israel was larger. The religious demonstrators' main charge was that whenever the public were divided in a debate between the religious and irreligious population, the Supreme Court' interfered on the side of the irreligious. They judged in their favour, and adopted an ideological standpoint in line with one of the sides in Israeli politics. There were also complaints from the religious side about the composition of the Supreme Court, which was composed of those representing the secular-liberal stance, whose influence on decisions involving Jewish religious values tended to be negative.
A counter-demonstration in support of the Supreme Court was set up opposite this demonstration, numbering 50,000 people, the majority of whom were irreligious, but it was a demonstration organised by the established organs of the state. The question may be asked: Is this not one of the signs of a religious war waiting to erupt? An additional and separate question may also be raised: Doesn't the Israeli Supreme Court and its supporters comprise one type of political unit, and the ultra-Orthodox (*Chareidi*) another?

In the context of these questions, it seems appropriate to analyse the issue of 'civil religion' from a universal perspective while broadening our analysis when dealing with the Israeli-context. This analysis will enable us to shed some light on the issue.

Using as a backdrop the decisions of the Supreme Court on religious matters, as will become clearer in the course of this discussion[3], an important and honest question can be asked by those who see themselves as critics of the Supreme Court. This question is multifaceted and can be formulated thus: Whom does the Israeli Supreme Court represent and whom does it serve? What role does it play within the ever-widening ideological and political split in Israel? Is the religious protest legitimate when it not only criticises a specific decision but rallies against the political legitimacy of the Supreme Court in its present composition and world view that it embodies? Is there any basis to the claim that today's Supreme Court acts as a political player?

The discussion on civil religion in Israel and in the Supreme Court will raise questions, from a broader perspective, similar questions, i.e.: To what extent is this Supreme Court a government institution that serves the aims of civil religion? An institution that tries to realize the goal of imposing civil religion as law in the State of Israel and to turn Israel into a "State of all its citizens" nullifying any of Israel's inherent centrality to the basic interests of the Jewish People? To what extent does the court make it difficult for those whose lifestyles and voluntary organisations are intimately connected to the Jewish religion? To what extent does the court play a role as a political rival (willingly or inadvertently) to those who continue today to support Israel as the Jewish State?

Further on it will become clearer that the religious-ultra-Orthodox demonstration reflects a real problem that does not solely affect the ultra-Orthodox (*Chareidi)* community. It is a problem that goes to the heart of our discussion.

What is religion and what are the types of religion according to this definition for the purposes of this discussion? General overview according to the stages of development.

For the purposes of this discussion religion will be defined as "the framework of beliefs and social behaviours built on the belief in a thing that is impossible to prove, an ideological and organisational framework, that has its own rituals, and which usually has its own institutions." In the course of analysing the evidence it will become clear to what extent this definition stands up to reality.

---

[3] See a Section 4 of Chapter 2 of Yehuda Cohen's book *Who's afraid of a Jewish State? A Constitutional and Ideological Perspective (*Tel Aviv: Law Society Publication, 2001), and also see section 7 of chapter 3, and section 4(c) of chapter 6, *Ibid.*

From the beginning of the existence of humankind, man has acted as a social creature; he has managed social organisations that are run in accordance with the rules of social behaviour. In order to counteract the insecurities that surround him and the lack of knowing what the forces of nature have in store for him, what unforeseeably great dangers lurk before him, man strengthened his spirit in the powers of his imagination, which provided him with justification for setting up rules that he constructed in his mind and that he sought to harness in order to help him. It was this setting that produced *inter alia,* for example, the Totem institution; this according to research gathered in Australia, Africa, America, South East Asia and other places that studied primitive societies, which research was conducted using scientific surveys combined with the teachings of Sigmund Freud and Durkheim.[4]It seems that what is discussed there is a wholly universal phenomenon in the origins of human nature. There is only one kind of human temperament, which is invariable to man's cultural setting or timeframe. Human nature acts within a universal phenomenon. This universality expresses itself *inter alia* in the following: (1) The prohibition of sexual intercourse and mating between a son and his mother, between brother and sister, though this prohibition does not extend to the father-daughter relationship (2) The prohibition of a son harming his father (3) Tribal affiliation obligating mutual aid between a man and his maternal relatives, but not his paternal relatives. Thus even if a man lived in the same place where a group of his father's relatives dwelt, he is under no obligation to give them aid. At the same time he is obligated to help his mother's family, even if they live far away from him. All these rules applied universally on all the continents and faraway lands where there was no contact between their respective human inhabitants since they lived under primitive conditions. For the sake of comparison- a Jew establishes his race through his mother- not through his father. What Freud does, is to explain how this uniform prototype of human lifestyle came into being amongst people who had no means of communicating with one another. Even if it were said that all primitive tribes originate from one progenitor or from a pair of progenitors, the question may still be asked as to the source of this prototypical lifestyle. This prototype was ingrained in man through his different tribes (or through the progenitor couple as the source of all the tribes- according to Freud's understanding) in such a strong fashion until it took hold of man and determined his modes of behaviour right until contemporary times. In the words of Freud, this prototype exists today not only among savage and primitive tribes, but also amongst us, the bearers of modern culture. It therefore seems that

[4] Emile Durkheim, *The Elementary Forms of the Religious Life* (Translated by Joseph Ward Swain, George Allen and Unwin, 1967, first ed. 1915); *Emile Durkheim on the Division of Power in Society* (Translated by George Simpson, The Macmillan Company, 1933); *The Basic Writings of Sigmund Freud* (Translated and edited with introduction by Dr. A. A. Brill, The Modern Library, 1938)

what was said previously is correct, that the general common traits shared by all cultures and during all periods of time is connected to human nature and for the purposes of analogy, are "programmed" into man from the beginning of his existence.

It needs to be added that according to Freud's analysis these mental prototypes that he speaks of, are not the only prototypes that are ingrained in man (as in Darwin's approach) or that were ingrained in man (as in the traditional religious approach)Man is ingrained with other tendencies:

i. The inclination to help the weak by virtue of them being part of the human race.
ii. Thoughtful curiosity based not merely on physical feelings but also, and primarily on human reasoning.
iii. A human tendency to generalise personal matters.
iv. Constant wavering of man between "good" and "evil" as a basis for establishing his social behaviour. This wavering caused philosophers, moralists and religious sages to interminably argue the question whether man's inclination is inherently good, or whether by nature man is evil. This last-mentioned dilemma found expression in the book of Genesis where it speaks of man choosing between good and evil.

This complex mental configuration of man led to the Totem institution, as it led him to other rules of behaviour connected with Totem. These components together with Totem are the progenitors of Theistic religion, that which is centred on the belief in any deity (and in our concept of belief, included for this purpose of our discussion the concept of idolatry). Religion is the most organised and sophisticated form of the Totem institution- and it should be added-the Totem institution predates the institution of idol worship, from which Theistic religion originated. (Theistic is used in the broadest sense of the word). It is patently obvious that as a result of the Totem institution and from the trends and rules of behaviour connected with Totem a social lifestyle was formed, which today has been formalised in the modern state. As will be demonstrated later on, civil religion was a later development of this process. Within the framework of the development of these social rules it is possible to encounter early on societies that lived according to moral values and Theistic statutes-morals and laws that are affiliated with all types of deities and with any ordinances that were received from that deity.

The connection between religion and fear is investigated by Casirer[5] who relies on Bergson,[6] whom he quotes approvingly, and who connects the phenomenon of fear with the phenomenon of religious adherence. This, not only in relation to the subject of Totem in which man tricked nature while at the same time communicating with the forces of nature, but also in the belief of eternal life and communicating with ancestors, whom, in their belief continue to exist even after they have died. Fear of death was alleviated from man by relying on the idea of a life after death, which belief was reinforced by reliance on myths. There what was discussed was the connection between special ceremonies connected with these mythological figures and the overcoming of fear. Casirer also speaks about the Dynamic Religion, which is driven by the forces of attraction and the Static religion, which is powered by various pressures. I suggest adding to this data, the question, how and why religion came into being amongst men. In Part 1 I elaborated upon it, but here I will deal with it briefly. I spoke there of the Static Religion which predated the Dynamic Religion. I described within that framework primitive man seeking to protect himself from his fears including his fear of death., his fears of forces that are beyond his control and that derive their power from a transcendental reality, and his communication, with the help of his vivid imagination, with a thing or force which is also from a transcendental reality, which force will come to his aid. I also spoke of the willingness of man to obey the commandments of this force, which is superior to man and to his reality. It is at this juncture that moral imperatives make their appearance; they are superior to reality and to base interests. In this way, rules of morality come into being, which are superior to, stronger than and inimitable to any base interest, and which impose duties (not rights) on man.

Theistic laws (laws which man assigns to any kind of deity) controlled society's lifestyle in the religious era, which was an offshoot of the primitive era (before there was organised religion in the full sense of the word), and which ceased to affect our lives the moment a civil religion came into effect. The reigns of power have been handed to civil religion in most Modern Day States, excluding those states which subject themselves to any kind of Theistic Law, like Iran and Saudi Arabia, who have subjected themselves to the rules of the Islamic Religion as did the Ottoman Empire in its time.[7] An exception to this rule is Franco's Spain,

---

[5] Ernest Casirer *Measure of Man: Prelude to the Human culture* (Am Oved, Tel Aviv, 1956), pp. 96-99.

[6] Bergson, *The Two Sources of Morality and Religion* (tr. R. Ashley Audra and Cloudesley Breton, New York, Holt & Co., 1935) II, 25, 26, 30, 42, 28, 48.

[7] That practised, in the area of civil law and property law, the *Majla,* which is an anthology of Islamic Religious laws (*Sharia)* and which also practised religious law in the areas

which is a subject in and of itself, and where civil religion reigned over a country whose state religion was Catholicism. As a matter of principle then, civil religion does not disapprove the existence of a Theistic religion within its borders, neither does it automatically seek to disenfranchise Theistic religions of their political status, nonetheless civil religion does have a strong tendency to seek exclusivity in the political realm.[8]

Civil religion as a concept is mentioned in the writings of Rousseau which he associated with the religion that predominated during the French Revolution, a time when the Catholic religion lost its control over the day –to- day life of the state and on the laws that had prevailed in France. One of the foreboding indications of this "religious revolution" (the crowning of civil religion over Catholicism) was the practice introducing the Sabbath on the tenth day in place of the seventh, as was the practice in Catholicism. (This innovation was short-lived' but is useful as an indicator of the revolutionary spirit which shows the French revolution, from an ideological perspective, to be a "religious revolution") French civil religion replaced belief in the Holy trinity into belief in the civil triad "*liberte, egalite et fraternit*'." [9]

The civil religion fashioned by the French Revolution believed itself from the start (and to a great extent continues in this belief today) to be superior to Theistic religion. In contrast, the American civil religion according to the First Amendment to the American Constitution, introduced two guiding principles meant to co-exist despite the possibility that they partially contradict each other:

i. Freedom of religious practice for all citizens
ii. Neutrality (non-interference) of the government in relation to religions (i.e. Theistic religions as defined above). [10]

---

governing the familial status applying the specific religious law on their respective religious communities, an institution that continues to have partial application in Israel.

[8] Cases in which the extreme zealousness of civil religions has prevented theistic religions to play any role in the political field include the communist civil religion in most of the communist countries (excluding Poland) and the USA and France.

[9] D.G. Charlton, *Secular religions in France 1815-1870*, (Oxford University Press, 1963).

[10] Judges in United States explain the First Amendment as intended to distance the government from all religions, but do not include in this prohibition American civil religion. Had they included civil religion within the framework of separation of state and religion they would have created a very real problem of disallowing any ideological activity or groundwork within American politics. It is patently obvious that the US Judges did not deal with this assault to equality, which is a founding principle of the Constitution, an assault which has been realised in the USA from the very fact that the US does not put

This latter principle entrenched and encouraged the principle of separation of state and religion.

Religious institutions and Religious Rituals, their Essence and their Importance

Religious and pseudo-religious ceremonies and rituals that centre on Totem, from the primitive era- even before organised religion came on the scene- strengthened the spiritual and mental faculties of man as did too the very idea of forming a society. As society and its constituent individuals progressed to higher standards of culture, its lifestyle and rituals become better organized, which resulted in a more fixed religious regimen. As will be seen further on, man is unable to live a life of security and inner strength without religion, including civil religion. Emanuel Kant's crusade against Theistic religion could have come about as a result of his dismay with this religion because of his youthful disgust of having religious ceremonies and prayers forced down his throat.[11] It is logical to assume that many others like him underwent similar experiences in their attitude toward the Christian religion of their day. Nonetheless, the wider community only accepted Kant's moral theories because of Darwin's scientific discoveries that refuted the Judeo-Christian version of creation.[12] There was a need for a strong and alternative anchor with which one could substitute the moral anchor that kept the Christian religion in place and which held sway over the lifestyles of the European nations. This new anchor was provided by the scientific branch (especially Darwin's theory) as well as civil religion per Rousseau. In France deep hatred for the Church which was seen as an ally to the monarchy was an additional factor in adding weight to this new anchor. For the ramifications of this look at the Soviet Communist regime (excluding Poland) as an example, it also forbade or generally limited Theistic religious ritual, in order to remove any competing and dangerous, in its assessment, political powerbase.[13]

---

civil religion on an equal footing with theistic religions. Theistic religions are prevented from taking part in American politics, at least not directly, whereas civil religion reigns supreme. It **is** the political regime.

[11] As appears under the title "Kant, Emanuel" in encyclopaedia *Judaica*.(Hebrew)

[12] As described in a book that analyses six intellectuals whose philosophy and writings were widespread and whose theories were formulated to refute theistic religion, See Lewis White Beck, *Six secular Philosophies, Religious Themes in the Thought of Spinoza, Hume, Kant, Nietzsche, Williams James and Santayana* (Thoemmes Press, 1960, 1997).

[13] The talk in Israel nowadays is that the presence of religious parties (Jewish) is a bad disease and that (Jewish) religion should be excluded from politics. This has been given expression by immigrants from the FSU who were fed from an anti-religious education

In France the rebellion against Theistic-Christian –Catholic religion expressed itself in a number of practical innovations, including the enactment of civil marriages, the seizure of Church property and the establishment of a 10-day workweek.[14] But what of the institutional void left by the removal of the church's role as lifestyle regulator as well as the diminishing centrality of the church based organisations and activities, which once controlled organised life of the State? It was Civil Religion then that filled this void.

It is probably correct to assume that in this new regime the wedding ceremony would have been conducted by a state appointed marriage officer rather than a church ordained priest. The institution of marriage was conducted under the auspices of a government ministry connected to the civil religion, since the state government was the civil religion and the state was fully "in possession of" the civil religion. A similar changeover occurred with regard to religious law, whereas previously each law had to be approved by the papacy, which was then the legislative body of the state, the French National Assembly now became the organ of civil religion. Through this lens and by describing in detail the functionaries and institutions that ran political life – it is possible to view the state institutions, one by one as institutions of the civil religion.[15] That French national patriotism replaced religious faith is as an axiom that is impossible to prove but which every

---

that was indoctrinated into the FSU immigrants by their dictatorial Soviet regime. When such talk- of excluding Jewish religion from politics is sounded by Jews who arrived in Israel from the liberal West- the question may be asked as to the liberal educational background of these Western immigrants. Is it liberal to prohibit political organisation which has a religious leaning but to allow political organisation based on other interests or positions? It is possible also to explain the pioneering Zionists'- who came here after the Bolshevik Revolution- antipathy to religion in terms of their being primarily socialists. Therefore those who support separation of state and religion in Israel were influenced by the Soviet attitude towards religion, and based their logic on their desire to create a "new Jew", who is not from the exile. A defining symbol of the exile is the connection to the Jewish religion. What are being discussed therefore are factors not really relevant but which hide behind the demand to oust religion from politics.

[14] It reminds us of the early Christians who changed their Sabbath from the Jewish seventh day (Saturday) to Sunday.

[15] See Charles S. Liebman and Eliezer Don-Yehhiya *Civil Religion in Israel: Traditional Judaism and Political Culture in the Jewish State* (University of California Press, 1983), p.10. Even if the main points of this book does not deal, as will be explained later, with the trend of the adherents of civil religion to turn state institutions into their own and to exploit those institutions by imposing civil religion onto the state government the words of Liebman and Eliezer Don-Yehhiya still have application to our book.

Frenchman believed in.[16] The French example became a paradigm for modern day Western countries as well as for most of the modern world.[17] Therefore, and owing to this fact, France turned the Church- run religious courts into obsolete institutions, which were replaced by State courts, and not just as representatives of the state governors but also as representatives of civil religion, whose precepts were the only ones acceptable in the halls of justice. This was the only way the authorities could ensure that Catholicism loses its hold on the French way of life. It was this process that similarly developed in the American version and in its different metamorphoses applied partially to a good number of other countries. The new hallowed slogan was separation of State and Religion. State organized (civilly religious) military parades became the ritual to replace religious processions, even if they did not manage to completely rid themselves of these religious processions. Sports games generally, and international sport fixtures in particular encouraged the ritual in which the modern socialized individual viewed his national team's victory as his own. Educational institutions affiliated to the state became institutions that educated the young generation in the nationalist patriotic spirit encouraging loyalty to the state and its values- i.e. the values of civil religion. In this way the modern state education system, to the extent that it was run by the state, was turned into a religious institution, an instrument of civil religion. Independence Day or Bastille Day became ritualized by civil religion and given legitimacy politically by state administrators. Nevertheless it must be said that the above-described phenomenon symbolizes the importance of rituals to man, even in the Modern Era. It bears repeating that the tendency of man to fortify himself from situations of uncertainty (and these situations have been present from the beginning of the creation of the human race until our days) leads him to

---

[16] And see in this regard the definition of religion in the beginning of section 2 *supra*.

[17] Even in France itself, there has been in recent years a compromise allowing religious schools to be partially subsidised by the state according to certain criteria. A different approach to the French example is the totalitarian regime of Franco in Spain where the civil religion extraordinarily was the Catholic State Religion. This is because of the unique relationship that existed in Spain where Catholicism was instrumental in enforcing a totalitarian regime under Franco. In Canada too, religious education continued to be taught since at its inception as a Federation, religion was deeply entrenched into Canadian life, a situation that with the passing of time has been taken over by a growing secularism which has undermined these religious schools. It is possible then to say that Canada has begun the journey away from being a Federation based on a Godly covenant where the government relied on Theistic principles of law and slowly become influenced by civil religion, which in turn tries to sweep away theistic religion from the corridors of power. In this discussion the focus will be on the growing secularism of civil religion, which has become the battle cry for adherents to civil religion. Since the most basic requirement for the blooming of civil religion is the enticement of others to lose their Godly faith, civil religion has been much stronger in secular circles than it has among those who still believe in God.

lean on religion- in all its forms-including civil religion. Testimony to the negative effects of civil religion may be found in fascist and authoritarian regimes that sprouted from civil religion, and which aided in changing the regime's facade into that of a monster's. Nationality and nationalism are stark expressions of civil religion. Cosmopolitanism- including the international communist, as well as multinational religions as seen in Radical Islam[18]- is the enemy of civil religion, since it subjugates man to a faith and an alternative loyalty which clashes with civil religion, which is a national religion, as will be elucidated later.

4. Religious Wars, Civil Religion and its hardships

The French Revolution, then, was among other things, a religious war. The concept "war" from a more esoteric perspective, from the perspective of religious faith, is a much wider concept than the physical concept "war", which describes a blood soaked armed struggle fought between two states. Nowadays war has become ever more sophisticated in all its forms and in every context, so that the concept of "war" has undergone a metamorphosis. In the field of international relations, in the last decades, the experts spoke of a "cold war" between countries joined to NATO and those affiliated with the Warsaw Pact, a war in which the militaries' possession of weapons of mass destruction was decisive, even though neither side made any use of them, they were "static". No shot was ever fired. Satellite surveillance and spy rings were the most active elements. Already at the time of British Imperialism, the term "imperialism" was expanded, and whereas before it was synonymous with the expansion of sovereignty over land conquered by military force, Prime Minister Disraeli viewed British imperialism as the extension of the Empire's influence beyond areas under its political and military jurisdiction.[19] Nowadays they are referred to as "economic wars" as opposed to "economic treaties". In the same vein when referring to the issue of "religious wars" it does not necessarily imply a war accompanied by bloodshed.[20] Religious wars are taking place in our days as they have been in the past, every day and every hour. And when at war one needs to act the part. The concept "with good

[18] The connection between (the destruction of) the World Trade Centre and the war in Afghanistan that came in its wake, demands an explanation, which will not be discussed at this juncture.

[19] See under the entry "imperialism" in Encyclopaedia Hebraica.

[20] Overstating the matter when it came to expanding meanings of concepts, the Israeli Supreme Court termed an outcome of their interpretative opinion as a "constitutional revolution" while handing down their verdict in the *Mizrachi* case. I mention this not to support an act of constitutional creativity but to show to what extent the modern man has been led by his fertile imagination in managing political life.

advice conduct war,"[21] whose source is found in the book of religious insight, applies also to our situation of religious wars. A common strategy is the dissemination of misinformation and denial. It is possible to make gains in a war without even acknowledging that a war is taking place. It is possible to set up religious institutions without actually admitting that they are in fact institutions spreading religion. It is possible to set up institutions for the advancement of a certain sector in society while oppressing a different sector and simultaneously claiming that it was performed for the good of the whole. It is proposed that in this spirit the American Constitution be investigated as to what it has to say about religious affairs and how this is actually applied in the everyday American life. This investigation will not accept everything that is declared as the irrefutable truth. It will be seen whether it is not only the message of liberty and freedom that is spread by the Constitution, but also a declaration of war against any successful (Theistic) religious influence in the political arena by relegating such influence to the churches and other marginal institutions. Perhaps it is the message of war that is being spread by the constitution. In this way Theistic religious influence is minimised and their political freedoms are put down.

Suppressing Theistic religions in the USA follows a basic American interest.[22] Individuals of different faiths, who also were from different national ethnic backgrounds, founded this Federal political entity. The declared goal in forming this new entity was to strengthen its inhabitants by forging a new nation. Emphasising the difference amongst Americans themselves, in the context of their different religious and ethnic backgrounds was bound to endanger the formation of one grand nation. The drafters of the Constitution, then, cannot be condemned when they made the amendments; neither if they consciously intended to unite the People, and nor even if unity was not the stated purpose but rather to put a distance between (Theistic) religion and politics. Nevertheless it should be remembered that the Israeli example, which will be discussed below, is diametrically opposed to the American model. Here one People is discussed, the Jewish People, which was in exile dispersed around the globe for 1900 years, and which then regrouped and returned to their original land. In the Israeli case, of a Jewish State, the Jewish religion is not a dividing factor, but its polar opposite. Religion has a very unifying aspect to it. Without religion, the forces of separation would be on the rise, especially taking into account the fact that Jews dwelt in very different cultural

---

[21] Proverbs, 20:18 (Translation from *The Jerusalem Bible* [Koren, Jerusalem, 1983], p. 816.

[22] Even though the very existence of theistic religions help the internal stability in the different states (the fact that religion flourishes does not mean it plays any role in the political sphere) See *The Religion of the Republic*, (ed. Elwyn A. Smith, Fortress Press, Philadelphia, 1971), p. 155.

milieu. How does the Jew coming from Yemen bond with the Jew coming from Romania? It is in this case scenario that Theistic religion (Judaism) alone plays the role of unifier.

At this stage it would be fitting to define what exactly constitutes civil religion. It seems improper to broaden the concept of civil religion into the same universal cosmopolitan terms, as usually defines Theistic religions. Theistic religions generally (with the notable exception of the Jewish religion) are not confined (by their definition and by their essence) to one entity, country or political society. Why, then is there a need to confine the structure of civil religion to one kind of political society? Why do we not claim it to be based on the same principles as democracy, for instance, so that this ungodly religion can be viewed at universally? This last-mentioned possibility is in fact the view of Charles Liebman and Eliezer Don-Yehhiya.[23] This broad definition should be rejected. There are three reasons for this- semantics, internal substantial factors and external substantial factors.

Semantic reason: "Civil religion" is closely related to the word "citizenship." A citizen (or civilian) is such by virtue of his being a citizen of a specific country. There is (still) no legal concept of a "citizen of the world." Though in legal and political literature "citizen's rights" are oft though of as part of the greater concept of "human rights", and this theme continues to develop in the definition of universal man- that is to say- every citizen in every state possesses according to Natural Law and according to the law of Nations, the same rights, even if they rights stem from the very fact that he is a citizen of that country. Notwithstanding, when a citizen of a specific country invokes his citizen's rights, the address for doing so is the authorities of that country. When a citizen is charged with fulfilling his duties as a citizen, it is the state of which he is a citizen that has sole jurisdiction to make such a demand and not any other international organ. The political authorities of his country (specific and concrete) are the only address for him.

Substantive Reasons from an external perspective: As civil religions developed- they developed in each and every country- the central focus for those practising the civil religion was the specific state and its symbols which were thought to have

---

[23] Charles S. Liebman and Eliezer Don-Yehhiya *Civil Religion in Israel: Traditional and Political Culture in the Jewish State*, (University of California Press, 1983), p. 3. It seems there that the authors view fascism and communism as manifestations of civil religion, as well as including it in their definition of the term "civil religion" in a later part of the book.

intrinsic value and not the broader idea of building states, nor the humane idea behind the functioning of a state in general.

It is true: the idea of civil religion stemmed from a general idea, the fruits of Rousseau's philosophical toil whose author did not intend to aim his words at the French alone. The political philosophy behind civil religion is a very broad idea, aimed at humanity in general unrestricted by geographical boundaries. Yet this idea was meant to establish rules and principles. Architects, the world over, learn the principles of technical drawing, as well as the general rules of engineering. These principles and acquired knowledge are common to architects around the world. However the structure that is eventually built in line with these principles is a concrete structure, belonging to one very specific place. The building suits this one place and does not simultaneously feature in any other place. Every structure has its place, every building its special community destined for it, who in turn put it to local use as they see fit. Every structure has its own building laws that apply to it. So too is the case with civil religion. Every civil religion comes to regulate the relationship and loyalties that are very specific between the state and its citizens. Every state has its specific citizens' community attached to it. It is possible that the relationship that exists in France between the state and its citizens is used as a role model in Senegal, Africa who copied the "model" of Civil Religion, French style. Yet the loyalties of the Senegalese citizens will be directed toward Senegal, not France. Their focus of loyalty will be exclusive. It is on this basis that the Senegalese civil religion is able to create a focal point for the special spiritual and emotional ties between the citizens of Senegal and their country. This focal point of loyalties competes with other foci of loyalties and emotion that are and were present amongst these citizens-whether it be between them (or a part of them) and a kind of idolatry, Catholicism, tribal affiliation, ideology (Communist or democratic) and similar ties of loyalties and emotions. It is very likely that the same Senegalese citizen will remain a Catholic, a tribal member and be waving the flag of democracy and the like. It is also possible that the Senegalese authorities will not prohibit these things and may even encourage them. It is also likely that conflict of interests will not exist. The whole problem of conflicts is a subject in and of itself that deserves separate discussion. But for the purposes of defining "civil religion" it should be noted that it relates to a specific country's society, and therefore there is no such thing as an "international civil religion" but every civil religion in each and every country must be treated separately. So far the substantive aspects from an external perspective have been dealt with.

Now the substantive reasons from an internal perspective will be discussed.
Looking at it internally means looking at the internal mechanisms of religion, each country's underlying reasons and intentions. The difference between internal and

external aspects is similar to the difference between internal and external functions of a motor car. To the question why a motor car is a land vehicle unsuitable for air or sea travel, it is possible to answer on two levels. Speaking on the level of its external features it can be said that that the motorcar does not have any wings, is not lightweight and is not hermetically sealed and therefore it is impossible to fly in it or to use it to sail on water. Speaking on the level of its internal features it can be said that that the motorcar was not designed with wings, nor was it made lightweight and was not planned to be hermetically sealed since its manufacturers were looking to provide a solution for those consumers seeking land transportation exclusively. Had they been asked to provide something suitable for air travel or sea navigation they would have built it differently and then in addition to it transporting people across land it would also be able to transport air and sea travellers.

Likewise the answers will change when speaking of civil religion, only they will be much more complex than the motorcar example. As was described in section 2 above, the motivations for forming a religion (and before that Totem) lies in the fears that humans experience, the emotions and insecurities that he feels and the impossibility of dealing with these problems by tangible means alone. Because of his nature and makeup, and owing to his limited depth of understanding, man feels that there are things that exist beyond the reality that he can grasp with his physical senses, things that he will never be able to fully solve. Since it is human nature for man to use his powers of imagination he can create an imaginary world, an unreal world, and to cling to these imaginary things so that they serve as an aid for him. This idea is present in the Jewish Prayer books. Anyone who glances at the actual prayers that Jews recite will find requests for help, expressions of faith in redemption, care for the aching soul and healing for man's soul. Everything is directed at the God of Israel, who that same Jew never sees with his human eyes, but the results of his supplications he knows well. It is not by chance that Jews are found praying to the Lord. It is not coincidence but an internal need, which internal need flows from internal motivations described above.

This need does not disappear the moment a Jew loses faith in the existence of a Master of the Universe. The need still persists in him, and therefore this same Jew needs to find an alternative to his God. This alternative might be offered to him by his state, the State of Israel. This is not to point to the physical state, or its delegated officials: the IDF, the police, the courts, the ministers, and the members of Parliament: they do not enable him to discover spheres beyond his reality, transcendental spheres. Nonetheless the State of Israel remains the focal point of his identity with the idea and the concept of ultimate loyalty, the recipient of his desire to help, as if it were something hallowed, as a vision which has a message attached to it, as something just, as an expression of solidarity with the state's citizens, as something for which soldiers sacrifice their lives, something which will never pass from this world and will not be nullified, something which belongs to that Jew and many like him uniting everyone into one body where his friends feel the same feelings towards national holidays, where everyone in the state celebrates those things that the state has hallowed, a uniting factor, a spiritual factor- the special spirit that flows from this state, lifting up the spirit of the state's citizens so that the latter are prepared to give above and beyond their legal obligations that have been enacted in State Laws. At this point what emerges is the concept of the "intrinsic citizen" and the "intrinsic people" that was analysed in depth in my book on the Jewish State.[24]

Therefore, as a result of fear and out of a desire to free oneself from it and because it is the state that provides its citizens these with these intangible ways out, man must inevitably lose his faith in his God in order to establish this civil religion. Had civil religion not existed man would urgently need to invent it.

Since the entity to which the civil religious practitioner relates is his specific state, there cannot be an international or supranational civil religion. There can only be each country's specific brand of civil religion.

Going back to the American example and to its brand of civil religion, defensive things will certainly be sounded off about American civil religion and about its attitude towards Theistic religions. At a scientific symposium, snippets of which will be presented later, things of this nature were said, regarding the attitude towards minority groups within the Anglo-American legal tradition.[25] This was at a seminar that centred on the opening and closing statements of Professor Aviam Sofer with the added participation of Professors Alan Aids, Milner S. Bull, Carol Weisbrod, and Sir Geoffrey Palmer, the last-mentioned being the former longstanding Prime Minister of New Zealand. Sofer noted the abandonment, by today's American Supreme Court, of its protections over minorities, which it had previously enforced prior to its present tenure. In his reply to harsh criticism sounded off by Aides, Sofer prefaced his defensremarks about the American Supreme Court and his claim that the Supreme Court does in fact protect minorities, including religious minorities as follows: "Have faith in the secular religion." In his view, so it would seem protection over minority groups and over Theistic religions is a central tenet of the American secular religion and of the

---

[24] See note 3 supra, Chapter 6, section 1.

[25] As it appears in Washington and Lee Law Review, Vol. 48, Spring 1991, from p.381.

beliefs which this religion upholds.[26] It seems from his words, even if he does not express them in such a way, that the principles of the American secular religion are one and the same with those of the American Constitution, and that this secular religion is not especially anti Theistic religions rather it acts in defence of its majority, lest this majority be discriminated against by these other religions.

Weisbrod, one of the seminar's participants, describes modern American society as a society in which the individual can create his environment at will. Included in this is the individual's family status (as is expressed in the possibility of divorce or adoption) determined by the individual concerned. The Court does not interest itself in merely investigating the legal status or jurisdiction of this or that, it rather deals with judicial discretion which is the formation of a new social reality in the United States. This it does through judicial fiat and through the creation of a new (judicial) lexicon. As to the repeal of laws by judicial censure, as Sofer remarks, the question- according to Weisbrod- is complex and conflict ridden- since it is just as important to protect the minority from the majority as it is to protect the majority's fundamental principles which are at times impaired by the minority. An example of this latter protection is when a minority group discriminates in its membership requirements on grounds of gender.

Palmer, another participant of this seminar, relates his New Zealand experiences. In New Zealand there is no judicial discretion. He argues that the only way to protect minorities as has been shown in New Zealand in its attitude towards its Maori minority which makes up 12% of the population, is through the court system which works very well in New Zealand, even if the judges do not have judicial discretion which is not practiced there. He gives examples showing how the courts avoid basing their decision on judicial discretion both in New Zealand and in Britain where the legislature are encouraged to enact legislation safeguarding minority rights. He argues further that the American system of judicial discretion hampers the legislature in taking steps to protect minorities. He also sees a link [from both directions of the scales- upwards and downwards- Y.C.] between judge made law that uproots a parliamentary initiative and a parliamentary initiative that renders judicial legislation superfluous. From what he says, it appears that the secular religions in Britain and New Zealand are no worse off in their protections of minorities than is the American system (which Sofer has qualms against, especially when he reports about the changes in approach recently

---

[26] Sofer replaced the expression "civil religion" and instead came up with "secular religion"- this alludes to the close relationship that these two concepts enjoy, and also the possible confusion in this area. The confusion arises in relation to an analysis in this section of the reason for the establishment of civil religion.

adopted by the US Supreme Court). He (Palmer) argues that there are two possible bodies safeguarding minorities, the courts and the electorate, and the courts are not the sole defenders of minority rights. The courts, for their part, have two options open to them, the first does not include judicial discretion, and the second does. As to the system that prevails in Britain and New Zealand (no judicial discretion) Palmer explains that they act in accordance with the rule of law. The rule of law in turn is a strong supporter of the both minority- and human rights.

Weisbrod's words, mentioned above, it should be noted, echoed those of one of today's most important thinkers in political philosophy, Richard Rorty, who presents the battle between American civil religion and Theistic religion , as will be demonstrated below, as one fought at all costs, and one which goes against any grain of logic. In this way he exemplifies the extent to which this war waged by American civil religion against Theistic religion is fought out of obstinacy and desperation. Rorty, in the footsteps of Kant and Nietzsche continues this war of civil religion against Theistic religion in the ideological plane. If Theistic religion used God's words to act as the criteria for human behaviour, Kant and Nietzsche together with Rorty come to free man and society from Theistic religion, as will be elaborated upon below.

Rorty speaks of human language as forming reality. This he argues accords with Nietzsche's view that it is within man's powers to create for himself his own image, his environment and even his world. Rorty relates this power to language, and does not accept that a language is merely a means of expression or form of communication. Rorty bases his views on the argument that one cannot search for objective truth and that subjectivity is no more inferior to absolute objectivity. Going even further along this line of thought he argues that there is no such thing as objective or absolute. He argues that men invent truth, they do not reveal it. Truth is only relative and depends upon man's inventive powers, whether in the scientific field, in the artistic world, or issues dealing with morality and social behaviour. In matters of truth he makes no distinction between science (which quite clearly discusses what is truth) and art and morality [and as I have remarked concerning Rorty- when relating to art and morality Rorty does a disservice when illogically connecting it to truth, since art is a matter of aesthetics and emotions while morality is a value judgement of social behaviour, mixed with aspects of emotion and logic- Y.C.] Rorty[27] does not offer a logical explanation for his stated position. He does not explain why the objective approach needs to be rejected. The only justification he provides is that the liberal behavioural values have furthered

---

[27] Further on Rorty's views see Richard Rorty, *Contingency, irony, and solidarity* (Cambridge University Press, *Ibid.* the first three chapters.

the causes of those ascribing to liberal society. This is the reasoning he employs when giving preference to liberal positions over national ones (the latter of which he describes using radical Nazi imagery in presenting it to his liberal readers) and over religious standpoints (which are those that were used in religious wars). Rorty debates with Michel Sandal, a person who, although liberal, preferred (like those holding religious or national views) the objective approach as truthful to the subjective approach held dear by Rorty. Since there is common ground between Sandal and those holding religious or national views, that objectivity must come up trumps against relative truth, Rorty combines all three approaches into one, presenting them all as Nazis or religious warriors (i.e. disgraceful in the eyes of his liberal readers). In this way, by confusing different standpoints, by meshing natural science together with arts and human mores, he explains why he favours the liberal approach of relative truth over any other viewpoint that supports objectivity. Thus, Rorty prefers liberal values and language to any other approach, with the reasoning that they are better and more appropriate for liberal society. He makes the case that what is good for man or society is also the truth for them. In this way he identifies truth with interest. Whatever serves me is the truth.

What links Rorty's outlook with that of Weisbrod's is a whole moral perspective that bases itself on the interests and on the "good" of the society that they describe. This is a view which hooks up well with Kant, who, although believing in and favouring objectivity while discarding the personal interests and biases of man, nonetheless placed man at the centre, because of man's pure consciousness and his ability to create objective truth through this faculty.[28] Kant's innovation sought to replace the religious and naturalist notions that both centred on something superior to man. They placed before man the challenge of reaching a higher plane, an ambition to improve oneself. The challenge of self-improvement does not stem from utilitarianism or from a chief desire to better man's predicament, as is the objective of Western cthat was headed off by Kant.

Instead of man upholding the tenets of natural- or any kind of religious morality, he lifts his eyes heavenward searching for truth, the attribute of objectivity, which (from his perspective) is the Supreme Being. Thus, the liberal man according to Rorty (like the reasonable man in Kantian thought) becomes (in his own eyes) the replacement for God. That is why Weisbrod puts the liberal community's interests

[28] The absurdity in the position taken by Kant stems from the fact that (subjective) man through his consciousness (which cannot be objective since it comes from man) discovers objective morality only after that same consciousness before this discovery created this objective morality. An absurdity then arises in the thought of Kant, first the creation of a thing in the mind and imagination of man, and thereafter the discovery of the very same thing, as this objective reality is suddenly revealed to man.

and guiding principles on a holy pedestal. This line of thinking arises from her supposedly balanced thinking, which is informed by the interests of the community she represents. She will only consider the interests of the minority as long as they do not clash with the interests and principles of the majority.

Therefore, Sofer's qualm with the US Supreme Court's present composition is not based on principle, but deals with the factual question: Do Theistic religions harm the cornerstones of American civil religion? It is a debate that is conducted within the confines of the liberal community and relates to the role civil religion's interests play. The supremacy of civil religion over Theistic religions is never in question.

Another position, more methodical, and also more explicit, pertaining to America's religious war, can be seen in the theory of **John Dewey.** This theory exemplifies the hardening of positions in the political wars (in the area of governmental influence) waged by American civil religion against Theistic religions, over American national interests. This war is fought while showing a modicum of respect towards theistic religions. Most Americans, in addition to being practitioners of American civil religion are also affiliated with theistic religious communities. The religious belief in a Deity- as a central theme- regardless of the theistic religion- is entrenched in the United States more than in almost any other country.

During the 1950s Dewey developed a moral code that disposed of religion and its absolute values both which predominated during the era just prior to modern science's appearance (hereafter "the pre-scientific era"), and which had guided social behaviour (morality). His system introduced in their place a stable and controlled resource, trustworthy and safe, through which norms and mores would be eked out, ensuring that (theistic) religion's status (Theistic) as spiritual guide would come to an end- either directly (through the cessation of religious commandments) or indirectly (through it no longer being a reference for moral values.)

His most fundamental writings on this topic are found in *Reconstruction in Philosophy*, published in 1920. A second edition was released in 1948 and by 1950, two years before Dewey passed away, The New American Library of World Literature Inc. republished his book with an expanded introduction wherein

Dewey explains his core ideas.[29] It is possible to find in this introduction Dewey's last will and testament and an overall summary of his lifework.

Dewey's contribution to his generation's notions of morality cannot be underestimated, and even today his theory remains important. Dewey engraved his signature on American causes for more than sixty years, and his sphere of influence spread beyond the confines of American soil. Contemporary post-modernist thinking can also be considered entrenched in Dewey's theory and flowing from it. Both schools of thought argue that just as science has proved that there are no unshakeable truths, and that everything is relative even in the exact sciences, human morality too must be relative.[30]

Dewey makes mention in his introduction about the doubts and wavering that have gnawed away at the notion of American morality,[31] and for the need then to destroy it and rebuild an American (and also western) morality. He admits the fact that those who believe in religious values and its trustworthy normative source

[29] John Dewey, *Reconstruction in Philosophy* (New York, N.Y.: Mentor Book, The New American Library, 1950)

[30] It is patently obvious that this argument *prima facie* is groundless. It is human **knowledge** that is uncertain and non-objective, not the object of the knowledge's curiosity-laws of nature.

[31] Dewey does not plumb the depths in trying to discover why these doubts and instabilities arose, just as he assumes these questions arose exclusively among the secular population and not the religious. Obviously and in light of what has been seen above it appears that the whole moral question is not entrenched in anything other than insecurities and human fears which no longer receive comfort from finding spiritual solace in the unpredictable transcendental spheres, the very power that caused the insecurity and fear in the first place. Morality is the outcome of a lifestyle for those who believe in a transcendental provider who commanded his believers to act according to its precepts and because the author of this morality hails from a higher reality so too the substantive morality will be higher than self-interest and materialism. Thus what Dewey identifies are the agonies of the American secular individual who has not managed yet to internalise a transcendental support base suitable enough to replace the God he no longer believes in, a replacement that American civil religion pretends to fill. Therefore Dewey's system, based on cold science cannot last long in providing a cure for the ailing Americans, as the results speak for themselves, as can be seen by the post-modern trend following that is rife in America. What Dewey is unable to discern is that the stimulus for clinging to religion is triggered by emotions (like the emotion of fear) and the cure provided to the believer and practitioner is also, by definition emotional, as is seen in the moral code of the believer which is engulfed by emotion. Part of morality's primal emotions is the preparedness to emotionally immerse yourself in such a way until you abnegate all interests. Herein lay the stark differences that divide morality from self-interest.

(i.e. moral code) do not face any dilemmas. For the secular individual this dilemma is left unsolved so long as moral virtues rely upon the old morality, of the pre-scientific period.[32] He then proposes that by using science and his system, not as a supporter of the prevailing morality and not even to partially amend it but rather as a total alternative to the prevailing standard and as a resource from which a new and faithful moral code can be drawn. Dewey believed, even if he did not explicitly say so, that if he succeeded in his mission, civil religion, which already then had been adopted by the political regimes of western states would be cured of fault. This would in turn relegate the position of theistic religions (the first being Christianity), which continued to attract the lion's share of adherents and which were the effective alternative for the ruling elite's civil religion.[33]

Dewey attempts to structure his theory on logical analysis. He goes about doing this in stages, common to each is the fact that they are so completely ungrounded in logic, so that it has to be asked why so many thinkers were duped (and still are) into following him.[34] Dewey begins with the premise that morality and science are in fact very closely related. This he shows by the fact that both science and politics underwent revolutions in the last few centuries. He asserts that moral values are created by the human intellect (just as any scientific endeavour-Y.C.) but at the same time disagrees with Kant that this is the same as pure consciousness. Morality is empirical [as is science-Y.C.] and does not presume to contain absolute truth [like in modern science-Y.C.] Politics like science and industry dismiss the effect of old theories to assist in creating new ones. It is true that philosophy deals with the human condition, but it does not confine itself to this study. While humans interest themselves in science, the universe, reality, truth-

---

[32] It is very odd that Dewey speaks to Americans as if they were a secular people, whereas it is well known that your average American believes in God.

[33] The fundamentalist-democratic regime in Iran serves as an odd example of this alternative, especially since it is a democracy dependent on the unpredictable polling stations in general elections which are held regularly. Less stark examples can be found in any democracy, which has religious parties in elections, and *Shas* in Israel is no less interesting an example of this type. Also the fundamentalist victory in Algeria is a very interesting example, and the reluctance of the west to try and prevent a religious Islamic victory in Algeria sheds some light on this issue in relation to its international aspects.

[34] One possible answer is to say that the interests of the ruling class (in their political thought and their political regimes) are so desperate, until they are willing to be led by any reasoning, so long as it upholds the basic principles to which they hold dear. This isn't only about the first half of the twentieth century. The burning desire of many in the USA, including those living now, to prove that the Divine Biblical morality is no better than modern liberaldom's version and that quite the opposite is correct can be seen *inter alia* in *Biblical V. Secular Ethics: The Conflict* (edited by R. Joseph Hoffman and Gerald A. Laure, Promtheus Books, 1988).

things of permanence, unconstrained by time, that are eternal- it is philosophy [which also deals partly with morality] that is responsible for the development of the natural sciences. A situation then arises where it is not quite certain whether a certain subject is of a scientific nature or a philosophical one. Darwin's theory then may be considered philosophy, since as a theory it does not have application to anything concrete, and by definition philosophy too does not relate to concrete facts. Works that are philosophical by nature and cannot fit under the rubric of science play an important role in facilitating the study of certain new disciplines.

Dewey explains that from these new disciplines "scientific" theories were formulated that philosophically challenged religious values and moral codes that were prevalent until then in Western Europe. In the past it was science that had led the war against religion, but those events that in the past were called wars were in fact fought by a science in the narrowest sense of the word. They ignored all the other lifestyle issues-- whose origin is in the world of science- including family status, the status of women and children,[35] education, the arts, political and economic relations –whether they originated then or whether they only affect modern life,

When relating to the "war" (in his opinion and by his definition) between religion and science that took place in the west, Dewey concludes that the war ended with an unfair compromise. State employment was divided into higher domains - issues of spirituality (which science surrendered) and lower physical domain that were handed over to science. This according to Dewey's narrative represented the partition between materialism and spirituality. Whoever was forced to accept this partition soon realised that science rises above its assigned realm redrawing the boundaries between the physical and spiritual. This caused a feeling of disarray and insecurity, which in turn sparked off and continues to inflame feuds and emotions. While relating this worldview Dewey makes the claim that he does not want to express an opinion on which side is right. Nonetheless he agrees that there is disarray, insecurity and confusion, and in an attempt to diffuse these issues he proposes reconstructing the whole moral code network instead of the old structure that is in place. Science will then come to his aid to supervise this simultaneous destruction and reconstruction. In this way, at least according to Dewey, science will repay to philosophy that which philosophy thus far had endowed it with.

---

[35] He does not explain from where he took all these allegations. One can certainly query whether the structure of the family and its inner complexities has its source in science? In light of the fact that emotions are so central to the family makeup and to morality in general, in what way does science deal with this, what tools does it have at its disposal to deal with a world of feelings?

In his telling description Dewey locates for us the formation of secularism. He says that the separation of powers between morality and the old religion, which continues to deal with the spiritual sphere, and science, which deals with more material matters, and which - aided by certain philosophical disciplines- crossed the boundaries in its criticism of religious supervision over spiritual matters, caused confusion. This whole episode brought about the phenomenon of secularism, which, because of its inherent bleak outlook on the future of humankind caused many to lose direction in life. Those able to look upon the old morality as absolutely rooted in firm ground [Dewey means by this, the religious person- Y.C.] are also able to resolve any of their doubts. Others however need to embark on a more intensive search in order to pave for themselves a new way. It is Dewey himself who can offer this new solution [for the secularists- Y.C.], one that is based on scientific empirical evidence, and one that would provide a new and wider foundation for morality than the one it has stood on prior to this discovery.

In addition to the last edition's introduction by Dewey- the book's body[36] details how it is that science can create a new moral code. He sees the construction of this endeavour having the same application as it has in other fields of scientific research. He opines that morality and ordinary scientific research share very similar characteristics. In his detailed analysis he enumerates certain shared features: the basis for investigation and discovery in both fields; experimentation through processes of elimination; axiomatic reasoning in logical thought; different laws and criteria for what qualifies as a springboard for arriving at a result, all these apply equally to the exact sciences as they do to morality. He also states that they share a common phenomenon; after analysing a certain matter they may conclude, on the one hand that they are bound by its findings, while realising on the other, that a past practice or long-held principle is no longer relevant. These common features according to Deweyan logic make it possible to draft a moral code in the same way as one would a scientific thesis, i.e. through theoretical and practical research. When speaking about democracy and the link between it and his system[37], he sees the role democracy plays in his new morality as creating an exclusively liberal climate. Within this climate, democratic regimes are vested with the authority and rights to institute and to choose political appointees to educate the masses to be more productive, to be more ambitious and to create wider room for manoeuvre. Within this newly created atmosphere Dewey's system

[36] *Ibid.* pp.139-140.
[37] *Ibid.* pp. 161-162.

can be put to better use.[38] Dewey does not suggest that his new code of morality be based on democratic decisions. It is obvious why he does not recommend this, especially since he favours destroying the old and rebuilding anew. If he was to rely on designing a moral code of binding norms underwritten by the democratic process, it would be in conflict with his central idea of a new way. Since already by the time Dewey hit the scene there was nothing new about democracy- and Dewey wanted something completely innovative. Nevertheless by harbouring these reservations toward democratic decision making (though he professed to be a sworn democrat) Dewey weakened the foundations of his theory, as will be demonstrated below.

Viewed in its entirety, Dewey's narrative portrays a known truth; those who do not feel bound by religiously ordained moral constraints-because of their secularism- are perplexed by the problem of defining for themselves a moral code. It is quite clear that Dewey's solution is inappropriate for those who have a close connection to religion and as a result thereof feel compelled to fulfil their moral commitments, which historically are entrenched in their religion. It is quite evident from the analysis portrayed by Dewey that the chain of events that induced western society to undergo mental change went hand in hand with the widening impact that civil religion was to have on their collective mental consciousness.

In contradistinction- if morality by its very essence is not merely a matter of consciousness and intellectual comprehension- i.e. empirical, but rather a set of values and emotions, science- neither intrinsically valuable nor very moving - is unqualified to formulate ethical norms *ab initio.*

From reading Dewey's words the question left begging is whether the logic of a scientist can substitute for a debate of values traditionally held between scholars of the humanities. What about the values that morality demands its adherents to live by? From where are these carved out? And if what is discussed has been

---

[38] In this way Dewey comes across to us as an educator. Dewey died at the age of 93, and his first most striking work was in the field of education. As a scientific person he was active from the end of the 19th century until the middle of the 20th and his innovations in education remain as refreshing as they were then- The education of children was based on the idea of viewing them as complete individuals, the school then has to treat them as people with genuine needs, and should not look upon their education as merely preparing the groundwork for adulthood. He was active in the USA, Japan, China, and the Ottoman Empire, where he was an educational advisor in educational matters. As was pointed out above, his theory of relativism in morality can be considered as a pre-emptor for today's postmodernist movement, without taking away from him his reputation as one of the fathers of American pragmatism.

empirically proven, is it possible or even proper to set moral rules based on an empirical statistical report on the social behaviour of a specific society, without even holding a debate on the values of that society? Without knowing how the *weltaunshaung* of the members of that society and of its thinkers determines the correct social behaviour? Dewey fails to explain how he can hope to make a connection between scientific research and value systems. What about the emotional aspect that plays such a large role in laying out the foundations for a moral system (whether as a positivist innovation within the framework of parliamentary institutions or as a means of communicating with God and of emotionally performing his commandments)? How are emotions measured in the Deweyan laboratory for moral research? What kind of remedy does dry scientific justice offer man's soul and how will a body of cold scientific thought alleviate man from his depressions and fears? It should not be forgotten: morality was always intimately connected with religion, and religion always came to relieve man from his oppressed state. Just like man's torment stemmed from an unreal place where logic has no meaning, so too morality, coming as it does from religion, always distanced itself from reality and from self interest. Science, in contradistinction, works within the bounds of reality, the tangible, existential interest (materialism).

An additional question begs to be asked, concerning the invalidation of the existing morality. The whole idea of absolutes that run at the core of morality is an Achilles heel to Dewey's system. He himself admits that modern science does not support objective truth and so is forced to deduce that the morality that comes as an outgrowth of his scientific system will also not be objective and will be subject to amendment. If this is what Dewy is offering us (and indeed that is what he is offering) the question left begging is what good tidings has Dewy imparted? In what way is this new morality, relative and variable better than the old morality, whose source is God and faith in Him? What is the special message and advantage in the Deweyan system? Where does the system ultimately lead? Is the main purpose of the system to destroy existing systems, to rebuild them anew and then to destroy them once again when they become established so that an ongoing process of destruction is formed ensuring dynamic change?

The last question that emerges relates to Dewey's take on civil-secular religion[39] and his war on theistic religion and call for the removal of theistic religion from

[39] Dewey's theory reflects a closeness between civil religion and secularism, even though in the USA most of the supporters of civil religion are also affiliated with one or other Theistic religion, together with their being politically mainstays of the civil religious regime and in support of distancing theistic religions from the American political arena.

the state's administrative affairs. Dewey points out that his recommendations are there to help the secular population. If so, the question is why does Dewey relate to the American people, most of whom stand firm in their beliefs in God, as if they were a secular nation waiting and ready to wage war on theistic religion? And how is it that this nation accepted Dewey's theory that was meant for a secular audience? Was it in the interests of American unity, which obligates all Americans to display common purpose by politically severing themselves from any divisive factors like the various religious factors?

An answer- at least partial- to this question- can be found in Dewey's system as it relates to the educational sphere. He promoted the idea of having an American public school system where all the students, no matter their religious or ethnic background would intermingle with one another, in order that they develop a common belief system. By preaching such co-existence he hoped that these students when they eventually enter adulthood would join together harmoniously in their pursuit of common happiness. The trend was, then, to turn the schools, which were religious- on the level that they had features that were common to all western religions- into schools that were predominantly secular. Although the trend had already started by the end of the nineteenth century and it continues until our day, in 1950 an attempt to stem the tide of secularism was quickly repealed by the Supreme Court. A brief episode[40] erupted in the 1950s and 1960s with a failed experiment of conducting Bible reading classes in the public school system following the Protestant custom. The court ruled against this custom rejecting the claim that Christianity was the law of the land in the USA. Previously they rejected an appeal to allow the promotion of a general faith in God, even though the appeal did not ask for the recognition of any specific theistic religion.[41] This approach of the American Supreme Court is a part of the trend to turn America into a country where religion will be totally crushed, because of its divisive effects toward internal American life. This is a trend that promotes secularisation. The trend to seal off theistic religion had its precedent in America more than a century before, when the public schools and most academic institutions promoted this action. This could only be done with the active promotion of Dewey's ideological thought. If despite all, most Americans stubbornly attend church services; this is a sign of the vitality of theistic religions and the powerlessness of civil religion,

[40] The eventual retreat reflects the struggle of the Protestant religion that wanted and tried to be the USA State religion. The experiment was blocked by the Supreme Court, which acted as a civil religious state authority, an authority that sifts out any Protestant influence from the corridors of power. The public school system supported the court's vigilance on behalf of civil religion.

[41] See Robert Michaelson "Is the Public School Religious or Secular," in *The Religion of the Republic* (ed. Elwyn. A. Smith, Fortress Press Philadelphia, 1971), p.30.

although it does not mean that the latter has totally lost their way. Still at some level civil religion does contain transcendental elements, which bind Americans together offering them some type of spiritual solace.

Generally speaking it is true that the political trend of any country is reflected by what is relayed in primary and secondary schools. In Israel too schools reflect politics, which can be seen when comparing the educational institutions with the prevailing party/political ideology. American civil religion likewise fits into what has been said. From an historical perspective the same is true of Canada, a nation that originally based its formation on a theistically religious covenant, but has since developed a secular religion, similar to that of the older member of this sorority, the USA.

Contrary to what has been said by those favouring the American system of judicial discretion, the following needs to be stated. In the USA a limited war rages between civil religion and theistic religion- a war that has been confined specifically to the field of political influence, though, considering our cautionary note above, and looking at it from a long term historical angle, this limited war has much wider repercussions. Entering the debate as representative of civil religion is the US Supreme Court. Within the framework of legislative interpretation, the US Supreme Court goes out of its way to unnecessarily impose hardship on theistic religion via its decisions relating to the educational system.[42] It is possible to view this topic by comparing the situation with that of Canada. In Canada the ruling party has been associated with the interests of the Protestant majority in the federal parliament, interests that are in opposition to those of the Canadian Catholic minority, a minority which in the province of Quebec is actually a majority. It is possible to pinpoint the struggle between these two religions, which has turned a religious battle into a cultural and linguistic war involving in an intimate manner these two religions. In the Canadian experience, the French culture and language is taken up by the Canadian minority which is in fact a Quebecois majority, while the Anglo-American language and culture is taken up by Federal Canada's majority and Quebec's minority.

In the United States the situation is different. American justices conduct themselves as representatives of the American civil religion, which is not a Protestant-Catholic, battle, or vice versa. The American civil religion in the United

[42] It is perhaps possible to understand this from the very central position accorded to the US Public Education system, which is designed to relay over the ideology of the state in a unitary alternative manner. See "Introduction," *The Religion of the Republic* (ed. Elwyn A. Smith,) Fortress Press Philadelphia, 1971.

States competes politically with all historically theistic religions, fighting against any hint of a connection between religion and the state government. Theistic religion in the USA may only be practised on condition that it confines itself to the church and synagogue. Accordingly the main practitioners of civil religion are the courts themselves particularly the US Supreme Court. The latter allows theistic religions to thrive on condition that it plays no role in the halls of power. In this capacity, the Supreme Court does not play the role of a judicial organisation concerned with all religions. Rather it represents the civil religion of the government, zealously fending off the political ascendancy of any other (theistic) religion to the extent that that religion is viewed as dangerous in its ability to exert any kind of political influence.[43]

In this spirit it is possible to understand the strange judgement in the Kirias Joel Satmar Chasidim case.[44] Here the justices showed no pity over thirty mentally disabled children whose special arrangement by the authorities to alleviate their suffering was discussed and struck down by the learned justices. The arrangement reached by the authorities had no other practical consequences yet it was criticised by the court and accordingly struck down. The Supreme Court Justices placed before them the hallowed principle of complete separation between (theistic) religion and state, and for reasons of demonstrating their longstanding ruling authority invalidated a humane and pragmatic solution. The American justices reached a similar decision when discussing raising the salary of Catholic schoolteachers in the *Lemon* case.[45] In contradistinction to these two cases the willingness of the justices to excuse the Indians[46] and Amish cult members[47] is rather striking. In both these last instances the justices saw no inkling of a threat over their authority or any seed of competition that would sprout in the future.

---

[43] The need for those who support a united American nation excluding religion from the political playing field is exacerbated by the fact that certain conservative religious communities in the US, who demand a conservation of the superior position of the white Protestants in the US and a concomitant downward slide among their black population, would like to exert influence on internal American politics. These communities dress themselves up as religious communities, in this context as theistically religious.

[44] The judgement involving special needs children in the Satmar community was handed out recently by the US Supreme Court. See *Board of Education of Kirias Joel Village School District v. Grumet*, 512 US 687, 129 Led 2d 546.

[45] See *Lemon v. Kurtzman*, 403 US 602, 29, Led 2d 745

[46] As was raised in the symposium when discussing the attitude of the United States Supreme Court towards minorities in the US, especially in connection with what Sofer had to say about Indians in *Washington and Lee Law Review*, vol. 48 Spring 1991, beginning at p. 381, and especially 402.

[47] For the Amish case see *Yoder v. Wisconsin*, 406 US 205 37 Led 2d 15.

As to Canada, the religious issue relating to the Protestant and Catholic power struggle reared its head after cases involving legislative amendments to the Quebec Education Act and constitutional amendments to the Newfoundland educational system were decided in the Canadian courts.[48] These decisions reflect a struggle over control of power. This struggle was carried out there, unlike the USA, by politicians rather than by the courts. In Newfoundland there were two constitutional amendments which for obvious reasons were supported by both Houses of Assembly, the provincial and federal. These amendments were also supported by the Protestant majority both of the province- Newfoundland's- and of Canada's federal parliament, allowing them (the amendments) to be applied to the (provincial) constitutions. It should be clarified at this point that each of Canada's Province's constitutions requires the approval of both the Provincial House and Federal parliament for an amendment to be effected. In the province of Quebec its majority also requested amendments to the religious education system. But the situation in Quebec was different to that of Newfoundland: Quebec's majority was Catholic and the amendments affected the rights of Protestants, while all along as mentioned above, the federal parliament was dominated by Protestants. Therefore the amendment in Quebec could not be passed as a constitutional amendment but had to be done in the framework of legislation which could be passed exclusively by the province and did not then require approval from Federal Parliament. The constitutional background to the educational problems was the same in these two provinces (Quebec and Newfoundland). According to the Canadian Constitution and according to Canadian custom both before and immediately after the Federation came into being the educational system was religious. There were mainly Protestant and Catholic schools. The Catholic schools focused primarily on the religious instruction element and the Catholic school was chiefly a doctrinal institution. The Protestant schools, on the other hand, placed a greater stress on studying content and less on indoctrination. These two approaches, doctrine versus scholarship squared up against each other. In both Quebec and Newfoundland a

[48] See *In the matter of the reference re the Education Act S.Q 1988, c. 84 The Attorney general of Quebec* also see *Ryan and Teanner-D Audet-Grenier, Renelle Grenier-Gagne,* File Nos. 22112, 22119, 22124, and 22129. Rempel, *Justifying Constitutional Change: The legislative History of the Newfoundland Denominational Schools Senate Committee report,* at 18-19 which mentions Canada *inter alia.* Question, 1922 to 1997 (not Commons debates 35th Parliament, 2nd Sess. At 3244, per Rock (31 May 1996) Newfoundland House of assembly Debate 42nd Leg., 3rd Sess., at 1381, per Fitzgerald (19 October 1995) at 1304, per Wells (17 October 1995). Canada Senate Debates Vol. 135 at 569, per Senator Doody (6 June 1996). Canada Senate Debates Vol. 135 at 640-41, per Senator Rompkey (11 June 1996). Senate Committee, majority report, at 7, dissenting at 34-35.

certain degree of secularisation had taken place, nonetheless, on the eve of these amendments the educational bases for both these provinces remained religious. The Newfoundland Protestants, who were the majority sought to make the study-oriented approach more efficient, in light of the technological and scientific progress, which rendered the acquisition of knowledge so vital. They strove then to amalgamate the smaller schools and to create larger schools, which could then develop and accommodate a wide-ranging curriculum. The request was out of a need to make the object of acquiring more knowledge more effective. In the beginning they were willing to reach some type of compromise solution with the Catholics. They sought ways of making the change not too drastic in advancing the study and knowledge acquisition approach at the expense of the (religious) indoctrination approach. This solution has and had always suited the Protestant approach. The Protestants who were in the majority claimed that both the Catholic and Protestant religious education were being affected since the dominance of both these religions had already been undermined. They claimed that the Protestant religious education system would be equally affected. This claim was disingenuous in light of the fact that Protestants had never stressed religious instruction in the same way as the Catholics had. The (provincial) government held a referendum on this first amendment and after the idea was approved (by a slight majority and with the participation of a very small amount of those eligible to vote) the Protestants passed this amendment in the Provincial House of assembly, after which ratification from the Federal Parliament was a mere formality. Following this the Catholics took legal action claiming that the procedure was unconstitutional. The Protestants met this with a thorny and radical reaction. An additional referendum was called in which the Protestants increased their margin of support (though also in this referendum –as before- a minority of eligible voters took part) and again both legislative houses, the provincial and federal, ratified the results. The second amendment was significantly more radical than the first and it deeply harmed Catholic education in the province. In the broadest sense of the word the struggle between these two population groups who preached very different ideologies may be viewed as a religious war. In this war the majority ended up overreacting towards the minority disrespecting its worldview in the process. Pushing ahead with the materialist agenda of the (Protestant) majority resulted in the spiritual lifestyle of the (Catholic) minority being crushed underfoot. In Quebec the struggle was centred more on cultural differences than on religious ones. The protagonists in this battle were the province's Catholic majority and its Protestant minority. The clashes made it to the headlines in the press. They centred on signboards that were placed in public places and places of business and which were written exclusively in French. The French cultured elite intended on taking on their Protestant English-speaking minority, who were supported by the majority of

Canada's Federal parliament (which was majority Protestant). As has already been explained, because of the predominance of Protestants in the Federal Parliament Quebec's Catholics were unable to change the educational system by means of constitutional amendment. They were then forced to opt for the legislation route, which would not require ratification on the federal level. Since Quebec, like its fellow province Newfoundland, was undergoing a process of secularisation, the only way for the Quebecois to unite under one banner was to exploit the language barrier. Language was a more effective tool in uniting the Catholic French cultural elite than was religion. Therefore, the new Quebec Education Act replaced the clause prescribing a religious standard for Provincial educational institutions with a clause demanding a language requirement. It would be pointless at this juncture to enter into a detailed chronology of how both these provinces enacted their respective amendments. What will be discussed are the motives behind forcing through separate education systems in Canada. The background of the struggle over a separate education system, like in the USA, is entrenched in the political/ regime struggle over religion or over issues that are rife with religious connotations.[49] Over the course of time, the infighting that has

[49] This struggle exemplifies how different Canada is from the USA that can be seen in the different educational systems that cater for the very young in these two independent states. In the USA the State run educational system has adopted the civil religious approach enabling this (civil) religion to spread its net across the country. In Canada the educational system has been divested from the two religious communities, Catholic and Protestant, and has been used to strengthen the hand of the Protestants against the Catholic minority. In Quebec the tables were turned against the province's Protestant minority in favour of the Quebecois Catholics. In both instances (USA and Canada) it is the schools that have determined what regime governs the country, is it a regime of unity or one of growing divisiveness. In both instances the strength of the religious motive is displayed, whether it is theistic or civil, both have shown religion to be a strong emotional element exploited by the authorities and gaining a powerful hold over society. In so far as it pertains to the State of Israel where there are various and separate educational streams for the ultra-Orthodox *chareidim*, the national religious movement and the secular Zionists as well *as* the general Arab population (combining Muslims and Christians) as well as the specific Christian Arab education system together with the recently set up *Sephardic chareidi* network of *Ma'ayan ha-Torah*, the great sectarianism along these lines is witnessed, especially among the communities themselves. Examples are Agudath Israel, Shas, the settler movement from the militant Zionists, the irreligious Zionists and among the Arabs, those with a Palestinian heritage versus those with the Israeli heritage of being part of a minority who are not taken into account as part of the Palestinian nation beyond Israel's borders and who participate within the political framework of Jewish-Zionist parties. Within this morass the standing of (a non-Zionist) civil religion would appear to be poor, nonetheless as will be demonstrated such a religion continues to grow. This growth is due to the ever-depleting Zionist content in the (irreligious) State educational stream. Therefore the state regime is

taken place within these two great countries has resulted in the interests, worldviews and emotions of the minority groups being crushed underfoot and being disrespectfully treated. This kind of attitude toward minorities prevalent even in liberal countries can be explained by the fact that the religious motive plays a very powerful emotional role. Religion is so strong a factor because of has been said already about its ability to deal with emotional elements of fear and insecurity of the supernatural by claiming itself to possess supernatural elements that alleviate that fear. Therefore it inevitably propagates a tough stance. Knowing this to be true, it is difficult to accept without any reservation Rorty's claim, as stated above, that dirty play is the exclusive domain of theistic religious wars, and that the contemporary liberal American record opposes these tactics. [50]

Regarding the United States the question may be posed as to why the parents of a child who attends Catholic school receives less financial support for their offspring's tuition than the they would if their child attended a state- run public school. In what way would equal treatment of both these educational systems (in both cases religion is taught- in the Catholic school it is Catholicism and in Public school it is [American] civil religion) impinge upon some or other important principle? How can those professing the American civil religion justify this budgetary discrimination between Catholic and civilly religious schools in a country whose courts strive to uphold equality before the law? Those wishing to explain away this conundrum point to the fact that it is not only the Catholic and religious schools that do not receive state aid but also private irreligious schools. This however fails to satisfactorily deal with the question. It is too easy to make do with the formal excuse that says that all private schools be they Catholic or otherwise are treated equally and thereby absolve the inherent inequity between Catholic and civil religious schools. This reasoning is not a strong enough alibi to the charge that the true aim of this inequality is to marginalise Catholic education. If the issue of Catholic education is being discussed (and likewise Jewish Orthodox education in the US) it is appropriate to speak of the Canadian model,

---

one rife with internal cracks, disunity, riddled by internal struggles which at times seem irrelevant or fed by mere hatred between the various communities. The picture is indeed bleak, and it is this book which attempts to contribute to an overhauling of the very foundations by addressing the constitutional problem. A complete recovery can only come about once the education system is purged by the joining of various elements together at the first stage and by uniting the institutions (Jewish and Arab separately) in the second stage. This healing process cannot be included for discussion in this book. A discussion such as this can only be carried out after full research has been devoted to the exact goings on of the education system.

[50]One can easily argue that the engagement in US philosophy with high theory of justice abstaining from dealing about huge economical differences in the US itself is hypocrisy.

where the state does provide assistance for Catholic education. American (like Canadian) Catholics devote a central part of their education on inculcating values. These values are at variance with those held by the liberal democratic state, while for Protestants the values they hold are not that much different to those which are acquired through state education. Therefore a special religious education system is more important for Catholic adherents than it is for Protestants. special classification system for schools that are not state- run does great harm to Catholics, but doubtfully causes any trouble to Protestants. In practice what is being conveyed is a form of religious coercion. The very fact that Catholics require their children to be inculcated with a special value system, part of which is not taught by the state is the key to the whole debate. It is a source of contention between civil religion and Catholicism, more intense than that between civil religion and the Protestants[51] (who have no need for a separate educational system within the US).

The constitutional basis upon which America draws its lifeblood, as recorded in the American Constitution (not in its draft form but as interpreted by the courts from the end of the 19th century) is the result of a bitter political battle between the state and theistic religions[52], differing from Canada's constitutional history. Canada's unification of its provinces kept in place the existing religious education systems, which the Canadian Constitution preserved intact. Though the prevailing spirit in both Canada and the US are very similar, and the liberal democratic tradition is the most viable ideology in both countries, Canada differs in its handling of religious affairs. It proves that a modern state does not need to be by definition anti-religious (theistically speaking) to the extent that it infringes upon the space of religious activity, especially in respect of education, as has been shown above.

For the sake of balance it would be well advised to take heed of Ernest Koenker's[53] narrative of how both democratic governments (including that of the

---

[51] Because of the fact that the majority of US citizens practise the Protestants religion, there are those who claim that there are parallels between the Protestant faith and civil religion. This is merely an optical illusion and is similar to claiming that because the majority of crimes in a certain country are committed by a specific ethnic group that ethnic group must be guilty of criminal conduct.

[52] This in context was completely justified, as I have shown above.

[53] Ernest B. Koenker, *Secular salvation, The Rites and Symbols of Political Religions* (Fortress Press, 1965), pp. 11-19.

US[54]) and Hitler's regime exploited Christian obedience, viewing Christians as politically tools for strengthening the government's grasp over the population. He quotes there a minister from the period of the French Revolution who claimed that when heavy taxes were imposed, the ranting of the masses against the government could be quelled by increasing the amount of religious study classes. His reasoning was that the more learned in religious subjects the masses were the more malleable they were towards the regime.

5. The hypocrisy of US civil religion in its manipulation of the justice system: A comparative study with France, Canada and Japan.

The court system in the United States refuses to accept any blame for consistently interpreting the constitution in a way that severely prejudices theistic religions. In essence there is no one who dares point the finger in its direction, apart from the writer of this book. That said, it is a fact that when the abortion debate in the US raged on, there were books written, discussions held and angry demonstrations led against the harm caused to religious morality which is opposed to abortion. This sense of morality managed to infiltrate the political spectrum and succeeded in causing legislation to be passed forbidding abortion or at least toughening the conditions. The central claim against the court's judicial activism that they were engaging in "constitutional revision" or "writing a new constitution" (without in any way mentioning the religious issues involved) can be found in Lusky's[55] treatise on the subject. This book, though like other polemical works, fails to single out civil religion as the chief opponent against theistic religion. The US

---

[54] On the topic of America's political attitude towards theistic religions and to exploiting them for the purposes of broad American interests see Ernest B. Koenker *supra* at pp. 14-15:

John Dewey conceded no value to religion except as it expresses the fundamental unities of life. His common faith bears certain resemblance to the common faith which inspired the German nation under Hitler. Many saw in the "new deal", the vast social reconstruction undertaken under Franklin Delano Roosevelt, the final realization of Christian beliefs in American social life. Usually, however the goal envisioned in such faiths is that devotion be transferred from the Christian faith to some forms of the democratic ideal. There have been not a few voices raised to urge that democracy be the real object of devotion in American churches and synagogues. Public schools too, should teach the democratic ideal as American religion; they should be teaching a community religion whereas the churches would instill private religion. According to J. Paul Williams' proposal, both churches and public schools would be teaching democracy as the ultimate metaphysical truth.

The scent of religious coercion of civil religion wafts through this idea.

[55] See Lois Lusky *By What Right? A Commentary on the Supreme Court's Power to Revise the Constitution* (1975).

Supreme Court is not attributed with discriminating against theistic religion due to the latter's adversarial position towards secular religion. Apparently this fact goes against the claims made during the debate. Nonetheless it is advisable to be aware of the "blurring campaign" taking place in American politics by its cynical exploitation of religious symbols painting civil religion with the same brush as theistic religion. In a list compiled by Robert Bellah[56] he analyses the political style of the United States presidents and traces certain phrases used in the public discourse on the Bible. Examples of this include referring to America as the "Promised Land", professions of trust in God by each president, and similar expressions, especially when taking the oath of office. Though, that is really what American civil religion is all about, it is unaffiliated to any one specific theistic religion. That may be the reason why in the United States more religious communities have blossomed than in most of the other Western countries. Generally speaking however these communities tacitly accept the premise of separation of religion and State. Only a minority of churches tries to influence the internal American political system, but this minority is itself attacked for being reactionary, a charge easily made in light of these communities' often blatant racist ideology.

In France, the birthplace of civil religion, and the initiator of the idea of separation of religion and State, Muslim women were for many years forbidden to wear headscarves even though their religious convictions demanded that they be attired with such. This Constitutional government's policy was for long regarded as progressive and enlightened- despite the fact that it contained clear elements of religious coercion- until a compromise solution was found and the restrictions were eased.

In Canada, where religious education[57] was the first issue to be constitutionally challenged, secularism proved itself victorious.[58] Even in Quebec, where the regime was mainly Catholic, the secular trend crept in causing the Catholic legislature to change its criterion for educational institutions from one based on religion to one based on language. The war cry for the Quebecois Catholics

---

[56] Bellah, R. N., "Civil Religion in America" in *Beyond Belief* (Harper and Row, New York, 1970) Ch. 9.

[57] In the States at the time of Independence and later when the constitution was drafted and the confederation was turned into a federal republic, there was no formal primary education system in place.

[58] After this Canada effectively changed from being a theistically religious state (Catholic or Protestant where Quebec adopted the former and the rest of the provinces the latter) to a civilly religious state. This possibly explains Quebec's reluctance to carry out its plans to fully secede from the Canadian Federation.

changed into a battle over the ascendancy of the French language and not the Catholic religion. Canada's Federal Government's institutions have not come out directly against religion per se, rather it has merely come out in favor of a State based education (which nowadays is becoming increasingly more civilly religious) over Catholic- run educational institutions. In this way theistic religions are receding from power especially in the educational sphere. Also as a general belief system, religion has been overtaken by a growing liberal democratic secularism which reigns supreme in Canada, owing to the quiet, gradual and unremitting cultural revolution, which is disconnected from the regime.

In Japan the Americans succeeded, during the military occupation of that country at the end of the Second World War, to set in place a new Constitution, ratified in 1952, on the eve of their departure. In this new Constitution, in contradistinction to the Imperial Constitution, its predecessor, the Shinto religion ceased to be the State religion and the principle of separation of state and religion was enshrined. Shinto, which many doubt its authenticity as a theistic religion and which has a direct link with Japanese nationalism (especially that aspect of Shinto, which played the role of State Religion during the Imperial period) has, in the minds of many, parallels with the more well known western theistic religions. Its cultural characteristics are typical of the Far East societies. Shinto deals with higher forces of nature that link man with deceased spirits (similar to the primitive religious tribes in Africa) and with other natural phenomena. Shinto adopted Confucian philosophy, which was the philosophy used to dominate society and culture in China and its environs, including Japan. Because of this and because of its cultural and historical ties to Japanese village life, it managed to create a Japanese status quo that demanded absolute compliance with all duties imposed upon the individual. Consequently Shinto is not interested in the procurement of human rights. From this perspective Japanese culture is at variance with modern western cultures that are an outgrowth of the rebellion against the past Christian hegemony over the West.[59] Official Shinto also received the emperor's stamp of approval, turning it into a State Religion[60] spiritually binding the People of Japan with the State of Japan.[61] The Americans viewed Shinto as no different to any of the other

---

[59] It is quite obvious that by substituting God with man at the centre, it was natural that they would move in the direction of expanding human rights.

[60] Like Judaism

[61] All of this is elaborated upon in Shiloni's book *Modern Japan* (in Hebrew). Also see *Law and Society in Contemporary Japan* (ed. John Haley, 1988), pp. 8, 43; Lawrence W. Beer and Hiroshi Itoh, *The Constitutional Case Law of Japan, 1970 through 1990,* p. 53; Itsuo Sonobe, "Comparative Administrative Law: Trends and Features in Administrative Law Studies" *(Japan) Administrative Law: Trends and Features,* Volume 19:40, 1986, p. 45.

well-known western religions. Out of a desire to weaken the position of Japan's emperor- who traditionally symbolized theistic religion and was not merely considered a political ruler- and out of ideological motivations (inspired perhaps by civil religion?) they instituted separation of State and religion in the new Constitution which was forced upon Japan. This Constitution was imposed by force, until the Japanese voluntarily agreed to accept it, in the course of compromise agreements between them and their American occupiers. Nonetheless the Japanese never really came to terms with the fact that America had dictated its terms to Japan. The Japanese courts ratified, despite the constitutional amendment of enforcing separation of state and religion, the granting of municipal funds to Shinto priests, who oversaw events that the local authorities designated as promoting the general public interest, but which were not exclusively Shinto. Religion has also infiltrated the political process so that nowadays it is so powerful and influential, to the extent that Japan's Prime Minister (apparently because of religious influence)slipped up by referring to Japan in the characteristically religious, and culturally entrenched term as "holy ground." An utterance such as this from the mouth of the premier shocked Japanese political circles. It also aroused fierce opposition among anti-religious circles (practitioners of civil religion) in Japan who view religion as a hindrance and stumbling block to progress. The background to this eruption is the fact that in Japan a battle has been brewing between those who practice this new civil religion, a product of generally western and especially American influence, and between those who observe traditional Shinto. Owing to the fact that state institutions were never fully taken over by practitioners of civil religion, the state has never taken a side in the conflict. This has always been the tradition of Japan, never to adopt an unambiguous stance, but rather to always accord some respect to traditional faith.

6. The National and International Aspect of Civil Religion: Will all followers of civil religions unite?

Civil religion is an imaginary entity that owes its allegiance to a concrete political regime and is therefore confined to a specific country's political framework[62]. Theistic religion on the other hand has no intrinsic link to any specific State and

[62] Apart from the emerging civil religion which has been integrated as part of the lexicon of the national liberation movement. Zionism during the pre-State period does not fit this category, since from the very beginning of the fledgling State's existence it had an established and large Arab minority, and because Zionism was in essence the Jewish national movement it could not incorporate this population group. Therefore the Zionist parties that are represented in Knesset confine their civil religious ideology to Jewish secularism alone. Things will become clearer below.

may predominate in a number of countries simultaneously. [63] Nevertheless in almost all modern western style states there is a specific civil religion suited to it, which the country and its institutions frequently belongs to. This civil religion elevates the state institutions to a higher status specially designated for this religion. Superficially there does no appear to be any foreseen enmity between the civil religions. If this prediction has not been made in vain it creates an interesting phenomenon. Every country has both an internal and external policy, the latter, which is part of its international policy. It is natural then, if not inevitable, that there should be a treaty between groups of states, which share a similar form of government and ideology. At the end of the scale it would be expected that there be friction between countries which have opposing forms of government and ideology. It often happens that external interests of a civil religious country force it to take positions that are contrary to the spirit of its own civil religious beliefs. Nevertheless they will do so if in the process they manage to suppress a competing theistic religion or alternatively punish a country governed by theistically religious values. Civil religious practitioners are terrified by the idea that a country governed by theistic religious principles will spread its values to their own borders. So, for example, most of the western democratic countries were forced to support a secular military dictatorship in Algeria even though it had suspended a popular Algerian religious movement from taking part in the country's democratic elections. This meant that even though these civil religious democratic regimes hallow the principle of democracy they were willing to support a regime that was intentionally suppressing democratic regime change. This situation was replicated in the western opposition to Iran, which had proved that internal relatively democratic change could alter key elements of the Khomeini regime. The Khomeini regime, even prior to the last democratic elections, was itself democratic in the sense that it accurately represented the feelings of the majority of Iranians. In its time it was carried on a wave of the widest popular support. Nonetheless although Iran's latest election results were considered a stepping stone towards full democracy in that country the western States continue today as they did in the past to denigrate Iran's regime (even after democratic elections). Taking the above into

[63] The Economic union of western European states which long ago extended its interests way beyond exclusive economic affairs, and has formed itself into one political entity, almost a State, is a good example of the process of uniting disparate States into one large State. In consequence thereof a process of unifying the national civil religions into one has also taken place. Loyalty has appreciably changed from loyalty to Holland, France or Portugal to loyalty to the EU. It will come as no surprise if the growing closeness of Russia and the US as well as the unity between Eastern and Western Europe results in one large state of the Christian white man, which will result in one, unified civil religion. It should be stated that when speaking of the white Christian I am not referring to Christianity as the theistic religion but am referring to the specific culture that began with Christianity.

account and considering the whole Algerian fiasco it behooves us to probe the question whether civil religious democratic regimes are not only two-faced in relation to theistic religion when it affects domestic politics, but also in regard to foreign policy. Maybe the essential difference between its domestic and foreign policy is that in the latter it is easier to sense this inequitable phenomenon. The common thread in its internal and external dealings is the fear that those professing belief in God will infiltrate the regime. Seen from this angle the facade of western morality is finally unmasked and what is revealed is its hypocritical power-seeking but immensely terrified spirit, fearfully wondering whether theistic religion which it had previously deposed would regain the reins of power.

It is possible to argue that depriving theistic religion of any role in internal politics is a necessary evil. It could be legitimately claimed that civil administrations have always allowed their subjects to privately lead any (theistically) religious lifestyle they please, whereas theistic religious regimes have not accorded the same privilege to those of its subjects wishing to lead a secular lifestyle. The response to this charge is simple; western theistic religions are no longer fundamentalist and do not even attempt the abolition of liberalism. As proof of this it is possible to raise the example of western states where religious Christian political parties play an important political role without in any way infringing upon the liberal regime's basic principles. Also in Israel there are no Jewish religious parties that seek to introduce a *Halakhic* state, as is oft claimed by those wishing to scare off Israel's secular majority. For the sake of balancing our approach the principle of separation of religion and state should on the one hand be annulled, and on the other, any possibility of political freedoms being tampered with should be removed, whether exercised by the religious or by the secular population.[64] The budget of the state should be used to foster religious lifestyles (unlike in the US where this is forbidden) in the same way as it is used to finance sporting and cultural events. A fortiori it should be clear to everyone that when theistic religious institutions run enterprises that lighten the burden imposed on the state (like Catholic schools in the US) there is no justification to withhold state aid from these institutions. There is no logic that justifies a Catholic parent whose tax

---

[64] The historical experience of the last century is filled with examples of religious regimes blocking off any influence of other religions, but as a counter example to Iran which is the paradigm of a theistic religious state is the example of Russia and the other Communist bloc countries (excluding Poland) , the fascist regimes of Germany and Italy, and for a long period Greece (an exception to Fascist opposition to religion is Franco's Spain which viewed Catholicism very favorably) The fact that examples are sparse and that these regimes no longer exist strengthens the opinion that says that there is no justification for the anti-religious stance adopted by the Western civil religious states, to the extent that such bias still prevails.

money goes toward running a state school being disentitled from enjoying equal funding for his child's Catholic school. It is therefore clear that the approach accepted in the US is unbalanced as it relates to theistic religion in the educational sphere.

With regard to foreign policy issues our discussion does not single out civil religious countries for any specific criticism. Rather it leaves these matters hanging in the air without any firm conclusions save to question the regular hypocrisy that accompanies any international relations, entangled as it is in so many competing interests. The civil /theistic religious debate is no exception to the usual complications involved in forming a foreign policy.

7. Particular Aspects of Theistic religions; each religion on its own and the degree of mutual co-operation.

There are very few countries governed by theistic religion. Examples include Muslim states such as Saudi Arabia, the Persian Gulf states, Iran and Sudan. Excluded from this group is Syria, which although constitutionally defined as a Muslim state where only a Muslim is eligible to be Prime Minister; since religious law is not the law of the land it is not a religious state.[65] It is patently obvious that Britain is not governed by theistic religion even though the head that is bedecked with the royal crown- the symbol of sovereignty- is also the head of the Anglican Church, the (national) Church of England. The British monarchy after all is merely symbolic of a glorious past. It is a remnant of a reality that no longer exists, a remnant that is preserved because of British conservatism. A country that is truly ruled by theistic religion is one where theistic religion is constitutionally determined to be the only law, and therefore such a phenomenon is rare. It is unrealistic to speak of any mutual co-operation between these religious states. External relations between these states reveal that in fact a significant degree of non-co-operation takes place. Iran, for example exhibits a noticeable degree of hostility towards its fellow Muslim states of Saudi Arabia and the Persian Gulf. This hostility has much to do with the fact that Iran practices Shiite Islam whereas the other Muslim states practice the Sunni variety. Since the death of the founder of Islam, the prophet Mohammed, Islam split itself into these two factions, each of which competes for the title of true Islam.

---

[65] In reality, the ideology of the Ba'ath Party- the single party reigning over Syria- is a secular ideology, similar to Iraq. What is interesting is the fact that the Khomeini Regime in Iran maintains very hostile relations with Iraq while at the same time treating Syria as a fellow ally; though in both countries the leading ideology is overwhelmingly secular. This fact reinforces a well-known fact that in foreign policy national interest trumps ideology.

In conclusion it may ·be cautiously said that the glue binding together civil religious countries is no weaker than that which binds countries practicing the same theistic religion. In fact, it appears that the opposite is true and that civil religion binds states together much more effectively than does theistic religion.

8. A Survey of Publications that deal directly with Civil Religion

Ilana Shelach penned a very comprehensive publication that deals head on with Israeli Civil religion while actually referring to it as secular religion[66]. Shelach and

---

[66] See Ilana Shelach *Effects of Secular Religion on Israel,* shortened version of thesis submitted for the degree of M.A, Hebrew University Library Faculty of Arts and Social Studies, Mount Scopus, Jerusalem. In the book written by Charles Liebman and Eliezer Don-Yehhiya, *Civil Religion in Israel,* published by the University of California, "Israeli Civil Religion" is not referred to, as it is by Shelach, as Secular Religion.
Nonetheless I have not found it useful to follow the lead of books written by Liebman and Don-Yehhiya, even though the volume on civil religion is all- encompassing, dealing with all the fundamentals of civil religion in the Israeli context. That said, it is premised on certain basic defects and errors: (A) the book fails to deal with the *raison d'etre* of religions in general and the link between this raison and the necessity for civil religions amongst those who do not believe in God and who are secular. (B) In the book (*ibid.* p.215) states are divided into welfare states on the one hand, and those states that are founded on some moral message on the other. It is contended that there is no need for a civil religion in Welfare States whereas within states with a moral message, civil religion must, by definition, be created. The authors straight away admit that their proposed classification is more theoretical than practical and it is only brought as a demarcation of the two extremes whereas all states in reality fit somewhere between these extremes, no one state fitting perfectly at either extreme. Despite the immediate clarification, the division as it exists contains within it a basic error, the failure to realize that every individual has an inherent need for civil or any religion, and because of this need, religion exists. Religion does not exist because the state wants it to exist. It is true that religion is an important ingredient in the make-up of any state, but it is not the need of the state that determines the founding of a religion. A state society like a religion comes about to answer the needs of individual man. That is why these entities are created. The result cannot be confused with the reason. Furthermore, implied in what the authors state is another basic error. A country, which is set up for welfare purposes alone without any other feature that binds its citizens together, is one destined for disintegration. It is not merely **another political** entity that is possible to identify, rather it has no "intrinsic citizens" and therefore no "intrinsic nation", and as was discussed in Chap 6 of this book, this state is in the process of disintegration. On the other hand there is no such thing as a state whose whole foundations are solely based on a moral message. A state with a moral message but with nothing emotional to offer is destined to the same fate as the welfare state, which is

extinction. Liebman and Don-Yehhiya divide the time periods into three: from the end of the First World War until the establishment of the State of Israel, an interim period between 1948 and 1956, and the last period that extends from then until today. Their survey is confined exclusively to the Jewish population, without discussing Arabs who inhabited Israel and who were later its citizens .Nor do they deal with the issue of Canaanism. The authors raise important facts that show that although in the first period, Jews in Israel had completely or partially severed ties with their Jewish roots, in the last period under discussion they have tried to reconnect with their Jewish past. This reconnection to their past roots is referred to as a type of "new civil religion". In this last statement they have erred irredeemably, having been trapped by a fundamental fault in their reasoning. A religion whose basic adhesive is Judaism has from the beginning right until contemporary times been referred to as the Jewish Religion, even if members of this religion no longer profess a belief in God. The authors define the Jewish religion of religious Jews, who are loyal to the state as a secular religion, since in their definition loyalty to the state is the sole qualification of a civil religion. This definition cannot be accepted. Judaism defines a Jew as one who is born to a Jewish mother, and even to qualify as a religious Jew only requires the observance of religious precepts, without actually worrying about that individual's theological doubts, should he have any. Even if a Jew does not observe the precepts, he is still a Jew whose membership in the Jewish religion is unquestioned. Associating a deep connection with generations of Jewish history with Israeli civil religion as Liebman and Don-Yehhiya attempt to do is erroneous. The connection is really an emotional element of Judaism. It is one of the internal factors of religion as defined in section 2 above. It comes to answer a religious need, as was elaborated in section 2, a need that in effect creates the phenomenon of religions. Therefore the mistake that is made in this otherwise all encompassing book of Liebman and Don-Yehhiya is indeed fundamental. They describe a certain kind of Judaism (even in its secular form it is still a legitimate version of Judaism) but term it "civil religion." This special kind of Judaism that split away from the Judaism that associated itself with the God of Israel, was also entrenched in Jewish history, but the focus of allegiances was never the State of Israel that has existed since 1948, but rather the People of Israel. Viewed from this perspective it must be said that it is Judaism and not civil religion. One of the characteristics of civil religion is its accessibility to all loyal citizens of the state, and therefore in the Israeli reality, its civil religion, by definition must be Canaanism- which embraces both Jewish and Arab offspring by virtue of their being citizens of the State of Israel. Therefore Liebman's and Don-Yehhiya's book can in no way contribute to our discussion.

(D) A fourth error that cannot go unnoticed is their placing of civil religion beyond the boundaries of nationality, as is obvious from the title of the book *Civil Religion in Israel* and not *Israeli* Civil Religion. The erroneous title comes from an outlook that views civil religion as an international phenomenon that *inter alia* exists in Israel. This does not view each state's civil religion as distinct from each other. This mistake is also found on p.214 of this book. There they speak of a universal morality that is not unique to each state; rather in their view what divide states is their local and particular interests. Absent from the authors' minds is the fact that religion is not an outgrowth of one or other morality system, nor the result of a state's national interests, whose interests alone are not even motivations for establishing a state.

(E) A fifth mistake is the author's premise that religion equals regime, and that **the very act of setting up a** religiously unaffiliated **political regime, creates a civil religion** (*Ibid.*, p. 266). This claim stems from the authors' superficial viewing of religion in terms of function rather than of motive and of emotion. In accordance with this opinion, King Saul's reign over Israel created a new civil religion so that two competing religions coexisted- the theistic religion of the Prophet Samuel and the civil religion of King Saul. This absurd reading of events places the motive for the Israelite's obedience to King Saul on the fact that he was a Jewish king who had led his people into war against their enemy. It makes no connection (as it should) to a national Jewish motive to preserve the existence of the Jewish religion.

(F) The authors themselves admit that their classification of the phenomenon taking hold of Israel after 1956, whereby Israel's Jews looked to Jewish sources as a guide to running the state's affairs, as a new civil religion is an idea not found in any of the literature dealing with civil religion. It must be pointed out that this idea, as it stands (and not just because no one has imitated it) is simply unacceptable. This type of nomenclature cannot even be adopted. In our discussion civil religion is related to those whose emotional ties to and identity with the State of Israel is unrelated to Jewish history, severed completely from it. It of necessity leads to Canaanism and a new religion, which is neither Jewish, nor Moslem, and acts as a unifying factor for all those citizens loyal to the state regardless of their ethnic, racial or (theistic) religious background. Some American literature on this subject also suffers from certain defects in discussing this subject, since the discussion there tackles civil religion from a superficial and not internal angle. They go into a description of the rituals, beliefs, moral institutions and codes that are shared by a certain community and to the extent that they are unique to that community, assert (from a superficial perspective) that that community" belongs" to a certain religion. This is like analysing the phenomenon of Swiss snowfalls by looking at the external factors that accompany them such as the effects these have on both the Swiss inhabitants and on the tourists as well as the fluctuations in tourism and the extent to which profits from tourism trade are affected. This analysis will be incomplete and only partially true as it relates to snowfalls- if indeed the purpose of the analysis is to deal with snowfalls as an important topic in its own right- if the climactic factors causing snowfalls are left out of the discussion. Or- as another example, when discussing the migrations of storks and dealing with the question of when these migrations take place, what travel paths they follow and how this information helps hunters track down storks in a certain area. The discussion will be incomplete-as it relates to the migration of storks if that is an important discussion in its own right-if it does not include the stork's needs and ordeals, the impact the weather can have, and the need to procreate, as factors that contribute to migrations. The same rule holds in a discussion of religion in general and civil religion in particular. A discussions revolving around beliefs, institutions and rituals, all point to superficial signs that aid us in identifying the existence of a religion. Even a discussion pointing to the important fact that religions impact positively on the formation of societies in general and political entities in particular does not do sufficient justice to an analysis of religion. Emphasising the nature of religion in "creating" a moral code as an exemplar of its importance manages only to scratch at the surface of the phenomenon of religion and its identifying marks that impact on human society. What is lacking in this discussion is a serious study as to the kind of distresses and type of deep-seated need that causes man to search for religion. What are the special qualities of religion in general or a certain religion in particular, that indeed are able to alleviate distress and fill the needs described above, and to what extent are religions in general or a certain religion in particular successful in their mission? A genuine discussion will not put the cart before the horse. By this I mean that discussing the benefits yielded by civil religion or any other religion towards a state's coherence or its ability to create loyalty of the state's subjects towards the state and its institutions places the state at the head of the discussion and not the individual. By doing this some basic truths are being ignored. Individuals created society in order that each fulfils his personal need. Likewise human being as a means of being resolved with personal distress created religion. Religious experience in turn caused man to create a moral code so that he could deal with the uncertain and insecure feeling that the world as it is would never fully contain all the forces surrounding man and influencing his life. The solution to the most fundamental questions cannot be found then within the present reality that surrounds him but has to be based on a "past". This "past" is transcendent, and he has no way of getting there, of acquiring the knowledge and strength of dealing with these "past" things. He therefore creates with his powerful imagination that he is blessed with and that he is formed by- a world of religious faith. In order to procure the support of this world with its proximity to the" upper" worlds, he is prepared and even interested in accepting upon himself the rules of this "lofty" game. These rules do not necessarily proclaim a connection to the reality that surrounds him, or to the self-interests that are within his strength to overcome. Rather they deal with a superior spiritual reality of morality surpassing narrow self-interest. Researchers who have studied civil religion have not yet undertaken a full study of these factors. See John F. Wilson "The Status of 'Civil Religion' in America" in *The Religion of the Republic,* (ed. Elwyn A. Smith, Fortress Press, Philadelphia, 1971) p.1. See also Robert N. Bellah "Civil Religion in America" *Daedalus,* vol. 96, no. 1 (1967), p. 1. They discuss questions like "What *did* American civil religion contribute to American society? Obviously this discussion cannot adequately answer the deeper questions that apply to a full discussion on the topic of civil religion, or on the topic of what constitutes religion. The discussion then is premised on a mistake, which is fact a double mistake. (A) They look there at the results of an already existent civil religion, its characteristics, rituals, beliefs and institutions to locate the essential benefits bestowed by this religion on society especially upon its moral code by which society is run. Their discussion does not touch upon the formation of religions in general and civil religion in particular. They do not deal with human needs and other emotions, which working together brought about civil religion. (B) Civil religion was created in the private domain for personal reasons and to fit the private lifestyle of the individual, not for society or its needs, or for its structures. Society is after all the outcome of the individual's needs. The individual needs for his own sake to live within society and for that reason society exists. The individual needs to be able to receive solace from his transcendental fears, which arise from a place that is beyond his reality, and he therefore creates a supernatural existence that acts as his support

her husband were killed in Russ Burka in the Sinai desert while hiking there with their children. Ironically the assailant was an Egyptian soldier, very obsessed with his religion. Ilana's family and ideology was closely associated with the Canaanite denomination in Israel, which obviously viewed itself as very secular. The intimate ties that this researcher had to secularism in Israel are proof that her interest in the subject was aroused by her familiarity with secularism and not with religious Jewish life. Because of her personal bias, so it seems, she does not speak of a civil religion but of a secular religion. Nonetheless after reading her work one realizes that she is in fact dealing with civil religion especially its secular religious character. And indeed if one thinks of the unique background to Israeli civil religion as will be relayed in the pages to follow, there is no real surprise. Secular religion is an offshoot of the Socialist Zionist movement, which pioneered resettlement of the land and which was under the influence of the anti-religious stance preached by the Soviet Communist ideology. Western immigrants similarly brought with them the spirit of the French Revolution which also opposed religion and supported separation of State and religion, as was adopted in American parlance. Therefore Shelach's secular religion must be related to as if it were civil religion. Shelach proves in her detailed analysis the existence of a secular-civil religion within Israel's boundaries. Her conclusions are different from what was raised here only in so far as they relate to the question of whether institutions exist for the promotion of Israeli secular-civil religion.(These by definition[67] must relate equally to practitioners of the Jewish religion, the Christian religion and Islam where each of them identifies himself with the state of Israel.) Shelach is of the opinion that Israel has no institutions of civil religion. Shelach's conclusions are contrary to the conclusions of our discussion in this part of the book, before surveying her writing, where it was concluded that in many different countries where civil religion has reached the level of monopolizing government, institutions of civil religion flourish. While the state's institutions are always identified as self- owned, the rituals and ceremonies carried out in the name of the

---

system. Man <u>needs</u> to feel spiritually whole so he creates a world of morals that is qualitatively superior to a self-interested world and that contains supreme moral values. Society, religion and morality all come to fulfill the needs of the individual, not the needs of society. Society was created for man. Obviously the inverse is untrue. One cannot say that the individual exists because society needs him to exist. As with society so too with morality and religion, man cannot afford to be without any of them. They are the offspring of his needs, and for that reason alone they exist. When speaking of religion it must then first deal with the reasons for it entering the universe, its characteristics and its essence before dwelling on the repercussions and outcomes of its predominance.

[67] This point will be made much clearer below, in a separate and especially devoted section.

state become rituals and ceremonies of the civil religion. As has been said Shelach only deals with the State of Israel, whereas our discussion thus far has been much broader and includes other states and deals with the underlying principles. The particular Israeli problem has not yet been delved into. Shelach does not ponder the question whether civil religion has taken control in the state, but it can be assumed from her claim that Israel has no institutions of civil religion, that she would argue that civil religion in fact has no control over the state. An analysis of her claim yields the following equation: if it can be proved that the reins of power in the state are not exclusively in the hands of those practicing civil religion, it must be concluded that state institutions are not institutions of civil religion. However to this line of thought must be added the fact that those who practice Israeli civil religion perform rituals and ceremonies which are exclusive to the State of Israel both officially and unofficially. (Israel Independence Day; Memorial Day for Fallen Soldiers; Support for the official Israeli sports team [which in Hebrew are referred to as "Israel's Chosen,"]; Hiking the breadth of the land; and any other activity which carries with it the scent of patriotism toward the state of Israel and adoration toward the Land of Israel, even those activities not officially recognized as "national" events) The fact that all these above rituals are properly associated with practitioners of civil religion on the one hand, together with the fact that none of the state institutions are in the hands of the civil religious population on the other is bound to create an imbalance. Those, whose religion, literally, is worship of the state, and who draw their strength from the existence of the state paradoxically have no real power to determine how that state is run. This situation of a loving child whose love is never really reciprocated, creates a tragic enough situation, which is at variance (if in fact it is true) with the accepted practice in the world.

Reinforcing this true but tragic impression is the fact that efforts to produce a Constitution that has equal application to Jew and other nationalities alike have proven fruitless. As I have noted in another of my writings[68] the basic constitutional principle of the state of Israel is that it is a Jewish State, which negates any possibility of it being affiliated with civil religion, which by definition cannot be Jewish. As was proclaimed in the founding document of the establishment of the State, the state of Israel is the natural successor to the Jewish State that was always situated in this geographic locale throughout the nation's history. Since concepts such as Jew and Judaism are concepts that have both religious and nationalist connotations, detaching the Jewish religion from the state is gnawing at the state's raison d'etre of being a "Jewish State". The ideological

[68] Part 6, *infra.*

outlook of the majority of Israeli Jews shares this perspective.[69] The official Declaration of Independence is the "birth certificate" of the state. All that it confirms with regard to the rights of non-Jewish citizens is the fact that all citizens- including non-Jews- are entitled (privately) to equal rights within a particular framework that is detailed there. It enshrines only the principle of non-discrimination against private citizens (excluding a national or ethnic group) on the basis of religion, sex, culture, language, and race as well as non-discrimination with regard to political rights of every citizen to vote, and be voted, for public office in any state institution.[70] This declaration does not speak of equal status of nationalities, since after all it declares Israel to be a Jewish State and not a Jewish-Arab State.

In light of the situation, Shelach only manages to achieve what she set out to do in the individual domain; with regard to the group domain her mission was doomed from the start.[71] The fact that the state in its essence is Jewish bars Canaanite ideology from infiltrating into the political and constitutional spheres. A Jewish state cannot allow a new group entity to invade its political domain (as opposed to its cultural domain), an entity which distances itself from the Jewish People and from Judaism; an entity which has severed itself from the past, from Jewish history and from the ties that bind the Jewish People with the territory which today forms the State of Israel. Shelach does not conduct a constitutional discussion. Her research is confined to sociological aspects. This part (of our book) does not hide the fact that Shelach managed to confirm through her research the very existence of Canaanism, which is synonymous with civil religion, within the borders of Israel.[72] That this phenomenon exists is not in question, but to what

---

[69] This is also raised in a discussion in my book *Who's Afraid of a Jewish State? Constitutional and Ideological Aspects*, note 3 *supra*.

[70] A more elaborate discussion on the constitutional status quo in the State of Israel, in the same spirit as what was said here, can be found in Part 6 *infra*.

[71] It will be shown later on, howvere, that she did not point to certain processes that took place in the Israeli Supreme Court that turned this court into an institution intimately linked in some of its aspects (as will be shown below) to civil religion. It will be seen later that this process, currently taking place in Israel's new reality, is contrary to the Constitutional status quo of the State of Israel forming an unconstitutional breach which in principle should make it unenforceable. All these issues will be discussed later.

[72] However it is unclear from Shelach's writings if there are two parallel civil religions- one for Arabs, the other for Jews- or is there one religion for both. Shelach's research is imprecise on this point. Nonetheless even if she is speaking of two civil religions, both of them are severed from their ethnic Diasporas who dwell outside the state- the Jewish and Palestinian Diasporas. Looked at it this way, Canaanism is faced with two alternatives, but since it has no historical or national roots that identify it with either Arabs or Jews, even two separate civil religions would over time merge together to form a common

extent does it exercise control over state institutions? To solve this question it needs to be split into two. First, the problem of whether constitutionally such control is possible has to be dealt with, and after having answered that, it still needs to be established whether in any event such control could actually emerge. Clearly there are no constitutional grounds for allowing this actuality. Yet it still needs to be clarified whether control of this sort could or does take place. After analyzing the (theoretical) constitutional question the practical situation must be referred to, lest there be a difference between what is practically permissible and what is constitutionally proscribed. After all there may well be an unconstitutional deviation in the present Israeli political reality.

Jewish religious parties are almost a fixture at both the executive and legislative branches (the Knesset) of government. Because of this, even if civil religion has a presence it has been unable to make it fully felt at the level of government. The Supreme Court with its liberal-secular ideology is quite a different story. Owing to the system of appointing Israeli judges to the bench the ideology prevalent in the court continues to enjoy prominence. So long as this system remains in place there is no chance the court will change biases that have remained with it for decades.[73] It cannot be expected that Supreme Court Justices would sanction any change to their ideological views by approving the appointment of new judges who think that parliament is the vehicle for promoting a vibrant state democracy. The (justices of the) Court argues that they may flex their muscles even without prior approval from the Knesset. As a result of this thinking the Supreme Court has been able, not only to overturn decisions of the executive, but also, to repeal statutes of Knesset. In this way our Supreme Court Justices have ensured that their status is elevated to the highest rungs of the regime. This Court is run by those whose worldview is very close to the principles of the Israeli Civil Religion. Therefore civil religion practitioners, even if not in total control of, are very intimately connected with the most authoritative institution in the land. It is this new way of seeing events, discussed in the last few pages of our discussion, which forces us to reach different conclusions from those reached by Shelach.

There is no one specific style that countries controlled by civil religion use to impose the said religion. In the U.S. the style is brutal and uncompromising[74]. In

---

Jewish-Arab civil religion . Therefore Israeli Civil Religion later on will be related to as a religion that unifies former Jews with former Arabs under one rooftop.

[73] The possible objection of a solitary Supreme Court Justice who opposes the liberal-secular trend cannot be taken into account, since this has no influence on the court's final judgment.

[74] The appointment of Joseph Lieberman to run as Democratic vice Presidential Candidate for the United States should not mislead us; even though Lieberman is an Orthodox mitzvah- observant Jew. His Jewish religion served merely as an adornment to the

France, with regards to education a compromise has been reached, just as it has in Britain. In other states such as Germany, Italy and Japan the style has been moderated by the fact that parties with theistic religious leanings are allowed to participate in the political field without any constitutional bars. Through these parties theistic religion is allowed a political role alongside civil religion. Since judges, with the constitutional authority to overturn legislation, are appointed by representatives of these political parties, democracy has the final say, and not a judicial oligarchy. Therefore the extent to which civil religion exercises control over these countries is to a large extent dependent upon its influence over democratic, party- political arrangements. In a country then which bars theistic religion from participating in elections for public office it is civil religion which controls the state apparatus and which converts state institutions into its own playground.

Dr. Haman Shelach, like his wife Ilana, also researched civil religion from an anti-theistic religious perspective. His research was conducted within the framework of his doctoral dissertation. He studied the United States situation, not Israel's, and even then he did not deal directly with civil religion managing only to skirt the issue when discussing the attitude of the American Supreme Court towards American [theistic] religions.[75]

American Civil Religion which tries to show itself to be non-discriminatory towards theistic religion, as if it holds by the principles of belief in God. This is all merely technical wrangling by a party seeking to promote its political clout by displaying (from a political-governmental perspective) Judaism, Islam and various strands of Christianity in one large beautiful glass cage. After his appointment Lieberman's words about belief in God as a value which enriches politics caused a storm of protest; he had crossed a red line by addressing matters of religion in a political forum. This whole episode obviously strengthened the desire of radical Protestants who have always wanted to draw their religion into the halls of justice, but these Protestants are not powerful enough to effect what is to a large extent a very revolutionary change.

[75] Haman P. Shelach, *Freedom of Conscience and Religion*, doctoral dissertation submitted for the degree, Doctor of Laws. In *Freedom of Conscience and Religion* there are various essays in memory of Haman. P. Shelach, published jointly by the Citizens Rights Association and Hapoalim Library, edited by Professor Ruth Gavison, at page 23. On page 88 Shelach concludes that "the principle of separation of state and religion was constructed, in order to prevent a reality wherein state and religion merge, as was the reality then in Europe and especially in England. The last-mentioned based itself on a broad conception of religion and on the religious establishment thereby contriving a principle that was not duly flexible in relating to the continuing evolving circumstances, resulting, then, in unjust and undesirable results in so far as religion and freedom of conscience are concerned and causing inconsistency amongst the various decisions" Shelach does not really discuss the real need behind separating religion and state. Our

9. Perspectives as to the essence of Israel: as a Jewish State or as or a State of all its citizens as shown by the actions of the Israeli Government Authorities.

When discussing Shelach's thesis on Israeli civil religion and when pointing to the only living proof of an **Israeli Civil Religion**, the existence of Canaanism[76] was raised. A state's civil religion has to be equally applied to all those of its citizens who see themselves as patriots to that state, and who maintain all the ideas connected with that patriotism and with the attributes of that state. Practitioners of the American Civil Religion who fiercely uphold the principles of the American Constitution, and who by virtue thereof are liberal, will cling to America's national history and its founding fathers and will create for themselves an image of the American nation, as evidenced by their ritualistic celebration of Thanksgiving Day. Their families' national religious history prior to arriving on American shores plays no part in the civil religious framework. Participation in this *Americanness*, in this American civil religious experience, is not limited to Protestants. The United States of America, in the eyes of the American Civil Religious practitioner, is a multi-racial and multi-ethnic nation. America's black population is not debarred from playing a role, especially since the American Constitution was designed to accord all its citizens equal treatment. The American civil religious practitioner will never disqualify an American citizen from participating in American civil religious rites based on his racial/ethnic background. The key for opening doors and gaining entry to this community-oriented American civil religion is American citizenship. The American president is the president of this civil religion and the American government, its (i.e. civil religion's) government. American public state institutions are this religion's institutions in the same way as institutions connected with the Catholic Church including the pope and the Catholic administrative headquarters in Rome are considered the institutions of all

---

discussion on the other hand addresses the need for its application in the context of today's reality, and to vigorously protest civil religion's domination over states' governments without making way for theistic religions to have their say.

[76] This was a small movement formed by secular Israeli Jews as a political movement that wanted to use the concept of Israelite- regardless of the racial, linguistic or religious background – to refer to those who lived by the new culture offered them by the State of Israel, and who viewed their attachment to the Land of Israel completely unconnected to any one nation's history. Though it would seem that this movement has had its life source drained from it, in reality it is a living, breathing organism. The immigration of one million immigrants from the Former Soviet Union, including a significant portion who have no connection to the Jewish Religion and its traditions, is bound to breathe new life into this movement in one or other forms, and quite possibly that process is already taking place in practice.

Catholics worldwide. Nonetheless from its very beginnings American citizens had dual loyalties. In the antebellum years they were loyal primarily to the U.S. Federal government, followed by, and of secondary importance, the individual state government. In the post-bellum period Republicanism gained the upper hand and ethnic ties overtook individual state loyalties to take second place behind an overall loyalty to the United States as a whole. Ethnic loyalties can be seen in cases where for instance Italian immigrants living in the US try help their kinsmen[77], just as in the case of other ethnic minorities. The total rupture within America whose final form was shaped by the outcome of the American Civil War and the renewed direction American nationalism would take is all discussed in Leah Greenfield's writings.[78]

Owing to the fact that no two countries are alike, each country has its own unique way of consolidating the loyalties of its citizens. A multi-ethnic state like the Indian Federation will for certain struggle against dual loyalties, since the Federal government's only loyal supporters will be those who harbor similar loyalties towards the ethnic group to which the government ministers belong. In Switzerland, as is obviously the case, secondary loyalties are split between local cantons and parties that speak the same one of the four constitutionally recognized languages as that citizen. . In Belgium it is very acceptable to owe allegiance to one of the two language groups, the Flemings or the Walloons, without affecting overall loyalty towards Belgium. Therefore civil religion which is completely affiliated with the state and its institutions cannot forbid secondary loyalties so long as they are subject at all times to an overall state loyalty.

Considering the above and taking into account what I said in my book about the Jewish State[79] wherein I concluded that Israel is the State of the Jewish People in all its dispersions and that through its citizens, both Jew and Arab, the Jewish People are loyally served, three primary questions arise.

(I) Does the Knesset as the State of Israel's parliament operate on behalf of the State of all the dispersed Jewish People or is it the parliament of a state of all its citizens? (As would fit the ideology of the civil religion)

[77] See Michael Walzer *What it is to be an American* (New York: Marsaio), pp. 23-49, at p. 28.

[78] See Leah Greenfield, *Nationalism, Five Roads to Modernity*,(London: Harvard University Press, 1992), p. 480. See also the opinion of Robert Palmer as it appears in Seymour Martin Lipset "The Newness of the New Nation," in Vann Woodward (ed.) *The Comparative Approach to American History*, (NY: Basic Books, 1968), p. 64.

[79] See *Who's afraid of a Jewish State?,The Ideological and Constitutional Aspects, supra* note 3, *ibid.* Chapter 6, Section 2.

(II) Does Israel's government act as if they are the executive authority for the State of the all the dispersed Jewish People or are they the executive authority over a state of all its citizens?

(III) Does Israel's Supreme Court act as if it is the highest judicial authority for the State of the all the dispersed Jewish People or is it the highest judicial authority for a state of all its citizens?

The Knesset: The composition of the Knesset reflects two different trends but in actuality it operates with one clear mindset. The Law of Return and the Law of Foundations of Justice,[80] as well as other Laws, encourage an ingathering of the exiled people. These Laws also provide a budget for creating areas demarcated for Jewish settlement in order to prevent the existence of an Arab majority in the Galilee as well as ensuring separation between Arabs living in the disputed territories and those in the Israeli Wadi 'Ara. All these actions either rely on legislative acts or have to do with the character and composition of the governments that have been approved by the Knesset. The Knesset upholds individual equality of all its citizens by not discriminating between Jews, Arabs, Druze and other minorities. On the national level however the object of their attention is the Jewish national group that is intimately linked with the Jewish Diaspora. To summarize, the Knesset acts most decidedly as if it represents all of the Jewish Diaspora, which can be most clearly demonstrated when it deals with immigrant absorption.

The Government: The government's composition is made up almost exclusively of Jews (with the exception of one instance which lasted for a very brief period) who in relation to the question of representation are even more one dimensional in their attitude than the Knesset. There were some prime ministers who on the rhetorical level spoke of the "people in Israel" as if Israel was a "State of all its citizens" and as if there was one Israeli nationality not based on its Jewishness, but on its citizenship. Yet beyond these verbal declarations, that always seemed to pop up close to elections and were uttered in order to garner support from the Arab vote, the governments have always acted as if they were preserving Israel's prime interest to remain a Jewish State. As for the nationalist significance of a Jewish state the government has always acted- both on the level of rhetoric and pragmatics as heavily focused on the Jewish idea. Like Knesset, the government has also sought to accord equal rights to its Jewish and other citizens as it relates to the individual on the municipal level. In this regard, however, it has not been careful to prevent discrimination against the Arab minority when it comes to employment opportunities, municipal budgets, hiring of public servants,

[80] See Chapter 7 of my book *supra* note 3

development work etc. This discrimination has nothing to do with our being a Jewish state, since the State's Jewish identity is in no way associated with discriminating against non-Jews. As to the different attitude with regard to the Jewish State's national aspect as opposed to its religious one, the uneven funding by every government, regardless, of religious and ultra-Orthodox educational institutions as opposed to those of a more general nature, comes as a result of coalitional pressure rather than of any inner convictions that this is the right path to follow. Other budgetary considerations that touch on religious matters involve mainly similar pressures. Since "Jew" is a concept which has both religious and nationalist considerations and the Jewish religion is a national religion, the designation "Jewish State" must refer to both these planes simultaneously.

The governments of Israel have never done anything for the "Jewish State" in its religious context out of an inner desire or conviction that they should work towards this goal. There has never been a positive impetus urging furtherance of religious causes; all that has been done in this regard is the result of negative pressures and stimuli. It follows then that Israel's governments that have displayed a good measure of sensitivity towards the nationalist aspects of the Jewish State have not displayed similar sensitivity in regard to its religious aspects.

This point of delving into this subject is not to suggest that the "Jewish Religion" per se is coercive. Yet beyond circumventing religious coercion there is a much wider field of operations upon which Israel's governments have paraded, to a great extent against their will. As a consequence of following this policy which it has been compelled to adopt, the government has eroded Israel's status quo on religion so that it is lopsided against the Jewish religion (in its non-coercive form, obviously). This erosion owes much more to Israel's government than to its Knesset.

In any event, as a final summation of what has been said, all of Israel's governments, as a rule, have reacted negatively to the concept of a "civil religion". Though they display a positive response to the concept of a "Jewish State", that is only as it relates to the nationalist connotations. Contrarily they have exhibited no special enthusiasm for its religious character.

The Supreme Court: At the initial stages of its tenure the Supreme Court acted like the court of the Jewish State and in its promotion of equal rights on the individual level did not oppose the policies of the Knesset or the government when it came to issues of national importance.

The Supreme Court from very early on consistently expressed its reservations with regard to the issues surrounding the religious connotations of the State of Israel being a Jewish State. An exhaustive list would be too long to reproduce here but landmark decisions include the *Shalit*[81], *Rufeizen*[82], *Kaplan*[83] (admittedly this was decided in a lower tribunal, but the fact it was not appealed against in one of the higher divisions is proof that it was commensurate with the judicial policy of the Supreme Court) *Jezeramcus*[84] and *Shakdiel*[85] cases, along with a long line of other judgments including the whole *Bar Ilan Street* episode.[86] In all these judgments the Supreme Court decided against the status quo on religion and even against the values that are accepted in those countries that impose strict separation of state and religion, akin to the United States. Any semblance of religious coercion is immediately repealed by the Supreme Court so for instance, a law relating to the closure of public places of business on the Sabbath, recognized as constitutionally grounded in the United States, was rejected out of as invalid. This was after the local municipality democratically sanctioned this provision by including it in one of its local by-laws. The closure of Bar Ilan Street, which passes through the center of the Jerusalem *Chareidi* (ultra-Orthodox) neighborhoods and which closure caused Sabbath travelers, at most, a few minutes delay, was deemed from the outset to be coercive. Furthermore a permit issued by a Public Committee in terms of which the street would be closed during a specially allotted time was discarded when the court began its debate on the issue. It was only after much arm twisting that the permit was finally approved. At the time of handing down its judgment approving the permit the court informed the *Chareidi* community that if they were to make any more demands or if they would engage in violent activity the court would weigh the options of retracting the permit. Such a statement coming as it does in the middle of a court judgment was equivalent to taking sides in the secular/religious debate. If the ruling was motivated by a desire to strike a fair balance there would be no place for threatening one of the sides that in the event that they "do not act nicely" or if they "come with more demands" an evenhanded decision would be overturned and replaced by a decision lopsided

---

[81] High Court of Justice (H.C.J) 58/68 *Benjamin Shalit v. License Registrar* P"D vol. 23(2) p. 477. [in Hebrew]

[82] H.C.J. 72/62 *Rufeizen v. Minister of the Interior*, P"D vol. 16 p. 2428. [in Hebrew]

[83] *Criminal Court (Jerusalem) 3471/87 *The State of Israel v. Kaplan*, PS"M 1988 (5748) (2) p. 265. [in Hebrew]

[84] *Court of Appeal 217/68 *Jezeramcus v. The State of Israel* P"D vol. 22 (2) p. 343 [in Hebrew].

[85] H.C.J. 153/87 *Shakdiel v. Minister of Religious Affairs*, P"D vol. 42 (2) p. 221 [in Hebrew].

[86] H.C.J. 5016/96 *Chorev v. Traffic Supervisor* P"D vol. 51 (4) p. 1 [in Hebrew].

against them. It is patently obvious that Supreme Court is completely negatively attuned to any issues that relate to religious aspects of the Jewish State.

When dealing with the nationalist aspects of the Jewish State, the Supreme Court Justices, until the end of the 1990s, were active in preventing the release of "captives" who in fact were prisoners of war, within the context of the war between the State of Israel and the Hezbollah. They were also very vociferous in joining Israel's demand for the release of Ron Arad from the clutches of the Hezbollah or at least for some information as to his fate. A similar patriotic stance was in evidence when the Supreme Court decided the extent of physical pressures that could be legally exerted against a Palestinian terrorist who is deemed a "ticking time bomb" (the torture case). The Court similarly backed the government, when, basing itself on the principle of reciprocity withheld the rights from two senior Hezbollah members- Mustafa Dirani and Sheikh Obeid to be visited by Red Cross personnel until similar visits could be arranged with Jewish captives held by the Hezbollah. However by the end of the 1990s this trend ended. This is strikingly demonstrated in the Katzir episode, discussed under title of the *Ka'adan* decision, in which Arabs demanded the right of abode in a Jewish hilltop settlement that was established by the Jewish Agency as a buffer between Arabs living in the Territories and those living in Wadi Ara.[87] The Court held that so long as no new settlements were being specifically designated for Arabs there could be no new settlements built for Jews. Following this reasoning specific land could not be allocated to the Jewish Agency since it was an organization that practiced discrimination against Arabs by setting up exclusively Jewish settlements. All these kinds of decisions reflect a trend that asserts that Israel is a State of all its citizens while denying the idea that State of Israel belongs to the People of Israel and is a realization of the Zionist enterprise.

The court's ruling, delivered in the Katzir case, is a clear example of how it conforms to the spirit of civil religion. While it is true that it still employs the terminology of the "Jewish State" and is not yet ready to use alternative language that the rest of the world uses i.e. a "State of all its citizens", it only does so for strictly legal and semantic reasons. According to this Court the rules of the game are defined in the Basic Laws, enacted in 1992, and since these Laws pay lip service to the constitutional idea of Israel as a Democratic Jewish State[88], the court

[87] H.C.J. 6698/95 *Ka'adan v. Israel Lands Administrator* (unpublished and in Hebrew), the verdict was delivered on 8 March 2000.

[88] It is foreseeable according to an assessment that will be presented later, that the court will in the future swing full circle and pronounce and lay down that a "Jewish state" means in fact a "State of all its citizens" just like the President of the Supreme Court pronounced lately that Zionism also includes Arab settlement alongside Jewish settlement.

follows suit. In practice the decisions of the Supreme Court Justices have already downgraded the Jewish character of the state so that it is only of symbolic, abstract value, devoid of any particularistic attributes. The state's democratic nature on the other hand is given detailed application. Paradoxically if the principle of a "Democratic State" were to be followed - a principle that has no constitutional value save for its reference in a few Laws[89] and which therefore awaits constitutional classification-it would be discovered that it is always a secondary feature which exists only in the abstract.[90]

By rights the principle of a "Jewish State" should occupy prime position, however it is the lower ranking principle, that has not been constitutionally enshrined- that of our being a "democratic state" -that our Supreme Court has declared, through its various judgments, that trumps everything else. Owing to democracy's supreme value it empowers the Supreme Court with the authority to change the structure of all existent Laws and to strike down any of the governments' administrative acts , its delegated legislation or the by-laws of the local authorities, on the grounds that they are all expressions of a democratic regime.

In the eyes of the Supreme Court circa 2000, all citizens enjoy equal rights not only in their capacity as individuals- which no one in Israel would question- but also in their capacity as members of various nationalities. Therefore Azmi Bishara's candidature for Prime Minister cannot be invalidated. That is what the Supreme Court believes, and that is the ideology that is mandated by members of the Israeli civil religion who observe religiously what Ilana Shelach defined as the Israeli secular (civil) religion.

The Israeli Civil Religion is then – as it emerges from our previously conducted analysis-one religion that cannot be split into two. It is not possible for a Jewish Israeli Civil Religion to operate alongside an Arab Israeli Civil Religion. To speak of the *Arabness* or Jewishness of a member of the Israeli Civil Religion is pointless. That is the situation in civil religions across the globe and there is no reason why Israel should be any different especially since citizenship is "born", so to speak, without any heritage or history that pre-existed that State. If members of the Israeli Civil Religion who are descendant from Jews cease to identify themselves as part of a larger Jewish Diaspora that lives outside of Israel's borders,

---

[89] This emerges in the analysis conducted in my book *Who's afraid of a Jewish State: Constitutional and Ideological Aspects* note 5 *supra*.

[90] It was declared so by Barak, before his appointment as President of the Supreme Court, when he was one of the justices of this court, in a published article. See Aaron Barak, "The Constitutional Revolution: Human Rights Protected" (in Hebrew) *Law and Administration* vol. 1 1992, pp. 9, 30.

they have to, perforce, cut themselves off from their antiquated history that serves to unite them with Diasporà Jewry. Continuing along the same lines it must be concluded that there is no reason why they should separate themselves from those whose roots go back to the Arab-Palestinian nation but who also practice Israeli Civil Religion.

The Israeli Civil Religious practitioner, as he has been defined, does not bow down to the Jewish State. Instead he worships a State of Israel that has burnt all bridges with the Jewish religion, its history, and its nationalist aspirations. It does not deny the right of Judaism and Islam to flourish in Israel, yet it regards the State as an emotional mainstay, and as a central focus for expressing personal loyalty by the individual citizen to that, that was created on 15 May 1948, with no past, just a present and a future.

In light of the judgments delivered by the Supreme Court, it would be correct to say that this court is an institution of the state of Israel that is very careful not to be associated with any one of the nationalities or religions that exist in Israel. This makes it an institution that is very close in spirit to the Israeli Civil Religion. In the opinion of this institution, as it emerges from what is contained in its judgments, not from the declarations or terminology that is used there, Israel is a "State of all its citizens". According to the most recent President of the Supreme Court, there is no real difference between the concepts "Jewish State" and "a State of all its citizens" especially when the former has been relegated (in his opinion) to contain elements only very broadly relating to it, while the latter (which he prefers to refer to rhetorically as a "Democratic State") is embodied with concrete and particularistic meaning. The State of Israel in his view is a "Jewish State" only to the extent that this concept is construed to be identical to a "Democratic State". Yet Barak would disagree with the opposite proposition i.e. that the State of Israel is a "Democratic State" only to the extent that this concept is construed to be identical to a "Jewish State".[91]

---

[91] See Aaron Barak, "The Constitutional Revolution: Human Rights Protected" (in Hebrew) *Law and Administration* vol. 1 1992, pp. 9. Also see *ibid.* at 230 where he goes into great detail on the principle of a Democratic State as conceived by the Court's judgments.

10. The contrast between associating oneself with Israeli "civil religion" and a worldview that sees Israel as a Jewish State.

The world-view expressed by the President of the Supreme Court, Aaron Barak is the same that dominates the court's thinking in the latest judgments. Present day court rulings in Israel will not present arguments that oppose Barak's world-view, and will certainly not rearrange things so that the principle of a "Jewish State" gains the upper hand over the idea of a "Democratic State". Only a small minority of cases dares to plead equality between these two concepts by blurring the differences between them.[92]

According to the principles of freedom of religion as spelled out by the founding document of the State, the Declaration of Independence, civil religion is granted equal religious standing in so far as the individual's rights in Israel are concerned (which according to the concepts of the Declaration is the citizens' rights). By contrasting the idea of equality on the individual level with the preferred [collective] idea, which is the essence and raison d'etre of the state, of a "Jewish State", and by locating the points of friction between the two concepts, the differences between civil religion and the principle of a "Jewish State" can be seen. When balancing the values of a "Jewish State" versus a "Democratic State" and when discussing how the points of friction between these two are eventually reconciled, three possible outcomes must be borne in mind, i.e.

(i) A preference for a "Jewish State" over a "Democratic State"

(ii) Equal value for a "Jewish State" and a "Democratic State"

(iii) A preference for a "Democratic State" over a" Jewish State"

Possibility (a) is commensurate with what has been said thus far in the discussion in this part of the book[93]. Possibility (b) is the opinion of Menachem Elon, while possibility (c) reflects Barak's views.

---

[92] See the reaction of Menachem Elon in Menachem Elon, "The Way of the Law in the Constitution: The Values of a Jewish and Democratic State in light of Basic Law: Human Dignity and Liberty "(in Hebrew) in *Judicial Activism*, p. 202.

[93] See note 3 *supra*.

In accordance with the view in (a) that holds that a "Jewish State" trumps a "Democratic State" it should be said (following the trend of the Declaration of independence) that in a private sense, on the level of the individual, any citizen who feels a common identity with the spirit of the "Israeli Civil Religion" or "Canaanism", is allowed to set up voluntary organizations and together with others he can establish institutions that enable him to undergo the Canaanite experience, so long as the Jewish religion has complete (and unequal) precedence over civil religion or any other religion for that matter. As to (b) Menachem Elon would see both concepts as vying for the same thing so that they are of equal value. According to third way of looking at it, that of Aaron Barak, level (c), the Jewish religion has no advantage whatsoever over any other religion in Israel. All religions are equal and are eligible for equal treatment, so held the court in the decision of the "Women of the (Wailing) Wall."[94] According to this third possibility practitioners of civil religion are entitled to the same burial rights as those practicing the Jewish religion and therefore there is no legal impediment to civil burials conducted by an organization which is not under the control of Jewish law or any other religious laws[95]. These practitioners are furthermore entitled to a mandatory order by the High Court of Justice to enable the establishment of their own religious institutions with a state budget allotted to them as is the case (which is equally applicable) with the Israeli Chief Rabbinate. The Knesset can expect to receive an order mandating it to enact appropriate legislation; otherwise the H.C.J. will set out constitutional guidelines mandating the same. In addition it is expected that the H.C.J. will order budgets set aside for civil religious educational institutions to which its members are entitled. This means that civil religious clubs will be set up that unite Jew and Arab while blurring the differences between the two. Additionally it is envisioned that a joint Arab-Jewish educational system will be put into place which will encourage intermarriage between Jew and Arab, following the new tradition of introducing the ideas of the Israeli Civil Religion or sect to the unsuspecting public. Members of this new religion or sect will be entitled to the same budgets that are presently given to synagogues, churches, mosques and religious educational institutions. Members of this religion or sect will be entitled to all of this if they only ask for it.[96]

---

[94] See Verdict B, H.C.J. 3358/95 *Anat Hoffman and others v. Administrative Head of Prime Minister's Office and others* (in Hebrew). This judgment was delivered by a court made up of the following three justices: Matza, Strasbourg-Cohen and Beinish on 22 May 2000 (unpublished).

[95] As has already been decided but was put in practice even before this decision.

[96] However it is doubtful if a request will be made in the near future, apart from those who request it in order to provoke and to stigmatize the recipients of budgets destined for Jewish religious purposes in Israel. As regards to the more distant future it is very possible

In light of the interpretation presented in this book when it discusses the constitutional situation in the State of Israel the last mentioned possibility cannot be implemented by virtue of its being unconstitutional. However in practice the Israeli Supreme Court does not follow this line of thinking.

11. Relevant Judicial policy in Israel.

The judgments rendered in the *Katzir* and "Women of the Wall" episode conform to the liberal, democratic, secular and egalitarian agenda that is found in the United States and its Constitution. The Israeli Supreme Court Justices are in the habit of adopting American terminology and case law without carefully discriminating between the constitutional situations that prevail in either country. Generally they do not even bother to mention that America has a written Constitution and case law is decided specifically in accordance with the American Constitution. The impression created is that Israeli law is linked to the American Constitution, even if the Israeli justices do not believe this or do not want others to think that that is the case. They imbibe the American ideology to such an extent that they are unable to deal with the constitutional differences that separate the two countries; a result, simply, of the approach that they have of late adopted.

The ruling in the *Chorev* (Bar Ilan Street) case was delivered in this same spirit. In an article that appeared in the supplement to the *Ha'aretz* weekend edition[97] the Israeli Supreme Court President Aaron Barak was called the "[Hassidic] *Rebbe* (literally: Grand Master) of the Secularists". This description seems an appropriate title heading for the purposes of our discussion in this part of the book. Does the Supreme Court-like its President- make up the leadership of the Israeli Secular Religion? And to what degree is this court "relevant" to the State as a whole?

In the *Chorev* case the Justices viewed the interests of the Chareidi residents to be emotionally driven and they juxtaposed this with the interest of freedom of movement of the secularists taking into account the fact that Bar Ilan Street was a quicker thoroughfare than any other, so that it cut travel time by a few minutes. If so the emotional impairment suffered by the religious population, which is not on

---

that the scenario described above will come to fruition especially if the trends and power of the present court, as they are today, will be allowed to develop further.

[97] See Supplement to *Ha'aretz* New Year's Eve Edition 5759, September 1998.

the same level as a basic right of every citizen, did not fare well against the basic right, so to speak, of the secularists, especially since the right of "freedom" , in this case freedom of movement, is always preferred. The very fact that the problem was framed in such a manner just goes to show how ignorant the justices are when it comes to their understanding of observant Jewish lifestyles. An observant Jew is indeed concerned that "the whole Jewish people" observe the precepts of the Creator of the World, but more than this, much more than this, the observant man is worried about the education of his children- that they be educated in the religious spirit. Exposing the children of the neighborhood to massive traffic violations on the Sabbath and Festivals frustrates his ability to preserve a consistent education for his children, in the spirit that he chooses. In any event it is not simply hurt feelings that are at issue. The concept "emotions" is one that belongs to the secularist lexicon, and not to the Jewish religion. An observant Jew toils in order to fulfill the precepts and obligations that are incumbent upon him, not for the sake of emotional fulfillment. This typifies the difference between the Western world's penchant for focusing on rights on the one hand and the religious Jew's penchant for focusing on duties, on the other. The expression "emotional impairment" reflects a secularist thought process and not a Jewish religious way of thinking.

The *Chorev* case is similar to litmus paper which helps us identify whether a problem exists. Indeed the problem has been identified as existing on two levels:

(i) On the level of principle, i.e. being the arbitrator
(ii) On the communicative level

On the level of principle, i.e. being the arbitrator, it would appear that those principles that guide Supreme Court Justices do not dictate to them any duty to help observant and religious Jews create an environment conducive to their religious lifestyles. Connected to this is the matter of a Jewish State supporting and aiding Jews who want to fulfill Jewish religious precepts and providing them with the tools, atmosphere and conditions that will make it easier to realize their aims. On a matter of principle the aid that is extended is based on the very essence of the State, in that it is a Jewish State, whose central mission is to spread Judaism to all of its Jewish inhabitants who simply request it, within reasonable limits. This mission is the number one task of the State which precedes all others, and cannot be pushed aside by the principles of democracy as in "freedom of movement" especially in the marginal definition of that concept when speaking of a few added minutes of Sabbath travel time. The standard for evaluating interests and aims of the Jewish State are different from the standards employed by the justices in this instance. On a communicative level the justices in the *Chorev* case were unable to

construe the Chareidi language. The Chareidim, it is true, did breach the bounds of behavior, but that was not because there is something uncouth about them. The reason they resorted to lawlessness was because there was no one from among the highest authority of the land (which for all practical purposes is the Supreme Court) who understood their needs. The Chareidim spoke of their needs and the justices understood this to mean their feelings. It can be confidently said that the sides suffered from serious language and communication difficulties.
All this is reflective of a certain estrangement that leads to discrimination in practice and in deed.

12. Summary: The possible and the desired future.

In Israel the prevailing judicial trend is to separate religion and State, even if this trend is unable to prevent the continuing registration of marriages and divorces by religious authorities or the institution of a chief rabbinate and religious council. The court, when interfering with the composition of and appointments to the religious councils, acts beyond its obligations, as a correct reading of the Law reveals. Similarly when it comes to interfering in questions regarding kashruth, they often needlessly clash with the religious councils or with legislation of the Knesset.[98]

In these circumstances it should come as no surprise that the religious and Chareidi communities are increasingly turning to the ecclesiastical courts for a ruling though the status of such a ruling is only on a par with arbitration. In the future this trend will be broadened further especially if the courts continue down the same path. It is foreseeable that Chareidim will put forward political demands asking Knesset to legislate changes in the Law that will make way for ecclesiastical authorities to be recognized as a separate judicial system on par with the judicial system presently in place. >From a political-moral perspective such a demand would be difficult to object to, and could only be faced off if the present judicial system altered its thinking to the extent that it emphasized its duty to act within the framework of a Jewish State, notwithstanding its democratic nature.

Doubtless neither the Israeli Supreme Court nor the majority of those, consciously or not, affiliated with Israeli Civil Religion actively seeks to introduce marriages between Jews and Arabs. In any event the idealists from either side of the spectrum will not deny this marriage option to those who seek it. In a similar vein

---

[98] It is for this reason that Knesset felt compelled to amend the *Basic Law: Freedom of Occupation*, knowing that if they did not fix it up this *Basic Law* relating to the import of kosher meat, the Knesset Law dealing with this matter would have been overturned.

many liberals who are not homosexual or lesbian do not deny the right of those who are so inclined to follow their inclinations. They also noisily object to any hardships the state places in the way of the gay community in contrast with the services and recognition granted by the state to straight families. Therefore just like the accusation cannot be thrown at these [straight] liberals that they undermine homosexual and lesbian activity within society so too the Supreme Court Justices cannot be accused of undermining intermarriage within society, even while acknowledging that these justices do not consciously serve the court as representatives of the Israeli Civil Religion or even attempt to further its cause.

The forecast presented here on the future awaiting Israel and on the links between the Supreme Court and Civil Religion will certainly put the backs up of any one of the Supreme Court Justices, in the event that they hear of this claim. Israeli Civil Religion is not a religion that has recognized leaders with a fixed and known membership list neither does it have established institutions that formally protect its membership. The subject of this discussion is made up of an ideology that is multi faceted and divided, but which binds many people together who in practice are generally unaware of the fact that they are members of this religion or have even heard of this religion's existence. What unite the members of this religion are a common ideology, culture and ritual. A distinguishing feature of civil religion in states whose populations originate from many different lands (like the USA, Canada and Israel), is the members' total severing of emotional ties with the history of the countries or people that they originated from before arriving in their new country. In the USA, Australia and Canada the matter speaks for itself, in Israel this is not at all clear. A Jew who emigrated from Poland to Israel and who joined the Civil Religion is distinguished first and foremost by his keen interest in things that happen in Israel, and concomitantly by his total break with Jewish Polish events that are presently occurring. Furthermore: in order to sincerely join this new religion he must for instance prefer American ideals that have been absorbed in Israel, which account for the similar lifestyles and living standards enjoyed in the US and Israel, over and above the principles enunciated by his Jewish heritage.

Indeed this is the direction that seems to be unfolding in the Israeli Supreme Court's rulings that have rejected any attempt at embracing the "Jewish Heritage" as a normative source for judicial review as was the case when the legislator mandated such an inclusion in the old *Law of the Foundations of Justice* ,5740 (1980). Apart from their rulings the tendency of Supreme Court Justices to view the concept of a "Jewish State" as something vague having no concrete value, of very broad conceptual application can be contrasted with their clinging onto the smallest particularistic details of what is called for by the principles of a Democratic State.[99]

The Supreme Court Justices, all of them, will mock any idea that suggests they have any political link to-or patronization of- any section of the Israeli public sector in general or Israeli Civil Religion in particular. They confidently believe with all their heart and soul that they are free of all and any prejudice because when they sit in judgment they have no ties to the people involved and are thus able to dispense justice to all. About them it must be said that intentions of the heart are not at issue, but deeds, a reality embroidered by their hands and the exact product of their pens. The Israeli Supreme Justices (those who are Jewish, that is) obviously believe that they are good and loyal Jews faithful to the Jewish religion. And behold they are being told here that they have links to a new religion which intends wiping away Judaism from the Jewish State, and that in practice they are strengthening the hand of the civil religion which is bent on taking over the reins of the State and depriving the Jewish religion of any influence over the governing process.

Like these Supreme Court Justices so too the majority of Israel's Jews feel that they are good and loyal Jews (the same thing can be said with regard to Israeli Arabs who wholeheartedly believe that they are loyal Palestinians). Nevertheless looking at the principles that many of Israel's citizens rally behind, combined with the ever diminishing emotional ties to that part of Israeli life that connects them to their ancient and well worn heritage, to the point where they are almost cut off from it, and without them even being aware of it they have left the old religion, and their antiquated feelings of nationality, and have created in its place a new religion, even a new people has been formed thanks to their active help. Another segment of the population has adopted two religions, one of them being civil religion. They practice one or another theistic religion in their homes and are members of the Israeli civil religion outside their homes, i.e. in the political lives they lead and in their relationship to the State. This is exactly the way the majority of Americans are, they look up to the USA, without at the same time giving up membership in this or that theistic religion.

Just like the Israeli Supreme Court Justices defended the rights of the "Women of the Wall" to realize their egalitarian aspirations by their loud chanting of the Torah portion next to the (Western) Wall while all time being wrapped in (male) religious garb, *talitoth*, so too continuing along this path our Supreme Court

---

[99] See Aaron Barak, "The Constitutional Revolution: Human Rights Protected" (in Hebrew) *Law and Administration* vol. 1 1992, p. 230.

Justices in the future will look favorably upon those non-profit organizations who will increasingly demand that they receive a state budget to set up an educational system imparting values, completely severed from what is unique, independently, to the Old Testament, to the Koran and to the New Testament, as well as those values that are common to all. Instead they will teach western, liberal- democratic values, with patriotic leanings to the State of Israel, and it is completely possible, even probable, that they will not raise any objections to marriages taking place between Jew and Arab, especially since the student body will be composed of both Arabs and Jews. In practice this chilling scenario that makes your hairs stand on end, is taking place right now in the most clear-cut way in Neve Shalom, which is in the Latrun district, where a mixed settlement has been set up for the express purpose of integrating Arabs and Jews.

The root of the problem is embedded in the high prestige that is given the Supreme Court Justices in Israel.[100]This status allows them to determine who will succeed their place on the bench. These Justices have become an authoritative body that is immune to any harm and that has the "final word", after the legislator has had his say. Even when the legislature amends legislation which the court's judgment disapproved of this amended piece of legislation is returned to the table of the Supreme Court Justices who again add their interpretation to it as they see fit.[101] Such a scenario has already

---

[100] On the silence of the legal community to utter any criticism against the Supreme Court and on that community's response of standing at attention as if they were clerks of the Supreme Court justices occupying their places to right hand side of the Supreme Court, see the "Books" supplement of *Ha'aretz* 1 September, 1999 edition. There is a book review by Ronen Shamir (an academic, not connected with law, who teaches in the Sociology and Anthropology Department of Tel Aviv University) coinciding with the release of the book *The Court: Fifty Years of the Judiciary in Israel* published by the Court Administrator in conjunction with the Ministry of Defense, and under the title "The H.C.J. and the country that encircles it" Later on *Ha'aretz* conducted an interview with Professor Ruth Gavison who severely criticized the Supreme Court, which was an exceptional incident, and which caused her colleagues to severely criticize her for publishing such remarks.

[101] Israeli judges mainly follow the line of thinking of American judges and at times adopt the thinking of other liberal countries such as Canada which itself is heavily influenced by the USA. See for example Michael Seymour, *Rethinking Nationalism* ed. Jocelyn Coutre, Kai Nielsen (Calgary, Alberta, Canada: Canadian journal of Philosophy, University of Calgary Press), p. 57. The accepted opinion there is that a nationality that makes up for the majority of a liberal state cannot define that state as having the culture of that majority nationality, which would then adopt the idea of "national culture" rather what must be followed is the system of multi-culturalism, in order that minorities or those people who do not have the same culture as that of the majority are not offended. Following this it is

happened as in the *Harris* case in South Africa[102] which is described in my book on the Jewish State.[103]

possible to understand Supreme Court President Barak, who wants to interpret the concept a "Jewish and Democratic State ' in a way that the word Jewish has none of the same detailed application as has the word "democratic".

[102] *Harris v. Minister of Interior* 1952 (2) SA 428; *Minister of Interior v. Harris* 1952 (4) SA

[103] In my book *supra* note 3, *Ibid.* Chapter three, Appendix II.

PART 4:

Ethnic Groups as co-builders with religions of nations

Opening Remarks:

In this part of the book, the standard definitions of the term 'ethnic group', and in relation to it, the terms 'ethnicity', 'nation' and 'nationality' will be reviewed. New definitions will be suggested, though not in the standard fashion used in the last decades of western thinking (hereinafter: The Main Stream). The term '*group of origin*', as will be shown, is not defined in writings on the subject of nation, and will be defined here, within the same framework (hereinafter: The Suggested Theory). The unique definitions of these terms will be the basis for the comparison between the United States and Israel, in relation to the phenomenon of 'inter-group help' [this term will be defined in this part of the book through self evidence]. The similarities and the differences between this last term and that of 'favoritism' will be defined, as they will be found partially congruent. All this will lead to a somewhat surprising conclusion regarding the title of this part of the book.

The term 'nation', and its definition is not, in itself, crucial to the subject of this part of the book, yet it is indirectly essential, by its connection to the terms 'ethnicity' and 'ethnic group'. It is essential also by its role in differentiating between the term 'ethnic-group' from the term 'group of origin'. These three terms: nation, ethnic group, and group of origin are terms of tangent definitions, and for that reason are the focus of extended discussion in this part of the book.

And now to elaborate a little – for the brunt of elaboration will follow in the body of the paper – to pave the way, so to speak, for the extended discussion to follow. This little elaboration contains only the major principles, and no sources of confirmation, for these will come in the body of the paper.
The term studied extensively, much more than the other two above, is that of Nation. This part of the book claims that western thinkers of the mainstream have, unknowingly and meaning well no doubt, set a biased definition of the term. This biased opinion at the base of western thinking is partly due to the weak and difficult grasp of western political leaders (some more than others) of the concept of national identity, and to the resulting 'cover-up' approach to the difficulty at hand , when dealing with the subject. This difficulty has arisen from the internal closeness of western countries, their interchangeability in ethnic and religious matters, and lately the acceptance of English as an international language in many

socioeconomic classes. Another cause is the rising apprehension and estrangement – to varying degrees – felt towards Islam and its culture.

The two world wars – which were mainly internal struggles within the white, Christian culture (with the Ottoman Empire, China and Japan, as appendages to the conflict) have shocked the Christian world of Europe, and led it to the conclusion that they were largely unnecessary – a kind of inter-familial feud. This uniting of the cultural makeup of the Christian world is comparable with the unifying of the United States after the Civil War. It would appear that national unity can be caused not only by a common enemy, but also by past **internal** strife. To make a domestic analogy: a couple surviving a terrible fight is stronger in its union.

This intimacy within the Christian world means, that whatever the actions of their leaders, its people recognize each other as belonging to the same one (albeit diverse) national framework. With this in mind, one can see the mobilizing of the Christian world[1] that followed the attack on the World Trade Center and the Pentagon on Sep 11th 2001, as one more link in a process that began at the end of World War II. Others were the forming of the EU, the warming of Russo-American relations, the break-up of the Soviet Block and the joining of some of its former members in the NATO alliance.

There is an assumption, that all British citizens are of one nation undivided by more than one nation, while assuming the same about the French, Germans, Danes, Italians, Dutch, Spaniards etc', despite the local myths of different ethnic identities, religions, of different group histories, of different wars and different futures. These myths may be common to citizens of two different countries, or to the majority of one and the minority of another. Such is the case with Transilvanians of Hungarian descent, who share the same myths of citizens of Hungary, even though Transilvania has been a part of Romania for years. Writing of people under this assumption would be to write within the mainstream. I do not intend to follow this mainstream, even though it is the dominant and respected

[1]Even though many non-Christian countries have joined the fight declared by the U.S., including Islamic countries fearing fundamentalism, and even Pakistan, these are partly the 'appendage' alliances such as the earlier example of Japan, and partly the actions of regimes disassociated from their populace in their pro-western policies. This undemocratic state of affairs is looked upon with favor by the Christian world, because of its fear of the anti-western uprising that would probably ensue if a true democracy were enacted. It is therefore with fear of just such an uprising that these regimes support the U.S. coalition. At any rate, the U.S. coalition is basically a cultural struggle between the Christian World, and the Fundamental Islam.

strain in literature on the subject nowadays. Another problem is that even those who stress the common group origin, or the historical and religious differences within a group, from within the Stream, do not follow the primordial dimensions alone, but, under the influence of the Stream, as Geertz would say, add non-primordial elements to their work. I will therefore stray from devoutly following the Central primordial writing, and only head in its general direction.

Conforming to the discussion so far, and to the definition of the term 'Nation' in this part, it should be established at this early stage, that Hungarians living in Hungary, Romanian Transilvania, Slovakia and Serbia, are all part of the same nation. In the same way, French of French descent are a nation (excluding Islamic French citizens of North African descent), Romanians not of Hungarian descent are another nation, the British nation does not include the Catholic Irish of Northern Ireland, despite their British citizenship, and that Palestinian Arabs are not part of the Jewish nation.[2] Every nation is recognized by its unique population of common and historically established ethnic myth, and by its homeland (National Territory).[3] Every nation has its expatriate population, that confirms its association with it by its very will to be part of it.

The mainstream, however, is held back by the different concept, that the entire population of every current country in the Christian world in general, and specifically in Europe, is a nation. It will therefore reject the ancient idea of common ethnic myth, history and religion, and seek alternative ideas that conform to its original concept. It is for this reason, that the mainstream will talk about language, problems of inequality within a country, and the recognizing the civilian population as a nation. Civilian population is recognized with nation, and as result, so is the country, as it exists today. Claiming that "the state is the nation", as the mainstream does, is the equivalent of the king of France claiming "the state is me".

Any west European holding to this concept, may have as well looked at his neighboring countries, taken stock of their various and diverse elements, and titled them - 'a nation.' This ironic description is not so far from the truth. We are dealing here, with a concept that precedes the scientific gathering of facts, hypothesizing, and arriving at conclusions in this field. This concept has blinded

---

[2] Under the assumption that it is a sub-nation of the Great White-Christian nation, the same as Saudis, Iraqis, Yemenites, Egyptians, Moroccans and Palestinians are sub-nations of the Greater Arab nation. The subject of sub-nations will be only partially addressed in this part, though it deserves its own discussion.

[3] The term of National Territory will also be addressed later, as part of defining a nation.

western thinkers to the possibility of nations in Europe before the Reformation. And so, taking their concept with them when examining the rest of the world, they have arrived at the amazing conclusion, that there were no nationalities, or nations, in the world before the European concept of the same.

There were no nations in the world earlier than four hundred years ago!

This last opinion holds no water. There was a sense of national identity[4] in the Israelites and Jewish people of millennia past. This type of National-Religious Identity was common with the Assyrians, the Amonites, Moavites, Edomites, Phenicians, Hellenists, Romans, Egyptians, Persians, Medians, Japanese, Chinese, Hungarians, Armenians, Khazars, Arabs (before Mohamed and after), Poles and countless others. The fact that this type of identity was led by priests, nobles or writers of the time, doesn't change the fact that it prevailed throughout different classes of the same national group. Even today, such identity is widespread, in part, thanks to the relatively high levels of literacy. Those Arabs who stormed new territories on horse-(and camel)-back, were probably not the great thinkers of their society, but they did have a united group identity, along with a myth of their common origins, histories, and goals. The Israelites fled before the Moavites, whose national identity was strengthened by their king Mish'ah's sacrifice of his own son to the (national) god, and the zeal for battle that ensued. Mainstream thinkers were probably familiar with this tale, as it is mentioned in the Old Testament, but were still blinded by their preconceptions. This is but one of many cases where intellectuals have been misdirected by the interests of their time and place[5].

---

[4] National-Religious Identity of course, as culture was defined by religion in those days.

[5] I have elsewhere elaborated on the morality of western philosophy, starting with **Kant**. Having removed God from his moral throne, and crowning Man in his place, it has sought to build a system by which Man is validated and encouraged by the absolute power and righteousness of his arbitrary morality. Obviously, this was a political necessity – after all, if morality were easily challenged society would collapse and government would topple. If ruling until now was done objectively 'by the grace of God', something just as powerful would have to be invented by intellectuals – for the sake of political stability. So did **Emanuel Kant** with his 'practical and pure consciousness', meaning: If God was objective, and Man is subjective, then pure and practical thinking must be objective, and therefore obeyed. **Thomas Hobbs** came up with the idea of social convention: Agreements must be honored, and everyone agreed on a king as a way out of the pre-monarchy days of chaos and banditry. This idea (which was supposedly uninfluenced by concerns of flesh and blood) sanctified the rule of monarchy and discouraged rebellion. **Jeremy Bentham** extolled 'the common good' as a basis for a system of government.

A fine example of such misdirection, caused by the interests of the local government, was Lord Akton, who described the British, and Austro-Hungarian Empires as positive vessels for national identity, as opposed to the nation-state.
The ample interest in nation is not just the result of 'The Spring of Nations' of 1848, and its subsequent civil unrest and breakup of the Austro-Hungarian Empire into many ethnic-based nation-states (a term I will discuss further later).
This philosophical interest is also the result of the self interests of European rulers, which existed long before 1848, and long after to strengthen their countries by developing a unique country-specific culture in various ways. Unique historical myth was in the best interests of any government. One instrument to this end was the establishment of a country-specific and pro-current-government church to give said government a non-self serving and spiritual aspect. Examples are the establishment of the Anglican Church in England, the adoption of Catholicism in Franco's Spain, or the forming of the 'State Religion', replacing the divine entity with the concept of The State, in other cases.

The nurturing of national feeling as a method of government was used well before the Spring of Nations by the Monarchy of France, which enforced the Parisian language on its outlying Gallic provinces. It would appear that the Germanic Saxons dwelled not only in the area known to us as Germany, but also in England and were even the backbone of the feudal monarchy in France. In addition to political maneuverings, the advent of the print industries has had a big effect in establishing common languages in large areas, according to Anderson's research. Seeking bigger profits in establishing a wide range of readership, the industry worked to unify related languages into common languages, which then began to form ideas of common nation within speakers of the same language.
Many factors were eventually responsible for the state of affairs in the late 20th century – that of many European countries that are not based of common histories,

---

John Stuart Mill pressed the superiority of the spirit of man, and the indispensability of freedom. **Jean-Jacques Rousseau** promoted the rights of the state community as precedent to those of the individual. **Ronald Dvorkin** explained the impotance of the individual over the community as opposed to **Charles Taylor, David Miller, Michael Sandel, Merilyn Friedman,** and **Amy Gutman,** who sanctified the community above the selfish needs of the individual. The **Post-Modern** current arrived after all these. According to **Richard Rorety**, modern man has grown used to putting his interests over everything else. Following **Nietzsche,** objectivism has been abandoned in favor of subjectively following the needs of a liberal society: if a certain liberal society acts in a manner it feels to be right, according to its own interests, it will set its own irrefutable morality.

centuries old, but on groups-of-origin of certain ethnic origin (in the sense of blood-relation in congress with a group religion, language and history which are special and separate from other neighboring groups). In Belgium, the common denominator of both the Flemish and the Volunians is the Catholic faith. Their ethnic backgrounds and languages are different, even though there did exist a brief period of common group history. Britain consists of four groups, three of which are Protestants, with a common language. Their common history is merely average-length on a historical time scale, and the diverse ethnic origins, and the dominance of the English group definitely stand in the way of any feeling of unity. In Germany there is a common ethnicity, but alongside the ruling Protestantism there is a significant Catholic population. Group history is not homogenous, and filled with many splits along the time line of government. Despite the unified German language and culture there is a certain inter-mingling with the English ethnic background. The north and south of Spain are ethnically very different, as are the corresponding regions in Italy. Scandinavia has a common group history, but is split by differences in language and culture.

Western Europe can be seen as one culture, divided only by its myriad languages, and that used to be, before the Reformation, a single Catholic entity, under a central, Latin-speaking leadership. The split has ensued in the ruling and priest classes, rather than in the masses. These two leading castes, along with other interest groups (a prominent one was the print industry) are the ones who designed the national diversity, solidified the separate governmental frameworks, and convinced the masses of their national uniqueness, based in political guidelines.

True, the Protestant churches have led the masses to believe in recognizing their own history and uniqueness within their state framework. In England, and later in Britain, there formed a unique identity of being 'the chosen' people, and of a 'divine mission' of 'the free man' to involved himself in government via parliament. The existence of a national-religious enemy: the Catholic French was no less important in forming this identity, than Protestantism itself. In this respect, the English (and later the British) 'nations' were built 'from the bottom', rather than by governmental direction or by the interests of the printing industry. Reading the Bible had become a hallmark of British culture, not because the print shops were seeking profit by printing it in English, but vise versa, the printing industry, as an effect, rather than a cause, profited by this English habit.
In the same sense, the wars on the invading Catholic French, were not part of some 'scheme' of a monarch seeking to solidify his/her rule by unifying his/her subjects under the flag of war.

Nationality[6] is a belief of the members of a group who define themselves as a nation, and who seek autonomous political rule in a specific territory. This definition is only legitimate if this subjective belief stems from objective factors that 'grew from the bottom' in a spontaneous fashion. This growth must happen on a long-enough period on a historical time-line, with the framework of a group ethos of the existence of common origins [which is the Ethnic Ethos, on which I will elaborate later]. In addition, it is preferable that there be common cultural factors, such as a common religion, and that along said historical time-line, the aforementioned group have a common goal, and even a common enemy. One last condition, is that these historical conditions be relevant in the present, and are expected to continue in the foreseeable future. Once again, this is not the popular definition in the accepted literature on the subject of nation and nationality. I disagree with said literature, and feel free to dispute it, even though I may quote from it occasionally, for the simple reason that it was heavily influenced by the interests of western culture, from whence it comes. It will be necessary for me to analyze this main stream of literature, before I dispute it, but after disputing and justifying the dispute, I shall be free to carve out new definitions, by the strength of my explanations.

In light of the new understanding I will propose, that of the above 'growing from beneath' view of true nation, the definition must be complete, with regard to the ethos of a common origin, as an ethnic ethos. This will bring us to understanding ethnicity, and the definition of an ethnic group, as well as a group-of-origin (which resembles an ethnic group but lacks the ethnic element).

Western writings on the subject of nation, have always used the term 'ethnic group' within the context of 'nations', and therefore I will not follow its example, as I reject the popular definition of a 'nation' [not including the primordial current, which may share some common terms with my work]. Considering the essential connection between the definition of 'nation' and ethnic ethos, and considering that this definition implies that an 'ethnic group' is one seeking independent governmental definition, it becomes self-evident, that the difference between a 'nation' and an 'ethnic group', is that an ethnic group is a group with a common origin ethos, and which does not seek self-rule within a specific territory. Seeking such self rule would turn the ethnic group into a nation. To put it in a mathematical way: Ethnic Group = Nation – Will for Independent Statehood. In other words, a nation that loses its will for independent statehood, becomes an ethnic group. So considering the reality of Europe's economic union, it can be

[6] And here I introduce and summarize what I will prove later, so as to push the discussion in the right direction.

said that once France loses its coin, it will also lose its ability to run separate foreign or defense policies, other then those of the EU, and bend its laws irreversibly to the regulations of the common European market. It will become an ethnic group.

An ethnic group[7] is a group, whose members believe in their unique common origin. As mentioned above` if it develops a longing for self-governance, it becomes a nation. But what about those who believe in a common origin, but do not see themselves as separate from other groups with other origins? If it is inconceivable that any of them wish for separate self governance, they become one nation, or one ethnic group. One nation (or group) which is divided internally into different groups of origin. An excellent example is that of the Israeli citizens of different ethnic origins, such as Romanians, Moroccans, Yemenites and Poles. All live in Israel and consider themselves a part of the Jewish Nation. A single ethnic group, a single nation - despite its diverse origins. It seems to me, that since it is unlikely that Jews of Romanian origin would ever wish to form a self governing entity within – but separate of - the state of Israel, they should be considered a group of origin, and not an ethnic group.

A special question is raised by the status of the different immigrant peoples which form the citizenry of the United States, and who see themselves as members of the American Nation. They are unlikely to ask for self governance, and therefore should be considered to be groups of origin, rather than ethnic groups. Yet the contact which they keep with their countries of origin is quite different from that of Romanian Jews living in Israel. Romanian immigrants do not consciously consider Romania as their nation-state, nor do they feel they have changed their nation by immigrating to Israel, for they see themselves as having been members of the Jewish Nation before their immigration. In this they are different from Christian Romanians naturalized in the US, who have changed their nationality in the process. In this part of the book, we will discuss weather these American groups are ethnic groups or just groups of origin.

Chapter A:
The term 'nation' as defined by Western thinkers

The mainstream of western thinkers see 'nation' as a new type of creature, born in 17th century Europe. According to this strain of thought, there was no nation in previous human history. This presumption molds the term of nation into a shape that does not use the ethnic myth a foundation. In its place they assume media, economics, interests, language and other causes that indeed play a part in the

---

[7] Here too, I precede summery to discussion, in order to focus the discussion to come.

forming of a nation in Europe and North America – though, as I will suggest, the latter are but partial successes, which are already undergoing a process of deterioration, having failed to supply a well founded base of national feeling, in the face of difficulty through history.

A marked difference is to be seen between the established nation of the Jewish nation on the one hand, and the French nation on the other. The Jewish nation has faced the difficulties of exile many times, for centuries, waiting for the proper time to gather its expatriates to the very territory that has rested in its collective awareness as the national home. Using its well rooted image of nation it has resurrected its ancient language and set up home in its motherland. It is inconceivable, that the French nation could withstand such trials. What is more: the French nation has shown a certain slackness in this respect in the years after World War II, by assuming the part of a White-Christian cultural entity in western Europe. This entity is gradually accepting governing roles [partial at this stage] so as to put forth the following question – Are the French not going through a process of national image, through which their national identity moves from being French to being West-European? With the exceptions of Belgium, a Canton of Switzerland, and Qu bec, the French language is the national language of the French nation, a crucial ingredient, in addition to French culture and Catholicism (though this nation encompasses about six million Muslims, a small number of Jews and practitioners of other religions). The French territory is fairly well defined, despite its ill-fated attempt to stretch across the sea.

On this occasion of delineating the mainstream of western thinking and criticizing said stream, I will also present theories about the United States, which in my opinion, is part of the great White-Christian nation, which potentially even stretches across the steppes of Russia. A sign of this can be seen in the wondrous attraction between Washington and Moscow, despite an era of abysmal rivalry, and even a nearing of social and economical philosophies in the US and Russia.

The nearing of these two separate countries, as that of all White-Christian countries, is instrumental to their internal organization, on the basis of 'Civil Religion' – that which separates divine religion from government and holds the government to itself [a kind of fundamental zealousness, which stands – after the attack on the Twin Towers of 9/11 – indirect conflict with Islamic fundamentalism, as will be explained later].

The very idea that nation was formed in Europe in the modern era qualifies as an amazing kind of blindness – which in itself provides clear proof of the skewing of mainstream western thinking (hereinafter: the mainstream). This skewing has probably come about innocently, in the same way that Israeli Supreme Court judges are certain of their honesty, while adopting a line of judgment that makes them supreme rulers on Israel[8].

Now, the prominent figures of the main stream will be reviewed:

Ernest Gelner [9]

Gelner claims that man has gone through three stages of development – Pre-agrarian, Agrarian and Industrial. The first has no political organization, in the second it is possible and it is essential to the third. The problem of nationality does not come into play so long as there is no state. Belonging to a state is not an essential part of being human, but has become one today.

Gelner gives two alternative definitions to the term Nation:

1. **Objective-Cultural:** Two people are of the same nation only if they are of the same culture. Culture is defined as a system of terms, signs, associations and behavioural and communication patterns.
2. **Subjective-Intentional:** Two people are of the same nation only if they recognize each other as such. In other words, nation is caused by man. Nation is the product of human beliefs, loyalties and fraternities. The condition is that they all recognize mutual responsibilities and rights among them.

According to Gelner, the agrarian society is ruled by a minority, besides which literacy is rare. A class of author/priests is established (eunuchs in some societies), which mingles little with other classes. In the Islam, author/priests had the missionary role of conversion. This enabled a certain openness of the class, although in practice only a few actually infiltrated it.[10]

On the subject of industrial society, Gelner disagrees with Webbers opinion of the relationship between Capitalism and Protestantism, but agrees that rationalism is an important component of such a society, in addition to the regularity and efficiency that lead to said rationalism. This society is built on productivity,

---

[8] See: **Who's afraid of a Jewish State? A Constitutional and Ideological Look,** by Yehuda Cohen (Tel-Aviv: The Attorneys' Publication 2001)

[9] Ernest Gelner, **Nations and Nationalism** translated to Hebrew by Dan Daor (Tel-Aviv: Open University, 1994, originally printed in 1983)

[10] Ibid. pages 31-37.

changing work distribution (though not through blood-ties, as in agrarian society) and economical mobility. This society is based on equality and freely available education. In this respect, the whole society becomes one big author/priest class, where communication is frequent and precise, culture becomes mobile, common and homogenous. State and culture are intertwined, and it is through the identity formed around this axle, that a nation of all the states citizens is formed.[11] An industrial state cannot function, unless it has a mobile, literate and culturally standardized population. The state organizes different ethnic groups and unites them. Thus are nations born. (Divine) Religion has lost its status because priests have only taken to preserve rituals rather than social unity. This society cannot be looked at through a divine prism. That having been said, this new society has its own ailments: Society becomes anonymous, and individuals are turned into changeable atoms. Members of ethnic group A may be cast aside while members of group B hold central and ruling positions. When this happens, the previously unimportant ethnicity comes to life and members of group A seek independent statehood.[12]

By digressing from the industrial niche and moving to cultural development, Gelner is saying that higher societies tend to become the basis for a new nationality (as in Algeria) while before the appearance of nation, it was mainly religion that defined the underprivileged from the privileged. An Algerian nation, according to Gelner, would not have existed, without the national awakening in the 20th century. There would have been an Islamic community, with some smaller communities around, but there would have been no definition of Algerian Muslims as group in and of themselves. The same has happened with the Palestinians with regard to the land of Israel (Palestine), where language and history serve as a national adhesive. He goes on to say that with regard to (divine) religion, the Islamic culture in the agrarian age is an obvious example of his theory (Gelner's), in that agrarian cultures do not tend to use culture to define political groups, and do not therefore, tend to be nationalistic. The loose guild of the *Olamah*, the educated-attorneys-theologians, that set the tone in the Islamic world, and ruled it morally, has crossed ethnic and political boundaries, and was never attached to any state.[13]

Gelner sees, with regard to the status of old religions in the modern age, three different modes of development, regarding Islam, Confucianism, Christianity in the West, and he even addresses the situation in dark Africa.

---

[11]Ibid, pages 38-61.
[12]Ibid, pages 79-90.
[13]Ibid, pages 105-106.

Western Christianity has retreated from the throne, since there was a transition from the agrarian age to an industrial one in the Christian world. This transition included setting a common language in relatively wide political territories and raising the culture level, processes which brought about a process of secularism, excepting Franco's Spain, that adopted Catholicism as the state religion [Gelner doesn't say so specifically, but it would seem he is saying that the economic-capitalistic-ruling interest created a secular unity in each country in the form of a civilian religion in that state]. Gelner says that the reformation in North-Western Europe turned society as a whole, at first, to a class of author/priests, and unified the spoken language with the language of ritual.

The Education Movement turned this big author/priest class secular, and the language became a national language. In general, he is talking about the industrial age being based on economic growth, which in turn depended on the cognitive growth established by Descartes, which stated that any meaningful claim about the world cannot be absolute, and that all proclamations must be tested by criteria outside any system of belief. This approach is the reverse of the absoluteness that characterizes divine religions. It is the secular approach of doubting everything. And indeed subjectivism and doubt have become the hallmark of the secular West, instead of the sureness and faith that marked the rule of religion over mankind.[14]

The Islamic world, according to Gelner, was spared the western subjective doubts, because the Islam, unlike Cristianity, showed great internal flexibility. Islam developed two faces. One faces the more severe and individualistic educated urbanites. The other faces the people of different countries and groups of religious and social diversity. The Islam therefore, was not rooted out, but has taken root even deeper in the nationality of Islamic people.[15]

The culture of the Far East, under the influence of the hierarchal Confucianism, could not stand the equality dictated by the modernism. Confucianism was fine for the agrarian way of life, but not for modern life.[16]

Dark Africa has not adopted the Western way of national unification within each state, and even the acceptance of global religions has not aided the process. The process of a local culture being adopted as the culture of a whole state hasn't

[14] Ibid, page 108.
[15] Ibid, page 110.
[16] Ibid, page 111.

happened either. There is no unity in dark Africa. Dark Africa is an enigma to Gelner.[17]

Benedict Anderson[18]

Anderson (henceforth: the author) defines a nation as an imagined political community, whose imaginary boundaries are the result of three factors: the specific territory, the concrete political sovereignty and an identifiable community. This would be, then, a fantasy held within a real triangle. The described sides of the triangle are present and well-known in the familiar European reality, but it turns out, through the writing, that if the author means in 'imaginary' something that is an antithesis to 'real', his definition runs into a problem later on, as will be explained.

The author correctly identifies the decline of religion with the rise of nationality, but why does he fear seeing these two as cause and effect? Had the author adopted a sociological or anthropological approach, he would not have had difficulty connecting his remarks on the human suffering caused by religion[19] with the psychological support derived by belonging to a nation. I suggest that religion, despite its occasional aiding to the design of nation, as it did in England, was removed from any central political position. I believe that this removal of religion was the result of a feeling of its power and of the principal that there is no room for two kings in one kingdom. There was a need to choose between religion and nation, the latter being served well by the 'civilian religion' which worships the state in the same way divine religion worshiped the standard deity. This exchange of divine religion for civilian religion is also dependant on diverting ethical thought, ethics being the main conditioner of human behavior by right of the human process of integrating ethical codes into their being. In view of this evidence, western philosophy has sought to replace emotional-religious-divine ethics with secular, or scientific-secular ethics, in the likes of Dewy's system, which I will review later.

The author explains extensively the spreading of Islam through Arabic writing, in which the Koran is written[20], or the verbal duplicity of Christian clergy, who spoke both Latin and the common tongue of their region – a duplicity intended to show Europeans the clergy's direct access to God, whose language is different from that

---

[17] Ibid, pp. 112-113.

[18] R. Benedict Anderson, **Imaginary Communities,** Tel-Aviv: Open University Publishing, 2000, translated into Hebrew by Dan Dower, Second Hebrew Edition. Original published by Verso, New Left Books, London, 1983.

[19] Ibid, page 40.

[20] Ibid, page 42.

of Men, and that only priests can speak, read or write it. Thus, according to the author, did the clergy prove the authenticity of their rhetoric as the direct word of God.[21] The author compounds this with the reason for the decline of religion in the west. According to him, this happened because religion existed on an imaginary plane, removed from real life. Nationality rose as an imaginary concept better linked to reality than religion.[22] The author speaks of the changing character of the novel, and of the characteristics of the newspaper, as better conduits between man and reality.

The author speaks of the phenomenon of relationship between people who do not know each other. This relationship is like a common framework of consciousness. All these people, who do not know one another, form, in their opinion a single nation. This, in the author's opinion, is an action of the imagination. What the author doesn't address in his paper is that the imaginary relationships formed by the novel and the newspaper did create a feeling of nationality, but not as a building with no foundations. Rather, the foundation existed long before the existence of the novel or the book (an imagined framework, granted, but with very real foundations of historical facts) in the form of ancient ethnic background and history. The new nation was built on some form of existing foundation. These foundations, and even the old myths, have been intertwined by some ancient blood-relation, some ancient historical events, part imagination, part actual.

Why has Anderson ignored all these? Why did he build a theory completely disconnected from the old framework?

Using a current example from the reality close to the state of Israel, it is true that the Palestinians adopted a national consciousness out of conscious stimulation from the Jewish nation that invaded their space, but this is not enough to deny the old roots that existed long before the Palestinians could define them in terms on nation.

Members of the Palestinian nation that live part in Judea and Samaria, part in the Gaza strip, part in Jordan, Syria, Lebanon, Israel and other places, have all a common ethnic background, history, language and emotional makeup that separates them from other people and they characterize all Palestinians. Their future is bound together, and they have a common enemy [although only partially, as most Palestinian Israelis do not see Israel as their enemy]. According to this example, their conscious definition as a single nation is based in reality, not

[21] Ibid, page 46.

[22] Ibid, pp. 53-54.

fantasy. Therefore, changes in the writing styles of novels can only effect (national) imagination partially.

According to the description the author gives of the forming of national languages, it is usually not by governmental decree, but by the forming of languages 'from below' and their amalgamation caused by print house-managing capitalists seeking to expand their industry by printing to a wide section of people. This brought them to assemble related languages into single, printed languages. But, contrary to the author's opinion, it should be remembered, that the existence of a language is not an imaginary fact, but a circumstance that creates the opportunity for discourse within a populace. It has nothing to do with imagination. Discourse is a fundamental element of establishing emotional contact between people. A national relationship is an emotional one. Emotional contact is not fiction, but fact. In the same way that familial relation is no figment of the imagination, so is the case with national relation. If we follow the author's reasoning, my belonging to a certain family has, until today, been only my imagination, and my relationship with my parents, siblings, children and grandchildren fiction. This theory has no basis in reality. For my (emotional) belonging to my family to be fictional, so must my relation to them be.

It would be well to add a remark concerning the role of television today, to the author's theory on the development of languages. Since televised reviews are international, emotional language becomes international, and the national ties separating nations from each other must weaken. International discourse, including UN resolutions, international forces, international organizations of various (for human rights and other subjecs) – all these contribute to the creation of a generic inter-human 'nation'. This may not come about soon, but it is an ongoing process, and we are part of it. Even American movies and culture - including the morality which may be leading us to this 'human nation' – are turning the world into a global village that erases separate national emotional differences – albeit slowly. Of course, if there is any basis to the method I prefer (following primordial thinkers), then the vision of a global nation should never be realized.

Ernest Haas [23]

Haas says that a nation is a group of people who seek to establish a framework of self definition (a state) and that these people are held together by origin symbols. The dismantling of nation is possible, and likely, when the people realize these heretofore unique symbols are shared by other groups. A national state is a

[23] Ernst B. Haas, **Nationalism, Liberalism, and Progress,** vol. I Chapter Two (Cornell University Press) pp. 22-60.

political entity, whose inhabitants consider themselves to be a nation and wish to remain within a separate political framework. The nation is sustained from the existence of a common enemy, common values and logically arranged institutions. Logic is the principle guideline in many areas, including nationality. It is even involved in the establishment of a national ideology. In this case, nationality leads to modernization, linking science to industry, educating the masses, social mobility and identifying the state with the nation. This development leads to over-adherence to state laws, extensive involvement in state political activities and the prevention of the concentration of wealth within a minority. Haas says nation in the west is liberal, but that nations exist, in the east and Latin America, that aren't. Haas mentions Nagata, who published a paper in 1981, defending the idea of ethnologically-based nations. The paper claims that national identity is built on a mixture of feelings and interests. Haas criticizes this approach, saying it is too vague, and that it replaces the theory of nations with a theory of ethnic 'gut feelings'. Instead of ethnicity, Hass proposes the element of discontent as a catalyst of nationalistic claims. In other words, ethnic relations do not create nation, but feelings of discrimination can lead to the emotions necessary for political separatism. The equality motif plays a part here. The effort to better the income of a group, the demand for better opportunity for a group, the demands for canceling segregation and equality in the eyes of the law – are all key elements in the area of nationality and national separation. The demand for equality defines the borders of group solidarity, and sometimes does so in relation to symbols of group culture. Sometimes, class distinction plays a part in the area of nation, sometimes there is a correlation between a certain occupation and a national identity, such as the Welsh identified with coal miners in Britain, the Untouchables with street cleaners in India and Blacks with household staff in Brazil. Status, in the cases above, serves as a measure of identity, which in turn confirms to the issue of nationality. In conclusion, Haas says that equality is a sign of group solidarity.

Thus he puts solidarity on the same level as self interest.

Haas goes on to say that spoken language and common culture play a part in the area of nation. As for the ethnological element, Hass asks why the Soviet Union and Yugoslavia broke apart along ethnic-national lines in 1991, but Spain, Britain and France did not. He arrives at the conclusion that in some places the elite of a group enjoys economic prosperity, and that this elite status is relatively easily gained, and this is the reason for the difference. To primordial thinkers he says: 'How is ethnicity different from any other cultural ingredient?' Therefore, Haas does not accept the difference between social national identity, and ethnic national identity. Haas defines a national ideology as one founded by a group of thinkers and burdened with a political agenda. This ideology has a plan of action. The existence of more than one national movement in the same group means a failure of the logic behind them, in that it could not bring the whole of the group into one, successful plan of action [in this, Haas attaches national emotion to intellect and reason, and confirms the superiority of intellect over emotion, as far as he is concerned]. When a certain ideology is successfully integrated with the entire state, it becomes a myth. As for national ideology, Haas, following Gelner, sees the subject as a developing process, strongest in the agricultural society, and leaning towards the principals of logic in the industrial society, with liberal ideology as the peak of development. There is a difficulty, according to Haas, with an ideological, illogical revolution. He mentions in this context the liberal Whigs and Jacobites, the former (such as John Stuart Mil and Nehru), who spoke of continuing historical legitimization, and the latter who spoke of cultural homogenizing form earlier generations. Nevertheless, both currents agree that the ideal relationship between liberal nations is peace, while both justify war and conquest by a liberal state against a non-liberal state, using the false justification that it is for the good of the conquered. As a rule, Haas finds that logic being the rule in politics is self-evident, in that national rulers always worked to further their own interests, preferring them to their ideology. The co-existence of divine and civilian religion is impossible, according to Haas, for one is the mortal enemy of the other, and that civilian religion, in the form of nation has won.

However, Haas maintains that as long as religion remains private (out of public and political affairs) it is tolerable. In this vein, there should not be any danger in American congress members paying regular visits to their respective houses of worship. The winning state religion is secular. Haas notes that in the U.S., civilian religion is fed both by Rousseau's ideas of a civil religion, and by the divine-religion concept of transcendental linkage, and says that the Christian-Jewish morality absorbed into American culture has founded the civilian religion there, as did Catholicism in Spain. Haas goes on to say, that liberalism was founded in the lap of nation, and could not have evolved without it. As for the future, Haas predicts a transformation from single-nation states, to a more cosmopolitan future. His prediction is based, he says, on the state of affairs in Western and North-American countries, and in Japan. Logic demands such a prediction, as global economic circumstances do not hold a future for loner states. The organizing of states could be known as a 'social contract', according to Haas, or a 'New Society'. At any rate, the direction for humanity is that of the loss of financial sovereignty for different states.

Michael Hechter [24]

Michael Hechter has contributed the idea of Internal Imperialism to the discussion of nation. According to him, every country in Europe was originally populated by different cultures, and eventually one predominant culture expanded at the expense of its peripheral neighbors. Even though the influence was mutual, Hechter claims that central influence was the greater of the two, setting the standards in law, family relations, agriculture, religion, administrative government and lifestyle. The danger lies in an imbalance favoring the center, especially during periods of modernization and industrial development. Lacking a cultural merging of the center and its peripheries, there is little wonder when discrimination against the peripheries results in movements of national separatism.

The solution of overexposing the different cultural elements within a country sometimes backfires in the form of intra-group hostility. A cultural merger is easier to achieve in industrial societies, within the economic framework of the state. The recommended solution would be to raise the cultural level of the peripheries, thus increasing the mobility of the periphery towards the center, thus softening the contrasts between center and periphery. A gradual equalizing will also aid in eliminating the discrimination against the periphery.

What arises from this approach, is that 'the curse of nationality' should be handled by preventing the short-changing of various ethnic elements in a state that has ethnic or national diversity. Ergo, the ethnic 'demon' can be restrained with economic and other special interest measures, such as the prevention of partiality on other than purely economical levels. Hechter does not see nation as necessary, but rather as a hindrance, and believes that it can be countered by self-serving measures.

J. C. D. Clark [25]

Clark claims that there was no nation in the Anglo-Saxon world, on both sides of the Atlantic, in the years 1660-1832, but that a progress towards nationality was taking place. This progress was furthered along by the French revolution, and the romantic reactionary movement that followed it. It consisted mainly of factors such as the establishment of the Church of England, which separated England

---

[24] See: Michael Hechter, **Internal Colonialism - The Celtic Fringe in British National Development, 1536-1966** (Berkeley and Los Angeles, University of California Press) pp. 3-43.

[25] See J. C. D. Clark, **The Language of Liberty 1660-1832, Political discourse and social dynamics in the Anglo-American world** (Cambridge: Cambridge University Press, 1994) pp. 46-62.

from other protestant countries, and above all, despite the faith in English ethnicity, the combination of Law and Religion. The feeling of a great unique group-oriented religious mission that developed in England, was carried on by the Puritans in America. Myths surrounding the Protestant enclaves during the Catholic reign of Queen Mary, also contributed to the building of the English sense of group. The myth, of the English being the first to accept Christianity in the true spirit of the scriptures, and of England being the first to welcome the Protestant reformation was created. Fox, who held no particularly national-oriented views himself, dubbed the English: 'the chosen people'. Law, too, had a role in the development of nation, in the sense that English law set the standard for the sovereign-subject relationship after the mold of Deity-believer, or father-son hierarchies. It was a legal ruling that established what parliament refused to proclaim: that anyone born in Scotland after the sixth union with the English Crown, as the English termed it, under James I (1603), will be considered to be a subject of England, as though he were born to English parents in England. It was of this, that the connection between loyalty and obeisance, and from the latter principal rose the link between loyalty and citizenship – which stands at the root of English nation – nation as a form of loyalty to the king. It has been repeatedly stated that the link between king and subject is as the link between mind and body, a link that requires total devotion – this concept is very clearly based in religious imagery. By separating the English from the rest of Christian Europe, who were under Roman law, English law has made the English unique in their own eyes. This pattern of thought left little room for discussion of ethnicity or language, which, while still hanging in the background, was of lesser importance.

As for North America, severing the link to the English king in 1776 and the French king in 1789 has forced a new structure of self-identity. This was achieved slowly and arduously, on the basis of common language, culture and, partially, common ethnic background. Loyalty was surrendered to The State as an abstract concept. After their independence, Americans demanded a declaration of loyalty from all immigrants, and considered it to be a sort of secular contract that replaced the concept of loyalty to the king. The concept by which a man was free to offer his loyalty to a new country was developed, and on its foundation, the concept of territorially-based loyalty, or the love of the land, a concept much encouraged by the Protestant church of England. This too, contributed to the solidifying of the American local nationality. American nation was raised in the lap of the Bible, which was full of national concepts readily adapted to American needs. It also drew from the concept of personal freedom that evolved in England during its 17th century rebellions. Even so, back in 1776 there were no real differences between the English in England, and the Americans, and so the rebellion against the

English crown did not really result in a new American nation. Benjamin Franklin wrote in1760, that a union of the 14 colonies against Britain was futile, since each colony had its own laws, interests, religious practices, customs and system of local government, but once the rebellion had started and succeeded, a new spirit emerged, and the concept of 'America' rose to sweep them all in.
Clark compares the aforementioned situation in America, to the situation in France, which, in his opinion, shared many similarities with the former. The French spoke of common religion and customs, and passed over ethnic origin and the problem of language differences. The French even defined the Catholic sovereignty in their country as a unique element of France – the French king was thought of as the most Catholic of them all, which set the French apart and nurtured their own special consciousness.

These descriptions of Clark's reflect the difficulty in the establishment of a nation in England and in the United States, where the ethnic motive has no real part, and other motives that were to be found were decidedly thin – yet there was, in all this, a will to create a nation. One of the signs of this almost desperate attempt to form a nation were the songs sang by English soldiers, such as *God Save The King* and *Rule Britannia*, which surfaced mainly in order to accent the difference between English Protestantism and Hanoverian Protestantism, a difference not easy to define. To summarize, Clark conveys, in his writing, the difficulties accompanying the Anglo-Saxon world to this day.

Linda Colly[26]

Colly attempts to confront the issue of designing the British nation, which includes the Welsh, Scots and English, from the time of the law that united Scotland and Wales under the English crown, until the beginning of the Victorian period in 1837. She stresses Britain's military victories over France as a constructive factor to Britain's nation. The beginning of the period was difficult, since in 1778 the French helped the Americans break away from British rule, and the Americans, in turn, declared themselves to be better, more liberated, and more Protestant than the British. In Britain itself there was much internal strife, beginning in the first half of the 18th century, with the Jacobite supporters, and those opposing the war with the Americas after 1775, and with those who supported peace with the French republicans, or with Napoleon after1793. War with the French had special significance for the British. They found the French to be superstitious, militant,

[26] See: Linda Colley, **Britons, Forging the Nation 1707-1837** (London: Yale University Press, 1992)

decadent and constrained. In their own eyes, the British fought to preserve their freedom. They constructed myths for themselves, based on their island-bound status, and believed that they were designed by God as a self sufficient people, destined to be separated from the rest of Europe. They nurtured their own special brand of Protestantism.

Up to 1829, British Catholics, could not vote for, or be members of either of the two houses of parliament, and were even burdened with penal taxation. The 1689 tolerance law made things easier for non-conformist Protestants but not for Catholics. This ease was conditioned by the said Protestant's acceptance of the Holy Trinity. National holidays linked to Protestantism were established, as was a prayer commemorating the execution of King Charles I. The return of the monarchy in 1660 is still celebrated today, as is the induction of King George of Hanover in 1714, William of Orange's coming to England in 1688, and the combined prevention of war by both parliament and by King James I, in 1605. These patriotic holidays were celebrated by British protestants as a thanks to the Lord keeping his vigil over Britain, and aiding it, thus proving that she is unique above all other countries. Hatred of Catholics unified the English, Scots, Welsh and especially the lower classes. 1892 saw the Welsh petition march against Catholic emancipation. Huguenot refugees, persecuted for their Protestant believes, made the English ever more aware of Catholic ruthlessness, and thus compounded their own hatred for Catholics.

The 18th century Spanish Inquisition was also active against Protestants. Treatment of Protestants within the Austro-Hungarian Empire in the beginning of the 18th century was also very harsh. All this only strengthened the British faith in its own Protestant Church, its nation, and its current treatment of Catholics. Fox's book about martyrs during the reign of Catholic Queen Mary was met with great popularity. The British linked their success in World War II with their Protestant Church, and spoke much of the divine providence that watched over British soldiers evacuated in private boats from Dunkirk. The famous picture of a Protestant church standing unscathed among the rubble after the German Blitz bombing, symbolized Britain's sacred status as a people chosen by God. It is recorded, how the audiences attending Handel's concerts behaved in a church-going manner, holding their programs like prayer books. The British public believed that it was blessed with its Church, with more freedom and wealth than any other nation, and ignored the fact, that London housed more prisons than any other city in Europe. Even though 19th century Britons were poor, they still believed they had more than the inhabitants of any other country, certainly more than the Catholic French. There is the story of a Scottish priest visiting a Catholic church in Spain, who heard a weeping sound as he approached the altar. He scornfully describes the Catholic priests seeing this as a miracle, and claims it is proof of their idiocy. There were, though, a few objective facts supporting Britain's advantages. In the years between 1700 and up to the French revolution, France suffered no less than 16 cross-country famines, and there was at least one starving county in France every year during this period. Britain knew no famine during those years. Britain had fewer land tenants than France, and was doing better commercially. Trade was brisk in Britain, and coupled with a steady urbanization, it made Britain (excluding Wales for this matter) unique among 18th century Europe.

Britain was also doing better in the area of the printed word. Edinburgh had become a world center of the printing industry, which later spread to London and Wales. Whereas French journalism began in the last quarter of the 18th century, Britain's firs newspaper came out in 1702. Newspapers drove the idea of their being part of Great Britain into the consciousness of British readers, and instilled in them a sense of pride. Britons knew that Catholicism meant blocking the mass access to the Bible, and trusting to the priesthood to explain and decipher the scriptures to the people as it saw fit. Being able, and required, to read the Bible in independent fashion, Britons saw themselves free of clerical intervention in their worshipping, and thus, that their widespread literacy set them above Catholic nations. It was thus, that the British concept of loyalty was transferred from King to Country. So much so, that the King was now required to be loyal to Britain.

In summery, Colly manages to explain how reading of the Bible gave the British a sense of freedom, which led to public interest and involvement in Parliament, which, in turn increased the sense of freedom and a self controlled destiny, and the concept of loyalty to the State, rather than to the King. A wide base of literacy developed not only the printing industry, but also trade, social mobility and urbanization. A successful economy raised the sense of nationality, and of divine providence, in the sense of a chosen people, not unlike the children if Israel in the widely-read scriptures. All this led to the establishment of a proud, thriving and even successfully modern Britain. Regarding the question: What creates nation? Is it the distant past, or events of economical and military value? Colly leans towards the latter. The question of how long can such nation survive has been discussed above already. Colly is undoubtedly part of the Christian main stream in the sense of understanding the term 'nation'.

Michael Lind[27]

Lind sees the question of American nationality as an unsolvable problem, with no real characteristics, apart from its being crisis-prone, and it's adopting of new ideologies after each crisis. He counts three revolutions so far: 1) The war of independence of 1776, 2) The Civil war, which ended in 1865 and 3) The civil rights revolution that ended in 1972. He predicts another revolution: 4) The revolution of merging races and classes, to happen at the beginning of the 21st century. Lind raises the question: Are Americans a nation, or are they a nation of nations, in accordance with their internal diversity, which can be compared to a group of different nations? To those who say that the U.S. is a Western culture, one could answer that a good look at its Latino-American population makes more of a Latin-Christian culture, in the sense of Ancient Rome, than a Western Protestant country, in the sense of other Protestant countries.

Universalists believe, that the U.S. is not a nation state, but rather a nation-less, Conceptual State, based on abstract, democratic and liberal philosophies. Others fear the Balkanization of the US and the eruption of conflicts between the mix of races, cultures, and nations that have made the US their home. While others counter that a nation can comprise various races, cultures, ethnic groups, ideologies, and national goals.

It is difficult to establish a nation on an idea, all the more so an idea that is not unique to that nation, but that is shared by many nations.

It is also problematic founding a nation on a mission. A nation may devote itself to a particular mission, but this mission cannot define it. While many Americans would certainly claim that they are a nation, their position may only reflect a fear that an answer to the contrary would lead to the conclusion that the US has been fractured by the multitude of cultures living in its midst.

A common government also does not sustain a nation indefinitely. Rome, the Ottomans, the Hapsburgs, and the USSR all turned into prisons for their nations until ultimately they collapsed.

A true nation is a specific historic community that exists in reality, defined first and foremost by a common language, customs, and culture. These aspects have already existed for the Americans for hundreds of years. What interferes with US nationalism is its negative attitude to Nazi German nationalism, and their fear of nationalistic, despotic regimes that stems from events of WWII.

Most Americans reject any definition of the American nation that is based on religion or race, but accept one that is founded in liberal ideology and an American

---

[27] See Michael Lind, **The Next American Nation: The New Nationalusm and the Fourth American Revolution** (The Free Press, 1995)

way of life that were deeply rooted in America long before America gained independence. In this respect, the American nation has existed for generations before America won its independence and will continue to endure even after the American government no longer exists.

Even though the American constitution has not been replaced since its ratification in 1789, American history can be divided into three periods in which there were three different republics – (1) The Anglo American period (1789-1861) (2)The European-American period (1875-1957) (3)The American period of multiculturalism (1972-the present). In each of these three periods, there was a particular consensus that characterized the American community, civil religion, and political principles.

In the first period, the community was defined as Anglo-American or Anglo-Saxon, the civil religion as Christian Protestantism and the political principles as federalism. It is completely unclear whether an Irish Catholic, let alone a Jew or Black, could have been considered a true American

The American Civil War established a second republic, in which – as a result of the European immigration, the community was defined as Christian-European immigrants (this included Protestants, Catholics, and Jews), and the political principle was a republican federation. Within the framework of the second republic, the community could be comprised of any one of five possibilities individually – White, Black, Hispanic, Asian, and American. The civil religion promoted a secular philosophy that allowed sub-cultures according to race, gender, and religion. The political system was democratic, multicultural, and characterized by discrimination against non-Whites, segregation of Blacks and Hispanics, and a small upper class that controlled politics and the economy and enjoyed low taxes. The fourth revolution, hopefully, will not require bloodshed, but will entail advancement of the middle class at the expense of the upper class, and hopefully – racial integration. This projection should be viewed not as a prediction of the future but as a manifest calling for a revolution.

This is an ideological article that raises doubts whether an American nation clearly exists and is unclear about America's future since its internal state is socially and nationally unstable. The hope – from a national perspective – is that hundreds of years of life in the US and the development of a local culture will strengthen the internal structure of the US, create a uniquely American way of life, culture, historical events, and myths, and nurture some entity with a unique character and primordial roots.

Ronald Rogovski [28]

Rogovski claims, that in the view of many sociologists, social scientists and historians, nationality appears very illogical, in the sense of ancient feelings of ethnicity and aggression (as Geertz and Connor), and that Marxists have a more rational approach to the subject – as they see nationality as emerging from the desire of the bourgeoisie to take over local markets, and as a tool of capitalism in using imperialistic conquests to gather support among the working class for their own interests.

Rogovski proffers, instead, that nationality is a compound consisting of three elements:

1) The result of the search for higher ideals.
2) (almost always) The balance between personal interests and social reality.
3) An intimate connection to the distribution of labour, and to changes in said distribution.

Rogovski defines a nation as social unit characterized culturally, capable of sustaining an independent and unified framework and striving for territorial independence.

Rogovski assumes that one adopts a nationality out of calculation – the path that offers the most benefits and the least dangers and disadvantages. This utilitarian view of nationality would explain the following:

1) The decisions of individuals in adopting the dominant nationality in their environment, and also the social phenomena of assimilation, isolation, apathy as well as the phenomenon of national resistance in a minority, as described by Benton in 1980.
2) The decisions and choices of individuals between different cultures and even the invention of a national identity, as described by Bates in 1974.
3) Personal decisions between adopting a certain nationality to supporting an element opposed to that nationality, as described by Rogovski himself in 1980.

---

[28] See: Ronald Rogowski, "Causes and Varieties of Nationalism: A Rational Account", in **New Nationalisms of the Developed West**, pp. 87-108.

Rogovski's general assumption is that whatever the decision, it will be the one best advantageous to the deciding individual.
The adoption of a nationality by a group will be done in the manner that best takes into account the conditions of reality at hand, and when said group can independently supply, or acquire, the skills and services within a national framework.
Whenever an inferior group exists within a national framework, those of it who manage to climb the path to success, will usually tend to be assimilated by the superior group. An inferior group that avoids acculturation, will usually turn into a nation. Within these principals, Rogovski discusses different examples and developments and reviews the mobility between different groups within the same state, but his outlook, that advisability causes all, remains.

Avihu Zakai [29]

Zakai explains, in both of his articles, how influential religion is in the general context of Reformation, and particularly in the context of England, and Puritan Protestantism in England and America. He discusses the relation between these processes and consciousness and historical investigation in general, and in particular between them and national consciousness and the forming of nationality.
According to Zakai, and in accord with the sources he presents, the Lutheran Reformation had to defend itself from attack by the Pope, Christ's emissary on Earth. The Lutherans searched for, and found, ancient writings from the dawn of Christianity, in which could be sought (and found) authorization that all historical developments are by Devine mandate. From the Annunciation to the Apocalypse and the promised return of Christ, all developments are watched over by the Almighty. It is within the framework of this vigil, that they found sanction for their own path in the ancient writings. It was this revolution – seeing history as a development, and both part and future as a part of it, in addition to assuming a direct relationship with the omniscient Providence – that allowed the Lutherans to break free of the Papal theocracy.
The Reformation, says Zakai, happened concurrently with advances in education and knowledge in the Christian world. While Francis Bacon saw the successful combination of the two processes as an unexplained act of Providence, Zakai reveals that on the contrary, this was no coincidence, but a need – the need that

---

[29] See: Avihu Zakai, "Religion and Revolution, The contribution of Puritan Rhetoric to Democracy in America" from the book: **Democracy In America** , Zmora Bitan Publishing (as yet unpublished). Also, Avihu Zakai, "Reformation, History, and Eschatology in English Protestantism", in **History And Theory**, Vol. XXVI, No. 3, 1987, pp. 300-318

pushed the Protestants, defending themselves from the well-educated arguments of the Papists, to greater efforts in their research. Research which, in their opinion, was indeed aimed at studying the historical development of Christianity.
At any rate, the theory of Providence brought with it much intellectual excitement, and in England, the practice of historical research from a Christian viewpoint received reinforcement after the 1530's, as well as after the crowning of Queen Elizabeth I, and during the Puritan revolution. A joining of Protestant exiles fleeing England to European cities with main-land Protestants pursued in their own countries. The idea was, that since the words of the prophets are destined to come to pass, knowledge of history can help understand the prophecies themselves (a back-to-front reconstruction). This path seemed clearer than that of Martin Luther's changing of beliefs to match the new interpretation of the prophecies. Using historical comparisons - the fall of the Roman Empire with the all of Babylon, the Turkish invasion with the war of Gog and Magog, the Pope with the Anti-Christ - this research arrived at the conclusion that Protestantism has come at last days before the Apocalypse. Thus was the Protestant Reformation linked to the prophecies of the Apocalypse.
Prior to the Reformation, Christianity existed outside of time. Christianity busied itself with the legacy of the founders of the Church, such as St. Augustine, and placed the date of redemption at some indeterminate point. St. Augustine himself had shunned history and its moves, being incomprehensible to him. According to St. Augustine, all history is homogenous from the revelation of Christ to the end of time, and if there are any events within it, they have no bearing on the Divine Revelation, and are not explained by it.
The Protestant historiography had put meaning back into history, and ruled out St. Augustine's dual attitude toward secular history versus the world of religion. With the Protestant historiography's rejection of the Papal Church, and its abuse of the theocratic powers at its disposal, Protestantism turned towards expressions on nationality, and so showed interest in Poland, Bohemia, France, Denmark and Sweden, building national histories for each of these.

England had a long series of struggles against the theocracy of the Church of Rome, and talk of the Church of England had begun, and of the importance of the English nation in history as it progressed towards redemption. Thus was revolutionary historiography established in England. It was claimed, that it was the Church of England, that was true to the Divine Word, and that the Church of Rome was no more than an outside exploiter of the Holy Writ. Zakai explains how the English saw the English Reformation as an important event in English history. He explains that this view helped establish the English Puritan expectation of the Messiah, an outlook that stood at the base of the Puritan revolution. Zakai quotes John Bale, who claimed that the books of the New Testament are an explanation of events, rather than the opposite. What Protestant historians did was to read the Bible in a literary, formal and historic manner, and then attach the prophecies within to the events in history.

One who greatly advanced English historiography was John Fox (1516-1587) that defined the English Reformation as national and spoke of national faith and holy history. He proposed, in his writing, that the Protestant Reformation is a part of the history of The Promise, and a direct successor of the Church established by Christ. In his opinion, the histories of England and of Christianity were inseparable. He described the downfall of Queen Mary and the ascension of Queen Elizabeth in her place, and the subsequent renewal of the Reformation of the Church of England, as a climax that would reveal England's part in bringing about the fulfillment of The Promise, and consequentially, as an affirmation of the English as The Chosen People [which is a national sort of proclamation – YC]. Within this hypothesis, Fox describes how, in 63 A.C. the word of Christ reached England and the Church of Christ was established. According to Fox, Christianity has remained in England ever since, and it was an Englishman of the 14th century [preceding Luther – Y.C.] who christened, so to speak, the Protestant Reformation. Protestants in England were occupied with calculating the time remaining until the Apocalypse and the return of Christ. This task was undertaken by Thomas Brightman, whose writing greatly influenced the Puritans, of both the Old, and New worlds. By his calculations, the Apocalypse was due by the end of the 17th century.

Zakai's second article, about the religion and revolution of the Puritans, continues the basic explanation of "The Chosen People theory" as developed by the Puritans of New England – the people chosen by God and delivered to his Promised Land with a sacred mission to the New World. Zakai, in the footsteps of other researchers, reveals the central role the Puritans and their special brand of Protestantism played in the American Revolution. Zakai even mentions the U.S.'s uniqueness as a largely religious country, with a religious circle on the rise, as opposed to the opposite process in other countries. Also mentioned are the recent survey showing that 96% of Americans believe in God, and Robert Bellah's opinion (from his book *Civilian Religion*) that within the framework of the many symbols and values spanning the scope of all religions, churches and institutions in the U.S., there persists the belief that the Americans are the Chosen People and that America is the Promised Land. This Civilian Religion, in both Bellah's and Zakai's opinions has its own theology, ethics, holy days and places and system of symbols and rituals. Among the more obvious of its manifestations are reciting the Pledge of Allegiance to the Flag in schools, the singing of the Star Spangled Banner at sporting events, and a list of national holidays, such as The Fourth of

July (day of independence) and Presidents Day (celebrating the birthdates of presidents Washington and Lincoln) side by side with purely religious holydays, such as Easter. One other element of the civilian religion [of Puritan origin, as arises from Zakai's words – Y.C.] is a Messianic grasp of politics and history.
Zakai explains that Puritans accept the principals of Devine arbitrary sovereignty over the world, the corruption of man, and an ancient selection between the righteous and the wicked embedded with Devine Justice. Puritans emphasize the internal and personal religious experience or the change of heart, proving openly the redeeming mercy of God, and the uncompromising demand that all aspects of life be based in Devine laws and commandments. Puritans believe in the concept of The Covenant, according to which, those who have managed to lead a life of extreme piety will be rewarded in the afterlife. By the same Covenant, the Puritans are the Chosen People. The Puritans have denied the Divinity of the Anglican Church, and therefore the validity of the clergy. For this belief were their movements were restrained within England, and so the Puritans emigrated to America and settled in New Haven, Connecticut, Rohde Island and Massachusetts. Due to their devoutness and religious reading of the Bible, no society of the 17th century rivaled New Englanders in literacy. The Puritans had established the universities of Harvard (1636), Yale (1702) and Princeton (1746), and had ordained 1600 clerics through these universities by the American Revolution. Indeed, during the Revolution, about 600 of these clerics had worked toward American Independence by spreading the spirit of rebellion against the British, and the ideals of freedom. The same priests were instrumental earlier, during the Seven Year War (between Britain and Prussia on the one side, and France, Austria and Russia on the other), in rallying the Americans to the aid of the failing British campaign in North America, as they saw any war on the Catholic French as a Holy War, and indeed, aided by the settlers, the British had won, and conquered Canada. With the end of the conflict, the heavy taxes imposed by the British had caused the American Revolution, where, once more, the Puritan zeal played a central part through the widely circulated sermons of its clerics. The victory of the American War of Independence was considered and portrayed in New England as a victory of Providence, as seen by the Puritan faith.
Zakai's writing is, in the conceptual sense, primordial writing, as it uses a national historical mythos bound in religion as the foundation for the building of national recognition.

Lea Greenfeld[30]

Lea Greenfeld tries to construct a meaning to the term 'nation' that corresponds to the term 'any and all citizens of country X'. She does this in her book, which corresponds to her doctorate thesis. This review includes only five countries: England, France, Russia, Germany and the United States. The factors working on the forming of said nations – according to Greenfeld – are mostly undirected by government, though some are.

ENGLAND[31]

At the end of the 15th century, the English belonged to the King, and their loyalty came from an advantageous approach: helping themselves by helping the King, and also from the natural love of one's homeland. The King, recognizing himself and his people as one entity, had a dual purpose: enriching himself while obtaining prosperity for his people. For the 150 years between 1500 and 1650 the English terminology took a distinct turn toward nationalism, in such terms as: *The Sovereign People of England, country, The Commonwealth, Empire, nation, The Commonwealth of This Nation*, while the last expression implies that the Commonwealth no longer belongs to the King. As of 1530, the machine of government was infiltrated by talented people, despite their middle-class origins, not only was the governmental mechanism infiltrated thus, but also the noble class itself was soon opening up. The term "public will" was accepted as a just and logical thing. Following the breakup with Rome, this new nobility was buying Church property at bargain prices. In 1540 much of the land belonging to the Church was sold to finance the war against France. Thus did many talented people enter the aristocracy, which expanded and grew richer. This social change in the years 1540-1640 influenced politics. The middle class grew, and there was a constant movement up and down the social ladder. In the year 1640, the number of MPs in the House of Commons with higher education reached an all time record, which would not be topped until 1970. The significance of this fact is evident when considering that, at the beginning of the 15th century there were no more than six scholars and one meager library in all of London. The ambition of social climbing was strong, and the idea of a nation attracted commoners and aristocrats alike. Henry VII won his crown in battle, but relied on Parliament to authorize his taxes, and was known to justify many of his actions by claiming "the good of the people". Henry VIII showed respect to the people, its representatives

---

30 See: Liah Greenfeld, **Nationalism, Five Roads to Modernity** (London: Harvard University Press 1992)

31 See: name, pages 29-87.

and the law of the land. His withdrawal from the Church of Rome was carried out on the wings of national patriotism and the resentment of foreign rule in England. Henry VIII flattered the representatives of the people by addressing them as 'wise' and 'learned' and was favored by their national sentiments. He promoted the printing of the Bible in English. The English translation of the Bible contains changes that reflect the independent outlook of the English, and is the single most influential translation for several reasons, among which its arrival at the time of the Reformation, and the rising importance of literacy in the approach to education – a change with ramifications far beyond the religious. The persecution of Protestants, and the martyrdom of the persecuted saints during the reign of the Catholic Queen Mary had left their impression upon the English. Many accused the Catholic government of using religion to bleed the people dry, and believed they could understand the meaning of the scriptures very well on their own. The martyrs were few, but they included prominent figures who by dying, pushed forward the recognition of the English nationality, and caused an illegitimatizing of the Pope's power in the commonwealth. The best of English patriots were among the persecuted expatriates. The idea of a nation had lowered the King's status to one whose power came from the people and was therefore obligated to their best interests. It became legitimate to overthrow a king whose actions went against the people as a tyrant. The exiles combined nationalism with Protestantism, to form the conclusion, that England's imperial status owed its existence to England's being a nation, and to the English's uniqueness as Protestants. Nevertheless, the house of commons was predominantly Catholic, and Protestants were still subjected to criticism for their support of the corrupted rule of King Edward. With the death of the Catholic Queen Mary, and the coronation of the Protestant Queen Elizabeth things changed. The Archbishop of Canterbury promoted theories that proved the prevailing uniqueness of the Church of England, and patriotism in the form of Protestant garb was encouraged. While Elizabeth I did not consider herself to be a national person. but rather a religious one, she did find her people's national feelings useful, and so Protestantism prevailed in England for the 50 years of her rule... national and religious feeling became synonymous. The English became a nation because their Protestantism proved to them that they were the chosen people, a world elite, yet by the end of the 15th century, nationality usurped Protestantism, such as was the case with the war on Spain, when the cry went out to die "for Queen and Country", and English of all faiths were called to the service. Nationality had penetrated all classes and levels of society. English of all classes, both rural and urban, were shaped by the literature and art of the Elizabethan era, even to the extent of winning England praise in those areas. The 17th century saw a retreat of King and Church before nationality and parliament. The first kings of the Stewart dynasty had offended

the national feelings of the English, but it was when they had offended their unique religious feelings, that the puritan uprising was brought about. The ensuing revolution helped the people understand what was essential for the national existence, and what was merely an extra – and made it clear that the right to participate in the government was essential. The monarchy was removed, but so was the religion stripped of its unique elements. It was said that England was a free country, and that this led to its shaking off the royal yoke. It was said that God had given people both religion and freedom, freedom being the interest of nationality, and that one cannot have one without the other. There was even talk, such as Milton's, preaching a civilian religion. When the monarchy returned, religion had lost a great deal of its status, and the monarchy itself was not really back to its former glory – it had learned not to go against parliament. In the 17th century, the belief in reason and science had taken the place of religion. The belief in an equality built on the merits of knowledge and education was developing. Science had marked the superiority of the modern age, and so scientific accomplishments by English scientists added to the strengthening of the national feelings. The English chose to specialize in science, in which they could excel, rather than literature, which was where the strength of other nations lay.
Grinfeld summarizes by saying that England emerged from the 17th century with two major ideals: 1) A national pride 2) Political freedom and equality, based on individualism. Religion was tossed aside, and the issues of personal freedom and political equality – both based in man's divinity - took center stage. The decline of nobility and the fluidity of the class system (despite the efforts of those attaining a higher class to keep it), all helped this take place. Religion may have helped nationality on its way, but when the latter was strong enough, it joined with politics to kick out its predecessor.

FRANCE [32]

In France, the unique national identity – the uniqueness felt for centuries only by the ruling and elite classes of France – was first formed through religion, and then through its culture and establishments. Being independent of foreign rule, as it was at the time, was helpful in forming France's unique consciousness. The term "State" only appeared later, during the ministerial office of Cardinal Richelieu, but still, ever since the first of France's two transitions – the one from Christian theocracy to political monarchy with only obscure religious aspects – through to the 18th century, all was built on the loyalty to the crown. France had had just two changes in government in total, the first being the Devine Appointment of the French King's direct rule, substituting for his rule under the patriarchy of the

[32] See: Name, pages 91-113.

Church. The second transition would be that of the State replacing the King. The common element in both transitions, is the drawing of the new phase upon the old one for strength and expanding on it.

The first phase, then, was that of France as a Church of faith and piety. The Gauls were native residents of region before the Germanic conquest, which established itself as a ruling class. After the dividing of Charlemagne's Empire between his sons, the Franks and Germans were once again separated in the 9th century. Caught between the Holy (German) Empire, and the Papal seat in Rome, the Frankish Kings found uniqueness in piety, and pride in over-devoutness. The King of France was, at the end of the Middle Ages, considered to be "the most Christian" of kings, to his great esteem, and was rewarded by the Pope with an official declaration of his being God's chosen. The French flaunted their independence of foreign rule as proof of this Devine mandate. The crowning of the kings of France was considered to be an act of God, and rumors were cultivated of a special royal link to Christ himself. The Hundred Year War was brought about by belief that God has chosen a bloodline, rather than a specific person, people or territory, so that the War was waged between members of the bloodline, each of whom claimed inheritance. By the same reasoning, many French saw nothing wrong with supporting a contender who was, at the time, the King of England. In this respect, the French patriotism of Joan of Arc was an aberration. This belief in the bloodline made royal marriage a holy affair. Adultery by the Queen would be an act of treason with political consequences – the royal blood was taboo. Loyalty to the King carried with it religious overtones. In this respect – France was united.

Loyalty to the crown was entwined with spiritual sentiment, military service became a sequel to the crusades. The uniqueness of the French King projected a uniqueness of the French entity, his spiritual superiority reflected in the French language, as well as the laws and culture of the French. The French language was, in fact, spoken only in the county surrounding Paris, where it had developed between the 10th and 12th centuries, but as of 1148 it became the international language of the elite, making a barbarian out of anyone who didn't speak it. French became the language of the crusades, and in the 13th century, it was adopted by the courts of England, Germany and Flanders. French was in contest with Latin as the language of literature and religion, but gradually forced its way in during the 16th and 17th centuries as the official language of the government, which included the language in which marriage contracts were written, and baptisms were performed. As of the 13th century, French had replaced Latin as the teaching language in schools and universities.

In the 15th century, being French not only meant being the subject of the "most Christian" of kings, but also being literate in French, and respecting the Sallic law.

This dates back to the pre-Roman era, and embodies the Germanic traditions of inheritance, which served, during the Roman conquest, as an expression of local independence and ownership of the land within the Empire. While the focus of loyalty had shifted from loyalty to the Church, to loyalty to the King who ruled with the Church's permission, one cannot say an actual nationality was in effect. It began to sprout when the French kings started to break apart from the Church. In 1516, a manifesto declaring the French King the head of the Church of Gaul. This was to be followed by a definition of "state" as a "political area", though in 1593 it was understood that Religion, not Nationality, was counted when crowning a monarch. The claim, that the French monarchy was the result of a choice made by the Franks and the Gauls in the spirit of cooperation, was to be made. Inheritance of the crown was done by custom (rather than by Sallic law), and so had overtones of being dependant of the silent approval of the people. In a certain respect, Kings were chosen by the people, who never gave up their sovereign rights, or their ancient right to observe the government of the three-council-state: King, Nobility and People. The three classes represented the entire community, and the idea that the community, as an entity, had its own spirit and will began to take hold. Mornay opined that two contracts were in effect: one between God and King, and the other between King and his People. The first says that there must be a King, while the second states the basic rights of the people, in which the King's rule is anchored. This second contract allows any individual to oppose an unjust or ungodly sovereign, though this right may lead to the dictatorship of many individuals. This implies that the Protestant method alone could not ensure the rights of individuals.

In 1584, with the death of the Duke D'Alenco, the Huguenot Henry de Navarre contended for the throne. This began a religious struggle between the Huguenots and the Catholics over the rule of France, which served as an occasion to revive the idea of the King's Devine Sovereignty and of the religion embedded in the Kingdom itself. The divinity of the French throne became a direct link between the crown and a non-corporeal entity – free of the Roman hierarchy. The next logical step, that of the secularism of government, would only come a century later, with the French Revolution.

Sovereignty and Territory had combined to create the Republic – a living entity of mind (sovereignty) and body (territory).

Cliford Geertz [33]

When speaking on the subject of groups, Geertz does not see ancestral lineage as the sole defining element of the group within the state. According to Geertz, the phenomenon of grouping is diverse, and often based less on lineage and blood-ties, but more on custom and tradition such as case is in Morocco, tribal affiliation such as in the Congo and Iraqi Kurdistan, racial origin as in Malay, religion as in India, regional territory as in Indonesia, a combination of religion, language, race, region and social customs as in Ceylon (Sri Lanka), religious branch of Islam as in the case of the Sunni and the Shiites in Iraq or language, as in Laos and Thailand. Cross-African national movements are based on racial origin, on language in the Shan states.

Geertz sees a duality in nationality:

(1) The aspiration to building a spiritual construct reflecting the common desires, hopes, opinions, ambitions and deeds.

(2) The aspiration to building a modern, efficient and dynamic state.

The first aspiration of spiritual aspect is connected to the search for identity and man's place in the world.

The second aspiration of practical aspect deals more with the search for progress, a rise in the standards of living, efficient political order, social justice, and taking part in political influences.

Analogous to these two aspirations, is the conflict between the desire for ethnic nationality, and the desire for modern living.

Such ambitions are received differently by different cultures in different times and places. For example – in modern states the ambition for ethnicity and common background is viewed as pathological, and so the tendency is more towards the civil framework that suppresses ethnic diversity, be it by force of police, or be it by rhetoric. The primordial background is based on blood ties, race, language and customs. In Ceylon, it was the Premier's initiative of reviving the traditions of the Sinhalese majority, that caused the ethnic dispute, i.e. when the effort was to make the transition from a civil framework to a more ethnic one, that violence broke out. In Jordan, King Abdullah was assassinated after trying to organize his country as a civil state, and for negotiating with Israel – both endeavourers had hurt the Pan-Arabic elements in his kingdom. Geertz gives more examples of the conflict between ethic organization and the completely civil state – as mutually exclusive forms of national organization. He suggests the policy of civil nationality while maintaining a sensitivity to ethnic issues. His proposal makes it clear that ethnic

[33] See: Clifford Geertz, "The Integrative Revolution: Primordial Sentiments and Civil Politics in the New States, in **The Interpretation of Cultures**, pp. 255-310, see pp. 256-7

elements should never be ignored or suppressed, but rather 'tamed' and integrated into the proper political structure, and thus neutralize their harmful effects.
Geertz goes on to say that new countries are influenced by the primordial element to a great degree, a fact which has its effect of the early stages in their legislation, at times to a disproportionate extent. He gives detailed examples and concludes that the transition is, on the whole, a peaceful one from primordial grouping to a civil society with different attributes of grouping in the different countries (region in Indonesia, race in Malay, language in India, religion in Lebanon, custom in Morocco, blood-ties of a sort in Nigeria). It is a transition, then, from an ancient group structure, based on common and different attributes of culture, to a civil society in which ethnic groups become parties within the same unified national framework. It is a conversion of group nationality into a group-based party system within one unified national, civil framework[34]. Geertz realizes then, that the meeting of the need for a modern state, and the need to hold onto one's identity leads invariably to an integration of the two[35].
To summarize Geertz's (who specialized in South-East Asian countries, and Morocco) approach, it is an approach to the subject of nationality that does nothing to undermine the mainstream approach to the subject, but that comes to explain to western readers (who form Geertz's own background) that in the East the playing field of nationality is inherently different, as it incorporates primordial elements – but offers a reassuring promise, that with a little understanding, the latter will also come to embrace the advantages of the civilian society, be it with the occasional modification to symbolize a connection to the roots of pre-civilized statehood. Ergo: Geertz does not dispute the opinion of Western thinkers, who ignored the ethnic element, as far as it concerns the Christian world, and built an idea of nationality based solely on the identification of nation with state. He does explain, though, that the 'backward' people of the East act not only upon intellect, as do their Western counterparts, but also on emotion.
I do not intend to adopt Geertz's approach. It appears to me, to lean too much toward the interests of western countries, whose nationality, built on unstable ground, is now falling down about them, as I have mentioned before.

---

[34] Name, page 307.
[35] Name, page 309.

Jurgen Habrmas [36]

Using the Marxist assertion that the bourgeoisie is essential to the formation of nationality, Habrams describes the atmosphere in Capitalistic West-European countries with a well developed bourgeoisie, as a primary condition for nationality, as a transition from the atmosphere in which the monarch's palace' or the noble's home would be the scheduled place for non-private meetings.

The term 'public', as opposed to 'private' was already in use in feudal times, when any noble had a representative-public side to his life, in addition to his private life, which, by feudal mandate meant his representation of his subjects. Anything done publicly was considered to be done by and for all his subjects. Titles such as 'liege' or 'grace' represent this aspect of nobility. A symbolic publicity is always present at any congress within the feudal monarch's palace. The Church was also considered to be a public place until the Protestant Reformation made each man's contact with his God a 'private' matter, and terms such as 'freedom of religious practice' came to emphasize that fact. Market places, newspapers, a stock-broker's and certainly governmental bureaucracy, be it regional or federal, were considered public places' and it was generally assumed that there would be some kind public regulation of the above, in the form of rules and regulations' seeing as the government would have an interest in their operation. In the same respect, articles published at university were subject to review. 'Public' also includes the meeting places of 'private' people, when they meet as a crowd, such as the meeting places known as 'Caf 's', or 'Salons', the patronage of which had bloomed in England of the 1680's through the 1730's. In Britain and France, the above institutions had replaced the royal and noble courts as public meeting places, but while Salons were frequented mostly, but not exclusively by women, Caf 's were exclusive to men. Germany also saw the establishment of similar meeting places, but, due to the lack of proper cities in the 17th century, such places were organized by literary and academic societies, and similar organizations.

The recognition of a group as a nation cannot occur without internal discourse within the aforementioned group. How could the Britons know they were a nation? They would have to exchange ideas, be it through literature, conversation during trade, private meetings or even on the street. Those who had come to have a recognition of their nationality, got it through such discourse, rather than through personal motivation or meditation, a method which, while possible, is rare and incapable of sweeping large numbers of people. Newspapers were fairly common

[36] See: Jurgen Habermas, **The Structural Transformation of the Public Sphere – An Inquiry into a Category of Burgeois Society**, translated by Thomas Burger with the assistance of Frederick Lawrence (Cambridge, Massachusetts: Thde MIT Press) pp.1-39

in this period in England, but not in France or Germany. At any rate, Habrams' article, discusses caf''s and salons as public meeting places of the bourgeoisie, which is why Marxists saw the bourgeoisie as an important phase in the formation of a nationality.

Michael Waltzer [37]

Weltzer, a Jewish American, says that Americans do not refer to their country as their 'Homeland', and that for many an American, the concept of 'mutual commitment' usually applies to blood-relations and members of the nation from which they immigrated to the U.S., and which they still see as their provenance. What matters more to the American than their state is their ethnic group, race and (Devine) religion.

An American who inwardly chooses to forfeit his pre-American origin is welcome to do so, but this will merely make them ethnically anonymous, and in no way a better American. It has been said of Americans and their ethnic origins, that try as one may, no American can replace their Grandfather. For the American, ties to an ethnic past are not supposed to disrupt or hinder one's loyalty to the United States or her ideals.

There was, however, in the 1850's a movement of opposition to the catholic immigration, especially the Irish immigration, a movement called "know nothing", whose New England center also opposed slavery. This movement fought the teaching of the immigrant's native languages with community funds, as well as the teaching of their religion, in an effort to homogenize American society.

A completely different movement, in the 1910's and 20's, lead by Jewish American Horace Kallen, worked to minimize assimilation to the narrow definitions of politics and economy, claiming that there was no happiness to be found in abandoning one's culture. Kallen spoke openly of a dual loyalty, leading the opposition to the Republican movement.

Kallen had two points:

1. Ethnic and religious groups may only practice politics for the protection of their own interests, but not for imposing their culture or values on others. The U.S. is not a unique nation or a strictly Christian country.
2. The duty of the private citizen is to only to defend the democratic framework which allows him to implement his own group's activities. This does not conflict with loyalty and patriotism.

---

[37] See: Michael Walzer, **What it is to be an American** (New York: Marsaio) pp. 23-49.

Kallen saw ethnic groups as 'organic groups', and claimed that as interest groups they can and should work toward the acquirement of material and social goods that any population needs. It is up to every group to take care of its own.
Kallen, who found ethnicity and religion to be of the outmost importance, was know to say: "**It id the center at which [the individual] stands, the point of his most intimate social relations, therefore of his interest emotional life**".

Wletzer states his own opinion, that this approach is a little too extreme, but goes on to add Kallen's opinion that there are emotional areas, where politics cannot, and should not interfere. These areas are governed by the organic, or ethnic groups, as well they should be. At any rate, no attempt, peaceful or otherwise, of the state, to interfere in such matters can ever really succeed.
Wltzer explains that Kallen was not ignorant of the strong forces in the U.S., who sought, and not necessarily by oppressive means, to put the populace through the famous melting pot. He was aware of the budding power of the mass media. He foresaw what became later, in the 50's the mainstream of social criticism. It is unclear, however, weather he predicted accurately the submission of the pluralistic, ethnic conservatism to the soulless, superficial Americanism, that sought the destruction of any ethnic luster or depth. At any rate, he was confident in the ultimate survival and victory of the ethnic pluralism. He believed in American mutual internal coexistence.
Weltzer speaks of the Jews of France, who had to give up their rights as a group, in order to gain rights as citizens, following the French Revolution. The price of emancipation for Jews in France, was assimilation, as per Rousseau's strong national approach toward the United States. In the U.S., the situation was completely different. Despite the Republican current, which demanded assimilation, there is a tolerance in the U.S. of groupings, ethnic and otherwise, and dual loyalties are possible. Understanding the essence of American citizenship is diverse, and many different approaches are legitimate.
Weltzer describes the conflicting trends in America, concerning ethnic grouping, and says that "**America is still a radically unfinished society**". He says that the U.S. has a political center alongside a decentralized government, in which the center does nothing to curb the diffusion of governmental authority, nor does it oppose the ethnic grouping, or even question the legitimacy of the phenomenon. In fact, it seems that American politics is pluralistic by nature, and could use a little clarifying.

This part of the book contributes to the understanding of grouping, and shows it to be a legitimate phenomenon, despite the chagrin of some Americans.

Salo Wittmayer Baron [38]

Salo Wittmayer Baron describes how religions throughout history had created nations. He proposes that even today, one cannot understand the courses of modern history, without first understanding religion, and its relationship with the state. Baron describes how it was the adhesive of religion that united the Flemish and the Vulonians in Belgium, and how religion has acted as a solvent in separating the Serbs and Croats, whose ethnic origin and language are the same (the Serbs and Croats are also separated by their choice of alphabet, but this is a result of the influences of religion). Baron goes on to say, that it was the rigor of trying to unite two separate religions in Germany, Catholicism and Protestantism, that the only solution was the creation of a particularly extreme form of nationalism – the Nazi party.

And so, using Baron's mirror of religion, it is impossible to make sense of conflicts around the world today without the taking into account the religious factor. Examles are abound in such cases as Chechnya, Ireland, Cashmere, Israel and it's various Arab neighbors, South Sudan and the internal conflicts within Egypt.

On the other hand, in places where there are no major religious or ethnic differences, there is today a strong tendency towards unification and the creation of singular Super-Nations of the nations involved. Such cases can be found in Western Europe, in the various member nations of the Arab League, which are taking on an aspect of unity within the League, as well as in the organization of African states which has assumed the task of uniting the black race under one main national entity, within which each African country forms its own nationality according to the civil society in question. More examples are the American ultra-political union of mainly Latino-American countries, under the framework of which do the individual nations take definition according to the guide lines set by the native societies in South-Central America and the Caribbean. The attempts to form a common framework for East-Asian nations, and, in a way, the uniting of Islamic nations under the banner of the super-nation of Islamic peoples are further examples of this trend. Following this trend, many nations will become merely ethnic groups within one national framework. First on this road are the peoples and countries of Western Europe, in creating the European Union. Nowadays East-European countries are joining the Union, and there is a pronounced warming

---

[38] See: Salo Wittmayer Baron, Modern Nationalism and Religion (New York and London: Harper & Brothers, 1947) p. 21

of Russo-American relations. The trend may go as far as to create one super-nation of White-Christians. White Christian man now fears the Islamic fundamentalism on the one hand, and the growing power of China and Japan on the other. These are fears of the ethnic-religious playing field, and religion is – as mentioned before – a primary ingredient of ethnicity.
It therefore seems appropriate today - as it was in earlier periods of history since the Islamic and Turkish conquests, the Crusades and the religious wars in Europe – to assign to religion and ethnicity a primary place in the understanding and defining of the term nation and nationality. The above must be taken with emphasis on the attempts of various regimes to adopt an ethos of ancient ethnicity, in order to form a well rooted nation around it.[39]

Summery: The definition and understanding of the term Nation

Considering that a nationality is based on what people feel, one should award emotion-based factors, and especially ethnicity and religion, a leading place in the definition of the term 'nation', and its understanding.
A nation – it would seem – is an ethnic group that forms a desire for political independence within a certain territory, to which it is historically and emotionally attached. By this definition, the Curds in Turkey and Iraq, the Irish in Northern Ireland, the Chechens in Russia, the Albanians in Kosovo, the Muslims in Cashmere and the Thamilians in Sri Lanka (or Ceylon), are all nations.

---

[39] As for the expression "a well rooted nation", see Yehuda Cohen, **Who's afraid of a Jewish State? A Constitutional and Ideological Look,** (Tel-Aviv: The Attorneys' Publication 2001), pages 132-127. There, the terms "rooted citizen" and "rooted people" appear. The term "rooted people" used there refers to the willingness of an ethnic group to contribute to the state beyond the requirements of the law, as a measure of extreme loyalty to the state. Still, the basis for such loyalty is the feeling of identity that binds the said ethnic group to the state, the introduction of the state into the national ethos of the group, and the existence of an historical bond between the two. In this context, it is obvious, that a regime would like to create a "rooted people", on which it could rely. In fact, the motivation of most regimes – as discussed in this part of the book – to deepen the ethnic ethos of its citizens, is directed towards binding said ethos to their state and turning the resulting ethnic group into a "rooted people", as the term is used in the aforementioned book.

Chapter B
Ethnic group vs. Group of Origin, and their connection to the Nation

The route to defining the term *Ethnic*

We encounter the ethnic question as far back as the French Revolution, as mentioned in the writings of Jacob Talmon[40], where the arguments by Seye's call for the removal of aristocrats from French politics on the basis that they are more than just a separate class, and that "these privileged classes are foreign, a burden, a wasted appendage. Let the aristocrats return to the marshes and forests of Francphonia, of which they are so proud, and let them leave be the sons of the ancient Roman race. Among these, will they prove their being a superior race!" Nowadays, there are different approaches to the subject of ethnicity. Cynthia Enloe speaks of the main influence and cause of differences in the grouping in a society, ethnic blood-relations on one hand, and religious affiliation on the other, both within a unique culture. But before going into detail regarding these two forces, she generally states that:

> There is no consensus on what constitutes ethnicity but there is growing agreement that it is both objective and subjective. Ethnicity involves cultural attributes that can be observed, but those attributes must be of a conscious value to a collection of people to amount to ethnicity. There is a growing agreement among scholars that ethnicity requires a sense of belonging and an awareness of boundaries between members and nonmembers, however vague and mutable those boundaries may be from situation to situation or from time to time. Ethnicity is difficult to define because it is composed of an intertwining cluster of attributes and not a singular cultural characteristic. Language, religion, territory and custom - by themselves - are insufficient to identify, or sustain, an ethnic group. Moreover, the cluster of attributes assigned a collective value by a group will vary. A common language is a typical component of the ethnic cluster, but it is neither necessary nor sufficient to distinguish ethnicity.[41]

---

[40] See: Jacob Talmon, **The Beginning of the Totalitarian Democracy** (Tel Aviv: Dvir Publishing), p. 68.

[41] See: Cynthia Enloe, "Religion and Ethnicity", in **Ethnicity**, edited by John Hutchinson & Anthony D. Smith (Oxford, New York: Oxford University Press, 1996) p. 197

Max Weber[42], who was active at the beginning of the 20th century, sees as ethnic groups those groups who believe they have a common origin. This belief stems from either anatomical similarities, likeness in customs, or shared memories of emigration or settlement as group. This belief in blood-relations within the group doesn't have to be real. A group ceases to be a group, once this belief is gone. Weber sees language, religion, shared rituals, dining habits, distribution of labor between the sexes, clothing and living conditions as factors supporting this main element.

Weber speaks[43] of ethnic relations paving the way for possible emulation and mutual influence between different parts of the group, including the areas of religion and customs. This argument is reminiscent of Yehezkel Koifman's theories[44], which speak of monotheism as a communal and national creation of the Jewish People. He sees religion as the creation of a group, rather than the fruit of inspiration of certain specific individuals, and in this, is in line with Weber's opinion. Both Koifman's opinion and Weber's is reflected in the public opinion, that more than religion, but also language, culture, customs, dress and even traditions of facial hair maintenance, are the communal creations and designs of groups of origin, bound by common historical events, by common enemies. By this formula, the basic element of an ethnic group is the common origin as defined by blood-ties, and forged in the fires of shared hardships and histories. The hypothesis ties in to this line of thinking, that even internal warring within the group should reinforce, rather than weaken the ethnic experience. If a group could not really be said to be an ethnic group before it's internal conflicts took place, such an internal war could serve as a catalyst for certain social processes, which would, in time, and through successive generations, transform it into an ethnical group.[45]

---

42 See: Max Weber, "The Origins of Ethnic Groups", in **Ethnicity**, p. 35.

43 See: there, p. 38.

44 See: Yehezkel Koifman, **The History of Israeli Faith – From Ancient Times to the Destruction of the Second Temple** (Jerusalem: The Bialic Institute and Dvir Publishing) p. 30-31.

In relation to Koifman's opinion, that monotheism is an Israeli invention, see Deuteronomy 29-5, where it is described how the Israelites have reached the required level of spirituality – through their group behavior – "לחם לא אכלתם ויין ושכר לא שתיתם למען תדעו כי אני ה' אלהיכם". By this method did the Israelites reach, during their torments in exile, the spiritual requirement for monotheism.

45 This is Lea Grinfeld's opinion, in her book: **Nationalism, Five Roads to Modernity**, Harvard University Press, London, 1992, p. 480, an opinion shared by Robert Palmer, as reviewed by Seymour Martin Lipset, "The 'Newness' of the New Nation", in C, Vann

Around the issue of cognation, as it is attributed to the ethnic group, there exist also the elements of race, language, religion and customs, as they are described by Geertz.[46]

As pointed out by John Hutchinson[47], new countries, such as the United States, Canada and Australia, seek to paint themselves with a coat of "Ethnic Seniority". The reason behind this governmental desire, is giving the citizens in question the feeling that they live within an ancient framework, based on an ethnic foundation, which, having survived to date, will undoubtedly survive for countless further generations. Such a belief inspires optimistic faith in one's country, strengthens the internal adhesive of the society, and thus, indirectly, strengthens the government. On the other hand, older, or better defined ethnic groups within the new country tend to "spoil the party", in Hutchinson's words. Apparently, being an ethnic group comes with its own form of distinction, a distinction jealously sought after by those who do not possess it. It is from this phenomenon that the term 'fictional ethnicity' stems.[48]

Religion has bearing on ethnic affiliation. It has the power to create ethnic awareness through generations. It can expand one ethnic group, at the expense of other ethnic groups, by merging them into one ethnic mother-group. This process was exemplified within one generation – abnormally fast for ethnic processes – in today's Indian federation, when different ethnic groups, all sharing Hinduism as a religion, but speaking different languages, began adopting the Hindi language as their own, in sympathy with the Hindu group, that was the spearheading the religious struggle against Islam. These groups, despite receiving independence and autonomy which allowed them to develop their own languages, began, through the initiative of their members, to adopt the use of the Hindi language, and many of their members have joined the Hindi Ethnic Party. By doing this, they have basically declared affiliation with the Hindi ethnic group, which is different from their original ethnic identity. As illustrated here, through the Maithili example, practitioners of the Hinduism were divided by their native languages up until not too long ago. By adopting the Hindi language, many ethnic groups lose their diversity, and become one, big, Hindi ethnic group.

Woodward, ed., **The Comparative Approach to American History,** Basic Books, NY, 1968, p. 64.

[46] See: Cliford Geertz, **Primordial Ties,** p.40, foot-note 40.

[47] See: In the aforementioned **Ethnicity**, footnote 40, p. 374, John Hutchinson, "Ethnicity and Multiculturalism in Immigrant Societies".

[48] See: In the aforementioned **Ethnicity**, footnote 40, p. 164, E'tienne Balibar, "Fictive Ethnicity And Ideal Nation".

Example: Urdu is the language of the Muslims within the Indian Federation, while Hindi is the language of the largest Hindu ethnic group in the world. The Mithila ethnic group practices Hinduism, even though it has its own unique festivals – apart from the festivals common to the larger Hindi group. Basically, the main difference between the Maithils, and the Hindi, is their language – the Maithils speak Maithili, which uses its own alphabet and writing system, while the Hindi speak Hindi. In light of the increasing conflict between the Urdu speaking Muslims and the Hindi speaking group governing the Federation, the Maithils had to choose sides in a conflict which began to take on the characteristics of a struggle between languages, a struggle between Urdu and Hindi. The Maithils speak neither Urdu nor Hindi, but felt the need to support their fellow Hindus - and so many showed this support by preferring that their children be taught Hindi at school. Simultaneously, the Congressional Party - with its approach to a civil nationality devoid of ethnic elements - was losing power, to the growing power of the National Hindi Party. And once again, the Maithils felt the need to take a side in the most prominent political struggle in the Federation, that in which the National Hindi Party carried the anti-Islamic flag. It was clear to leading Maithils that they must support their fellow Hindus in this matter, and so many have joined the National Hindi Party, whose basis and ideology are rooted deeply in Hindi culture, but to which the Maithils felt a religious affinity. In much the same manner, many other ethnic groups subscribing to Hinduism have gathered under the flag of the National Hindi Party, which subsequently became the ruling party. Thus the phenomenon of religious struggle, whose outward appearance was that of a linguistic struggle, managed to gather under its flag many ethnic groups, many of whom were significantly different and unique in their own right. The result of this was that the Hindu religion soon became an ethnic nationality in its own right. The Hindi ethnic nationality grew progressively, and gradually, religion and nationality became congruous[49]. The Hindu religion turned (and is still turning, at a slow, but steady, pace) many language-groups into one language group, and thus, many ethnic groups into one ethnic group, creating within the Indian Federation one nation based on a unified ethnicity.

As per the Indian example, 16th and 18th century English history, as well as American Colonial history stress the role religion plays in the forming of a nationality, and in the longer run, the forming of a unified ethnicity. The effect in these cases came about from Protestant customs, such as the reading of the Bible, from the struggle against a common enemy, in this case, the Papist French, and

[49] See: Robert H. Bates, "Modernization, Ethnic Competition and Rationality of Politics in Contemporary Africa", in **State Versus Ethnic Claims,** pp. 152-171.

from the sympathy to fellows members of the same religion, specifically the Huguenots, some of whom, persecuted for their Protestant beliefs in France, fled to England.[50]

Ethnicity crystallizes around a belief in blood ties through generations, which in turn depends upon special behavioral and visual elements, among which religion plays a leading role. As shown in the Indian example, this one important element can be powerful enough to create ethnic changes within a relatively short period of time.

The Jews who came to Israel from across the globe, with the purpose of realizing their belief, held though generations of exile, that they were one people, had a strong awareness of blood ties, and a belief in a common origin – the basic ingredients of an ethnic group. This is why, though spread over many different countries, they have always been one ethnic group. Even if it were ever proven, that not all Jews have a common origin, and that there is absolutely no relation between Polish Jews and those from Yemen, it would make no difference at all. It is the awareness what matters. Subjective elements have much greater power that the objective truth. With ethnicity, what matters is belief. Despite any sentiments Israelis have for the respective countries from which they came to Israel, their first attraction is always to the state of Israel. It is therefore correct to say that the Jews in Israel consist of many groups-of-origin, none of which realize the potential of becoming an ethnic group. These are different groups-of-origin, that all branch off one race, which serves as a unified ethnic group. Judaism, as an ethnic group, has realized its desire for political and territorial independence, and has become a nation.

---

[50] See: Avihu Zakai, "Religion and Revolution, The Contribution of Puritan Rhetoric to American Democracy", in **Democracy in America**, Zmora Bitan Press, pending publishing. Also J. C. D. Clark, **The Language Of Liberty 1660-1832** (Cambridge University Press) pp. 46-62, and also John Pocock, "England" ' chapter IV, in **National Consciousness, History, and Political Culture in Early-Modern Europe**, editted by Orest Ranum (Baltimore, Maryland: The John Hopkins University Press, 1975) pp.98-117 and also Linda Colley, **Britons - Forging the Nation 1707-1838 (New Haven and London: Yale University Press, 1991) pp. 1-53** and also Avihu Zakai, "Reformation, History, and Eschatology in English Protestantism", in **History And Theory**, Vol. XXVI, No. 3, 1987, pp. 300-318 and also Liah Greenfeld, **Nationalism - Five Roads to Modernity** (London: Harvard University Press, 1992) pp. 29-85, 399-484.

Group-of-Origin, is a term for which I could find no definition in past or current writings. Objectively, I propose that any group with a unique and separate origin be labeled a group-of-origin, while in the eyes of the members of the group, their group is no different, ethnically, from any others making up the local ethnicity. In other words, a group-of-origin is a subdivision of the ethnic group into smaller groups of different origins, without this different origin being enough to create a different ethnicity on its own.

Use of the term 'ethnic' in Western writing is usually not accompanied by a definition of the above term. For example: Donald Horowitz [51] makes liberal use of the term 'ethnic' when speaking of groups, even when members of the group in question do not see themselves in this way, but consider themselves members of a super-group, of which the discussed group is a part. The case of the Cantons in Switzerland is a clear example of this, as Horowitz refers to the different cantons as ethnic groups, while the Swiss regard themselves as simply Swiss.

Horowitz himself mentions that objective definitions are not as important as the subjective outlook of the people in question.

This approach, as in Horowitz's case, is quite common, and therefore, when there is a lack of any clear definition by the author in question, one should not take the term 'ethnic' in the writing as an assertion by the author, that he, or she, believes that people who share a language or area of residence are, in fact what should properly be called an 'ethnic group'.

In other words: One should not jump to the conclusion of ethnicity wherever uniqueness of language or residence is in evidence. 'Ethnic' is a broad definition, and one should not believe it to be the premise of every author who uses it. The aforementioned conclusion thins the available sources for the definition of the term, and is the primary reason for the small number of sources I could find for this very paper. Due to the relative lack of resource material on this subject, and the linking established between the terms 'ethnic' and 'nation' and also following the disposition of the terminology of nationality as explained earlier, I find that I must hew a definition for 'ethnic group' with my own reasoning and examples. Under the circumstances, I propose to return to my own point of origin, in the definition by Max Weber I had brought earlier, and based on the arguments put forth so far, and make a sort of midway summery to the effect that: Any group of people holding a belief common to a significant number of people around it – significant if it can reasonably be called a 'population' – and that the belief in question is composed of such elements as an ancestral lineage of the group, a

---

[51] See: Donald L. Horowitz, **Ethnic Groups in Conflict** (Berkeley, Los Angekes, London: University of California Press) pp. 3-54

common destiny, a common desire, common feelings about certain historical events which in turn are kept through tradition, common rituals, ceremonies and patterns of social behavior and a common emotional tie to a specific territory – any group that falls within these parameters can be classified as an 'Ethnic Group'.

Usually, as we have seen before, religion, or a branch of a religion has a major role in the creation of a specific identity in an ethnic group. One more attribute of an ethnic group, is that it becomes a nation once the group consciousness is compounded with a desire for self rule within the emotionally charged territory.[52]

Once this point of view of ethnicity has been proposed, we should continue to examine it correctness in the writings of thinkers on this subject. Indeed, Cliford Geertz, for one, doesn't see ancestral lineage as enough to justify the use of the term 'ethnic group'.[53] According to Geertz, ethnicity is varied, and in most cases its dominant element is not the presence of blood ties or ancestral lineage, but customs, as is the case in Morocco, tribal affiliation, as in Congo and Iraqi Kurdistan, race in Malay, religion in India, religion as in India, regional territory as in Indonesia, a combination of religion, language, race, region and social customs as in Ceylon (Sri Lanka), religious branch of Islam as in the case of the Sunni and the Shiites in Iraq or language, as in Laos and Thailand. It should be pointed out to Geertz's argument, that in most of the above cases, there is, at least,

---

[52] In this respect – using the example of the Jews – Jews were an ethnic group throughout their exile, despite whatever usual term is applied to their group, usually by misjudging the strength of the relations between Jews in different reaches of their exile. The international trade between Jews was based as much on their solidarity and close relationships as on their common language. One Jew believed in another simply because he was also a Jew. Jews would pay ransom for other Jews, even if they were strangers from a strange community, or were taken in faraway places. When the Jews of Yemen were in trouble, they turned to the Rabi Moshe Ben Maimon , who sent them a scroll of spiritual encouragement. They, in turn, sought his religious guidance and saw him as a spiritual leader. Only members of a common ethnic group treat each other in this fashion. Jews would correspond over great distances, and vouched for one another. They had a common dream and a common vision of rebuilding the fallen kingdom of Judea. If the prayers of the Jews were to be translated and seen for the very real desire for political and territorial independence – what we have is a nation. At any rate, the arrival of the Zionist movement, and the accumulation of enough Zionists to justify the term 'population', the Zionists and their followers became a nation.

[53] See: Clifford Geertz, "The New Integrative Revolution: Primordial Sentiments and Civil Politics in New States, in **The Interpretation of Cultures**, pp. 255-310, see pp. 256-7

the presence of *imagined* ancestral lineage and blood ties, which, real or not, was the basis for whatever criteria now holds the ethnic group together. It is quite possible, that the aforementioned elements of ethnicity were originally there to preserve the blood-ties in question. It is appropriate to mention here the opinion of Pier Van Den Berge, who sees the network of blood-ties as essential to the structure of ethnic groups.[54] With respect to the points brought to bear so far, one can cautiously agree with this opinion. The strongest social unit that there ever existed is the blood-based family unit. The family, as a social institution gives an excellent example of the strong ties between the newfound definition of 'ethnic group', and the nature of man.

Linking 'Ethnic Group' and 'Nation':

The term 'ethnic' can be seen as the base of the term 'nation'. A nation, as it occurs naturally, with no artificial involvement from any specific government, is based on ethnicity.

Ethnicity and (ethnic) nationality are abutted. The more common approach to the difference between them is that a 'nation' is formed once the ethnic properties of a group are joined by a desire for political independence. This approach is self-evident in the writings of various thinkers on the subject of nationality, who speak of the possible awakening of political desires within an ethnic group, such as is the case with the oppression of peripheral ethnic groups. As Hechter[55] describes it, this oppression is handed out by the center, which isn't part of the discussed ethnic group.

In the literature of ethnic disputes, ethnic groups are seen as groups built upon lineage, and which are more or less qualified for nationhood, but which do not wish to assume leadership of their country, and which are content in letting another ethnic group do the ruling.[56]

---

[54] See: Pierre L. van den Berghe, "Race and Ethnicity: A Sociobiological Perspective", **Ethnic and Racial Studies**, vol. 1, no. 4 (October 1978) pp. 401-411.

[55] See: Michael Hechter, **Internal Colonialism,** chapters 1-2. See also Marx and Engles' opinion that: "modern nations are ... what we today call 'nation states': ethno-cultural and linguistic communities with their own state. In much the same way as Ephraim Nimni puts it in: Ephraim Nimni, "Marx, Engels, and the National Question", in Will Kymlicka ed., **The Rights of Minority Cultures** (Oxford: Oxford University Press, 1995) p. 57, 64.

[56] See: Donald L. Horowitz, **Ethnic Groups in conflict** (Berkeley, Los Angeles, London: University of California Press); Michael Hechter, **Internal Colonialism - The Celtic Fringe in British National Development, 1536 - 1966,** (Berkeley and Los Angeles: University of Los Angeles Press).

Summery: Defining the Ethnic Group

An ethnic group is, therefore, a group of people sharing a common perception, which states that all members of the group have a common human origin, or ancestry. Such a group has an awareness of a common history, a common culture consisting of elements relevant to present day life, such as religion, language, social customs, a typical mentality, common and unique legends and myths, a feeling of shared destiny and a willingness to assist each other, a common commitment to preserving the uniqueness of the group, a shared vision of the future, most often a common enemy, an emotional tie to a specific territory and a tendency for marriages within the group, or the adoption of those who marry into it. So long as the above are not compounded by the desire for self-rule, the group is an ethnic group, rather than a religion. In this respect, the Kupt in Egypt, the Maroon Christians in Lebanon, the Druze in Syria, the Shiites in Iraq, the Maithils in northern India (before their assimilation into the Hindi ethnic group), the Welsh in Britain, the Vulonians and the Flemish in Belgium, the Italian, Irish, Ukranian, African, Japanese and Chinese in America, the Palestinian citizens of Israel, the Berbers in Morocco, the Zulu in South Africa (as well as most other black races in Dark Africa) and the Gypsies, spread as they are through many countries – these are all ethnic groups, who have not achieved the status of nations.

Chapter C:
Groups of common origin within the United States, and among Israeli Jews

The examination of social conditions and developments can be done either externally or internally. One could also perform this examination both ways simultaneously. An example of the external view is Gershon Shafir's party, which sees the essence of Zionism as colonialism, through finding similarities between the efforts of Zionism and examples of European colonialism.[57]

[57] See: Gershon Shafir, "Land, Labor and Population in Zionistic Colonization: General and Specific Aspects", from **Israeli Society – Critical Aspects**, edited by Uri Ram (Tel Aviv, Breirot Press, 1993).

The Zionists, as opposed to Shafir, saw their entire endeavor from an internal view point [in the Hart sense[58]] which they, as engineers of this work have been, and still are deep into, the view of national resurrection and the gathering of a scattered people. Indeed, through the external view of historical processes and events the world over, one cannot find examples of national resurrection in the form of such a gathering. The process taking place in Israel for one hundred and twenty years now – when compared externally to world events – can only be compared to the processes of colonialism. One cannot compare the Zionist endeavor to other gatherings of scattered peoples as a form of national resurrection, because none exist. The proper approach to examining a unique phenomenon is through the internal view, because an external view, lacking any reference points, would fail to correctly interpret the phenomenon. With apologies for the next example – and by no means with any disrespect to Zionists, of whose number I have always wholeheartedly been – in a world where there are only males and females, there can be no understanding of the androgyne – it cannot be understood by being compared once to males and another to females. Comparison is useless. One must research the androgyne's view of his/ her self. **He** or **she** must be asked. This is the internal view. It is therefore hard to accept the UN's judgment of Zionism – which is external, but not objective – that it is synonymous with racism.

An external view will seek, and not find, external assurances. Therefore, the examination of the gathering of exiles must be taken with the internal view, which is the correct view, when one cannot understand matters from the outside. The internal view gives a unique perspective, which cannot be acquired any other way. The forming of groups as it occurs amongst Jews gathered in Israel – in the case of groups of origin – is unparalleled in the globe. When attempting to discuss favoritism within these groups, one needs, first and foremost, to define these groups. Using the external view, of other immigrant countries, such as the United States, Canada, New Zealand and Australia, these groups may be called 'ethnic groups', but in the above countries the situation is that of people of different nations immigrating as individuals, while the situation in Israel is different. If the term 'ethnic group' in the above countries is used in the sense that the members of different *nations* have given up the desire for political independence in their countries of origin and thus have turned, in their new home, from nations into ethnic groups – then the term is used in the sense that an ethnic group is a nation lacking the desire for political or territorial independence. A transition made

---

[58] See: H. L. A. Hart, **The Concept of Law,** Second Edition, Edited by Peter Cane, Tony Honor'e and Jane Stepleton (Oxford, England: Clarendon Press, 1961. 1994, 1997) p. 98

willingly with the immigration. In Israel, the immigrants – from Poland, Morocco or Romania – who are all Jews – had no need to give up a desire for political independence in their country of origin, because they never had such a desire. They were not supposed to turn into a new nation along with other ethnic groups, but rather they were – before their coming – one nation. Not only this, but the new immigrants, arriving from places around the world, all saw themselves and their fellows – prior to the immigration itself – as one ethnic group, which is one nation.

The immigration to the U.S., Ethnicity, and ethnic and religious favoritism

The United States were born as a singular political entity largely against their will. The residents of the thirteen rebelling colonies did so, after being laden with heavy taxation without representation. This took place after the war between Britain and Prussia, who won, and France and the Austro-Hungarian Empire, who lost. But alas! The winners, namely the British treasury, was deep into heavy debts due to the costs of war, some of which it sought to balance by charging the sums necessary from the British colonists residing in America, who were called - merely as an abbreviation – Americans. The Americans were no different in any national sense from the equally abbreviated British. It was one nation, part of which - the part residing in the ancestral home the nation - could impose taxes, using its elected Parliament, on the other part, which resided across the Atlantic, and could do nothing about it, for lack of any representatives in said Parliament. The Americans, being aware of their freedom rights as any other British citizens would be, made every effort to reach a compromise and modus vivendi, and when these failed, they resorted to rebellion.

So with the independence of the American colonies, there were two parts of one nation under two different and separate political and sovereign units. The Americans began the building of a separate national awareness of their own. This process went on at least until the American Civil War, meaning it took nearly one hundred years (1783-1860). There are even those who say that it was this very Civil War that gave birth to the unique[59] American nation with its own characteristics and history. There are those who say that Americans are still building their nationality, and that this nationality is still at its early larval stages.

---

[59] This is the opinion of Liah Greenfeld, **Nationalism, Five Roads to Modernity** (London: Harvard University Press, 1992) p. 480 ;As well as the opinion of Robert Palmer as reviewed by Seymour Martin Lipset, "The 'Newness' of the New Nation", in C. Vann Woodward, ed. **The Comparative Approach to American History**, Basic Books, NY 1968 p. 64

Among the means to solidify the American nationality were the drive west, towards the Pacific Ocean and the war with Mexico. They even include the immigration itself, which held a very important place in the process, because it helped to increase the diversity of Americans, and further differentiate them from their British origin. America was not established **for** its immigrants, quite the contrary: **The immigrants had built and strengthened the unique American nationality**, which until then was part of the British nationality, and is still undergoing development today, as is covered elsewhere in this part of the book. The immigration came from different European countries, but later on consisted mainly of Latino-Americans. The internal migration of blacks, turned from slaves to free men, greatly diversified the American nation, and gave it a strong and unique color.

The nature of immigration to the America was essentially that of individuals and families, even if these same individuals and families later congregated into communities according to their countries of origin, their religion or their former nationality[60]. Every immigrant did so for his or her own good. They did not come to America for any objective designed by group, nation, culture or religion, nor for the purpose of establishing an American nationality. The forming of the American nationality was not at the base of the immigrant's motives[61]. The Ukranian immigrant did not come for the purpose of forming a Ukranian ethnic group within the U.S., nor to create a haven for the Ukranian nation. The Jews, who arrived as people with no homeland, rather than trading one for the other, came, too, as individuals, for themselves. The United States was, to every one who immigrated, or planned to immigrate to it, a place of liberty, of liberal government, a place free of persecution, where there is a basic and principal equality among citizens, a political entity where the individual rights of the citizens are all the same, a land of unlimited opportunity, a land of individualism and self-interest. Incoming immigrants had no expectations of anyone helping them out in their first steps of assimilation[62], or that anyone would feel obligated toward them. On the other hand, they did expect that no special obstacles would be placed in their way, and that every immigrant would be awarded the same opportunities, on the basis that

---

[60] See: Moshe Sharet, "Examinations of the Problem of the Gathering of Exiles", from **Immigrants in Israel – A Study**, edited by Moshe Lisk and others (Jerusalem, Academon Press), p. 25.

[61] The arriving immigrant did not come to America to create a 'civil society'. Individualism and the rights of the individual were at the center of the immigrants' ideals. Every one sought to enjoy their own right to liberty.

[62] See footnote 59 – Moshe Sharet.

any immigrant is equal to any other citizen under the eyes of the law[63]. They knew very well that by coming to the U.S. they must pledge their loyalty to the U.S., and that they will belong to the great American nation. Still, a dual loyalty was never unknown in the U.S., a fact clear not only to veteran citizens, but to the new immigrants. In the beginning, before the Civil War, loyalty was to the country, and to the state, but after the Civil War, loyalty to the state was replaced by one's loyalty to one's ethnic group, or the American's group of origin[64]. The various (devine) religions were gradually, during the 19th century, removed from any involvement in politics and public education[65]. The devine faiths served, alongside the ethnic groups, a focus of belonging, a focus of the community. Thus were formed American communities based on religion. The American would 'belong' to the United States as a political entity, and in addition, he legitimately belonged to other entities. With liberal individualism as the main force in American culture, it was the dynamics of the ethnic group, and or those of the religious group, or church, which provided the American with spiritual and moral support, or offered him any real form of mutual assistance. Living in the atmosphere of liberal individualism, this support was really important to the American. Whenever the American felt alone, or in need of moral support, he knew he could always turn to his support group, a fact which served to strengthen the position of ethnic and religious groups in the U.S. The ethnic grouping came to serve a purpose which the American government did not provide, nor see as its duty to provide – that of support for the lonely immigrant facing the difficulties of assimilation, sometimes completely broke[66]. It is of small wonder, then, that many

---

63 Although the political rights within the state would not be awarded every immigrant immediately, and there will be a waiting period involved, his federal rights as an American citizen are not delayed.

64 See Grinfeld's book, footnote 6.

65 Dewey's opinion has greatly contributed to the abolition of the reading of the Bible in public schools – a profoundly Protestant custom. In general, the public school was a valuable and powerful instrument in the shaping of the 'American Civil Religion' and has helped – alongside American Supreme Court rulings – in the separating the (devine) religions from governmental politics and the from the state.

66 In the United States, the government had no national attitude toward incoming immigrants – before their arrival. Immigrants were not American until they had actually arrived in the United States, and were naturalized. This is quite different from the situation in Israel, where the government sees immigrants and Jews – prior to their immigration – as members of the very nation for which the State of Israel was founded. It this entirely different approach that stands behind the governmental Office of Immigration and Assimilation, which is regularly supplied with a respectable budget, for the purpose of

ethnic groups had developed the need to help their fellows[67]. This moral support awarded to the American by his ethnic or religious group is likened to the financial support given to the economically struggling Mexican, as mentioned in the study, which will be reviewed later. In both cases, distress or hardship on the one hand, and the reassurance within the group on the other, have instituted this phenomenon of mutual assistance. The strength of the churches as communal and social centers in the United States, is that due to the moral support they afforded, they created a wider interest in the needs of the public, in the eyes of Americans. In this way, civic duty and obedience of the law was put into a positive context. It is therefore evident that ethnic and religious sympathy has had a positive effect on public life in the United States.

With this in mind, one can see the special care taken by Americans, to assist member sof their ethnic group in life, or employment, as a definitely positive phenomenon. The obvious price to be paid for this phenomenon, is that of the deepening of inter-ethnic differences, following the favoritism within the group at the expense of members of other ethnic groups – seems a minor price to pay, in relation to the blessing it brings to the ethnic groups. It is therefore possible to accept Michael Walzer's description of ethnic favoritism in the U.S. as a good thing[68].

The story is similar to Bates' description of favoritism among tribe members in Dark Africa, who, having moved to the city and away from tribal life, continued, and still continue to support their fellow tribesmen, to set up educational institutions and professional unions, all dedicated to a particular tribe[69].

This special treatment of fellow members of one's ethnic group in America (and in Africa) should not be seen as contrary to the basic puritan ethic core of equality in America. The same can be said for Mexico, as will be illuminated later. In this respect, even favoritism towards family members, practiced around the world, Israel included, is a positive aspect of the fabric of emotional relations surrounding the family.

This form of favoritism seems to be detrimental to the organization of the body politic, when it is found within the management of public offices, and when it

---

supplying new immigrants with loans and other aids in their assimilation. Such an office does not exist in the United States of America.

[67] Within civilian society.

[68] See: Michael Walzer, **What It Means to Be an American?** (New York: Marshio)

[69] See: Robert H. Bates, "Modernization, Ethnic Competition and Rationality of Politics in Contemporary Africa", in **State Versus Ethnic Claims,** pp. 152-171

comes at the expense of the equal treatment of citizens by the said public offices, which should be run according to strict ethical guidelines.

Public services are, by definition, public property, and therefore, favoritism enacted within them is tantamount to making private use of public property, which is why any proper state should not allow it. Favoritism cannot be tolerated from people who represent the state.

Yet socially, the defining picture is not quite as sharp. So when dealing with the daily decisions in the life of the individual and his or her own conscience – rather than a person appointed by the state to uphold the law – then one cannot, and should not limit one's self to the narrow perception of ethics that is required of officers of the law. As for the internal viewpoint of the business of the community, the person and his or her private affairs, mutual assistance within the ethnic group is actually a blessing. In a country where there are no governmental institutions to provide a similar support, this is a vital phenomenon which should be praised. It is what gives the society its required internal strength.

The forming of groups in the U.S. of the 19th century

Alexis de Torquiville, a Frenchman visiting the United States, was impressed by the multitude of organizations that were there for the citizens in need. He saw the American society as immune to tyranny, because of the constant support and protection its citizens receive one from the other, which makes their situation better than that of their counterparts in France, or the rest of Europe.

Current Jewish assembling in Israel:

On introspection of Israel, one can see that the beginning of political life in Israel was already abound with intermediate institutions for supporting the individual, from the very beginning of the Jewish settlement in Israel, through the period of Ben Gurion's influence[70], and up to this day and age.

Ben Gurion's war for a municipal centralization took its toll on the sectorial method and concentrated the care of personal welfare in the hands of the state. The same effort is still in place today, when any attempt at favoritism is subject to

[70] The man who gave up his political power, and who gave up the power of the distribution of labor using party tokens, the power of entitling those with party memberships to governmental favors, who dismantled the separate military organizations (specifically the Hagana and the Etzel), who gave up the special labor education network, who (with partial success) worked towards a civil service standard removed from the party system – the man who resigned for his beliefs and principals, and his sense of mission.

exposure, condemnation and preventative measures. Today such group support can be found in small sectors, in the Shas religious-political party, for familiars of select party members (support in the form of providing a low-cost education network, and working to have it recognized by the state), by the Judaism of the Torah party, in relatively the same manner, as well as in the courts of religious leaders and communities.[71] Occasionally, and irregularly, such phenomena are seen as the initiatives of individual volunteers or non-profit charity organizations, as is the general custom of philanthropy in the Western world, and indeed, volunteering is a wide-spread phenomenon, which is encouraged by ceremonies and tokens of appreciation held for the benefit of said volunteers – but individual volunteering, as well as isolated acts of philanthropy, are not a group phenomenon. What sets the action of group support apart, is the sense that both giver and receiver of the assistance have, that it is given because they are both members of the same group, and thus, that the receiver is not alone. It is a feeling of power. This phenomenon has its negative side, and that is the phenomenon of xenophobia. Xenophobia, and bigotry, was present in the southern states of the U.S. in the 19th century, among those of white ancestry, but little or no property, who felt they had a group relation to the property owners, and consequentially, a superiority to and racial hate of the black slaves. In this fashion, they confirmed their belonging to the white group on the one hand, and their exclusion from the black group, on the other. In this manner does the negative aspect of grouping come into play, when support should be its main feature. Vagueness of familial status and affiliation can also cause severe problems, another element that arose during the period of slavery in the United States.[72]

The differences in the degree of assembling, between the US and Israel

The feelings of alienation and estrangement between Jew and Ukranian, both of whom immigrated to the United States, would surely have remained as strong in the new country as in the old. They were present before the arrival in the new land of freedom. Intermarriage between the two peoples would be extremely rare. A

---

[71] Arranging the free rental of wedding dresses is common practice among religious Jews.

[72] One of the difficulties that arose was the phenomenon of female slaves bearing the children of their white masters. The offspring were definitely not considered part of the white group, yet were usually treated better than most slaves, or even set free. Most social difficulties emanating from this problem were solved by the freeing of all slaves in the wake of the civil war. The problem remained later, in the sense, that when one's group affiliation is unclear, one encounters social problems.
See Dan Brega's **Race and Ethnicity**, page 408, 2nd upper footnote.

union of families between German Protestants and Dutch Protestants in the U.S. could theoretically come about without too much difficulty, though the occasions are rare. It is therefore safe to postulate, that every group of immigrants in the U.S. brings with it a trail of relationships of different kinds with people of different nations, which, in the new country, are converted from relations of nations to the relations between ethnic groups within the same nation. While border disputes between the parent countries will no doubt no longer be relevant, well rooted emotions will not soon fade away.

Immigrant Jewish families coming to Israel, one from Rumania and the other from Hungary, surely do not drag with them the mutual hate and contempt so typical of non-Jewish families of these people immigrating to the U.S. There has never been any kind of special strife between the Jews of Hungary and those of Rumania, and if any of them felt something of the kind, it quickly disappears on arrival in Israel. Therefore there is no trail of rivalries trailing behind Jews coming to Israel as new immigrants. Mutual contempt could very well be, though. There is record of relations of contempt and disparagement between Jewish immigrants of different origins in Israel, for instance, the contempt held by the Western-educated Jews of Baghdad toward the Jews of Morocco, and even those of Iraqi Kurdistan is well documented. While there are many well-known instances of this kind, the problem is not deeply rooted. Families of immigrants from different backgrounds have been known to familiarize, and many intermarriages are known, with the passage of time since the immigration. The disdain held by a Baghdad Jew towards a Jew from the remote villages of Morocco, is the same as his contempt towards a Jew from the remote villages of Kurdistan – that is, there is no real history of national rivalry or hostility between the two, as one might find among the Christian immigrants from Rumania and Hungary in the United States. Jews, whatever their whereabouts, have no traditional history of animosity with Jews of other countries. Quite the contrary – there is an ancient tradition of mutual help and ransom payments – a sense of a common fate. The immigration to Israel itself was raised in the lap of the common national vision, and so the depth of estrangement and alienation is unlike what is the case among Christians arriving in the United States from different countries. An Indian Hindi, and an English Christian, both arrive, upon immigration and naturalization in the U.S., with a history of coming from a dominated nation, and a dominating nation, respectively. A Jew, and a Muslim Arab of Syrian origin – both American citizens, carry the burden of the conflict taking place outside the borders of the U.S., doubly so, in the case of a Jew and Arab of Palestinian origin. In the case that the above immigrants return to their countries of origin, they will resume their age-old rivalry, and feel no camaraderie, even if they do retain their American citizenship while reassuming their older nationality. A Protestant North-Irishman, and a Catholic North-Irishman, both of whom have lived, and been naturalized in the United States, along with their families, would, if they should later return to Northern Ireland, retain the old rivalry of their families, be they both American citizens. Jewish American citizens from Rumania and Hungary, two countries with a historical rivalry, upon returning to their respective countries of origin, will feel no particular animosity toward each other or each others families, as there was none there before the immigration to the U.S. – moreover, if the two ended up in Israel, their sense of camaraderie would be even stronger, regardless of weather they both now possess Israeli citizenship, or American, or any other citizenship for that matter.[73]

With all this in mind, one should note that the attempt to settle, in Israel, Jews from Yemen and from the Indian province of Cochin, fell through to such a degree, that immigration and naturalization authorities in Israel have since strived to settle only members of the same group in any new settlement, and rather than mix immigrants from different origins, they created 'bunches' – different settlements, each populated by people from a different country.[74]

In Israel, unlike in the U.S., Jews have no dual loyalty, one to their political entity, and the other to their ethnic group. This is due to the simple fact – which was in place long before the immigration to Israel – that we Jews are one people, with one desire for bringing our different congregations together. It is because of this, that - with the exception of the two main religious parties: 'Shas' and 'Yahadut Ha-Torah' – there is no desire to further any group-of-origin as a separate political entity from all other Jews in Israel. The nationality of Jews in Israel is stronger than the nationality of Americans in the U.S. in general – and this is true in all variations and connections of the families involved and their countries of origin.

---

[73] As a rule of thumb, one should separate citizenship and nationality, and bear in mind that citizenship does not imply loyalty. Nationality, on the other hand, does project loyalty, as it covers the wide range of objective circumstance and subjective feeling, while the term citizenship refers only to objective formalities, and has no bearing on the subjects feelings.

[74] See comments by Moshe Sharet, in the above footnote No. 13, pages 28-29. On the same note, enforcing a group structure appears to be a difficult task. Settleing the Cochins along with the Yemenites was a declaration of superiority by the authorities: 'you look alike, therefore the is no difference between you'. In my opinion, this is the worst kind of condescending insult. A proper linking should come by through voluntary decisions by those involved, if it is to prosper.

The main reason is the greater ethnic depth of the Jewish people, from an historic point of view, the extreme tempering of Jewish nationality through the Jews' many trials and the stronger common vision possessed by the Jews. The Jewish nation is internally stronger than any other, since it has existed in one form or another for so long, it is certainly stronger than any nation with the historical depth of a mere two or three centuries, and definitely stronger than a nation, which has not even a full century behind it, such as the Congo, or Sierra-Leon, if the term can be used for these.

Lea Shamgar-Handelman's research[75], when compared to Larissa Lomintz's study[76], the one done in Jerusalem, and the other in Mexico, reveals different data regarding mutual support and favoritism among families with blood-relations. The mutual help among such families in Mexico is intensive when these families live in dire conditions. In such conditions, there is no great financial difference between the assisting and the assisted. In Mexico – and not only among the financially distressed – a man's promotion through politics or government office is usually done so that when the promotion is achieved the beneficiary of the assistance will return the favor and promote the interests of those who supported him. The assistance can take different forms when there is no blood relation or even acquaintance involved. The difference is that where previously the assistance was given freely, it will now be given in exchange for bribery. The unwritten golden rule, is that one does not accept bribes from relatives, but rather one is fulfilling a social duty. Apparently the above is practiced in Mexico by men, and that women are not involved in the process. It is mentioned in the Mexican study, that assistance with no bribes is common also in the United States and Peru, but in Mexico, by comparison, the custom has developed among the financially distressed, since they are dependent on such mutual help for their very survival. Due to the serious unemployment situation in Mexico, when the head of a distressed family is out of work, the others support him through the difficult period.
The Jerusalem study reveals that in Israel there is almost no trace of these procedures. The mutual help found in Israel is mainly between parents and their

---

[75] See: Lea Shamgar-Handelman, "Social Advancement And Social Networking Among Jerusalem's Families 'who need care', from **Social Networking in a Forming Society – A Study of Social Networking and Its Contribution to the Understanding Processes of New Immigrants – A Parley**, edited by Ora Ahimeir and Yaron Idan (Jerusalem:The Jerusalem Istitute of Israeli Studies), pages 33-55.

[76] See Larissa Lomintz's notes from the above title, pages 5-20, under the note entitled "Social and Familial Networking in Southern America"

married children, and very little between married siblings. In Israel the mutual help is a private matter, while in Mexico, favoritism is a widespread element of public conduct.

The difference, with regard to ethnic classification, between Jews in Israel and groups of origin in the United States

The above discussion reveals a difference in the group structure between the United States and Israel, that is mainly a difference of depth of feeling. The question remains, though, weather, according to the definitions given in this part of the book, can it be said of groups-of-origin within the United States, that they are groups-of-origin after the Israeli fashion, since it is of low practical probability that any such groups in the U.S. will actually develop a vision, that demands that the group seek unique and separate political independence. Should it be said that groups-of-origin in the U.S., like their Israeli counterparts, lack the internal emotional requirements for seeking separate nationhood for themselves?
While the answer cannot be given with any certainty, the coin must be tossed, and tossed correctly – there can be no half-answer. According to the predictions of the various thinkers, than American nation is stronger than its country, has been around since the first puritan immigrants, and will continue to exist even if the present form of government does not.[77]
Considering all that has been said here about the United States and the American nation, this prediction seems to be bit on the optimistic side, in relation to the inner strength of the American nation. In fact, the claim that this nation is still forming, and may not even be worthy of the title yet, is not without merit. Though the nation did strengthen considerably after the civil war, its definition of three republics, with the impending fourth yet to come and cure it of its growing pains seems quite plausible according to many sources.[78]
Is it possible, that this country - that began as a federation of states, and which saw a shifting in loyalties, from country first, and state second, to country first, and ethnic group second – is immune to further shifts in this area? Does the United States' position as a continually forming and evolving nation – still – leave no room for the formalization of one's loyalties to one's group-of-origin, to the degree of legislation or even constitutional amendments to this effect? Is the formalizing of autonomy, cultural, or otherwise, for any particular population group not possible? Let us not forget, that even as we speak there is talk of

[77] In much the same way that the Jewish nation continued to exist throughout, and in spite of, its long exile.
[78] See Michael Lind, in this review.

segregation – even territorial, as in separate neighborhoods – for different races within the United States. There are ghettos for Blacks and Hispanics. Jews and Catholics have their own education networks. Private schools exist, whose sole purpose is separating white man from his multi-colored fellow countrymen. The demographic takeover by Hispanics is strengthening. One town has already declared Spanish as its official language. The white population already feels that it is on the defensive – at least many who consider themselves as 'white' do. There are those who claim that the government serves only the interests of a small, rich, white minority. Some claim the president is the 'prisoner' of such a group. The situation described is far from stable, and is unlikely to continue without some form of revolution taking place. It is therefore not implausible to assume that groups-of-origin may yet have their day, and that it very well may hold independent political management of cultural elements, which every group-of-origin will wish to preserve.

It is therefore not unlikely, that the historical nationality based on the countries of origin of the citizens of the United States, is due some comfort in time. The question, at any rate, remains open.

Additionally, considering that the American nation is a 'fresh' nation, one cannot exclude the possibility of total breakdown, in which case there may be parts of the old U.S. who will look for a way back to their old nationalities.

Under the circumstances, I propose to see the grouping by countries of origin in the U.S., especially when compared to the groups-of-origin in Israel, as a grouping in which ethnic elements are powerful, to the degree that former separate nationalities may re-emerge – and not necessarily through dissolution of the American government. It could very well come about as a result of internal restructuring within the United States government itself.
One should now say: Groups-of-origin within the citizenry of The United States of America can be seen as ethnic groups, while groups-of-origin within the citizenry of Israel cannot be seen as ethnic groups.

Ideals vs. a pragmatic atmosphere
Is there any difference between the favors obtained by 'Shas' (Eastern Religious Jews) and 'Yahdut Ha-Torah' (Western Religious or Ashkenazi Jews) for those in their sphere of influence, and the favors obtained by the JSA settlers? Indeed both cases manage to obtain government subsidies for their relatives at kindergartens, which is the most obvious example - others are low city taxes and a subsidizing of new apartment prices by contract realtors. On the other hand, subsidizing for the

JSA group is not connected to any particular group-of-origin. It is part of a national political movement to advance a distinctly political agenda of colonization and settlement, in areas which the JSA group sees as their prime target for settlement themselves, and are therefore able to obtain through organized lobbying at government offices. It is not a favor for its own sake, but a favor used to promote a political cause. It is similar, in this respect to the favors awarded by the settling institutions that predated the independence of the state, to those settling the country with the national cause in mind.

Another question is how to treat the favors awarded by the religious parties to their relations. It appears that these favors are also for the benefit of an ideology, similar to the political, or national agenda in the case of the JSA people. The ideal in this case is the spreading of particular religious ideals. The religious parties in question have a very particular vision of religion, and by spreading support among those who share it they ensure the spreading of their vision as well. This is not a union of benefit for its own sake, but a union for an ideal – in this case, a religious one.

Brief summery of a brief subject

The favors and special treatment awarded in the U.S. by members of ethnic groups to their fellows are for the sake of the benefits themselves, not for any ideal, unless one defines the helping someone else an ideal. Therefore there is a crucial difference between the American case and the Israeli one. Does the difference lie in the difference between a practical society, whose whole way of life is based on usefulness and pragmatism, and a society of ideals? This subject is worthy of another book in itself.

As for the question of relating the favor in question to grouping according to countries-of-origin, the JSA settlers organization is affiliated with any particular origin. The division between 'Shas' and the 'Yahdut Ha-Torah' parties, is mainly (and roughly) that of origin, in the sense that 'Yahdut Ha-Torah' embraces those falling under the category of Ashkenazi Jews in its widest sense, and 'Shas' those immigrants from Arab countries. The Rabbinical [Sage] Courts, also adhere, though vaguely, to immigrants of particular origin. While the guiding rule for all three organizations is the adherence to the rules of the Torah, there is a strong link to countries of origin present in the background.

Chapter D: A Broad Summery

Israel is a country of immigrants, the same as the United States.

On the other hand it seems unlike the United States, in that it has no ethnic groups, except for the minority of Israeli Arabs. Israeli Arabs are an ethnic group, rather than a nation, because they have no desire for an independent country of their own, and they do not wish for separation from the state of Israel – rather they desire an equality of rights within Israel, be it as individuals, or as an ethnic group seeking treatment equal to that of the Jewish ethnic group. Though literally, representatives of the Israeli Arabs call for 'Equal National Status', not 'Equal Ethnic Status', considering the definitions discussed in this part of the book, and considering that Israeli Arabs do not demand political independence, the situation is more that of an ethnic group with quasi-national demands, seeking equality with the ethnic majority in the same country. By the same definition, the Jews in Israel are a nation, since most of them want to live in a Jewish country, at least in the sense that they want Israel, the country they live in, to be the state of the Jewish people, a state intended for Jews. Any Jew who does not see Israel in this light, and who sees her as a 'State for All Her Citizens', or a 'Duo-National Country', would also have to agree to canceling the Law of Return (which guarantees citizenship and residential rights to any Jew applying for immigration), and would possibly also have to agree to the return of all Arab refugees, who left Israel in 1948.

The Jews in Israel are not divided into ethnic groups, but belong – albeit partially – to groups of origin. Partially – because many Israeli Jews do not consider themselves to be part of any group of origin, either because they feel themselves to be purely Israeli in every sense, or that they objectively belong to more than one group of origin, due to intermarriages in their lineage.

As for the comparison to the United States, it would appear that out of the Zionistic-Jewish-National urge Israel has created a political society which stands somewhat differently from the U.S. on the subject of social favoritism – in the sense that it is present in immeasurably small amounts. This element represents the national over-integrity of the Jews in Israel, and that is an ingredient of national inner strength.

Also: so long as there is no direct aversion to intermarriages between the different groups of origin in Israel (which is generally the case nowadays) group favoritism is an irrelevant issue. It would appear that the equation is true on both sides: On the one hand, so long as there is no prejudice against inter-group marriages among Jews in Israel, group favoritism is irrelevant, and on the other hand, the lack of group favoritism in Israel indicates the lack of ethnic groups, which in turn is the reason why there is no prejudice against intermarriage among Jewish groups of origin in Israel.

Part 5:
Morals and Religion

Western and Jewish, Secular and Religious Morals

Preliminary:
Logic and Emotion (An Anthropological Perspective):

The philosophical ideas presented in this part of the book are the fruits of reflection and contemplation. These ideas were omitted by anthropological science as is reflected in the words of Clifford Geertz,[1] a well-known anthropologist who wrote, regarding the anthropological subjects he had studied, "I never successfully got to the bottom of anything I ever wrote about, neither in my essays here nor elsewhere."

---

[1] See Clifford Geertz, **Interpretation of Cultures,** translated into Hebrew by Yoash Meisler (Jerusalem: Keter, The book was published originally in English in 1973), p. 38. On p. 37 Geertz writes that "The role of theory in ethnography [a branch of anthropology – Y.C.] is to provide the wealth of terms by which it will be possible to express what the symbolic action [the action which is the subject of the ethnographic article and the anthropological study] has to say about itself, in other words about the role of culture [the particular one that the anthropologist is investigating– Y.C.] in man's life. On p. 35, however, after depicting the primary work of the anthropologist as 'thick description', Geertz writes: "We are unable to write a general theory of cultural interpretation." Perhaps, we can, but it appears that the potential benefit is negligible, since the primary purpose in constructing a theory in our field [the field of anthropological science – Y.C.] is not to derive a formulation for the simple repeated action but to facilitate a thick description, not to include the individual cases [to find the common denominator that connects the anthropological facts into a broader understanding of the subject of research – Y.C.], but to include within them [to develop a 'thick description' in which the facts that emerge in the study connect at the low theoretical level, and not at a general fundamental level of understanding that even allows us to draw general conclusions – Y.C.]. On p. 36, though, Geertz explains that the emerging theory must be consistent with already existing as well as future findings, yet still the actual concept of theory is limited.

In contrast to Geertz's approach, this book seeks to construct a theoretical understanding of human group behavior within the framework of broader human societies. There are many questions that have yet to be asked and some that have been asked but yet to be answered in philosophical literature, such as: What characteristics are shared by all modern Western moral theories and what distinguishes them from moral codes that are based on belief in God? Why did human beings look towards worlds beyond the reality they knew for forces that ruled and could rule over their societies? Why did modern man, after usurping God's reins over moral and social behavior, base new rules of social and moral behavior on reason rather than on emotion? What differences are there between moral codes predicated on logic and those predicated on emotion, and what is at the root of their differences? Does man need to believe in something that is beyond his reality and that is not verifiable, and how does he acquire such faith? Can man exist without such faith (defined in the previous section as belief in God)? What connection is there between all these questions and the question that has engaged the attentions of the legal world and political circles in Israel regarding the Jewishness of the State of Israel? These basic questions receive short shrift in academic scholarship of the 20th century. Geertz, in his book (p.44), concedes that the prevalent view during the Enlightenment according to which man's civilized behavior is a consequence of his fundamental inherent nature – is accepted also today. Nevertheless, he notes (p.45) that, "There do not exist people who are not molded by customs of particular places…It is particularly difficult to differentiate between what is natural, universal, and fixed in man's nature, and what is conventional, particular, and variable." Geertz offers the example of trance states that are common in some societies and rare in others as proof that all people do not have the same fundamental traits. This is a specious argument, however, since it is not man's nature that hampers certain societies' success in achieving these trance states, but rather their ignorance of the proper technique and the absence of a conducive atmosphere. Additionally, Geertz's opinion regarding the difficulty of differentiating between what is natural, universal and fixed in human nature to what is specific, conventional, and variable among different cultures does not negate our contention that there are in fact basic universal traits common to all humanity. On page 46 of his book, Geertz speaks of the danger of abandoning man as a force behind his culture – and his consequent fall into one of two traps – the relativism that perceives man as a captive of his time, and the historic determinism that began with Hegel that leads to the idea of cultural evolution. The approach taken here avoids both of these traps, and seems to be the golden mean, the only path without obstacles. Geertz (in his book pp. 48-52) challenges Kluckhohn's theory of universal forces that determine certain common perspectives to all cultures, and suggests alternatively that there are three preconditions for a fundamentally uniform culture. These conditions are not relevant to this part of our book, as our theory which is reasonably consistent with Kluckhonhn's, does not relate to the uniformity of the products of various cultures but rather to the uniformity of the physical and emotional factors that affect the fundamental direction every human society takes in its cultural developments. Similar sources of influence can produce different cultures or different religions.

The issues examined in this part of the book are well-known. They are basic ideas that logically follow the first part of this book – 'Why religion,' and that focus on human nature. The heart of this section challenges the approach that man is a predominately intellectual creature within whom emotion plays a secondary or negligible role, arguing instead that man is by nature a logical **and** emotional creature. Man is a social creature by nature, blessed with a desire to comprehend the details he observes by finding links that connect them. This inclination is a gift that was given only to man and it has enabled man to achieve greater heights than any other creature. Man not only seeks to grasp how the natural phenomenon he observes interconnect to form the laws of nature, but also the technological details of these laws. He then employs this knowledge to accomplish his own technological feats. This inclination to categorize and classify led man, in the social realm, to establish rules of behavior, and to deduce from them appropriate behavior in every specific case.

Man is 'programmed' by his Creator with traits that precede him, so that he can succeed in the grandest of endeavors, as he in fact does. Despite all his 'technical' achievements, man could not have risen to a level qualitatively different from all other of God's creations, if not for his emotions. Without his intellect, man would be incapable of action, but without emotion, man would be unmotivated to act. The combination of these two forces enabled man to contribute to this world. It is emotion, and not intellect that is man's compass. When the emotional position is defined and clear, then emotion will always prevail. Reason arbitrates between options only when emotion is ambivalent or apathetic. A person who allows his child to drown after rationally assessing that if he attempts to save him, he will also drown, is acting based on reason, because his emotions are torn between his will to live and his love for his child. Reason only steps in when there is an emotional void.

Whoever lacks these two components of reason and emotion is not human.
Whoever possesses these two components – is God's helper and agent – the only helper God has in this world.

This book calls for a revolution, that is in fact a counter-revolution, for it comes to counter and rectify the results of the revolution described in this author's book about the Jewish State,[2] a revolution carried out by the Israeli Supreme Court. This book advocates the adaptation of a certain philosophical social approach specifically with regard to Israeli society, an approach that differs from all Western ones that are common in Western democracies including Israel. Yes, Israel, is in many respects part of the West; its norms as well as its secular-liberal Supreme Court rulings are typically Western. This reality, however, is intolerable, and problematic from both a moral standpoint, as well as from the legal one that is binding today in the State of Israel though not implemented. This book, however, in contrast to the one mentioned above,[3] will not deal with the legal issues involved, but rather with the moral and national ones.

The goal of this work, both in presenting the religious view and in attacking accepted Western theories, is not to prove the superiority of the religious viewpoint, but rather to divest secularists of their smug attitude toward the religious whom they consider primitive and ignorant. Once the religious position is at least no longer viewed as inferior – it will be possible to conduct an evaluation and discussion without being hampered by preconceived notions.

One of the main subjects this section will discuss is that of '*Moreshet Yisrael*', Jewish heritage, a tradition whose roots are in a divinely based morality, which according to the "1980 Basic Law" is the basis for Israeli law.

Debunking Myths (A View of the West):

One should never presume the truth of conventional ideas, and this includes Western ones. In critiquing Western theories, attention must be directed to the principles they are based on. This work reveals their structural flaws and undermines this foundation in order to make room for a new one. Before beginning the actual critique, this work surveys the historical development of the sources of social moral codes in human society and offer a new perspective on historical facts. It divides the history of the evolution of human societies into three periods: primitive, religious, and secular, according to changes in the source of moral guidance. The roots of the Jewish tradition are fixed in the religious period. There are many flaws in the traditional analysis of the motives behind the transition from the religious to the secular period that everyone seems to ignore. The arrogance involved in transferring the source of societal behavioral norms

---

[2] R. Yehuda Cohen, **Who Fears a Jewish State? An Ideological and Legal Perspective** (Tel Aviv: Lishkat Orchei Hadin Publications, 2001).

[3] Ibid.

from God to man has caused the instability of the entire Western moral structure. Even if one assumes the secularist position that also in the religious period, it was not God who charged man with ethical norms but rather human beings masquerading as divine messengers, secular man still exhibited greater conceit when he proclaimed himself as the source of morality than did religious man who attributed his ideas to a higher being. This book discusses the weaknesses and pretensions of Western thought in its evolution from the rule of God to the rule of man, evaluating and critiquing the ideas of Kant and Rawls among others.

There is injustice in the system Rawls speaks about and his theory of justice. The democratic system, allows a nation to turn whatever it chooses into incontrovertible law; it is a wild offshoot of secularism that began with Rousseau in the eighteenth century in France, followed by Sieyes during the period of the French Revolution. The philosophical connection between "human desire" and "human right" should rightly be viewed as the beginning of the fall and the source of the deviations that sprung up in society. These wild offshoots resulted from the translation of the sanctity of the general human will (according to democratic principles) to the plane of the individual's will; the individual, like the general public wishes to see his will followed. The individual reckons: If the general public can legislate whatever it desires, why can't I also find justification for my personal desires? Why can't I say that since what I want is proper in my own eyes – it should also be respected and considered legitimate by others? This perspective ultimately develops into a belief that 'it is coming to me,' a view strengthened by the individual's sense that it is fitting that he should get what he wants as compensation for something positive he has done. This is the transition from general will to personal will, both very human feelings. This belief of 'it is coming to me' has developed in modern days within the framework of liberal individualist thinking, which favors the individual's legitimate interest over the interests of the general public, and even condones certain deviant behavior for certain individuals. A father may be of the opinion that 'it is coming to him' that he should be obeyed. Use of violent means to achieve what 'is coming to him' is often the next obvious step.

Who is Supreme?

This section presents the bird's eye view of human social development, not only in the plane of ethical norms, but also regarding human progress in the realms of science and technology and social behavior. Man is portrayed as driven by his inherent nature, by the way he was programmed, a nature to which he owes thanks for enabling him to surpass all other creatures. Presenting the development of humanity in this manner emphasizes the true inferiority of man, and demonstrates to all Western secularists who scorn 'primitive religious people' that there must indeed exist 'something' greater than man. It forces them to recognize that man acts and achieves only because a greater 'force' 'programmed' him with these capabilities, and that we are indebted to that same greater force that programmed us all for all of our achievements including our ability to engage in debates such as this one. This understanding will impart a bit of humility and proportion to the discussion.

This discussion begins with the topic of "human rights' since this is a key factor in the field of societal behavior in the modern world.

Chapter A:
The Basis of Rights

Sie'yes' Theory:
The term "right" seems self-explanatory until one attempts to define it or to examine its development and its relationship to other concepts. The concept of rights is one of the legs upon which the normative social structure stands. It is a key player, in Western societies, in both the ethical and legal realms. Sieyes', a theoretician of the French Revolution, and one of the first French philosophers to discuss the realm of jurisprudence,[4] deals with the question of who has the right to establish law. He posits that the very existence of the national wills warrants it being made into law. All other wills, in contrast, do not turn into binding norms, except within the framework of what the national will and law have established. Only the national will and the nation can establish law;[5] one's personal will can become a legal right only and on condition that it is consistent with the national will (constitution) and all statutory law. The individual's will, according to Sieyes, differs in this way from the general will. According to Sieyes' approach, the will of the national government (which is to be differentiated from the national will of the nation) can become normative only if it is consistent with the nation's constitution, which should be remembered is determined according to the national will. National rule or government is not synonymous with the 'national will' of the nation, even though the specific persons ruling in a democratic country must be elected in accordance with the nation's will.

---

[4] Emanuel Joseph Sieyes, **What is the Third Estate?** Translated by M. Blondel and edited with historical notes by S.E. Finer, Pall Mall Press (1963), p. 126.
[5] Ibid. p. 119.

Choosing Between Rights and Benefits:

In the moral realm, consider the following perspective regarding the development of social norms before there were established countries in the world, and then later once there were national entities: Man was endowed with certain traits. One of them is his inclination to live within a social framework. Man does not seek the company of others in order to enjoy the benefits of societal living but rather because he is by nature a social being. The advantages of societal living were not the cause but rather the consequence.

In modern days, as a result of the development of Western ethical social thought, much of the clarity and sharpness which characterized these ideas during Sieyes' lifetime, has been lost. The consequent muddle and ambiguity are apparent in the ideas of Avishai Margalit, a professor at Hebrew University and student of these schools of thought. Margalit[6] claims that rights are matters that are in one's self interest, a claim that is problematic for two reasons:

1. Does the mere fact that I am an interested party (that it will be beneficial for me) confer rights regarding the object of my interest? Does my interest in getting a 90 on an exam entitle me to that mark? Of course not, and certainly Margalit did not mean to imply otherwise.
2. Could it be that I have a right to speak, even if I have no interest in doing so? The answer of course is yes. It is possible that I have the right to the empty seat on the bus, but that does not imply that I have any interest or desire to exercise that right. I many inherit something I never wanted and am indifferent to. I may bear a child not to my liking, and through this merited the right to participate in his education, though I have no interest in doing so.

Margalit defines a benefit or self-interest as that which it is fitting for a man to desire. Its existence (a potential will) does not imply that man will necessarily make it real (a will in practice). Yet this definition still leaves cause for wonder: is the mere fact that it is fitting that I should desire something sufficient or requisite basis for my right to that thing. From where did Margalit draw the connection that in his opinion exists between rights and self-interest? It seems likely that this stemmed from Western thought's placement of man, his interests and rights, in the center, in place of the dominant conception during the religious period that viewed God and his commandments as the source of behavioral norms. In the context of this discussion, which is more expansive than the question that prompted it, the concept of rights in Western vs. Jewish thought will be analyzed, preceded by an

---

[6] A. Margalit, **The Decent Society** (Cambridge, Massachusetts: Harvard University Press, 1996) p. 38.

anthropological perspective. "Rights" will be examined, not only vis-à-vis the more narrow question of the connection between it and self-interest (as Margalit contends), but also with regard to the general roots and sources of the concept of rights. This section will grapple with the question of what preceded both rights and self-interests and in what order they developed, first examining the beginning of the development of morality and then addressing the moral distinctiveness of the State of Israel.

Man's Natural Tendencies

Man is programmed not only with the desire for social living, but also with the characteristics required to establish a society,[7] and thus certain basic ethical principals are common to all human societies and communities, as if they were all patterned after a single prototype. In a primitive society, these will simply be moral rules, while in a national alliance, these rules will be legislated laws. Thus, all human societies show concern for the weaker members of their society. This trait is common also among dolphins and even among far less developed creatures. Pigeons take turns watching over their eggs and they feed their fledglings until they learn how to fly. All human societies forbid murder and theft and expect their members to honor their promises. Man's right to life and to having promises made to him honored are universal rights, rights which by definition obligate all people not to murder and to keep their promises.

Eradicating Emotion:

Almost all modern Western philosophers rejected emotion as a correct or possible element of the moral systems they hoped to build. Warnuk rejected the notion of

[7] R. Yaakov Bronovsky, **Sources of Knowledge and Imagination – Witchcraft, Science and Culture – Two Series of Lectures**, Translated from English by Sarah Yertzki-Kahanski (Tel Aviv: Am Oved, Ofakim Library, 1983, Published in English in 1978). There on pp. 22, 25, 29, 41, the idea is proposed that over the last million years, man essentially created himself by developing his brain, and that man's understanding of things in nature is more a product of receiving mechanical sensory information according to a conception that matters of import must be able to line up. Man's imagination guides him more than reality. Man's ability to understand nature depend more on his ability to interpret sensory information than on factual information. On page 79, it is claimed that man's world view is dictated by his biological makeup and on page 82, it is explained that every scientific principle is subject to modification based on new understandings and research. On page 76, man is depicted as a hopeless optimist who searches for new principles every time his old system of principles collapses.

the centrality of emotion that is basic to the emotive movement in philosophy.[8] Kant, similarly, seeks to purge morality of all natural inclinations and to deny man's emotions, establishing rational tools by which man can design moral principles. Since man is a 'rational creature, his actions have value, according to Kant, only if they are the product of his 'pure intelligence' and not of his personal inclinations and emotions. Thus instinctive behavior is virtually worthless. Behavior motivated by one's emotions similarly has no moral value, even if it is consistent with the principles of 'pure rationality'.[9] Only pure rationality stripped of any hint of instincts and emotions will enable man to design moral principles that as products of man's autonomy, will be equal to laws of nature and as binding upon man.[10] Rawls[11] set up a similar system by which a society establishes principles of justice and morality through neutralizing all actual existing individual interests and all acquired differences of knowledge and skills, thereby creating a state of absolute impartiality regarding every individual or sectoral interest. Both Kant and Rawls, therefore, seek to create moral codes in a (unnatural) state untainted by "real" life.

---

[8] Jeffrey G. Warnuk, **Modern-day Moral Philosophy,** Translated by Shaul Chanani, Ed. David Had, (Magnes Press: 1987, 1992), pp. 59-60. He writes: "Even though the emotives weighed the effect of moral dialogue on the standpoints, their explanation was incomplete, or in actuality completely misleading. The problem stemmed from certain imprecision in the explanation of the term "standpoints". Their goal was to associate standpoints with feelings – to identify, for example, my disapproval of Mr. Smith's behavior with the repugnance or recoil I am likely to feel when I witness it. This is not, however, a simple mistake but rather a most serious one. For the result was...my disapproval with Mr. Smith's behavior was identified with a completely different occurrence – 'of getting something off my chest' with regard to it. My desire to change Mr. Smith's viewpoints turned into a mere attempt to 'work' on his emotions. This is the source of the fallacy that moral expressions hold 'emotional significance', for if let my emotions out and 'work' on your emotions, aren't I using emotional language? From this we are led to the final conclusion that moral dialogue is fundamentally irrational, a product of psychological pressure and not rational argumentation, a matter of effective manipulation and not reasoning." See also Graham Wallas, **Human Nature In Politics - with a foreword by A. L. Rowse** (London: Caonstable and Company, 1948, first edition 1908) pp. XIII, XVII, 21,114.

[9] Kant, **A Premise of Metaphysics,** Magnes Press.

[10] Further on, Kant's motive in formulating this philosophy will be analyzed, an explanation that will connect Kant's philosophy with the transition from the Age of Religion in the areas of morality and law to the Age of Secularism in the development of society.

[11] John Rawls, **A Theory of Justice** (Oxford: Oxford University Press, 1972).

The exceptions to this school of thought in the modern Western world were philosophers from the Romantic period at the end of the 18th and beginning of the 19th centuries, adherents of the emotive movement of the 20th century, as well as three psychologists: -Sigmund Freud, Richard Lazarus, and Victor Frankel and the anthropologist Clifford Geertz.

In their book, Emotion and Logic, Richard and Bernice Lazarus describe the deviation from logic's domination of Western philosophy that took place during the Age of Romanticism at the end of the 18th and beginning of the 19th centuries. The Lazarus couple, following in the footsteps of Spinoza who preferred that man's emotions, rather than his intellect guide him, denies the supremacy of logic over emotion and advocates instead a synthesis of the two. Geertz, too, in his anthropological perspective (in his book cited in footnote 1, pp. 82-84), views emotion as the key to human behavior, saying in accordance with Hobbes and Thomson, "Man is not only the most rational being but also the most emotional...man is incapable of functioning effectively, in the absence of a constant significant emotional force...mental activity is the primary force that determines the nature of our encounter with the world around us...our concern is no longer resolution of problems but rather clarification of emotions." This work will not examine the effect of the mind on emotions, as it seems clear that intuitive emotional responses that guide man – are emotions and should be related to as such.

Emotion and Logic:
The synthesis of logic and emotion, both of which are inherent to man, create human morality. When logic and emotion clash, then it is emotion that rules. For example: Can one logically persuade a mother that she should kill her child and eat his flesh, thus providing herself with meat, as well as saving herself the irrational burden of raising him? Conversely, can a person's love for his children impel him to give them all his possessions when they become adults, leaving nothing for himself? If that person does hold himself back from distributing his wealth, is it because logic dictates that it is unwise that he put himself in the position of needing to rely on his children's generosity in supporting him when he is old. It is logical to retain whatever one will need in old age so as not to become dependent on others, including his children. If his wealth runs out in old age, then he won't will any to his children. The view taken here, however, is that it is not logic that competes with his love for his children but rather an opposing emotion – his will for self survival, self sufficiency, and self dependence. In this situation when two emotions are in conflict, then logic will prevail. Consequently, despite the dominance of emotion, most of man's behavior is ultimately guided by reason since logic determines which of two conflicting emotions will triumph. For

example, man has an emotional interest in making a living that goes beyond his practical-physical interest. The question of what is the most effective way of achieving this emotional goal will be determined by man's reason, assuming that several means of providing for his livelihood are compatible with his emotional desires. Logic will only select, however, an option that is in the running emotionally. Thus, if a certain means of making a living is emotionally oppressive to man, it is unlikely that he will choose it, even if logically it seems ideal.

The existence of the driving forces of reason and emotion within every person, as well as the regular dominance of emotion are proof that these are not the products merely of nurture and education, but rather inherent forces within man, which came into being when he did. Further on, this book will examine other innate tendencies such as familial loyalty, a propensity for communal life, and a desire to organize details within the framework of general principles both in what man encounters in the reality about him, in nature, and within his family life and society, in his behavior within these frameworks. This section, however, will focus on the roles reason and emotion play. Man was blessed with these two guiding forces, as well as the inclination to use these forces in a 'humane' manner, and thus emotion will generally prevail over logic.[12] Thus when man establishes moral principles, obligations and rights, emotion determines the guiding principles, while logic fills in the details. Emotion will resolve that it is imperative to help the weaker members of society; reason will determine what percentage of one's income one should contribute to this cause. Social communities and nations function in this respect just like the individual: dominant sentiments which reverberate within the nation will determine the nation's fundamental goals and positions. A country will organize as a social democratic state in accordance with their feelings, while reason will determine the details, how to reconcile social democratic principles with sometimes conflicting economic considerations. Moral principles are primarily the product of emotions, of a perspective that sees the forest more than the trees, while specific laws passed in a certain country's legislature are a product of reason and cold calculation. Basically, laws are rules of social behavior that come into existence over a relatively short period of time through a formal process. Moral principles, on the other hand, evolve through an informal prolonged process. Principles of law can be divided into two categories: rules of conduct and legal rights, and law enforcement, which include sanctions for infractions of the first category. Most laws will include both types, sometimes

---

[12] See Victor Frankel, **The Unknown God, Psychotherapy and Religion** (Jerusalem-Tel Aviv: Devir, 1985 – Translated into Hebrew by Shimon Sevi), p. 37. The original is in German, its 3rd edition was published in 1979 and its first in 1948. Speaking about the roles of reason and emotion in directing human behavior, Frankel writes, "Man's emotion has the ability to be far more sensitive than his reason has to be logical."

in separate sections, sometimes in one, with the legal sanctions generally enforced by or via the state. Moral principles, in contrast, are imposed through social rather than legal sanctions.[13] The common denominator between moral and legal principles is that both seem to advance a higher cause. Yet there is a wide range of views on what defines a higher cause. Liberals who consider man's individual rights more important than the common interest will claim that these rights promote each individual's self fulfillment, the highest of values. Those who support social values and the interests of general society will describe communal goals as higher than narrow-individual ones. They will claim that since man is a social being he has no business protecting individual rights, without concern for their affect on the general interests, which ultimately serve also the individual. Religious people who consider their deity the supreme value, will speak about advancing the will of their God, or alternatively about developing man's spirit so that he will better comprehend his creator and the will of his creator, and be more capable of emulating his attributes.[14]

Man's Inclination to Devise Underlying Principles:

Man's inclination both in the scientific as well as normative-societal behavior realms is to formulate overarching principles. In the scientific realm, scientists tie each natural phenomenon into the laws of nature.[15] Through discovery of the underlying laws, man establishes scientific laws that facilitate technological advancement. In the normative realm, man establishes principles of behavior, normative principles, which help him organize social-national life. Man's natural tendency to search for principles in both these fields promotes human progress, enriches man (physically and spiritually), and naturally creates rights and self-interests. These are self-interests that are linked to rights that were in practice acquired in the way depicted above, and rights – in potential – that man dreams of and achieves with the help of an imagination that is not possessed by other creatures. Therefore, rights, and benefits – are the products of the natural qualities

---

[13] H.L.A. Hart, **The Concept of Law** (Clarendon Press, Oxford, Second Edition, 1994) pp. 185-200.

[14] Further on, this work will present the difference between the approach that places man and his traits as a goal onto itself (as the center and supreme goal) held by Aristotle and Macintire on one hand, and an approach found in Judaism, that views man's traits as the way to get closer to God. It will be shown that Aristotle and approaches.

[15] Kant describes the connection between existing laws of nature that man uncovers and behavioral (moral) laws that man creates in his book cited in footnote 9, on pages 78-79. On page 91, he elaborates on man's tendency to formulate principles as well as on the objective root of moral principles. The generality and objectivity of moral principles is the reason, according to Kant, that man is obligated to follow these principles. See pp. 103-105 of his book.

with which man is programmed. It is not his interests which produce the principles, but the reverse. Geertz describes man's tendency to devise principles. He explains that man by nature cannot tolerate chaos. This was religion's hold on man – it offered him a system that explained the mysterious, that made sense and order out of his universe, and that offered him answers that gave meaning and reason to his life.[16]

Geertz and Anthropological Studies:

Geertz[17] claims that "man so desperately seeks symbolic sources of inspiration such as these (systems of cultural checks such as principles and directives, as he explains on p. 53 of his book – Y.C.) in order to find his way in this world. Among lower primates than man, patterns of behavior are part of their physical makeup, at least far more so than they are for man. They act according to genetic instincts. Man, in contrast, inherently possesses only the most basic reactions, which allow far more flexibility and complexity, and in those rare cases that everything is running as it should – also far better results. They do not, however, precisely regulate his behavior... Without the direction of cultural norms, the system of meaningful symbols, human behavior would be absolutely ungoverned. It would turn into chaos and pandemonium of meaningless actions and emotional outbursts. Culture, in its cumulative totality of patterns of this type, is not a mere adornment of humanity's existence, but an essential condition, and as such the basis of its uniqueness."

Further on, Geertz explains that according to earlier anthropological studies that were popular until the beginning of the twentieth century (his book was published in 1973), cultural development paralleled the physical development of man's brain, a fact that leads us to conclude that man's ability to learn, the fact that man can't function without 'an educational system' advanced his genetic development, since "man is an imperfect incomplete creature, and the difference between him and sub-humans stems less from his ability to learn (as great as it is), and more from the quality and quantity of the things that he **must** learn in order to simply function...man's physical existence came into being as a result of regular methods of genetic mutation and natural selection, until his anatomical structure reached approximately the level of perfection of its present state. At this point, cultural development began. An incidental genetic mutation of some form that occurred at a certain point in the development of the human race, endowed man with the ability to create a culture and to sustain it. From that point on, his genetic instincts became fundamentally and almost exclusively cultural responses. When man first

---

[16] See his book cited in footnote 1, chapter IV. On p. 136 he describes the 'impulse to find meaning in his experience, to give it form and order."

[17] Ibid, p. 54.

spread out all over the world, he wore fur skins in cold climates, and a loincloth in warmer climates; but he didn't change how his body reacted to different temperatures. He devised weapons in order to enhance his genetically inherited hunting skills and began to cook his food in order to make more foods potentially edible. Man became man, the story continues, when in crossing a certain mental Rubicon, he attained the ability to transmit to his descendants and neighbors through teaching and to acquire from his ancestors and neighbors through learning – knowledge, beliefs, laws, ethical principles, and customs (like Edward Taylor's definition of classical culture). After this miracle occurred, the advancement of Homo sapiens almost completely stopped being dependent on cultural development, on the growth of conventional practices."

According to the most current studies, he explains, "Evolution of Homo sapiens began approximately four million years ago...the beginning of culture preceded man by more than a million years…It was an overlapping period…the ice age – in which the initial steps of cultural history took place…Culture became a primary guiding force in the evolution [of man]…invention of tools, development of organized hunting and food gathering, beginnings of family units, discovery of the uses of fire…growing reliance on systems of meaningful symbols – language, art, myth, ritual – for purposes of orientation, communication, and self control – all these created a new environment that man needed to adapt to…the same creature who started out as a prehistoric Australopithecus with a diminutive brain became a large brained totally human Homo sapien… Man created himself in the simple sense of the word, even if he did it unconsciously…This is the period in which the human brain expanded, especially the forebrain, to its present incredible proportions…What happened in the Ice Age was…we had to rely on cultural resources – on the growing wealth of meaningful symbols…Symbols of this sort, then are not simply expressions, instruments…of our biological, psychological, and social existence, but preconditions. No doubt, without men there is no culture, but to the same extent and more significantly, without culture there are no men. The gist of the matter is that human beings are imperfect or unfinished creatures who perfect or complete themselves through culture…through very specific individual forms of culture, Dubai, Java or Italian culture, high or low culture, academic culture or business culture…people build dams and shelter, find food, organize their social groups, and find a mate according to directives hidden in flow charts and blue prints, in hunting traditions, in systems of morality and in esthetic judgment. We live in what is incisively described as an "information gap" – between what our bodies tell us and what we must know. And we fill it with information (or false information) provided by our culture. The line between innate and culturally learned behavioral limits is not well defined…we do not need cultural guidance in order to know how to breathe any more than does the fish. Our ability to speak English, however, is without a doubt cultural. To smile in response to a pleasant stimulus and to frown in response to an irritating one is definitely genetically rooted behavior to a certain extent…a cynical smile and a sneering frown, though are essentially cultural…"

This progression, as described by Geertz, relates to motivations – What led man (the term man also includes lower species from which man developed) to use skills other than biological ones, to fill voids essential for his existence? How did man's brain develop as a result?

Geertz fails to address certain issues, let alone to solve them. He overlooks the source of skills man acquired to compensate for the deficiencies that were inherent to him, and whether these skills developed out of paternal skills and motivations. He also ignores the source of the secondary skills, which created language –the inclination to connect, to make order, and to find underlying principles. He ignores the maternal-motivation, the emotional tendency that joined people together and caused them to cooperate and to communicate in a manner that would transmit information from generation to generation, traits that served man not only by linking different generations, but also different societies and ethnic groups. Diamond cut diamond. No matter how hard Geertz tries to elevate man to the level of self-creator, he cannot avoid the question of who and what trait enabled man 'to create himself.'

Man demonstrated an inclination to search for connections between individual facts, to attempt to link isolated events, to find the common denominator to different natural phenomenon, to establish a code of social behavior that doesn't address every specific case but rather offers underlying principles, to not limit himself to solving each and every problem separately as it arises but to strive to find an all-encompassing solution. The social developments and relationships that developed that were predicated on feelings and on sympathy for the weak, traits lacking in other creatures must be viewed in light of these inherent tendencies. All these, according to the approach that Geertz develops, are paternal-influences that directed man on the path that he described. These influences will be examined in the next chapter.

Chapter B:
Three Periods in the Development of Morality

The Primitive Age:

From the beginning of social living, the natural tendencies that guided man and his actions benefited him greatly. One can imagine that in a pre-society (organized society) period, family units were very small, composed most probably only of a couple and their offspring. These units were the expression of. man's natural instinct to mate and to raise children, an instinct that is predicated on natural inherent feelings called love, with which man is blessed still today and which he continues to develop. Just like the inclination to establish underlying principles and to associate with others, feelings of love necessarily, naturally, and logically led the couple living without a wider social framework to establish certain rules of behavior to govern their relationship. Rules that applied to their children ostensibly followed from these. Here too then, is an example in which self-interest did not guide man – to find his mate, to establish mutual rights and responsibilities between himself and his mate and their children. Self interest was not at the root of these developments, it was not their cause, but rather a consequence of primary forces that stem from human nature. In this book, this historical period of man's narrow societal structuring into couples and families will be called – **'The primitive age.'**

The Age of Religion:
The second period of human social development is one that falls between the 'primitive age' and modern time – a period that will be referred to here as 'the Age of Secularism' since during it a kind of 'secular religion' developed throughout the world. In this interim period – 'the Age of Religion', social frameworks developed and the dominant factor in the establishment of societal behavioral norms was religious belief. These norms were established in an environment of religious faith, even if this faith was not the sole influence. The 'Age of Religion' will be examined at the beginning from a Jewish viewpoint. In Jewish way of life until the modern era, Torah laws played a primary role. This Torah included an Oral Law that Jews believed God also gave to Moses at Sinai, as well as religious rulings and Jewish doctrine.

Religion and religious statutes played a central role in this period also among other nations.

The transition from the Age of Religion to the Age of Secularism was marked in England by a markedly new view of the role of Parliament. The English Parliament initially functioned as a law court that offered the king counsel regarding the law but did not legislate. In other words, just as a court must identify what the laws are in order to adjudicate according to them, the Parliament similarly identified the laws, just more broadly and not in relation to a particular case. This perception of the Parliament stemmed from a belief in a divine origin of the law - the king had no authority to establish law but only to interpret divine laws and to apply them to the needs and problems of his time.[18] Parliament was given authority to approve taxes that the king required to run his country or fight his wars. In England, a Common Law developed alongside the religious law. It was only with the spread of secularism that the Parliament began **legislating** changes in the Common Law, and Parliament gradually evolved into a legislative body in the modern sense of the word.

The one thing that distinguishes a religious ethic from a secular Western one is that the religious ethic is built on obligations while the Western one is built on rights alongside obligations. There are no rights, essentially, in the divinely based ethic, as it exists today (this include Hinduism, Buddhism, Confucius' system, Judaism, Christianity, and Islam). An ethic whose source is from above, from a transcendental being who has influence over the world and who determines how man should behave, is a hierarchic system of principles imposed from above on man who exists down below. It is not man, but rather the transcendental being who imposes a binding ethic, who is supreme. Therefore, the Biblical injunction that a Hebrew slave goes free in the Sabbatical (seventh) year obligates the master to free his slave while granting the slave the right to go free only as a by product of the master's obligation. The Torah commands the Jews to set Hebrew slaves free in the seventh year, to love the foreigner, to judge him impartially, and to treat the orphan and widow with kindness. It instructs those who are more fortunate to act with charity towards those who are less fortunate; it does not turn to the recipients of this charity and inform them that they have a right to this treatment. In Confucianism similarly, the master is commanded to treat his worker in a certain way (eg. with tolerance) and the worker must listen to his master. There is no declaration of the worker's right to this treatment but rather only an obligation imposed upon the master. This is generally the case regarding all divinely based systems of morality. Obligations, not rights are established both upon the individual and as is common in Hinduism and Judaism, upon the group. There are certainly some today who wish to prove that Judaism confers and always conferred rights, in order to make Judaism more palatable to those for whom human rights are a supreme value. The beauty of the divine ethic, though, in contrast to Western morality in which man – by definition – has no higher authority to emulate, is that man does not see himself as supreme but rather aims to raise his level of morality.

---

18 M.J.C. Vile, **Constitutionalism and the Separation of Powers** (Clarendon Press: Oxford), pp. 24-25.

The Age of Secularism:

In the 'Age of Secularism', through the process of developing a kind of 'civil religion', Western philosophers searched for a source of morality or ethics. Initially, they attempted to anchor normative principles in objective sources. The transition from the Age of Religion to the Age of Secularism was bound up in a search for a new legitimate source that would be as objective as the divine source and thus could replace it. Objective, in their eyes, implied 'truth' and truth was compelling, worthy of being followed. Hobbes, Sieyes, and Kant each offered a different justification for their ethical systems.

Hobbes and the theory of a social contract found validation in the accepted principle that 'agreements should be honored.' The democratic movement, as expressed in the modern period by the ideologue of the French Revolution, Sieyes, and his followers, found legitimization in the notion that the nation is sovereign and the legitimate landlord of its country. Just as a landlord may do as he will with his own property, the nation has a binding lawful right to exercise its will over its own property. Therefore, if it is their will to choose for themselves a legislator who will create a constitution and pass laws, these laws will be binding because they were legislated by a legislator of all the nation's choosing.

Kant found legitimization in the 'truth' and 'objectivity' that are within subjective man's only objective possession, namely his reason. Pure practical reason, unsullied by man's subjective elements, is the objective ideal by which truth may be discovered. Practical reason can take one of two paths in order to uncover the truth. It can follow the course of natural sciences, physics, and 'find' the true laws of nature (that exist) or it can follow the course of morality and virtue and create ethical principles, a creation ex nihilo. Kant sought to offer man freedom, freedom from laws of nature, a freedom that alongside the objectivity of the rules that his intelligence would establish, would motivate man to adhere to those same rules as a free man. This was a freedom that man in the 'Age of Religion,' who was bound by religious precepts, never enjoyed. Kant did not seek a source for morality in nature; if man's pure practical intelligence had 'revealed' such a source, and adhered to its laws, man would see himself as constrained by natural laws that he did not create. Pure practical reason, however, belongs to man, and since it created principles of morality and laws autonomously, man's compliance with these laws does not constitute enslavement, but rather the epitome of freedom. Consequently, man will willingly obey these laws. The legitimization of (secular) laws of morality was thus based on a truth that was derived from objectivity, and the freedom that is inherent in following these laws.[19]

---

[19] Kant, in his book cited in the previous footnote, on page 110 explains, in the context of why man should heed laws of morality that he himself (and not an objective source such as God or nature) creates, that adherence to the laws of 'pure practical reason' that man

Kant sought (unconsciously) to solve one of the problems Rousseau raised regarding the transition from a religious moral system to a secular one, by establishing a new 'objective' source for moral commandments,[20] namely that of 'pure practical reason.'[21] Kant posited that one must not establish behavioral norms based on man's [subjective] feelings, on his practical needs and desires, and on his aspirations. None of these are suitable sources for moral commands for they are all dependent on man's whim. Morality's authority lies in its objectivity. This trend toward objectivity, as will be seen, exists also today according to Rawls.[22]

---

autonomously designs make man 'free in regard to all laws of nature and bound only by those laws that he himself gives.'

[20] Jean Jacques Rousseau, **On the Social Contract** (Magnes Press, 1996), p. 64. He writes there: 'This is what compelled heads of state throughout the ages to rely on help from God and to give honor to the Gods, attributing to them their own wisdom, so that the nations bound by the laws of their country as they were to laws of nature, recognizing that the same force itself created man...will willingly heed and eagerly bear the burden...This exalted principle, which is beyond the understanding of the masses, is that the legislator put his decisions in the mouth of the Gods in order to suppress by divine decree anyone not stirred by human authority.' Isaiah Berlin in his book **Four Essays on Religion,** translated into Hebrew by Reshafim Press in 1971, writes on page 189, regarding the transition from the Age of Religion to the Age of Secularism: 'In it's apriori version, it is a secular form of Protestant individualism, in which a rational approach replaces God...' It is clear to all that reason replaced God in the Age of Secularism. What we seek to explain and emphasize is the reason why reason was chosen in these circumstances. In Kantian philosophy, reason is objective, and therefore it became the incontrovertible anchor that replaced faith in God.

[21] Kant, **Basis of Metaphysics**, cited in footnote 9, pp. 99,117,124-131, 143-150, 159, 167-170.

[22] One may view liberal individualism as a decisive transfer of the crown to man. After it had rested on the head of the deity during the Age of Religion and been passed through three secular stations that provided refuge from claim of non-objectivity in other ways, man forgot about the Age of Religion. The problem of legitimization ceased to disturb him, and it was finally possible to crown man with the same crown with which it was inconceivable to bestow upon mortals in the Age of Religion. But see: Hermann Cohen, **Religion of Reason from Jewish Sources** (Mossad Bialik Press and the Leo Baeck Institute (1971) written by the religious liberal Jew Hermann Cohen in the beginning of the 20th century. His writing reflects the strong influence of Kant, and in fact Cohen builds a moral theory based on man's reason, but not in opposition to religious morality but rather as the product of his system that marries what is in existence (nature) to what is desirable (morality) to form one unity directed by the scepter of a God who created man so that he might join between these two using his powers of reason granted to him by God. According to this, truth is the union between what exists and what is desirable and its chances of success depend on God. This union produces the true religion which all people

The connection between the transition from the Age of Religion to the Age of Secularism and the fundamentals of Kant's theory of morality and his idealization of pure reason, need not be interpreted as pretentious calumny of Kant and his philosophy. You may protest: 'How dare the author of this book accuse Kant, one of the central pillars of the philosophy of morality, of distorting and twisting his theories in order to bolster secular philosophy? How can he suggest that Kant tailored his philosophy, which was intended to be theoretical truth untainted by any subjective interest, to promote secularism? What right does he have to charge Kant with such dishonesty, thus detracting from the value of his theories and the inner truth they hold?'

To this we respond that this work never meant to imply that Kant deliberately misled his followers or that he did not believe in his own philosophy. Kant, like all philosophers in every generation, was a product of his environment. He experienced the problems of his time and of the community in which he lived. Thus, though his theory of objective morality seemed to him to be free of any personal interest or bias, and as such he represented it in his writings, it was unconsciously influenced by his generation and country.

This is one of our primary criticisms of Kant's theory, a theory that has been critiqued by many including Rupert Emerson who attributed hidden motives to all German philosophers from Kant until the rise of Nazism in Germany.[23]

Chapter C:
The Moral Helm is Transferred From God to Man

Utilitarianism and Law:

Over time as secularism struck roots, ideas about political and social entities developed, and the movement that placed man at the center grew stronger, the

---

will eventually come to follow. This is the 'religion of reason' that Hermann Cohen finds backing for in Jewish sources.

[23] Rupert Emerson, **State and Sovereignty in Modern Germany** (New Haven: Yale University Press, 1928), chapters I & II. An analogy is drawn there between cultural and political events and developments in the internal government and the different systems. Though great German philosophers were leaders until today in the development of moral and political thought, Emerson depicts them as prisoners of the reality in which they lived. They developed their theories as answers to the problems of the reality they were familiar with. This supports the thesis of this book regarding the weaknesses of secular Western philosophy, which despite its hopes to reach the skies with its 'objective' study, was mired in the sludge of the ever-changing reality

attraction of this external secular force faded for some philosophers, the desire to imitate the objectivity of divinely based morality ebbed, and theories that did not strive so much for 'objectivity' arose. Man himself, the subject, without the mantle of objectivity that would jar him out of his innate subjectivity (eg. through the practical pure reason that Kant spoke of) became a source of legitimization. It began with the social-utility theory that searched for the magic formula in the form of the greatest good of humanity. One of its proponents, Bentham,[24] constructed formulas by which the general social good could be calculated if the society was viewed as a single man. This theory of utilitarianism metamorphosed into a theory of individual utility, which was particularly popular in the 1970's in the philosophy of Rawles[25] as well as Kimlika and Dworkin. This philosophy valued the individual and his rights and interests over the goals and interests of the general society. It favored the static rights of the individual over general society's dynamic needs. This approach, which had budded far before the twentieth century, anchored individual civil rights into the constitutions of many countries, in an effort to check the pragmatic legislation by elected officials that accorded with the general variable interest. The clash between the individual's constant rights and the pragmatic fluctuating interests of the general public as represented by the public's constantly changing elected officials was the driving force behind a constitution, a rigid permanent set of laws that took legal precedence over legislated law. Advocates of this constitutional system believed that a particular generation could define basic desires and rights according to conceptions of their time, and impose them on later generations, regardless of how needs and ideas changed, leaving only an escape hatchet of a complex amendment process.

Liberal Individualism:

Proponents of a liberal-individualist philosophy argued against a communitarian morality, a non-objective morality that varies from society to society. How can we, they asked, condone the caste system in India since it conforms with the ethical code there, when it is inconsistent with an objective truth.[26] Though undeniably, liberal-individualist philosophy has raised awareness of the value of fundamental rights of the individual, it is a problematic view. It demands the state's neutrality on one hand and non-intervention of one individual in the affairs of another, on the

---

[24] J. Bentham. **An Introduction to the Principles of Morals and Legislation** (Athlone Press: London, 1970), ed. by J.M. Burns and H.L.A Hart.

[25] See footnote 10, J. Rawls, **A Theory of Justice** (Oxford, New York: Oxford University Press, 1972).

[26] See a description of Rawls position in footnote 30, **Communitarianism and Individualism**, p. 5.

other hand.[27] Though proponents of liberal-individualism will deny it,[28] by putting the individual at the center and his will as the basis of freedom and rights, this philosophy weakens man's natural inclination to live in a society and his commitment to it, and hampers society's ability to serve as his moral compass.[29]

Modern Communitarians and Their Criticism of Rawls

Modern communitarians, such as Michael Sandel[30] opposed individualist philosophy. Sandel asserted that Rawls' theory of a social contract minus the personal interests of those forming the agreement was similar to Kant's state of 'pure reason', and that Rawls simply 'translated' Kant's theory into terms palatable to Americans today. Kant's source of moral norms, the state of 'pure reason' was compatible with the German culture of his days, but it was not, according to Sandel, compatible with twentieth century American culture. In America's business culture, the concept of a 'deal' was far more agreeable as the basis for an ethical code. Thus, according to Sandel, Rawls apparently[31] possessed an inner moral conscience, which he sought to convey to Americans using terms that would speak to their hearts. From Rawls' own words, it is clear that he felt an affinity for Kant's theories. Thus he simply modified them for twentieth century Americans, his greatest change being the marriage of American business with Kant's objectivity. He proposed eradicating the self-interests that by nature do not lead to consideration for others or justice (just as Kant had 'eradicated' feelings and tendencies), by viewing normative questions and social principles through a 'screen of ignorance' through which those defining principles of morality do not

---

[27] See the comparison between the political community and the domain of integrative feelings and accountability of the individual within it, as described by Dvorkin in his book in the previous footnote, pp. 211-213.

[28] See Ronald Dvorkin, "Liberal Community" in **Communitarianism and** Individuqalism, edited by Shlomo Avineri and Avner De-Shalit (Oxford. New York: Oxford University Press, 1992) 205-224, in p. 219, where Dvorkin claims that a liberal who lives in an unjust society will feel that his quality of life is diminished as a result. He will develop true sensitivity of civil republicanism. These individual citizens must fuse their interest and personality within the communal politic. Dvorkin argues that this approach will blossom only in a liberal community and that only a liberal is capable of merging political morality and his own interest and personality. Dvorkin ignores, however, the limited framework in which the liberal will exercise his involvement in the national society, the framework of the activities of the 'neutral' establishment that does not restrain individuals in the country from behaving in a manner that the communitarian ideologue considers contrary to his values.

[29] See footnote 11, Rawlesp. 560.

[30] Sandel Michael, "The Procedural Republic and Unencumbered Self", **Communitarianism and** Individualism (Oxford: Oxford University Press, 1992), Avineri and A. De-Shalit ed., Political Theory 12, pp. 81-96.

[31] Apparently, but not in reality as will be demonstrated in Part V of this book.

recognize their own interests and thus all concur as to the moral fundamentals. Since this matter will be carried out under 'just' conditions, it will produce a 'just' ethical system. While a thorough critique of this theory must wait until Part V of this book, it will be noted here that it is clear that this imaginary scenario in which the participants mask their eyes and thoughts with a 'screen of ignorance', which blinds them to their inner moral and rational senses is impractical. Even Rawls never claimed that this situation could be practically implemented but rather only that man could reconstruct it in his imagination and based on his reconstruction sketch the correct principles of justice.

Based on Sandel's critique, it becomes apparent that Rawls, like Kant sought 'an objective source' of morality as a kind of substitute for God. Rawls combined his modified version of Kantian philosophy with a watered down version of Hobbes' social contract. He did not speak of a constitutional social contract that establishes (like Hobbes) a new society, but rather of a means of improving a society's already existing rules. Rawls lived at a time when 'secular religion' had already taken root; therefore he was not driven by the same motive as Kant, a desire to legitimize principles of justice, which had been divorced from God, a common objective for people accustomed to the idea that truth could issue only from God or nature. Nevertheless, Rawls adopted the fundamentals of Kant's philosophy regarding the objectivity necessary in devising binding ethical rules.

Ascendancy of the Community and the Social Contract vs. Ascendancy of the Individual and Liberal Individualism:

Margalit's theory equates self-interests with rights, a connection likely to be drawn by modern Western philosophers (Rawls included). It views rights as the product of self-interests. People achieve rights according to their interests (whether communal or individual). The entire social system and its functioning is dictated by interests. A person's self interest is what will motivate him to seek this right and then ultimately to implement this right. A right allows the fulfillment of an interest, and an interest is protected by a right. Whoever believes in liberal-individualism, as Dvorkin depicts it (and as Barak does in his rulings) believes that at the center of man's being is a blueprint in which are linked the connections between will and right, between right and interest, between interest and will, and so on and so forth.[32] This is in essence the opposite of Sieyes'

---

[32] This is manifested in countless examples. For example: Ronald Dvorkin, "Liberal Community", California Law Review, Vol. 77 [1989] 479, p. 485. Dvorkin clearly distinguishes between circumstances which are clearly in man's interest whether or not he recognizes, such as good relations with one's children to man's understanding of their value. Dvorkin advocates society's non-intervention in areas that are autonomous to man. He argues that society has no right to interfere on paternalistic grounds and to force man to appreciate the importance of his relationship with his children and thus improve his

philosophy. Instead of saying that only the will of the **nation** can by virtue of its very existence turn into law (or right) – Dvorkin's liberalist theory emphasizes the supremacy of the **individual** over the 'good' (interest) of the general society. Modern day Western communitarianism (in contrast to modern day liberal individualism) also associates man's self interest with his will. Communitarians view man as the center and purpose of ethics and morality,[33] but since they view the individual as a social creature, they speak of the community and society. In this way both liberal individualism and communitarianism in our days relate to the tension between the supremacy of the individual's right and the 'good' (interest) of the general society. The common denominator between these two theories is the **centrality of man's self interest**. This is the issue that distinguishes both of these theories from an ethic[34] based on religious Jewish faith. This will be the subject of the following chapter.

Chapter D:
Jewish Morality

An Edifying Jewish World View and the Laws of the State of Israel

Before continuing, it is important to examine the Jewish perspective on morality, its place in Jewish philosophy, and to demonstrate the uniqueness of the Jewish religion in comparison with other divine religions, including those monotheistic religions that were an offshoot of Judaism: Christianity [35] and Islam. Yeshayahu Leibowitz[36] identified two categories of believers in a divine creator. There are those who believe in a God who metes out justice in his world, who rewards those who fulfill his commandments. Serving this God is ultimately self-serving and

---

relationship – even if this intervention is intended to help the man himself and to further his interests. This assistance is objectionable since it involves interference in an individual's private affairs.

[33] **Communitarianism and Individualism** [edited by Shlomo Avineri and Avner De-Shalit, Oxford University Press, p. 3. They write, "Both communitarian and individualist theories begin with the image of the individual.

[34] This book distinguishes between the words morality and ethic. Ethic refers to already existing principles of behavior while morality refers to appropriate principles of behavior. Ethic is the implementation of morality in a certain time and place. Morality, according to a communitarian perspective, can be appropriate for a specific society at a certain time, while according to a liberal view, it will be applicable at all times and in all societies. A third possibility, is that it is the suitable moral code for a particular generation. These three viewpoints will be analyzed further at some other time.

[35] Not including the Jesuites and monks, to a certain extent, as will be clarified further on.

[36] See Yeshayahu Leibowitz, **Five Books of Faith** (Jerusalem: Keter, 1995), pp. 23-24.

thus there is an element of utility in serving this creator. A second category shares the type of faith that Avraham, the forefather of the Jewish people, manifested particularly in the story of the *akeidah* (the binding of Yitzchak). His love of God did not depend on reward. His love of God was bound up in fulfilling God's commandments. Even when God's commandment essentially negated all prior divine promises (regarding the nation that would emerge from Yitzchak), Avraham remained silent. He did not reproach God for breaking his promise, but took his son Yitzhak to offer him up as a sacrifice on Mount Moriah, as God had commanded. Through this act, Avraham distanced himself from all materialism and utilitarianism and drew closer to his God in his love of him. There are groups in certain non-Jewish religions, such as Jesuit monks who have retained some of these sparks of worship, and shun all materialism or personal benefit in this world – but they do anticipate reward in the world to come.

After this digression, let us proceed. A Jew is commanded to emulate the noblest of traits, which are embodied by the Creator. Every Jew has a purpose in this world. He is not the center of the universe, and his needs and self-interests have import only if they serve higher loftier goals. Humility is as esteemed as happiness, and mercy is greater than both. A Jew adheres to the commandments that are incumbent upon him, for their fulfillment is his means to spiritual growth. A Jew takes care of his body so that he will have the strength to fulfill God's commandments. This perspective should be the basis for how Israeli courts interpret Israeli law laws, as will be demonstrated further on. This is not because this work advocates religious coercion. The term "law" itself, however, contains an element of coercion, and a world-view that arises from the law is binding upon a judge even if he does not personally share that view. For example: the laws of the State of Israel absolutely prohibit corporal punishment in the schools. While it is quite likely that a specific judge in Israel will deem it appropriate to hit a student under certain circumstances, the laws of the state obligate him to rule against the teacher who hit his student. That judge would be absolutely unjustified in claiming that the law constitutes coercion of a world-view.

The same holds true regarding the Jewish view that esteems spiritual values over personal interest. Since judges are required to rule according to Jewish values, they must rank dry material interests much lower than higher values, such as teaching people the importance of returning lost objects. The case of Handels vs. Kupat-Am Bank involved interpretation of Israeli law regarding the restoration of lost objects.[37] When a bank customer found an object on the floor of the vault and the owner could not be found, a legal dispute ensued over rights to the object. Barak ruled, in accordance with American law, that the bank (who owned the

---

[37] See D"N 13/80. Handels vs. Kupat Am Bank Inc.. Supreme Court Law Reports Vol. 35 (2), p. 785.

vault) had rights to the object, while Alon ruled according to Jewish law in favor of the finder. The difference in ruling depended on interpretation of an Israeli law. Both judges had already given their reasons in detail in an earlier round of the case.[38] Alon based his ruling on the goal shared by the Israeli legislator and Jewish law – that of encouraging the person who finds a lost object to try to return it to its owner – by reporting it to the police according to Israeli law or by searching for its owner according to Jewish law. The knowledge that he may acquire the lost object, if despite his best efforts its owner is not found, may encourage the finder to fulfill his lawful obligation. It is now in his self-interest to do his duty. This is a perspective that views self-interest not as the goal but only as a means of encouraging fulfillment of an obligation. The obligation and mitzvah to locate the owner shapes our interpretation of the law. Virtuous behavior on the part of the finder is encouraged by offering him a potential reward, the chance to earn the lost object for himself, if he fulfills his obligation to search for its owner. There is no need to encourage the owner of the place where the object was found, since he does not face any moral challenge. This is an example of an interpretation of law which considers the edification of man and development of his character as central to the legal system. Barak's interpretation of the law, on the other hand, gave precedence to ownership and rights, not virtue, and since the object was found on bank property, it belonged to the bank. The virtue that is spoken of is not the virtue that Alasdair Macintyre refers to, one that **places man and his self interest at the center,**[39] but rather a Jewish conception of spiritual virtue (in accordance with the

---

[38] See civil appeal 546/78, Supreme Court Law Reports Vol. 34 (3), p. 57

[39] Alasdair Macintyre, **After Virtue A Study of Moral Theory**, second edition (University of Notre Dame Press: Note Dame, Indiana, 1984), Chapter XIV "The Nature of Virtues", p. 187. Macintyre enumerates three steps in the development of virtue: a)practice (in contrast to theory) b)way of life c)moral conduct. He distiguishes between external 'goods' bestowed upon man by external sources and internal 'goods' who possess excellence in 'practice'. He differentiates between institutions (such as universities) who award degrees, external 'goods', and exceptional 'practice', which is an internal matter. In defining the 'practice', he opposes the labels of good and bad. A wonderful pianist, Macintyre writes, may possess negative personality traits (p. 193). Yet, he establishes that the 'practice' must be one that benefits society. Excellence, Macintyre writes, must include three elements: justice, courage, and honesty. Different societies may have different codes of justice, courage, and honesty, and man must be judged according to the yardstick of his society (pp. 192-193). Macintyre discusses the element of gratification there is in 'practice', and he posits that this pleasure from the action and the action itself are one and the same (p. 197). He doesn't rule out the possibility of action leading to iniquity. Virtue, he writes, may be linked to activity that has no redeeming value and that is not positive, and therefore one must differentiate between the excellence of man's action and the virtue regarding the morality of the action, since the question of morality lies independently in the realm of moral law. In general, Macintyre adheres to Aristotle's approach, and he notes

view of the Rambam who adopts a similar understanding as Plato, one that is not popular in Judaism today), one that does not hold man at its center, one that is not utilitarian, and whose characteristics do not seek to improve him as an ends to itself but rather as a means of drawing him closer to the attributes of the Creator. Hermann Cohen refers to the commandment in Deuteronomy, "Behold I have placed before you today life and good, death and evil...therefore choose life," and deduces from it that God limited himself when He gave a Jew freedom of choice, since though He commanded him to choose the just path, God will not prevent him from choosing otherwise. Cohen develops from here the constraints of a God who does not interfere either in man's intellectual reasoning (by which man establishes laws of reason) or in his moral reasoning (by which man's behavior is guided, and which is responsible for, among other things, a Jew not only fearing God but loving him). Fear distances man from his God while love draws him closer and impels him to strengthen his connection with his Creator by emulating Him. This ambition is a far cry from Western philosophy's goal of man's 'self fulfillment', that focuses entirely on advancing the secular man who sees himself as the source of all norms. Though Hermann Cohen calls man the goal, he in actuality views man's good deeds as the goal.[40] The objective here is not religious coercion, but rather entry into a world in which man and his traits are viewed as the "corridor that leads into the dining hall."

An In Depth Examination of the Jewish Perspective:

The Babylonian Talmud in Tractate Brachot[41] cites the Biblical commandment to send away a mother bird before taking her eggs, explaining "that he considers God's attributes as stemming from mercy. The Gemara there asks why we must silence the person who attributes this Biblical Law to God's mercy and answers (one of its two answers) because this person errs in attributing God's laws to mercy when in fact they are decrees. The Maharal[42] analyzes Rambam's reason for this mitzvah. The Rambam, in contrast to the Ramban and other Jewish philosophers,

---

that not only in Aristotle's philosophy (who seeks to cause man to help himself), but also in other schools of philosophy that relate to man's character, like Plato's (who seeks to motivate man to help society), the New Testament (that seeks to draw man closer to a certain destiny as a believer), and of Franklin (who seeks to motivate man to achieve the greatest benefit from his actions) virtue is not a goal onto itself but rather a means to a certain goal. Macintyre embraces Aristotle's position, but when we search for the system most in line with the trend in Judaism that we are presenting in this book, the New Testament is the closest. The Rambam's view will not be examined in this context except to note his divergent interpretation of the mitzvah to send away the mother bird away.

[40] See Hermann Cohen in his book cited in footnote 22, pp. 431-432.

[41] Tractate Brachot 33b.

[42] In his book Tiferet Yisrael (Jerusalem: 1972), Chapter VI, pp. 21-24.

did not believe that the purpose of mitzvahs was to develop man's spiritual traits so he would more closely emulate God. He is more in line with Plato's view that the improvement of one's traits is an inherent good, not necessarily connected to the mitzvahs. The Rambam, therefore, in contrast to the perspective in Judaism that we will be presenting, did not think that the commandment to send away the mother bird before taking her eggs was intended to teach man to be more merciful. As a result, the Maharal rejected the Rambam's opinion, preferring the Ramban's view instead. Nevertheless, as he explains in his '*Hilchot Deot'* compiled by Dr. Zifroni and published by Omanut in 1968, the Rambam agrees that a Jew seeks to develop his behavioral traits in order to draw closer to God. *De'ot* is synonymous with *techunot*-attributes and in fact the subject of this book is not ideas (an alternate meaning of *de'ot*) but rather attributes. The book is primarily directed toward a 'wise' man, a man, as the Rambam describes on page seven of this book, "whose attributes are moderate and temperate." The Rambam elaborates on page six saying: "The just path is one of moderation in every trait that man has, so that each trait is equidistant from either extreme and not close to either. Therefore the early sages commanded that man should put [contemplate, as Zifroni explains according to Sota 5b] his traits constantly and direct them to the middle road, so that he will be complete in his person. How so? He shouldn't be an angry person, easily incensed nor like a dead person who is insensate, but rather moderate: angered only by important matters that deserve his wrath, so that he won't be inclined to do so another time. Similarly, he should desire only those things his body cannot live without as it is written : "A little bit is good for the righteous person. He should not seek more, nor should he squander his money, but rather he should give charity according to what he has and loan money to one who needs. He should not be foolish and giddy nor gloomy and miserable but rather cheerful and contented all his days, with a pleasant countenance." The Rambam cites as support for his advice the verse in Deuteronomy 25:9, "You should walk in His ways" and the Gemara in Sota 14a, "Just as He is merciful, you should be merciful, just as He is compassionate, you should be compassionate, just as He is holy, you should be holy." On page eight he lists God's attributes as He was depicted by the prophets (long-suffering, merciful, righteous and just, perfect, strong and mighty). He writes that the prophets sought "to advise us that these are good and just paths and that man must follow them and undertake to emulate Him as best as he can." The obligation to emulate God is incumbent upon all of humanity, and not only Jews, as is logical, since it doesn't relate to a religious commandment but rather directly follows from the recognition that there is a creator. Since the Rambam lived among religious Muslims who shared a belief in monotheism, his premises were different from those of Plato's or Aristotle's. A different section of 'Hilchot De'ot' is dedicated to the Jew specifically. There (page 24), he relates an explicit mitzvah in Torah to a Jew's moral behavior, even though generally the Rambam does not link man's traits to mitzvahs. The Rambam writes there: "It is a mitzvah incumbent upon every person to love each and every Jew as himself, as it is written, 'You shall love your neighbor as yourself.' Therefore, he must relate his praises and watch over his property just as he watches over his own property and desires honor himself. And one who rejoices in his friend's downfall has no part in the World to Come. The obligation to love of the stranger, who has come under the wings of the Divine presence, stems from two positive commandments, one because he is included among 'neighbors' and two because he is a convert, and the Torah commanded us, "You shall love the convert." The Torah commanded us to love the convert just as it commanded us to love God himself, as it is written, 'You shall love Hashem your God.' God himself loves converts as it is written, 'and He loves the convert.'

The Maharal preferred the Ramban's view over the Rambam's. The Ramban was of the opinion that, "the reason [for the mitzvah to send away the mother bird] is to accustom us to act mercifully so that we won't act cruelly to living creatures...And God decreed this attribute as well as all other commandments in order to inculcate man with good traits and they are decrees upon man." The Maharal quotes Rabbi Yochanan ben Zakai who in reflecting on the entirety of the mitzvahs concluded that, "The Torah comes to improve us, but the commandment is a decree that He decreed, and this is the meaning of the statement – that he considers the attributes of God mercy when they are in fact decrees." [In other words: the decrees that God ordained, are to improve our traits – Y.C.] The Ramban[43] writes regarding God's commandment to Avraham to go to the Land of Canaan, "This section did not explain the whole matter, for why should God tell him – leave your land and I will do for you good unlike any ever done in the world, without prefacing that Avraham worshipped God or was a perfectly righteous man, or explaining that his reason for leaving his land was to go a different land that was closer to God." The Ramban here is of the opinion that Avraham's rewards for fulfilling God's commandments are unimportant since only his closeness to God mattered. The Rambam, in his commentary on the introduction to Mishnah Avot,[44] writes: "Man must subjugate all his mental faculties to reason, as we wrote in the previous chapter, and he should always keep before his eyes one goal, and that is comprehension of God, to the extent that a human being can comprehend Him, and he should direct all his actions, his movements and his breaks and everything to this goal, until none of his actions

[43] In his book **Commentaries on the Torah** (Mossad Harav Kook Publications: Jerusalem, 1959), Volume I, Genesis, Exodus, p. 76, Genesis 12:2.

[44] As cited in Rambam's Introduction to his Commentary on the Mishnah, ed. and explained by Mordechai Dov Rabinovitch (Mossad Harav Kook Publications: Jerusalem, 1961), p. 184, in his reference to chapter V of Shmoneh Perakim.

have any element of futility, in other words any action that does not lead to this goal..." The Kuzari[45] writes: "Our Torah is divided between fear and love and happiness. Draw close to your God through each of these for your submission on a fast day does not draw you closer to God than your rejoicing on Shabbat and festivals...What we learn from this is that we can approach God only through his commandments..." In the Zohar[46] it is written regarding the verse in Isaiah 42: "R. Abba began and said, 'Sing to God a new song, and His praise from the end of the earth...' How beloved are Israel before God for their rejoicing and their praise only come to include God and His divine presence within it, as we learned in the Mishnah – Any rejoicing of Israel in which they do not include God, is not rejoicing..." [This teaches that even man's joy, even his personal intimate joy should be done with the ultimate goal in mind. Man's willingness to rejoice only if God rejoices with him demonstrates significant restraint and humility]. To this we should add the array of mitzvahs, which besides accustoming man to follow God's commandments, yield no benefits through their performance, and their sole purpose is the training and refinement of man's soul.[47]

The question this work will address regarding Israel's existence as a Jewish State is the following: To what extent does, and to what extent should, an ancient Jewish principle, that is the creation of the Age of Religion in Judaism, of an ethic that is not constricted or constrained by the narrow framework of self-interest, apply? The term 'self-interest' here also includes the interests of the weak, the foreigner, the convert and the widow, for these are also human interests, as well as certain elements from prophecies of the prophets, concerns that are definitely extremely positive, and which still fall within the broader definition of 'interest': To what extent do we find in Israel the desire to emulate God expressed similarly to the way Judaism relates to this goal?[48] This is not a question of the application of

---

[45] Sefer Hakuzari in five articles with the two well-known commentaries of Kol Yehuda and Otzar Nechmad. First printing by R. Yitzchak Golman , Warsaw. Reprinted by Hadran Pub. In Israel, 1959. Attributed to the Sage R. Yitzchak HaSangari. Second article, p. 115 and on.

[46] Zohar on Torah (Yosef Lugassi: Jerusalem, 1959), p. 362.

[47] Sefer HaChinuch, 7th edition (Mossad Harav Kook Publications, 1966), authored by an anonymous Jew from Barcelona in approximately 1407 who due to his humility wrote under the assumed name of R. Aharon Zalhahan. First published in Venice in 1523.

[48] Sefer Hachinuch (Mossad Harav Kook) examines each of the 613 mitzvahs, generally finding within them a connection to education of man and improvement of his traits. R. Dr. Shimon Federbush's in his book **Morality and Law in Israel (Mossad Harav Kook)**, also writes about the value of morality and law according to the Jewish perspective, emphasizing the development of spiritual attributes by the Jew who trains himself to love others and yield to their wishes. He writes that the Jewish legal system does not accord with Iharing's perspective that it is morally incumbent upon every man to seek justice for

Jewish law but rather a question that relates to man's essence,[49] to a moral orientation that relates to man's personal and social behavior through a conception that arises from Jewish religion without necessarily a connection to specific religious precepts,[50] as demonstrated in the Handels case. Man's estrangement from the divine source of rules of behavior led many Western philosophers to concentrate on the 'procedural' question of 'how to derive ethical principles' while

---

every legal claim in court because by conceding, he weakens moral foundations and promotes injustice. Quite the contrary, one finds in all of Talmudic literature sharp criticism of those who sought judgement according to the strict law and praise of those willing to compromise, who behaved mercifully and leniently to others...This is the crux of the difference between Western philosophy and Jewish philosophy – Western philosophy will value social order and society's interest even at the expense of the development of the individual's character while Jewish philosophy is more concerned with elevating man and his traits, drawing him closer to God than with correcting the way society functions.

[49] It is clear that the contempt for the weak and for morality in general and for morality towards the servants in particular, that are the basis of Nietzche's philosophy, reflect just how low we are liable to sink when man stands at the center of our moral systems.

[50] Kant 'borrowed' one of Judaism's principles of faith in order to justify an estrangement from religion and in order to build a secular moral system. He adopted the principle by which man should "act only according to that maxim by which you can at the same time will that it should become a universal law." This principle is in fact a reformulation of Hillel the Elder's statement, "Whatever is despicable unto you, do not do unto your friend" which was his interpretation of the verse in Leviticus, "Love your neighbor as yourself." Kant took this verse that exhudes love and feeling, and distorted it, formulating in an utterly dry unfeeling manner. This principle, thus lost its primary moral force and it is easy to identify its weaknesses. Jeffrey G. Warnuk, in his book **Moral Philosophy of Our Times**, translated into Hebrew by Shaul Chanani (Magnes Press: Jerusalem, 1987, reprinted 1992), pp. 81-82, refers to a similar idea to Kant's, developed by Hare of the perspectivist movement, that the author of any moral statement must always be willing to have the statement apply also to him. Warnuk writes: "The callous landlord, about to turn his elderly, ailing, and indigent tenants out into the cold, is likely to agree that not only will they not appreciate such treatment, but also that he wouldn't appreciate it more if he were in their place. Nevertheless, he is likely to claim that it is still just to evict them just as it would be to evict him in a similar circumstance. The degree of satisfaction or dissatisfaction is irrelevant; the point is that a deal is a deal and that a financial agreement must be kept. In other words, a consistent defense of the fact that I ignore the interests of others, doesn't require me to go so far as to positively desire that my interests be overlooked, or even my equanimity when others disregard them. All that is demanded of me is my agreement that failure to take my interest into account should not prompt feelings of moral repugnance, and this isn't a perversion of justice or inequity. This is the principle that lies behind self-reliance, the unrestrained competition of captitalism – a message that no matter how unpleasant was adopted by many reasonable people."

abandoning their search for the **content** of these principles.[51] Basically, the transition from a religious morality to a secular morality involves not only the transfer of the source of law from God to man, and in Judaism and the religions that stemmed from it, from the spirit that transcends man to human materialism,[52]

---

[51] See Warnuk's book in the previous footnote, beginning on p. 84.

[52] One should not confuse the relationship between spirit and material to that of liberal individualism ('rights of the individual') and communitarianism or utilitarianism. Placing rights above self-interests is not the triumph of the spirit that this book speaks of. This book is not referring to man's spiritual needs, to his freedom of speech and thought and other basic human rights. All these are examples of man's self-interests, though they may be spiritual interests. This book refers rather to spirit in the meaning of that which man aspires to, not that which man already possesses and should not have stolen from him. The first is an existing spirituality, that wishes not to be trodden upon and aspires to grow and develop. The second is what we identify as a higher value that we aspire towards, though only very few will attain it, since it is extraordinary and exceptional in relation to human nature, and it is common particularly among religious people who distance themselves from materialism. Examples of the first are freedom of thought and expression, man's dignity and freedom, free scientific inquiry. The second is exemplified by an unassuming nature, humility, submissiveness, lack of greed and violence, and self sacrifice at critical moments. An example of the first is Mill's philosophy. See "Toleration and Mill's Liberty of Thought and Discussion" by David Edwards, Susan Mendus ed., in **Justifying Toleration** (Cambridge University Press, 1988), pp. 87-113. There, he speaks of the inherent value of individualism, that goes beyond the anticipated benefit to society. When he says this, though, he means that individualism is in the interest and to the advantage of the individual person, and not only to society. Mill is still referring to human benefit; he is simply distinguishing between general and individual benefit. In contrast to this popular Western apporach (that Mill is expressing), according to the Aristotelian system that the Rambam developed, and in later generations, also Yeshayahu Leibowitz developed (in his book on five books of faith, Keter Pub: 1995) a Jew is obligated to fulfill religious commandments without any connection to self-interest. This is illustrated in Rambam's Mishneh Torah, on Mada, Ahava, Zemanim, printed in Israel, on page 40a, where the Rambam relates to the view that mezuzah holds practical benefit. The Ba'al Haturim holds this opinion as he writes that, "the mezuzah will cause Moshiach to come into your houses" for if you shall "preserve [the commandment]" "God is thy keeper. God is thy shade upon thy right hand. God shall preserve thy going out and thy coming in… (Psalms 121)." R. Avraham takes a similar approach towards the mitzvah of mezuzah, viewing it as having practical value as he writes, "In addition to the laws…given regarding mezuzah, the world is accustomed, in order to increase the security of their home, to write at the ends of the lines certain marks and names of the angels, and these do not detract but they are also not a commandment, but simply added security." In Gaonic literature we find similarly regarding mezuzah, "It is written only on Mondays and Thursdays, during the fourth hour, in the beginning of the light at the time when the angel Anael administers, and all tefillin, mezuzahs, and amulets written at these times bring luck with the will of God." The Rambam, however, takes issue with these opinions, writing, "Those who write inside

but also a redefinition of the terms 'good' and 'right'. While during the Age of Religion, 'good' was what was 'right', in the Age of Secularism – utilitarians defined the 'right' as what was 'good'.

Western views vs. Jewish Views:

In Judaism, in general, and regarding modern Western theories of morality, in particular, there are varied opinions and approaches. The question arises – what should Israel's approach be, considering the fact that it defined itself at its inception and also in its constitution as a Jewish state. Should Israel embrace individualism or communitarianism or perhaps an entirely different approach. Is the new approach that was revived in the 1970's that relates to man's character and to virtue consistent with Jewish beliefs? Wewill establish immediately that though they appear similar, they in actuality are fundamentally different. The point of reference in Western thought is man and its goal is to improve man's inner essence. Thus, even Western theories that are opposed to utilitarianism are in fact also utilitarian in this broader sense. Even though Sieyes' ideas about national will are generally not associated with approaches of the twentieth century such as utilitarianism, liberalism, communitarianism, emotivism, perspectivism, they all in fact revolve around one and the same thing – namely man (either as an individual or a social entity). In Judaism, in contrast, the focus (even according to the Rambam) is external to man and unconnected to will or personal interest, concentrated rather on God and fulfilling one's responsibilities to Him. In short, the quality utterly lacking in Western philosophies is modesty. This is an attribute that follows naturally from many of man's instincts – for preferring his emotions over his reason, for desiring social company, for finding the underlying principles – both in the realm of morality and social behavior and in the realm of science and technology. Even the 'pure reason' with which Kant sought to 'rescue' man from his enslavement to nature, was implanted in man by his Creator. Our constitution and the adherence to 'Jewish tradition' that is mandated by the constitution, as well as the entire principle of a 'Jewish State'- all seek to set us apart from other nations. This legal and moral obligation that connects us to spiritually-blessed generations of Jews should not be renounced. As the author of this book explained

---

names of angels or holy names, or a verse or mark, are included among those who have no portion in the World to Come. For these fools have not only forfeited a mitzvah, but they have also related to an important mitzvah of making God's name one, serving and loving Him, as if it were an amulet of their own making..." The Rambam, therefore, rejects any connection between a commandment and benefit or enjoyment. This is a rejection of the utilitarian approach, a rejection that was adopted in Judaism, and so from the time of the Rambam on, people stopped adding names of angels to the parchment of the mezuzah.

in an earlier work,[53] Supreme Court decisions that direct otherwise, contradict the legal basis of the State of Israel, disregard Knesset legislation and thus are not morally binding. There is a higher command than the directives of the Supreme Court judges, besides Israel's constitutional law and that is the command of Jewish history which is immersed in a moral system that is of no lesser stature than Western moral systems.

Chapter E:
Synopsis

In 1980, Israel passed "The 1980 Fundamental Law." As was explained in Chapter VII of my previous book,[54] this law was meant to cause a virtual 'revolution' in the area of Israeli jurisprudence. It determined that Jewish heritage should play a significant role in determining the norms of Israeli society. Israeli Supreme Court judges, biased by their personal ideologies (as demonstrated in Chapter VII of my previous book) managed, however, to effectively table this law.
Connected to this fundamental law is the fact that Israel is a Jewish State as was established by Israel's Declaration of Independence, a legal document that possesses paramount legal force. In Part VI of the book,[55] the circumstances by which the State of Israel was established as a Jewish State belonging to the Jewish nation are described at length. Azmi Bashara's last attempt to run for Prime Minister of the State of Israel is and the legal blunder involved in not disqualifying his candidacy are examined. The election of an Arab prime minister is a step toward national suicide and is therefore an illegitimate action on the part of the Jewish State. This step reflects the view that Israel is a 'state of all its citizens' (a fundamental denial of the Jewishness of the state) – a view that may be held by some Israelis but which contradicts the principle that Israel is a Jewish state. A **Jewish State** cannot be governed by non-Jews - the majority of the Knesset, as well as the Prime Minister himself must be Jewish.

This chapter therefore, seeks to establish three things:

1. Morally-politically, Israel is meant to be a Jewish State, which preserves democratic principles so long as they do not conflict with its Jewish ones.
2. Israel should adopt, both in the political administration of the country and in its legislation, Jewish values of freedom, justice, honesty and peace. In

---

[53] See Yehuda Cohen, **Who Fears a Jewish State? A Legal and Ideological Perspective**, cited in footnote 2.
[54] Ibid.
[55] Ibid.

this realm, intentions and education are no less important than actions, and as such the laws should be interpreted.

3. The basic approach of political morality in Israel should be distinct and compatible with the concept of a 'Jewish State'. Despite certain similarities to communitarian theories as well as Western ideas of virtue, this approach will differ in all fundamental respects from these theories.

Chapter F:
A General Perspective

The evolution of the role of the British Parliament exemplifies the first basic distinction between Jewish morality and Western morality. Originally, the British Parliament functioned as a court of law. Its role was to establish law ,through interpretation of already existing law, and not through actual legislation. This perception of Parliament stemmed from the prevailing religious view of the time according to which only God had the authority to ordain law. A king's authority was limited to interpretation of God's will via the agency of the Parliament.[56] It was only with God's fall from power, that man, in other words – Parliament – was given the royal power to legislate. With this the Religious Age, the reign of God, ended, and the Secular Age – the reign of man – began.

The divine source of religious morality not only creates a technical difference between religious morality and secular morality, but also a very fundamental distinction. Religious morality, because of the nature of the relationship between God and man, is predicated on obligations. Secular morality, in contrast, is based on rights. God doesn't need rights; only man does. In this lies the second distinction between religious and secular morality.

The third underlying difference between religious and secular morality lay in the creation of government rights alongside individual rights. These rights promptly turned into democracy.

Within the framework of divine morality, there are no rights, only obligations. These obligations, of course, benefit many others, but a benefit does not imply a right. This holds true in Hinduism, Buddhism, Confucianism, Shintu, Christianity,

---

[56] M.J.C Vile, **Constitutionalism and the Separation of Powers** (Oxford: Clarendon Press) pp. 24-25.

Judaism, and Islam. Thus, in contrast to secular systems, the Biblical injunction that a Hebrew slave goes free in the Sabbatical (seventh) year obligates the master to free his slave while granting the slave the right to go free only as a by product of the master's obligation. The Torah commands the Jews to love the foreigner, to judge him impartially. It instructs those who are more fortunate to act with charity towards those who are less fortunate; it does not turn to the recipients of this charity and inform them that they are entitled to this treatment. The same holds true regarding the orphan and widow. The Torah commands us to treat them with kindness, justice, and love. It imposes an obligation upon the stronger members of society; it does not confer a right upon the weaker members. In Confucianism, the master is commanded to be lenient and magnanimous to his servant. This behavior is incumbent upon the master, but the servant does not possess a right to this treatment. Similarly, though the servant is obligated to obey his master, his master does not have a right to he be obeyed.

In Hinduism and of course Judaism [57],these obligations are sometimes imposed upon the group – a communal responsibility or accountability.

A legal system, in which man, not God, designs the rules, is a system in which rights play a central role [58].It is man who determines the law and it is man who implements the law. Man is supreme and there is no force greater than him. Since all men, by definition, are supreme, it follows that they are all equal. This brings us to the fourth premise of secular morality – the principle of equality. This right is derived from utilitarian ideology and the concept of 'it's coming to me.' It is a right that is non-executable and utterly hypocritical. There never has been equality and there never will be.

The Jewish commandment' to love one's neighbor as oneself,' on the other hand, may not be more executable, but it is more enlightening. It reflects less conceit than the principle of equality, and greater truth. It turns to the one who should be giving, not to the one who should be receiving. My love for my neighbor does not necessarily result in equality, and thus it is more likely to be realized. The Biblical injunction addresses a person's attitude and intentions rather than his technical superficial actions.

---

[57]Eva Hellman" ,Dynamic Hinduism – Towards a New Hindu Nation ",in **Questioning the Secular State – The Worldwide Resurgence of Religion in Politics**, edited by David Westerlund (London: Hurst & Company) p. 242.

[58]The distinction between obligations and rights should not be confused with the totally separate issue of the possible benefits latent in the fulfillment of religious commandments that constitute obligations.

The beauty of religious morality is that man does not see himself as supreme, but rather strives to elevate himself and to raise his moral stature. The inherent problem with Western secular morality, in contrast, is that man has no higher authority to emulate. The potential for improvement that religious morality holds for a religious person combined with the obligations it imposes upon its adherents, create the potential to rise above the level of utilitarianism (assuming the divine commandments are not designed to simply benefit those who fulfill them or someone else of their choosing). This potential is not realized in every religion, nor in every religious system, but it does exist to some extent in the world of religious Jewish thought.

The spirituality of which Jewish sources speak, refers to the spirit of God that man seeks to emulate in order to draw closer to his Creator. This spirituality is not to be confused with the spirituality referred to by Western philosophers, such as John Stuart Mill. Mill refers to a matter that belongs to man, an inalienable right. It is a form of acquisitiveness, a spiritual utilitarianism. It is a spirit of man that seeks not to be crushed or suppressed, that wishes to grow and blossom. In Judaism, emulation of God's attributes through one's love of Him, is not man's inalienable right, but a goal a Jew is commanded to strive towards, an obligation – he seeks to fulfill through his love for God. This commandment is an obligation, not a right. It is a much higher, deeper, more elevated spirituality that is far closer to the truth. Even those who try to find the latent benefits within the reasons for the commandments, concede that this spirituality is not an asset that belongs to man by right, but one that he has an obligation to strive towards.

Western man also exalts freedom of thought and expression, human dignity and freedom, free scientific inquiry. All these are Western man's possessions, though they are spiritual possessions. In Judaism, Christianity, Islam and Hinduism, spirituality is a product of submission, humility, of a renouncement of greed and force – and thus it is a far more elevated spirituality.

Western secular systems, in contrast, safeguard material and spiritual assets in similar ways. They establish laws for the benefit of the individual and for the benefit of the group, for the good of the physical and the good of the spiritual – but the common denominator – is fortification of man's property. Man fortifies himself, while in Judaism, the Jew fulfills his destiny by going out to meet his God.

As a result of Western-secular man's inability to rise above his acquisitiveness- in both material and spiritual matters, certain inclinations towards: hedonism, exhibitionism, sexuality, and aggression have colored his everyday behavior. Some of the products of these inclinations are:

1. Pornography
2. Immodest dress that only promotes a view of women as sexual objects rather than subjects with the ability to influence their environment
3. Latent hedonistic competition – who threw the most ostentatious party, invited the most distinguished guests, or owns the biggest car - without regard for their host's or owner's emotional connection to them
4. Violent children's games often based on a struggle between the forces of good and evil where good is equated with powerful and is thus victorious over evil
5. Gum chewing – perpetual eating
6. Use of force also in the political arena

In summary, Western secular morality is based on the supremacy of man, on rights, democracy and equality. Religious morality (what is common to all religions) is based on the supremacy of God, obligations, hierarchy. It has educational advantages for it emphasizes self-improvement. It sets realistic goals based on love and kindness, in contrast to secular morality that possesses hollow slogans and less regard for the individual. Secular morality apparently is intent on scientific, economic, and technological achievement, on the discovery of new distant physical worlds, while religious morality is more concerned with purifying and elevating mankind. Western man is more closed and focused on his achievements while *homo religiosus* is more spiritually receptive. Religious man should not feel compelled to bow to Western man.

SPECIFIC SOCIAL PRODUCTS

Voliume III: Specific Social Products

PART 6:
Black Africa, Primitive Religions Tribes vs. state, emptiness of nationality

Chapter A: A Comparison of Africa and the West

Horton's anthropological perspective on African traditionalism and Western modernity:
Horton, the one of the few Western anthropologist living permanently in Black Africa today, seeks, in his article on the topic of tradition versus modernity, Black Africa versus the West, [1] to probe this issue and to determine to what extent tradition and modernity are merely two sides of the same coin. Africans may have no greater fan than Horton, yet we will see that he is locked into Western thinking, incapable of defending tradition except by proving its high quality based on Western modern criteria not on its own criteria.
Horton calls man a social being, but speaking about patterns in creativity and approach, he describes him as a solitary being, and does not view him as a social

[1] Horton, "Tradition and Modernity Revisited," in Robin Horton, **Patterns of Thought in Africa and the West, Essays on magic, religion and science** (Cambridge, Massachusetts: Cambridge University Press, 1993) , pp. 301-346.

individual. He conclusively determines that man transmitted and transmits his ideas, his philosophy, and his creative works within the society that he lives, an inter-generational transmission, but he doesn't address man's motivation for engaging in these matters. He speaks about man's possibilities, not about his reasons and motives. He depicts man as an intellectual, not emotional being, an approach as we have seen in earlier sections of this book that this is typically Western. We know our nature. We act due to internal and external incentives –not because we possess the ability to do so. Ability is the limit of possibility, but without a reason and incentive to act we would do nothing, not even examine our capabilities.

In comparing modernity and tradition, Horton does not perceive that modernity was achieved in a secular environment while tradition is preserved in a religious one. When he notes that tradition is remarkable in that we receive a tradition handed down from earlier generations without argument, Horton neglects to ask – whether this isn't because – being religious - we ascribe the tradition to a divine source? Isn't the modernistic approach that exalts competition of ideas and approaches an inevitable consequence of the loss of a divine source of action. Isn't it because we lost a divine authority that we felt free to search – from the void that we found ourselves in – for new truths, without feeling a sense of obligation to uphold a previous 'truth.' No truth possessed inherent holiness, since every new 'truth' came from us, from our consciousness, and 'the mouth which decreed can also retract.' This is what distinguishes a religious individual – who is traditional because he believes in a deity (or in Africa in idolatry, which is within the definition of deity in this book). The deity sanctified the truth it imparted to us, and only it can sanctify an alternate truth; it and not we. Therefore, Horton does not probe deeply enough when he notes that Africans cite tradition as the reason they adhere to their own truths. We should recognize that the African who insists that his unqualified reason for action is 'that this is what was passed down to him by is fathers' is in effect saying that this custom is sacrosanct, since it was commanded by deities and passed down to him by his fathers.

A summary of the critique of Horton's approach:

Therefore, when Horton speaks about African traditionalism vs. Western modernity, and when he notes that during certain eras, traditionalism ruled in the West, it would not be a distortion of the truth, if he asserted that Africans today are not only fundamentally traditionalist, but also fundamentally religious. For part of them this religious source is a primitive one but also for the most of them that are Muslims or Christians the origin of their traditional medicine is from primitive religion. Westerners today are not only fundamentally modernistic, but also secular. Their thinking is shaped by secularism and by the freedom that secularism offers them, a freedom that Westerners did not enjoy during eras in which religion governed them and their actions.

Another separate question is how does the secular modern individual grapple, emotionally with this situation. He has lost his divine guide and now must find a substitute within himself. It is difficult for him and also burdensome.[2]

An alternative possible thesis consistent with the writings of other philosophers: One can view the transition from traditionalism to modernity, of which Horton speaks, as a shift from religious belief in a deity to secularism, as we will see later on, Horton also deals with the topic in his own way. According to the approach that is suggested here, belief in a deity is belief in a supreme or transcendental force, in a force that is effecting from its supernatural standing. This force has its first incarnation in man's consciousness, as a fatherly spirit, such as I described in the first section of this book. We speak of that same father that saved him when he was a young child from beasts of prey and from natural forces. Now, that the father has died, the son who has grown up looks around and sees nature renewing itself. His father's death, he realizes, was not the end; his connection with his deceased father has not been severed. In his imagination – analogous to nature which does not disappear or end, which is infinite and regenerating – the son creates his father's spirit, from which – he believes – salvation will spring forth. Since his father's spirit is not part of his reality, it seems to belong to a world that is beyond – beyond reality. Being transcendental, this spirit can influence reality[3] and being a spirit, it exists in the formative world, and not in the world that is formed (this world) – and accordingly and in accordance with his desire, his

---

[2] Part 3 of this book develops the discussion of civil religion. It shows how modern man managed to find a partner beyond his reality who could replace God. This partner was the notion of a state or nation, two values that existed even before the modern era, but that were enlisted due to modern man's immense difficulty coping with reality alone, along with a home in the form of each state's 'civil religion' – analogous to each primitive ethnic group's ethnic God. These became sanctified valued ideas linked to the supernatural, and which turned transcendental. These 'fabrications' did not succeed as well as divine religion (a term which includes here also idolatrous religions, but not civil religion), despite these ingenious measures which were the product of man's healthy intuition.

[3] In developing this theory, there is room to relate to primitive man as a rational being who grasped – what we grasp today – that there are limits to our abilities, and that no factor found in reality is a primary cause, since it too was created and affected by another. This led man (primitive, just as modern) necessarily to the conclusion that there is something beyond reality, something that is not affected, that is not created, that cannot be manipulated. It is something that influences, something more powerful than reality.

father's spirit can save him. His father has always been ready to help; this is the image of the prototypical father.[4]

This same image, in its evolution later on, in the age of modern religions, ascended to a higher sphere, to embody the entire world, a God that symbolized unity and that was credited with creating the world. This evolution to an exalted eternal religion parallels the transition Abraham underwent when he shattered, according to the Midrash, his father's man-made idols. It is a transition to something more spiritual, that is not 'manmade.'

In the era that follows – the modern era - modern civilization comes and proclaims 'God's demise.'[5] In place of God – who until that point had governed man's fate – man instates himself. It is now man who sits on the throne – he will, from this point on, lead himself, using his own intelligence and understanding.[6] This is apparently the transition from the age of sentiment to the age of reason. (This is what transpired, but as we will describe further on, luckily it failed and emotion continued to govern man's fate due to man's atrophic intelligence.) In effect, after human civilization moved on from primitive religion, of manmade idols, to a spiritual religion, that was not a product of his own hands - after Abraham shattered the idols, (modern) man reverted back to the age of idolatry. Only this time he instated himself in place of an idol that was the work of his own hands. Just as the idol was subjective, and specific to a certain ethnic group, and just as God, in the early Biblical period, was viewed more as a national God than as the creator of the heavens and earth, the post-modernists with their moral relativism came, and instituted moral relativity. They rejected any notion of an objective Kantian truth and declared that morality would be determined according to the inclinations of a group of Western liberals.

If we now return to our broader understanding of primitive man's adoption of the father figure, as described above, this understanding, though not the only

---

[4] One of its marks, found till today in the Jewish prayer book within the Jewish liturgy – a prayer recited upon taking out the Torah scroll – "Father of compassion, do good with Zion according to Your will; rebuild the walls of Jerusalem. For we trust in You alone, O King, God, exalted, and uplifted, Master of worlds" – a paragraph that follows another that sees God as universal, "There is none like You among the gods, my Lord, and there is nothing like Your works. Your kingdom is a kingdom spanning all eternities, and Your dominion is throughout every generation..."

[5] R. Roni Aviram, "The secularist as the forerunner to the last man: a critique of Friedrich Nietzsche's modernity" in **Bein Dat Lemussar,** edited by Daniel Stateman and Avi Shagya (Ramat Gan: Bar Ilan University, 1996), pp. 75-94.

[6] According to Kant.

possibility, seems closer to man's nature than Horton's model that represents man's change through a logical process, in which emotion played no role. Man, however, is not by nature merely a rational being, as Horton depicts, but also an emotional creature, as described by Otto, James, and Luther, and as described at length in the first two sections of this book. In contrast to Horton's depiction of the solitary man as the sole cause of the evolution of religion, we claim that man is a being that operates in a social framework, that his accomplishments are the product of a group effort. This is Kaufman's view, and a view that seems correct even though exceptional men of spirit have stood out throughout history. The individual's spirit and his wisdom have always sprouted from fertile soil, the soil of human society, a soil enriched by wisdom passed down by those who preceded him.

The theory that I offer as an alternative to Horton's is not only consistent with the philosophy of Otto, James, Luther, and Kaufman. It is also consistent with the view that the primordial ethnological groups shared a father spirit that represented the unity of the relevant ethnological group that adopted this belief and did follow it. This group joins with, and creates, an ethnic society that is larger than the family unit and even the extended family. This group, preserves a symbolic blood tie through their connection to the primordial father figure, a tie that exists even between people who do not know each other and who would not feel any emotional attachment if not for the primordial father figure they share.

Relating the alternate thesis to anthropological studies:
This theory connects to something that Horton does not deal with, though it seems central to the topic, more central than Horton's secondary theory of medical or technological benefits. I speak of the formulation of a moral code[7] – a code specific to each social group, and one of the central components in determining each society's unique nature. A society or group of people bound themselves to the commandments of their deity – the primordial father. Without this code of conduct, it is impossible to sustain an organized society.[8] Man's emotional tie to the primordial father figure, that rescues him developed and later on into the image

[7] Morality in this book refers to rules of social conduct ingrained within the hearts of the society – in contrast to a law which comes from the government. Therefore – morality in a specific society does not have to be "inherently moral" from the perspective of members of a different society.

[8] Laws alone cannot sustain a society. Enforcement of legal principles cannot rely only on governmental power but rather the society must be fundamentally ready to obey the government. Therefore, the rules that exist in people's hearts are a precondition for the establishment of a society. Laws only help achieve this goal, making a society more organized and directing the social behavior in a particular direction.

of God or a deity that the man and the group all turn to for salvation. This appeal, made in time of distress, is an emotional appeal, and consequently so is the adherence to the command of the primordial father or deity or God. This is the earliest connection between morality and emotion, and it is the basis for man's generally emotional approach to moral principles even when he is not facing misfortune. Modern man loses this tie to emotion if he foregoes not only his God but also religious morality. It seems strange that religious morality should still govern man's life even in the modern age, even after God has been banished from his reign.[9] Presumably, modern man, due to some healthy instincts he still possesses, is unwilling to allow religious-divine morality to desert him completely, leaving him all alone. In spite of all his rational, dry, a-emotional morality that modernity has introduced him to, modern man continues to cling to the emotional, ancient morality – that speaks to his heart.

This theory – that I offer as a possible anti – thesis to Horton's, is also consistent with a fact, proven by anthropological studies,[10] that man from his inception was a social being bound by an ancient established (social) code of conduct.[11]

Incontrovertible authority to command indisputable principles – could only come from an external source, and not from within the society itself. Naturally, the possibility arose that the source of these ethical principles – that comprise the code of conduct – would be supernatural – and that is how God was "discovered." In general, cause and effect are related. If my courteous behavior has favorable consequences, it is likely that my courteous behavior from its outset was intended in order to achieve those results. Similarly: if courteous conduct brings positive results to a particular person, it is likely that he will be motivated to behave courteously. Therefore, if cleaving to the father spirit resulted in social bonds and alliances, the implication is that the spirit shared by the group – the father spirit – was intended to enable them to bond as a society,[12] or that, post factum, as a result of the blessed consequences of social bonds, they clung to the idea of a father spirit. Religious faith served both directly and indirectly as a uniting force through: a)direct divine intervention to the social group that sought a divine sign after creating one in its consciousness b)indirect divine assistance through creating an emotional familial bond between the members of the group based on their common tie to the primordial father spirit c)additional indirect divine intervention

---

[9] A perspective and understanding that are reinforced.

[10] Meyer Fortes, F.B.A. **Rules and the Emergence of Society** (Royal Anthropological Institute of Great Britain and Ireland, No. 39) p. 2.

[11] Ibid, pp. 3-6.

[12] Further on, I will speak about two additional effects of the appearance of God, physical deliverance from a threatening or difficult situation and emotional support.

in the form of a divine command to adhere to a code of conduct that facilitates societal life d)offering spiritual support for the members of the group, an address to turn to in times of distress, since the mere existence of the God-primordial father, even before he actually offered any tangible help, provided emotional succor.

On the relationship to Hinduism from Horton's perspective:

Horton speaks about the world of the first theory. This world is the invisible, hidden world.[13] The hidden world is the part of the world that is concealed, while the real world is manifest to all. Both are parts of one world, therefore it is natural to draw, according to Horton, analogies to these two parts of the world, that are together one unity. This idea of Horton's is reminiscent of the 'dharma' in Hinduism. The 'dharma' is an eternal, universal, constant value that unites the divine with everything in existence.[14] The dharma reveals 'individual divine providence' over the individual's deeds that takes into account the individual's behavior, as well as 'general-social providence' over the lives of the entire Hindu community.[15] One should recall, the other theory I presented verges on a philosophy that holds of the existence of a transcendental being, a deity who has created everything, who influences and is not influenced, and an understanding of whom can be attempted through analogy between him and reality, futile as it may be. Primitive man, according to the approach that I am suggesting, does what his God requests of him. He does so in order to demonstrate loyalty to God's word and in order to adhere to his commands, and also to prove the purity of his intentions in turning to God and beseeching his help. Yet, the religious believer cannot forcibly influence the deity. [16]The ultimate question, therefore is, what did primitive man think? Did he think he had the ability to manipulate his God, or did he recognize that he was dependent on his God's good favor, that his God had no obligation to help him, but that he would help as he saw fit. When a Roman commander offered a sacrifice before battle, he knew what God said to him, but he couldn't direct God's will. This approach is similar to one that I propose, but not to Horton's. Almost anecdotally, we mention Horton's overstatement when he suggests that primitive man came to an understanding of the revealed and hidden

---

[13] In Horton's article cited in footnote 1, pp. 322,326.

[14] Eva Hellman, "Dynamic Hinduism: Towards a New Hindu Nation," in **Questioning the Secular State- The Worldwide Resurgence of Religion in Politics**, edited by David Westerlund (London: Hurst & Company) pp. 237-258. Take particular note of p.240.

[15] It recalls the Jewish notion of personal responsibility vs. general responsibility and the consequent relationship of the deity to the individual and to the community.

[16] This idea is connected to the perspective offered by Evans-Pritchard in Evans-Pritchard, **Nuer Religion**, pp. 197-228.

from his attempts to hurl a spear while he was concealed behind a shield.[17] Horton, it seems, forgot, that primitive man had neither spear nor shield. Did Horton really suppose, that in a time before the totem pole, the beginning of religion, the beginning of primitive religious faith found man when he was throwing a spear and taking cover behind a shield.

A comparison between modernity and traditionalism that ignores the role of religion – and its shortcomings:

Horton explains that the similarity between the modernistic approach and the traditionalist approach is that both are searching for what is most useful and advantageous to them. Both seek to understand incomprehensible matters, to predict events and to control the progression of events.[18] Traditionalists that Horton speaks about them, that its source is in primitive culture of African Tribes, presume that the means, methods and approaches adopted by earlier generations proved effective, else why would they have continued following a particular approach. Modernists assume that knowledge in general is constantly advancing. They think that is the way of the world, the wisdom of the past was less refined and of inferior quality to wisdom in our days, and in the future people will certainly discover knowledge even more beneficial than that which exists in our days. It is a Darwinian approach according to which the fittest and best will certainly survive. Therefore, one should not suppress new ideas and understandings that come to replace the old.

Horton overlooks, however, the source of knowledge. He neglects to mention that the traditionalists – we speak about the primitive ones – were people who believed in God, who attributed their knowledge to God, and who believed in the divine origin of traditions passed down through the generations. African tribes embrace their fathers' traditions - since according to their beliefs these traditions originated from a God or from the primordial father's spirit. Horton overlooks a basic fact, that the 'primitive peoples' believe in a God, while modern man lost this faith, or abandoned it the moment they needed to solve a concrete problem in their lives. Modern man who is religious will say: 'Of course I believe in God but what does religious faith have to do with the practical problem I'm facing.' Once matters are portrayed in this way, then the reason for the difference between traditionalists and modernists and their differing approaches becomes clear and simple. This way of

---

[17] In Horton's article cited in footnote 1, p. 326. He brings examples from his research that show that the African does not expect that he will be able to manipulate the spirits to whom he sacrifices, and that he offers sacrifices only to prove his faithfulness and the seriousness of his intentions.

[18] Ibid p. 329.

portray is the only one which does not omit a basic fact, that of the primitives' faith in God, a faith they possessed and which modernists have lost. Horton's analysis, therefore, is incomplete, and his equation of the traditionalist and modernist approaches, is patently false. There is no parallel here, but rather a basic difference.[19] As we mentioned earlier, Horton's Achilles heel is his focus on logic, as the source of man's actions, when in fact man is an emotional creature, first and foremost.

The Western theory of impersonal justice vs. the primitive's personal (adulterated) theory of justice:
Horton's view[20] is false, since justice is not coldly-logical but rather humane-personal-emotional. When we compare the primitive African tribes to Western modern people, we are not comparing a subjective personal, unjust notion of justice to a pure impartial justice. Western morality is ailing, and the symptom of its illness is its attempt to uproot emotion and to act only according to logic. The primitive African tribes' morality is one which draws on religious faith, and as such is more emotional than that which Westerners espouse. Fortunately, the analytic morality Westerners champion does not successfully eradicate from their hearts the morality that is connected to emotion – a blessed consequence of Western morality's failure.

Modernity's difficulty in relation to in relating to traditionalism that contradicts science:
Horton attempts to defend traditionalism, but he uses modern tools in order to do so. He argues that basically traditionalism has the same goals as modernity, but that it is less successful in achieving them because it is handicapped by certain false notions – eg. that something that has withstood the test of time has proven itself...that in order to derive the maximum benefit... - a modern concept imposed on traditionalism against its will and spirit – it refuses to discard old practices. Horton fails to appreciate the emotional succor that a traditionalist draws from religion. He refuses to recognize that the traditionalist desires to derive emotional support in times of distress, no less than he does actual physical support. In a later writing, by Robert Hind,[21] the question is raised (through modern eyes) how is it that modern Western people embrace religion, when the particulars of their

[19] Therefore, Horton's comparison of the totem and taboo system to the aggressiveness of rival modern approaches cannot bridge the gap between them since a basic conceptual difference separates them –the religious world possesses a given accepted truth while the modern world is searching for the truth.
[20] Ibid p. 327.
[21] Robert A. Hinde, **Why Gods Persist – A Scientific Approach to Religion** (New Yor, Routledge, 1999), Chapter I.

religious faith are not scientifically proven. Hind considers the possibility that religion provides emotional support and that it even encourages self sacrifice, social-communal discipline and compromise, and even social responsibility. Many of his insights are good, but since his perspective is external, rather than internal, he fails to attain the understanding that I suggest in this book.

The difference between technology and morality:
It should be absolutely clear that all criticism here is directed toward the realm of morality and not technology. There is no debating Horton's proof of the technological advances made possible by modern ideas of progressivism and competition, two philosophies that advance by working together. They raise modern man's physical standard of living – from this perspective – modernity is unquestionably superior.

In the ethical realm, the modern world is also not inferior, but this is not thanks to modernity but rather in spite of modernity. The failure of modernity's secular spirit to present an alternate moral path that would replace the religious-divine approach – is a blessed failure.

Chapter B:
African tribes vs. ethnic Indian groups

Background and purpose of the chapter:
Robert Bates[22] developed a unique theory regarding the relationship between tribal loyalty and nationalism among African black tribes south of the Sahara (Africa) who left behind tribal dwelling patterns to move to the cities (the city dwellers in Africa). According to Bates, the African city dwellers are first and foremost loyal to other tribe members and they feel an obligation to promote, to the best of their ability, the interests of tribe members who live in their city (tribal loyalty). No sense of nationalism gets in the way of this tribal loyalty. Therefore, it is common - that members of a specific tribe that live in the city and work in a certain profession - will organize a trade union open only to members of their own tribe, establish vocational schools for that same trade open only to members of their own tribe, and in their workplace work towards general advancement of their own tribe members. African city dwellers demonstrate the same attitude when they are faced

---

[22] Robert H. Bates, "Modernization, Ethnic Competition and Rationality of Politics in Contemporary Africa," in **State Versus Ethnic Claims,** pp. 152-171.

with an opportunity to shape public policy in areas that will potentially impact tribe members in their native tribal lands – outside of the cities. A tribe member who is in the position to promote regional development or the establishment of factories in different regions in his country, will favor the region in which his tribe lives, in order to improve their economic state. Bates doesn't discuss the loyalty of African city dwellers to the country they are citizens of, and whether or not such loyalty exists. Nevertheless, it is clear from his writings, that tribal loyalty supersedes loyalty to the State, if and when it exists at all.

In contrast to African tribalism, we have the various sectors according to language, ethnicity, religion, and nationalism in the Indian federation, as Paul Brass describes in his book[23] on the relationship between - the central federalist government in India, controlled originally by the Congress party, that advocated 'civil religion,' and later by the Hindu nationalist party, that promotes ethnic Hindu nationalism – and non-Hindu ethnic groups, who do not speak Hindi but practice the Hindu religion. What emerges from Brass' book, is that in general, non-Hindus who simply speak a different language but practice the Hindu religion, integrate into Indian society in contrast to non-Hindus who are also a religious minority (Sikhs or Muslims) who fail to integrate. Both groups preserve their unique language and culture, but the minorities based on language and not on religion are less resistant to allowing Hindi to infiltrate their schools, in the hope that knowledge of Hindi will help their children advance.

What is common to both India and Africa is their varied cultural mosaic. In India, the Hindus themselves are a minority, concentrated in the northern part of the federation. Both India and Africa were for many years under colonial rule that was considerate of this mosaic and even stressed it when it served their interests. Factionalism became even more entrenched once they gained independence and in the period leading to it. In India there were population shifts connected to the division of the continent between Muslims and non-Muslims. Similarly, the Indian federation was organized from the outset based on language and cultural differences within the federation.

In this chapter I will focus on Bates' theory – in his study of Africa and the loyalty of the different groups to their own members, and the advantages of this loyalty (traditional tribal loyalty) over nationalism.

---

[23] Paul R. Brass, **Language, Religion, and Politics in North India** (Cambridge University Press, 1974).

What defines a nation?

I list here 22 salient features of nationalism, some of which we will find are key to the formation of a nation, and others that we will find are more peripheral:

1) Geographic boundaries inhabited solely or predominately by the particular group
2) A distinct language or dialect and script
3) A separate political framework
4) A distinct religion
5) Internal ethnic bonds
6) Common enemies
6) Forging through internal struggles
8) Distinct myths
9) Special heroes
10) Distinct rituals
11) Unique problems
12) Unique rituals
13) Literature, music, song, folklore
14) Particular etiquette and attitudes toward children's educations and caring for the elderly and infirm
15) Unique lifestyle and means of interaction
16) Unique national or ethnic consciousness shared by all the members of the group or by the overwhelming majority
17) A desire for national independence with specific geographic boundaries
18) Common mission or destiny
19) Shared ideals and values that are distinctive
20) A unique way of life in ways other than those detailed above
21) Other characteristics of the culture – assuming they are unique and common to all or most of the members
22) Anything else particular to this group.

It is possible that the existence of these criteria or others will lead to an ethnic alliance that is not nationalistic. In instances when one of the aforementioned criteria is common both to a group being studied and to another group or groups, that may or may not be geographical neighbors, one should examine whether the groups in question do not constitute a joint *'kevutzat Av'*, either ethnically or nationally.

In fact, both in the Indian Federation and in Africa – many of the aforementioned criteria listed are common to many groups. The difference lies in that in the Indian federation, all the groups are part of one state, though it is federative, while in Africa there are many separate States with much in common.

Nationality and ethnicity[24] : important components in the Indian federation – a comparison to Africa and other comparisons:
I enumerate here important elements for national or ethnic alliance.
Cultural civil war:

In conjunction with this comparison, let us consider Western Europe which is uniting economically, and which shares both a common (if varied) culture and history (of wars which could be considered civil wars). When we note how European nations from the former Eastern-Soviet bloc have joined the EU and how the US and Russia have grown closer, it doesn't seem unreasonable to predict a process of national unification of the white man – a process that began with both World Wars since they functioned as civil wars that encouraged unification, just as the American civil war increased nationalism in the US.[25] We can view civil war within a common culture as a process of internal alliance, similar (though not equivalent) to a married couple whose relationship is stronger after they successfully grapple with a crisis typical of marriage. A civil war does not necessarily erase the differences between the two sides that opposed each other – eg. Americans today are still very conscious of the South vs. North divide, and Bush's election to president in 2001 was viewed by some as the election of one of few 'Southerner' as opposed to the many 'Northerners' elected in the past.

In India, as Brass describes, the Mithyali Brahamins preserve their ethnic identity yet maintain their distinctiveness from other sects of the Mithyali ethnic group.[26]

---

[24] As will become clear further on, an ethnic alliance differs from a national alliance in that the ethnic group does not seek autonomy. Otherwise, they are similar. A non-ethnic union differs from an ethnic one in that the non-ethnic group (eg. a tribe that is not an ethnic group) has none of the characteristics of a nation and also no history of self government.

[25] This is a view developed by Liah Greenfeld in **Nationalism, Five Roads to Modernity** (London: Harvard University Press, 1992), p.480 and also by Robert Palmer surveyed in Seymour Martin Lipset, "The 'Newness' of the New Nation," in C. Vann Woodward, ed. **The Comparative Approach to American History**, Basic Books: NY, 1968, p. 64.

[26] In Brass' book cited in footnote 23, on page 56, Brass writes how the Mithyali Brahamins refrain from marrying non-Mithyali Brahamins, in this way preserving their distinctiveness and connection to the Mithyali ethnic group - despite the fact that these Brahamins – like Brahamins who belong to other ethnic groups in India all descend from foreign conquerors who ruled over the Indian sub-continent. At the time of this conquest, all the Brahamins banded together - preceding their division among different Indian ethnic

Brahamins, therefore, do not marry other Brahamins who do not belong to the Mithyali ethnic group, but at the same time, they also do not marry Mithyali who are not Brahamins. The Brahamins do not detach themselves from the Mithyali ethnic framework and in fact in the example brought,[27] the Brahamin leader is also considered a Mithyali leader, though it is questionable whether leadership that is inherited is as powerful as that which sprouts from below. In truth, the Brahamin leader, Maharaja of Darbhanga, in our example, has little power. Be that as it may, the detachment that exists reflects a nationalistic or ethnic bond that formed within the framework of the State, despite conflicts and civil wars that became part of its history and strengthened more than weakened the States` internal bond. Conflicts and wars that occurred throughout history become myths that inspire nationalism, rather than division. And thus the European Union can be composed of Germans, French, and others, though in the past – which today is considered irrelevant – they fought against each other. The same goes for the French and British who also fought one another, and for that matter the eleven tribes of Israel who almost annihilated the tribe of Benjamin in a civil war, and only shortly after united under King Saul – a king chosen (intentionally?) from the tribe of Benjamin. It may seem like a distant dream – but is it a fantasy – to envision Americans and Russians serving in a new union of the white Christian nation with a common culture.

Language and alphabet:

Anthropologists discuss the centrality of language in the development of civilization and of culture.[28] The French people experienced a revolt that shaped their culture and language according to the Parisian model, molding a people with a uniform and unifying culture – the basis for French patriotism and French nationalism. The government as well as the printing industry, in their efforts to create as wide a market as possible, played a major role in this standardization of different dialects of the language.[29]

Morality:

We concluded already in the first section of this book that a common morality – which until the modern age was always a product of religion was central to formation of a society. All those who read literature and newspapers published by

---

groups – to form one distinct ethnic group separate from all the ethnic groups being conquered.

[27] Ibid, p. 59.

[28] Meyer Fortes, F.B.A., **Rules and the Emergence of Society** (Royal Anthropological Institute of Great Britain and Ireland, Occational Paper, No. 39).

[29] R. Benedict Anderson **Kehilot Medumyanot**, (imagined societies) translated from English to Hebrew by Dan Daor (Tel Aviv: The Open University, 2000), pp. 69-113

a particular source adopted the moral sense and consciousness of that same source, came to share the same likes and dislikes, to condemn the same actions, etc. When man began attempting to form a 'rational' ethics using reason, intelligence, and a study of truth then his morality became feeble, unable to withstand the test of time. Anthropologists[30] attempt to establish oral and written language as the conduit of the society's moral principles. Language, however, is a matter of the mind and of reason, while ethics is primarily based on emotion, (resulting in the failure of most of modern man's attempts to create a rational morality). Therefore, it follows that anthropologists – who are products of the modern 'rational' age - have attempted to stress the value of reason over the value of emotion. Their effort, however, is doomed to failure.

Divine religion plays a key role, not only in formation of society (via the moral principles it created) but also in the development of the state and of nation. Language, we will see, plays a more limited role, generally following lines drawn by religion. In Yugoslavia, for example, the Serbs and Croatians speak the same language, but the Serbs use the Cyrillic script, as is consistent with their religion – the Eastern Orthodox Christianity, while the Croatians use the Latin script, as is consistent with their religion, namely Catholicism. Language distinguishes the different parts of the Swiss nation -Switzerland is divided into cantons according to the different languages and so too the Supreme Court's judges are chosen to represent the different language populations. This in no way, however, threatens a breakup of the Swiss nation. In Belgium as well, though states are generally organized along linguistic lines, neither the Flemish nor the Walloons desire autonomy but rather only the opportunity to live separately and remain distinct. These two ethnic sectors are actually so united, that recently when the Walloons began moving into Flemish districts and attempted to establish a French school system there, the Flemish and Walloons worked together in the legislature to foil this attempt. They declared, in other words, that in order to discourage this assimilation of cultures and language outside of the capital city (where it was permitted), they would make it difficult for a person who dared move to a different ethnic group's district, to educate his children.

Brass' starting point, in his book, is that language has the potential to divide, and to unite different sectors. He questions why the Mithyali who speak Mithyali gradually abandon their language and begin speaking Hindi instead, while the Sikhs and Muslims in the Indian Federation zealously guard their distinctive tongue. He concludes that it is religion that causes people to tenaciously cling to their own language while rejecting their country's official language. Brass

[30] See footnote 5 above.

demonstrates how in India too, religion plays a key role in drawing the lines in the conflict between the Hindus and Muslims. Since Mithyali follow the Hindu religion, like the Hindus who speak Hindi, while the Muslims speak Urdu, the Mithyali identify with the Hindu side in this religious-nationalistic conflict and even wind up having their children adopt the Hindi language.

Let us consider what would happen in Israel to the Arabic language that is the mother tongue of the immigrants from Arab countries if a bitter struggle were not taking place between Jewish and Arab nationalities. It is likely that under such circumstances, Jews emigrating from Arab countries would have continued speaking their native tongue much longer, as in fact was the case with German immigrants in the 1930's and with Russian immigrants presently. The Arab Israeli conflict played a major role in motivating Jewish immigrants from Arab countries to renounce Arabic, though there were additional factors that influenced also European immigrants.

Common enemies :

Enemies or political opponents, such as the Muslims are to the Hindus, or such as the French were to the English, Scottish, and Welsh (leading them to unite and form one British nation) –also play a key role in fueling nationalism, though in both these cases the common enemy also followed a different religion. The terrorist attack in the Dolphinarium in Israel that killed many Russian-speaking teenagers, had a similar effect on many Russian immigrants, strengthening their connection to and solidarity with the State of Israel.

Common religion:

The Iran-Iraq conflict is not simply a conflict between two nations who have different cultures, language, and history, but also between distinctive religious denominations. Iraq, ruled by Arab Sunites (and not by the Iraqi Kurds or Shiites), oppresses the predominately Shiite Iran – primarily because it suspects they are loyal to the Shiite faction in Iraq, even though ethnically there is no connection between the Iraqi Shiites, who are Arabs, to the Iranian Shiites. The Yugoslavian conflict between Muslims and Eastern Orthodox Catholics is another prime example of the role of religion in defining nation and in national conflicts. The strained relations between Irish Catholics and the Protestant British government compared to the cordial relations between the English, Scottish and Welsh – who are all Protestant, is an additional example of the internally unifying, and externally segregating force of religion. The Israeli-Palestinian conflict and Israel's conflict with its Arab neighbors also is built in great part on religious differences. Israeli Arabs participation in Arab-Israeli conflicts and in the two intifadas reflects that as long as they did not fear for Islamic holy sites (on the

Temple Mount), they passively and indirectly helped the Israeli effort against Arabs outside of Israel.

Modern religion and armed struggles:
Religion serves as a force that infuses people with a war fervor – such were Islam's wars of conquest and the Crusades as well as the Moslem Christian war in Spain. Even in the modern age, after the purported separation of Church and state, religion when it is merged with nationalistic forces, serves as a particularly strong motive for war – eg. – in our days - the wars in Yugoslavia, Chechnia, Ireland, between the Arabs and Palestinians and the Jews in Israel, Kashmir, Iraq-Iran, civil war in Sudan, and in the distant past –Turkish wars to conquer Europe, and Serbian and other nations wars in the Balkans to kick out the Turks.
One needs to distinguish between territorial wars, such as these, that are perceived as a religious mission, either to spread one's religion or to conquer 'holy lands' for one's religion,[31] and between territorial wars that have no religious goals, such as the Roman conquests and establishment of the Roman empire, the Greek conquests during the period of Alexander of Macedonia, colonization in America, Africa and Southern Asia.[32] Economic ends (economic hardship, the pursuit of war booty, slaves, and new peoples to tax, the quest for natural resources such as gold, the desire to expand one's trade borders and to gain control of new territory that would secure sea travel, etc.) were the primary motives behind these wars.

What is striking is that all the wars that were religiously motivated were waged by 'advanced' religions whose God was not a deity specific to one nation but rather a God who had created and now ruled over the entire world. It was a religious imperative for those who believed in this God to act on his behalf, to spread his messianic message.

This point sheds light on our comparison of India and Africa.
A religion that revolves around a God that rules over the entire world, who created the world or was involved in its creation, demands – because of its very essence – from its followers to aggressively seek dominion over the entire world – in the name of its God and to seek to spread the word of their God. Such was the primary goal behind conquest of Latin America, and the reason why the Indians in Latin America mostly survived conquest by the White man while the North American Indians did not. Therefore the religious struggle between Hindus, Muslims and Sikhs – according to the definition of God that each of these religions possesses -

[31] Like the Crusades.
[32] Even though the English felt a sense of mission on behalf of their Protestant faith.

is a never-ending battle, as long as there are still believers left in the area where the war is being waged.[33]

In contrast – the primitive African religions are not essentially covetous. They don't believe in missionizing or in the supremacy of one religion or another. The totem or ethnic father spirit does not seek to expand the boundaries of his religious rule. Therefore any conflicts or competition between different African ethnic groups, each of which is connected to a different idol, is based on personal interests, and not on religious differences. It is a material, not ideological struggle. Therefore, it can be mediated and compromise is possible. This is in contrast to a conflict of deities – a spiritual ideological conflict over religious 'truth', which no 'payoff' or physical compensation can resolve. Therefore, rivalries and clashes between African ethnic groups should be more rational, more solvable. They should be, but in reality aren't, as evidenced by the Ibo tribe in Biafra, the Tutsi and Huttu tribes, and the Somalian Ethiopian clash which I won't include, because of its religious elements. The question arises, therefore, how is it that ethnic cleansing occurred in these wars, despite the fact that the lines drawn in this conflict were not drawn according to religious affiliation. In Biafra, perhaps people died mostly from famine and the Ibo tribe in Biafra was Christian with those opposing them mostly (though not entirely) non-Christians, yet we still have a conflict which prompted ethnic cleansing even though no religious-messianic lines separated between the oppressed and oppressors.

Perhaps the explanation is that conflicts, in actuality, erupt based on a clash of interests. The dividing religious or ethnic line is only drawn later to justify the

---

[33] The argument that democracy is not aggressive is flawed, since the lack of aggressiveness and the dwindling desire to rule others- in democratic Western countries – is linked to rising secularism and the loss of a strong connection with religion, as well as the rule of civil religion. The big question is what role does this factor play – as opposed to the democracy factor – in the waning aspirations of Western countries to rule over other countries. Since the civil religion is a religion that belongs to the specific country, the moment a Western country is transformed from a country linked to a divine religion to one linked to a civil religion, the political horizon narrows to the country's borders. This is the reverse of what used to be. The English, for example, believed, that as Protestants, they were the chosen nation, with religion mission to fill in the world. This belief was one of England's and later Britain's motives for imperialist conquests, and it fueled the militancy of the English-British 'Chosen Nation.' Once this motive no longer existed, Britain easily ceded its magnificent empire. The same goes for other imperialist European countries, except for France. France established a unique civil religion, that viewed also territories across the sea as objects of this faith. Only when this belief began dying out, France relinquished, unwillingly, certain territories that it had previously insisted belonged to France.

violence. Analogously, prejudice against Blacks in the South in America was an ideology advanced until the American Civil War, in order to justify slavery, a product of economic interests. Racial prejudice did not create slavery, but rather economic interests related to slavery created a racist ideology. Thus, an "ethnic conflict" can take place between two sides separated by ethnic, and not religious boundaries, who are really fighting over economic interests, and only after the fact defined their conflict as ethnic in nature. This may explain the Nigerian conflict revolving Biafra. The Ibo tribe lived in Biafra, a particularly advanced tribe, also democratically, yet Nigerian independence made them an insignificant political player. When oil was found in Biafra, the Ibo declared independence, hoping to keep their newfound source of wealth to themselves. This resulted in a civil war that caused the genocide of the Ibo tribe. The line that separated between the Ibo and the other tribes confronting it was ethnic, but the true cause of the conflict was economic. A similar occurrence with scriptural changes occurred in the conflict between the Tutsi, a minority that was considered an elite in the colonial period, and the Hutu who were the majority and who therefore wanted to assume control of the government after they got independence. Under these circumstances, the conflict acquired an ethnic character, even though it was truly a struggle for power, a struggle that turned violent and resulted in genocide due to the absence of democratic traditions. Therefore, except for seeing the relationship between messianic religions that are aggressive and territorial, and ethnic religions (including primitive religions, that always belong to a particular ethnic or tribal group) there is no definite clear answer to offer, and we will not venture to do so.

It suffices for the purposes of our discussion, to see that religion, whether messianic or ethnic, is an important central force in shaping nationalism.

In addition to violent struggles, there are economic ones. In Africa, according to Bates, tribal rivalry more closely resembles the conflict of interests between ethnic groups in the US rather than irreconcilable conflicts in India. The African conflict of interests resembles, somewhat the internal protectionism in Israel between groups of Jews from different places of origin. Confrontations both in the US between different ethnic groups and in Israel between Jews of different origin are not conflicts between deities. In the Indian federation the harshest conflicts are religious in nature, both between Hindus and Sikhs and primarily between Hindus and Muslims in Kashmir.

A comparison of Israel and the US to Africa regarding the effect of religion on inter-communal relations:

In Israel, it is quite clear that there is no religious struggle between groups of Jewish origin, aside from relatively slight differences between the entrenched

secularism of the majority of immigrants from the former Soviet Union, and the far more religiously traditional Sepharadim. This is the primary reason – along with feelings of persecution by the established Ashkenazic elite – for the establishment of separate political parties for Russian immigrants and for traditional and religious Sepharadim.
In the US, God-based religions were barred from the halls and even the corridors of government. Only one religion was permitted entry – American civil religion.[34] The American God-based religions resigned themselves to this fate, a fate dictated by America's national interest in unifying Americans of different religions into one nation. As a result, protectionism developed in the US and ethnically based unions were formed, a situation paralleling Bates' description of Africa.[35].

The aggressiveness of modern religion in India:
We can learn about the aggressiveness of the all-embracing messianic modern religion that champions a God with global influence and power, by contrasting the prevalence of religiously based conflict in Africa and the Indian federation. Not one of the primitive African religions aspires, seeks, or encourages its followers to make it into the national religion, into the religion on which the laws of the State are based, into the religion according to which the State is governed. No political struggles take place because of or in the name of one primitive religion or another. In tribal-idolatrous Africa (this is the Africa we will be speaking of, in accordance with Bates' book, and not Moslem Africa or Christian Ethiopia), conflict stems from differences in tribal, not religious, views and aims.

Since inter-tribal rivalry in Africa, according to Bates, is economically based, a question of whether land will be developed in a certain tribe's region or another's,

---

[34]This topic comes up in the first section of this book, 'Why Religion,' and in section IV, on civil religion and the Supreme Court in Israel, as well as indirectly in the articles, Lior Barshack, "The court and civil religion," **Hamishhpat Law Journal,** College of Administration (Rishon Le'tzion: ed. College of Administration Law School, 2000), pp. 35-65; Lior Barshack, "The Totemic Authority of the court," in **Law and Critique**, 11:301-328, (Kluwer Academic Publishers, Printed in the Netherlands, 2000). Regarding African civil religion, see T. Dunbar Moodie, **The Rise of Afrikanerdom, Power Apartheid and the Afrikaner Civil Religion** (Los Angeles: University of California Press, 1975). Regarding Israeli civil religion see, Charles S. Liebman and Eliezer Don-Iyechiya, **Civil Religion in Israel, Traditional Judaism and Political Culture in the Jewish State** (Los Angeles: University of California Press, 1983). Regarding American civil religion see, Elwyn A. Smith, "The Voluntary Establishment of Religion" in **The Religion of the Republic,** edited by Elwyn A. Smith (Philadelphia: Fortress Press, 1971), p. 154.
[35] Michael Walzer, What It Means to Be an American? (New York: Marshio).

or who will be afforded an opportunity /for vocational training, rivalry is less complex than it is in the Indian federation. In the Indian federation, there are not only different religions (which revolve around universal Gods) but also castes within each ethnic group with different political and economic interests, and languages. When these differences coincide with a religious struggle, the result is irresolvable conflict. The Indian federation is built according to a federative model, in contrast to all African states, apart from Nigeria and South Africa. As the problems in India become more varied, the tribal protectionism and loyalty, discussed by Bates, that takes precedence over national loyalty, becomes weaker than in Africa. This comparison clearly, becomes less apt and significant as the number of factors increases. The fundamental difference between primitive and modern religions, compounded by the differences in social structure between Africa and India make it difficult to compare the role of religion in each country.

The effect of modern religions on India's languages populations:

The central government in the Indian federation is generally tolerant towards linguistic minorities who seek autonomy in order to safeguard their unique language. Such tolerance exists as long as the minority in question is not a distinct group since in that case, the suspicion arises that a latent desire to preserve their religious identity lurks behind their professed concern for their language. Such is the situation regarding the central federal government's attitude toward the various groups that make up its population. Conversely, it seems that the degree of allegiance linguistic-ethnic groups show to their native language is linked to their religious commitment. Those who are not religiously distinct, will generally even if given the freedom to continue speaking their own language, fail to do so (eg. the Mithyali people who speak Mithyali gradually adopt Hindi, the official language in India, as their own) while those who are also religiously distinct (like the Sikhs and Muslims) will jealously guard their distinctive language. What happens with the non-religious ethnic groups is that since they identify religiously with the ruling circles in the Indian federation (who are Hindus by religion), they feel duty-bound to support the Hindu government against the insurgent Muslim minority. As a sign of their support, they refrain from opposing the government on the language issue, and instead gradually stop speaking their own language, adopting Hindi instead. The non-religious ethnic groups are also motivated by the belief that knowledge of their country's official language will help their children advance in the workplace and increase their chances of receiving government positions (a poor rationale considering the fact that the federal government is quite tolerant regarding different language-populations and willing to give government jobs to non-Hindi speakers. What emerges from all this is that religion (modern) has tremendous influence, not only because of its inherently jealous-covetous nature.

Ethnic ties are favored over Western-style society:
Ashutosh Varshney describes in his article[36] how the Hindu Nationalist Party that replaced the Congress Party received many votes even outside of Hindu districts. Ethnic divisions, he writes, became blurred and "Hindu" came to include all ethnic groups indigenous to the Indian sub-continent, even Sikh-Muslims. From the beginning of the establishment of the Indian federation, the Congress Party had rejected a trend towards ethnic nationalism, and instead espoused the modern Western system of a civil society that included all of the State's citizens within a national body embracing the State. This party did not believe that ethnic nationalism or divine religion had any place within the framework of the country's government. The State was, for it, the transcendental value that parallels God in a God-based religion.

This revolution is evidence that religious and ethnic alliances create stronger bonds and ties than do the State and any secular values. In India, one witnessed, though, not only evidence of the resilience of ethnic ties, but also the growth of the Hindu ethnic group due to various religious struggles. Before we examine these religious conflicts, however, we must clarify an additional problem, that of religious and national identity in India. Mhatma Ghandi[37] wished to see the Hindu nation free of its roots in the Hindu religion, to divorce the nation from the religion. According to his approach, that was shared by many Hindus as well as Muslims in India, Moslems in India had two options. One, was to integrate into the Indian culture, a national-Hindu culture without the component of the Hindu religion, to which Indian Muslims had contributed immensely and significantly. The alternative was to close themselves off to Indian society. Mhatma Ghandi's approach was very popular, and many Muslims in the Indian federation even fought in the Indian army against Pakistan. In time, however, the Hindu religion proved its zealous nature. Hinduism is a supreme religion in which the deity is based on the concept of the 'dharma' – an eternal, universal, unchanging value that unites the divine with everything that exists,[38] and that has personal divine providence over the individual's actions. It is a religion that is concerned with both the behavior of the individual and of the entire Hindu public.[39] It is politically

---

[36] Ashutosh Varshney, "Contested Meanings: India's National Identity, Hindu Nationalism, and the Politics of Anxiety, in **Daedalus** (Summer 1993) pp. 227-261

[37] Ibid, pp. 240-241.

[38] Eva Hellman, "Dynamic Hinduism: Towards a New Hindu Nation," in **Questioning the Secular State- The Worldwide Resurgence of Religion in Politics**, edited by David Westerlund (London: Hurst & Company), pp. 237-258.

[39] It recalls the Jewish concepts of individual and general responsibility and the corresponding relationship of the deity to individual and to the community in Judaism.

ambitious, and seeks to determine also the political beliefs of its followers.[40] Therefore, the success of the Hindu Nationalist Party was the downfall of two alternative approaches – the first of a civil religion and a civil society based on the modern Western model, and the second of ethnic nationalism, a state not bound by or connected to religion. As we will see soon, it became apparent, that in the Indian federation, religion had the power to create nations and even to extend the boundaries of the nation. Religion in India, even caused, as we saw, certain language-populations to give up their distinct language in order to strengthen their religion against a rival religion.

How religious conflict spurred the growth of ethnic nationalism in India:
Urdu is the language spoken by the Muslim population in the Indian federation while Hindi is the language of the largest ethnic Hindu group. The Mithyali are Hindus by religion, though they observe their own distinct festivals – in addition to festivals common to them and to the main Hindu group. Essentially, it is language that distinguishes between the Mithyali and the large Hindu group, as the Mithyali speak and write Mithyali while the Hindus speak Hindi. When fighting broke out between the Muslims who speak Urdu and the Hindi speaking Hindus, the Mithyali who spoke neither Urdu or Hindi felt obligated to side with the Hindus, members of the same religion, even if their language was different. In order to show their support for the Hindus, the Mithyali began encouraging their children to learn Hindi in school. Parallel to this, the Congress Party, which espouses a civil society free of any ethnic components, began losing power to the Hindu Nationalist Party, a fiercely anti-Muslim party. The Mithyali opted in the political arena just as they had in the educational one, to side with fellow members of their religion, and so many Mithyali joined the Hindu Nationalist Party. Other ethnic groups who were also Hindus by religion, chose similarly to join the Hindu Nationalist Party, which subsequently came to power. The sides in the conflict aligned themselves according to religion, with most non ethnic Hindus identifying with ethnic Hindus simply because they shared a common religion. The result was, that for the most part, the Hindu religion became the Hindu nation. Religion developed into a nation. The Hindu nation grew and expanded because of a religious conflict.

Strong modern religion and weak modern religion - in India?
In the Indian Republic, there emerged a difference in the resilience of the Sikh religion versus that of the older Hindu and Muslim religions. Historically, the Sikh religion emerged, a little over 500 years ago from a union of Hinduism and Islam. The British, eager to bolster an ethnic-religious basis connected to militarism that

---

[40] See Eva Hellman's book cited in footnote 38, top p. 248.

had in the past opposed Muslim rulers in India and even briefly the British conquerors, encouraged the distinctiveness of the Sikhs, during their period of rule in India. The Sikhs demonstrated greater hostility toward the Muslims than toward the Hindus. They opposed the establishment of Pakistan, and deserted it for the Indian federation. When the Hindus opposed a firm demand by the Sikhs for national autonomy – just as they had opposed Muslim independence in Kashmir, the Sikhs rolled up the nationalist flag, and compromised on linguistic but not national autonomy. The Sikhs take a more flexible approach toward the Hindus than do the Muslims, evidenced by Sikhs' willingness to intermarry with Hindus (their children often consider themselves Sikh-Hindus) in contrast to the Muslims' refusal to intermarry.[41] In the absence of comparative studies regarding the difference of nationalistic fervor among Muslims and Sikhs in the Indian sub-continent, it seems reasonable to attribute the moderateness of the Sikhs' position to the fact that they are a much smaller minority than the Muslim minority in the sub-continent (they constituted less than 2% of the Indian Republic population when it was established). Additionally, it seems likely that Pakistan's backing of Muslim aspirations in Kashmir bolstered the Kashmir Muslims,[42] as did the support of the greater Muslim world. This was a major advantage that the Muslims had over the Sikhs. It seems reasonable to consider as a possibility that needs further examination that Sikh weakness and lack of determination stemmed from their religion's relative immaturity and lack of real distinctiveness compared to Islam. This thesis is supported by the weak ethnic standing that Druze have in the Middle East, whether in Syria, Lebanon, Jordan, or Israel. Their religion is a Muslim sect, and wherever they live, they adapt nationally to their new home, and even demonstrate basic loyalty to the ruling government. The Moslem Kurdish living in various Moslem countries: Iraq, Iran, Turkey, and Syria, demonstrate similar flexibility and irresoluteness in their national struggle. Judaism, in contrast, is an ancient religion. Thousands of years of history have forged a people with immense inner strength.

Religions stripped of their religious aspects:

Primitive religion (idolatry, associated with a regional local God and to a restricted audience) does not attempt to exert influence beyond the essentially limited and restricted bounds of its God. It is therefore not outwardly aggressive, surely not beyond its own narrow target audience. Even towards its own target audience, it is

---

[41] See Brass' book cited in footnote 23, p. 27.

[42] See Varshney cited in footnote 36, bottom of p. 237, where he describes how from the beginning Kashmir enjoyed far greater independence than other states in the Indian federation, nothing is left in Kashmir besides control over foreign affairs, defense, currency, and media.

generally not overly-jealous, since it views things as optional rather than imperative. A similar situation exists in the US today. There the ideology of a civil religion demands of its followers only that they follow a non-primitive religion. Which specific one they choose is inconsequential. A member of Congress may be Catholic or Jewish or Muslim or Budhist or Shintu – he is not obligated to be Protestant, though that might be most desirable. Furthermore, civil religion in America embraced certain Protestant holidays (Thanksgiving, Christmas), encouraging even non-Protestant American citizens to celebrate them, alongside American Independence Day and Memorial Day.

Under these circumstances, religious holidays lose to a certain extent their divine-religious nature. Add to this the principle of the separation of Church and State which de-legitimizes the participation of divine religions in the American political game, and you are left with divine religions that have been stripped of all goals other than a desire to preserve their customs – traditionalism for its own sake. Under these circumstances, Jews in America begin losing their Jewish distinctiveness. Catholics, too, are no longer like Catholics in manifestly Catholic countries. The unique color of each of the divine religions fades.

This situation is reminiscent of the Indian Republican in its early days and in the spirit of Mhatma Ghandi who viewed all Indians regardless of their religion as brothers. This approach, though, lost popularity in India, and was replaced by a desire for autonomy.

In tribal-idolatrous Black Africa, according to Bates` description, the tribes are equally un-aggressive regarding their religions. In this respect, it is more apt to compare tribal-idolatrous Africa to the US, rather than to the Indian Republic. In fact, when we return to Michal Walzer's description of every American's dual loyalty to America and his particular ethnic group, the US seems to resemble tribal-idolatrous Africa, while the Indian Republican parallels neither Africa or the US.

Summary:

The essence of the tribes in Africa today:

A tribe is a kind of ethnic group. It is a group of people who share an ethnic connection to the founding fathers of the tribe (a vertical bond – from the perspective of time) as well as an ethnic connection to others living at the same point in time (a horizontal bond). A tribe always lives in one specific geographical region or settlement.

In Africa, as a result of modernity's influence, even before they received independence, some of the tribal population left their tribal living patterns for the cities. The tribal system implies tribal rivalry, (even the true ethnic origin of two bordering tribes is similar) and leads to economic rivalry between the different tribal populations in the cities. We saw above how common enemies engender nationalism. A similar phenomenon exists between tribes. Geographic proximity leads to rivalry, even though geographic closeness naturally points to similar or common origin. Colonial rule often created tribal borders that had not existed previously, resulting in new tribal or ethnic groups – but these did not necessarily constitute a State.

A necessary characteristic of a nation is the desire on the part of an ethnic group to enjoy some form of autonomy in a particular land, an opposition to having a ruler who is not part of their group. This is what turns an ethnic group into a nation.

The route towards independence in Africa:

In Africa independent nations came into being more because of changes on the part of the ruling powers rather than because of changes experienced by those ruled. In other words, the imperialist powers, no doubt with some push by those being ruled, granted independence, at the point in time, when opposition reached a line – that the ruler preferred not to overstep. As we see from Israel's withdrawal from Lebanon, the decision to withdraw was made by Israel and related to internal politics, just as the decision to dismantle the Soviet Union was an internal political decision made by the leaders of the Soviet Union. In all these examples, including Africa's establishment of independent states in place of colonial rule, there was no bilateral process between the military powers of opposing sides. In the Indian sub-continent too, the underlying decision was made by the colonialist power, but in that case the internal structure was not tribal. We will compare India and Africa in this regard later on, even though nationalist aspirations were far more developed in India than in Africa. Consequently, nation-less African States were formed, ethnic-tribal groups.[43] What happens to a nation-less State?

[43]This does not relate to Anderson's writings about the illusions held by the overseers of colonial powers who, as a result of habits acquired while functioning as a colonialist state, they imagine the existence of the state with its colonial borders. When upon receiving independence, they acquired control of the government, they internalized this illusion, and their point of departure became the idea of non-contestable borders of the colonial state. This illusion was not shared by the general masses, and even when it did spread to the masses, a nation in the true sense – rooted in the deepest emotions of its citizens - was not formed. See in note 29 blow - Benedict Anderson, **Kehilot Medumyanot – imagined**

One can ask the same question about the US over 200 years ago. There, citizens of 13 states who had won their independence through war (definitely not by a process similar to Africa's) felt – at the time they achieved independence – like Protestant Brits in every which way even though –from the moment they rid themselves of British parliamentary rule – they needed to 'devise' a nation for themselves. What the Americans did at that time, and what the Africans are doing today is similar: they institute, first and foremost, dual loyalty. The Americans established loyalty to the state alongside loyalty to the federal government, while the Africans establish tribal loyalty alongside the state that the colonial government happened to form. After the Civil War, American dual loyalty shifted from the state to ethnic group. Africans, according to Bates, already felt this loyalty to their ethnic origin, to the tribe, from the beginning. In India, we see evidence of partiality to members of one's ethnic group, parallel to the US and Black Africa, but also a clear trend towards predilection towards members of one's caste

The power of nationalism vs. religion in India:
Varshney quotes Ashis Nandy regarding the growing trend in India towards radical nationalism. He writes that modern India does not demonstrate the same tolerance towards non-Hinduist religions as Hindus did towards the Jews, Zoroastrians, and the Christians. This trend highlights the difference between the Indian federation and African states regarding the relevance of Bates' theory.
This intolerance is a marked sign of national unification in India, as was the political displacement of the Congress Party with the Hindu Nationalist Party. We

---

Societies, pp. 143-163. In this context, I suggest rejecting Azmi Bashara's theory propounded in his article published by the Open University, 'A man wakes up one morning and suddenly feels he is a nation.' There he explains that the key to political achievements in the national arena lies in the precise definition one chooses for the concepts of 'nation' or 'people', or 'nationalism.' Bashara argues that based on a certain definition, the entire Jewish ethnic population across the world will constitute a 'nation' while the Palestinian people will not. After Bashara emphasizes just how connected the matter is to political 'national' interests, he seeks – as he did in his article in '*Tioriya Ubikoret*' where he sought to glorify the civil society in every place and to convey a message opposite to one he disparaged earlier regarding Jewish and Palestinian right to self determination – and though he doesn't say it explicitly, he is referring primarily to Israel. According to this, Bahara ultimately prefers the loyalty of Arabs and Jews in Israel to the State of Israel over their ethnic loyalty. It comes as no surprise, that in contrast to Bashara the pristine academician, unsoiled by any ethnic stain in his article, Bashara the politician does not hesitate to encourage the State of Israel's enemy, Syria, to organize a campaign of terror and war against the State of Israel, saying that though for the State of Israel Syria is an enemy, he personally as a Palestinian, cannot under any circumstances view Syria as an enemy. Regarding his article see, "Between Nations and Peoples: Reflections on Nationalism," ***Tioriya Ubikoret*** **6** (Spring 1995), pp. 19-43.

do not find such bolstering of nationalist feelings in Africa. It is questionable whether nationalism even exists there at all, in its true sense – meant to describe an ethnic group's aspiration to rule a certain country or to participate in its government as a group.

African emptiness as an indicator in a comparative view:
Therefore, it is specifically Black Africa composed of independent states lacking a national backbone, whose religious core is primitive and un-aggressive, in which a developed form of protectionism occurs, that is the void in which one can relatively clearly and transparently, examine other states to see the weight religion the state, and the political organization have in those states.

Part 7

Imperial China Vs. the West

The role of religions

China:
A Non-Aggressive Religious Approach
The West:
An Aggressive Religious Approach and the Revolt Against Divine Rule

Scope of this Part and the Leading Standpoint:
This chapter focuses on an event that never took place – the Industrial Revolution in Imperial (until 1911) China. In an effort to determine what were the obstacles that thwarted this revolution, this chapter compares Imperial China and the West – particularly 19th century America. This is an absolutely necessary comparison, considering the fact that until the year 1600, China surpassed the West in the field of technology. During the relevant centuries, China's geographical size and population were comparable to those of Western Europe. China possessed its share of large cities and an advanced culture. Chinese cities were larger and more developed than their Western counterpart and the Chinese society was very advanced.

China had embarked on exploration and conquest expeditions long before the West. Its ships had reached Africa and Arabia, but with one Imperial declaration, this fleet was recalled and China retreated within her boundaries . China outstripped Europe in both military strength and new inventions (paper, printing, gunpowder, compass), as well as in breadth and depth of astronomical knowledge. China wasunited and ruled by an Imperial government for most of the years between 221 BCE and 1911. Yet, beginning in the 14th century it ceased advancing; China remained an agricultural nationwith underdeveloped - industry did not develop. This chapter explores the reasons for this phenomenon, probing deeply to explain its causes. Thus, for example, it does not accept at face value, China's decision to recall its fleet – as merely an Imperial order. It delves deeper – to discover – not only what motives impelled the specific emperor to make the decision he made, and not only how China at that time came to be ruled by an emperor and what chain of events led to his assumption of the throne, but also how the Imperial dynasty began in China. It probes even further to determine how a system of government that allows no political contest or challenge affected China's development – when such a system began and how. It attempts to resolve certain questions: What characteristics of Chinese culture permitted one man or one family to seize complete power and to enjoy the loyalty and wholehearted enthusiastic respect of all his subjects. Why were the Chinese inclined towards a system of government that united all China under one ruler, in contrast to Western nations who revolted against such a form of government? How did China, with its vast population, equal to that of all Europe, maintain one single uniform culture? And finally, is there in fact a connection between the form of centralized government in China and parental authority. What role do the development of the nuclear family unit, and familial and ethnic-tribal loyalties play in creating the impetus and necessary conditions for industrial development and initiative?

The effect that pluralism and European divisions had on the development of Galileo's telescope offers us a clue as to the answers to some of these questions. Galileo was able to find numerous customers for his invention in the open European market. In China, in contrast, commerce was regulated by theimperial system (in many cases the emperor did not actually ruled in person) and restricted according to Imperial policies and interests. Thus a free market was permitted in China only as long as it coincided with Imperial goals. When it conflicted, however, then the emperor, as "head of the family" would intervene and severely penalize the offender, in a manner that reinforced his position of power.
This part of the book will also examine the liberating and broadening effects of division, controversy, rivalry, enmity, strife, and war versus the confining constricting effects of unity, harmony, and peace.

The one question that will not be addressed in this context is the one that demands a value judgment: which do we prefer – peace or war? Our personal inclination is to choose peace, but it is important to examine and know what is the price humanity must pay for the morality that we aspire to.

In this same spirit, this work critiques certain relatively new views on Chinese culture, such as those that appear in Dr. Yuri Pines' paperbook on the reasons why the ideal of the 'Great Unity' evolved in China[1]. Pines quotes opinion that this ideal was nothing but a myth, an unattainable dream of the archaic Golden Age, or

[1]Yuri Pines, " 'The one that pervades the all' in ancient Chinese political thought: The origins of 'the great unity' paradigm" in **Toung Pao LXXXVI**

a historical fabrication. Pines explains that this was a logical political method of resolving the constant state of political anarchy, and that the concept of unification was not a consequence but a precondition – an idea that preceded its realization. Pines claims that logic led to the establishment of Imperialism, a claim that may be partially correct but that is overly superficial. Pines describes how emotionally inclined, Chinese farmers were to accept upon themselves the rule of another, even when this rule absolutely suppressed their personal ambitions for power. This work will examine the relationship between fathers and sons in China and seek to determine whether there wasn't a connection between the benevolence of the father-son relationship and absolute Imperial rule. Perhaps a father searches for a benefactor, a patron, who will look after his interests just as he does for his son, and towards whom he will consequently feel such loyalty, that he will refrain from revolting against this patron. This discussion will be similar to the one regarding Galileo's distribution of telescopes to various economic and political figures in Europe and to the question of the logic and value of such an action. This chapter will address the various social and cultural factors that caused political and other division in Europe, forming the market that served Galileo so well, yet was completely non-existent in China. A complete analysis of the European side of the equation is beyond the scope of this work.

This introduction has hinted sufficiently at the solutions that will be offered. It is time to finally begin to try to prove the thesis.

The Father's Position in the Family and Compliance with His Will

Worship of early ancestors and attachment to an ancient father-spirit that according to their legends provided protection to those who were ethnically related, were common to all societies prior to the development of non-ethnically linked religions.[2]

---

[2] Taking into account the singularity of the Chinese, it is correct to draw this distinction rather than the one popularly drawn in academic studies between historic religions and religions connected to the periodicity of nature. See Mircha, **The Myth of the Eternal Old Age** – Archetypes and Review. Translated from French: Yotam Reuveni. Editing and notes: Ronit Nilolski (Jerusalem: Carmel, 2000), pp. 46-71. Within the scope of a discussion of a-historic religions, Eliade speaks about religions that conduct rituals in order to ingrain myths, reinforce their followers' inner confidence, and bolster their connection to the gods who watch over them. They imitate the deeds of the Gods, cutting off the foreskins of the Aborigines In Australia, memorializing historical events and personalities, events whose historical and personal characteristics are obliterated, transforming them into archetypes. This reinforces the belief that what was will yet be, because the deeds and wonders of the past do not belong only to a particular date, but continue to endure. A renunciation of history and belief in the renewal of time insure positive results in the

The distinction that must be drawn for the present discussion is between religions whose adherents viewed themselves as the descendants of early ancestors, and religions that were not based on any such connection – for this belief developed later into the concept of paternal respect. These early ancestors lived in the distant past, and were not limited exclusively to Chinese traditions.[3] The concept of ancestor worship and paternal respect, however, was emphasized particularly in China, and has existed there, according to Uri Pines,[4] for over two thousand years. Pines notes that over time decreasing use was made of the term 'Xiao.' Pines claims that during the Western Zhou Dynasty (1050-771 BCE), this term was more commonly used to describe ancestor worship, rather than parental respect, in

---

present and future. The ongoing periodicity ensures the replenishment of food reserves, the fall of rain, and the renewal of the periodicity of life. The elimination of the historical dimension implies that whatever happens today already took place in the past, and since according to their religion's folklore, the ancients successfully grappled with whatever transpired in the past, the religion's followers are guaranteed a successful end and solution in every endeavor. The system of historical religions cultivates the national consciousness and faith in the everlasting existence of the nation. The continued existence of the people signifies that the people – as a national entity – overcame until this point all obstacles, and therefore the presumption is that the people will continue to prevail and endure. What follows, though Eliade did not explicitly state it, is that from this respect, historical religions are religions that establish nations, while non-historical religions are linked to societies that seek to grow without the national component. Regarding historical religions, it is significant how much time has elapsed since the historical events took place in the days of the religion's patriarchs, while in non-historical religions, time is inconsequential, since whatever was will be. Buddhism, in this respect, to the extent it is a religion, is not a historical religion. Buddhism does not promote a certain nationality, and neither does Catholicism, whose key characteristic is salvation and the anticipated renewal of man's soul. Protestantism, in contrast, concerns itself with the historical aspect, and with academic historical study of holy and ancient texts, within the context of its efforts to prove that the Pope's word is not final, and that it is possible to escape his clutches. Protestantism sought sources more binding than the current Pope, in order to achieve independence. Thus, Protestantism was able to forge a new distinct nationality in different places and to impart a historical dimension to the local population (like in England). See: Linda Colley, **Forging Protestantism and the Nation 1707-1837**, T. Claydon et al, eds. (New Haven, 1992), National Identity: Britain and Ireland, c. 1650- c. 1850 (Cambridge, 1998).

[3]See Mircha Eliade, footnote 2 above

[4]Yuri Pines, Aspects of Intellectual Developments in the Chunqiu Period (722-453 B.C.), Ph.D. Dissertation by Yuri Pines, Submitted to the Senate of the Hebrew University 1997, pp. 367-384.

contrast to the usage noted by otherof this term by Confucius and other thinkers during the Eastern Zhou (770-221 BCE).

Pines describes the evolution from loyalty to the extended family structure to the more narrow-nuclear family structure. Before relating to this, it is correct to note that what is referred to in studies of religion[5] and also by Pines, is not religious worship that was based in the framework of the extended family and certainly not in that of the nuclear family, but rather worship linked to the ancestors. Ancestor worship was not directed at live human beings who were serving as the heads of the extended family but rather at those who were deceased. Pines too, regarding the concept of 'Xiao,' does not speak of sacrifices to the living. The authority and power given to the head of the extended family, was the authority to offer sacrifices to one's ancestors. The question is, whether this authority was given to the head of the extended family or to the head of each nuclearfamily or the founder of the extended family or the deceased fathers and grandfathers of the nuclear. Moreover, the meaning of the term itself changed (or expanded) whereas at the begging it means mostly worship later, after Confucius, one of its basic meaning was respect and care for the living parents and elders. The term 'Xiao' that Pines refers to, relates to this authority over sacrifices. Pines explains that the change in the meaning of the Xiao resulted from changes in governmental land distribution. Originally, the heads of the extended families received land, which they were entrusted with distributing to the heads of the nuclear families. When the head of the extended family died, the land returned to the king (this is during the pre-imperial period) and a new family head was appointed who would distribute the land. When over time the system changed, and the king began distributing land directly to the heads of the nuclear families, the status of the extended family head decreased significantly, and the authority for sacrifices, and the honor associated with it, also passed to the heads of the nuclear families. This chapter will examine the role this change played in the lag in Chinese industrial growth.

According to David Keightley, [6] cult worship in China cultivated legends relating to the family lineage beginning with the ancestral father. The Chinese viewed death as a phase in the life cycle of the family beginning with family or tribe's ancestral father. An individual, thus, lived on through his descendants.[7] This

---

[5]See Mircha Eliade, footnote 2 above

[6]David N. Keightley, "Early Civilization in China: Reflections on How it Became Chinese," Chapter II in Heritage of China: Contemporary Perspectives on Chinese Civilization, edited by Paul S. Ropp (Berkeley and Los Angeles: University of California Press, 1990) pp. 15-53.

[7]Ibid, p. 31.

perception made it relatively easy (in relation to the West) for them to relate to the notion of death, and explains why there is no Chinese parallel to the elegy recited by Gilgamash, frightened by Enkido's death.[8]

Beginning with the Sheng Dynasty (in the 16th century BCE and lasting until the 11th century BCE) the king also served as the highest religious figurepriest. Obligations owed to one's ancestors were transferred to the king, and his power grew, and the country became a unified religious-familial framework. As death became less tragic and difficult, and loyalty to one's ancestors and king, and by analogy to the master grew, it became customary to bury a master's servants along with him so that they could serve him even after death,[9] and thus human sacrifice became more common. Keightley notes that over the course of 150 years during the Sheng Dynasty, 5000 human sacrifices were offered in order to enable servants to continue serving their master after his death.

Keightley contrasts this perspective on death with Western dread and trepidation of the inevitable end. The heroes of Greek mythology, the source of so much of Western culture, are tragic figures who suffered great tragedies as a result of their efforts to carry out the will of the gods. Greek heroes were negative figures such as Achilles who killed the woman he loved, Oedipus who killed his father, and Antigone who committed suicide. In Western thought and in Christianity man was viewed as inherently evil, struggling alone in his life just as in his death. His strength was the strength of the individual, and from this derived the Western myth of the victory of the few over the many. The Chinese, in contrast, viewed man as inherently good; their mythological personalities are positive, and heroism and war are collective actions, organized bureaucratically. Even murder is perpetrated not as a result of greed but for the sake of family honor or to fulfill a divine mission and obligation. The Chinese hero is worthy of imitation. His deeds are bursting with optimism based on the belief that good character and deeds will be rewarded. The individual who obeys the bureaucratic governmental system is a common Chinese hero.[10]

The Chinese did not speak of the God's desire to harm man; no animosity existed between the gods and man, since one's ancestors lived together with the gods in

---

[8]Ibid, p. 33.

[9]Ibid, p. 28, but, later on there happened a retreat in that matter and fear overcame from being burying alive with the dead master.

[10]Ibid, pages 19-22.

heaven. Since no discord existed between the living and the gods, the issue of theodicy, of 'evil befalling the righteous' did not arise. The world operated as it should and its operation merited no criticism. While there were myths about angry gods, their actions were depicted as bureaucratic measures. Mainly, there was no myth in China about the origin and beginning of the world (there are but they are relatively late and not very important); thus there was no distinction between the nihilistic approach and the religious approach. According to Keightley, Western culture's concern over what the future held for them inspired the development of myths regarding the creation of the world. Since this fear did not exist in Chinese culture, these myths also did not.

This approach naturally led the Chinese to relate respectfully and uncritically toward their ancestors, leading in turn to the absolute prohibition against criticizing one's parents.[11]

Death, too was not depicted in China, as it was in the West,[12] as a process of decay and decomposition of the human body. Chinese love songs lacked any great lovers (as follows from the tendency towards the bureaucratic approach over the individualistic approach).[13]. Its depictions of parent-child relationships merely related the specific situation to established principles of conduct.[14] Even the attitude toward the ancient father was not based on faith in him (a personal approach) but rather on faith in his existence.[15] As a general rule, optimism and fidelity were common literary themes, rather than drama or social or political criticism.

All this engendered far greater serenity and calm than was prevalent in the West, an atmosphere that was also consistent with their system of government.

Chinese esteem for hierarchy and obedience were the natural consequences, according to Keightley,[16] of ancestor worship. Keightley claims that cities developed differently in China as opposed to the West, also as a result of all these factors. In the West, beginning in Mesopotamia, diverse populations, both religious and secular, inhabited the city. In Greece, the cities adopted varied forms of government, from dictatorship, to oligarchy, to democracy. In China, however, the city was built around the temple and was ruled primarily by the founding

[11] Ibid, page 36.

[12] Ibid, page 37.

[13] Ibid, p. 39.

[14] Ibid, p. 42.

[15] Ibid, p. 43.

[16] Ibid, p. 44.

families. Merchants and artisans who lived in Chinese cities were bound by the will of the ruling elite and permitted to play a very minor political role.[17] According to Chang,[18] in ancient China, everyone belonged firstly to a clan and secondly to a lineage group, both of which were related to an ancient father (but this changed dramatically with the begging of the imperial era). Political power developed based on these divisions. Every imperial dynasty associated itself with the most prominent lineage group in its tribe, and each tribe distinguished itself by one specific trait. Intertribal marriages were uncommon. Political standing of different clans varied, based on genealogy. New branches of the dynasty were established by sending one of the sons who was not next in line for the throne to a new settlement, along with a group of supporters. There, they would establish a new dynasty that was a branch of the central dynasty, but also independent – as was reflected by the erection of a temple in the new territory, a temple that eternalized the founder of this new dynasty.[19] Yet, Chinese society went through a very deep change during the last centuries of the first millennium BCE – in many respect this was a change from aristocratic (and thus depend on family ties) to bureaucratic (and thus depend on jobs) society. Although, family ties and family ideology was maintained and even became stronger in a non-aristocratic society.

Jumping way ahead to the 16th-17th centuries, it appears that association with the klan, even among non-ruling classes, continued to take place. Rubie Watson[20] surveys the various opinions on this subject. According to Friedman, collectivism developed as a result of the intensive labor needed in order to cultivate the rice fields and the need for cooperation in the defense of the border regions. Pasternak claims that a system of family based nepotism, which affected issues of inheritance, marriage, and residence, did not develop during the period of border infiltrations, but later when agricultural settlement had stabilized. Watson recalls Hillary Beatie's opinion that nepotism in China was less a function of one's residence and biological connection and more a function of economic and political factors. He describes a Klan that was established around a family temple in the Kapri region near Hong Kong around 1660 and which existed until its dissolution in 1751. The dynasty shared their temple with another family branch, yet they refused to include it in their dynasty. He compared this organization to a different

---

[17] Ibid. pp. 46-47.

[18] K. C. Chang, Art, Myth, and Ritual – The Path to Political Authority in Ancient China (Cambridge, Massachusetts and London: Harvard University Press)

[19] Ibid. pp. 9-17.

[20] Rubie S. Watson, "The Creation of a Chinese Lineage: The Teng of Ha Tsuen, 1669-1751," in Modern Asian Studies, 16, 1 (1982) (Great Britain: Cambridge University Press) pp. 69-100.

more homogeneous familial alliance in which the collective father included all of his descendants, and not only certain select ones. During periods in which there were no formal political establishments, these alliances increased the standing of its members in the region in which they lived. Donations to the temple also financed the purchase of ships that transported their merchants to distant markets, and even raised their status within the central government. At the end of the 18th century, the Chinese emperor, concerned that large families possessed so much power that they posed a threat to his throne, passed several laws meant to decrease their influence and to increase that of the smaller families. Watson notes the differences in resilience and internal strength of homogeneous alliances versus alliances in which certain native branches were detached from the main dynasty despite their natural bond. He describes how, periodically, different families merged, and claims that alliances of family dynasties based around the family temple were not only not the sole form of alliances in China, but that they did not exist at all.
Regarding this final claim, it should be noted that though these alliances almost completely did not exist in China from the first millennium BCE until modern times,[21] there is evidence that there were some in ancient times.

Moving ahead even further, to the end of the Imperial Age, T'ang Leang-Li, in an essay praised by the President of the University of Bejing, former Cultural Minister to China, Tsai Yuan-Pei,[22] claims that the most important institution in China was the family – whether in the meaning of an entire tribe that outwardly filled the role of internal civil and judicial government through the head of the tribe, the father. In reality, however, the government was not centralized and the head of the family did not rule alone, but rather the family's council determined policy, and the head of the tribe implemented these collective family decisions. The emperor seemed to preside over this hierarchical system, but this too was deceptive, since he was bound by the limits established by Confucius' principles, according to which – the people will obey the emperor and accept his authority if he punishes those who are dishonest, but will cease to obey him if he punishes those who are honest. The family was a microcosm of the State and its capital was the memorial hall to the original father of the family. Its members were obligated to respect the family's customs and help other family members in need. Rulings that were appealed could be brought before the local judge, but they rarely were. From familial obligations, rights - such as the rights to benefit from family owned

---

[21] See footnote 17 above.

[22] T'ang Leang-Li, China in Revolt – How a Civilization Became a Nation (London: Noel Douglas, reprint edition published in 1976 by University Publications of America Inc., Arlington, Virginia)

land that has not been sold (a right shared evenly by all the males and widows in the family) – were derived. Every child had the right to an education. If a family lacked the financial means to provide its children with proper schooling, the most talented of the children was given a formal education in order to bring honor to the family and ancestors of the family through his future accomplishments.

The entire familial system was based on worship of the ancestors who bring blessings upon the land. Thus marriage was viewed as a primary responsibility and so children were betrothed when they were still young. Chinese religion was humane in that the god was humanity itself. According to T'ang Leang-Li, the worship of man conquered death and oblivion. Most families, he claims, established rules regarding family matters. Even family members who had attained government positions were still bound by their family's conventions. When the males of a village, who consisted of the founding families, assembled, they exercised judicial authority and power over civil and religious matters, and wielded influence over the government authorities. In the cities, representatives of the various trade unions formed a council, with each representative having judicial powers both within his own trade and between the various trades. These representatives, along with government officials, and prominent authors constituted the urban elite that was responsible for what goes on in the city. This system of government kept crime levels incredibly low. In the city of Henko, for example, a city with a population **of one million people, there was only one homicide in 34 years. In** Chili, a country of 25 million people, only 12 people were sentenced to death in the years 1866-1867, and in China (excluding the district of Kwentung which was subject to foreign influences) only 581 people were sentenced to death in 1826.

With this background, this chapter can attempt to demonstrate the connection between the unique status of the fathers in Chinese society and - the position of the emperor and the Chinese adoption of one central government for the entire Chinese population. Once this is established, this paper will address the correlation between this system of government and China's failure to develop technologically along with the rest of the world.

The Connection between The Rule of the Head of the Family and Imperial Rule in China:

The cultural tradition of paternalistic rule in China was fortifying imperial rule at the same time that the prevailing philosophical system (Confucianism) and imperial legislation that had adopted Confucianism were buttressing paternalistic rule. Thus, the following four factors:

I. Paternalistic rule
II. Imperial rule
III. Confucianism
IV. Imperial legislation

mutually strengthened each other. In order to govern one's subjects, one must 'program' them, lead them to believe that it is both fitting and advantageous **from their perspective** to obey their rulers, and disadvantageous **for them** to overthrow their government. A government will only be stable if its subjects do not seek independent sovereignty because they believe that, both religiously and culturally, they all constitute one entity, and that no differences between them warrant a group of them seeking independence. Economic and social distinctions – differences that necessarily exist in any human society – are in fact proper and even desirable distinctions. It is advantageous that people will develop a sense of allegiance to a small intimate unit, and that these units will in turn develop ties with other units and broader circles, and between these circles, with loyalty ultimately focused on the leader, which in China was the emperor. In the West, this translates into a network of political parties with internal organizations based on narrower smaller factions and local leadership. In China, however, there were even more intimate associations of nuclear and extended families and tribes, and of trade unions in the cities. Chinese emperors built this intricate system of allegiance with great wisdom and foresight, despite a very diverse population and vast size. They definitely played a role, but their success was not due to certain extraordinary talents, but a result of the distinctive Chinese culture, structure, and beliefs. Chinese system of law and government constituted an important foundation, as well as the network of intellectuals and bureaucrats, philosophers, among them adherents of Confucianism, and the non-aggressive Buddhist religion, and traditional religions whose gods were chosen by the emperor. Daoism, too, even though it was not one of the institutionalized religions, posed no threat to the imperial form of government. Chinese Buddhism, which came to China at the end of the Han dynasty, and spread with the dissolution of this dynasty, during a period in which there was no centralized government, was a Northern trend of Buddhism that had come from India via central Asia.[23] This form of Buddhism did not cultivate a class of monks who would stand between its followers and the religious experience, but called upon each individual to endeavor through his own personal strength to fulfill the religious commandments and to enjoy the emotional succor that Buddhism provides. In this respect, this sect paralleled Protestantism, and it differed from the Southern more "Catholic" sect in which the individual

[23] The T'ang Code, Volume I, General Principles, translated with an Introduction by Wallace Johnson (Princeton, New Jersey: Princeton University Press, 1979) p. 7.

relied on the monks to intercede the gods on his behalf. Another characteristic – or additional consequence – of this Northern trend of Buddhism that dominated in China – was that no powerful class of priests-monks evolved that could pose a political threat to the government. In fact, the form of Buddhism that developed in China prior to the Tang dynasty, between the years 618-907, the philosophy of Confucianism, as well as the system of law, all supported the imperial government. Buddhism even managed to integrate with the two state religions that preceded it, Daoism and regional paganism.

All the imperial dynasties in China worked towards establishing one uniform system of law for all the people under their rule, and in conjunction with this goal, to creating a detailed legal constitution. Even before the establishment of imperialism, there were those, and in particular, Shang Yang in the country of Qin in the year 338 during the second half of the 4th century BCE, who pursued this goal.[24] The essentials of most of these codes of law whose influence continued even when the ruling dynasty changed, have been lost. One code that was preserved and continued to exert influence until the end of the imperial age (in the year 1911) was the code of the T'ang dynasty, an unusually comprehensive code. The reason for this is linked to the philosophy of Dong Zhongshu (who lived in the 2nd century BCE), which developed in China during the rule of the Han dynasty. According to this philosophy, man and nature constitute a holistic unity, with man's actions influencing nature and the emperor's actions affecting both man and nature. Theimage of the emperor played a critical role, in this system, and any slight to his honor was viewed as a threat to the entire world order since it would necessarily result in terrible catastrophes. According to this philosophy, five forces of one type within the holistic system (the sun, male, imperial mercy, spring, and summer) oppose five other forces (the moon vs. the sun, the woman vs. the man, the death penalty vs. imperial mercy, the autumn vs. the spring, the winter vs. the summer). Everything in this system is based on the number five: there are five colors, five directions (the middle is the fifth). When man sins, he must be punished in order to restore balance to the holistic universe, and his punishment must fit his crime, since both excessive stringency and excessive leniency prevent the restoration of holistic equilibrium. It is the job of the emperor to mete out appropriate punishment and to restore equilibrium. It is essential that the judge will impose a punishment in exact accordance with the code established by the emperor-legislator, and that there will be uniform penalties throughout the empire. This is why a person who falsely accused another would receive the exact

[24] Ibid. All descriptions, from this point on, of the legal situation in China, come from this book.

punishment that the accused was to have received, and similarly why confession to theft and restoration of the stolen property obviated the need for punishment.
Since the emperor held the most important position and link between man and the natural world, any crimes against the emperor and his family were considered the gravest offenses and resulted in the punishment of the offender's entire family, and the annulment of all standard procedural safeguards.
The result of all this was that the position of the emperor was secure. There were later periods in which it was not the emperor who governed, so much as the ruling circles who in effect ruled in his name (officials, intellectuals, and others), but none of this changes the fundamental fact that imperial rule wielded great influence, was involved in even relatively minor matters in the vast kingdom, and was aided by an intricate and large bureaucratic network. Power was centralized, except for periods in which the central government was weak, and the 'rules were broken' temporarily until the government regained its strength and vitality.

This system - of a strong centralized government entrusted in the hands of one ruler - was essential if the emperor was to restore nature's balance. Therefore, comptrollers were appointed whose job it was to insure that the law was implemented and that judges who erred in their application of the law were themselves punished. China considered itself pivotal in maintaining all of mankind and nature's balance. It viewed itself as responsible for the entire world, with the emperor having the greatest responsibility. As a result, both the system of law in China and compliance with the law were highly venerated. Whoever failed to conform to this system and with the authority of the emperor was considered uncultured and boorish.
The legal code in China served as the basis for the legal systems in Japan, Korea, and even Vietnam. China's influence over neighboring countries, undoubtedly stemmed in great measure, from the reputation they had earned as an enlightened people which itself resulted from the role Confucianism had played in shaping their legal system.

In light of the stability of their legal system which all the Chinese learned to protect, the emperors introduced into the legal judicial code and the system of law, elements that would reinforce imperial rule, in particular – Confucianism, a philosophy that from the time of the Han dynasty was introduced into every new territory that an emperor gained control over.

Confucianism demands that a son and servant respect their father and master. It is a system of obligations far more than a system of rights, discipline, and other factors that insure societal stability and prevent objections to economic and political differences. This philosophy was essential for Chinese emperors, and was the factor that prolonged their rule and enabled the legal code from the T'ang dynasty to survive for close to 1300 years. Man didn't dare implement changes in precise detailed laws that were responsible for preserving the world's equilibrium. Imperial Chinese laws secured the privileged status of those in positions of power in government as well as those that held these positions in the past or had inherited a title of nobility (all government officials – including judges). Every official had a certain number of points, up to thirty, according to his rank and achievement. In lieu of a punishment, he was permitted to trade in his rank, and in certain instances pay a fine, options that is not exist for a person who was not an official. He lost his position only temporarily, the length of time determined in accordance with the severity of the crime, anywhere between one to six years. Even during his period of suspension, he maintained his exemption from taxes and national service, two general civic obligations. Generally, after his suspension, he was demoted to a lower position. A job-related offense generally earned him a milder punishment than one that related to his personal life.[25] In general, officials received lighter sentences than common citizens for the same crimes, except in cases of deliberate burglary, abduction, bribe taking, and distortion of the law. Lower classes received more severe sentences than the average citizen. According to the accepted social structure of the T'ang dynasty, there existed three classes: higher, middle, and lower. In addition, there was a class of slaves and indentured servants. Crimes committed by a member of the middle class against a member of the lower class were considered one degree milder than those same crimes committed against a member of the same class. Similarly, crimes committed by a member of the lower class against a member of the middle class were considered one degree more severe than the same crimes committed against a member of the same class. The same rule applied, with the difference of one additional degree, to offenses between a member of the middle class and a slave.[26] Slaves and indentured servants were only allowed to marry a member of their own class. A slave who married a middle class woman was sentenced to a year and a half of hard labor. If the slave's master made his slave's wife part of his household staff, the master was sentenced to life long exile to a distance of 3000 li. This law was in accordance with the law's general perception of slaves as chattel.[27] A member of the middle class who married a slave woman received a lighter punishment than the above case. In cases of intermarriage, it was always the man and not the woman who was

---

[25] Ibid. pp. 25-27.

[26] Ibid. p. 28.

[27] Ibid. According to p. 29, this matter was established in section 92 of the T'ang dynasty code.

punished, whether he was a slave or a member of the middle class.[28] A woman and her family were punished if she was found guilty of witchcraft[29] or of beating her husband.[30]
Crimes against the emperor, the state, religion, or one's family (e.g. mourning customs for one's parents) were considered most serious of all. Collective punishments to one's entire family were meted out to those guilty of rebellion or attempted rebellion (including accessories to the crime). First-degree male relatives could be sentenced to death even if they had no prior knowledge of the crime. Other relatives were exiled and their property confiscated. There existed a wide range of punishments for these crimes, but the basic objective was as described above.[31]

The following law exemplifies how valued the family unit was, surpassed only by the importance of safeguarding the position of the emperor: a person was permitted to conceal a relative's crime, and even warn him of a government investigation taking place, as long as his crime did not involve the emperor. This law strengthened the family unit and encouraged family loyalty. If family members jointly committed a crime, such as theft, the oldest male was put to trial.[32] Stealing from a family member was considered a relatively minor crime, particularly if it was a close relation. Therefore, a son who stole from his parents would not be punished unless the value of the stolen object exceeded a certain sum, and even then the punishment was mild.[33]
What happened to nature's equilibrium when a person was convicted and punished, and then it emerged that he was falsely convicted? How did nature restore its balance? One thing is clear: if a person was falsely executed, nature simply had to bear the trauma, not only because there was no way to restore the man to life, but also because the emperor was by definition infallible, and death sentences were not executed without the emperor's consent. Thus, since the emperor could not have erred, clearly no disturbance to nature's equilibrium occurred and there was no need for repair. In other cases, the court acknowledged

---

[28] Ibid.

[29] Ibid, p. 19. Apparently, witchcraft is universally linked to women, as it is considered the weapon of the weaker elements of society.

[30] Ibid, p. 22. Women were generally not considered fit to stand trial. A case, however, such as witchcraft in which male authority was attacked, was considered an exception to the rule.

[31] Ibid, pp. 17-20.

[32] Ibid, p. 32.

[33] Ibid, p. 33.

its error and the falsely accused person was compensated, not by actually awarding him money from the Chinese coffers but by granting him tax exemptions. If he would have been eligible for a tax exemption for some other reason (e.g. his entire district received tax exemptions because of a drought), then his exemption was extended by a year.[34]

In order to reinforce internal family social order, the T'ang dynasty code of law[35] established that a son who hit his father or grandfather or designed to kill one of them was beheaded, and that a son who attempted through unlawful means to gain possession of the family's wealth during his father or grandfather's lifetime was sentenced to three years of hard labor.

One of the only crimes that resulted in collective punishment was the practice of Black Magic, or "Ku" (even by a woman), which resulted in the death of another or his going mad.

Rebellion against the emperor also resulted in collective punishment. According to the judicial code, the emperor equaled heaven and earth; he was the father of all his subjects. Thus any revolt against him was comparable to a natural disaster, which could be averted only by uprooting the source of the mutiny and this included the insurgent's entire family. This punishment had exceptional deterrent force, since eradication of the family was the harshest conceivable punishment in Chinese culture.[36] Thus the punishment for not participating in mourning rites for one's parent or grandparents was life long exile to a minimum distance of 2000 li.

In order to strengthen the family structure, assault of an adult numbered among the top ten most serious crimes in the T'ang code.[37]. The five degrees of family relation that pertained to mourning rites also constituted the basis for establishing different levels of punishment for crimes within the family. Even cursing a family member constituted a criminal offense. Laws regarding crimes against bureaucratic officials and religious figures were derived from laws relating to crimes against elder family members.

Though wives and concubines were considered inferior according to the judicial code, from relatively early on and continuing until the 11th century (when their status again declined, their status began to improve. The woman, and not her

---

[34] Ibid, p. 16.

[35] See footnote 1, Ibid, p. 21.

[36] Ibid, p. 20.

[37] Ibid, p. 31.

husband, managed all family and work matters.[38] Mourning customs for women were identical to those for men. The restrictions on women primarily related to where they were allowed to go, a distinction drawn, according to some, only to protect them.

One possessed the right to appeal a family ruling, but such appeals were extremely rare.[39]

As long as the families were relatively small and lacking political power, the family served as a center of loyalty and strength towards the government. Family institutions' support for the government completed the reciprocity in the positive relationship between the family on one hand and the law and government institutions on the other. Government positions were established by the emperor's court, upon the recommendations of local citizens and dignitaries, recommendations that were based upon the candidate's loyalty and respect for his parents, obedience to one's father, and level of education. Since these positions were awarded based on one's performance on exams in law, philosophy, and religion, it was common in many families to finance the studies of one child who seemed particularly talented, in order to enable him to earn a government position, thus glorifying the family's early ancestors.[40] Studies were financed in part by a government-awarded exemption form certain taxes, thus establishing semi-subsidized education.

It was common practice to use undividable family assets to fund quasi pensions to all family members above the age of 59.[41]

Villages in Imperial China were generally created by a few founding families who then formed the village's government. In the cities, the situation was similar, except that during certain periods, the government was run by local trade unions whose members were obligated to obey their union's leaders. The leaders of the various unions in the cities, along with government officials and prominent authors created a form of local nobility that assumed responsibility for all that took place in the city. In this respect, there was a kind of internal democratic rule.[42]

No civic book of law existed in China [only judicial law and administrative laws of the administrative government] perhaps because the imperial government

---

[38] See T'ang Leang-Li, China in Revolt (London: Noel Douglas, 1976) p. 24.

[39] Ibid, p. 25.

[40] Ibid.

[41] Ibid.

[42] Ibid, p. 26.

wished to leave the reins of the family leadership in the hands of the heads of the families and the leadership of the villages in the hands of the leadership. It preferred to see civic issues resolved through compromise and agreement between senior members of the family or families.[43] Within the context of this approach of family and group responsibility, collective punishments were established also within the framework of the trade union.[44]

How did the Chinese relate to the differentiation and discrimination of different social classes that was written into the code established by the emperor? In this lies the key to the Chinese system. Since:

1. The emperor was the only being who knew the secrets involved in the dangerous and delicate work of balancing between nature and man.
2. He had been responsible for this task for many generations.
3. The system worked.
4. No other being had the power to prevent the terrible calamity that would befall them if the emperor would desist from his holy work.
5. And the emperor had God-like status.

The Chinese accepted his rule and his way. The alternative was to rebel against the emperor and bring about utter devastation to the world. In order to avoid such terrifying consequences, the Chinese were willing to pay the price of accepting the imperial system and justice. Revolts definitely took place, but powerful elements worked to suppress them, elements that were strengthened by Confucian ideology that trained the Chinese to obey and submit to authority and by social forces of family and intellectuals who mollified and placated revolutionary spirits.

It is possible and entirely justified to suggest that Confucian values that emphasized order and hierarchy in the family and society were thoroughly assimilated into Chinese thought and accepted as part of the natural order. The more profound question is why did this take place? Evidently, by basing their code of law on Confucianism, the Chinese joined the social interest for which Confucius had created his system, with the imperial ruling interest, all alongside Chinese tradition which was deeply rooted in worship of one's ancestors and the status of the father and tribal head. The connection between the imperial government's interest and philosophy and law was highlighted during the

[43] Ibid, p. 29.

[44] Ibid, p. 31.

establishment of the Ming dynasty in 1368,[45] when the emperor chose to base his rule on the neo-Confucian system since it supported the imperial government.

Possible Reasons Why No Industrial Revolution Took Place in China:

1. According to T'ang Leang-Li there are some who claim that the family system that suppressed the younger generation and demanded their humility, impaired Chinese creative abilities, and prevented it from advancing in the field of technology.
2. T'ang Leang-Li, however, attributes their failure to advance, to the philosophical system of Dong Zhongs -Shu from the 2nd century BCE, which fortified the emperor's role, conferring upon him a critical delicate position that and linked man and nature. It later developed a similar cosmological view involving heavenly forces and energy – spiritual forces that connect with the land and physical matter. According to this philosophy, man must adapt himself to this union, and thus he himself must be perfect, before he works the land. Chinese man, therefore viewed labor as a holy spiritual endeavor, and shrunk from industrial work that demanded a utilitarian no-bounds approach to labor not sanctified by a long tradition – as was agriculture.[46]
3. Derk Bodde suggests an alternative approach[47] based on a detailed analysis of the scientific and technological development of Imperial China. He proposes that the reason industry failed to develop in China was the unchallenged status of Chinese intellectuals. Chinese scholars, in contrast to their European peers (whose status was challenged by the ruling class, the merchants, the military, etc.), saw no reason to promote scientific development since it was not necessary in order to insure their own good standing.
4. While Bodde's theory is possible, it is just as feasible that Chinese intellectuals engaged primarily in the study of spiritual loftier matters (ethics and understanding of cosmic forces) because their environment did not

---

[45] Edward L. Farmer, Zhu Yuanzhang and Early Ming Legislation, The Reordering of Chinese Society Following the Era of Mongolian Rule (Leiden, New York, Ko'ln: Brill, 1995).

[46] See footnote 35, T'ang Leang-Li's book, p. 36.

[47] Derk Bodde, Chinese Thought, Society, and Science – The Intellectual and Social Background of Science and Technology in Pre-modern China (Honolulu: University of Hawaii Press, 1991) p. 12. See also Chapter VII in Civin, Science in Ancient China (1982) which appeared as an article in Chinese Science 5: 45-66, entitled, "Why the Scientific Revolution Did Not Take Place in China – Or Didn't It? The article there posits that the reluctance of Imperial China's intellectuals to engage in the development of science, was one of the factors that prevented a Scientific Revolution from occurring in China.

radiate toward them a need for scientific and industrial development. In general, the direction and focus of people's efforts is in great part a product of the needs, pressures, and circumstances of their environment, and not merely a function of their ambition to improve their social standing. If there had existed in China, during the period of the final two imperial dynasties, Ming and Qing (1369-1911) competition between economic and ruling forces, as there was in Europe, and there had been a demand for technological development with anticipated dividends, then individuals – not necessarily intellectuals cultivated by the government – would have emerged who would have trained themselves to 'supply the goods' in accordance with the demand. In China – particularly during the relevant period that corresponds to industrial growth in Europe and the US – there was no competition between ruling forces for any significant period, and it was impossible to develop any serious competition between economic forces who were receiving encouragement from government powers or were involved in the government and in its power struggles. In China, a fleet of ships would be established by imperial command, and recalled – again by imperial command – all according to the interests of the one united government.

5. A fifth possibility is - that the last three imperial dynasties that ruled in China during the relevant period, between 1260-1911, were very conservative for reasons of self interest. The first was Mongolian and the third Manchurian and as foreign dynasties, they feared provoking opposition, and thus shied away from innovations and attempted to adhere to Chinese traditions. The second of these three dynasties, the Ming dynasty was established based on claims that the previous dynasty , Yuan, violated ancient traditions since it was a foreign dynasty. In order to make itself more palatable to the Chinese, more authentically Chinese, and also in reaction to past problems and internal problems that had developed in China as a result of greater openness and relatively rapid development, the Ming dynasty manifested absolute conservatism and avoided all innovations. This renouncement of innovation undermined the potential for scientific and technological development in China during these three dynasties, and is a possible reason why China did not advance in the field of industry and science.

6. Regarding the previous reason, it should be made clear, that it is not a cause or root, but rather a consequence. If the prevailing system in China had not discouraged all internal power struggles, then individual rulers (they or representatives who acted in their names) would not have favored considerations that would increase their domestic power over considerations that would improve their international image and position. Therefore, to a certain extent, reason #6 is connected to reason #4.

7. Of course, it is self evident that both the fourth and sixth reasons do not probe the root of the phenomenon - why was there an imperial uniform system of government in China. This leads us to consider the basic social structure, the nuclear family, the clans, extended family, native tribes, and ancestor worship as possible reasons for the Chinese predisposition to loyalty and submission and to uniting under one single ruler.
In comparing the West and China, the question arises as to what societal differences as well other factors caused an industrial revolution to take place in the West and not in China.

The seven possibilities suggested above are not sufficiently fleshed out to produce any definite conclusions. Therefore, further analysis of the related subjects and facts is necessary. This chapter will commence with the West, starting with the beginning of Christianity, and the research incentive that was the product of hermetic legends, and then proceed to the beginning of the age of scientific inquiry, focusing on Galileo and an understanding of the forces that promoted scientific innovation even in an environment of a patronage whose ruling powers sought to safeguard their own powers from competing elements and whose religious leaders censured scientific advancement. A sketch of the development of science in the West, with the emergence of a scientific community that oversaw and adjudicated scientific progress will follow this. The controversy between Hobbes, who represented the position that advocated the advancement of the scientific theory to empirical science, and Robert Boyle, who represented the school that advocated the advancement of experimental science that is responsible for scientific theories, will serve as a concrete example of this. This chapter will then move on to the role of Protestantism and the bourgeoisie in the development of capitalism, concluding with the US and changes in the American family that resulted from the Industrial Revolution. Following all this, this chapter will proceed to a comparison of the West and China.

The Roots of the Industrial Revolution in the West:

Hermetic Legends and Their Influence on the Development of Science During the Period of the Renaissance:
According to Frances Yates,[48] the urge for scientific development during the Age of the Renaissance stemmed in part from a tradition that originated during the Rise of Christianity, around a historical Egyptian figure named Hermes Trimigestos Who lived at the time of Moshe and the Exodus from Egypt and was also linked to

---

[48] Frances A. Yates, "The Hermetic Tradition In Renaissance Science"

the banishment of Adam from Eden and to man's creative powers. This legend intimated that man has the power to acquire knowledge and that it is his duty to perfect God's creation and to be a creator himself. The message of this legend was that labor is not contemptible, but rather noble since it has the power to refine knowledge.

Galileo and the Factors that Influenced Scientific Research During his Lifetime:

Galileo[49] was a Catholic from Northern Italy who lived at the end of the 16th-beginning of the 17th centuries. He studied physics and mathematics, focusing primarily on the celestial bodies. Coming from an indigent family, he needed the financial support of wealthy and often also powerful individuals, and therefore developed a relationship with the Great Duke of Medici and also with the Pope himself. Galileo's fame spread even during his lifetime, and his telescopes sold well throughout Europe, making him considerable profits. Galileo faced serious financial and religious pressures to develop his scientific theories in accordance with religious beliefs and texts. He refused to succumb, however, insisting that rather than tailoring his scientific findings to conform with accepted religious interpretation, religious writings should be reinterpreted in accordance with scientific findings. In other words, whenever these two contradicted each other, Galileo concluded that the original interpretation of the religious writings had been mistaken, and that scientific discoveries could facilitate a more correct understanding of the religious texts. The realism that had already begun to take hold of Europe, however, demanded that every hypothesis must be consistent with science as well as the Church's interpretation of religious texts. When Galileo was summoned to Rome to be tried by the Inquisition for his ideas, his theories were rejected on scientific and religious grounds. Galileo's belief that the earth revolved around the sun was considered both scientifically erroneous as well as absolute heresy. In order to avoid being punished as a heretic, Galileo recanted. Scientists – who were not Protestant and who did not live in such close proximity to the Pope,

---

[49] Edwin Arthur Burtt, The Metaphysical Foundations of Modern Physical Science, a Historical and Critical Essay (London: Routledge and Kegan Paul, 1924);
Pierre Duhem, To Save the Phenomena, An Essay on the Idea of Physical Theory from Plato to Galileo (Chicago and London: The University of Chicago Press, 1969, translated from French into English by Dolan and Maschler, the French original version written in 1908);
Richard S. Westfall, "Science and Patronage, Galileo and the Telescope" in Isis, 1985, pp. 11-30;
Mario Biagioli, "Galileo's System of Patronage", in History of Science, XXVIII (1990) pp. 1-62.

faced fewer restrictions on their scientific beliefs. The Protestant Tycho Brahe based much of his science on Copernicus' theories, with the support and encouragement of the King of Denmark who left at his disposal an island with various equipment including a sophisticated printing press.[50]Scientific research, during this time, faced not only the external censorship of the Church, but also internal, self-imposed censorship. Kepler, for example, who first published his findings in 1596 was a committed Protestant, who felt duty-bound to only publicize ideas that were consistent with religious texts. Galileo, in contrast to Kepler, did not concern himself with this issue, though he did attempt to reconcile his findings with religious texts.

Galileo lived at a time when the success of scientists depended on their ability to find benefactors and patrons. The patron would generally provide the scientist with a regular stipend or, as in the case of Brahe, with scientific equipment and supplies. A scientist's rank and status depended on the size of the stipend he received from his patron, relative to those received by other scientists.[51] No scientific community existed at this time that could evaluate scientific discoveries, as will be evident in the case of Hobbes discussed below, so patronage was the determining factor. The patronage of an admired leader conferred social status, and even sometimes enabled one scientist to organize patronages for other scientists, and thus prove his power and standing.[52] Patrons were common also in the fields of music and art in general.[53] The system of patronage insured that a scientist did not ignore scientific criticism, since it had an affect on one's own patron's standing among fellow patrons, and a scientist owed his patron respect.[54] The system motivated scientists to prove themselves, and to publish their discoveries. Galileo, for this reason, felt obliged to follow in the footsteps of Copernicus, to take upon himself the difficult weighty task of fighting for his beliefs, a fight, which ultimately landed him in the dungeon of the Inquisition.[55] The scientist and his scientific method, during this time period, were thus pawns in the hands of opposing social forces.

---

[50] Elizabeth L. Eisenstein, The Printing Revolution in Early Modern Europe (Cambridge, UK: Cambridge University Press, 1983), p. 216.

[51] Westfall, footnote 49 above, p. 17.

[52] Biagioli, footnote 49 above, pp. 1, 10.

[53] Ibid, p. 4; and it is common knowledge about musisions, mainly in Germany for a long period; one may even suggest that most Universities are supported today and that is a modern form of patronage.

[54] Ibid, pp. 26-37.

[55] Ibid, p. 44.

According to Elizabeth Eisenstein,[56] the dearth of scientific research by Protestant scientists in the year 1640 stemmed from Luther's declaration against scientists and against Copernicus' theory and all proponents of his theory. Luther asserted that according to Biblical texts, it is not the earth that moves, but rather the sun, and thus it is not conceivable to suggest the opposite. Luther's views had influence, for some time, over Protestant scientists, just as the Catholic Church's opposition to Galileo had influence over Catholic scientists. Thus, around the year 1640, Protestant scientific activity declined, until with the passage of time the weight of Luther's declarations diminished, and scientific activity resumed.
It emerges from this description that a range of conflicting, competing factors existed in Europe that affected the development of science. These factors were apparently essential to scientific development, and it is logical to suppose that similar factors had influence later on in history, and even today.

The Emergence of the Scientific Community to Steer Scientific Research as Exemplified by Hobbes and Boyle:
In the case of Hobbes,[57] controversy took place in the years 1660-1670, in England, between two scientists, Hobbes and Boyle. Hobbes supported the philosophy of the natural sciences while Boyle advocated scientific development through the method of experimental science.[58] Boyle designed an air pump that was recognized and applauded by the royal scientific community in London, and by which he proved that vacuums are possible, at least under laboratory conditions. Hobbes also was recognized and venerated for his achievements – in the realm of society and morality – for his book, Leviathan,[59] while in the realm of natural sciences he was censured, and even accused of plagiarism.[60] Hobbes did not realize that in criticizing Boyle's air-pump, he was criticizing an invention and a person who enjoyed the status of a national hero, and who was a source of national pride for England.[61]

---

[56] See Eisenstein in footnote 50 above, p. 230.

[57] Steven Shapin & Simon Schaffer, Leviathan and the Air-Pump – Hobbes, Boyle, and the Experimental Life (Princeton, New Jersey: Princeton University Press, 1985).

[58] Ibid, p. 7.

[59] Ibid, p. 19.

[60] Ibid, p. 83.

[61] Ibid, pp. 8, 32, and 36.

Hobbes claimed that, in contrast to Boyle's experimental approach, proponents of a philosophical approach to science are members of an elite class of true intellectuals and scholars, and not mere laboratory assistants. This statement peeved those who were meant to adjudicate between Hobbes and Boyle, members of the royal scientific community, individuals who held Boyle's methods in great regard. They considered Hobbes' words a vilification of a British national hero and a denigration of his means of employment. Hobbes refused even to submit to the judgment of the royal scientific community, insisting that they were biased in the matter, a claim that implicitly accused them of corruption. Hobbes' attitude alienated the scientific community and caused them to reject his scientific methods, even though theoretically both Hobbes and Boyle's methods both possessed their share of flaws.

It is fitting to include here the words of Thomas Kone,[62] a writer at the beginning of the 20th century who described the role of the scientific community in the acceptance of Western scientific theories. His book, which earned the approbation of that very community about which he spoke, claims that when a majority of scientists are persuaded as to the truth of a new theory, then it replaces an old one, only to be replaced itself when a newer theory becomes popular in the same way. This is a limited social process that is not dependent on natural forces, but rather on the bias and predisposition of members of the scientific community. Thus, the social game played a significant role in the development of science in the West.

Protestantism, Bourgeoisie, and the Industrial Revolution

Max Weber,[63] noting that Western man gloats in the fact that he surpasses Eastern cultures, explores the reason for this phenomenon. Leaving aside the possibility that the cause is anthropological, and observing that Western Protestants outperform Western Catholics, he discusses differences between Protestants and Catholics, and the development of a form of capitalism that is based on rational organization of free labor, steering of the production according to free market and separation of the business from family maintenance as well as logical bookkeeping and a clear system of law.[64] In his opinion, Protestants have succeeded in these

---

[62] Thomas S. Kone, The Structure of Scientific Revolutions (Tel Aviv: Israel Institute of Poetry and Semitics, University of Tel Aviv, 1977) translated from the English by Yehuda Meltzer.

[63] Max Weber, The Protestant Ethic and the Capitalist Spirit, translated from German by Baruch Moren (Tel Aviv: Am Oved, 1984), original published in 1920.

[64] To the extent that it pertains to Zchina, these statements are true. The judicial system in China, throughout the Imperial Period, included only elements of criminal and

areas more than Catholics because Protestantism demands more of its followers than does Catholicism.[65] It imposes ethical duties, including diligence and honesty, as is most apparent in New England, the home of the Puritans and Protestants,[66] and in contradistinction to Catholic values from the Middle Ages and earlier.[67] According to Protestant, and specifically Puritan teachings, though every individual should be paid according to his output because otherwise productivity will decline,[68] financial compensation should not be the motivating factor but rather the view that one's job is a religious calling. Protestants, in general, and Puritans, in particular inculcate their children with such a work ethic,[69] and this education has resulted in a serious approach towards work, a willingness to make do with little, and an attitude that one is fulfilling a religious calling through one's work, a calling that has its dividends, and whose dividends are reinvested in the factory, over and above the factory owner's needs. He must invest these profits in his factory, in order to expand his business, and in this manner a 'capitalist spirit' developed. The constant attention and effort that the business demanded ultimately became a life force, and man began to live to work, rather than the reverse.[70] Protestantism deemed the pursuit of profit - which Catholicism so denigrated, as described in the writings of Thomas Maquines - extremely laudable.[71] This approach began with Luther's reformation, and his emphasis on fulfillment of national obligations, from which the notion evolved that all honest labor finds favor in God's eyes.[72]

Weber speaks at length about the Calvinists, a sect that branched off from Protestantism, which taught that man must prove his faith by working the land.[73] While Thomas Maquines, according to Catholic theology, claimed that man's place in the world is random and haphazard, Luther believed that the classes and professions of man are the products of the historical objective order, expressions of the divine will, and thus it became a religious imperative to remain in one's

---

administrative law, and none of civil law. See footnote 23 on the code of the T'ang Dynasty.

[65] Catholicism is built on confession and pardoning by the priest, while Protestantism places the individual directly facing God.

[66] See Weber, footnote 63, pp20-22.

[67] Ibid, p. 23.

[68] Ibid, p. 25.

[69] Ibid, p. 26.

[70] Ibid, p. 30.

[71] Ibid, pp. 31-32.

[72] Ibid, p. 36.

[73] Ibid, p. 59.

preordained class. The Puritans already affirmed man's right to change occupations, even for the sake of increased financial reward, since personal wealth is considered an acceptable goal, as long as it does not lead man to slothfulness and sinful pleasures,[74] and as long as society ultimately benefits too. Calvinists and Baptists took these convictions one step further, believing that through their industriousness and diligence, they fulfilled a divine obligation.[75]

Over the course of time and the development of capitalism in the West, the religious component was lost, and only bald latent utilitarianism remained. Western philosophy has always been permeated by the motif of utilitarianism, whether personal or communal, material or spiritual. This process began with Kant, continued with Bentham's theory, until the liberal communitarianism of today, Rawls and post-modernism.

Weber's description contrasts sharply with Chinese culture, which was based on Confucianism, on loyalty to the emperor, father, and master, and on the generosity of these individuals to those beholden to them. In such a system, there is no concept of man trying to better himself or aiming to raise his social standing, since there is no higher good than fulfillment of obligations in general, and faithfulness, in particular.[76]

Fathers and Sons and Division Between Family and Work

Weber already spoke about how the bourgeoisie was built on a division between one's work and employment on one hand, and family life on the other. He did not, however, relate to changes in family relations that resulted from this split. This chapter will explore this issue, in particular the status of the mother-wife in the narrow family unit, and the changes that transpired in father son relations in the US during the 19th century, as a result of the Industrial Revolution and urbanization. John Demos[77] describes how - the shift from an agricultural life, in which the entire family, including the children, participated, to an alien, even precarious atmosphere, in which the father-husband concentrated on providing financially for his family, and the mother-wife concentrated on the education of her children and on domestic affairs – affected family dynamics. A son's connection with his mother intensified and became intimate, while his feelings towards his father became emotionally estranged and competitive. A son sought to

---

[74] Ibid, pp. 78-80.

[75] Ibid, p. 88.

[76] Tung-tsu Ch'u, Han Social Structure (Seattle and London: University of Washington Press, 1972) pp. 251-305.

[77] John Demos, "Oedipus and America: Historical Perspectives on the Reception of Psychoanalysis in the United States", Chapter III in

prove himself equal or superior to his father, while possessing warm, intimate, almost sexual feelings towards his mother. These feelings were so strong that when soldiers went out to war, they would sing songs proclaiming their desire to fight 'for the sake of their mother,' for whom they were willing to even sacrifice their lives. Towards their fathers, however, they felt they owed nothing.

Demos considers the Industrial Revolution one of the factors that caused the father-husband's disconnection with the family home, in 19th century American society. Perhaps, though, Demos has reversed the cause and effect. Perhaps the changes in the family (that stemmed from urbanization, and the perils of city life that drove women to seek the shelter of their home, leaving their husbands to make their way on the outside alone) enabled the father-husband to work in industry and factories. Perhaps the son's sense of competition with his father and need to prove himself, impelled him to aspire higher than his father, to excel in his work and perhaps open his own business or factory.

The mother-wife's role in the home became primary, while the father-husband became somewhat of a peripheral, alienated factor, responsible for "bringing home the bacon," but playing an absolutely secondary role in the home. The mother's increased authority and influence in the home, and the sense of estrangement the son felt towards his father, distinguished Western culture from Chinese culture. In Imperial China, disrespect of one's father was inconceivable. Respect for one's mother was also valued, but it was secondary to respect for one's father. A child in 19th century America had far greater freedom to forge his own way than did his counterpart in China. This factor, among others, had a major impact on the development of industry, or lack there of, in America and China.

Religion

The term 'religion' in Imperial China has a different denotation than it does in the West. In China, religion refers to Buddhism, Daoism, and various other regional and national religions, that are all connected with idols or spirits and demons. Moism (Of course, not that of Chairman Mao) that lasted for about 250 years, until the second century BCE will be discussed separately. Buddhism and Daoism (and also Moism, in its time) were based on writings and theories. Confucianism is a moral code that served as a basis for life in Imperial China, beginning in theeven before second century BCE. The founder of Taoism established a number of gods that corresponded to the range of traditions, and Daoist priests were permitted to add gods, in defined roles, and varied hierarchical positions. Every political figure in the Chinese government possessed a spiritual-pagan twin whose bureaucratic function paralleled that of the actual political ruler, and whose existence strengthened the rule of the actual leader.

Already, during the period of the Sheng Dynasty, from the 16th century BCE until the 119th century, the accepted belief was that the spiritual world operated according to established rules that served as basic conditions for the existence of bureaucratic rule in the physical world. National religions had a hierarchy of spirits and demons, just as there was a hierarchy of gods in Daoism. A spirit could be attached to a particular family and some had established temples that were open to the public.[78]

Buddhism seemed almost modern, in contrast to all these religions, but Buddhism, itself, was associated with an idol – the Buddha. The roots of Buddhism were found in the ancient religions of the Indian sub-continent Hinduism -, polytheistic religions that did not speak of pure transcendentalism. It was based on dharma, a concept that fuses the physical world with the transcendental world.[79] Buddhists in China performed ceremonies reminiscent of the bureaucratic operation of government institutions. The primary moral system that the Imperial state generally recognizes, did not emerge from the religions that were mentioned – though Daoism and Buddhism do contain moral principles – but rather from Confucian moral philosophy. Daoism and Buddhism have holy writings, and in this respect they are progressive religions.

The Chinese, like the Japanese and Thai, did and do not consider it inconsistent to accept all the religions and philosophies that one is familiar with. Thus, it is quite common that a Chinese person will be simultaneously a Buddhist, Daoist, follower of Confucianism, and a believer in spirits and demons. The situation in Japan is similar, as Ben-Ami Shiloni writes on page 301 of his book, 'Modern Japan,' "The nature of Shintuist ceremonies is on the whole communal nature, while that of Buddhist ceremonies is familial. Most couples perform only a civil ceremony of marriage, though there are some who conduct also a religious ceremony in a Shintu temple or Christian Church. Most of those who marry in a Church opt to do so only because of its beauty and the organ music that is played, without any connection to Christianity. Thus, it happens that many Japanese will celebrate their birth in a Shintu temple, marry in a Christian Church, and be brought to burial in a Buddhist ceremony – without viewing their actions as inherently inconsistent."

The dominant religion in the West is Christianity, a religion rooted in Judaism. In its early stages, Christianity was Catholic and afterwards also Protestant It is based

---

[78] Unruly Gods – Divinity and Society in China, edited by Meir Shahar and Robert P. Weller (Honolulu: University of Hawaii Press: 1996), pp. 1-13.

[79] Eva Hellman, "Dynamic Hinduism Toward a New Hindu Nation," in Questioning the Secular State, The Worldwide Resurgence of Religion in Politics, edited by David Westerlund (London: Hurst & Co.), pp. 237, 240.

on the Jewish belief in an unseen God who transcends reality, who is not corporeal and has no body, fused, from its inception, with a belief in a son of God, Jesus – a belief with definite pagan influence in the idols of Jesus and the Holy Virgin. The Pravoslavic sect even added certain pagan symbols and images from different Eastern countries in which the Pravoslavic religion had spread. With the advent of the Protestant reformation, the various offshoots of this sect of Christianity became less pagan, more transcendental, though they retained their faith in Jesus, the son of God.

Despite the pagan impurities that adhere to Christianity, it is a religion that is less pagan than Chinese religions. Christianity is absolute and severe in its demands, in contrast to Chinese religions. Confucius' philosophical-moral teaching, the central moral system in China throughout most of the imperial periods, is considered a secular philosophy, though it teaches that a spiritual world parallels our own. As Bodde explains, such a belief is convenient for the ruling powers because it lends support for the existence of hierarchical privileges and it values literary culture.[80] Confucianism, known in China as 'the intellectuals' school of thought,' was from the outset popular primarily among Chinese elite. This system propounded respect and deference for the emperor, and was adopted by many imperial books of law. In this manner, and in accordance with imperial directives, this system expanded its influence in popular circles too, though national religions still remained dominant in these groups. Confucianism's rival philosophical system for approximately 250 years, was Moism. It spread primarily among populist circles, and in its time, was as widespread as Confucianism. Moism was a moral code of behavior, established in China by Mozi Tzu (5th century381-479 BCE) that always had a spiritual leader, a community of loyal believers, holy writings, and an explicit code of law. It taught that man should love all his fellow men equally, though politically, inequality existed in the form of higher and lower classes. It called for belief in spirits and demons that observe man's actions, and reward

---

[80] See Derk Bodde, footnote 47, p. 169. There are those who define Confucianism as a secular philosophy, while others characterize it as a religion, since it entails a recognition and belief in a divine being. This book relates to Confucianism as a philosophy, and not a religion. Confucianism's belief in a divine entity parallels American civil religion's general belief in a deity and in religion, without choosing a specific one. In both systems, God, and not man creates moral laws. Civil religion in America has always adhered to the first amendment's insistence on separation of Church and State, and the prohibition against the involvement of religion in American politics. Confucianism does not prohibit the performance of other religious rituals, and its point of origin is that the guiding principles by which the State will run are not divinely ordained. What follows, though not explicitly, is separation of Church and State.
The Religion of the Republic, edited Elwyn A. Smith (Philadelphia: Portress Press, 1971).

those who believe in them, primarily Maoists, and punish those who deny their existence. It promoted the value of honest labor and efficiency, extreme asceticism, and concentration on logic and on very specific topics, including the science of light, mechanics, biology, and defensive military technology. Imperialism rejected Moism apparently, because of the asceticism and economic equality that it promoted, its uncompromising nature, its logical inconsistencies and lack of realism.[81] During the early imperial era – the Qin and Han dynasties – Moism was uprooted as popular movement because of the threat it pose to the centralized bureaucratic system and its anti-Confucionists ideas.
With the exception of Moism, there was separation of religion and State in China, aside from short limited episodes, the most prominent ones being the rise to power of two messianic Daoist movements after the fall of the unified Han dynasty, in the year 184. One of these movements lasted a mere few months, while the other survived 31 years.[82]

Derk Bodde[83] discusses the role religions in China played in preventing an Industrial Revolution. Buddhism, especially, is thought to have played a significant role, since it is based on a distinct world perspective that can be harmed through study of the universe. Bodde claims otherwise, suggesting that Buddhism was never a serious force in China. He quotes C.K. Yang, an anthropologist who discovered that traditional Chinese in the 19th-20th centuries, in Southeast Asia and Latin America demonstrated an ability to develop industrial and commercial factories. Bodde presents this as proof that the roots of the lag in China's industrial growth lie not only in the Chinese system of values, but also in the makeup of Chinese society and its partiality for the upper social-political class of intellectuals over the social class of merchants.

This idea constitutes a seventh possible explanation of the lack of an Industrial Revolution in Imperial China, though it also raises certain questions:

1. While it is true that most Chinese intellectuals did not study natural sciences, there is nothing remarkable about this fact. Most teachers and students in the West today and during the time of the Industrial Revolution do and did not study natural sciences, and many do and did study philosophy, literature, sociology, law, history, anthropology, and other classical subjects.

---

[81] Ibid. pp. 166-169.

[82] Ibid. pp. 164-165.

[83] Ibid. pp. 158-159.

2. One chose one's occupation in Imperial China freely and directly. Perhaps the one 'above,' guided one's choice, for he possessed the power to prevent any activity that was not consonant with his ruling interest, as will be demonstrated below, in the discussion of the merchant class.
3. Does occupation not depend on financial backing – both in the form of research and study grants, and in the form of economic markets for one's designs? Even if a society's social structure promotes the study of literature and not science, won't people engage in scientific research, when there is a 'market' for scientific inventions? Garbage collection may not be considered the most dignified occupation, but since there is a demand for it and a willingness to pay for the service, there are garbage collectors. Social standing is only one form of possible compensation. Money is the other.
4. Regarding the claim that Chinese social structure didn't promote a positive attitude to exact science, the question arises – whether any social structure in any country actually promotes scientific research. Perhaps the aspect of social structure that encourages scientific research only came into being as a result of changes in this structure that occurred as a result of scientific research.
5. As will be discussed further on, commerce developed in Imperial China at a time when the government was weak and it made no attempt to impede scientific development. Once the government ceased erecting barriers, social structure also ceased presenting a barrier. Thus clearly 'social structure' alone does not have the power to hamper an industrial or scientific process. Nevertheless, combined with other factors, and in specific circumstances, it definitely plays a significant role.

Bodde adds that had Daoist philosophy prevailed over Confucianism in China, China would have been more likely to experience technological and industrial development, just like Western Europe.[84]
In general, according to Bodde, religions in China, being polytheistic, lacked central structure and the ability to demand the same general responsibility as monotheistic religions.[85]
Bodde notes that in Tibet, Mongolia, and Japan, religion played a decisive role, even though it was not monotheistic, and thus concludes that polytheistic religion in China was a secondary, and not primary cause of China's failure to develop scientifically and industrially. The primary reason is tied to the institutional air that prevailed in Imperial China.

---

[84] Ibid, p. 169.
[85] Ibid, pp. 171-172.

While this reason deserves to be pursued further, one should not underestimate the significance of the difference between monotheistic and polytheistic religions. In monotheism, a single god rules over the entire world, and therefore his rule is absolute in every place. A monotheistic religion is therefore, total and absolute, while a polytheistic religion is less rigid and more tolerant. It, naturally, lacks the ambition for political rule, and poses no threat to the government. Thus, a government can confidently permit the practice of many varied polytheistic religions. Pagan religions generally do not get involved in government or in development of industry or science, though one notable exception is the role played by Daoism's search for a drug that would give eternal life, in the advancement of science and chemistry in China.

What emerges from all this, is that if Protestantism played a significant role in the rise of the bourgeoisie, capitalism, and rationalism, and in the economic and industrial development of Europe, as Weber claims, then no such development could even have been anticipated in China. Though Moism 'officially' supported the concept of technological development - since it was a pagan religion, the actual motivation to develop technology during the Han dynasty did not suffice to insure real change and revolution, like in the West.

The roots of the absolute nature of the governments in Japan, Mongolia, and Tibet, can be found not necessarily in the religious dimension of the government, but rather in non-religious, civilian causes and circumstances. Due to the expansive nature of this specific topic and our belief that it will not contribute significantly to our discussion, we leave further examination of it to a different time.

Merchant Status in Imperial China and Conclusion:

An examination of the status of merchants in Imperial China will reflect the influence of centralized government on social structure and economic developments in China.

DenisTwitchett[86]examines the revolutionary change that took place in Chinese political institutions, economic organization, and social structure during the years 750-1000 CE. There was immense growth in commerce, the general money system, and urbanization, as well as changes in government bureaucracy.[87]

Until that time, the scholars were tied to the government, by their common ideology and because they served as their scribes. The status of anyone who displayed any rivalry toward them immediately suffered. The military elite was treated contemptuously, and the scribes who recorded the history of the time regarded the merchant community even more negatively. There were four classes

---

[86] Denis Twitchett, "Merchant Trade and Government in Late T'ang," in Asia Major, 14 (1968) p. 63.

[87] Ibid, p. 63.

mentioned in recorded history: the scholars and bureaucracy, the farmers, artisans, and merchants.[88]

The government favored the farmers, since they paid taxes and served in the army at a time of war. The merchants were considered a threat to the established order. They were disparaged because in their pursuit of wealth and material gain, they violated Confucian principles that emphasized service of the civil and military state.[89]

Though there was consensus that the merchant filled an essential role in bridging distances between sellers and buyers, he was nevertheless considered as lowly as the artisan, in addition to being viewed as uncreative and a divisive force. The government struggled to find a way to monitor their activities. Some people were of the opinion that they should be isolated in order to avoid rousing the farmers` jealousy.[90]

The merchant class was already accepted by the time of the Chin and Han dynasties as a necessary evil, and merchants enjoyed a free status according to law. During the T'ang dynasty, two policies pertaining to them were established:

1. A prohibition against turning them into an elite class based on their wealth, a class that would rival the governing and intellectual elite. The intention was only to prevent the merchants from parading their wealth, not to prevent them from amassing wealth.
2. Financial activities and expenditures, including style of dress, type of vehicle, residence, furnishings, ornaments and their involvement in social events were to be regulated. All these regulations and the taxes they were subjected to would highlight how lowly their status was compared to the bureaucrats and scholars.[91]

The merchants were even the first class enlisted in a time of war. Each merchant was obligated to register and pay for a place in the market. He, his sons, and his grandsons, were disqualified from government positions. Despite all the limitations, the merchant remained a free man[92] and he was exempt from all civil obligations. A special government agency established work conventions and

---

[88] Ibid, p. 64.

[89] Ibid. p. 65.

[90] Ibid.

[91] Ibid, p. 66.

[92] Ibid. pp. 67-68.

hours, monitored the quality of the merchandise, issued licenses of sale for livestock, slaves, and land, and ensured fair honest business practices.[93] Independent markets that operated in the capital city catered to the needs of the ruling elite, the clergy, and the emperor's court.

Foreign trade was conducted, all the way until the Middle East, Manchuria, and Tibet. There were various checkpoints along the way in which written licenses were checked, and tolls and even bribes were paid.[94] The government itself competed with the merchants, buying up large quantities in times of bounty and selling them at discounted prices in times of scarcity. The government's intention was to help the needy, but this policy significantly lowered the merchants' profits.[95] During the T'ang dynasty, the government issued coins whose value was lower than the price of their copper, as well as stockpiled in its warehouses silk cloth that they sold at prices that prevented the merchants from making excessive-profits. Inspectors from the merchant class itself worked in cooperation with the merchant unions that registered merchants and set official prices. The government employed other merchants to collect taxes. It would entrust money usually in the hands of certain wealthy merchants, who would pay a set interest rate and could then use the money as they chose, loaning it to who they saw fit, and keeping the difference in interest. The local, not central government, was responsible for all this.[96]

All this changed in the year 755, with the revolution of An-Lu-Shan.

At the end of a multi-year process, the only areas that remained under direct imperial control were the areas around the capital and the southern regions, while all the other regions maintained only a tenuous connection with the emperor. Some of the southern districts were destroyed and became desolate. During the revolt and the battles that took place, the government gained control of approximately a fifth of the merchants' assets. The manufacture and marketing of salt remained primarily under the emperor's control, and a monopoly was created that paid the emperor taxes, an arrangement that continued for the duration of the dynasty. Salt merchants attained an elite status among the general population of merchants. After the year 760, every semi-independent region paid an annual tax to the emperor, and the regional government imposed taxes as it saw fit – but taxes were

[93] Ibid, p. 69.

[94] Ibid, p. 70.

[95] Ibid, p. 72.

[96] Ibid, pp. 72-73.

paid using currency, and not merchandise, as had been formerly the norm – causing a serious shortage of copper currency.[97]

Hebei and North Henan were now independent and thus paid no taxes. They were the primary source of silk, so money replaced silk as valuable change, weakening the power of the imperial government. Various copper mines and their copper fell into the hands of private individuals, lowering the value of the copper currency that the imperial government issued. As a result of this situation, private banking began to develop in the year 760. While all these changes were occurring – also manufacturing began to expand, early agricultural machinery and irrigation tools were developed, and a population shift took place – all of which led to a growth in commerce.[98]

The cities that were home to the governments of the semi-independent regions grew and prospered, particularly in the regions of River Hiang-Che and Henanonaan. The growth of commerce affected the process of urbanization. Markets became particularly active in the cities of the region. The government no longer interfered in the markets in rural regions, where commerce was originally seasonal, but ultimately became almost daily. In the 9th-10th centuries, these rural markets became commercial cities, and the regional government's administration was established in them. Trade initially took place through a system of bartering, but eventually currency was used instead. The old system of government-controlled markets gradually disappeared, and centers of trade even began to operate outside the markets, in separate quarters that each specialized in a particular line of merchandise.[99] The special status previously enjoyed by foreign merchants, relative to local ones, declined. Commercial taxes were no longer imposed on a regular basis, but rather only in times of emergency. During the years 844-878, during the reign of Chao-Tsan, direct taxes were levied on buildings, and certain merchandise (like tea, wood, and polish), a government monopoly existed on liquor, and a 20% sales tax collected by the merchants' union. All the taxes were repealed, however, in the year 785. In the year 793, a tax was reimposed on tea, a product that enjoyed a wide market and which enriched anyone who traded in it. Both the imperial government and regional governments occasionally imposed taxes on the merchants.[100]

The prevailing attitude was no longer that commerce was a necessary, but inherent evil, and close supervision and regulation of it was abandoned, now that it

[97] Ibid, pp. 74-75.

[98] Ibid, pp. 74-76.

[99] Ibid, p. 77.

[100] Ibid, pp. 78-79.

provided a source of income for the government. Nevertheless, 'lip service' was paid to the agricultural heads, since agriculture was viewed as the backbone of the economy.[101]This completed the changes that resulted from government uprisings combined with changes in economic needs. The height of this process took place in the 12th-13th centuries, but subsequently, in the later imperial period, there was a return to the conservative attitude that opposed commerce and consequently impeded the development of science and industry.

Conclusion

For hundreds of years, the Chinese progressed and even overtook the Europeans in the field of technological inventions,[102] such as the paper and printing industry, gun powder, large battleships, manufacture of silk, astronomic studies, and the manufacture of iron. During the period of the final two dynasties, primarily beginning with the 15th century, however, all progress halted. Astronomy, from the beginning, had only served the interests of the royalty in China, providing the emperor with background for astrological predictions regarding his empire. The building of cannons did not progress past cannons that fired arrows (probably because the imperial government had no imperial aspirations, and needed only to protect itself against invaders).[103]

As is evident from examination of the development of industry at the end of the T'ang dynasty, in the year 755 C.E., Chinese commerce and economy expanded as

---

[101] Ibid, p. 80.

[102] Joseph Needham, Science and Civilization in China (Cambridge: Cambridge University Press).

[103] Beyond the purview of this book is an examination and comparison of the nature of Chinese imperial conquests vs. European and Arab conquests of wide expanses outside of the geographical and political borders. Arab and European conquests were generally – aside from their conquests within Europe – conquests that involved the subjugation of those conquered. Occasionally captives were also taken and turned into slaves, when the Arabs adopted the system of enslaving anyone who would not accept Islam, and the Europeans transformed conquests in Africa, Asia, and America into colonies. Chinese conquests and some of the European conquests (particularly in America, Australia, and New Zealand) became frontier land or penal colonies. The Chinese – as a rule – only conquered land in order to settle it with their own people or to impose their culture on those conquered. During the Han dynasty, the emperors enforced Confucianism within all conquered territories, and the Chinese laws that were implemented in these areas made adoption of Confucianism a legal imperative. It may be claimed that the imperial system could not have endured over the vast Chinese territories, if all the people they conquered had not accepted their culture and the Confucian system that emphasizes the critical role of the emperor in maintaining the equilibrium that is necessary in order to avert terrible natural disasters.

a result of the partial collapse of the imperial government. Similar economic development, including industrial and commercial growth, urbanization, changes in the social structure, system of taxation, and ownership of agricultural land, as well as changes in the status of the farmers, occurred over 1,000 years earlier, as examined by Hsu Cho-Yun.[104]

All this demonstrates the critical role - that the system of government, its structure, power, and interests – play in halting, or encouraging and facilitating economic and social changes, and the effect they in turn have on the government. In examining the reasons for the lack of an industrial revolution in China, taking into consideration the centrality of the government in all that goes on in the State, it is important to take into account the unity of the Chinese government and the trend to one unified government in all of China, as depicted by Yuri Pines. This was a trend that prevailed in China throughout the relevant periods, and it played a significant role in the endurance of the imperial form of government whose authority and jurisdiction extended to all of China.

The question is, why specifically China? Why not Europe? Why not India? Why not Africa and America? Why not the Arab world? Why didn't the Roman Empire survive as long as Chinese imperialism?

Imperial government could not be sustained indefinitely simply by military legions, as is evidenced by the reign of Alexander the Great and the Roman Empire. What failed, though, in Greece and Rome, succeeded in China, namely the attempt to imprint in the hearts and minds of the Chinese citizens the perception that the emperor was a father to all his subjects, and that all his subjects were a single nation, bound by one faith, one worldview, one tradition, and even one (written) language. The Chinese considered themselves one family, and this perception, whether historically accurate or not, caused the Chinese to view themselves as one unity, rooted in hundreds and thousands of years of common history. The Chinese, very successfully achieved that which so many –the French, English, German, and Italians – sought largely unsuccessfully to accomplish. Only they were able to create the perception that their nation was one great unity. As a result, even when a foreign power ruled China (the Yuan dynasty that ruled China for approximately one hundred years, and the Manchj'urian Qing dynasty that ruled for close to amore than 250 hundred years), the government lasted for many years. The key to such successful government lay not within successful rulers, but within successful subjects – the Chinese.

---

[104] Cho-Yun Hsu. Ancient China in Transition – An Analysis of Social Mobility. 722-222 B.C. (Stanford. California: Stanford University Press. 1968. original printing 1965) pp. 107-108.

Why were the Chinese such successful subjects?
As seen in Chapter I, the father's status in the family, the obedience that was shown him, the connection between his position in the family and imperial rule in China, the ancient rituals, and the deep interconnection felt not only by the nuclear family, but frequently, also by the tribal-family – are linked to the figure of the emperor, and to the Chinese desire for unified government. The Chinese were indeed linked by their common worldview and basic beliefs, and even by the destiny that was shared by 'anyone under the sun' (a reference to the Chinese). They shared one father – the emperor, the only person with the power to maintain nature's equilibrium.
Several reasons were suggested in Chapter III as to why no industrial revolution took place in China. We have now provided enough background to properly evaluate these reasons:

Reason I: A familial system that repressed the younger generation - if industry had developed in China and then collapsed because of the absence of a workforce, then this reason would seem more pertinent.
Reason II: The Chinese reverence of agricultural labor is discounted for the same reason.
Reason III: The uncontested status of Chinese intellectuals that eliminated their need to prove themselves through scientific achievements, in contrast to the competition that motivated Western scholars - seems historically inaccurate. There is no evidence that Western scholars competed with the military or merchants, but rather only among themselves. In any case, competition between the classes was not the driving motivation in the West, but rather the inventive spirit – so markedly lacking in China - that comes with market demand and sources of funding.
Reason IV: The divisiveness and internal rivalry within the government that led to economic competition and growth does appear to be a primary reason.
Reason V: The conservative nature of the three dynasties in China does seem to have had a major impact, but this quality was the result of another cause, that also must be examined.
Reason VI: The general nature of the imperial system that for internal considerations sought to avoid creating concentrations of economic strength within the empire was a reason no industrial revolution occurred in China, but not the root cause, the primary cause.
Reason VII: The emphasis on paternal respect, the attachment to the spirit of the ancestors, and the willingness to submit to leadership, and the resultant humility – are in fact the root causes behind the loyalty and commitment to the imperial system.

Yet, this still does not answer why the Chinese sought to establish a unified government for themselves. This apparently resulted from the view that was shared by the Chinese and advanced by their philosophers and emperor – that the emperor played a critical role in balancing between natural forces and human forces, a balance that is essential if no natural disasters are to occur and if life is to be tranquil and fruitful. This belief gave them good cause to seek the endurance of the imperial form of government.
This belief was coupled with the recognition that all the Chinese constitute one unity, one nation, and that no national differences exist between different regions of China. Any conflict over control of different sections of China was simply the personal business of the rival rulers and it carried no import for the citizens of these areas, since they felt no greater loyalty to one ruler over the other. There was no true ethnic-tribal division between the residents of different areas ruled by different rulers, since the institution of the traditional Xiao doesn`t support division in the existing government. Even the various rival rulers could not justify the split in government, and it was clear to each of them that only one of them could rule, and that there was no option to divide and share control.
Under these circumstances, there existed in China the aspiration for national unity, an aspiration that was linked to ancient ritual, which in China was strengthened by the relationships within the nuclear family, and particularly the principle of paternal respect. The discussion of the root reason behind China`s lack of industrial growth relates to the study of the internal changes in the bourgeois family in Europe and in the family structure and intimate relationships within the American family in the 19th century.

Europe is presently undergoing a similar process to the one that China underwent so many years ago. This process explains their desire for unification. In retrospect, both World Wars seem more like clashes within the family of White Christians, a family whose bonds of common tradition, culture, and faith, are much greater than their differences. Europe endured great tragedies before it came to its present realization, which most Europeans believe will provide them with security. Most Americans and Russians feel basically the same way. It is even reasonable to foresee in the distant future a unification of all White Christian men as one nation that even joins Europe with North America. Many Americans of European descent, who see themselves – in the not so distant future – becoming a minority in their own land – would have reason to support such a union. Christianity is a much more aggressive religion than Buddhism or Daoism, and consequently it constitutes a strong traditional-ethnic component that can unite White Christian European man, just as the Chinese united. The French today are primarily the descendants of farmers from diverse origins and cultures. A few hundreds of years ago, they considered themselves completely distinct from each other, and most did

not even speak French. Their unification resulted from a strong aggressive rule of a Parisian princess who joined various conquests under her rule, and imposed the Parisian tongue (which became French) in all the provinces under her rule, and in this manner the French nation was born. Benedict Anderson, describes similar unification processes throughout the world. Regarding Scotland, he quotes Siton-Weston who describes the evolution of the Scottish tongue:
" It developed from a fusion of Saxony and French, though less of the latter and more from the South from Celtic and Scandinavian sources. They spoke in this language not only in Eastern Scotland but also in Northern England. Scottish, or 'Northern English,' was the language of the Scottish court and the social elite (that either spoke or didn't speak also Gaelic), and also the language of the entire population in the southeastern lowlands of Scotland. It was also the language of the poets Robert Henryson and William Dunbar. It could have developed into a distinct literary tongue in modern times, if the unification in 1603 hadn't caused southern English to prevail, penetrating the royal court, the administration, and the upper classes in Scotland."[105]
Recognition of the distinct European 'nationalist' identities[106] began in England in the 17th century, and the process was complete in Europe by the 20th century, a relatively short time period. Chinese national consolidation took longer, over a 1000 years, and their nationalism after it was achieved has endured for over 3200 years. The Europeans – in contrast to the Chinese – are presently forming a joint European Union, after attempting over the course of 100-350 years to form distinct nationalist entities.

Reason IV above already relates to Bodde's theories about the Maoist religion that endorsed technological developments, in contrast to Confucianism that promoted the study of literature over technological research. Reasons V and VI above relate to the expectation that Moism had the potential to encourage Chinese intellectuals to develop science and industry. Since this development conflicted with imperial interests, there were two choices – either Moism would be stronger than the imperial interests and would prevail, or the Maoist idea would be forced to 'bow' to the imperial interests. Though the possibility that the emperors would have adopted Moism over Confucianism is merely a theoretical possibility, it should be recalledthat:

---

105 Benedict Anderson, Illusory Republics (Tel Aviv: Open University Publications, 2000), trans. Dan Daor, the original was published in English in 1983).

106 There was no definite sense of nationalism yet in either France or England during the period of the French national heroine, Jean Djark. The revolt of the nationalities took place in the middle of the 19th century, while the unification of Germany was only at the end of the 19th century.

1. Moism was a kind of religion deeply immersed in spirits and demons, and 2. Polytheistic religions are classically non-aggressive. The combination of these two factors makes it likely that in a confrontation between a pagan religion like Moism and a vital imperial interest, the imperial interest would have prevailed.
Answer I: In Both China and Europe, developments in the nuclear family unit proved dominant, and responsible, though indirectly, for the occurrence of the Industrial Revolution in the West and not in Imperial China.
Answer II: According to SCivin,[107] the answer, to a question as basic and fundamental as ours, cannot be simple. Thus, while the previous answer already provides a solution to the question, it is fitting to offer an additional answer that does not detract from the first one, but only comes to supplement it.

Western man was ruled, until the middle of the second millennium, by Christian religion, institutions, and law, and even kings sought the Pope's sanction. The rule of Christianity was aggressive and powerful, definitely by Chinese standards that did not attribute any ruling power to religion. As Christianity's influence began to decline, Western man needed to find an alternate source of morality and code of behavior, and the governments of the time sought and found new sources of legitimization. Man found himself seated on the royal throne, but it was patently obvious that in contrast to the absolute truth and absolute morality that were attributed to a divine source, man does not possess absolute truth, morality, and legitimacy to rule.
Kant's 'pure practical reason,' Hobbes' 'social contract,' nationalism such as that awakened by Protestantism in England, Rousseau's democratic principles, as well as Bentham's theory of utilitarianism, all came to replace the divine 'objective' source of morality. Kant's theories were advanced further by Darwin's theory of evolution.
As part of their liberation from the rule of religion, Western intellectuals built up modern science, and developed new sources of strength that came to replace those that secular man had rejected. One of these sources of strength was physical science and industry, products of the scientific and industrial revolutions. Scientific and industrial-economic motivations were as strong as the religious impulses they came to replace, and they yielded incredible far-reaching results.
Another aspect of the religious revolution was the establishment of a civil religion, as foreseen by Rousseau, and as developed in the United States, and then spread throughout most of the world. Nationalism also grew stronger, and more radical, leading to the rise of fascism and Nazism, and even in its liberal form, as in the US, it manifested radicalism. This paralleled the characteristic reaction to the

[107] In Chapter VII of his book cited in footnote 47.

radical religious structure that existed in Western China before the civil revolution due to its distinct tradition, a widespread tradition even in countries that, because of Chinese influence, did not adopt such radicalism. Thus, the dethroning of God obligated science to seek to emulate the precision of God, His omniscience and perfection, and to build a strong economic and political force that would empower the new ruler, man, who had unseated God. Thus, it was not only competition between various sources of power that fueled scientific and industrial development, but also rivalry with God, and man's need and fate to replace God. This tragic destiny of man led to his fanatical excessive ambition, of which development of science and industry and aggressive colonialism were the most prominent signs. Western man needed to undergo an Industrial Revolution, and to conquer space in order to prove his potential in these areas.[108]

---

[108] There are in fact those, such as Weber, who claim that Protestantism, and Puritanism, in particular, preached the industriousness that led to capitalism and the development of science and industry –

Max Weber, Protestant Ethics and the Capitalist Spirit (Tel Aviv: Am Oved, 1984) Translated from German by Baruch Moren. The original was published in Germany in 1920).

The growth of industry in Europe, not only in Protestant regions, but also in Catholic ones, and the achievements of Copernicus and Galileo – who were Catholic – demonstrate that religious motivation did not cause scientific and industrial revolutions, but rather only bolstered these revolutions, serving as a supportive but not critical force.

In: Carlox H. Weisman, Reversal of Development in Argentina, Postwar Counterrevolutionary Policies and Their Structural Consequences (Princeton, New Jersey: Princeton University Press, 1987), Weisman describes the decisive role that the ruling class in Argentina, seized by irrational fears of a Communist revolution, played in thwarting an industrial revolution. This example illustrates the critical role that political forces and rivalry played in preventing, and presumably also in promoting an industrial revolution. Rivalry and competition are basic motivating forces in the development of mankind, which also exist in the realm of man and God, as is evidenced by the secular revolution in the West. Nevertheless, Weisman's claim is flawed, since as he describes, the failure of the Argentineans to develop industry following the War was due to high prices and inferior quality, and thus the human factor was responsible for the project's failure, and not a government decision (that was cut off from reality). It is clear from Weisman's book that Argentina had no chance of developing industry that could compete with the vastly superior industry in England. The Argentinean government insisted on trying to catch up with England's hundreds of years of development, over the course of just a few years. Had it, instead, progressed more gradually, and emphasized education, the results would definitely have been different. It is important to also note that there is no comparing the conditions of unrestricted industry in the 20th century to the restrictiveness of China during the Imperial Age, just as there is no comparing China which for hundreds of years developed a far more advanced culture than England's, to Argentina under Peron.

Chinese culture did not need to compete in these ways. It did not rebel against God. God had never ruled her.[109]

In other words, religion in China was non-aggressive – and when there was concern that Buddhism was becoming a threat to the government in the 9th century, the government immediately dispersed their monks and stripped them of all their belongings. Therefore, no revolt against the rule of religion took place in China. The religions wielded great influence over the society and the government indirectly, through a system of values that was transmitted directly, and even more so indirectly, through the channels of Confucianism. This indirect influence of Chinese religions, especially that of ancient customs, was primarily responsible for the developments described in this section, and to the preclusion of a scientific or industrial revolution in China.

Christianity ruled in the West, a religion that seeks to missionize, an aggressive religion relative to Eastern religions in general and to Chinese religions specifically. The political rebellion against the Christian religion and the enthronement of man in the place of God were the primary causes of the scientific and industrial revolution in the West.

In short, the differences between Christianity and Chinese religions are key to understanding how and why science and industry developed as they did in different areas of the world.

---

[109] Meir Shachar, Chinese Religion (Ministry of Defense Publications: 1998), pp. 17-18.

Part 8:
Latin America and North America

Foreward:

From the beginning of European settlement in Latin America, a highly developed mutually beneficial patronage relationship evolved (patron-client relationship). This relationship was characteristic of societal ties in Latin America (the American countries from Mexico southward, until South Chile). According to Luis Roniger,[1] the patron-client or patronage relations, existed between landowners and peasants who did not own land, or between both peasants and herdsmen - and - merchants who controlled market practices. They also existed between labor leaders recruiting the support of their followers for political figures – and - those politicians themselves. This relationship was based on the understanding that if the politician was elected, he would channel resources to union members. Patronage relationships were also formed between powerful individuals who controlled positions of power in agrarian societies - and – urban political leaders, a relationship created in order to reap the benefits of ties made in the bureaucratic system, either directly or with the help of an influential intermediary.

The common denominator between all these forms of patronage relationships, according to Roniger, is their fundamental dissimilarity to the formal relations that are characteristic of the Western organizational model. Patronage relations, in their basic and essential form, Roniger claims, were not similar to the relations between castes in India, for example, since the relations between the castes were rigid and inflexible. Patronage relations differed also from corporate relations established within families or wider communities. The patronage, essentially and basically, differed from other forms of economic and political relations in its exceptional flexibility and reliance on personal relationships.

Roniger explains that contrary to the ancient antiquated view that perceived patronage relations as characteristic only of backward societies that still need to develop ('developing nations'), it became clear to researchers from the 1960's on,

---

[1] See Luis Roniger, "Variations of Patronage Patterns in Mexico and Brazil" (Doctoral dissertation in Philosophy, submitted to the Hebrew University in Jerusalem in June 1984) pp. 1-3.

that these relations were and are common also in developed modern societies. They should not be viewed as an institution that belongs only in the past, that has no place in the modern world, and that is about to disappear completely. Sociologists, anthropologists and political scientists have realized that the patronage relationship was a bond based on power and influence, which allowed people to wield their power and influence over society based on asymmetric channeling of a society's resources, inequality, and hierarchical relations. [2]

According to Roniger's definition, any representative of a person or group before the government or any other organization, political, economic or social, that is based on trust is a patronage. This includes the personal trust that a person has in the lawyer that represents him in court, or in his trade union, or in the workers' committee or candidate that citizens choose for local council or parliament. This relationship existed in feudal society in the vassal-feudal relationship. What distinguishes modern patronages is that they are relatively weaker, lacking in personal connection, and not based on the strong personal trust that characterized patronages in the past. Roniger cites the views of the early sociologists Durkheim, Weber, and Marx, to illustrate that a precondition for the division of labor, in any organized society, is basic trust between the different sectors, including peasants, manufacturers and distributors of various goods. These relations are pre-contract trust-based relations, without which it would be impossible to begin establishing a patronage relationship.

This definition underscores the continuing relevance of the institution of patronage. It belongs to a group of institutions that do not deny the reality that human society was never equal and is by nature unequal – a reality that the North Americans (from here on: the Americans) as opposed to the Latin Americans - wish to refute through the power of a liberal-democratic-equality ideology, by which they claim to live.

This subject will be expanded upon further on, within the comparison between North America and Latin America regarding the differences in the origins of their ideology, their histories of genocide, and the practices and ideologies established by the Europeans in these two parts of America. Within this discussion, the differences that emerge from this comparison will be evaluated.

Alongside the patronage motif, in the broad sense of the word, and that of hierarchy, two motifs that are closely related to and define the Latin American

[2] Ibid, pp.4-5.

region, is the motif of revolutionism that developed from Latin American distinctiveness, and from the specific conditions and historical developments that produced Latin America's problematic attitude towards democracy and nationalism. Analysis of these motifs will help us better assess the current situation and Latin America's future prospects.

This chapter seeks to demonstrate that combined factors of the basic homogeneity of Latin American lifestyle in the different countries in this region, and the existing pressures and problems, as well the current realities in the world and America, are likely to result in the creation of one large Pan Latino nation. This political entity would be composed of 25 countries, all bound by one history of a Spanish - Portuguese occupation. They would be divided administratively and operate by uniform guidelines, within the context of the Spanish imperialistic entity and within the framework of a European nation The nation would include Brazil, Spain's neighbor, Portugal whose culture, language and religion are not that different from those of Spain and the small insignificant areas near Holland, France and Britain.

Latin American countries all achieved national independence within a short span of each other, and they resembled one another quite closely. At the end of the 19th century, after achieving independence, and as was characteristic of "sister countries," all the Latin American countries convened to establish principles - of mutual respect for each other's independence and borders, for settling confrontations peacefully, and of nonintervention in each other's internal matters. They raised the possibility of eventually establishing a joint committee that would deal with political issues and with settling confrontations within the special context of Latin America.

Each of the Latin American States sought and still seeks to achieve a distinct national identity. Each country has its own specific circumstances, but they share certain similarities and common denominators. The motifs of patronage, hierarchy, revolutionism and democracy, as well as a fifth motif of nationality all weave together a unique fabric with the distinct characteristics of Latin America. The order of presentation will not be as mentioned above but according to the pedagogic needs that will be outlined later. Discussion of these five motifs will raise questions regarding human nature that will remain outside the realm of the current discussion. North America, especially the U.S., will be examined at length, however, since this discussion will shed light on Latin America.

Chapter I includes a general survey of Latin America but primarily focuses on the unique circumstances of four Latin American countries, Brazil and Mexico which together contain almost half of the Latin American population, and Argentina and Venezuela, each of which will paint Latin America in a different color. Chapter II presents a historical-ideological comparative analysis of Latin America as one entity vs. North America, with distinction being drawn between Canada and the US. The chapter highlights the characteristics that distinguish Latin America vs. those that distinguish North America. Chapter III will discuss the hierarchy motif and in its connection to labor unions in Latin America, highlighting the four Latin countries that are the subject of Chapter I. Chapter IV examines the transitions from revolutionism to democracy in Argentina and Brazil. Chapter V discusses the different forms of nationalism in America and chapter VI deals with the institution of patronage in Mexico and Brazil.

Chapter A:
General Background and Close Analysis of Four Latin American Countries

General Background:
According to Roniger, America, in the 16th century, gradually came under European control. In Central and South America (Latin America) this occurred primarily as a result of the Spanish and Portuguese invasion. In North America the British and French predominately assumed control, and the Dutch, to a lesser extent. In North America, as a result of an agreement that concluded an internal European war in which the British defeated the French, at the end of the 18th century, the British achieved almost absolute control.

The following elements characterized the domination of Latin America:
Primarily European males participated in the conquest, assisted in most cases by local divided Indian populations. This divisiveness facilitated the Spanish take over.
The Catholic Church, in many cases, served as the pioneering force in the conquest, with priests being the first ones to enter new areas, engaging in religious missionary work and establishing churches. An Indian village that accepted Spanish rule was established around each of these churches.
Massacres of Indians did take place, and they were driven out of areas taken over by the Europeans, but as a rule there was no systematic annihilation of the Indians.
European men married local women (Indian) and produced offspring, creating a large class of hybrids and the blurring of ethnic borders.

The government attempted unsuccessfully to reorganize the population, to identify groups - including hybrids - and assign each group a profession and unique dress. Many fled the centers of government where ceremony, stratification and hierarchy were rigidly defined. They escaped to peripheral areas were greater social mobility was possible, creating a new less severe hierarchy.

The Spanish granted privileges to the Indian tribes that helped them gain control, and even recognized Indian aristocracy rights that preceded the Spanish invasion. The criteria that determined one's social status changed, with 'contribution to the conquest' replacing ethnicity. The character of the aristocracy changed as well and became more European, emphasizing the importance of education, adoption of Spanish lifestyle and being cultured by Spanish standards.
In the process, the government allowed the Indians to switch from forced labor that preserved social distinctions, to salaried work that permitted blurring of social classes and encouraged social unification.[3]

Roniger explains that following the Napoleonic wars and Napoleon's conquest of Spain and Portugal, changes took place in Latin America. Black slaves revolted in Haiti and freed themselves. Wars for independence broke out in other Latin American countries that were under Spanish rule, in which black Africans that had been brought earlier as slaves, and descendants of mixed marriages were recruited. When independence was achieved, the slaves received some freedoms as reward for their contribution. When there were conflicts between Liberals and Conservatives in the Andes region of South America, in the 19th century, the Blacks again participated in the war, thus earning their freedom. The last country to free its slaves was Brazil since no war of independence took place there. This was because Napoleon's conquest brought the Portuguese king to Brazil. His son who ruled after him established a legal monarchy that ultimately achieved independence and became a republic, obviating the need for internal conflict. The Brazilian case will be expanded upon in a separate analysis of Brazil.

Even before the wars of independence, Spanish rulers feared an uprising of the lower class, comprised mainly of Indians and Blacks. This weakened the principle of ethnic distribution, a weakness only highlighted by the wars of independence. Ethnicity – whether Indian or Black – was determined not simply based on origin, but rather on social class, culture and the ability to adopt the Spanish colonial lifestyle. Therefore a black or dark skinned man who worked in cotton and became

---

[3] See Luis Roniger, "The Disintegration of the Spanish Empire and Collective Identity Construction in Latin America", S.N. Eisenstadt (ed.). (Jerusalem: Van Leer: 1990), pp. 55-60.

rich was considered 'white' even before independence was achieved, though this phenomenon intensified afterward. This principle applied also in Portuguese-ruled Brazil. The meaning of 'race' became cultural and did not involve discrimination between different ethnic groups.

Gradually new terms were adopted that did not exist under colonial, Spanish or Portuguese rule, but were imported from modern Europe. The old terms of national sovereignty were integrated into new structures of: representative government, distribution of power, citizenship, political rights, freedom of expression and press. However, a gap developed between these burgeoning ideas and the reality of the existence of elites, the same elites that initiated the war of independence and seized control of the government from Spanish colonialists. The new countries wrote constitutions that established representative government, yet the societies remained hierarchic and divided. So the new rulers-'the independents'- ruled with a firm hand, establishing, in the 19th and 20th centuries, autocratic and presidential regimes, which sought to lessen the people's participation in government. This created a gap between the new ideals on one hand and the political reality on the other. The revolution essentially altered the identity of the rulers without actually transferring power to the people. The liberalism, of which the ruling elites boasted, was attended by discrimination and annulment of the property and land rights of agrarian populations. Therefore, the 'technical' infiltration of European culture occurred earlier in Latin America than in other places, but its implementation in the political arena was incomplete and primarily in name only, and when it did exist, it created or strengthened the social hierarchy in the different countries. [4] What occurred was that though common national identity lacked much basis in reality, there were still some people who sought and seek to belong to this inclusive, illusive, national identity. [5]

As an overview, in the 1970's, 15 out of 25 Latin America countries lived under authoritarian, militant regimes. They relied on the support of the army or were one-party countries, like Cuba. During the 1980s this number decreased to only two, but the populations of most of these countries believe that a military regime will eventually return or at least that a military regime was no less successful than a democratic one. In practice, there were authoritarian nations, like Brazil and Chile, that pursued successful economic policies, and there were and are democratic nations that failed in their economic policies, the most striking of these

---

[4] See at end of discussion on Argentina the three conclusions connected to Roniger's opinion.

[5] See Roniger, note 3.

countries being Argentina, though the last military regime there also pursued unsuccessful economic policies.[6]

Mexico:
In 1522, King Carlos I of Spain, in recognition of Cortez's conquests, appointed him governor of 'New Spain', eventually renamed Mexico. Prior to the Spanish conquest, the Aztec tribe, known for their practice of human sacrifices, lived in Mexico. Between the years 1520 and 1620, the Indian population in Mexico decreased from 22 million to less than one million – primarily as a result of exposure to viruses that the Spanish had introduced to the region, to which the Indians had no immunity.

From 1545 until the 19th century, Black slaves were brought from the Antiles and Africa, many of whom married Indian or *mestizo* spouses and were absorbed into the diverse population. They were called *Castas*. Many Blacks also died of diseases from European viruses. The colonial government divided the Whites into two hierarchical groups: the *Gachopins*, born in Spain, who held government, church, and army positions or any other position that involved loyalty to the throne, and the Creoles - Whites born as Whites in Mexico itself. While these two groups were in theory equal, in practice, the Creoles were banned from important positions. The Indians were perceived as inferior but the government prohibited selling them as slaves and made it compulsory to pay them for their work. *Mestizos* were required to pay a special tax, and it was forbidden for them to study certain subjects, such as law. Like the Indians, they were not allowed to carry weapons and to live in certain areas. Nevertheless, in the army *Gachopins*, Creoles and *mestizos* (mixture of white and Indian) all served together.

Towards the end of the 18th century, Europe's Enlightenment ideas began filtering into Mexico, prompting a reassessment of Indian heritage and the Spanish conquest, and inviting a Mexican nationalistic identification with Indian symbols and myths such as 'the *Guadelopa Virgin*'. In the second half of the 18th century, as a result of the American and French revolutions, Creoles began to identify more as Mexicans.

In 1808 a French king was crowned in Mexico. The *Gachopins* identified with the local military J'unta and the Creoles claimed that sovereignty had been restored to the people. A race war broke out. 1823 the Mexican congress assembled and

[6] See The Hebrew Encyclopedia, "Latin America", Supplementary Volume III, 1985.

ratified a federal constitution, which appointed a president who freed the slaves, abolished aristocracy titles and limited church owned property. The *Gachopins* fled, in this period, to Spain, taking much wealth with them and initiating a long period of economic deadlock and politic chaos. A civil war took place in which the church played an integral role since it opposed Mexico's secular constitution. In 1876 a president was elected who established a stable government that cruelly suppressed the Indian uprising. The regime was firm and brutal, and responsible for election fraud, yet the economic state was stable and foreigners began investing in Mexico. Initially, church lands were distributed in order to build big estates, peasants were dispossessed of their land and the ruling class was comprised of Creoles.

Meanwhile, the number of *mestizos* grew. In 1912 a civil war broke out which ultimately led to the separation of Church and State, the renewed distribution of land, and the establishment of schools in agrarian regions. The 'Nationalist Revolutionary Party' was established in 1929 to protest a halt in land distribution. This party became the only real political force and in 1934 the distribution of land was renewed with vigor. Since then the government in Mexico has been stable and based on a culture that is a fusion of three elements - Indian culture, Spanish culture, and modern Mexican culture.

The Mexican is characterized by his incongruous nature. He loves and respects tradition, appreciates honesty and proper etiquette, is usually friendly and discrete - but sometimes he can become cold and aloof. His temperament is unstable. He does not pursue his goal with sufficient dedication and commitment. He wants to know and try everything and at times will be unruly. He is quick to grasp things, yet violent. He loves life, children and partying above all.

Beyond this, the Mexican lives with a profound awareness of death, an awareness tied to the Aztec myth of creation. The bullfight represents the celebration of death. The bull symbolizes death that sometimes takes us by surprise. On November 2nd every year, children play with skull shaped toys – an activity that makes the concept of death less foreign to them. This distinctively Mexican motif of death fuses elements of Spanish and Indian culture.

Mexicans consider coexistence and integration of the races an ideal state and from this stems the prohibition in Mexico against writing down a person's origins. This attitude developed as a consequence of civil wars in which both sides sought the alliance of the Indians. This is why the revolutions were connected to the apportionment of land and redressing the injustice that was done in confiscating Indian land.

Pregnant women refrain from killing animals since there is a Mexican superstition that the soul of the animal may enter the body of the baby, as well as a myth connected to the *Talopha Matphic* virgin.

Breaching one's godfather's trust is considered one of the most serious offenses, an attitude whose roots are in Spanish culture, a fusion of hierarchy, patronage and intimacy.

As a result of all these factors, the Mexicans lack any clear ethnic connection. Their language and religion were bequeathed to them by their Spanish conquerors while their primordial traditional heritage is Indian in nature. Thus, culturally, they are Spanish and Western, while emotionally they are Indian – a synthesis that is distinctly Mexican.

The Mexican definition of nationalism dates back less than 70 years old, from the time political reforms were introduced in the year 1934. Their definition is a late 20th century one and is based on the principle of inclusion of all classes, including the Indians, and on political equality. In practice, Mexican society remained hierarchical and based on patronage, as Roniger described.[7] Roniger defines hierarchic patronage in its most expansive sense, which goes to the root of these basic concepts in Latin American society. Patronage is intertwined with accepted societal norms in various ways. The most common is when employment opportunities are offered in exchange for one's support in an elections. A patronage relationship may be formed when politicians have the means to guarantee a loan, a spot in a high school, or a bed in a hospital to their friends, to friends of friends, and to mere supporters, and public officials have the ability to grant preferential care - in exchange for political support. People seek a connection with a powerful person in order to secure political protection, or in order to raise their social status. Arrangements, such as these, would be illegal in modern Western countries but they are a standard accepted norm in Latin America, in general, and in Mexico, in particular.

These are some of the factors that create a nationalism that is a mixed weave of modern and ancient, where equality is theoretically and fundamentally part of the democratic ideology but is not personified in social conduct, where races and ethnic classes are meant to preserve their distinctness and in practice intermingle with each other. Mexico, in contrast to the US, does not deny the racial inequality

---

[7] Luis Roniger, **Hierarchy and Trust in Modern Mexico and Brazil** (New York: Praeger, 1990).

that exists in its country, though in practice, racial integration takes place, and is gradually even becoming an ideal.

Brazil:
In contrast to Mexico, where the Indians comprise 12.4% of the population (and combined with "half Indians", they make up the majority of the population), in Brazil, the Indian population is estimated at 0.2% of the total population.[8] Brazil instead grapples with its policies towards its black slave population from Africa, a population group that was particularly central to public life in 1870 and 1880, as will be described presently.

Beginning, however, with the situation at the end of the 20th century, the ongoing economic crisis impeded the government from playing an aggressive role in society and from providing basic services to its citizens.[9]

The first presidential elections in Brazil were conducted in 1985, but the election reform that had been instituted by the military faction in power on the eve of the elections, mandated consensus between the parliament and president, denying the president any effective authority without the cooperation of the legislature. The elected president received only 5% of the votes in Parliament, and refused to include the Parliament in the government. He also committed various crimes that ultimately led to his impeachment and to his replacement by his vice president, Itamar Franco. In 1995, President Cardozo was elected.

Until Cardozo's election, the situation in Brazil remained difficult, with 38% of the population in favor of restoring military regime. Many people were killed in the conflicts, and the government continued to refrain from meting out justice to criminals, except in isolated cases, and this only when a well-connected person was murdered. The police would summarily execute any violator of the law – though this did not increase general compliance with the law. Government officials regularly violated the law, without fear of impunity. Inflation grew. Yet memories of life under the military regime and lack of military support for a revolution prevented the outbreak of a revolution.

---

[8] Deborah J. Yashar, "Indigenous Politics and Democracy: Contesting Citizenship in Latin America," Prepared for delivery at the 1996 Annual Meeting of the American Political Science Association, The San Francisco Hilton and Towers, August 29 –September 1, 1996.

[9] Juan J. Linz and Alfred Stepan, **Problems of Democratic Transition and Consolidation, Southern Europe, South American and Post Communist Europe** (Baltimore, Maryland: The John Hopkins University Press, 1996) p. 167.

Returning to the 19th century, there is a parallel between Brazil, Mexico, and the US, regarding the evolution of nationalism in each of these countries. Mexican nationalism evolved only following a bitter internal struggle, as a result of which the lower Indian class was freed, just as the US nation fully developed only following a hard bloody Civil War, which freed American slaves.[10] Brazilian nationalism, similarly, began to take shape, only after its slaves were freed, and a bitter civil war was fought in the 1880's, 20 years after the US fought its own civil war and freed its own slaves.[11] At the start of the process of the liberation of the slaves, the Brazilian legislature served as a forum by which the elites could safeguard their own interests, included in which was the preservation of slavery. Certain compromises were achieved through this forum, which were accepted by all members of the elite class, including slave owners – such as the liberation of all slaves by the age of 60, and the liberation of second generation slaves at the age of 21 in exchange for financial compensation by the government. Slave trade and importation were legal and legislated by law. Rural and urban regions in Brazil developed different attitudes towards slavery as a result of disparate economic needs, just as the Northern and Southern states in America had done.

Differences between the Brazilian Civil War and the American Civil War reflect fundamental differences between Catholic Latin American culture, a culture that is built on direct personal relationships that are often hierarchic and not always democratic, and Anglican Protestant North American culture, which is predicated on select democratic institutionalized relations and a system in which problems are solved according to formal established principles rather than intimate personal connections. This distinction was also responsible for the American Civil War being the bloodiest war in American history, while the liberation of the slaves in Brazil was essentially bloodless, and the product of a consensus created through spirited public debate alongside political debate in the newspapers.[12]

---

[10] This is the view held by Liah Greenfeld, **Nationalism: Five Roads to Modernity** (London: Harvard University Press, 1992) p. 480 and by Seymour Martin Lipset, "The 'Newness' of the New Nation," in C. Vann Woodward (ed.) **The Comparative Approach to American History**, NY: Basic Books, 1968) p. 64.

[11] Leonardo Avritzer, "The Generation of Public Spares in Brazil: The Role of Abolitionism," in **Globality and Multiple Modernities – Comparative North American and Latin American Perspectives**, Luis Roniger and Carlos H. Waisman (ed.), (Brighton, Portland: Sussex Academic Press, still being edited, projected publishing date 2002).

[12] Ibid.

Towards the end of the 1860's in Brazil, members of the movement for the Liberation of the Slaves began forming associations to promote their goals, and the Brazilian parliament began debating the issue. In 1871, a law, meant to begin the process of freeing the slaves, was enacted, and 6,500 slaves were freed over the course of three years and their owners compensated by state coffers. This rate was too slow to satisfy the opponents of slavery, and so efforts were made to transfer the process to local levels of government, and in 1883 private foundations were established to finance the liberation of slaves. Even prior to this, in 1880, organizations were formed to help badly abused slaves escape from their owners. In 1882, a movement began that harshly protested the importation of slaves. In 1884, as a result of public pressure, a place named C'eara was declared slave free – all present slaves there would be liberated, and slave importation to there was prohibited. The opponents of slavers advertised in the newspapers one day, that they would be concentrating on two streets in the capital city, and over the next few days, they went from house to house in those blocks, and found 12 families who still owned slaves. They persuaded these families and all the rest of the residents of these blocks to sign a statement pledging to desist from slave labor. The government stepped up enforcement of the clauses of the law that prohibited the mistreatment of slaves, clauses that had been virtually ignored until then. A law was passed that prohibited beating a slave with a whip. Opponents of slavery protested the law that granted slaves their freedom only at the age of 60, claiming that property rights must yield to the right of liberty. In 1887, slaves began fleeing from their owners, by the masses. In a number of states in Brazil, laws were passed by which slaves were freed without compensation to the owners. The media and public opinion encouraged free expression regarding the issue. The debate promptly reached the Parliament, where discussions focused on questions of morality, rather than economic interests. People met face to face and persuaded others – including slave owners – of the immorality of slavery, until slavery expired completely and was unconditionally terminated in a formal and legal manner.

This overwhelming victory for public opinion was exceptional in Brazil. The reality of the arrangement of internal forces in Brazil could not lead to any decisive changes in Brazilian society beyond the liberation of the slaves and the establishment of a national community in Brazil that included the lower classes, and the African slaves. After the slaves were freed, the State's interests (embodied in the army) joined forces with proponents of capitalism, and supporters of positivism – the Brazilian equivalent to Western and North American liberalism. These three groups formed a cohesive force that opposed public debate, democracy, and liberalism. This force continues to wield influence in Brazil today,[13] even after a completely democratic system of government was instituted. Yet this does not diminish the greatness of the Spanish legacy of patronage, of personal relationships and debate – which enabled the Brazilians to achieve the bloodless social revolution that shaped their nationalism. This historic moment represents the power of personal contact, a power that can even promote positions that are not consistent with self-interest, and which stands in sharp contrast to liberal-democratic North American hypocrisy that emphasizes values over personal relationships.

Argentina:
In regard to ethnic origin, Argentina differs from both Mexico (where the majority of the population has some Indian blood) and Brazil (where there is a significant African population). Argentina is populated almost exclusively by people of European descent, with only 1.5% of its population being of Indian origin.[14] Most emigrated from Spain, with a significant percentage from Southern Europe, particularly Italy. Considering the makeup of its population, the question arises as to why Argentina did not advance technologically at the same rate as the US and Canada.[15]

According to Carlos Weissman, events in Europe had an effect on Argentina's economy, freedom, and political crises.[16] This refers to both the cutbacks in British importation of meat from Argentina, as well as to the Russian Bolshevik Revolution that led to a strict authoritarian regime in Argentina in an effort to prevent revolution from breaking out in Argentina. Weissman's claims are both unpersuasive and superficial. Authoritarian regimes existed in Latin America for 500 years, long before there was any fear of a Bolshevik revolution. Passing temporary factors do not need to be examined, when deeper long-term reasons are involved. Fear of communism was stronger in the US than in Argentina, yet the wave of McCarthyism passed and the essentially liberal nature of the government in the US remained. Britain's cutbacks in meat importation were virtually irrelevant, contrary to Weissman's claim otherwise. As Weissman himself describes, the governments in Argentina maneuvered to establish mutual trade agreements with other countries besides Britain, thus increasing the amount of meat exported from Argentina. The global meat market is far wider than Britain

---

[13] Ibid.

[14] See note 8 above.

[15] Carlos H. Waisman, **Reversal of Development in Argentina – Postwar Counterrevolutionary Policies and Their Structural Consequences** (Princeton, New Jersey: Princeton University Press, 1987).

[16] Ibid.

alone. Finally, the question arises – why Argentina focused only on meat and meat products. The answer to this question addresses the root of the matter, and is linked to Argentineans ability to develop industry, an ability that is connected to motivation and inner strengths found within the Argentinean people and the internal relationships that exist between them. Venezuela, as will be seen further on, developed much more advanced industry than Argentina – perhaps because of the natural resource, oil, that it possessed – that encouraged the growth of industries connected to oil, and because of which, it saw a large European immigration in the 1940's. A contrast, nevertheless, emerges between Catholic man's ability and motivation to compete in demanding fields involving skilled labor and Protestant man's ability and drive. This relates to Max Weber's comparison of the dedication and ability of Protestants and Catholics.[17] This chapter will focus presently on the specifics of the Argentinean case, leaving in-depth examination of these issues to later.

Argentineans perceived themselves as people of Spanish descent who were born locally (Creoles, by their Latin American name). They permitted immigration from Europe for utilitarian reasons, since the new immigrants were willing to work in areas of labor, such as agriculture, that the Creoles disliked. Class distinctions were made between "old timers" and new immigrants. Voting laws made it difficult for new immigrants to become citizens and gain voting rights, making it easy to expel any "undesirable" non-citizen. This was a product of the hierarchical nature of the system, previously described.

Throughout the generations, there has been significant emigration from Argentina that clearly stems from Argentina's failure to develop into an industrialized nation, a reality that must be examined.

Between 1821 and 1932, 6.4 million Europeans immigrated to Argentina, fewer than immigrated to the US (34.2 million) or Uruguay (7 million), but more than Canada (5.2 million), Brazil (4.4 million), and Australia (2.9), and percentage-wise (of the former population) the most of all countries. In 1914, 30% of all Argentineans had been born outside of Argentina (In America, during this period, the percentage never exceeded 15%). In 1914, new immigrants constituted 90% of coastal populations and vineyard regions, where 77% of the total population lived.[18] New immigrants made up 66% of factory owners, 50% of factory workers, 74% of merchants, and 45% of craftsmen. A significant portion

---

[17] Max Weber, **The Protestant Ethic and the Spirit of Capitalism** (Tel Aviv: Am Oved, 1984), Original published in German in 1920.
[18] Ibid, 53-56.

of the middle class in general, and of industrial workers was new immigrants. Nearly half of the immigrants were Italian and close to a third were Spanish. The Italian immigrants brought with them a different political culture than the Spanish immigrants. The immigration to the US, in contrast to Argentina, was primarily from northern and central Europe.

In a comparison of the rates of growth (or decline) of agriculture and industry in various countries between 1940 and 1978 it emerges that: in Argentina, agricultural workers decreased from 33 to 14 % and industrial workers increased from 28 to 29%, in Italy, agricultural workers decreased from 47 to 13%, and industrial workers from 27 to 48%, in Spain agricultural workers decreased from 52 to 18%, and industrial workers increased from 24 to 43%, in the US, agricultural workers decreased from 18 to 2%, and industrial workers increased from 32 to 33%, in Brazil, agricultural workers decreased from 67 to 41% and industrial workers increased from 13 to 22%, and finally in Mexico, agricultural workers decreased from 65 to 39%, and industrial workers increased from 13 to 26.[19]

Country	Agriculture 1940 (%workers)	Agriculture 1978 (%workers)	Industry 1940 (%workers)	Industry 1978 (%workers)
Argentina	33	14	28	29
Italy	47	13	27	48
Spain	52	18	24	43
US	18	2	32	33
Brazil	67	41	13	22
Mexico	65	39	13	26

These statistics demonstrate that Argentina lagged behind the other countries in developing industry, and that Italy surpassed Spain. Therefore, there must have been some fundamental impediment to the growth of industry in Argentina, that inhibited its growth despite strong immigration from industrially – successful Italy. Mexico and Brazil both exceeded Argentina in growth of industry, despite the fact that they have large Black populations who do not have a tradition of industrial growth, while Argentina's population is nearly entirely of European descent.

Prior to WWI, standard wages in Argentina were higher than in Italy, France, and Germany, though lower than in England and the US. The standard of living in

[19] Ibid, 59-60.

Argentina was relatively high which explains the mass immigration to there. Trade with Britain provided Argentina with the materials to construct railroads, slaughter and packing- houses, while Spain and Italy supplied her with all the labor she needed. Everything began to change in Argentina during the worldwide Depression of 1930, and Argentina has yet to recover fully from it. The military seized control of the government, an event that was typical of the attempts of various classes in Argentina (first-the land owners, then the middle class) to take control of the government with the help of the military, maneuvering the minorities to their own advantage, using manipulation, military force, and pseudo-democratic games.[20]

Argentina, in the years 1880-1930, was a democracy in the Wig style, where until 1912, the electoral system left control of the elections to a minority of landowners. In 1912, an electoral reform conferred voting privileges also upon the middle class, and in 1916, the radical party that represented this position actually won the election. Despite all their promises, the new government did nothing to change the financial status quo, and occupied themselves only with extending the right to vote.[21] The global economic crisis that also shook up Argentina terrified the landowner class. As long as the radicals did not threaten their assets, they allowed the radicals to play whatever democratic and political games they desired. When they erroneously determined, however that the radicals were planning to change the economic status quo, concern for their wealth and the political status associated with it impelled them to ally with the conservative party that prodded the military to revolt. Apparently, the army promptly restored democratic rule, transferring control of the government to the liberal party, a party that then sought to retain control by repressing other parties, such as the communist one. While democratic rule was theoretically restored during the years 1930-1943, in practice there was no opportunity to alter the identity of the ruling party. Thus, Argentina - until 1943 – was bereft of the democracy that had not led to any real change even before then. Such was the nature of hierarchical Argentinean society, that democracy was to a certain extent simply a political game, rather than actual power. Until 1930, everyone, besides the radicals, supported Argentina's inclusion in the world economy, as an agricultural nation since agriculture had been shown preference over industry. The radicals did not dare to change the status quo even though they were in control of the government.

During 1930-1943, extensive social change took place. New bourgeoisie rose from the lower middle classes, while farmers arriving from agricultural regions became

---

[20] Ibid, in Weissman's book.
[21] Ibid, 78-79.

the new lower middle class. Two groups of middle class developed – one of new immigrants and one of natives, with the latter group considered higher class and possessing connections to foreign capitalists. A split formed also between immigrants and native Creoles. Labor unions and the labor class rose in stature.

In 1943, following an economic crisis that resulted from a partiality to agricultural interests and a lack of financial resources to support this policy, a military insurrection occurred that sought to introduce true democratic rule.

The winner of the elections, Juan Peron, attempted to unite different classes, particularly workers and members of the middle class. As a result of his connection with the workers, factories were nationalized. Prices were set, salaries raised, and financial incentives were offered to factory owners who couldn't compete. Agricultural produce was sold on the local market, instead of exported, and markets were closed down. No land or assets, however, were expropriated. Within a few years, Peron realized that his policies had curtailed production and decreased exports. The economy suffered, and the alliance between the classes that supported Peron dissolved. Even the workers who had backed him abandoned him the moment their salaries froze and even fell.

In the year 1955, the military again gained control of the government, and from the fall of the Peronists in 1955 until democracy was restored in 1983, the government changed hands many times, but always with connections to the military.

In 1983, after the economy had completely deteriorated and even the army's plans for the Faulkland Islands - intended to salvage the government's image – had failed, the army restored control of the government to the people. The economic depression, however, continued, and Argentina did not recover from the crisis.

The chapter of Argentina is a tragedy of failed attempts to establish democratic rule over a society of European immigrants who never successfully formed an integrated nation and who squandered any economic opportunities. Relationships were founded on the basis of hierarchy, without the personal dimension that was characteristic of the patronage tradition. Without, a feeling of connection and unity, class struggles were inevitable. What we have here is the combination of two evils from two opposing systems, the Hebrew-Catholic hierarchic model on one hand, and the Anglo-Protestant democratic one on the other. This can be formulated in the following manner:

1. Excessive hierarchic leadership that is more radical than the Iberian (Spain and Portugal) tradition, that lacks the institution of patronage, the upper class' charitable support of the lower class, and the lower class' political support of the upper class – as a result of all the classes having the same ethnic and racial (White European) background.
2. Playing political games with democracy without adopting its true principles – accepting the name of democracy without its inner content.
3. The establishment of a national framework without forming a true national identity, because of internal disparity and divergence.

Venezuela:
The following reflects the difference between Venezuela and Argentina: the Argentineans disaffiliated themselves from their European connection, yet they didn't have sufficient will or means to build a new distinct unified Argentinean nation. Venezuelans, on the other hand, according to Coloca and Ben-Zeev,[22] have considered themselves since the 16th century an inseparable part of the Western world. The myth of a thriving North Atlantic world, as well as language and culture have drawn them closer to the Western world, though they are still attempting to forge a uniquely Venezuelan nation.

The pivotal event in the formation of this nation was the discovery of oil in 1940, which prompted the immigration of many Europeans and their integration within the technological elite upper class – a smooth integration that blurred or even obliterated original ethnic differences.

In Venezuela, there are no ethnic community centers, though it would be inaccurate, according to Coloca and Ben-Zeev, to attribute this unity only to the discovery of oil and its consequences. As proof, they cite the case of Saudi Arabia where the discovery of oil has not united the specialists who came to the country with the Saudis. This argument doesn't seem relevant, but Coloca and Ben-Zeev's second reason is simpler and more comprehensible. They claim that even before the 1940's, a process of unification began in Venezuela. Every individual in Venezuela, already during the colonial period, had the potential to climb the social ladder and secure for himself the privileges of the White class, by improving his economic status.

[22] Eliora Coloca and Efrat Ben Zeev, "Ethnic Groups in Venezuela," Term Paper submitted to Dr. Luis Roniger of Hebrew University in Jerusalem, Included in Roniger's Anthology in the Library of Sociology and Humanities in Jerusalem.

Coloca and Ben-Zeev describe how all survivors of the racial genocide suffered by the Indians underwent a process of assimilation, and were then considered "Lanneros."

In contrast to the Indian population that has essentially vanished, people of African blood and ethnic origin, including slaves, Blacks, and dark skinned individuals, comprise approximately 60% of the population (particularly in coastal regions). They actively participated in their war of independence. They do not perceive themselves as a distinct group and have not even formed any separate societies. A wealthy Black easily integrates into a White society (though he didn't during the beginning of the colonial period). Slavery was banned in 1854 – before the US and long before Brazil. Venezuela's democracy from its inception was open to all shades and colors. In the 1940's, with the discovery of oil, it was natural to develop in Venezuela a cosmic-political society, which is the basis that characterizes the region's brand of nationalism and which distinguishes it. While Whites may stand at the top of the social ladder, others are an integral integrated part of the society.

Regarding the historical process in which the Spanish gained control of Venezuela, initially the Spanish oppressed or slaughtered the Indians from coastal regions. The Indians in Venezuela were far less cultured from those in Mexico. Catholic missionaries assumed control over them, influenced them to accept Christianity, and established churches for them. The conquest was religious-cultural, rather than military. The Indian tribes before then had not shared a common religion or framework. The tribes lived separately from one another and even spoke different languages. Coloca and Ben-Zeev claim that it is quite likely that the missionaries' activities lent the Spanish conquest a peaceful character, a character that ultimately bred the unity that characterizes Venezuelan society. This unification process persisted throughout the 16th, 17th, and 18th centuries, and it resulted in the expansion and growth of Venezuela under colonial rule, and gradually to the creation of an independent nation. In Coloca and Ben-Zeev's opinion, it also paved the way toward Venezuela's war of independence, through which the Venezuelan nation was formed.

By and large, the Indians ultimately disappeared as a result of their inability to adapt or adopt new agricultural methods, and due to assimilation and illness.[23]

---

[23] According to a study conducted by Devorah Yashar, there are 290,000 Indians in Venezuela today, who constitute 1.5% of the total population. See note 8 above.

As a result, the new Venezuelan culture, in contrast to the Mexican one, did not derive inspiration from Indian culture. It is a fundamentally Spanish culture, with strong tendencies toward modernity. Democracy reached Venezuela only in 1960, before which time Venezuela was ruled by military regimes and was characterized by successive coupes.

Chapter B: Latin America vs. North America – Differences in Ideology and Practice

Anglo-American Culture in the US

Louis Hartz discusses the deep-rootedness of democracy in American society.[24] He praises the Americanism of US citizens (North Americans), who besides personifying certain extreme tendencies (individualism, aggressive capitalism, American doctrinarism, the purest form of capitalist democracy), managed to complete a successful stable historical process, in which they fought a civil war without producing an oppressive regime, and through which they developed an enlightened moderate liberal ideology, and adopted an enduring constitution.[25] He adds that North American liberalism existed even in the colonial period, and thus the War of Independence was not in the colonists' perception a revolt against accepted conventions, but rather a pursuit of the values that they had derived from their native country, England. In their opinion, it was the British royal government that had veered astray, and not they. The American democratic system was based on fundamental beliefs and feelings. Thomas Jefferson who was supported even by religious leaders of the American Revolutionary War, such as Jonathan Mayhew from New England, initiated a process towards secularization, an adoption of natural law, which paved the way toward individualism.

Individualism is based on a belief in a natural right that is not derived from God. Thus it differed fundamentally from feudalism, a system based on a divine right. This natural right existed both among Canadian Catholics and Latin Americans.

---

[24] Louis Harz, "United States History in a New Perspective," in **The Founding of New Societies – Studies in the History of the United States, Latin America, South Africa, Canada and Australia**, by Louis Hattz et. Al (New York: Harcourt & World, 1964) p. 69 (chapter IV).

[25] Ibid, 71-72.

The difference between natural and divine rights is at the root of the differences between Latin and North America.

North Americans followed the philosophy of Locke, and not Rousseau. Rousseau and other French philosophers represented the break with tradition – a rift North Americans could avoid because of their liberal ideology. The society they built, already during the colonial period, was elastic, diverse, and inclusive of everyone from the governor until the poorest of peasants. The religious diversity and social equality of the Americans contrasted sharply with the French Canadian nobility and Spanish Portuguese aristocracy in Latin America.[26] Protestantism, with its emphasis on the importance of the individual, played a significant role in forming the character of America. The individual stands before his God without the intercession or intervention of a priest. He has direct obligations and responsibilities to his God.[27] This contrasts with Spanish Catholics treatment of Creoles and the general political passivity of French Canadian Catholics.[28]

These differences explain why independence produced no change in North American traditions, while in Latin America it caused significant change. Republicanism in Latin America constituted a break with Latin American tradition, and as such was accompanied by acts of violence, such as the slaughter of the Malukans in Mexico. According to Hertz, the strong tradition of liberalism in the US is reflected in the fact that the Constitutional Convention that convened in Philadelphia managed to come to a compromise regarding slavery, an undoubtedly controversial issue.[29]

At the time of the Philadelphia Convention (in 1776), slaves were not considered part of American society, a state of affairs that persisted until the American Civil War and the liberation of the slaves in the South in 1861. The Anglo American nation was formed by the American Civil War, both as a result of the terrible shared trauma of a civil war and the liberation of the slaves and their inclusion within American society and the redefinition of the American nation. This process parallels similar developments in Mexico with the Indians, the liberation of the black slaves in Brazil, and the peaceful integration of the Indians in Venezuelan society through the agency of the Church. Apparently, a national trauma and the

---

[26] Ibid, 73-74.

[27] Ibid, 75. It should be noted that priests, not bishops came to Anglo American settlements, since according to Protestantism the priest was only a guide and religious life was not hierarchic

[28] Ibid, 75.

[29] Ibid, 80.

integration of lower classes into the nation are critical steps in the formation of a nation.

This same phenomenon is apparent in the experience of the ingathering of all the Jewish exiles since the establishment of the State of Israel, during Israel's War of Independence and immediately following. All Jews from all the exiles were accepted as part of the nation that was now returning to its homeland. The presumption was that all these people were members of one nation, a conception that guaranteed from the outset the national consolidation of the Jewish people into not merely one religion but one nation, despite differences in culture, language and social class.

This trend can also be linked to the development of European nationalism and the growth of democracy in this continent. The connection between democracy and nationalism exists also in nations that gained independence in Africa and Asia. The mere cooperation of all the classes and ranks in establishing a democratic government helped form a single nation. The unification of the higher and lower classes turns them into one nation. According to this principle it appears that Argentina's failure stemmed, at least in part, from the absence of different sectors and classes that it would be possible to unite – and thus the lack of a social mission.

The question is whether the similarities in the process of forming a nation between the US and Latin America should cause us to view them as one entity in terms of democracy and equality, according to the English liberal version. It will become clear that the answer to that question is negative.

Latin America's Entanglement from Democracy

James Malloy[30] surveys the different views on the social and governmental structure that is characteristic of Latin America. He writes that according to Douglas A. Chalmers, the political parties in Latin America struggle to offer legitimate backing for the authority of their country's rulers because the hierarchic, elitist and bureaucratic nature of these parties prevent them from reflecting class struggles and revolutionary changes. They even lack strong connections with the masses. Malloy also cites the opinion of Howard J. Wiarda who claims that the political parties lack any real power in Latin America, and that it is the private corporations and economic elites that wield the real power.

---

[30] James M. Malloy, "Authoritarianism and Corporatism in Latin America: The Modal Pattern," in James M. Malloy (ed.) **Authoritarianism and Corporatism in Latin America** (Pittsburgh: University of Pittsburgh Press, 1977) p. 3.

Without disputing either of these opinions, Malloy claims that in Latin America there are two hierarchic institutions – corporatism and clientilism (patronage). Latin America, he maintains, differs from Europe, the US, and parts of Asia and Africa in that in Latin America class based unions did not form, but rather corporatism and patronage. The Latin American system eschews free market competition, instead granting monopolies to bodies involved in the single government bureaucracy controlling the country. This stands in stark contrast to the competition that developed between autonomous unions in America and other countries. The corporative method suited the colonial system and it served the central government well, even later, in places like Mexico, Brazil, and Chile, by producing unions of workers that served the government more than the unions themselves.

Malloy cites Eric Wolf's opinion regarding the symbiotic relationship between corporatism and patronage, in which the patronage tempers the formal rigidity that typifies corporatism. Corporatism and patronage are two central components in the Latin American political arena, both sources of power and support for elected officials, and as such, substitutes for political parties. Alongside these, stands the institution of the 'statesman', a deep-rooted Latin American institution, from which parties developed.

Regarding the power of the corporations, Malloy writes that in Brazil and Mexico the corporations have no power over the government.[31] The government can do as it sees fit, even disbanding parties it disapproves of, though in Brazil there are select brokers who have methods of influencing the government, and businessmen who wield influence either directly or by means of these brokers. In general, in comparison to Latin America, in countries in which a political arena exists, workers' unions attach themselves to parties from the understanding that support for a victorious party will benefit the union. Thus the relationship between workers' unions and the parties resembles a patronage of sorts. Regarding the power of workers' unions, Malloy writes that in Venezuela, Argentina, and Chile, workers' unions managed to stand up to a dictatorial government. In general, he writes, collaboration and partnerships encourage greater political activism, which in turn promotes greater democracy. Based on this, Malloy expresses his hope and belief that democracy will develop in Latin America.

The question is how realistic Malloy's optimism in fact is. Democracy is an institution based on the equality of citizens, not on the efforts of the lower ranked individual to curry favor with a higher ranked individual. Democracy is a system

[31] See Hertz, note 24, pp. 94-98.

in which social forces meet and struggle with each other on a level playing field, where no team has any unfair advantage over the others, other than size. The Latin American playing field isn't level and the rules of the game do not award victory to the will of the majority. Whoever is on top rules, even if he is an insignificant minority, and whoever is on the bottom bows his head in submission, even if he is the majority. Thus, there can be no talk of replicating the democratic system from the British parliament in Latin America, as long as it doesn't divest itself of its culture predicated on hierarchy, an unlikely possibility, and not even necessarily a desirable one. Democracy in Latin America can be compared to a man dressing in a bear-skin or a bear wearing a dinner jacket – it depends on one's perspective. The same can be said for the adoption of the principles of faith and reliance on one another that characterize Latin America by their North American neighbors. While this could take place on the official formal level, these attitudes are unlikely to be imbued by the average citizen. Americans do not possess a deep faith in man's fundamental goodness and honesty. Their constitution, in fact, was based on an underlying distrust of man's fundamental nature, and therefore incorporated a system of checks and balances.

American Fundamental Values and Their Influence on American Government

The Indians and the Blacks: A Comparison of the US and Latin America

The Indians in the US

According to Hertz's description,[32] Anglo-Americans slaughtered the Indians as a matter of policy, stole their land, sometimes through legal sophistry. The 1987 Dawes Severalty Act, for example, professed to be an agricultural reform, whose goal was to distribute small plots of land to individual Indians at the expense of the general tribe's land, but in light of Indian apparent apathy, in actuality allowed the theft of Indian land and its distribution to white farmers. The European immigrant was not accustomed to problems of discrimination in his native country, while the British immigrant had learned about equality and about treating everyone equitably. European immigrants-colonists of other continents did not, as a matter of policy, engage in racial genocide. Yet in America, in contrast to other settled countries, and certainly as opposed to Latin America, a policy of appropriation of land through slaughter of the Indians was adopted. Even those who were not killed

[32] Michael Walzer, What it Means to Be an American? (New York:Marshio).

were isolated in closed reserves – all so as not to include the Indians within the egalitarian white society.

It was a hypocritical racist hierarchic policy. Hertz claims that European ideologies do not deal with races, but immigrants from a feudal world needed to confront the issue of a non-Western mother, the different classes of Indians and Blacks. The Anglo American solution during the period of slavery was to exclude Blacks from the human race, thus allowing the existence of 'liberal slavery'. Hertz doesn't explain, however, why this was the Anglo American solution to the Indian 'problem, while in Latin America, the attitudes and policies towards Indians that developed were entirely different. He doesn't offer reasons; he simply describes the facts. He writes that while many Indians were in fact killed in Brazil, that was a function of a religious mission to eradicate idol worshipers, rather than an act of racial discrimination. Indians who were not exterminated in Brazil and other Latin American countries integrated into the societies there and partially assimilated. Though the immigrants-settlers related to them according to the hierarchic system that was typical of their culture, they – ultimately – admitted the Indians into the general society.

Indians and Blacks in Latin America

In contrast to the liberal hypocrisy reflected in North America's liberal society's refusal to accept certain groups within its midst, it emerges from the discussion until this point that Latin American society admitted all Christians and everyone who adopted Latin culture and joined it, without distinctions of race or ethnicity - through a process of wars and upheavals. The question is why Latin-Catholics accepted within their midst whoever embraced their principals (cultural and/or religious) while the Protestant Anglo-Americans (the founders and those who came after them) adopted a different path, including many who were not true Anglo-American Protestants, even Jews – but only as long as they were of white European ancestry. All these who were assimilated into this culture adopted the political culture of the Anglo-American Protestant founders, and for the purposes of this discussion, they too will be called Anglo-Americans. Even if they were not Protestant, they accepted political principles that were derived in part from the Protestant religion, such as individualism, human liberties and rights including every person's right to a democratic republican government that represents him and his interests. This Anglo-American society sought to create a single Anglo-American nation.

Latin American society, in contrast, strove to create numerous national identities, according to the number of Latin American countries. The question is what fundamental difference between Protestant Anglo-American society and Latin

American society resulted in the North American annihilation of the Indians and the isolation of the ones that remained in remote reserves, on one hand, and Latin American assimilation of the Indians in every Latin American country, and their tolerant, sometimes even positive attitude toward intermarriage?

The lack of political equality between North American Indians living on reserves and other US citizens starkly manifests itself in the limitation of their right to vote to presidential, and not congressional elections. The Indians remain outsiders in the Anglo-American political society.

Blacks in the US

Before endeavoring to answer the question raised above, this chapter will examine the differences between treatment of Indians and Blacks in the US. The Anglo-American liberal was willing to absorb a limited amount of Blacks that would neither critically change the nature of his society nor harm his economic interests. Thus North American states had no particular problem with the Blacks who lived there, and laws were even passed in those states regarding the annulment of slavery. In Southern states, however, whose economy was built on the forced unpaid labor of Black slaves, there was bitter public controversy over the idea of prohibiting slavery. At the time the constitution was written, Southern representatives managed to have their slaves count for 2/3 of a person for the purposes of determining population for state representation in Congress, even though slaves did not possess the right to vote. It was also decided that no changes would be allowed in the slavery laws for twenty years.

Over 80 years passed, and still slavery in the South had not been annulled, until the Dred Scott case rocked the country. Dred Scott was a slave who had moved to a Northern state and been freed by his master, yet he insisted that legally he was a free man even without his former master's consent. The US Supreme Court of the time - ultra-conservative and presided over by a Southerner - ruled that a slave is to be considered property, not a human being, and thus possessing no more rights than a beast to petition the court. This racially discriminatory decision provoked great public outrage that did not subside until after the end of the Civil War, that broke out shortly after.

Why is the American Civil War considered the greatest upheaval in American history? Of course, the enormous number of casualties and the fact that civil wars are always more traumatic to a nation than external wars had a lot to with the severity of this trauma. Yet also significant – was that in addition to the humiliation and defeat that the South suffered, they were also forced to politically absorb the Blacks into their midst. Approximately 100 years later, the Brown vs.

Board of Education Supreme Court decision also required them to integrate their schools, but this chapter will deal with the trauma experienced by the generation of the Civil War. The enforced changes were so disturbing because they forced Southerners to accept into their midst people they considered not only foreign but strange – people whose culture and appearance were different, even if not their religion, people who despite the legal ruling that made them part of the "family" were really not family. The trauma the South experienced is comparable to the trauma that would be experienced in Israel if Jews were forced to accept Palestinians as part of their nation (even if Palestinians would convert to Judaism), instead of maintaining distinct national entities. White Anglo-American's slaves were suddenly – from the political perspective, and later from a social standpoint – transformed into part of the White national entity. This radical social change combined with the devastation it wreaked on the South's economy completely shook up the internal structure of Southern society.

An additional change was the transference of loyalty to the State to ethnic alliances; in both Northern and Southern states in the US primary allegiance was shown to people of the same ethnic origin.[33]

To summarize, it appears that the fundamental Anglo-American attitude towards Blacks for the most part resembled its attitude towards the Indians, though they ultimately played themselves out differently. The Blacks never fought against the Anglo Americans; they couldn't be forced into reserves – there was nowhere to remove them to (though the US returned those who wished to go to Africa, thereby creating Liberia). Since the US was a liberal nation, there was no option other than to include them within the Anglo American people and to grant them all the democratic privileges of American citizens. Even if by law Blacks were equal citizens, they could still be discriminated against, but after serving and sacrificing their lives in two World Wars, Blacks developed a sense of the fundamental rights that were basic to Anglo American culture, and began to demand and receive equal and even preferential treatment (affirmative action - reverse discrimination). It is a process which took over a hundred years and which is not yet complete, as reflected in the fact that the minority of neighborhoods are mixed, and that Black infiltration into a neighborhood will often promptly drive the Whites out.

---

[33] S.N. Eisenstadt, "The First Multiple Modernities: Collective Identities, Public Spheres, and Political Order in the Americas," Chapter II in **Globality and Multiple Modernities – Comparative North American and Latin American Perspectives**, Luis Roniger and Carlos H. Waisman (ed.), (Brighton, Portland: Sussex: Academic Press, to be published shortly).

A Comparison of Fundamental Latin American and Anglo American Characteristics

The two main centers from which people immigrated to America (Britain and the Iberian Peninsula) were vastly different and cultivated major differences in the cultures of these people, differences that only intensified when these people immigrated to America.

As Samuel Eisenstadt explains,[34] Spain and Portugal were characterized by an insistence on the uprooting of all sectarian groups, a prohibition against points of view that did not conform to Church dogma, and a great stress on hierarchy. The culture that Anglo Americans brought with them and developed allowed and facilitated the existence of multiple different religions alongside the British government and the Anglican Church, which only played a secondary role. The government in Latin America, in contrast, did not permit self-government on any level higher than the municipal government. As opposed to the Anglo American colonists who acquired for themselves a status of aristocracy or gentry, and ran most public affairs in freedom, the Latin American colonists were generally adventurers or people seeking advancement in the colonial administration and Catholic Church, both of which played an important role. In the area that became the US, the Anglo American colonists developed their own culture, though in the more northern area that became Canada, the colonists sufficed with adopting European culture. The institution of Spanish-Portuguese hierarchy became more entrenched in Latin America than it had in the colonists` country of origin.[35]

Eisenstadt doesn't offer an explanation for this last phenomenon, just as he doesn't explain the reason why independent culture developed in the US but not in Canada. Regarding the issue of hierarchy in Latin America, presumably Eisenstadt doesn't relate to it explicitly because it is clear to him that the existence of Indians and then Black slaves in Latin America naturally prompted a particular emphasis on hierarchy, as a means of allowing the colonists to express the supremacy of their culture and government over that of the Indians and slaves. As for the cultural difference between the US and Canada, this relates to a lack of political initiative on the part of the French Canadians, a quality that stemmed from Catholic doctrine that imposes no personal religious responsibility, as does Protestantism, but rather revolves around the priest and Pope. Ostensibly, the high percentage of French Catholics in Canada shaped the Canadian culture.

---

[34] Ibid, 11-12.

[35] Ibid, 12.

Eisenstadt notes that there were areas in Latin America where there was some inclination toward democracy, such as Argentina, Uruguay, and Brazil, but the inclination was weak, and considered more of a problem than a solution.[36]

In general, Eisenstadt claims, that cultural differences within Latin America led to a redesign of local customs, languages, and communities, and a blurring of distinctions between the colonists and the natives, while differences between local culture and that of the native countries caused serious tensions. This stands to reason since the Latin American colonist had far greater association with local customs, than with those from his country of origin.[37]

Eisenstadt claims that in the US, in contrast to Latin America and also Canada, there was a strong emphasis on equality and on the objectionable nature of hierarchy.[38] Eisenstadt doesn't explain the reason for this, but it seems relatively self-evident. Once the colonists annihilated the Indians, there was no one to learn the principle of hierarchy from, and in any case there was no longer a multicultural multiracial population in which to establish this hierarchy.

Eisenstadt claims that this lack of hierarchy manifested itself, among other ways, in the absence of an official religion. An official religion is declared only when a hierarchy exists, in order to establish a hierarchy also among the different religions. In this, Eisenstadt makes a serious error, as a dominant religion did develop in the US, though not from the beginning but rather from the end of the 19th century – namely the civil religion.[39]

Only this religion is permitted to participate in the political realm, while all other religions were expected to remain separate from issues of the State. The Anglo-Americans needed to develop a new religion that they hadn't brought or adapted from Europe, or learned from their Latin American brothers. This need didn't exist before America declared its independence from Britain. It stemmed from the very fact, that until the eve of their independence, American colonists were part of the British nation, loyal British subjects, who derived their sense of nationalism from British history and tradition, and who had no interest in altering this situation. The American colonists did not revolt because they felt separate and

[36] Ibid, 14.
[37] Ibid, 15.
[38] **The Religion of the Republic** (Elwyn A. Smith (ed.), Philadelphia: Portress Press, 1971).
[39] William H. Rehnquist, **All the Laws but One – Civil Liberties in Wartime** (New York: Random House, 1998).

distinct from Britain. They revolted for economic reasons, because of a British fundamental principle that there is no taxation without representation, and American colonists did not have representatives in the British Parliament. Upon achieving independence, the colonists were like a ship without a sail – they had won independence from their own nation. The Anglo American colonists needed to forge for themselves a new nationality that would unite their ranks and unite and distinguish them from their British brethren across the sea. Thus, they couldn't adopt Protestantism as a civil religion for two reasons, neither one corresponding to Eisenstadt's claim:

1. Protestantism was the backbone of the British nation.
2. Protestantism was not the religion of the new immigrants, who were not necessarily British.

Nonetheless, it was difficult to declare secularism the new State religion, when almost all Anglo-Americans were religious people.

Thus at the end of the 19th century, a fundamental change took place in the US. Until then students in the public school system had Bible class daily, a custom that was at the base of Protestantism. At the end of the 19th century, court rulings were passed that prohibited the reading of the Bible in public schools. For the purposes of this book, this fact along with the general background outlined until this point are sufficient to demonstrate that the American civil religion preserved a fundamental monotheistic faith, while denying its specific agents any rights to participate in the elections or in any government role, in a religious role and in the name of religion. A Protestant, Jew, or Catholic that runs for office does not do so in the name of his religion, but in the context of the American civil religion that is at the heart of Anglo-American nationalism. This was the new hierarchy that Anglo Americans created.

A separate question is whether Anglo Americans created a cultural motif of strong central government that was not intended by the early colonists. Civil religion was promoted by the Anglo American nation both by the citizens themselves in order to develop their culture by strengthening their sense of nationalism, and by the government – since the Supreme Court's ruling regarding the reading of the Bible in public schools was an act of the central government. The central government again took a strong position regarding the integration of Blacks and discrimination in the Supreme Court case of Brown vs. Board of Education, as it did in the detainment of Japanese Americans during WWII, and again recently in the black out in the media of details of the military action against the Taliban and Bin Ladin. The latter decision may have been supported by public opinion and enjoyed the cooperation and patriotic self-imposed restraints of the media, but it was nevertheless an act of the central government. We witnessed the same phenomenon that Renquist describes during the American Civil War when the right of habeas corpus was temporarily suspended.[40]

According to Eisenstadt's description, Anglo-Americans emphasized acquisitiveness alongside democratic rights.[41] This focus resulted in a difference in material wealth between Anglo Americans and Latin Americans, in the significant disparity between US economic success and its sisters south of it, and even partially in the political unrest in Latin America. There are other factors at play here too, however, in particular the trust in one's fellow man that characterizes Latin American society, that is at the basis of the institution of patronage, and that is essentially lacking in Anglo American society.

Eisenstadt, in analyzing Anglo American culture, speaks about the elimination of any need for hierarchy in the relationship between the government and the governed, since the individual has access – using democratic tools – to the government. He also refers to the phenomenon of weak government found among Anglo-Americans.[42] While he is definitely correct in his assessment that the American government in its early days and in colonial days was weak, this trend was true also in Latin America. If not for this fact, the Spanish government would never have needed all the local patrons or the oligarchies it fostered in order that they help enforce the rule of government in areas not under the domination of the Spanish colonial government. Strong government is characteristic of modern democratic nations. None of the kings in Europe were able to achieve control over the private lives of their subjects. It is democracy that made government strong. In Latin America today, there appears to be no strong government - the Brazilian government is incapable of enforcing public order throughout greater Brazil, and a similar situation exists also in relatively small Latin American countries. It seems that Eisenstadt is not referring to a government that imposes its will and laws in every single place under its jurisdiction, but rather to its aggressiveness and resoluteness. The American government was aggressive and resolute in its treatment of the Indians, and quite naturally solicitous and considerate of those upon whom the government depended – the voters. This is not a phenomenon that was unique to Anglo Americans, but rather one common in all interdependent societal relations. In the entirely theoretical scenario that true democracy were established in Latin America, it is probable that the government would be

[40] See Eisenstadt, note 33 above, p. 15.
[41] Ibid.
[42] Ibid. 20.

considerate of its citizens. Until today, wealthy individuals in Latin America manage quite well to have influence over the government, often with no need for any middleman, union, or party, to mediate between them and the government. The situation in the US is quite similar with the affluent exerting their influence over the politicians in exchange for bankrolling their election campaigns.

Regarding this point though, Eisenstadt adds that the hierarchy that operates in Latin America led to presidential type regimes, in which the president is a quasi father figure who is served by a central bureaucracy. In this respect, Latin America and the US resemble each other considerably, since also in the US the presidency is a prominent institution. The difference is that the US constitution established checks and balances that limit the president's powers. It was inevitable that after years of being ruled by a king – whether Spanish, Portuguese, or British, that Americans would establish a presidency in their country too. In the US, however, where there was no underlying culture of faith in man, a system of checks and balances was created. Therefore, the correlation between the institution of hierarchy and the system of government in Latin America is tenuous and questionable.

Eisenstadt claims that the equality that was a legacy of the Puritans influenced societal interrelations, which in turn had an affect on public and private lives, family and places of work, and on the entire concept of equal citizenship. In Latin America, in contrast, absolute hierarchic principles existed side by side with a blurring of societal distinctions, an inconsistency that led to a legislative-formal blurring too. On the surface everything is equal while in essence, everything is hierarchic – a reality that creates an irreconcilable tension in Latin America.[43]

According to this description, a certain hypocrisy exists then in Latin America that contrasts with an Anglo-American genuineness, a Latin American double talk vs. Anglo-American sincerity. This description is not consistent, however, with American policies toward the Indians and toward the Blacks until the Civil War and even after. Utilitarianism does not always coincide with honesty, just as patronage relations that are based on trust sometimes are connected to sincerity, to the diametric opposite of the 'two facedness' that Eisenstadt attributes to the Latin Americans. The Latin Americans have claimed repeatedly, especially in their

---

[43] Enrico Rodo, Manuel Ugarte, and Jose Vasconcelos draw similar conclusions in the article, "Has it Really Been 500 Years Since the Discovery of America? Historosophy and the Struggle over the Shaping of Latin American Consciousness," Printed in Roniger's anthology located in the Library of Sociology and Humanities in Hebrew University Library in Jerusalem.

philosophy and literature, that they feel spiritually superior to the Anglo-Americans.[44] In fact, Eisenstadt confirms that the racial issue in the US, since it is hierarchic by nature, creates a problem for the ideal of equality. In Brazil, however, ethnic relations pertain to a man's personal sphere, while in the public sphere, Brazilian heritage is viewed as a story of three morally equal races that together create the Brazilian nature. Brazil, consequently, can possess characteristically White, Black, and even Indian traits all at the same time – African rhythm and spirit together with Indian obstinacy and ties to nature, along with White language and government institutions. It combines wholeness, inclusiveness, and hierarchy. Racial ideology is just one of its components.

The situation in North America stands in marked contrast to this fusion of races that characterizes Latin America. The Black and Latin American must adopt the Anglo American culture if he wishes to succeed in the US. Everyone ultimately learns to play by the rules that were written by the "Anglo Americans", whether out of necessity (in political life), out of expediency (in economic life), or as a means of integrating into and being accepted by American society (in leisure). A true look at Latin America and Anglo America must make us question whether the representation of Latin America as a symbol of a hierarchic dictatorship and the US as a symbol of freedom, liberalism, and openness, isn't a reversal of the reality in these countries.

Perception and Fact: Racial Genocide, Equality, Supremacy and Hierarchy:

A short synopsis of basic facts on both halves of the American continent:

1. The Anglo Americans developed a theory of equality, which they don't in fact practice towards new immigrants, preferring instead to completely assimilate them into their already existing political, economic, and social culture.
2. Latin Americans may declare their belief in hierarchy, but interracial and inter-ethnic marriages are more common among Latin Americans than among Anglo Americans.
3. The ability to establish a government whose declared purpose is preservation of equality and of the rights of man was based on the annihilation of the Indians.
4. The US prospered economically because of a culture that encouraged personal achievement and success.
5. The Anglo American's desire for success stands in contrast to the Latin American' aspiration for respect and personal connection.

---

[44] In his book cited in note 30 above.

6. Based on the previous distinction, Latin American thinkers assert the moral supremacy of Latin Americans over materialist Anglo Americans.
7. Autocratic aggressive resolute government is possible and natural in a society that is not democratic. True democracy is not practiced in Latin America, while it is in the US. This is one possible reason while autocratic regimes can exist in Latin America. Another factor is their hierarchic structure that is consistent with Catholic ideology but sharply deviates from the equality promoted by Protestantism.
8. The main difference between Latin and Anglo Americans is that Latin Americans will often be personally intimate with individuals who are on a different hierarchic level, while Anglo Americans preach absolute equality but preserve a distance between races by encouraging personal elitism. Paradoxically, there seems to be greater equality among the former than among the latter.

Chapter C:
Hierarchic Practices in Workers' Corporations in Latin America

The corporative, as seen above, is one of two institutions that express the hierarchic spirit that pervades Latin American society. Within this context, this chapter will discuss workers' unions, focusing on the situation in each of the four countries that were chosen in Chapter I: Mexico, Brazil, Argentina, and Venezuela. Latin America will be studied as a whole, and not each country separately.

Malloy,[45] in his discussion of workers' unions in Latin America, describes how businessmen in Brazil wield both direct and indirect influence over the government, while the workers' unions lack real power to influence to government, even though their contacts with it afford them an image of power. In Columbia and in Chile, the unions are more powerful and have at times even managed to veto certain governmental appointments. As a rule, ties exist between workers' unions and certain parties, with the two offering mutual support and even

[45] Ibid, 127.

sometimes exchange of members. This situation strengthens the trust between the two sides that is the basis for these relationships.[46]

In Argentina, Chile (until Pinochet's military regime), and Venezuela, the workers' unions displayed strength and determination against the government. In Venezuela, the unions opposed Marcus Perez Imenes' dictatorship. The powerlessness of the unions in Mexico and Brazil stemmed from the central government being dominant and not dependent on the workers' unions. As a result, the percentage of workers in these two countries who are members of the unions is approximately 20%, in contrast to 68% in Venezuela, and 34% in Argentina.[47] These statistics definitely reflect the power of the unions in the different countries.

Malloy claims that in Latin America a presidential regime exists which decides certain issues behind the closed doors of the government, but that social groups and workers' unions are involved in some way or another in deciding certain more fundamental issues.[48]

Despite the powerlessness of the unions, the central government in Mexico in the 1920's engaged in the widest land distribution in history (in the history of the White man, but not including Imperial China in which larger land distributions took place – Y.C.). Unions also did not play any role in creating the governments' strong orientation to development of industries and encouragement of investments and initiatives in Mexico after the great land reformation, and in Brazil during the military rule after 1964. All this reflects the limited powers of the workers' unions in Mexico and Brazil in the latter half of the twentieth century.[49] Even more so, it demonstrates the lack of interest political leaders showed for populism and for the will of the people, when they were confident that their policies were in the best interest of the State. This was characteristic of Mexico and Brazil upon the rise of strong government – in the period being surveyed -- in contrast to Latin American countries – such as Uruguay - that were dependent on the masses, in which democracy was a powerful force. In Uruguay, close to 30% of the labor force is employed by the central government, and bureaucratic institutions are so developed that up to 30% of the population lives off of government pensions, and

[46] Ibid, 133.
[47] Ibid, 136.
[48] Ibid, 139.
[49] Ibid, 140.

many are employed in cushy undemanding positions. The general approach there is to give something to almost everyone.[50]

Malloy concludes his analysis of government powers and the corporative by saying that it is utterly ludicrous to claim with regard to Latin America that the existence of a despotic government is inevitable. It is precisely the confrontation between groups that create the corporative and patronage in Latin America. The political parties are not absolutely irrelevant, but they are also not key players in determining the nature of political and social life. Many other institutions, including unions and patronage related powers, as well as administrative ruling powers that are not based on personal relationships help define political and social life.[51]

The government maintains careful control over the considerably influential union to insure that they remain friends rather than foes. The various laws pertaining to this matter that have been passed in the different Latin American countries can be divided into three categories:

1. Establishment of unions by the State.
2. Subsidization of unions by the State.
3. Supervision of union activity by the State.

In a study of laws passed between 1905-1974 in ten Latin American countries, laws were found that mandated the membership, in recognized unions, of people who were not at all members of these unions. In this manner, these unions were given the monopolistic right to represent the workers in specific branches of labor. Other laws established forums of union representatives of different areas and classes, State financing of union activities, as well as legal guidelines regarding government supervision of union demands, union elections, and direct involvement and supervision over union affairs.[52]

The actual relations between the government and workers' unions depend upon the extent of the government's need for the workers' support. In Argentina, therefore, in the period post-1943, workers wielded considerable influence over the government because Juan Peron's regime relied on their support. The degree of their influence also depends on how industrialized the country is becoming, since workers' unions in Latin America help strengthen paternalistic relationships

[50] Ibid, 142-143.
[51] Ibid, 494.
[52] Ibid, 500-502.

between workers and management. In the context of these relations, it has transpired in Latin America that workers demanded and received a portion of the industry's profits.

The strength of the unions grows when they succeed in acquiring an exclusive monopoly over representation of the workers in a certain area of labor. The government will occasionally grant a right of representation to a specific union, and not to others. Connected to this phenomenon, is legalized compulsory membership in a specific union. Such laws placed certain unions under its protection, and of course insured that their activities were consistent with the loyalty they owed to the government. The government also granted subsidies to union leaders and unemployment payments, in efforts to increase loyalty and dependency. The government attempted to achieve this goal also through opposite means, by limiting the right to strike, establishing who may serve as union leader, and mandating the right of a government official to participate in and run union meetings. All these laws, combined with prohibitions against certain unions, granted the government significant power in different Latin American countries, a quasi-self-established patronage that was consistent with concepts of patrons and clients so deeply rooted in Latin American culture.[53]

Chapter D:
The Transition from Revolution to Democracy in Brazil and Argentina

Brazil:

According to Linz and Stephan's description,[54] the military government in Brazil that was established on March 31, 1064 collapsed. The military generals were simply incapable of running a country, certainly a mammoth country of millions of inhabitants and vast territories such as Brazil. In 1974, General Ernesto Geisel was ceremoniously chosen to be president of Brazil. He declared his intent to find partners for his government from within the civilian population in his country, a goal, which he then implemented while checking any excessive assumptions of freedom. Yet once democracy saw a crack, there was no stopping it, and presidentialelections were held. On March 15, 1990 (a symbolic date for democracy, the day the Emperor Julius was murdered in Rome for the sake of

[53] See Linz and Stepan's book, **Problems of Democratic Transition and Consolidation**, in note 9 above.
[54] Ibid, 166-172.

democratic rule), President Fernando Kolor De-Melo entered office. Six years prior to this democratic election, civilian parties, which had organized under the platform of 'Direct Elections Now' were engaged in political debate with the united hierarchic military regime. The military agreed to a gradual transfer of power but adamantly insisted that direct elections not be held. Thus indirect elections were held in 1983 and in 1985, when the elected president quit before entering office. The vice president, who was a member of the party that supported the military, and had been the compromise candidate, became president, though 75% of Brazilians wanted him to leave office. Six cabinet ministers were military officers so in essence the military ruled together with the president. An anti-government strike was held, and the military considered sending military forces to break the strike. Under pressure from the military, the relevant committee ratified a constitution that preserved the military's autonomy and established the branches of government in such a way that that the president was dependent on parliament, similar to the French constitution in the French Fifth Republic.

Kolor, elected through the new system, received only 5% of the votes in Parliament, yet he sought to govern against their will, thus creating an impasse in the government. When Kolor was found guilty of various criminal offenses, the Parliament ousted him, and his vice president, Itamar Franco, considered an uninspiring personality, replaced him until the 1994 elections in which Cardozo was elected. Cardozo was more successful in working together with the Parliament.

Considering this background, it is no wonder that in 1992 only 42% of Brazilians preferred democratic rule, while 46% either preferred military rule or were impartial.[55]

Linz and Stepan blame Brazil's failure to emend its constitution on the interests of small parties, which dominate in the Parliament. They don't examine the Brazilian people's apathy in this matter, which starkly contrasts to their efforts to abolish slavery over 100 years ago. This inaction seems to stem from a lack of national unity and confidence. Abolition of slavery was a much simpler feat since it was consistent with the interests of most Brazilians. Brazilians were inspired by America's abolition of slavery and also were able to realize their own desire to free themselves from oligarchic rule by freeing the slaves. Now that democracy has officially been established in Brazil, there is no longer anyone against whom to revolt and Brazilians feel insufficient impetus to collectively work towards

[55] Ibid, 190-204.

extracting themselves from the political mess that small interest groups, like the military, have entangled them in.

Brazilian political torpor has been so great that Brazilians even failed to free themselves from military rule and instead waited for a decision by the military. Their continued apathy even after they became a formally democratic country should be viewed as a general internal national weakness that is linked to weaknesses in their democratic education, an educational system that lacks any great appeal.

It is reasonable to posit that Latin Americans, as they are represented by Brazil, are more interested in their practical personal lives than in the political arena – in sharp distinction from their Anglo-American cousins. Latin Americans may perhaps be described as people who miss the forest for the trees while elitist Anglo Americans may be depicted as people who miss the trees for the forest.

Argentina

According to Linz and Stephan's portrayal,[56] a military regime ruled in Argentina between 1976-1983, which engaged in terror against its own citizens, in order to keep them in line and was ultimately also bankrupt from an economic viewpoint. Many people disappeared – in reality were secretly murdered. The military forbade the existence of any political parties and of course did not hold elections. It made no attempt to transfer control of the government to civilians, as was done in Brazil. Instead of engaging in any form of economic or political reform, the army sought to stir national Argentinean pride through a military operation in the Faulkland Islands. Their military operation, however, instead enabled British Prime Minister Margaret Thatcher to send in a British army that defeated the Argentinean army.

The Argentinean general resigned as a result, and his replacement, General Dimos became president until elections were held a year and a half later and a civilian president was elected. The military was tried for their many criminal acts. Between April 1987 and January 1990, four military coupes were attempted by middle ranked officers who did not want to accept the humiliation to the military institution. President-elect Alfonsin, in an attempt to focus on rebuilding the economy and nation, agreed to certain concessions that raised the military's morale. Alfonsin, who already suffered serious opposition from the Peronists who were very connected to the workers' unions, lost even more political power as a result of these concessions. In 1987, Alfonsin lost the majority that he had held in

[56] Ibid, 190-195.

Parliament. In June 1988, only 12% of the population continued to support Alfonsin, while 49% advocated restoration of the military regime. In June 1989, Alfonsin resigned at a time of 'hyper-inflation' in Argentina, though by June 1992, economic analysts declared that Argentina was finally emerging from a 60-year economic recession.

The newly elected president, Menem, began his term in office with a general pardon of the entire military. When shortly afterward, in October 1989, middle ranked military officers attempted to revolt, Menem joined forces with the army general, and together they suppressed the rebellion and tried the insurgents both for military insubordination and for treason. Menem was elected with 49% of the vote, yet during his first three years he enjoyed the support of the Peronists and workers' unions who refrained entirely from striking, after holding 13 general strikes during Alfonsin's term in office. At the beginning of Menem's term, 72% of Argentineans were hopeful about the recovery of the Argentinean economy, and only 15% advocated returning to military rule (in contrast to Brazil where the percentage was much higher). Menem also enjoyed the support of wealthy businessmen, and he attempted to introduce a new economic plan that was not to the liking of the professional unions who had been among his strongest initial supporters since it reduced their profits. Timing worked in Menem's interest – Menem took office just as the global economic crisis was ending and were searching for new horizons and investments. Menem dealt with the workers' unions in classic Latin American style, and as was particularly common in Brazil and Mexico. He used his presidential powers to determine which professional unions would be legal and which illegal, to break up unions that insisted on continuing to strike, and even to control and oversee union funds.

Yet, even though Menem faced only weak opposition from the unions, his economic plan was not much more successful than his predecessor's. In February 1991, fearing a second epidemic of hyper-inflation in his country, Menem chose a new financial minister whom he sent to Parliament to enlist its aid and the support of all the public and agricultural sectors in Argentina in the war against inflation. The Peronists held the majority in Parliament at the time, but public support for the government's economic policies rose from 16% to 68% in the capital city of Buenos Aires. In 1992, public optimism regarding the effectiveness of the Argentinean government also increased.[57]

Linz and Stepan cite the opinion of Guillermo O'Donell who describes the political battle in the years 1955-1966 as an impossible battle, since the Peronists

[57] Ibid, 196-200.

who were the majority received no political power once in government, while the radicals who lost the elections enlisted and received the backing of the military. This political trend came to an end when Alfonsin, a radical, won the elections, and Menem, the Peronist, demonstrated that he was not acting in the narrow interests of the workers' unions who had voted for him, but in the general interest. The military's strength was undermined by the events in the Faulklands. The workers' unions ceased supporting the president they had voted into office because of his disregard for their interests. The time had come for democratic politics that were not based on the Latin American system of unions and loyalties. The age of democracy had finally arrived.[58]

The crisis of 2002 demonstrated that contrary to Linz and Stepan's claim, Argentina could not completely sever itself from the Latin-American way, and adopt the Anglo-American approach. Argentina cannot deny its Latin American heritage, and personal relationships, and trust will always be more important to Latin Americans than economic success and advantage. Thus the 'unadulterated' democracy that Linz and Stepan propose doesn't seem compatible with Latin American culture.

Linz and Stepan present various examples in which President Menem circumvented both the law and the constitution. He took advantage of his expanded executive powers during a state of emergency to legislate various laws, which he was required to subsequently submit to Parliament for their ratification, but which he generally did not. He packed the Supreme Court with judges who shared his views. He turned a blind eye to the corrupt practices of close advisors. He established a new court with jurisdiction over all criminal activities of government officials including himself, and rewarded loyal friends with lifetime appointments to the court. The media didn't dare express much criticism of Menem, and the culture of fear that had existed during Alfonsin and ended in the beginning of Menem's term again ruled over the media. Though the Argentinean constitution prohibited electing a president to a second term, Menem convinced a Parliament in which he didn't have a majority to amend the constitution through covert means that included convincing his opponent to drop out of the race.

Linz and Stepan's description is a disheartening one that only seems confirmed by the economic crisis of 2002 that followed Menem's presidential terms. The question that remains to be answered is what future is to be anticipated for Latin

---

[58] Michael Hechter, **Internal Colonialism, The Celtic Fringe in British National Development 1536-1966** (Berkeley and Los Angeles: University of California Press).

America, and is it possible for each of the Latin American countries to develop independently, both economically and democratically.

Chapter E:
Nationalism in America

Primordial and Political Nationalism:
Most of Western writing on the subject of nationalism is a product of the 20th century. Very little was written on this topic outside of the West, except for what was written about Asian countries from a Western perspective.

Western writing has proposed realistic, material, utilitarian, primarily non-emotional causes of nationalism that have little to do with ethnic factors. Some examples are:

1. The model of internal imperialism, which is based in Max Weber's theory regarding the economically and industrially deprived periphery.[59]
2. The model of nationalism as a utilitarian system that a person either does or doesn't adopt depending on how well it serves his interests, which is led by the society's elites and not by all the members of the group that is to be declared a nation.[60]
3. The model of ability and economic interest as primary factors in the formation of a nation. According to this model, a nation is formed only if the group possesses the necessary economic capability, and the establishment of a distinct nation is in the group's interest.[61]

---

[59] Ronald Rogowski, "Causes and Varieties of Nationalism: A Rational Account," in **New Nationalisms of the Developed West: Toward Explanation** (Boston: Allen % Unwin, 1985) p. 87.
[60] Hudson Meadwell, "Ethnic Nationalism and Collective Choice Theory," in **Comparative Political Studies** (1989) p. 54.
[61] Ernst B. Haas, **Nationalism, Liberalism, and Progress** (Ithaca, NY and London: Cornell University Press, 1997).

4. The model of discrimination and discontentment that follows from Max Weber's system. According to this model, a group will establish a separate national framework only if overcome by feelings of group discrimination.[62]

The German Max Weber[63] who wrote in the beginning of the 21st century considered the roots of nationalism to be economic. He initiated a German national discussion that promoted German imperialism and disassociated itself from the issue of democracy. Ernest Gelner,[64] another notable writer on this subject, who wrote in the US in a later period than Weber, based his theory on economic forces that stemmed from modernization and from the development of industry on the basis of a democratic society with a modern advanced culture. He considered discrimination a necessary impetus in the formation of a nation. A later star in the study of nationalism who completed yet also opposed Gelner's theories, was Benedict Anderson.[65] Anderson claimed that the printing industry played a primary role in promoting nationalism by creating a uniform written language that was widely distributed and that unified similar dialects and languages into one language. The industry's goal was to increase its profits by widening the distribution of its printed materials. At the same time, it managed to create a single entity out of wider communities that were united by virtue of common language, common literature, similar ways of thinking, common likes, dislikes, fears, and objects of disdain, thereby facilitating the creation of larger national entities, which constituted the basis for the establishment of large modern states with populations in the millions. According to Gelner's theory, private business and industrial business interests created modern states. Anderson proposed the opposite theory of the modern state as the stimulus, which established advanced industries. According to this theory, the large and developed source of manpower that is essential for industrial growth can only be supplied by a modern state that has the means of establishing public school systems that offer a sufficiently high education to prepare people for these jobs. Therefore, the modern state supported industry and enabled the development of capitalistic industrial interests in the modern world. In this way, of course, the state itself became modernized, and was compensated with modern industry, that led the state to become modern and

---

62 "Max Weber and German Sociology," in Max George Weber, **Economy and Society, Vol. I** (London: Routledge, 1992) p. 385.

63 Ernst Gelner, **Nations and Nationalism** (Tel Aviv: Open University, 1994).

64 Benedict Anderson, **Conceptual Models of Societies: Reflections on the Roots and Spread of Nationalism**, Translated from the English by Dan Daor (Tel Aviv: Open University, 2000).

65 Seymour Martin Lipset, **Continental Divide – The Values and Institutions of the United States and Canada** (New York: Routledge, 1990) pp. 3, 14, 52, 53.

successful. All these political thinkers, as a rule, do not base the nationalism they have witnessed on ethnic-historical-emotional-or primordial sources – which will be referred to here as 'deep-rooted nationalism'. Deep-rooted nationalism can sustain itself even without economic and political interests and forces. The other form of nationalism will be termed here – 'political nationalism' since it comes about according to the interests of the state that seeks to strengthen its sense of nationalism. In the absence of a deep-rooted nationalism that corresponds to the basic framework of the state, the state promotes a sense of nationalism, whether directly or indirectly, whether as a bureaucratic act or whether by academics, writers, poets, and the like, all acting from different motivations, and not always with the awareness that they are helping create a nation that coincides with the civilian population in the state. Taking Israel as an example:

1. From the outset, the state was declared a Jewish state, a state for the Jewish people.
2. Representatives of the Zionist movement, the Jewish nation's national movement in the diaspora, and representatives of the Jewish settlement in the land in which the state of Israel was established, a population of people of Jewish descent living in the territory of the State, declared the establishment of the State of Israel in Israel's Declaration of Independence.
3. The state was established through the efforts of the Zionist settlers, the Zionists, and members of the Jewish nation's national movement.
4. The Jewish nation is an entity that lives in the consciousness of anyone born to Jewish parents, through the blood relation that has existed over thousands of years.
5. The Jewish people share a common distinct religion, a long history, a separate culture, an ancient tongue, and territorial aspirations to live in their ancient homeland (an aspiration that for many years was expressed only in prayer and no practical steps were taken to implement). This ancient homeland is located in the place that the State of Israel was established.
6. This state is inhabited also by Arabs who have lived there hundreds of years, and who began to experience a national awakening as the Palestinian people. These Arabs, along with neighboring Arab countries fought against the establishment of the Jewish state, while the Jews fought for its establishment.
7. Approximately 50 years after the establishment of the State of Israel, debate has ensued over whether an 'Israeli nation' exists that is composed of the citizens of the State of Israel (political nationalism), or whether two nationalities – deep-rooted ones, based on ethnic-religious ties (deep-rooted or primordial nationalism) exist in Israel. Those who claim and advocate a political nationalism cite the American-French idea of Israel being 'a country of all its citizens'. It

should be recalled that both the French people and the American people are 'synthetically formed' nations, which strengthen their respective States.

It thus emerges that the nationalism in all American countries is a political nationalism, with the exception of countries – like Mexico – which are united by some ancient tradition (in Mexico – Indian tradition). Further on, the question will be discussed certainly with regard to Mexico, of whether an approach that unites not only people with Indian blood but also those with Spanish blood is true deep-rooted nationalism, or in fact political nationalism disguised as deep-rooted.

In the context of this question it will be possible to identify – with regard certainly to specific Latin American countries – which type of political nationalism exists, and what factors led to it – discrimination, economic interest, domestic imperialism, or some other factor not previously suggested. This book will evaluate the nature of the nationalism in Latin America and also attempt to predict what lies in Latin America's future.

US Nationalism

This subject will only be dealt with briefly, since the focus here is Latin America, and the US is mainly discussed in order to contrast it to Latin America.

1. The English colonists in America had a need to create a distinctive identity that would distinguish them from the English in Britain.
2. Religion posed a problem for them, so they established the American civil religion.
3. The question of who should be included within the nation was a difficult one, which was ultimately resolved by the exclusion of the Indians and inclusion (particularly following the Civil War) of the Blacks.
4. They lacked a shared national experience – The War of Independence provided this factor.
5. They required shared traditions and legacies – and so legends developed around the writing of the constitution and the Philadelphia convention, the birthdays of great American leader became national holidays, Christmas became an American holiday, the national flag and American Independence day were stressed, and traditional parades were held.
6. English was chosen as the national language.
7. The Americans sought a unifying spiritual idea, one that was derived from English thought but had a distinctly American style. The democratic-political structure of government and legal institutions played an important role in this, and individualism and liberalism were advanced as aspects of the unique American spirit. The puritanical notion of a chosen land – America – and of a chosen nation

– the American people – as well of a spiritual mission – of America's role as the champion of civil rights throughout the world (from which followed its support for the establishment of the UN, the Korean and Vietnam war, and American involvement in Somalia and Bosnia) were all reinforced. These ideals, combined with Protestant influence and emphasis on reading and knowing the Bible, formed the basis for the development of Black spiritualistic music, and for basic support for: the State of Israel – as the tie between the American 'Chosen nation' founded in the spirit of the Bible, and the original Biblical Chosen nation, the Jewish people, and for the Jewish people's return to their 'promised land' (that paralleled America as a promised land). It is these ideas that lie behind Anglo-American support for Israel, and not material or political interests.

This last issue is the source of the differences between American government policies towards Israel and Western European ones. Western Europeans did not need to form a new nationalism, since they already had one. The question of whether what is being spoken of is separate French, German, Italian, Dutch, and Belgian nationalities, each around 200 years old, or of a 2000-year old unified culture and tradition (as emerges from the economic and political unification of Western Europe) is not within the scope of this book, though in general in relates to the broader discussion of political nationalism vs. deep-rooted nationalism.

Canadian Nationalism

Strong Catholic influence existed in Canada, in comparison to the US. Therefore, the political approach that developed there was more consistent with French-Catholic hierarchy and loyalty to the British crown. Canada also developed around a certain conservatism and belief in the divine source of group rights and liberties (in contrast to the individual rights and individualism promoted in the US) that prompted groups to seek to preserve their distinct traditions (French Canadians in Quebec even sought to distance themselves from French activities in France that went against their religion[66]). There is a theory (that will not be examined at length here) that does not seem implausible that Canada is an alliance of two religions, Protestantism and Catholicism. The school system is built religiously, as a dualistic separate system, in which each of the two religions has a separate educational system for itself. The Anglo-American belief in separation of Church and State was not accepted in Canada. Thus, while in the US, parents of a Catholic child attending a Catholic school must pay full private school tuition, in Canada such schooling would be paid for by the State. An element of fundamentalism, of religiosity, therefore, exists in Canada – an element that didn't

---

[66] Ashutosh Varshney, "Contested Meanings: India's National Identity, Hindu Nationalism, and the Politics of Anxiety," in **Daedalus** (Summer 1993) pp. 227-261.

develop as a means of creating a distinct Canadian national identity, but which does define Canadian nationality and is one of its components.
The form of government between provinces is also a product of the same alliance of religions, and it too serves as a natural, genuine aspect of Canadian tradition.
The connection to the British monarchy, and the idea of a government appointed by the British king or queen – though by the recommendation of the Canadian government – also plays a role.
The distinctiveness from the US is also a fundamental one, part of the Canadian national tradition. Fundamental to the process of nationalism is the act of distancing the arising national entity from some external body. An enemy nation will inspire the greatest instincts for natural disassociation and national distinctiveness, yet any foreign entity can suffice. The British nation was formed in this manner, with the French king being a historic enemy from whom the British felt estranged since he was Catholic. Though the US did not represent an enemy nation to the Canadians, Canadians did feel a sense of superiority to their Anglo-American neighbors.

Mexican Nationalism
The Mexican nation was formed approximately 70 years ago as a fusion of Indian and modern traditions. Their conception of death has Indian and Spanish roots, while their legends of creation are Aztec and their stories of bullfights, Spanish. The institution of patronage has its roots in Spain, though its fine points are derived from conquest and the conqueror`s feelings of superiority and from ethnic differences.

Intermarriage in Mexico is part of Mexican heritage. It was neither brought from Spain, nor in existence among the Aztecs, but it is rather a fundamentally Mexican phenomenon that developed in Mexico – not in order to create a distinctive Mexican national identity but because it is truly Mexican. Therefore, the legend of the maiden from Guadalope Is not an Indian story that was adopted by the Mexicans, since the Mexicans on a whole have Indian blood. The fact that there aren`t distinct races and ethnic groups in Mexico proves that their ethnic nationalism developed authentically. It still remains to be determined definitively, though, whether their nationalism is deep-rooted or political, since even though deep-rooted nationalism generally develops naturally and political nationalism is artificial and imposed, there is another factor that must be considered – that of age. Deep-rooted nationalism is generally particularly connected to an ancient civilization. A relatively new trend does not generally carry enough weight to have an effect on nationalism – a phenomenon linked to history. A nation would not be defined by a passing fad. Certainly a custom that is shared by a community, which has existed for a length of time that is not measurable by historical units of time, cannot be considered as defining a nation, for nationalism is essentially a historical term that can be quantified and measured – when the time comes – by the court of history.

For example: the Germanic tribes that reached France and Germany, in their migrations and in the process of their settlement, do not appear to be, from a historical perspective, nations or peoples. They served a function in the process of forming a nation. Though they all originated in the same place, those who settled in France are known as Frenchmen while those who settled in Germany are known as Germans. Regarding the historical dimension that is essential for the test of nationalism, it is even reasonable, as mentioned above, to view the French and Germans as members of a common nationality, along with the Dutch, Belgians, British, Italians, and Spanish, since from a historical perspective they resemble family members who have quarreled, but who share a common culture. After all the wars between them, including two 'world wars' that truly seem more like domestic wars of Christian White man than international wars, the European nations reached the conclusion that all their internal quarrels lack relevance. Thus, it can be said that the many wars fought between the English and French, like those between the French and Germans were not expunged by the conciliation but by the conclusion that the wars lack relevance.

According to this understanding, we will see that a Mexican nation exists, but that it is likely though far from certain, that it will be absorbed by an Pan-Latin American nation, the realization of a deep-rooted nationalism that can unite countries above the heads of their heads of State.

Venezuelan Nationalism

Similar to the US, it was not the culture of the Venezuelan natives that influenced the dominant culture in the country, but rather the European culture of the immigrants. Of course there are several differences between the US and Venezuela:

1. Europeans who came to Venezuela from Spain did not feel superior to immigrants who came from other European countries, and new immigrants felt no obligation to adopt any new cultural practices other than language. It is possible to attribute this to the fact that the Spanish culture of the immigrants was not elitist, and the immigrants who arrived in the 1940's and later were perceived as skilled professionals of high social stature.
2. There are no racial groups in Venezuela that are considered innately lower class (Indians, Blacks).

3. As a result of the Spanish culture's lack of domination, and the economic boom that resulted from the discovery of oil, it was quite natural for the Venezuelans to adopt aspects of non-European cultures, and thus an 'international' culture rapidly began to infiltrate Venezuela, a culture that seemed consistent with the modernization that had so captivated Venezuelans.

The first conclusion that follows is that an overwhelmingly natural process is taking place by which Venezuela adopts aspects that are a blend of cultural influences. This is a process that is unique though it its substance lacks uniqueness – since it adopts practices from varying sources, while mixing and blurring their roots. Considering Venezuela's connection to and solidarity with other Latin American countries, the question arises whether this diversity doesn't define the Pan-Latin American nation, a nation that is in the process of being formed. This is a topic that has far more questions than answers.

Brazilian Nationalism

Brazilian nationalism is now approaching its 120th birthday (from the time of the liberation of its slaves), making it older than Mexican nationalism, and closer in age to Anglo-American nationalism. The fact that Portuguese is the official language in Brazil, as opposed to Spanish, and that from the time of Napoleon, Brazil was not a colony but an independent country are other factors that distinguish Brazil from other Latin American nations. Brazil, again in contrast to other Latin American countries was not first settled with the goal of spreading Catholicism throughout the world. Its size, in terms of geographical dimensions and population are two other distinguishing qualities, all of which form a basis for building a nation.

Brazil's population is made up of Whites, who are the majority, and Blacks. Intermingling of the races is not ideologically mandated, but it is a reality. Patronage, a strong Spanish tradition, is a well-developed institution in Brazil. Brazilians are overwhelmingly pessimistic regarding the economic situation, and lacking in confidence that democracy will benefit them in this regard. They have little faith in the future, and except for carnivals and soccer, there is little that inspires strong feelings of unity. It is difficult to build a nation without an elevation of the spirit, inspiration, or a feeling of ascendancy, uniqueness, or mission. All these are lacking – for the most part – in Brazil. No individual or group possesses a sense of strength. The government is hierarchic as is common in Latin America, and there is no hope that the government or any other body has the ability to provide salvation. The small percentage of workers that belong to a professional union is a reflection of the lack of societal faith that exists in Brazil.

Therefore, despite the distinctiveness of the Brazilian people, no process of nation building has occurred. Brazilians are essentially citizens without a great deal of hope, and without a clear future, even though the central government has managed to reasonably stabilize the economy and there is no societal breakdown like in Argentina. A clear picture of the situation in Brazil has yet to be drawn, but any conclusive determinations will be left to the conclusion of the discussion of nationalism in Latin America at the end of this chapter.

Argentinean Nationalism

Argentina is a tale of class struggles and political conflict. The army has played a significant role in this story, enabling a minority to rule over the country for long periods of time. The collectivism that in other Latin American countries assumed a gentle form of currying favor with the central government, served in Argentina a basis for an internal rift. The population is almost entirely of European origin, the majority from Spain, and some from Italy. The absence of any obvious characteristic distinguishing one group from another, and thereby justifying hierarchic superiority has had a destructive influence, creating a hostile competitive atmosphere. The military too has adopted an aggressive confrontational approach, and the number of people secretly abducted and murdered by the army has only deepened the internal rift – not only between citizens, but also between the citizens and the army.

Nationalism is a sense of unity. To the extent it exists in Argentina, it does not manifest itself in a positive constructive manner, but rather in demonstrations of violence and superiority on the part of those who consider themselves the elite towards other classes who do not accept their authority or superiority.[67] The hierarchic structure of Argentina was thrown into confusion by policies adopted by President Menem, a Peronist who acted against the interest of the Peronist professional unions, who had voted him into office. He did so because of his connection to big businesses and his hopes to use them to pull Argentina out of a 60-year economic crisis – that had resulted from a sectoral government practices – both with landowners and the anti-Peronist labor movement. While Menem's willingness to break with the tradition of serving the interests of the sector that has offered him political support is commendable, his policies which were based on economic benefit rather than sectoral interest are more consistent with an Anglo-American approach than with a Latin American one. This fact was at the

---

[67] Luis Roniger and Mario Sznajder, The Legacy of Human-Rights Violations in the Southern Cone – Argentina, Chile, and Uruguay (Oxford, New York: Oxford University Press, 1999) pp. 236-237.

root of the last economic crisis, though plenty of economic crises took places under governments following the more traditionally Latin American approach.

Apparently, no system can succeed when there is societal discord and division. When a society is sick, its economy is doomed to failure, regardless of whether its central government is following objectively 'sound' economic principles or whether it is acting in the interest of one sector and with utter disregard for the interests of the general economy. It emerges that the true problem in Argentina is social, rather than economic.

Before a state can be run, a society must be run or built. Social leadership must firstly consider the social obstacles and demonstrate leadership in tackling them. The leadership must invest energy in inculcating the younger generation with the value of societal unity in a society that is fundamentally egalitarian, or with steering hierarchic values in a Latin American society towards charity to those who are considered inferior, as is done in Chinese society. Such generosity is compatible with Latin American values, as is reflected in Mexican and Brazilian efforts to free their slaves - but it has faded in recent generations particularly in Argentina.
Thus Argentina is ailing since it is a nation is in the process of fragmentation rather than unification.

What Characterizes Latin American Nationalism
So many Western, African and other countries are endeavoring to establish their own nations – not capriciously – but because feelings of nationalism are a country's source of strength, without which it is destined to disintegrate. Western Europe's efforts to unite, therefore, are a clear indication that the nationalistic sense in each of the individual Western European nations is in the process of crumbling or at least weak. Western Europe is seeking to revitalize itself by creating a political nationalism that can take the place of a non-existent deep-rooted nationalism.

1. A serious problem exists both with the imperialist borders that separate the African states and those that divide the Arab states. These states were not formed on the basis of deep-rooted social (primordial) differences, yet the states are very cautious not to open any Pandora's box by breaching any of these borders. This pretense is maintained because it is in the common interest of all the governments. This same pretense is maintained in Latin America and is reinforced by the many interconnected interests that exist within each state. Even the media is recruited in order to deeply implant this rootless, political nationalism.

2. There is an opposing side that must be considered also. It has been demonstrated here that the story of the Mexican people is not a façade, a popular invention, but a true story. The emancipation of the slaves in Brazil was a real event, not a fabrication thought up in order to create a nation where one did not exist. Yet even though nationalism is an abstract reality, a matter of faith, nearly almost every Venezuelan citizen will emphatically affirm the existence of a Venezuelan nation. His answer will be less clear-cut if asked his feelings about Latin Americanism, and about his connection to Latin America. There were political thinkers who shared Simone Bolivar's perceptions regarding the unity of all Latin Americans.

It is important to emphasize before taking this discussion any further that nationalism is a subjective conception that can not be established according to objective concrete facts [that is why there is no point in arguing that the Palestinian nation does not truly exist, since the very claim for its existence was made as the anti-thesis to an exclusive Jewish nationalism. The only relevant question is how do the 'Palestinian people' view themselves and feel?]. Yet, in addition to the determining subjective side, there is an objective reality that can be examined as a portent of what lies ahead?

In regard to Western Europe, for example, certain objective facts indicated that unification was likely, just as the ties between Bush and Putin are likely to be the foundation of an alliance that is part of the nation of White Christian man, and not simply the relations of two former enemies trying to reconcile. A careful reading of the world map, an analysis of potential common US-Russian enemies or factors that will threaten their economic supremacy, combined with an assessment of the ethnic-religious history that plays such a significant role in building nationalism, will demonstrate the great likelihood, or even certainty of such a possibility.

The same question applies with relation to Latin America, after comparing certain basic Anglo American fundamental concepts to Latin American ones – is it possible, and even very likely that Latin America is already in the midst of the establishment of one united nation.

When the US declared its independence, there were thirteen colonies that established a confederacy between them, or in other words perceived themselves as thirteen independent political entities, which shared one congress. The colonies had their differences and their separate interests. Some were more puritanical than others, some supported slavery while others opposed it – yet it was possible to ascertain at the time that their unification was not only possible but certain.

It is the institutions of patronage, corporatism, hierarchy, and a society built on personal commitments and trust and an estrangement from the English conception of democracy based on parties that do not necessarily act according to self-interest, the willingness to use the army to topple a democratic government in a time of crisis, and the preference for a presidential form of government- all in combination with the special mixes of Indians and Blacks and interracial marriages that do not contradict the feelings of hierarchy – all these aspects and more that create the uniquely Latin American rhythm that any outsider would have trouble comprehending but that will be the basis for a unified Latin American nation.

In addition, however, to the objective reality, there is the matter of internal national strength and ability to endure in times of trouble and turmoil. This internal strength is related to how deeply-rooted feelings of solidarity with the State are, and to what lengths the citizens of the State will go in order to contribute to the State over and above their civic duties – to what extent they are 'rooted citizens with a national consciousness and readiness to give to their country over and above what is demanded by law.[68]

An additional assessment that must be made is how well the citizens of the country have proven themselves in the past. Cuba, for example, showed great strength in standing up to the US, and in standing firm even when Russia withheld aid in the early 90's creating such an economic crisis that there wasn't even gasoline for cars to run on and they were compelled to start riding bicycles instead of automobiles and to adopt a system of food rationing of fewer than 2000 calories per person. Other Latin American countries have not held up as well as Cuba. While most maintained stability so long as the government had the means to provide a certain minimal standard of living to most of its citizens, as soon as economic problems arose that were far less severe than those Cuba endured, internal terror, uprisings, and riots erupted. In Cuba, in contrast, the people stood loyally behind their charismatic leader, Fidel Castro.[69]

---

[68] Yehuda Cohen, Who Fears a Jewish State?: An Ideological and Legal Perspective (Tel Aviv: Legal Association Press, 2001) Chapter VI.

[69] Mario Sznajder and Luis Roniger, Politics, Social Ethos, and Identity in Contemporary Cuba (Jerusalem: The Hebrew University of Jerusalem: The Harry S. Truman Research Institute for the Advancement of Peace, 2001, a publication no. 15 of Gitelson Peace Peace Publication, January 2001)

What Differences Are There Between US Nationalism and Latin American Nationalism?

Both nationalities are political ones, and both nations are composed of all the citizens in their respective countries. While a certain degree of 'discrimination' takes place in both countries, the Anglo-American seeks to deny the existence of bigotry in his country, while the Latin American feels no compulsion to do so.
It is likely, however, that this situation will change if and when the Latin American countries unify into one nation.
The conditions for inclusion in a particular nation will not be based on political borders, since the nation will not be the outgrowth of a certain country or countries, but of a culture, a tradition, a uniquely Latin American approach to social interaction, a common history, language, and religion. Since Latin Americanism will be rooted in fundamental traits, rather than political interests, there won't be a need for a system of separation of Church and State. Since Latin American culture derived so much from Catholicism, Catholicism will naturally become the dominant religion. The shared history is one of similar circumstances and realities that ultimately led to the establishment of military regimes, which were backed by the US because they suited her political global interests and her economic interests (the critical factor as always in shaping American policy).[70]

In general, nationalism that is based in deep-rooted fundamentals (ethnicity, integration of ethnic groups, a long shared history, significant events that constituted pivotal national experiences) is generally also connected in some way to religion. This is true in India, where in conjunction with the formation of a deep-rooted rather than political nationalism, the Congress party that supported political nationalism ceded control of the government to the Nationalist Hindi party. This nationality –initially a relatively small minority in India – attracted other cultural groups, which spoke languages other than Hindi – a fact that set them apart for a long period of time from those who were Hindi both in religion and language. A growing number of groups joined the new Hindi nation, many of which spoke different languages, but all of which shared the basic Hindi religion. As a result of these developments, the Hindi religion forms the very backbone of

[70] Wolfgang S. Heinz and Hugo Fru'hling, Determinants of Gross Human Rights Violations by State and State-Sponsored Actors in Brazil, Uruguay, Chile, and Argentina 1960-1990, pp. 16-17, 27-32, 48, 51, 85.
See also Peter H. Smith, Talons of the Eagle, Dynamics of US-Latin American Relations (New York: Oxford University Press, 2000) p. 61. A US general who served in Latin America is quoted there as saying in 1933 that he was disheartened by the lack of higher purpose in his service once he realized that his military service in Mexico and Nicaragua in the years 1909-1912 were only meant to benefit American business.

the Nationalist Hindi nation, though it did not attain official status. Thus the new ever-growing Hindi nation includes within it even Muslims, as Ashutosh Varshney depicts in his essays.[71]

All this seems to reflect that a unified Latin American nation is a realistic, likely possibility. It will be a nation rooted in Latin American values, culture, history, and customs. Any citizen of a Latin American country that does not share all these will continue to be a citizen of his country, but he will not belong to the Latin American nation. Most Latin American citizens, will in fact though feel connected to the Latin American people.

Since nationalism exists in the minds of those who feel connected to it and is not dependent on the objective conditions that simply serve as basis for projections regarding the likelihood of the formation of a nation, Latin American governments will not need to make any official declarations in order to make the Latin American nation a reality. No treaties between countries or formal accords will be necessary. All that is needed is that the feelings and thoughts of the people and their very way of life will turn this deep-rooted national sentiment into a living breathing reality. These beliefs must be rooted both in fundamental similarities and a pressing reality – in the form of a common enemy or civil war (like the US in its Civil War, and Western Europe and the World Wars, if it manages to unite). It is of course possible that political nationalism in Latin America will prove to be a bitter disappointment and result in a social crisis, like that taking place in Argentina, or in feelings of rootlessness and utter pessimism, like those felt in Brazil, that bring abject poverty and the dissolution of the family structure.

While in the past the solution to such hopeless situations in Latin America was revolution and military regimes, this option no longer exists. It seems likely, if not inevitable, that out of the ruins, a new nation will arise that will unite the forces, informally at first, and ultimately in a formal political manner.

There is a difference between a political (artificially constructed) nationalism and a deep-rooted (primordial) one. Though it is natural and anticipated that when an all-inclusive Latin American nation comes into being, initially there will be conventions, conferences, and even various academic institutions that will promote

---

[71] Rachel Sieder, "War, Peace, and Memory Politics in Central America," in **The Politics of Memory – Transitional Justice in Democratizing Societies**, Alexandra Barahona de Brito, Carmen Gonzalez Enriquez and Paloma Aguilar (ed.) (Oxford: Oxford University Press, 2001) pp. 171, 176, 178.

this nationalism, ultimately, a more formal stage, such as the one described by Simone Bolivar, will be reached.

Chapter F:
Patronage in Mexico and Brazil

Mexico and Brazil are both characterized by powerful central governments, which operate essentially as the patrons of their citizens, applying pressure granting favors, and carrying out threats. As a result of historical developments in the two countries, not only was the centrality of the government and administration established, but also the central elite managed to gain control over the regional elite by tying their leaders to the central elite.[72]

The process of centralization is linked to the discovery of gold and diamonds in the central Western highlands in the second half of the eighteenth century, and to the arrival of the Portuguese king upon Napoleon's invasion of Portugal in the beginning of the 19th century. His arrival and appointment of his son as king of Brazil weakened the movement – that had arisen in other Latin American countries – towards achievement of independence. Brazil's transformation from colonial settlement to independent state led to the expansion of the local bureaucratic system and the de-politicization of public lives, a phenomenon reinforced by the army's disregard for the influences and trends of a greater part of the society.

This situation strengthened the status of the landowners, who were given the opportunity to influence military appointments, and who together with the government bureaucracy constituted the ruling party. This was at the root of additional developments, including pressures to grant rights to the provinces (though not to the lower districts), the strengthening of the army and operation of the government according to the model of the old republic of 1889-1930 characterized by a weak opposition, and increased public involvement in politics – even though the percentage of voters did not exceed 3.5% of the population. In 1945, upon the onset of a multi-party period, the percentage of voters rose to 15%, following the establishment of countless professional unions from 1937-1945,

---

[72] Luis Roniger, **Variations in Models of Patronage in Mexico and Brazil**, in note 1 above, pp. 35-36.

during the period of 'the new state'. Groups connected to the bureaucracy established some of the modern political parties. In 1964, a military faction took over control of the government.[73]

In Mexico, as a result of local uprisings and military struggles with the US, the army and the central government became stronger, with the Congress and Courts serving mostly as 'rubber stamps' for the government's actions. The strength of the central government stemmed from its revolutionary ideology and political reforms that called for a more liberal distribution of land also to Indians and the agricultural classes. The central government's ties were not with the elite, like in Brazil, but rather with the masses, a connection formed as a result of the government's need for their support during military conflicts.[74] The most glaring common denominator between Mexico and Brazil is the corruption – the bribing of bureaucratic officials in order to earn political favors.

The basic difference between Brazil and Mexico is that in Mexico, the majority of the population has some degree of Indian blood, while in Brazil the Indian population was essentially wiped out, and the Blacks form a sizable minority alongside the European majority. The slaves underwent a process that eradicated all former tribal connections, and integrated them fully into Brazilian society. Assimilation and integration are far stronger forces in Mexico, as is their national cohesiveness.

The bonds of patronage, therefore, extend to the masses, while in Brazil, narrow oligarchic elites control the path to governmental preferential treatment. Income differentials are far higher in Brazil than in Mexico; 1:20 in Brazil compared to 1:9 in Mexico. Nevertheless, the central government in both countries tries very hard to maintain its ties to venture capitalists and foreign investors and to support industry, though most of industrial production is for domestic consumption. These activities, of course, are pursued at the expense of the lower classes, though the precise effects differed between Brazil and Mexico. In Brazil, they prompted an escalation of a process, which turned farmers into proletariat, while in Mexico, they followed massive agricultural reforms enacted in the first half of the twentieth century. In Mexico, the political system allows people in the administration considerable freedom to grant political favors, thus promoting and ingraining the institution of bribery.[75]

---

[73] Ibid. 36-38.

[74] Ibid. 38-39, 41-45.

[75] Ibid. 46-51.

In both Brazil and Mexico, intermediaries known as the Cossix in Mexico and the Colonels in Brazil used to – though they no longer do so – mediate between the government and the country's citizens. The Cossix may have enjoyed a less established position than the Colonels, and Mexican citizens may have possessed somewhat greater power vis-à-vis the Cossix than Brazilians did vis-à-vis the Colonels, but these were essentially parallel institutions.

Mexican Cossix possessed economic and political power over the local government and over means of law enforcement. They served their communities by acting as go-betweens between them and the federal and state governments. They served their governments by providing them with inside information and by maintaining the peace in their districts. They mediated between distant rulers and local farmers and appointed municipal officials. They maintained monopolistic control over agricultural production and commerce, and controlled the best lands. They maintained power even through unlawful means. Yet, like the Colonels in Brazil, the Cossix lacked any formal status or appointment, and it was not always clear who in fact was a Cossix. Public opinion was divided regarding the Cossix depending on people's personal experience with them.

Brazilian Colonels operated both on the regional level and through political parties. They basically filled the same functions as the Cossix, but their social status was higher, and even served as a substitute for titles of nobility – titles, which were unattainable by local elites.
Patron-client relationships today very much parallel those of the Cossix and Colonels and the citizens of their respective countries.

Summary

Latin American history, political and social state, lifestyle, and life values reflect a distinct society that despite internal formal borders and divisions constitutes one united entity. The parallel to North America, and to the US specifically highlights Latin America's singularity.

Latin America has experienced constant and repeated crises in its 200 years of independence – military revolts that are characteristic of Latin American hierarchy and attempts at democracy that reflect external influences, more consistent and compatible with North American values than with Latin American nature and character. Democratic values, which are generally associated with an impersonal anonymous approach, have not generally proven suitable for Latin Americans.

Latin Americans derived their fundamental principles from the European half of the Iberian Peninsula, Catholicism, and feudalism, modifying them according to the needs of the time and place, and fusing them with fundamentals from Indian culture. Some of these ideas promoted the intermingling of races, of Whites, Blacks, and Reds, alongside the hierarchy that was accepted in their culture. They never developed a complex about their hierarchic ideology that is interwoven with racial distinctions and racial mingling. They don't feel any pangs of conscience regarding the lack of equality in their lives, and they haven't internalized democratic values. They are fundamentally different from North Americans in these ways. Latin Americans have their own rhythm, language, and culture – they are a distinct human, cultural, and even national entity that does not belong to Europe. They drew considerably from the European past and from the past that predated White man's conquest of America, and even from African rhythm. Their culture and nationality are deep-rooted, not politically contrived, and they are a force whose future is before it.

It is crucial to examine the growth of nationalism from above, a bird's eye view that ignores the trees that make up the forest. From this view it becomes apparent that US leaders desperately needed, at the time of its establishment, to find ways to set America apart in order to unify the people. They were British citizens who had revolted against their mother country primarily for economic reasons. Thus they were in favor of immigration from Europe that mixed the English in the US with other Whites, creating a clear distinction between the British nation and the American nation. The Spanish who revolted against Spain, the Portuguese who separated from Portugal, and the Africans in the Caribbean did not need to take such a step since they had a tradition of interracial mingling – with the Moors and Jews in Spain, Orientals in the Philippines, Africans in the Caribbean, Indians in America – Aztec, Apache, and Pueblo.[76] Thus, American culture is fundamentally European (primarily Republican based on English tradition), while Latin American culture is generally deeply connected to Indian roots. The general-Latin American connection is thus stronger than those of the individual states, as is reflected in the children's literature that is intended for all Latin American immigrants in the US.[77] Both US and Latin American nationalism are deep-rooted, an essential criterion for a nation's success. Canadians also managed to deeply root themselves, by attaching themselves to the old British crown. All Canadians did so – whether they were Catholic or Protestant, French speaking or English speaking, even though one might have presumed that only Protestants would feel a connection to the Anglican-Protestant British crown. The French Catholics, acing on healthy instincts and from a desire to distinguish themselves from their French

[76] Smolen LA. Oriz-Castro V. "Dissolving Borders and Broadening Perspectives Through Latino Traditional Literature." in **The Reading Teacher,** 53 (7) 566-578. April 2000.
[77] Ibid.

brothers, distanced themselves from the French Revolution that separated Church and State. This search for uniqueness led the Catholic Canadians to accept the belief in divinely given rights and the divine right to rule, in contradistinction to the Anglo-American belief in a natural source of individual and governmental rights. This was also their connection to their neighbors – the Anglo Canadians, and the source of the bi-national, bi-religious, bilingual pact that was made in Canada. To a certain extent, this situation is similar to the cities in Switzerland, some of which are Protestant and some of which are Catholic, whose languages differ one from another, but who signed a treaty based on mutual support they offered each other against local rulers who attempted to conquer various Swiss cities. Strong external pressure and concern for survival even led, at times, to alliances between different religions.

In this context, the centrality of religion must be emphasized. Salo Wittmayer Baron[78] describes how religions throughout human history built nations. He claims that even in modern times, it is impossible to understand the currents of modern history without understanding religion and its relationship to the State. Baron describes how the religious bond united the Flemish and the Walloons in Belgium and divided the Serbs and Croatians who share both common ethnic roots and language, but whose religion is different. He claims that in Germany the unification of Protestants and Catholics within one state was so problematic as to result in the creation of a particularly radical nationalism – that of Nazism.

From Baron's perspective, it is possible to argue that the conflict in Chechnia, Ireland, and Kashmir, in Southern Sudan, between Israel and the Palestinians and the Arab nations, and the internal clashes in Egypt, cannot be understood without examining the role religion plays in the conflict.

Returning, though, to the example of Canada, there is an example of how different religions and languages will ally to form one nation in the face of an apparent powerful threat such as the US. When the threat ceases to exist, as in the case of the US, the alliance is likely to weaken – and that is why today there is strong support in Quebec for seceding from the Canadian federation. The absence of a common enemy is weakening Canadian sense of nationalism, and the only thing that is still holding the inter-religious alliance together is economic factors.[79]

---

[78] Salo Wittmayer Baron, Modern Nationalism and Religion (New York and London: Harper & Brothers, 1947) p. 21.

[79] The strong forces in favor of division, despite the economic incentive to unite, prove that even in modern days when religion's influence seems to be on the decline, the religious

Economic reasons, however, do not generally sustain a sense of nationalism, proving that nationalism is inspired more by emotion than by logic.

The example of Canada demonstrates that it is truly realistic to predict a future Pan -Latin American nation.

A further examination of US nationalism will shed more light on the future of Pan-Latin American nationalism. Though Europeans were involved in the formation of an Anglo American nation and integrated within that nation, this union faced real problems during the two World Wars, wars that were essentially internal European wars. In retrospect, these wars might truly have been civil wars of the European nation or of the White Christian nation. These wars were fought and decided primarily in Europe. What should a president like Woodrow Wilson do when US citizens essentially feel an alliance with both of the warring sides in Europe? Neutrality would have best preserved US nationalism. Yet the length of the war intensified the nationalistic-emotional connection felt by the Anglo American elite to its country of origin. As the war continued, the pressure mounted to join the war on the side of the British. Woodrow Wilson introduced legislation before Congress before America's entry into the war, as preparation for the perilous days that were to follow America's entry into the war – perilous not in terms of what would happen to the troops on the battlefield, but with regard to Anglo American nationalism. The 1917 Espionage Act, which established severe punishments (up to 10 years imprisonment) for protesting against the war, sought to protect America from this internal danger. Opponents of this law claimed that it violated America's sacrosanct freedom of speech, yet it was nevertheless passed,[80] out of concern for a rift in the American nation. It was quite symbolic that one of the people indicted on the charge of violating this law was a journalist for a liberal very influential newspaper in the US called *Nation*.

Later, during the Cold War between the US and its allies and the USSR and its allies, this threat to American nationalism did not exist at all, since America itself was a direct player in this war and there was no issue of direct loyalty on the part of Russian – US citizens. The only problem was an ideological one that related to the connection between the US and Latin Americans, a problem that stemmed from the different compositions of the Anglo American and Latin American nations. In the US, all the national myths and the roots of their nationalism were

---

factor is still a very significant one. Though it is surprising, the fact is that the religious spirit is still alive and kicking, even within people who consider themselves secular.

[80] William H. Rehnquist, **All the Laws But One** (New York: Random House, 1998) pp. 170-183.

(and still are) European, while in Latin America – they are Indian.[81] Thus, Latin American support for the US stemmed primarily from their foreign relations with the US, as their ruling elites were inclined in favor of capitalistic ideology and thus had somewhat of a fundamental connection to the US in the context of the Cold War. If they had not been inclined towards capitalism (like Fidel Castro's Cuba), it would have been very easy for the local government to ally with Russia. In other words, the determining factors were economic interests and strong bilateral primarily economic material relations with the US, rather than deep-rooted nationalistic feelings.[82] Latin America did not pose a threat to the Soviet bloc; it was not an economic rival – its economic power was neither great nor independent, or a political –ideological opponent since democracy was not a strong Latin American value. Latin Americans were always far more inclined towards human personal interaction rather than noble ideas and ideologies. Thus, the battle between Communism and Capitalism did not particularly interest the Latin American people like it did the Anglo American people. The Latin Americans did not demonstrate a great desire in getting embroiled in this conflict, just as they hadn't in the two World Wars that had so absorbed White Christian man.[83]

With the conclusion of the Cold War, a revolution took place in the world of nationalism.

Suddenly it became clear that the Western-European union was not intended for the consolidation of the Western-European nation, but that it was only a kernel in a much wider vaster unification of White Christian man. This consolidation is not some fantastical whimsical notion rooted in some globalistic ambitions, but is the result of two giants in the Far East, Japan and China.

The contest today is between yellow slanted eyed man who lives in an environment of non-jealous religions, a culture of paternalism and loyalty to family and to one's master, where responsibilities guide behavior – in contrast to White Christian man, whose culture revolves democratic liberalism that is based on rights of the individual and on excellence in performance and competition between individuals.

---

[81] See note 72 above about Latin American children's stories both in the US and Latin America.

[82] Peter H. Smith, **Talons of the Eagle – Dynamics of US Latin American Relations** (New York, Oxford: Oxford University Press, 2000).

[83] Ibid, 84-85.

It is a special form of a war of religions – religion referring in this context to that which man believes in, that cannot be proven, according to whose prescripts man acts on a daily basis, that motivates man, and even provides emotional succor.

This book will not attempt to predict what Canada and Latin America will do in the circumstances just described. This book deals with the formation of a nation, not with a country's behavior in the framework of global conflicts – for two reasons. Firstly, because by nature, nationalism influences a country's behavior. Secondly, because the approach that will be taken here to the development of nationalism in general, and to American nationalism specifically – since it is a broad speculative topic – will focus more on formulation of questions rather than on offering answers. Finally, this discussion will be based on a general understanding of matters, rather than an academic analysis anchored in proofs and citations.

As already mentioned, there is a basic difference between Canada and the US with regard to the State's obligations to its citizens. In Canada, the perception is that the States has obligations to groups of citizens, while in the US, the State is perceived as having responsibilities to each individual citizen.

Regarding the citizen's obligations to his country, the starkest contrast is between the Catholics who have greater influence in Canada than in the US, and the Protestants, who are more dominant in the US than in Canada, and most reflected in the differences in their educational systems. Catholic education emphasizes far more than Protestant education the individual's responsibilities to the general community, though there are certain streams of Protestantism that do stress personal duty in forming the community. Yet, nonetheless, it was most fitting that it was John F. Kennedy, America's only Catholic president to date who declared, "Do not ask what your country can do for you, but what you can do for your country," an ideology consistent with Catholic teachings. The behavior of American presidents at moments of truth, at times of crisis for the British in Britain, raise the question – of whether despite all Anglo American attempts to build a separate national entity, they aren't simply a limb of the British nation, and whether Britain's participation in the European Union won't be one more reason why Anglo Americans decide to join the united nation of White Christian man.

Returning again to internal American differences, it seems that Canada and Latin America have a common denominator with respect to man's relationship with the society in which he lives. Both advance a duty that precedes and takes priority over any right. While the institution of patronage in Latin America, an institution based on trust and personal relations, is very strong, it is interwoven with the institution of corporatism, which is a communal group concept. Without making any definitive statements about collectivism vs. individualism, the cultural differences between Latin Americans and Anglo Americans are greater without a doubt.

Latin Americans, it appears, bear close resemblance ideologically to the Chinese, who hold great respect for the father figure, have the utmost value for duties, and do not base their moral system on rights. The Chinese system draws greatly on Confucius' philosophy, just as the ancient Japanese culture does.

Despite this resemblance, China and Japan are foreign to both Protestant and Catholic Canadians, and also to Latin Americans. Canada and Latin America are similar, nevertheless, in that neither is threatened by either China or Japan since neither Canada nor Latin America– in contrast to the US - is competing for world hegemony.

Therefore, it seems unlikely that Latin Americans or Canadians will join the Anglo Americans in forming a nation of the White Christian man. Latin Americans have mixed racially too much with Indians and Blacks to allow them to join the race of White Christian man.

Another issue of great relevance is the high percentage of Latin Americans in the US and their high rate of growth. Latin Americans, in contrast to European immigrants and to a certain extent, even the Blacks, have not assimilated easily within American society from a cultural perspective.[84] They have preserved their own language, and in one case of a city that was almost entirely populated by Latin Americans, they even declared Spanish the city's official language. Latin American immigration to the US, therefore, is likely to serve as a catalyst that drives the Americans into the arms of the Russians and Europeans with the goal of forming a unified nation. American policy makers are already discussing the fact that within a few decades, Latin Americans will turn from the largest minority in the US (15% of the population), a minority that has struggled with and resisted adapting to American culture,[85] to a clear majority of American citizens.[86]

---

[84] Johnson K.R., "Melting Pot or 'Ring of Fire'? : Assimilation and the Mexican-American Experience," in **California Law Review** 85 (5): October 1997,1259-1313.

[85] Ardila A. Ponton, "The Future of Neuropsychology with Hispanic Populations in the United States," in Archives of Clinical Neuropsychology 14 (7): October 1999, pp. 565-580.

[86] Santoro WA, "Conventional Politics Takes Center Stage: The Latino Struggle Against English-Only Laws," in Social Forces 77 (3): March 1999, pp. 887-909.

If matters really develop in this manner, there is likely to be a rift between the US and Latin America, and this will serve as an additional reason or impetus to forming a Pan-Latino nation. The present existence of distinct nations in each of the Latin American countries is no reason to doubt the potential for a Pan-Latino nation. Under pressure, Pan-Latino unity will naturally occur,[87] predicated on common religion, among other factors.[88]

Of course, these are not absolutely certain predictions, but they are not baseless speculations either, and they should be considered as likely future scenarios.

The theory that these scenarios are based on has been alluded to already,[89] and will now be described more fully. Nationhood is a phenomenon that is conceived and exists in the heads of a large group of people who believe that they are a nation. This phenomenon is based on myths that developed from ancient traditions that were connected to the early fathers, traditions that evolved in a true natural and historical manner, that were connected to territory (a homeland), and were rooted in cultural and religious foundations and in emotional ties that connected the members of the group and prompted them to work together. A melding process is required, generally in the form of wars and common enemies over the course of hundreds of years. Generally, the group will share a distinct language, unique customs, and their own educational methods. A nation forms both because of internal processes and because of external pressures and threats. As long as the members of a group lack the desire to live cooperatively as an independent State or even autonomous one, it is an ethnic group, not a nation. The aspiration for independence is what turns an ethnic group into a nation. When the members of this group even lack a sense of identity and individuality, they are not even considered an ethnic group. It is will and determination that form a nation or an ethnic group, not action. The objective perspective is not a condition for the existence of an ethnic group or nation, though it can mark the way and indicate the potential for the formation of an ethnic group or nation. Objective elements – such as the existence of people who are likely to cultivate a desire for unification – must exist, but the determining factor will be the will and consciousness of the members of the group.

---

[87] Levitt P., "Local-level Global Religion: The Case of US-Dominican Migration," in Journal For the Scientific Study of Religion 37 (1): March 1998, pp. 74-88.

[88] Baia LR, "Rethinking Transnationalism: Reconstructing National Identities Among Peruvian Catholics in New Jersey," in Journal of Inter-American Studies and World Affairs 41 (4), 93, Winter 1999.

[89] In the manuscript to this book, **Why Religion?**

Many countries that came into being not on the basis of a distinct ethnic group and without a collective desire to turn their ethnic group into a nation, tried and are still trying to form some kind of nation that will be their backbone. Their nationalism is what is called 'political nationalism,' and its relationship to 'deep-rooted nationalism' is like that of a child adopted as a teenager vs. that of a child adopted as a baby. Let us assume two steps in the adoption process:

1. At the time of the adoption, the adopting family is wealthy and the baby's biological family is on the verge of starvation.
2. As time passes, the adopting family suffers financial difficulties, and it becomes clear that they did not grow to love their adopted child.

It is readily apparent without further analysis that the adoption agreement will be dissolved in the second stage.

If the US, for example, began to suffer such serious economic difficulties that its standard of living falls lower than the ones in its immigrants' countries of origin, what would happen in the US? Wouldn't many 1st and even 2nd and 3rd generation immigrants return to their native countries?

There is no need in fact to consider this hypothetical example, when Argentina serves as a real example of a country to which many immigrated hoping to reach the 'flesh pots' (in both senses of the phrase), but then left when their hopes were not realized.

In order to be thorough in our analysis of this subject, let us also consider the different waves of immigration to Israel. Even though Israel is a country, ostensibly based on a 'deep rooted nationalism', many Jews who immigrated to Israel before and after the establishment of the state returned to their countries of origin or emigrated to the US. This example does not seem consistent with the findings until this point, which seemed to indicate that 'political nationalism' is a kind of 'lame duck' that cannot walk without some form of crutches, while 'deep rooted nationalism' is a creature that walks on four solid healthy legs.

Upon further consideration, it becomes apparent that the case of Israel is not necessarily incompatible with the principles of nationalism that were being established here. Jews were dispersed in various places all over the world, with various cultures for approximately 2000 years. The Jews in the different lands followed different customs from each other, and spoke different languages, though they did share the 'holy tongue', a religious language, not used for the vernacular. They all followed one religion and prayed to return to the Land of Israel, but these prayers were generally no more than lip service, and most of the time only those fleeing persecution and oppression actually came to Israel. Of course, the realization of their abstract dream was thrilling, but since a great number of them in the recent generation were accustomed to secular life in a modern-secular country, and their attachment to Israel was a political but not deep-rooted nationalism, the difficulties of absorption process caused many to leave Israel in search of a higher economic standard of living.

Jews were not the only ones to immigrate to the US and other countries. Deep-rooted nationalists like the Chinese and Japanese also immigrated, proving not that 'political nationalism' has become stronger than 'deep-rooted nationalism', but only that an economically flourishing country attracts people from relatively poor countries.

If one considers all the examples, including that of Israel, China, Japan, and of course Argentina, one will conclude that the strongest nationalism is the 'deep-rooted' one.

Statements written by this author elsewhere regarding Israel apply and can enlighten us regarding the nationalism of every State and nation:[90]
"...Lord Devlin, expressing the traditional British position, says that a country is a home. Regarding this one should note that a country is not necessarily a home to each and every citizen – though it is so in the eyes of many citizens, who see their fate tightly and emotionally intertwined with it. A citizen who falls into the latter category can be called a "deep-rooted citizen."

This is a citizen who considers his country (and not only in his land) a homeland, which binds to it his national feelings, who cannot imagine a substitute for this country, who feels towards his country feelings similar to those a person feels towards his biological mother (for whom there is no substitute), and who does not view his country simply as a convenient place to live his life but who feels towards it unambiguous feelings of duty, which he is unwilling to show towards any other country. A person who considers his country the social republic to which he belongs, who does not consider himself connected to any other republic, who is tied to the country and nation who live in it with such strong bonds – that even if he leaves the country, he will feel similar feelings in whatever place destiny leads him – a citizen who feels like this, along with others who feel a national

[90] Yehuda Cohen, 'Who Fears of a Jewish State? A Legal and Ideological Perspective' (Tel Aviv: The Lawyers Association Publications, 2001) pp. 123-124 – what was written there regarding the State and regarding the nation that constitutes the backbone of the State.

connection like him – constitute the backbone of that country – a citizen such as this one can be called 'deeply-rooted.'

A deeply-rooted citizen feels attached to the society in which he lives, considers himself an integral part of it, "belonging" to it; he feels that the political society in which he lives is "his"; he feels shame or pride, satisfaction or regret, and also responsibility for the character of this society and republic. This idea is reminiscent of Jewish tradition's conception of mutual responsibility or of the idea that "All Jews are responsible one for another." It is reasonable to assume that a political society that does not have many deeply-rooted citizens is a society lacking in a "backbone." Woe to the country that does not have a deeply-rooted people; it is doomed, even if its citizens are yet unaware."

On the basis of this description it becomes clear that not every entity that is called a 'nation' – is truly a nation. The new countries that were established in Africa on the basis of colonial settlements, similar to US and the Latin America countries were not created as national entities. These were countries that sought to create for themselves, each one in its own plot – its own nation.

The genuine thing, however, is not what one seeks to forcefully create. It is like love, which is something that can fail to exist, despite the formal bonds of marriage, and which can exist even without the bonds of marriage. Love can bloom for a married couple (State?) during shared hard times and over the process of raising children. It can bloom and be real, but it doesn't grow according to instructions or commands or (in the case of a State) law.

Nationalism, in contrast to love, is a matter in which a large group is involved. At certain moments (such as critical points in WWI or WWII), it seemed as if the American president (be it Wilson or Roosevelt) acted not as the president of the political entity of the United States, but as a member of the greater British nation that comprises the dominant elements in both Britain and the US. That is the power of nationalism, similar to love, that sometimes it seems dead and extinguished, and yet it still lives and breathes.

Thus, the separate national existence of each of the countries – Mexico, Argentina, Brazil, and Venezuela does not imply that the matter is set. There is certainly room to consider whether a Pan-Latin American nationalism doesn't in fact exist.[91] Even if these inquiries leave us in doubt, that will still suffice.

Appendix

Klark[92]

Klark claims that between the years 1660-1832, no nation in the Anglo Saxon world on either side of **the** Atlantic existed, though there were steps in that direction, steps that were furthered by the French Revolution and the Romantic reaction that followed it. These initial steps included the establishment of the Anglican Church that distinguished England from other Protestant countries, and predominately, though the belief in a unique English ethnicity was significant too, the role played by religion and law. Puritans in America had a sense of collective mission, a belief that developed also in England. The myths revolving around Protestant residences from the time of Catholic rule (under Queen Mary) also built England collectivism. A legend developed that the first Christians were English, that the first country to accept the Protestant Reformation was England. Fuchs, who himself did not possess a national consciousness, called the English in his writings, the "Chosen Nation." The law also played a role, in that Common Law established a process of acquiring citizenship according to a theory that equated a king's relationship with his subjects to that of God's with his followers and a father's with his children – a hierarchic relationship. The ruling established what Parliament refused to establish, that whoever was born in Scotland after the sixth English king, known as James I according to his English name (in 1603) would be considered an English subject as if he was born in England to English parents. From this, developed the connection between loyalty and nationalism, a principle that established the conceptual connection between loyalty and citizenship – an idea that is at the root of the existence of an English nation based on loyalty to the English monarch. It was explained and developed that the connection between a

---

[91] And if a Pan-Latino-American nation will exist while differentiated Latin-American states exist, this will be only a temporal phenomenon, since there will be acting a common will of the existing and live Pan American Nation to live within a common political entity.

[92] J. C. D. Clark, **The Language of Liberty 1660-1832, Political discourse and social dynamics in the Anglo-American world** (Cambridge: Cambridge University Press, 1994) pp. 46-62.

king and his subjects is similar to that of the soul and the body, and it necessitates complete faith – an idea based on a religious conception. English Common Law set apart the English from the Christians living in the European continent who were bound to Roman law, and this set them apart also in their own eyes. All this left little room for the factors of ethnicity and language, factors that played a role, but a less significant one.

Regarding North America – severance of the connection to the English king in the year 1776 and to the French king in the year 1789 necessitated a new self identity, one that was formed slowly and with great hardship on the basis of common language and culture, and to some extent – common ethnic origin. Loyalty to the State was an abstract concept. After winning their independence, Americans required new immigrants to make a declaration of their loyalty to the American flag, a kind of secular contract that was a substitute for the idea of loyalty to the king. The idea evolved of a human right to choose to be loyal to a new country, upon which the idea of the connection of loyalty and territory and love of the land developed. This also helped form a loyal American nationalism. American nationalism translated Biblical concepts of nationhood to its own terms. American nationalism developed on the foundation of a consciousness of freedom that evolved in England over the course of the revolts that took place from the 17th century on. In 1776, there was no concrete difference between English and American ideology and culture, and thus the American revolt did not create a new nation in America. Benjamin Franklin wrote in 1760, that a unification of the colonies against Britain was impossible since each of the 14 colonies had its own distinct laws, interests, religions, customs, and forms of government. Yet when they did revolt, successfully, a new spirit overtook them and the concept of 'America' took hold.
Klark compares the situation in America to the situation in France, which in his opinion was similar in several ways. The French focused on common religion and customs, and disregarded differences of ethnicity and language. The French even emphasized that the French king was considered the most Catholic king, a distinguishing fact.
Klark's descriptions reflect the difficulties that were inherent in forming a nation both in England and the US, where the ethnic aspect played no real role and other factors were weak, and yet still there was a desire to form a nation. One of the signs of the nearly desperate attempt to form an English nation was a song that British soldiers sang which were meant primarily to emphasize the division between the Protestant British and Protestant Germans, a division that wasn't so easily drawn.

Michael Lind[93]
According to Lind, American nationalism is fundamentally insecure since it lacks any real defining character other than recurring crises and the ideological goals it adopts after ever crisis. He names three past revolutions – (1) The Revolutionary War in 1776 (2)The Civil War that concluded in 1961 (3)A Revolution for Human Rights that ended in 1972. He anticipates a fourth revolution, one of a union of races and classes that will take place in the beginning of the 21st century.

Lind questions whether Americans are a nation, or whether they are a nation of nations, a home to many diverse distinct nations. Its strong Latin American constituency makes it very different from other Western Protestant cultures. According to universalists, the US is not a nation at all, but only a conceptual State, lacking in nationality, which is based on a liberal broad democratic philosophy. Others fear the Balkanization of the US and the eruption of conflicts between the mix of races, cultures, and nations that have made the US their home. Others counter that a nation can comprise various races, cultures, ethnic groups, ideologies, and national goals.
It is difficult to establish a nation on an idea, all the more so an idea that is not unique to that nation, but that is shared by many nations.
It is also problematic founding a nation on a mission. A nation may devote itself to a particular mission, but this mission cannot define it. While many Americans would certainly claim that they are a nation, their position may only reflect a fear that an answer to the contrary would lead to the conclusion that the US has been fractured by the multitude of cultures living in its midst.

For more details about *Michael Lind and his investigation, see at part 4 of this book, chapter 1.*

Avihu Zakai [94]
Zakai describes in both his articles the role religion plays in reformation in general, and in particular in relation to Puritan Protestantism in England and America. He discusses the connection between these processes and historical consciousness and study, and especially to national consciousness and formation.

---

[93] See Michael Lind, **The Next American Nation: The New Nationalusm and the Fourth American Revolution** (The Free Press, 1995)
[94] See: Avihu Zakai, "Religion and Revolution, The contribution of Puritan Rhetoric to Democracy in America" from the book: **Democracy In America** , Zmora Bitan Publishing (as yet npublished). Also, Avihu Zakai, "Reformation, History, and Eschatology in English Protestantism", in **History And Theory**, Vol. XXVI, No. 3, 1987, pp. 300-318

In England, study of history through a Christian according to reformation perspective became popular after 1530, after the crowning of Queen Elizabeth in 1558, and over the course of the Puritan revolution. Protestants exiled from England to Protestant cities in Europe after religious persecutions allied themselves with Protestants already living there. The Protestants reasoned that since the words of the prophets ultimately come true, knowledge of history could help them to better comprehend the prophecies. They drew comparisons between historical events and prophetic descriptions, associating the invasion of Rome with the fall of Babylon, the Turkish invasion with the War of Gog and Magog, and the Pope with the antichrist. They concluded, as a result of this study, that Protestantism is the period of time that immediately precedes 'the End of days', thus linking the Protestant reformation to the prophecies about the End of days.
Zakai's second article, about the religion and revolution of the Puritans, continues the basic explanation of "The Chosen People theory" as developed by the Puritans of New England – the people chosen by God and delivered to his Promised Land with a sacred mission to the New World. Zakai, in the footsteps of other researchers, reveals the central role the Puritans and their special brand of Protestantism played in the American Revolution. Zakai even mentions the U.S.'s uniqueness as a largely religious country, with a religious circle on the rise, as opposed to the opposite process in other countries. Also mentioned are the recent survey showing that 96% of Americans believe in God, and Robert Bellah's opinion (from his book *Civilian Religion*) that within the framework of the many symbols and values spanning the scope of all religions, churches and institutions in the U.S., there persists the belief that the Americans are the Chosen People and that America is the Promised Land. This Civilian Religion, in both Bellah's and Zakai's opinions has its own theology, ethics, holy days and places and system of symbols and rituals. Among the more obvious of its manifestations are reciting the Pledge of Allegiance to the Flag in schools, the singing of the Star Spangled Banner at sporting events, and a list of national holidays, such as The Fourth of July (day of independence) and Presidents Day (celebrating the birthdates of presidents Washington and Lincoln) side by side with purely religious holydays, such as Easter. One other element of the civilian religion [of Puritan origin, as arises from Zakai's words – Y.C.] is a Messianic grasp of politics and history.

Zakai explains that Puritans accept the principals of Devine arbitrary sovereignty over the world, the corruption of man, and an ancient selection between the righteous and the wicked embedded with Devine Justice. Puritans emphasize the internal and personal religious experience or the change of heart, proving openly the redeeming mercy of God, and the uncompromising demand that all aspects of life be based in Devine laws and commandments. Puritans believe in the concept of The Covenant, according to which, those who have managed to lead a life of extreme piety will be rewarded in the afterlife. By the same Covenant, the Puritans are the Chosen People. The Puritans have denied the Divinity of the Anglican Church, and therefore the validity of the clergy. For this belief were their movements were restrained within England, and so the Puritans emigrated to America and settled in New Haven, Connecticut, Rohde Island and Massachusetts. Due to their devoutness and religious reading of the Bible, no society of the 17th century rivaled New Englanders in literacy. The Puritans had established the universities of Harvard (1636), Yale (1702) and Princeton (1746), and had ordained 1600 clerics through these universities by the American Revolution. Indeed, during the Revolution, about 600 of these clerics had worked toward American Independence by spreading the spirit of rebellion against the British, and the ideals of freedom. The same priests were instrumental earlier, during the Seven Year War (between Britain and Prussia on the one side, and France, Austria and Russia on the other), in rallying the Americans to the aid of the failing British campaign in North America, as they saw any war on the Catholic French as a Holy War, and indeed, aided by the settlers, the British had won, and conquered Canada. With the end of the conflict, the heavy taxes imposed by the British had caused the American Revolution, where, once more, the Puritan zeal played a central part through the widely circulated sermons of its clerics. The victory of the American War of Independence was considered and portrayed in New England as a victory of Providence, as seen by the Puritan faith.

For more details about *Avihu Zakai and his investigation, see at part 4 of this book, chapter 1.*

Michael Waltzer [95]

Weltzer, a Jewish American, says that Americans do not refer to their country as their 'Homeland', and that for many an American, the concept of 'mutual commitment' usually applies to blood-relations and members of the nation from which they immigrated to the U.S., and which they still see as their provenance. What matters more to the American than their state is their ethnic group, race and (Devine) religion.

An American who inwardly chooses to forfeit his pre-American origin is welcome to do so, but this will merely make them ethnically anonymous, and in no way a better American. It has been said of Americans and their ethnic origins, that try as one may, no American can replace their Grandfather. For the American, ties to an ethnic past are not supposed to disrupt or hinder one's loyalty to the United States or her ideals.

---

[95] See: Michael Walzer, **What it is to be an American** (New York: Marsaio) pp. 23-49.

There was, however, in the 1850's a movement of opposition to the catholic immigration, especially the Irish immigration, a movement called "know nothing", whose New England center also opposed slavery. This movement fought the teaching of the immigrant's native languages with community funds, as well as the teaching of their religion, in an effort to homogenize American society.
For more details about *Avihu Zakai and his investigation, see at part 4 of this book, chapter 1.*

Waltzer speaks of the Jews of France, who had to give up their rights as a group, in order to gain rights as citizens, following the French Revolution. The price of emancipation for Jews in France, was assimilation, as per Rousseau's strong national approach toward the United States. In the U.S., the situation was completely different. Despite the Republican current, which demanded assimilation, there is a tolerance in the U.S. of groupings, ethnic and otherwise, and dual loyalties are possible. Understanding the essence of American citizenship is diverse, and many different approaches are legitimate.

Weltzer describes the conflicting trends in America, concerning ethnic grouping, and says that "America is still a radically unfinished society". He says that the U.S. has a political center alongside a decentralized government, in which the center does nothing to curb the diffusion of governmental authority, nor does it oppose the ethnic grouping, or even question the legitimacy of the phenomenon. In fact, it seems that American politics is pluralistic by nature, and could use a little clarifying.

For more details about Michael Waltzer and his investigation, see at part 4 of this book, chapter 1.

RELIGION
AND THE BELIEVER

Volume IV
Religion and the believer

Part 9:
The Religion Itself
How it is revealed in one's mind? The attitude unto it

What is in this Part?

In this **Concluding part** there are two **chapters**. In the first **chapter** a **complementary** review is introduced that supplements the reviews that were introduced until this point in the book. The second **chapter** is the opportune moment for a summary that will flavor this entire book providing its underlying reasons.

The first chapter introduces the philosophical writings and opinions of those, whose discourses deal directly or indirectly, with the question of how people discover religion. This question relates both to the individual, and to groups or societies. Religion includes theistic religions as well as ideological ideas and beliefs (non-theistic religions). Yet - **belief** that does not dictate the actions of the public is not a religion. Whether they are theistic beliefs or non-theistic beliefs, they cannot be classified as religions if people do not conduct their lifestyles according to them. **That is true** either in the sense of leading a positive, active and obedient lifestyle or in the negative sense, leading a lifestyle that prevents certain acts from taking place, i.e. via ritual ceremonies- that fends off the occurrence of events that instill fear in people. The fear of demons, if people act in accordance with such fear, is religion. Therefore, the belief in a spirit that causes the sun to rise or set, or the rain to fall, is not a religion except if people who believe in this spirit direct their deeds in order to please it. It is also not a religion if no ceremonies or rituals are performed from which they seek support for their actions. Those who believe in the idea of liberalism and who steer their social institutions towards the liberal administration of the state, are members of a liberal religion. A member of the terror organization, *The(Palestinian) People's Front*, who believes in certain ideals- which from his perspective cause him to perform acts of terror- is a religious man.

Religion transmits power to man and to groups of human beings. Religion strengthens the soul and allows man to perform acts, which from his own private standpoint and personal well being, would be detrimental to undertake.

The question that the first **chapter** of this part focuses upon relates to the discussion of how people discover religion. Is it by way of revelation or emotion? Is it the outcome of a very difficult experience or that of a pleasant encounter? Is meditative thought and contemplation the creator of a new religion or is it the perusal of the principles of an existing religion and persuasive cogitation that religion is the truth, and that one should follow it? Does the way to religion pass through the path of curiosity or the path of concern? Which part of this wonderful path is paved with emotion and which part is paved with logic and intelligence?

Philosophers whose thoughts were swayed by their emotions will be presented in this chapter as well as those who did not act in this way. Philosophers who worked against their immediate surroundings will be adequately represented as well as those whose philosophical theories supported the political system of their environment –on this latter aspect matters will be presented not only be in relation to the different paths that lead to religion but also through the personal paths of those who swayed away from religion leaving the powerful hold that religion exerts on them. Religion is an exciting subject. Religion places itself at the spiritual core of man linking him with wonderful worlds whose plane ticket to them is found exclusively in the ticket booth of religion. The first chapter will seek to portray – if only circuitously –the image of this ticket booth.

The second chapter will be the concluding chapter not only for this part but for the entire book.

In the second chapter the religions will be classified, their genetic code located and the key to the relations among them will be found. Parental-religions will be presented that give birth to other religions, religions will be represented according to their type and beliefs and whose very function are to be 'forbearers'. This clearly derives from their natural character, and from the new religions that they produce, which after nursing from the life source of the religion that bore them, they devour the parental religion, either by destroying it or enclosing it in a glass cage, a pleasant cage that prevents the parental religion from continuing to exert an influence. The religion that was born declares its independence and does not wish not to receive other advice or directives from its parental religion.

An example of a progenitor religion in modern day United States that may be considered is the Protestant religion which from the [United States'] beginnings was in charge of many different things in the United States, all the way from morality to the educational network and finally to the capitalistic lifestyle. In compliance with Dewey's theory, however, Protestantism was forced to withdraw from all positions of influence, and to make way for American civil religion. The latter – also in compliance with Dewey, seeks to create rules of morality according to scientific yardsticks, and to get rid of the Judeo-Christian ethics that has controlled the lives of citizens and the government in the United States (the concept Judeo-Christian alludes to the parent – the Christian religion –to the grandparent – Catholic Christianity from which the Protestant religion emerged – and to the great grandparent – Judaism – from which Catholicism emerged.)

The review in the second chapter will be a summary overview for the whole book, but before presenting the contents in chapters one and two, the internal thread connecting the previous parts of the book will be demonstrated. These parts, at superficial glance appear as separate lectures that were grouped together without any internal reason or meaning. Indeed; there is one common main object to them all, the purpose of religion and its significance; that has emerged in the last mentioned sentences.

The path of humanity was studded with obscure images sought by man who was forced to cry out for their assistance – in order to overcome factors stronger than himself – factors that appeared to him to be controlling his reality, and therefore the source of his salvation had to emanate from outside this same reality that was controlled by them. Thus emerged primitive religion which was originally pursued in order to help with very specific problems having narrow application and which frightened and oppressed man. This was the pagan-religious period.

Man's outlook expanded and he comprehended – certainly at first from revelation – but afterwards from deeper contemplation- that there is only one factor which flowing from its power emerges all the laws of nature and all the winds that blow in worlds that are beyond man's control. Thus came into being the belief in one God. But the belief in one God did not come about from the beginning of time and did not penetrate man's consciousness from the beginning, since man needed a training period, in which he accustomed himself to the religious principle and idea, that was assimilated in him in the pagan-religious period, making him fit and prepared to approach the era of belief in one Divinity. The belief in one God is the belief in historical Divinity, that develops for the first time a vision of the end of days that is connected to one God – this end of days is the final continuum stretching from the creation of the world, whether that creation was believed to be *ex nihilo* (as Judaism believes, and its offspring, Christianity and Islam) or whether creation was not believed to be *ex nihilo* (as Hinduism and its branches – Buddhism, the system of Confucius and Shinto believe). In any case, just as paganism had paved the way for belief in one Divinity [1] so too did the original belief in one God prove capable of producing different and separate denominations.

One trend of the "birthing process" was the production of offspring that entered the world as a finished product, from which further offshoots would not be produced. This 'product' was the built-in capacity to create, a perhaps less sophisticated and less encompassing, set of ethics. Ethics begets neither religions nor rules of morality; they just develop into more refined and detailed rules of behavior.

Another trend of the "birthing process was the production of offspring that entered the world, capable of producing further offshoots. Mirroring the conception of the original monotheistic religion, which was generated within an atmospheres that believed in a multitude of gods, is the coming into being of the various monotheistic religions, where the singular monotheistic religion produced a multitude of independent offshoots. These usually did not repeal the original belief but rather added to it. (Examples are Christianity and Islam which emerged from Judaism; and Buddhism and the rest of the eastern religions that resulted from Hinduism).

A third trend, not really the result of any natural "birthing process", whose product is incapable of reproduction is the collective of non-theistic religions, ranging from nationalist to totalitarian ideas that govern society's lifestyle (e.g. socialism, communism, liberalism), and that came to fill the voids created by the death of theistic religions or by the latter being forced into hiding or being pushed into a corner. Nationalism- especially in its most basic ethnic form is a religion that was completely nurtured on the lap of theistic religion, but after weaning itself and being independently strengthened, following the example set by its ally in propagating ideas, totalitarianism, rid itself of its progenitor-parental, theistic religion. For all intents and purposes this theistic religion is synonymous nowadays with monotheism. This subject will be developed further in the second chapter, the summary chapter.

[1] From this perspective there is no clean break with the past since there are still the fibers of pagan belief and belief in forces that do not conform with monotheistic belief, which are remnants from the old pagan era

Chapter A:

A Review of the Opinions of Philosophers on the Origin of Religions

Ezekeiel Kaufman[2] differs from Durkheim's approach which seeks to understand and explain every cultural innovation as a result of the 'environment' (the milieu). Instead he says that if the source (for culture) had environmental conditions it would be a given that in every environment there would be a cultural innovation that would predictably follow one theme. The existence of multifarious innovations points to the fact, according to Kaufman, that the origin of cultural innovations stems from within the spirit of man and not from within environmental conditions.

Kaufman[3] also claims that monotheism, the belief in one God, is an Israeli national creation. But, in contrast to Kaufman's argument it can be claimed that the argument about religion as a spiritual innovation of man appears to contradict the claim that monotheistic religion is a nationalistic creation, since "the spirit of man" is an individual matter and not a national one. Is it conceivable that a group of people or a nation could have one spirit? Is it possible that a number of people 'will prophesize' in one spirit? After all 'environmental conditions' is a much better indicator of a group's common purpose than is the 'spirit', which is a more individual matter. Is it conceivable that a whole nation, comprised of many individuals, each with his unique free spirit, would simultaneously come up with the idea of monotheism, which is just one solitary religious system? In fact there should be a multitude of religious beliefs including various degrees of belief in various gods, whether each deity is universally all-powerful or whether each deity's power is fragmented so that its potency extends over a limited geographic or spiritual domain. On the face of it, belief in a multiplicity of gods or polytheism, in contrast to monotheism, is commensurate with range of spiritual yearnings, where each constituent individual of this society is able to create and develop a god for himself in accordance with his spiritual desires. Kaufman can therefore be taken to task for opining that belief in one God is a spiritual, nationalistic innovation of the people of Israel, and can be asked a very general question with regard to humankind within the context of monotheism – why did the heritage of mankind acuire a very limited number of monotheistic belief

[2] See Ehezkiel Kaufman, History of Israelite Belief from Ancient Days Until the End of the Second Temple (Jerusalem, Tel Aviv: Bialik Institute, Dvir, 1948), ibid, p. 22

[3] *Ibid*, pp. 7-8, and on p. 23 and onwards

systems representative of national and cultural groups, rather than creating a multitude of belief systems reflecting the overwhelming multitude of individuals.

Kaufman[4] says "the creative power of the spirit of man is the source of cultural innovation", where the concept 'cultural innovation' includes *inter alia*, religion and religious belief. Kaufman understands the difficulty this his words arouse, since they assume two things which must be proven at first, and they are mutually connected. It must be proven a) that the spirit of man indeed created this cultural innovation, that is, the spirit of man created the idea regarding the existence of Divinity and created the details of the message that this Divinity transmitted to its believers, and - b) that it is not possible that this cultural innovation emanates from another source– for example that the source is in fact that Divinity to which this message is associated –or that man discovered this same message by way of revelation or intuition.

Therefore, Kaufman[5] says:

"There are those who think that such an answer does not 'clarify' anything, since it is as if something vague is dependent on something vague. Yet there are natural sciences that assume a reality of 'forces' and "qualities" when analyzing data without further 'clarification'....indeed, the spirit is by definition a riddle beset by eternal questions as to its existence. .. After thorough investigation this riddle to is no more than a combination of raw material, space, time, movement, life, etc.... the spirit is an experimental phenomenon, in fact the most primeval experimental phenomenon. It is the first thing we get to "know" and it features primarily when making our assumptions about existence. And it is a **creative** force uncovering for us its revelations about human culture. This **creative force** is a result of the experimental dimensions of the spirit. Imagination, the intuitional genius, the capacity for invention, the skill for observation and contemplation, the ability to think abstractly by making essential connections between ideas and concepts, intellectual enquiry, moral evaluation for its own sake, the power of expression and signification, the ability to exert influence upon others – all these qualities cannot be explained in a vacuum extricated from their environment. The spirit in its capacity as creator, adds something of its own, drawing from its own reservoir, and therefore should be viewed as an independent source for creating culture, even if the spirit itself owes its existence to a specific set of environmental conditions."

If that is the case, Kaufman does not see embedded in the spirit of man the ability to discover concepts and to transfer them to another plane– and when speaking of

---

[4] Ibid. p. 22.

[5] Ibid

the religious domain this involves the transmitting of ideas that are beyond reality and translating them into real world concepts. Kaufman suggests that belief in the Divine entails an additional and precious human element* which imparts knowledge of the Divinity and likewise identifies messages as emanating from this Divinity. The difference between our knowledge relating to God and that which believers in Him are exposed to when it comes to the subject of Divinity is a topic categorized and developed in Judaism. In Judaism the well known idea that 'the Torah expresses itself in human terms'[6] concedes the fact that Divine matters are relayed to us in concrete terms so that we can relate to them from our perspective of reality. In fact the pure and unadulterated truth of the Divinity, as well as the depths of Divine purpose[7] can never be successfully grasped or fully comprehended.

Kaufman, although advocating the originality and authenticity of the Torah from the developmental-historical perspective, did not express Judaic traditional beliefs, that speak of the Torah that was given to the nation of Israel at Sinai, by revelation. Auerbach, whose writings will be presented at the end of this review, represents Judaism more correctly.

The argument relating to the question whether our knowledge of the Divinity is the product of our imagination or whether it exists independently of ourselves and was transmitted to our corpus of knowledge by way of revelation, is disputed in other belief systems apart from Judaism. Many different philosophers discussed this subject, and I shall discuss William James,[8] Robin Horton,[9] Andrew Nauberg,[10]

---

[6] And in this context I am not confining it to its narrow interpretation, of the Jewish religious law, where this expression, according to Rabbi Eliezer is used for a discussion on Jewish law in interpreting the words of the Torah according to Brachot 31(b) nor as Nachum Rackover interpreted the expression in his book 'Idioms of the Talmud', but according to the interpretation of the Ramban to the first chapter of the Book of Genesis, where he saw creation not necessarily as an accurate recounting of events but rather a big secret, whose revealed part only is written in the Book of Genesis.

[7] This conforms to what is written at the end of the Book of Job, where it turns out that no man – in this case Job – is capable of knowing and understanding in his limited and restricted consciousness the logic and intentions of the Creator of the world.

[8] See William James, Religious and Other Experiences – A Study of the Nature of Man (Jerusalem: Bialik Institute, 1968).

[9] See pp. 301-346. Robin Horton, "Tradition and Modernity Revisited", in *Patterns of Thought*, also Robin Horton, "African Traditional Thought and Western Science" in *Rationality* ,edited by Bryan R. Wilson (Oxford, England: Basil Blackwell, 1970), pp. 131-171.

Sigmund Freud,[11] Henry Bergson,[12] Max Weber,[13] Emile Durkheim,[14] Frederich Schliermecher,[15] Iliade, Fukuyama, Hocking, Otto, Hind, Frankel, Mart, Gellner, Spinoza, Winche, Weilson, Hollis, Robert Bellah, Shaul Shaked (on Hinduism),[16] Ephraim Auerbach.

William James, by admission a non-believer[17], and from this perspective lacking in religious encounters, delivered in the second half of the 1890s a series of lectures at the University of Edinburgh in Scotland, which included the diligently prepared and well researched subject *'Religious and Other Experiences, A Study of the Nature of Man'*. In the course of his presentation, he tried to provide an understanding as to the source of religious authority, the reasons and

---

[10] See Andrew Newberd, M.D., Eugene D'Aquili, M.D., Ph.D., and Vince Rause, *Why God Won't Go Away* (New York: Ballantine Books, 2001).

[11] See Sigmund Freud, Culture and Religion (Merchavia, Doar Afula: Kibbutz HaShomer Haartzi Publication, 1943) and also Sigmund Freud, *Totem and Taboo – and Other Essays*, translated by Chaim Isaac, appears in the original – *Writings of Sigmund Freud* – part 3, (Tel Aviv: Dvir, 1988), and also Sigmund Freud, *Culture Without Satisfaction – and Other Essays* (Tel Aviv: Dvir, 1988).

[12] See Henri Bergson, *The Two Sources of Morality and Religion*, translated by R. Ashley Audra and Claudesley Brereton with assistance of W. Horsfall Carter (Garden City, N.Y.: Doubleday & Company 1935).

[13] See Max Weber, *The Protestant Ethic and the Spirit of Capitalism* (Tel Aviv: Am Oved, 1984, translated from German by Baruch Moran, with an epilogue by S. N. Eisenstadt); Max Weber, *The Sociology of Religion* (Boston: Beacon Press, 1963 for the English translation. First published in Germany in 1922); and also Max Weber, *On Charisma and Institution Building, Selected Papers*, Edited and with an Introduction by S. N. Eisenstadt (Chicago and London: The University of Chicago Press 1968); and also Max Weber, *On Charisma and Institution Building* [in Hebrew] (Jerusalem: Magnes, 1979).

[14] See Emile Durkheim, *The Elementary Forms of the Religious Life*, Translated by Joseph Ward Swain, Introduction by Robert Nisbet (London: George Allen & Unwin, 1976).

[15] See Fredrich Schleirmacher, *On Religion – Speeches to Its Cultured Despisers*, Introduction, translation and notes by Richard Crouter, Carleton College (New York: Cambridge University Press, 1988).

[16] See *A Collection of Religions*, edited by Joseph Bentowitz (Tel Aviv: Joshua Chichik Publishing, 1963).

[17] See James's book in footnote 7 *supra*, p. 23

circumstances of the phenomena of religious encounters. James pointed to many instances of religious encounters that various people underwent and that were similar to phenomena of mental anomalies. Yet in later writings, after it was made clear that people indeed underwent religious experiences and their beliefs, in many cases, conformed to their religious experiences, he spoke of the personal interest as the source for the impulse that induces man to religious experience and to faith, as well as the impulse to carry out scientific experimentation. Where science is unable to provide the answers, man's drive to acquire knowledge may induce him to supplement his lack of knowledge by delving in mysticism which is linked to religious belief and experience. James advocated experiences that depend solely on our physical senses, yet he also held a deep belief of a reality existing above the realm of the human senses.

To summarize James's stated position on the question before us: what is the source for religious belief? James holds that self- interest and desire lie at the roots of man's belief. When circumstances exist where man does not succeed in reaching knowledge through "terrestrial" means he activates his desires so that he can communicate on the level of supernatural' intuition, communicating with transcendental objects that rise above human reality. Through experiencing revelation, man reaches out to his God, Who in turn exposes him to worlds of understanding and knowledge that cannot be accessed through natural means.

Robin Horton:

This integration of scientific pragmatism on the one hand and supernatural communication with supernatural forces, on the other, is investigated by Horton, who sees a logical application of this in the submission by primitively educated Africans to witchcraft. The impetus for submitting to witchcraft is as reasonable as the religious impetus found in western nations, especially since it is only undertaken for healing purposes, and is only embarked upon after a referral to a medical doctor, not a witch doctor, has yielded no tangible result. It is through this example that Horton understands the turn to religion which only occurs after more mundane irreligious methods have failed to provide aid. Religion, then, at least according to Horton's perception, is intended to facilitate those situations where no natural alternative exists.

Andrew Newberg

Within the framework of biological research published in 2001, Andrew Newberg and Eugene D'aquilli (the latter passed way during the experimental phase and did not live to see the published results) discovered very specific brain signals appearing during religious ritual encounters or other spiritual and meditative experiences. These signals were identical to those that appeared when a person found himself face to face with the truth. The conclusion that they hurriedly reached[18] was that religious experience paints a false picture of reality. They pointed to research that has revealed physical evidence of places where ritual sacrifice was performed that goes back to the beginning of mankind, which in their estimation is 200,000 years old. Newberg theorized that the reason the spirit of a deceased father was included as a religious motif was due to primitive man exercising his imaginative powers and comparing the smoke imparted from an extinguished bonfire with that that seems to be released from the cooling down of the corpse of a fellow tribesman. The extinguished bonfire is representative of the cooling process of a corpse, and just like smoke emerges from a fire that has been put out so too does the spirit of a person depart from the body of one who is dying and whose body warmth has been cooled in the process. Newberg presents another example of the power of the human imagination at work: the hunter, who senses the awesome might of his hunted prey, by using his imaginative and perceptive faculties, may figure out the idea that the power of the animal lies in his spirit. Since the animal when alive was a powerful force, the spirit of the animal, even if physically dead has its own potency. >From these examples there emerged the idea of belief in the power of the spirit. This powerful imagination together with an inclination to mysticism led man to form myths, and religions. The myths helped man to strengthen his spirit and overcome his fears. Newberg also speaks of the fact that in the modern era, science has been able to refute religious beliefs. At the opposite extreme, the immense power of religion and religious encounters, as has emerged from the biological experiments that examined the efficacy of religious experiences, as mentioned earlier, clearly demonstrates that the religious experiences man undergoes transmits false signals. The transmitted signals have an immensely powerful grasp and influence over man. Therefore, the religious experience is itself very persuasive and is not susceptible to being disproved.[19]

[18] My hesitant tone stems from the sparseness of evidence offered and the inability of scientific experiments to adequately reflect all of the world's religions at all times. The researchers relied upon very few experiments, e.g. one individual undergoing meditation, or the results upon one group undergoing what can be defined as a religious ritual, and then found that that in those experiences the observed subjects had a blurred view of reality. The researchers ignored the fact that rituals do not only take place within a religious framework and that democracy, for example, also has its own fair share of ritual ceremony. These ceremonies do not undermine the democratic process because of this fact. In a similar vein the authors do not question whether all of the world's religions have their source for observance in ritual, or whether ritual is just there in order to preserve an existent religion, and the founding principles of that religion are not, in fact, the outcome of meditative trances or ritualistic experience.

[19] See their book, *Why God Won't Go Away*, note 9, *supra*, at p. 160.

Newberg's study, which was partly undertaken in order to predict an answer as to the chances of religion surviving and being an active player in the day to day life of man, concludes by saying that man's connection to religion is based on man feeling oppressed and turning to religion which proved successful in offering support for his soul. He explains that the tools used to implement a religious situation are technical. These experiences are very similar in kind to the experiences we have of reality, and the way of achieving such an experience has nothing to do with true revelation but rather with grand manipulation, whereby man believes that his imaginary experiences are in fact real. Newberg predicts that religion will continue to play a role into the future. This is because religion is artificial and the product of manipulation. It is still deeply embedded in the distressed state of the primitive mind.

Newberg's book forms an appropriate part of the literature used by American Civil Religion in their "war" against theistic religions which is described in Part 3 of my book which deals with civil religion. His book was written in the context of contemporary American reality and appears to be the next stage in justifying the policy in the USA that promotes separation of [theistic] religion and state. This policy assimilates well with the experiments, carried out throughout the modern era, of certain philosophers who in the name of science, try and claim and even prove that theistic religion distorts man's vision of reality leading him to believe in things that cannot be verified. In one short sentence it is possible to summarize the opinion put forth in the research: religion distorts the minds of its believers and is untrustworthy. It exerts influence through self delusion. In the primeval period religions helped people find an outlet for their oppressed state. Religion perpetuates itself through promoting falsehoods, but has ceased to play a positive role. Phony revelation and empty fantasies lie at the source of all religions.

Sigmund Freud

Sigmund Freud also views religion as a negative phenomenon. He sees it responsible for producing unenlightened regimes which oppose cultural progress. Bearing this introduction in mind it is easy to understand why he uses emotions of guilt to explain ancient man's adherence to religious prohibitions that restricted his movements. In line with this thinking he explains the taboo imposed upon men forbidding them from engaging in sexual intercourse with female blood relatives of the first degree- mother and sister, and similarly, and for the same reason the graver prohibition of patricide. He relates over an event that occurred to the world's first father, who sired humankind. This father-according to Freud's speculation- did not permit the other males in his family to have sexual relations with the females, reserving that right exclusively for him, being the sole male who was allowed to engage in sexual activity. As a result thereof the sons united together and killed their father, but in order to prevent feuding between the brothers decided amongst themselves to ban sexual relations with their mother and sisters. It was this singular episode, according to the Freudian version, that caused this sexual prohibition to reach all the world's continents. Apart from this theory being odd and unserious, where the guilty feelings over the murder of a father proscribe the actions of all humanity of all different cultural backgrounds, living hundreds and even thousands of generations after this singular and solitary event occurred; it is difficult to look at feelings of guilt as being an important ingredient in the formation of religion or even in the distribution of universal ethical norms. Nonetheless, Freud did introduce an important concept, and that is the emotional element which indeed flavors the atmosphere surrounding religious ritual as well as playing a vital role in ensuring that moral rules and imperatives are followed. It is also true that the emotional element, which is prevalent in all societies everywhere, is the cornerstone of morality. The fact that Freud- who was wise enough to see the emotional dimension deeply embedded in religion-spoke only of the negative connotations of this dimension, I think stems from two basic reasons. (A) As a doctor of the soul dealing with psychoanalysis and mental disease Freud was more sensitive to and primarily aware of twisted feelings than he was of positive ones, and this approach affected his discourse on religion. (B) Basic to his theory is his outlook on religions as being all illusory[20], antagonistic to culture[21], mass hysteria[22], and whose days are numbered[23]. Freud said that even if claims are being made that religion ensures that "the world will never return to the same chaos which was removed thanks to thousands of years of cultural activity... for countless people religious laws are the only source of comfort in their lives and only because of their allure are many able to bear living ...at the same time it imposes an excess amount of guilt! Yet I am willing and able to destroy each and every [religious law], and furthermore to proclaim that a greater danger is foreseen to culture by keeping up its current relationship with religion than there is by completely halting it..."[24]

In contradistinction, in the course of a rather lengthy discussion on the Totem and the Taboo,[25] Freud elaborates upon the (religious) laws of the Totem and the Taboo praising their utility. He does not discuss there, the question as to how humanity came to draft these laws. It appears that the multi-pronged treatise on

---

[20] See his *Culture Without Satisfaction – and Other Essays* note 11 *supra*, at p.100.

[21] *Ibid.*, p. 103.

[22] *Ibid.*, p.132

[23] *Ibid.*, pp. 104, 110.

[24] *Ibid.*, p.101.

[25] In his book *Totem and Taboo – and Other Essays*, note 11, *supra*.

religious laws and mores- as it relates to the Totem- is attributable to utilitarian logic. He draws parallels between the childish imaginations of our modern world and the imaginations of the savages. He justifies this view by saying that just as today's children imagine their fathers to be some kind of beast who at times reveals himself to be violent , and at others to be loving, so too the relationship between savage and Totem wavers between two doctrines, teaching both a positive and negative relationship, on the one extreme protecting the Totem's life, on the other killing the Totem and devouring him[26].Freud fails to explain why ancient man sought to communicate with a father figure. It seems that, at least in this context, he does not delve into the root causes. He does not ask why ancient man wanted a relationship with a father figure, or why a father figure would be able to solve this person's problems. He just deals with technical explanations like which father figure was conjured up by primitive man. As previously stated, when speaking of the taboo that relates to the father and to the womenfolk, he does not contend with the fact that this taboo, which according to him is the result of a one-off event that occurred within a solitary family,(with the inherent premise that this one human family is genetically responsible for the entire human race, that dispersed itself over all the continents) was equally spread amongst all savages analyzed by anthropologists from Australia, Africa, far-off islands, and also America[27].

Henry Bergson[28],

-a Jew, whose father was Polish from a distinguished Jewish Warsaw family and whose mother was descended from British Jews, was a Nobel literature laureate and a member of the French Academy, who spent most of his life in France. Late in life he developed a strong affinity for Catholicism, yet at the time of the Nazi occupation he refused to accept any privileges that would exempt him from the laws that applied to other Jews, and insisting that he would suffer the same fate as his Jewish brethren, died as a Jew in 1941 at the age of 82. Bergson was Freud's contemporary, though a bit younger than him. He divided religions into two phases, the ancient religions he called Static and the more recent ones he termed, Dynamic. He says that human feelings and needs are the stimuli for Static religions. Religion came into being as a result of the personal needs of each individual as well as the needs of the societies that existed in ancient times. Religion came onto the scene under the heavy influence of human emotions, for

---

[26] *Ibid.*, pp. 115-119. Compare Shaked's analysis, where at the conclusion, he speaks of the identification between the sacrifice and the person who offers it as viewed by the Hindu religion.

[27] *Ibid.*, pp. 133, 138-143.

[28] See his book, note 12 *supra*

example: the idea that the spirit of one who has already died continues to exist was created to respond to the longings of those living relatives who still harbor powerful feelings towards the deceased. The idea of the spirit also serves society's needs; the need to believe and the need for natural continuity.[29] This all began with the idea of the soul of the departed and then turned into a religious institution evoking the influence that spirits exert on everyday events. In order to persuade the spirits to cause rain to fall man created the institution of myth and of offering sacrifices to appease the spirits. Bergson relates two incidents that he personally experienced and also quotes from a letter written by William James where the latter gives an account of what he underwent during the great earthquake that rocked San Francisco in April 1906. In all three of these events the impression created was that in each concrete situation there is a personal side, there is someone attending to these events, to the extent that in one of them the overwhelming feeling is that intentional evil is being wrought. Using these models Bergson concludes that ancient man attributed events to an entity that was not from the physical world, which after further processing of this idea he saw a kind of Divinity at play. Bergson explains that religion is more a reaction to fear than fear itself. Religion, in his opinion can be compared with witchcraft since both contain similar characteristics; science on the other hand has nothing at all in common with witchcraft. Generally he does see reason playing a central role in religion, which was formed out of a logically intuitive feeling that man's ability to comprehend everything is limited and that indeed there are things that exist beyond his reality that exert influence upon him, but about which he knows nothing.[30] Man did not choose the path of religion because he was a philosopher or great thinker, rather because of his general observation that he was a mere dot in a great universe, and because he basically understood that there was a universe; man sought the most helpful way of coping with this fact. The stimulus for finding a way out had much more to do with his vital needs than with any theological viewpoints. Man experimented different things, maintaining those things that were of value to him, and abandoning other things that he deemed worthless, or worse, damaging. It was reality that had the final say in man's decisions and his will to survive that dictated his actions. The idea of sanctity and Divinity was the end result of a genuine striving for value, and was reached at only after certain experiments and activities had proven its existence. This does not refer to the refined extraction of spirituality from material things. It was the result of a search for things that strengthen and support the spirit and desire of man, rather than man's striving to widen his understanding and enrich his spirit. Through this very elementary process of experimentation proofs were established pointing to

[29] *Ibid.*, p. 134.

[30] *Ibid.*, pp. 153-163.

witchcraft and magic and through this many different deities to whom prayers and requests were directed made their appearance. The path towards spirituality was paved with materialism and utility.

Continuing this line of thought and using the same theory, Bergson saw the development of religion changing from a static religion to a dynamic one. After starting off by ascribing a spirit to every "expressive" natural phenomenon such as a fountain or brook, and after having had a narrow conception of Divinity similar to that of the Totem, religion slowly devised deities whose reign stretched farther afield, so that it's boundaries were unlimited by local phenomena, as was the case with the Greek gods. This latter idea led to the abstract conception of a single all-powerful God, as is found in Monotheism. All these religious theories evolved through the same pragmatic and utilitarian avenues. They are all pragmatic, utilitarian, developmental, intellectual and empirical. Bergson talks about the myths and rituals that reinforced these religions. Sacrifices for example strengthened the bond between God and his believers since those offering it imagined themselves to be closer to God since they had fortified Him by offering up the blood of the sacrifice, the blood which is known to be the source of all strength. The meat of the offering was also meant to strengthen the Divine. Bergson deals with the basic question as to what sparked man's interest in God. He claims that man is the only living thing whose activities are tinged with insecurity, whose steps are hesitant ones, and who aspires for success while dreading failure, who feels the loneliness of one struck by a disease, who is keenly aware that he will eventually expire, and who knows that of all those in society, he alone is able to better his personal circumstances by looking out for himself and avoiding situations that carry with them a general risk to man. Amongst other beings that operate within their own societies, each individual member works for the betterment of the group since each sees their individual and group interest as harmoniously coexisting. Bergson claims that the unique conflict of interests that arises between the human individual and his society is the price paid for being endowed with reason, which in turn casts man into an atmosphere of uncertainty as to his future.[31]

---

[31] This is similar to what is recited in the Jewish New Year prayers, where it says *inter alia:*
On *Rosh Hashanah* will be inscribed and on *Yom Kippur* will be sealed, how many will pass from the earth and how many will be created, who will live and who will die, who will die at his predestined time and who before his time, who by water and who by fire, who by sword and who by beast, who by famine and who by thirst, who by storm and who by plague, who by strangulation and who by stoning, who will rest and who will wander, who will live in harmony and who will be harried, who will enjoy tranquility and who will suffer, who will be impoverished and who will be enriched, who will be degraded and who

When he eventually speaks about dynamic religions Bergson reveals an intimacy with Christianity, viewing it as the only true religion, while at the same time casting off any value from the other monotheistic religions. He selects three dynamic religions which are located at three different planes each ranking higher than its predecessor. First in line is the Greek Philosophical religion as practiced by Pluto who was said to have merged with the Divinity. The next ranking religions are those originating in ancient India: Brahmanism, Jainism, and Buddhism. The highest level is then "greater" Christianity, which by this is meant Catholicism.

In the first two rungs spirits played a central role, especially the second ranked religion, the Indian variety, as represented by Buddhism, which views gods and humanity occupying the same inferior plane.[32]Christianity also utilized certain features of static religion, such as naturalness [by this Bergson means the fundamentals of paganism, even if he does not explicitly say this- Y.C), yet the adoption of such features was done for purely tactical reasons, in order to "pass on" the Christian Gospel to the masses who were more accustomed to the pagan religions[33]. Christianity- according to Bergson the Jew- is superior Judaism. That this is correct can be gleaned from the fact that the Israelites exploited Judaism in order to preserve God for their own benefit through their role as His Chosen People; the special relationship to God was preserved through the conduit of nationhood. Christianity, in contradistinction, raised itself up a level allowing Godliness to infiltrate all of humanity. Judaism spoke in terms of a meticulous God who sits in strict judgment over those who believe in Him, whereas in Christianity, God spreads His love to all[34]. Admittedly the Prophets of Israel, who expressed themselves through mystical revelations and prophecies, were determined in their seeking out of justice, yet their message was defective for it only applied to a specific nation.

Bergson outlines the different stages of spiritual elevation traversed by religion and Greek philosophy. Philosophy developed in ascending order: (a) Dionysus

will be exalted. (*The Complete Artscroll Machzor, Rosh Hashanah* edited by Nosson Sherman and Meyer Zlotowitz, [New York: Mesorah Publications, 1985], p. 483.

[32] Bergson, p.222.
[33] *Ibid*, p. 238.
[34] *Ibid*, p. 240

philosophy, (b) Orpheus philosophy, (c) Pythagorean philosophy (d) Plato philosophy and (e) Alexandrian philosophy[35].

He explains that the stage arrived at by the Indians- the intermediate stage between Greek philosophy and Christianity- was preoccupied with human suffering, suffering that in the view of the Indians was caused by the human desire to live. Buddhism developed a solution to this problem. After the option of suicide was discarded because of the belief in the reincarnation of the soul, and the belief that in the case of suicide the suffering soul is punished by being reincarnated into another body ensuring that the person continues to suffer, an alternative solution was found. The problem of suffering would be solved by uprooting the will to live. After all the will to live is the source of all afflictions. Through using techniques of yoga which took man away from activating his thoughts and thus caused him to detach himself from the passion to live, man could distance himself from suffering. He could attain contentment.

What characterizes Christianity is its love for all. It is through this love that the elite of Christendom, who are possessed of a fiery willpower and who are thus capable of reaching the level of mysticism, are able to extend their influence. This mysticism, together with help from God, enables man to be perfect a very flawed character trait which flaw had been present at creation. This perfected character trait is the ability to love all human creatures.[36]

Christianity's main goal is imbuing humankind with mysticism. In order to succeed in this mission the messenger must be someone who has himself experienced the mysteries of mysticism. The whole undertaking is performed through religion, which in and of itself is merely a means, or an "external cover" for the hidden message. Religion is not important. Mysticism is important. After all religion predated Christianity, and had already existed during the period of the Static religions. Religion took the form of rituals and ceremonies. Christianity employed these religious aspects, although its essence was mystery, and many experienced Christianity in a concerted effort to feel the wonders of this mystery. This can be compared with the development of popular science which was designed in order to expose the masses to a real and practical science. Words, symbols and material concepts were resorted to, in order to attract the seer and to prepare the listener to take in their gospel to the extent that they are able. Mysticism can only be successfully experienced by a select few. But even this experience that these select few underwent was not unstained, and the only person to possess a crystal clear vision was Jesus himself, the first Christian famed for his

---

[35] *Ibid*, p. 220

[36] *Ibid.*, p. 234

Sermon on the Mount[37]. Even those who deny that Jesus even existed find it much more difficult to refute the contents of the sermon.

Generally speaking all the revelations and all the gospels in all of the religions, whether they are static or dynamic, are the outcome of an exerted effort and of willpower. From this angle, the development of religion mirrors that of philosophy. In this way[38] Bergson reduces all religions to a core product of human effort. Religion is not merely revelation unconnected with intellectual exertion, nor is it the outcome of pressures external to man, which as a result thereof he seeks spiritual elevation. Rather it is the result of an internal powerful desire that propels man to experience mysticism, an experience which only a select few will be privileged to undergo[39]. It seems that Bergson- who saw Catholicism as the ultimate religion- distorted his own sense of objectivity. This is quite starkly seen in his attitude towards Judaism- a religion that did not bow down to the graven images of Mary and Jesus which are so intimately connected with pagan worship or human Divinity-to which he gave no serious attention in his capacity as philosopher. Contrarily, it is specifically Christianity, known for rinsing its hands in the blood of Jews, especially during the crusades and inquisitions, which Bergson considers the harbinger of love of man solely by reason of man's innate humanness. In addition his excessive advocacy of Jesus' Sermon on the Mount as the only viable gospel, perfect and without fault; his insistence that the only true religion is Christianity; and his defensive posture towards Catholic Christian exploitation of pagan methods, taken together does serious harm to Bergson's theory.

Max Weber

-A German researcher who developed the science of sociology using an approach that combined economics and science, and who viewed social science as an exact natural science and as a science in which things could be dryly measured without being obscured by emotion. In his opinion it is possible to structure theories and systems that allow us to understand social processes, as well as providing us with the understanding of social phenomena through comparative studies in social science. Weber stressed that each person was endowed with his subjective and individualist viewpoint, but nonetheless he tried to incorporate these personal

---

[37] *Ibid*, p. 238-239.

[38] This is in addition to what Bergson already commented on with regard to primitive man who indeed did suffer from fears and insecurities and which therefore led him to draw closer to religion.

[39] It is patently clear that it was not Protestantism, which is available to everyone, that appealed to Bergson, rather it was the closed off world of Catholic mysticism

predispositions within the framework of typical behavior patterns. He died in 1920 at the age of 56. He introduced the idea of a link between the human spirit and a transcendental reality by taking up of the concept of "charisma". Charisma is a special mental state that is able to break free of the constraints of nature and to develop something else. A charismatic person is someone endowed with extraordinary powers, both of destruction and of creation; someone endowed with leadership qualities, who rebels against accepted norms but who is powerful enough to construct social institutions in place of those that he intends to do away with. This type of person is able to select a group of followers that he will be able to lead. A person blessed with brilliance is by definition charismatic, so too those privileged to experience Divine revelation or prophecy. Charismatic traits can emerge in any field of human activity, including science, culture, economics and management. Someone who is charismatic, generally speaking, will deny for himself life's daily pleasures. And indeed many of those possessing prophetic or artistic charisma never married.[40] Unsurprisingly, for the Jesuits celibacy is mandated as a precondition for priesthood in the church.[41]

Within the framework of Weber's theory, the creativity found in religious belief, including the birth of religions and their development, is the result of spiritual genius that penetrates the barriers of reality and becomes attached to those worlds that are beyond our reality. Notwithstanding the above,[42] the central feature that determines the development of the social environment is the economic factor. Weber explains that the Reformation in Europe created the type of person who was fiercely diligent and whose diligence was the consequence of a religious precept, and the profits that were yielded by this person's work were viewed by the worker as heaven's blessings and God's kindness in repayment for fulfilling his religious duty- that duty to be diligent and industrious. What happened when religion lost its allure was that rationalism and economic calculation replaced the religious precept of diligence, and utilitarianism took over as the motivating factor.

Weber, like his contemporary, Durkheim who lived at the same time and who also worked with him on creating the rules of the science of sociology, broke away

---

[40] See his book on charisma, note 13 *supra*, p. 13.

[41] See the *Midrash* on Moses that discusses with the verse: "the Ethiopian woman that you took", and the argument between him (Moses) and his sister Miriam who rebuked him for abandoning his wife. See also all the prophets of Israel and the bare mention given to their family life, which is even true in regard to the prophetess Deborah.

[42] In this way Weber's theory reinforces the analysis that was undertaken in this book on the difference between a utilitarian Western morality that is based on rights and on equality and a morality which has its source in theistic religion, which bases itself on duties and aspirations for spiritual elevation and the emulation of Divine qualities.

from the negative stance taken by his contemporary historians who dismissed viewing human history as the social development of human beings, which is determined by human action. This negation by the historians was merely a follow on to the previous wave of pro-Darwinists. They took Darwin's theory of evolution of the natural sciences and extended this evolutionary process so that it applied in equal measure to human lifestyles, and not only the lives of the other creatures of the universe.

Within the framework of viewing changes as the result of human activity especially in the field of human social interaction it was Durkheim who compiled anthropological studies of primitive tribes in Australia, which studies dealt with the degree of belief these tribes had in the Totem, and it was Weber who analyzed and compared the results reaching the overwhelming conclusion that man from the beginning believed in supernatural forces, just as from that very beginning he spoke using language and just as from his genesis he adhered to the rules of behavior that were included within the framework of the taboo. Weber's contention was accepted by all modern anthropologists from then on[43]. The opinion that casts doubt on whether there existed a world unregulated by natural events is relatively new and is the product of the modern skeptical culture.

Weber's discourse on primitive religions is commensurate with the above stated worldview, and is also commensurate with the trend of thought that sees religion playing a central role in the evolutions of society. Indeed- and quite apart from it being a stimulus for change- religion also has a stabilizing influence, especially looked at from the social angle, but Weber was not particularly interested in this aspect. What interested him more was religion's evolutionary impact upon human society, which alongside material interests and conditions played a defining part in effecting changes. In order to test his theory he initiated comparative studies in the field of world religion.

For the sake of measuring the influence religious factors exerted upon human behavior, Weber made a distinction between

(i) The witch/ magician who introduced rules of behavior that belonged to the taboo system, and

(ii) Those priests who introduced a broader religious ethic, which was able and did include as one of its components the taboo system.

---

[43] And indeed this opinion fits well with what is written in the first chapter of this book "Why religion?"

He also differentiated between

(i) Those details that are contained in (b) above i.e. the priestly rules of behavior that on the one hand are culled from a semi-covenant between man and the gods, whose covenantal conditions impose mutual obligations on both man and God, and on the other, are the product of a the supreme will of God to lead his flock by means of ethical mores, which themselves have a higher universal purpose, and between

(ii) Those rules having general application but which are endowed with an autonomous source of authority and though not the outcome of any covenant between God and man, strict adherence to them, reveals the believer to be assuming the highest degrees of responsibility. They cannot be changed using instruments of witchcraft neither are they susceptible to the witches` threat of punishment.

These three religious systems (encompassing rules relating to witchcraft, priestly rules, and rules of autonomous validity) evoke supernatural forces that endow them with supreme potency and through which they are able to influence society to introduce dynamic changes, including cultural change. In every human society, in his view, there are remnants of the influences of each of these supernatural systems.

The fact that religion is at one and the same time both a stimulus for change in society and a guarantor of its stability owes much to the influence of certain independent factors operating in tandem. In particular Weber includes intellectual capacity, the phenomenon of prophets, charismatic persons, and crisis situations. Intellectual capacity provides religious ideas with a platform; through its application man comprehends his mission and his destiny, ensuring that he give preference in his commitments to the duties that are imposed upon him over and above his earthly desires. Likewise intellectual capacity provides man with the malleability required for the performance of his duties, in order that he carries them out with a perfect faith and a pure will, since it internalizes the feeling of responsibility he has for fulfilling his obligations. Weber also speaks about prophecy and charisma as the motivating factors for the taking root of religion and for the changes caused as a result thereof.

Weber submits that religiosity is a vital component of the social lifestyle, performing a function similar to both that of blood ties in establishing ethnic groups and that of politics in managing social affairs. Weber, an economist by training and one who perceived economics to be taking center stage opined that the goals of religious activities are first and foremost economic ones. He added that most of behavioral patterns that are based upon religion deal with matters relating to our earthly existence. The first Divine images that we have, at least according to Weber's account of events, are inspired by spirits[44]. The imagery process began, in his opinion, by imagining that the spirit of an exalted hero continued to exist after his demise.[45] With regard to monotheism he held that only Judaism and Islam could suitably qualify as monotheistic religions, whereas Christianity and Hinduism must be excluded since both speak of involving the embodiment of the Divine and do not completely rule out spirits and demons from their religious frameworks. These declarations by Weber prove that he does not view Christianity in a favorable light. From this standpoint he is the polar opposite of Henri Bergson, the Jew who affiliated himself with Catholicism. Common to all religions- in accordance with the way Weber reads events- is deliberating over who will have the strongest impact on the individual's daily routine.[46] By making such a determination Weber proves once more that his approach is not an attempt to beautify religion but rather a far- reaching scientific study. This approach is commensurate with Weber's single-minded conviction that everything must be scrutinized under a social scientific lens, thus religion must be treated as a science and be observed and reflected upon in the same manner as one would natural scientific phenomena.

Although he speaks about the charismatic state of mind that allows those possessed of charisma to be in touch with supernatural worlds, when it comes to dealing with reaching such a state of mind, he explains that one would need a strong will to reach such levels, and similarly, then, for one who wants to communicate with a world that exists beyond our reality, a transcendental world, one would need to perform human acts and would need to will his mind to produce this extraordinary circumstance. When speaking about a prophet Weber explains that a prophet is one possessed of charisma, and he is granted these extraordinary qualities in order that he completes his mission successfully.[47] In this context Weber does not enter into the question how the prophet received word of his mission at the outset, but in another place in his book dealing specifically with charisma, Weber explains that the revelation witnessed by a limited and select elite is the direct outcome of the activation by each constituent individual of his high powered and strong willed mind. If we are to connect what has just been stated with that that was stated earlier, namely that everything performed in pursuit of a religious objective is primarily embarked on for economic attainment, it would

---

[44] See Weber's book *The Sociology of Religion*, in note 13 *supra, ibid.*, at p. 1.

[45] *Ibid.*, at p. 4.

[46] *Ibid.*, at p. 20.

[47] See *ibid.*, at p. 46.

appear- even if Weber does not so in as many words- that, as a rule, religion and faith in God are the products of man's own labors. Weber's central message is that religion is not the direct product of a Divine initiative; rather it is manufactured through the efforts and initiatives of man, who within the framework of (physical) human activity aims at achieving Divinity. Following this line of thought, it now makes sense why man calls out to his God much more frequently than the opposite scenario. Weber does not deal with the question whether the phenomenon of Divinity which comes about as a result of man's toil is in fact a true phenomenon. All that interests him is the result of the belief that the Divine indeed appeared. He deals with the extent of the impression made by the religious factor and its impact upon other participants vying for a prominent position in man's social arena, especially economic factors, like the struggle between farmers and shepherds, or political factors such as the military trespass over a neutral country in order to use it as a thoroughfare with all the resultant geopolitical aspects. All of these are enmeshed in religion and in turn influence the path religion will take.[48] This is even given expression in the type of deity chosen and the ethical norms attributed to him which are incumbent upon his believers. The class of merchants and of other men of wealth have no interest in obeying tough precepts that demand they part with their possessions, and therefore the type of god they will choose will fit this type of mindset, so that the ethical demands of these gods will be very limited, and at times will for all practical purposes be non-existent.[49] Through this analysis Weber proves his contention that religion and God come to serve the community according to its objectives and its needs.[50] There is even the notion that each class

---

[48] See *ibid.*, at p. 81.

[49] See *ibid.*, at p. 92. in this way God is malleable in accordance with man's whims, whether He be at times the result of a strong desire on the part of man or whether God becomes a vital element in man's life, it all depends on the independent situation of the individual in question

[50] We can reinforce Weber's contention by observing the various climatic conditions and vicissitudes of the Land of Israel, which requires therefore according to the Weber theory an all- demanding God like the God of Israel whose many, myriad and complex commandments suit a community whose lifestyle is agricultural and who are dependent on rain, which following the Land of Israel's weather patterns are not consistent or foreseeable. We can add to this the sacrifices made by man in those communities which are involved in difficult wars, where it is necessary to produce amongst the warriors a great and keen decisiveness to do battle. The readiness of the king to sacrifice his son's life arouses the sympathies of others and strengthens the battle, as can be seen in the episode of Mesha the king of Moab who when he was losing the battle against the Israelites, sacrificed "his eldest son that should have reigned in his stead and offered him for a burnt offering upon the wall. And there was great indignation against Israel, and they departed

within society is allocated its special religion, adding fodder to the idea developed by Weber on the link between economic needs and interests, and the content and scope of religious observance of its precepts and the preservation of its character, which are relative to the financial situation of the respective believers. Religion and its precepts, then, fit every social stratum in the same way as a tailor stitches a suit "according to size."[51] Sometimes, when a new religion does not suit the

---

from him, and they returned to their own land," as is described in the last verse of Chapter 3 in The Second Book of Kings.
(*The Holy Scriptures*, edited and translated by Harold Fisch, (Jerusalem: Koren Publishers, 1983), p. 444. See also the daughter of Jephte whose father swore an oath that he would sacrifice the first thing that he comes in contact with if and when he is victorious in his war against the Moabite king, a war which was expected to be very difficult. We can add to this the fact that apart from the democratic period, where the political significance of women improved because of the openness mandated by the democratic era and their resultant elevation in status- all religions that took over the reins of control set up rules that trampled upon the status of women, thereby entrenching the male interest, which was- from a social perspective- connected to the overwhelming imbalance of power that existed in communal affairs in favor of men over women. This status quo was taken for granted in secular society. This happened in Islam, where Mohammed declared that women cover their faces with a veil causing some kind of (negative) development in their personal status as opposed to their stronger position during the period of "ignorance" where a woman was able to marry a number of men at the same time and to annul her relationship with her husband out of her own volition, and more importantly she was also able to hold over family property. So too with Christianity, which for the period when it did not hold sway over government spoke to the woman's heart, but this disappeared very soon after they regained control. The same can be seen in Judaism where the denomination that managed communal affairs for hundreds of years, the Orthodox denomination, which even in the State of Israel holds some sway, does not campaign in the same way for the rights of women as does Conservative and Reform Judaism both of which have never held a position of autonomous authority within the Jewish communities, and because they have never been in positions of power, take a stand very similar to that taken by Christianity which in its early period acted very much in favor of women. The democratic and intellectual spirit with its commitments to women forced politicians in the West to agree to grant women the right to vote, and after this it was quite obvious that women's rights would grow, as did the power of their voting bloc. Orthodox Jewry still insists that those who are appointed overseers are men. The synagogue council and rabbi are therefore all male. Already at the age of childhood and adolescence Orthodoxy provides separate educational facilities for males and females, even requiring a high and more difficult study to be taught to the male gender at the same time assigning the bulk of the housework on girls and on female teenagers. It seems though that this situation will also become obsolete even in this last stronghold of male dominance reminiscent of an antiquated past that existed in generations gone by.

[51] See *ibid.*, at pp. 95-103.

communal needs, it provides the locally entrenched religions, which are capable of satisfying these needs, with a platform to assert their relevance, and in this roundabout way ensures that the new religion adapts itself to suit the community's needs.[52]This theory then sees religion as being accepted into society owing to its chameleon like ability to suit all circumstances. It is difficult to reconcile this outlook with the idea that it is revelation that is the source for religious belief, and it can only be squared if we accept that "revelation" is something we can plan ahead for, something that human exertion can make happen, and after trying really hard, can produce the desired result.

Weber expand this theory to such an extent that he is unable to accept that beyond concrete interests there are also pure spiritual forces that pave the way for the religious message to filter through, a message empowered with the ability to move a whole congregation of men to behave in a way that is contrary to their own interests. Weber's obstinacy is blatantly demonstrated when he tries to understand why the Jews who have been persecuted and who have endured terrible suffering while exiled in the Diaspora, cleaved to their religion. He seeks to know why the Jews refused to renounce their religion and assimilate with the ruling classes with whom they lived in close proximity. He combines this question with one dealing with the caste system in India where the lower castes have similarly refused to give up their low ranking, keeping their status intact. [53]Weber's answer is that the Indian low caste community believed in reincarnation of the soul and following this belief was convinced that should they assimilate with others they will lose the possibility that their souls will be reincarnated and will thus forfeit life after death[54]. With regard to the exilic condition of the Jews Weber speaks of the fear of having a black spell cast upon every Jew who converts to another faith. Weber does not take into account the fact that reincarnation of the soul in the Indian

---

[52] See *ibid.*, at p. 103.

[53] See *ibid.*, p. 109.

[54] Indeed this is the correct answer, yet it was motivated not by fear but by hope in the wonderful tidings with regard to the reincarnation of the soul. See *Anthology of Religions* (in Hebrew), edited by Joseph Bentoitz, with a foreword by R. Y. Zvi Werblowsky (Tel Aviv: Yehoshua Chechick Publications, 1964) at p. 65 it is stated:

> Through the Openishandot the idea of reincarnation had already been given expression. A person is being constantly reborn after his death in the form of one of the cosmos's existing creations, and his rebirth is dependent upon the type of deeds he performed and the life he had led in his previous incarnation ... one cannot conclude from here that the *weltaunshaung* of the Openishandot was pessimistic. Quite the contrary is true. Life was indeed uneasy since man was constantly looking to break free of it, yet the Openishandot had with them the great tidings that it was possible to break free and be liberated from life.

culture is a positive omen, not the cause of great fear. A member of the Tama sect believed with all his heart that if he faithfully fulfilled his duties as a devoted member of the sect, he would be reincarnated into the body of someone of higher rank. He viewed his present incarnation as a purely temporary state of being. Likewise Weber does not even take into consideration the more prosaic fact that the higher castes were in no way willing to sacrifice the destiny of a lower caste member, bearing in mind that each person's membership within a specific caste was public knowledge making assimilation amongst the various Tami castes not only socially unfeasible, but also unviable for the financial hardship such a move involved. Concerning the Jews, who were known for their spiritual superiority thanks mostly to their unique religion, it is odd indeed that Weber failed to realize that Jews felt their Judaism to be possessed of an inner beauty making it superior to all else. If Weber had bothered to research the tractates of Jewish prayer, he would have realized to what extent the Jews viewed themselves as superior to the nations of the world. Furthermore all Weber had to do was review the corpus of Jewish scholarly material- that turned the Jews into the "people of the Book" and not only because of the Book of Books, the Bible, but also because of the breadth and depth of study instilled in Jews at a tender age making them into a truly learned nation. Weber would then have to compare this with the feelings of superiority on the part of the English who prided themselves on their widespread Bible reading groups, which as a result of investing in this Bible reading venture, the English felt themselves freer than the Catholics, who in contradistinction were held hostage in their understanding of the Bible to what was told and explained to them by the Bishop in church. As a result of the abovementioned, England was able to enlarge their publishing houses and to multiply the amount of newspapers printed, which in turn ensured higher levels of trade which translated into a higher average standard of living especially in relation to France and Spain, so that the English felt that they were the "chosen people" entrusted with a "mission" which led to their setting up of a vast empire, which created the myth of an unified English nation, not to speak of a British one. In this way religion's positive elements were given recognition, not because religion helped in serving the economic needs of England, which has been shown in the above example, but owing to the fact that it was the Protestant religion that was responsible for creating the British People and by extension, the American nation.[55] Bearing this in mind and relating it to the Jewish experience, there should be no grounds for wondering why the Jews viewed it as great punishment to have to relinquish their cherished uniqueness, viz. their religion and their God. Weber discounted all of this, and while he may have perceived things correctly when they related to

[55] See the first part of this book "Why religion?" *Ibid* at notes 49, 50 and 51 of "Why religion?" as well as the various references provided there.

economic issues, viewing everything as dictated by pure interest blinded him from appreciating the full picture, including the beauty of spirituality that is found in religion, which light does not only provide material benefit to its adherents, but which also contains an internal magic. [56] His eyes were blinded to such an extent that he regarded the tendency of Christians living in the East to accept upon themselves the rites of Islam- the reigning religion- as something sensible and predictable. Weber's point of view on religions in general- an economic point of view which resembles natural science more than it does social science- is similar to the point of view expressed by an unmarried banker who in his youth was

---

[56] See Weber's book *The Sociology of Religion* in note 13 *supra, ibid.,* at p. 110 where it contains Weber's sarcastic description of the local Jews to whom God's promise of salvation means that at the appointed time of redemption they will not need to borrow money from others and will be able to lend to others, which earns them the right of being usurious money lenders in the ghetto. The Jewish belief, especially prominent at times of feelings of inferior status, in the coming of the Messiah, seemed to Weber,-who was the standard bearer for facts that were firmly implanted in *terra firma,* and which were calculable by economic measures- as a pathetic scheme. Weber's vision parodied what is written in the portion *Ki- Tavo* (lit: When thou art come [in to the land]) in Deuteronomy Chapter 28, verses 1 and 12-13, where it is stated:

> And it shall come to pass, if thou shalt hearken diligently to the voice of the Lord thy God, to observe and to do all his commandments which I commanded thee this day, that the Lord thy God will set thee on high above all the nations of the earth... The Lord shall open to thee his good treasure, the heaven, to give the rain to thy land in its season and to bless all the work of thy hand, and thou shalt lend to many nations, and thou shalt not borrow. And the Lord thy God shall make thee the head, and not the tail, and thou shalt be above only, and thou shalt not be beneath, if thou hearken to the commandments of the Lord thy God. (*The Holy Scriptures, supra,* note 50, at pp. 243, 244.)

This does not refer to free gifts but is repayment for someone who fulfills all the moral precepts that God imposed upon him, according to his observance so he will be worthy, at the end of his spiritual journey to receive this back payment Did Weber not even pause to consider the fact that a Jew who lent usuriously was wise enough to realize that he was not receiving some economic bargain based upon financial considerations that can be universally judged but rather realized that usury was a basic necessity for surviving a Ghetto life wrought with hardship and which money lending entailed great risk not only to himself but also to the other members of his household, but where he carried on being in a (forced upon) Jewish occupation for the sake of the spiritual promise of the end of days that, despite all, he overwhelmingly preferred to a [comfortable] Christian lifestyle? Had Weber extricated himself from the all too limiting arena of economics while trying to figure out the importance of the spiritual domain, the religious domain, and had he elevated himself to reach the spiritual level of that same Jewish usurious moneylender, who was seemingly interested only in calculating the interest owed him, he would have had a much more positive understanding of the whole religious aspect.

educated at institutions and not at his parents' home, and therefore, viewing family life through the eyes of a professional, and informed by his banker's *weltaunshaung* expresses wonder, why the female in the family is intent upon producing children from her womb and nurturing them, when that same woman as a professional first class surgeon can be earning a high paying salary, and owing to her pregnancy is bound to lose a good fortune, whereas if at the same time she were to adopt children, this adoption would save the household a significant sum of money. It is quite likely that this young banker would be quite qualified to analyze the financial aspects of running a family, but he has no expert knowledge on family life itself. After analyzing the way Weber discusses religion, it would appear that he did not undertake an internal perspective of the religious elements, and therefore his perspective remains utilitarian- economic.[57]

Weber's assessment of the role played by Protestantism in the advancement of capitalism is of course incomplete, especially since it predates surveys measuring the influence of traditionally Protestant Bible reading, by researchers who publicized their findings many years after Weber's death. Nonetheless Weber preceded those studies that were embarked on in order to assess missionary zeal, and which was later developed by English and American researchers influenced by Protestantism[58], when they speak of *beruf* in German or a *calling* in English.[59] Weber speaks about the development of this idea by Luther[60] who heaped criticism on the Catholic priesthood which through its idleness brings about the sins of a loveless selfishness and a shirking off of earthly responsibilities. Having exhausted his need for criticism, Luther did an about turn converting his words of rebuke into words of appreciation for working within a profession, seeing it as a depiction of love for one's neighbor. Luther developed this idea explaining that only through fulfilling all the conditions of one's earthly obligations can man derive God's will and therefore all the legitimate professions were equally good in His eyes. As Weber demonstrates, Lutheranism developed into many different denominations, the main ones being Calvinism, Pietism, Methodism and Baptism. Calvinism taught the believer that only a select few of mankind would be worthy of salvation of their soul, the rest were to be eternally damned, heaven's edict was against them

---

[57] See the distinction Hart makes between internal perspectives and external perspectives in his book, H. L. A. Hart *The Concept of Law,* Second Edition, pp. 89-91, 242-243, 254.

[58] As it emerges from what we have shown concerning the Bible reading by the English which was continued by the Puritans in the United States, as detailed in the first part of this book "Why religion?", in notes 49, 50, and 51 of that part, and as we have detailed the matter here.

[59] See Max Weber *The Protestant Ethic and the Spirit of Capitalism,* in note 13 *supra, Ibid.,* at p. 35.

[60] *Ibid.* at p. 36.

from birth and was unalterable, nothing could help this individual, especially since his fate was sealed in advance. Nevertheless a believer still had to fulfill his duties to glorify the hallowed name of the Lord. This is the most difficult predicament for a believer, so Weber alleges. Together with his obligation to belong to the "true Church" as a condition for salvation the Calvinist maintains his relationship with God via the deep solitude of the soul, which is exemplified in the depiction of Christian's behavior in John Banyan's book which was the most widely distributed book in Puritan literature. After it becomes clear to him that he is dwelling in the "city of destruction" he hears the voice beckoning him to embark on a pilgrimage to the "heavenly city" His wife and children cling to him, [not wanting him to leave], yet he is deaf to their pleas and runs towards the beckoning voice. This is a depiction of a man who lives with a sense of terrible isolation[61] whose behavior Weber projects onto those denominations which were influenced by the Calvinist and the Puritan traditions in their approach to individualism (which is connected to feelings of isolation) and in the serious and meticulous attitude towards fulfilling one's obligations, both with regard to work and with regard to loving one's neighbor, so that love of a fellow human being is not contingent with how much love one showers another member of society but rather upon the fulfillment of Divine commandments. Both in Weber's interpretation of Banyan's story and in his writings quoted earlier with respect to the difficult predicament into which Calvinism places one, knowing that one's personal fate is sealed from birth, Weber reveals a basic deficiency in his comprehension of religion and the way in which man relates to his God. Weber did know that a Christian, any Christian no matter what type of Christianity he subscribed to, believed that the Lord was a very kind God, and also that this Christian was taught when he was still at his mother's breast to love God without any thought of any reward that he might receive for showing this love. In order to understand this above principle that is given so much prominence in Christianity, but is in fact a principle followed in every theistic religion, exemplified by the binding of Isaac[62], it is explained that

---

[61] *Ibid.* at p. 51.

[62] This happens when Abraham obeys the Divine message "Take now thy son, thy only son Isaac, whom thou lovest and get thee into the land of Moriyya; and offer him there for a burnt offering" (*The Holy Scriptures, supra,* note 50, at p. 22), in contradistinction to the episode in Sodom, where he protests against the evil decree that has been declared upon the inhabitants of Sodom and argues with God: "Shall not the Judge of all earth do right?" (*Ibid.*, p. 18), trying to somehow soften the verdict. Abraham, according to Weber's theory was not meant to submit to God's commandment. in this instance (i.e. the sacrifice of his son), not because it was a violation of the Divine promise: "Sarah thy wife shall bear thee a son indeed, and thou shalt call his name Isaac: and I will establish my covenant with him for an everlasting covenant, and with his seed after him" (*Ibid.* p. 16) The reason, as Weber has it, is not because of a violation of an explicit Divine promise, but because there can be

humanity's behavior towards the Divine stems from the emotional realm, the realm of love. A man cleaves to his God because of his love towards Him and because of his yearning to do His will, which he will do even if that will has no ready explanation. Indeed he does it not for the sake of any reward he may collect in this world, and neither for the sake of reward that he may receive from a place which he truly believes exists, viz. the hereafter. Once this is comprehended it becomes quite clear that "the heavenly city" depicted in the story of Christ is not merely repayment, neither is it a matter of mere salvation, nor even the reward that man receives after his death, but much more importantly it is the fact that one is being placed in close proximity with the most loved thing of all, God.

Weber explains that the expansion and eventual branching out of Calvinism gradually introduced to its denominational members the belief that by working hard and relentlessly on fulfilling ones obligations and on behaving impeccably man assures for himself his salvation, and therefore the norm of relentless and hard work hard was reinforced, interpreted as it was as forming part of the ministering to God, in the event that "a Calvinist, like those in the business of profit making, assures for himself his own salvation"[63] Again: the explanation that Weber does not offer and which would complement his understanding and comprehension is the explanation of love of God. We can also ask Weber to explain the Calvinists' decision to leave France, to abandon their land and their homes, and to wander about with their portable belongings in England and Germany, without knowing what will eventually happen to them. Had Weber asked himself to explain this incident, it is difficult to say what he would have answered, what more had they accepted upon themselves the tenets of Catholicism these wanderers would have guaranteed themselves a safe "free passage" to paradise.

For the purpose of analyzing Weber's theory it is unnecessary to study the details of his explanations in depth, since we are not dealing here with the connection between capitalism and Protestantism. It is important, though to end this subsection by noting that according to Weber religions change according to the needs of their human followers. It follows from this- even if Weber does not explicitly say so - that his theory fits the worldview that says that not only the

---

no replacement (economic or tangible according to Weber) that can compensate for the loss to Abraham of his son Isaac. Abraham had nothing to lose [by refusing God?] and concrete calculations, according to Weber cannot explain Abraham's action with respect to the whole binding incident. The explanation can be found beyond the realms of which Weber speaks, as will be explained later.

[63] Ibid., at the end of p. 55.

development of religion serves the needs of the human race, but also the origins of religious faith and of religions themselves follow this pattern-.

Emile David Durkheim

-was a Jew, the son of a rabbi from Alsace. He lived between the years 1858-1917, and was a contemporary of Max Weber. He was active at the end of the nineteenth century and at the beginning of the twentieth, and was considered to be Weber's twin since both dealt with social sciences and religion. Both were thought of as the best sociologists of religion up until the middle of the twentieth century. Durkheim was a self-proclaimed heretic who dedicated most of his time to the study of science and logic, and believed that intellectual progress was buried beneath the thoroughfare linking religion with science. Despite this, in the course of his studies he formed the opinion that apart from the deep idea of sanctity- which in his opinion was an essential component of all religions- nothing can be of everlasting value to mankind. Sanctity and sociability according to Durkheim are two sides of the same coin and the difference between holy and secular is the most meaningful difference that has ever been observed in human thought. The concept "sanctity" as interpreted by Durkheim is similar to the "charisma" that is used in the Weber model. In his social philosophy he gave a lot of weight to the influence exerted by social factors upon human behavior.

Durkheim saw in religious rituals the tools that bind together the individual with his ethnic community and his social order. Religion is the source for those principles that allow human society to run its course, such as the principle of the sanctity of private property and the sanctity of contract.

Durkheim contends that religions multiplied with each new religion extracting principles from the religion that predated it, i.e. – all religions, so he thought, form one continuum that originated from one principal religion, and so in his estimation there is one basic and general thing that has been perpetually carried over in the various religions, yet in order to properly research each and every religion it is necessary to start by investigating the subjective motives of the (religion's) followers. He therefore studied religions by looking at the subjective viewpoint of the believer, and by delving into the latter's thought processes and emotions. Viewing his subjects from this observation post he did not agree with the opinion that says that the act of the believer turning to God is performed in order to fill a need in the believer to understand, to investigate, and to subsequently find the truth. In his opinion what the believer is seeking by drawing himself to God is the hope of receiving an inner spiritual strength. In order to obtain this, rituals are arranged and rites are performed. For man, rituals bring into sharp focus the concept of time, the concept of God, and the elevated reason and purpose of living. When taking sides in deciding who has the upper hand in the competition between religion and science, he prefers the scientific option in explaining the workings of the universe, but would back religion when it comes to many other areas, that are not under the rubric of technology or utility.

He argues with Robertson Smith, who sought to introduce into anthropological research the notion that offering sacrifices are not meant to appease God or to shower him with gifts, since in any event the subject of the sacrifice as well as everything else has always belonged to God, and indeed nothing would exist were it not for God's presence. Smith is of the opinion then that the offeror of the sacrifice would not have laid a hand on the offered beast merely for the purpose of handing over something to someone who in any event owns it and which is within His jurisdiction. Smith maintained that the offering up of a sacrifice was an act performed to promote closeness between man and his God. Durkheim argues with every one of Smith's contentions. Basing himself on sketches drawn by the primitive Australian tribes which depicted their sacrifices to the Totem, an act that reflected a very early form of religious communication, and in an era that predated contact with the gods and the spirits, Durkheim concludes that one cannot concur with Smith's theories. The reason underlying Durkheim's adamant rejection is the fact that the Totem was never considered being a deity, neither a Divine entity nor an idol, and nothing ever belonged to him. The Totem in fact is composed of subhuman and mysterious forces. If the sacrificial ceremony were to be terminated it would lead to the downfall of the Totem. Man is the very creature who sustains this "god", without man the Totem would cease to exist forever. Smith held that the offering of a sacrifice, which is comprised exclusively of food, takes place in order to guarantee man that he will never lack food, yet Durkheim reveals that in at least one of the sacrificial ceremonies, that of pouring water as an omen for rainfall, it was done prior to the offering of the sacrifice, and therefore it is illogical to assert that the sacrifice itself comes as a surety that he who offers it will be provided with sufficient quantities of food[64]. Therefore sacrifices can indeed be considered a type of gift that has been delivered at the time of it being offered up. When seeking an explanation for the root causes for the institution of sacrifices, Durkheim[65] suggests that the reason underlying it has to do with the community's perpetual insecurity, as instanced when someone questions whether the dry season with its withering plants will eventually pass and allow once more for the produce to grow, or when wondering whether the dwindling prey, which is very much a factor of seasonal and climatic changes will once again be

---

[64] See Emile Durkheim *The Elementary Forms of the Religious Life*, in note 14 *supra* at pages 336- 343.
[65] *Ibid.*, at p. 344.

replenished. A man earnestly seeks an ally, and by thinking that the prolongation of man's existence ensures the existence of the world and the existence of the gods, he turns to these gods as his natural ally with the claim that they have the same vital interest in the invigoration of nature, as he does.[66] Durkheim notes that people's souls are emboldened when faced with the opportunity of offering a sacrifice; the fact that religious ceremonies such as these take place in the midst of a popular gathering can only add strength to the individual participant. Durkheim summarizes his opinion on the matter by saying that both man and his gods reap the benefits of sacrificial offerings, and while it is a truism that man – in keeping with his faith- cannot live without God, it is also the case that God cannot function without the sacrificial offering, and therefore the most important thing that man can offer God are his reflection on God. God only survives in the consciousness of man. In this way man and God enjoy a mutually beneficial relationship. Durkheim continues this thesis of symbiosis when discussing a completely different matter viz. the relationship between man and his society. He reaffirms the principle that without society, man would be devoid of spiritual values, and obviously without the human constituent of society, i.e. man, society would never come into existence. The replication of this symbiotic relationship, found both in the ties that bind man with his God, and in those binding the individual to society was the stimulus for the idea of offering sacrifices. It then makes perfect sense that the ceremony accompanying the offering up of sacrifices joins together these (two relationships that are composed of) three participants, man, God, and society (the community that takes part in the ceremony).

Durkheim's theory in principle mirrors that of Max Weber's. Both refer to religion's utilitarian aspect and both analyze religion using social needs as their setting. This all makes sense if we bear in mind Durkheim's assertion that all religions share one common origin and each religion is the product of its predecessor.

Frederick Daniel Ernst Schleiermacher

-was a German Protestant minister who was also the son of a minister, and who entered the clergy at the age of 22. When he turned 28, at which time he became a minister in Berlin, he managed to pave his own way to fame through his series of lectures on religion that he delivered to an intellectual audience who were non-believing, within the framework of the disputations that were rife in the Germany of that time. These lectures were later published in book form[67] so that

[66] See the first part of this book "Why religion?" next to note 14. Also compare the above with the beginning of chapter 2 of the first part of this book- "Why religion?"

[67] The book was called, *On Religion, Speeches to its cultured despisers,* in note 15 *supra.*

his fame quickly reverberated far and wide. In this book Schleiermacher tries to prove the superiority of religion over morality and metaphysics which are anyway, in his opinion offshoots of religion.[68] The three fundamental aspects of the human consciousness, according to his system[69] are recognition, will and emotion. He structures these elements in a way that proves the superiority of religion above all else. He explains it in the following way:

Recognition- adapts abstract thought into reality, and into its natural objects.

Wilful acts - adapts reality into abstract thought expressing itself in the spiritual realm

Emotion- deals with God who is identified as the unifying force that binds together abstract thoughts and tangible reality, nature and spirit (where the material and spiritual converge)

This unity, which is God, allows humans the power of recognition but at the same time He Himself cannot be detected.

The result: God wields His influence, but cannot be comprehended, explains things, without being explainable.

Owing to man's adeptness at being able to describe complex facts, which skill is a gift from the Divine, the human spirit, the faculty of man's will, is able to adapt concrete reality into abstract thought, whereas the faculty of human recognition converts into nature that which it receives on the level of abstract thought. Within this theory there is some kind of balance and pecking order between substance and spirit, between lower and higher spheres, where the latter also joins together spirit and substance.

Theoretically Schleirmacher could have based his theory on the logical premise that the three spiritual entities whose source exists outside the parameters of reality, viz. morality, metaphysics, and religion, by definition had to have all originated from the same celestial plane, since one cannot imagine that there are a number of different and competing sources, which, in the absence of one unifying force, would cause our world to turn topsy-turvy. Since there is order in the universe we have to view everything as emanating from the source for creation of the world. The source for the creation of the world is by definition the source for the rules that govern creation, and thus we get to his definition of God. Since

---

[68] See *Ibid.*, at pp. 97- 99.

[69] As outlined in the *Hebrew* Encyclopedia under the entry that bears his name.

religion is by its very essence connected to faith in God, (in contradistinction to the other two spiritual entities that were mentioned), we should view it as being closest to the source, and therefore superior.

Yet Schleirmacher does not choose the route of logical persuasion, since he views God as the supreme being, that cannot be humanly comprehended, neither by comprehension through recognition (which has the power to discern nature, but not the Divine, and therefore adapts abstract thoughts into reality by observing nature) nor by human willpower and by the human spirit (which operates in the opposite direction, and which adapts reality so that it takes on the abstract form of human thought). Man can comprehend what is created and can contend with these things, but he cannot elevate himself to the extent that he comprehends the Creator. Man can grasp what has been created but not who is doing the creating.

There is no point then to try and prove the existence of the Creator, especially since doing so is beyond man's limited capabilities. There was therefore no possible way to logically prove to those cultured intellectuals listening to clergyman Schleirmacher's lectures, the truth of their contents. Instead they had to appeal to their own emotions, because only emotion can adequately contend with the idea of the Divine. In order to play on his audience's emotions, who, it would appear from the transcribe of the lectures posed difficult questions and disturbed the flow of the lectures, Schleirmacher threw things at them that were bound to have an emotional affect, like saying that he who denies the status of religion as the source for all customs is afflicted with boastfulness, hastiness, hating deities, and throwing insult at God Himself. Schleirmacher certainly captivated the audience that he was trying to convince in that he explained that religion and religious morality are predicated on the fact that each individual is free, and in this way, in contradistinction to Emanuel Kant, determined that every individual has his own personal morality which defines his humanity. In this way Schleirmacher managed to show respect for each of his listeners, which certainly helped the task that he assigned himself, to fight for the sake of religion in the midst of cultured and intellectual people, fellow inhabitants of his city, who at that specific time formed part of the upper class and whose opinions were held in high regard. Thanks to his powers of persuasion Schleirmacher succeeded to such an extent that he was considered the principal religious philosopher of Germany at that time.

Schleirmacher's manner of argument in favor of religion had mixed elements of intellectualism and raw emotion, and in order to implant in his irreligious and even religiously hostile listeners a positive attitude towards religion, he resorted quite quickly to making compromises, so that he said that in contrast to the religions themselves, which are established institutions each of which has their own *Code of Laws* that are standardized and that cannot be subtracted from, the individual practitioner is allowed to choose those parts of religion that he desires, while ignoring others which he deems inappropriate or which fails to tug at his heart.[70] This was said after he had already mentioned the whole episode with the holy trinity which included God being turned into a flesh and blood human being as the Christian religion believes. His aim could have hardly been made any clearer: if anyone of the audience of non-believers found it difficult to accept the fact of a transcendental God turning into the tangible image of Jesus Christ, he could nonetheless still be part of the Christian Church for which Schleirmacher had appointed himself, the spokesman, (that is for the Protestant Church in whose name Schleirmacher preached). The listener could accept upon himself a Christianity that did not include belief in the holy trinity, even if the Protestant Church itself was never going to annul or even retreat from the fundamental belief in the trinity that is an integral part of its hallowed teachings. This kind of compromise solution which ensures that everyone is satisfied, and at the least guarantees that a downward turn in the number of non-believers in Berlin is in the offing, is what Schleirmacher stood for.

In respect to the question which this book discusses, viz. how did religions came about, Schleirmacher does not dismiss the revelation route, which is central to the whole episode of Jesus playing the role of the Divinity which he reveals when proclaiming himself to be the son of God, yet Schleirmacher refuses to directly involve himself with the whole idea of revelation. Instead he turns to a discussion that mixes intellect with emotion, which fits well with his theory which is a sort of blending of the two paths through which one can attain faith in God- the empirical path and the intellectual path. In actual fact he suggests a third alternative, the emotional path accompanied by intellectual deliberation, as opposed to an emotional path where one plods through ritual and myth.

It appears therefore that there are four possible ways of attaining faith in the Divinity:

A. Via revelation; this is the most empirical.

B. Via intellectual deliberation.

C. Via emotion that is accompanied by intellectual deliberation

D. Via emotion through the means of ritual and myth

---

[70] In his book, note 68 *supra*, at p. 191.

Francis Fukayama[71]

- who had his base of operations in the United States and was active two centuries after the German minister Schleirmacher, developed the thesis that in some respects is a carry over of the latter's theory, from the perspective that Fukayama also attempted to promote religion by means of intellectual discourse, however in this regard Fukayama was a lot less tolerant of other religions, and in this respect may be differentiated from the German clergyman. The religion that Fukayama desired to promote (in the spirit of the broad definition of religions suggested in Part 1 of this book, that includes ideas around which men direct their behavior) was Liberal Capitalism.

Fukayama like Schleirmacher before him began his mission with a series of lectures that were later turned into a book. He delivered this series in the academic year 1988/9 in the University of Chicago. This was towards the end of Soviet domination and at a time where it was becoming ever clearer that Liberal Capitalism had relieved itself of its greatest enemy, the Soviet- Communist system, and as it would appear these lectures came to celebrate this momentous event and to formulate the theory of the supremacy of the Western political system.

Fukayama spoke about the Liberal –Democratic- Capitalist regime in terms of a cycle, as will be elaborated upon later on. Since there is an internal contradiction between his findings and his predictions, this analysis will begin by reviewing the earlier period of his writings at the time that he penned the opening remarks to his book. These earlier writings are then superceded by the writer's later remarks and thus a radical change in direction takes place so that the whole picture changes accordingly. If so, below are his main ideas, the first part of which can be seen in Fukayama's opening remarks.

Fukayama adopting the approach of Hegel viewed the history of humankind, in the sense that within that history a competition takes place between the leading political systems, with each system developing and reaching new heights until an optimal peak for each is reached. It is at this peak that the growth of each political system comes to a halt, and that system that is most useful for humankind is adopted by all. Therefore as soon as humans have found the best possible system,

---

[71] See Francis Fukayama *The End of History and the Last Man*, (New York: The Free Press, a division of Macmillan Inc., 1992)

no logical motivation will lead them to seek yet another replacement, and thus this type of ruling system will stay in place forever. In this respect- the end of history has arrived- which is also the end of the road for the further development of other systems that control the human lifestyle. Fukayama mentions that Marx also arrived at his conclusions by relying on the Hegelian system to explain historical developments; the only difference is that Marx thought that the most successful and lasting system would be communism.

Fukayama saw history following a progressive line, from the tribal system that was based on very basic labor and agriculture, through the religious reigns, then on to monarchies closely followed by the aristocrat-feudal system and finally arriving at Liberal Democracy with its ties to capitalism and to advanced science and technology.

Fukayama like Schleirmacher spoke of the joining together of spirit and substance, which merger man has always paid an interest in .He, too, selected three factors that take the lead in determining human behavior, though in his case, in accordance with Plato's philosophy, the three factors are:

Desiring- which refers to desiring after material goods.

Reasoning- this is the intellect, the cognitive faculty.

Desire for recognition- in the Plato original *–thymos-* this refers to the ambition to attain (a high) self- esteem.

It was the Liberal Capitalist system that optimized for man the first two of these factors, by opening up for him the world of science and industry. The exact sciences helped man conquer nature by outsmarting it and by exploiting the rules of nature. Science and technology which is a direct offshoot of the exact sciences helped man develop warfare with which he was able to develop the most effective defence for his country that would ward off any would- be attacker. In respect of economic progress it was science and technology that aided in man's accumulation of wealth, and which changed the world into a homogenous society regardless of the various cultural backgrounds of the different countries that make up the globe, and in fact each country mirrored the next one, so that their outer appearances were alike. In the same vein education and consumerism were standardized across nations so that places located far apart geographically started to resemble each other. While science managed to provide economic growth and material enrichment it failed to deal with the spiritual side of things, with the need for self worth; this had to be provided for by democracy. This is not the same democracy of which America's founding fathers spoke, viz. the freedom of all men to work towards self enrichment, nor did Fukayama have in mind freedom as a means (to achieving something else)- but rather as a goal in its own right. Economic development as a result of the Liberal Capitalist system had already instilled in man the ideal of self -esteem, since at its very essence, the capitalist system required its supporters to possess a broad academic background, and this fact aroused within the people thus educated a feeling of self-esteem leading many of them to demand a broad based democratization.[72]

Fukayama harbors an undisguised and intolerant approach to theistic religions and to nationalist corporations. He justifies this approach by explaining that a religious person seeks recognition from his God through the religious ceremonies that he performs, whereas the nationalistic person demands recognition of his language, his culture, and his ethnic group. These and similar demands according to Fukayama are less "logical" than are those of the inhabitants of the Liberal State, since the religious person's demands are based on the arbitrary claim that a distinction exists between the holy and the secular, while the nationalistic person bases his claims on a specific social group. He opines that religion, nationalism, and customs which have their origin in tradition will always act as a barrier that blocks the establishment of successful democratic political institutions, as well as stifle the flow of an economic free market.

Fukayama's utterances reveal an intolerance towards the self esteem of an ethnic group that desires to preserve a heritage, which it holds dear to its heart. In addition he shows himself to be prejudiced against members of a religious faith who want to fulfill the precepts of their religion and to nurture their religious ceremonies that are unique to their faith. "Self esteem" in Fukayama's learned opinion is only achievable by those who are neither religious, nor nationalistic and whose loyalties are directed towards a multi-cultural regime that exists in a liberal country like the United States, which contains people of various ethnic backgrounds and who are affiliated to a variety of churches and religions. That is the "self esteem that has been sealed tightly into a very exclusive box". This idea jells well with the discussion in part 4 of this book dealing with civil religion (for which Fukayama is one of its foremost spokespersons) and its oppressive attitude

---

[72] It is possible to support Fukayama's analysis by raising the whole issue of feminism. and to assert that the women's right to vote was achieved in Anglo Saxon countries only through demonstrating at polling stations and by sending questionnaires to the various candidates. The whole campaign was managed, obviously, by educated women. The very fact that these women enjoyed an academic background was crucial in bringing about the possibility of this type of feminist organization. After attaining the right to vote for women, further progress in other arenas became inevitable, thanks to the "woman's voice" that played a role in the electoral process.

to theistic religion for the reason, as explained there and as reaffirmed by Fukayama here, that the existence of a multiplicity of various theistic religions in an integrative country like the United States is an intrusive factor retarding the process of consolidating an American nation. [73] Fukayama's theory helps to promote the launching of a civil religion that has no association with the ethnic backgrounds or theistic religions of any of the state's citizens. Instead of having firmly rooted ethnic groups that practice an established religion, civil religion intends to uproot the world-wide responsiveness to faith in God. It is a new religion with no God, which according to Fukayama goes out on a holy crusade against any manifestations of Divinity and promotes exclusive self rule. Fukayama's grounds for justifying this are indeed interesting, as they are laced with emotions, and in this way quite paradoxically share a feature of Schleirmacher's theory (who using emotional methods worked towards achieving a diagonally opposite goal). Fukayama bases his ideas on the proposition that it is incumbent upon people of culture to have a sense of their own self worth with which they can assert their fundamental rights, and this they will never be able to accomplish in an area where theistic religion has been firmly entrenched.

What we have before us therefore is a new religion being formed; a religion that has no God, a religion whose highest value is man, encompassing his economic interests mixed in with a healthy dose of his self esteem. The three essential building blocks, used to construct the highway upon which modern man travels in order to arrive at this new religion, are:

(a) Desire (in relation to material objects),

(b) The intellect (a pragmatic mind directed to reaping material-economic profit)
(c) Feeling of self esteem,[74] reserved exclusively to those who raise the banner of a Liberal Capitalism that has no relation to any kind of Divinity.

According to the Fukayaman system, especially its first incarnation, that is, before it underwent a complete makeover- theistic religions have no place in the future. As to the status of theistic religions in ancient history, that was an episode that belonged to an antiquated stage of development, a stage that is too far down the

[73] At the moment this theory has been exported by the United states to the rest of the countries of the world, so that even Israel- a country that defines itself not as a collective of all different nationalities but as the Jewish State, as has been explained in Part 4 of this book that deals with Israeli Civil religion- has been similarly perverted.
[74] This is defined in the Israeli *Basic Law: Dignity of Man and his Freedom*-under "dignity of man"

scale to even be considered. Indeed, it takes second last place among the five stages of the development of the systems of human governance.

The picture, painted for us, up until this point is radically altered when Fukayama suddenly puts a completely different slant on what is being viewed. As opposed to his central thesis on the negative role that is played by religions and by nationalisms, Fukayama now presents things in an opposite light where he shows many examples where in fact it is those people who work within a religious society or an ethnic community who are most prone to display a high work ethic. It appears that the reason for this is attached to the fact that within a limited and exclusive national or ethnic framework as within a small community framework that bases itself on religious or ethnic ideals, man is provided with the recognition and encouragement to devote himself to the work allotted to him.

There are two things that to Fukayama appear to be moving in opposite directions. The first thing he defines as a leftist viewpoint, whereas the second he defines or names as a rightist viewpoint. The leftist viewpoint holds that although a liberal democratic state is able to be internally balanced and to accord equal treatment to all; external relations between states and nations are wrought with inequality. This inequality creeps outwards, outside the confines of the state and into the international arena. From a more rightward view, the picture one gets is of Liberal Capitalist regimes whose egalitarianism is responsible for creating a workmanlike morality, as envisaged by Nietzsche, i.e. a situation where the citizens feel complacent about their egalitarianism and tend towards a mediocrity which is the inevitable result of a society whose citizens accept the principle that each has the limited responsibility of performing his mutual share of the workload. In the process the citizen loses one of the most cherished character traits of the human race, viz. the incentive to receive critical acclaim for scaling the walls of excellence. Recognizing everything as equally valuable diminishes the desire to attain uniqueness, so that "the last man"- the supposedly perfect individual-the product of the liberal democratic regime, has lost all those constituent elements that mark him as a "man". Who knows, asks Fukayama, perhaps there will come a time when man will be so fed up with the unexciting, uninteresting mediocrity that the Liberal Democratic regime imposes upon him, that he will turn the tables and start waging new battles against this regime, just like the "first man" did, only this time he will be equipped with much more modern and lethal weaponry.

Do these words not cause us to wonder whether they are not the inner croaking voice of modern "post-religious" man crying out for having lost his God and ultimately having lost his soul in the process?

Stephen W. Hawking

,who became a legend in his own lifetime in that he was a brilliant scientist who had overcome very serious physical disabilities (he was constantly attached to his wheelchair and could never speak with his natural voice) wrote a very popular book in 1987 which he called *A brief history of time*[75] He presents the way in which the natural sciences contend with the basic claims made by each theistic religion in regard to the creation of the world. This is a book that surveys how the human mind, using its natural powers and relying on the strength of the scientific experiments carried out by scientists, copes with the fundamental questions of the universe. In undertaking this quest man has to stand on his own two feet- as is befitting the only creature amongst creation who has been self crowned- at least in the modern period- and who has placed himself on the throne of leadership determining without the help of God how each human being should behave.

In theory most of the book's sections support the claim of an existent God who created the world, and in this way may be considered as part of the school of thought derived from Jewish houses of study as well those of its various offshoots (Christianity and Islam) which all rally behind the idea of creation of the world as a creation which was *ex nihilo*, as opposed to the school of thought, as represented by the Hindu religion and its offshoots who hold that the universe always has and always will exist. The whole notion of the big bang raises the question- if in the beginning of time there was a big bang and prior to that time there was no world, who carried out this big bang and for what exact purpose?[76]

Therefore Hawking says[77]:

> The defining purpose of science is to provide one theory that can describe the whole universe. Yet, the approach opted by most scientists is to split

---

[75] Stephen W. Hawking, *A brief history of time: from the big bang to black holes*. Hebrew edition is translated from the English by Emanuel Lutes; scientific editor is Yakhin Una (Tel Aviv: Ma'ariv Library, 1989).

[76] See in this regard the article that appeared in the *Kol Ha'ir* weekly dated the 14/09/2001 at p. 98 under the title "There is a God", which reviews the personality and work of Gerald Schroeder, a nuclear scientist and author of the international bestseller *The Science of God* that proves, relying upon quarks and quanta, energy fields, and cosmic time, that the world in fact was created in six days, and using the premise of a "big bang" poses the question "what instigated this whole process?" For the boundaries between science and religion and the respective and various spheres of influence see A. Czerwinski *Between Science and Religion* [Hebrew edition] (Tel Aviv: Yehoshua Chechick) pp. 7 -17.

[77] In Hawking's book that is in note 75 *supra*, at p. 19.

> the problem in two. First, there are laws that tell us how the universe evolved with time. (If we can tell the condition of the universe at any specified time, these laws of physics can inform us what the condition will be at any time in the future). Second, there is the question as to the condition of the universe at its very beginning. There are those who are of the opinion that science needs to confine itself exclusively to the first question; whereas the question relating to how the universe looked at the beginning of time, they view it being more appropriately falling under the purview of metaphysics or religion. They hold that God, because he is all-powerful, could have let the universe run any course it fancied and in any form it wished. Perhaps this is how it was, but in that case God could have caused the universe to develop in a completely arbitrary fashion. However it would appear that he elected, instead, to cause the universe to develop in a very ordered manner, in accordance with highly specified laws. Therefore it makes more sense to speculate, that, likewise, specific laws were put in place from the very beginning.

In his opening remarks Hawking wants us to know that he has solid grounds for stating that God did not create the universe. The reason for this assertion is that the laws that followed on the footsteps of the big bang were very ordered, and the world was not created as a chaotic entity. From where did Hawking get the idea that God's intentions (assuming that He did create the world, whether via a big bang, whether via any other way) were to use arbitrary things to push start the creation and not base it on the ordered laws of nature. What is his justification? Hawking explains that if God is the one who "lets the universe run its course" (as he puts it) – he could have determined that the universe follow a completely arbitrary pattern. This type of justification makes no sense whatsoever; why should it be that if someone has the capacity to operate in an arbitrary manner this immediately precludes him from the possibility to choose not to operate arbitrarily- as he is able to- and to operate in a "very ordered manner, in accordance with highly specified laws" (as Hawking puts it)? It is not only this fundamentally flawed justification that is to blame for Hawking placing such a strong question mark (on God's existence), but it is also the result of a tendency and trend within him to exclude God from the whole story of creation.

Hawking raises the possibility that the big bang, the theory which he promoted for many years, can be explained as a "successful coincidence" that opposes the possibility that the Hand of God was behind it. After dismissing the theory of a "successful coincidence," he raises the possibility that there exist adequate explanations for the fact that the wondrous preciseness of creation, coexisting with tiny but necessarily inexact phenomena, is the fusion that is the only one poised for bringing about the formation of the human race. He explains that the various laws of nature can be explained through scientific theories, like the "classic laws of general relativity, the quantum laws of gravity, the classic laws of gravity, everything is explainable and thus there is no need to refer to the "Hand of God" in the story of creation. We are almost begged to ask Hawking a few questions, which he himself does not bother asking. Who directed and formulated all these laws and these veritable theories? Was it some higher natural law? And if so who created that higher natural law?[78]These questions however have become superfluous in light of Hawking admitting that at this stage not only is "the idea that space and time simultaneously capable of being finite and unbounded by limitations, merely a proposition: but also impossible to substantiate from any other principle" .There is therefore a conflict between the theory of relativity and that of quantum physics which so far no scientific theory has successfully reconciled.[79] In the latest edition of his work Hawking openly admits that he has abandoned the theory of the "big bang", which is based on invented timeframes and on assigning a starting point to the universe. He concludes that[80]:

> The possibility can be raised that what we have referred to as invented time is in fact real time, and contrarily what we call real time exists only in our imaginations. In real time the universe has a beginning and an end in that its uniqueness binds itself in the space/ time dimension whereby the laws of nature gradually disintegrate. But in invented time there is no uniqueness and therefore no boundaries. Therefore, perhaps what we call invented time is the fundamental truth, whereas what we think of as real time is just an idea that was invented in order to aid us in describing the universe in a way that we think it operates. But according to the approach that I discussed in chapter one, scientific theories are just a mathematical approximation that we produce in order to describe our vantage point: it exists in our minds alone. Therefore there is no significance to the question: what is more real, "real time" or "invented time"? The simple question is which description is at the end of the day more helpful.

In this way the scientific theory that seeks to challenge God is exposed, so that it is left naked in its birthday suit: the soul of a lost man seeking direction, but having no guide to lead him.

---

[78] *Ibid.*, at pp. 130- 131.
[79] *Ibid.*, at p. 132.
[80] *Ibid.*, at pp. 133 -134.

Rudolf Otto[81]

Protestant theologian and religious philosopher who was influenced by Kant and Schleirmacher (1869- 1937), and who saw in religion a type of numinous element (experiential –emotional) that is revealed to man by way of a prophecy of the heart[82]. Even though Otto claims that one cannot view religion only through its rational dimension and that a key ingredient of religion is the religious experiential and emotional component; he claims that the rationalism that one encounters in Christianity places it above all other religions.[83] He speaks about God as someone "holy", "awesome," "loved", "savior", "exalted" ,"hidden", "secretive", versus man who is "lowly", "filled with fear and trepidation."[84] Religious feeling is a complex mix of irrational (numinous) and rational elements, a complex mix of feelings on the one hand, of "exaltedness" i.e. a "holiness" that reaches the level of the "pseudo- eroticism" towards God, and on the other hand more elevated feelings of "holiness". Otto equates this complexity, by way of analogy, with human love, which is composed of elements of sexual desire on the one hand, with feelings of yearning and of affection that exist on a higher plane of true love[85], on the other. He equates the two polar opposites of the religious experience- irrational fear versus refined and rational religious belief- with the development of music from its simple primitive stage to its more advanced westernized incarnation[86]. The Divinity is also possessed of two opposing countenances, the exacting God versus Patriarchal God who is close to our hearts.[87] Otto says that religious belief began with expressions of faith in the dead and in rites that celebrated the dead, faith in souls and rites connected with the soul: witchcraft, the magi, legend and myth, idolization of natural bones that were either shocking or wondrous, fetishism and the totemic; and rituals that are connected with plants or beasts; yet common to all was that they were sated with numinous elements.[88] The first displays of religious feeling are manifested, according to Otto, in the idea of the "spirit" or demon, yet without there being any myths attached thereto. All these manifestations precede and are to prior to the onset of religion. They do not

[81] See Rudolf Otto, *The idea of the holy: an inquiry into the non-rational factor in the idea of the Divine and its relation to the rational,* Translated from German into Hebrew by Miriam Ron, (Jerusalem: Carmel, 1999)

[82]See the entry in *Hebrew* encyclopedia, and also see the review in this book, in part one, "Why religion?"

[83] See Otto, *The idea of the holy,* at pp. 8- 9.

[84] *Ibid.,* at pp. 38- 39.

[85] *Ibid.,* at pp. 56- 57.

[86] *Ibid.,* at p. 84.

[87] *Ibid.,* at p. 85.

[88] *Ibid.,* at p. 127.

explain, in Otto's opinion, religion or the fact that religious practice could come about. Latent in them however is origin of religious practice, viz. the first numinous feeling. Consequent upon these revelations, the real religions began to develop. Theologians therefore deal with the capacity for divination[89]; the capacity to distinguish when there is a genuine revelation of holiness , which is what Otto deals with, and which is what Schleirmacher also dealt with. This is the same as the "capacity to judge fairly," which Kant was referring to. In Otto's estimation, only those people who have a naturally "prophetic" profile are graced with this talent, and not just any human being, as the rationalists would have it, and certainly not, then, the "masses" who form a homogenous bloc. This perspective of Otto's shows him to be a follower of the Schleirmacher school of thought. That is the school of thought that rejected rationalism as a central element in religion, and turned instead to its emotional aspects.

Mircea Eliade[90]

-One of the greatest religious law experts in the twentieth century, who was of Romanian origin, and lived for a while in India where he focused his research on traditional societies. He taught in the University of Bucharest and after that moved on to Paris and Chicago, where he lived until his death in 1986. He explained that religions add an element of depth into their activities, and thereby articulate their central messages by means of symbols and myths.

According to Eliade's narrative[91] all Eastern traditional religions have in common a parallel between celestial transcendental concepts and between their terrestrial holy temples. Even cities are built using Divine prototypes, as an expression of their principles of faith, principles that in many of their details show an identity and similarity between the various religions in the East, which would include India and the Near East. This (city) structure is the expression of a symbolical and mythical meeting place between heaven and earth, or between heaven, earth, and perdition. Any kind of mountain is referred to as the centre of the earth, a holy area which represents an absolute reality.

---

[89] *Ibid.*, at pp. 151-154.

[90] See Mircea Eliade, *Le mythe de l'eternel retour: arch'types et r'p'tition* , translated from the French into Hebrew by Yotam Reuveni, with scientific editing and notes by Ronit Nikolsky, (Jerusalem: Carmel, 2000.)

[91] *Ibid.*, at pp. 11 -25.

Religions contain ritual practices that entrench their myths, and strengthen the inner faith of the believers, fortifying the bond with the gods that protect them. These rituals then are an attempt at imitating the gods' actions. Within this framework the foreskins of the male members of the Abuja tribe in Australia are circumcised; and ceremonies that commemorate the creation of the world by observing a weekly Sabbath resting day are performed by both Christians and Jews. Eliade talks about the a-historical nature of popular memory; the inability of the collective memory to commemorate real historical events and people, without it converting everything into archetypes that are devoid of historical context and ignore the real personalities of the subjects that are ritualised. By doing this they manage to strengthen the belief that that which was will always remain so. This is because the wondrous actions that are commemorated are not limited by any timeframe and therefore their potency remains in force up until present times. This characteristic of negating history and of renewing time ensures that the believers can expect positive results from their actions whether in the present or in the future. This element is starkly witnessed in the ceremonies that surround New Year celebrations; their symbolization of the replenishing of food stockpiles, of acclaiming good rainfalls, and of revitalizing the lifecycles.[92] The elimination of the historical dimension means that anything that occurred today already happened in the past-and since according to myth if something is in the past it means it has been successfully concluded – one is then assured that one's future will also yield a successful outcome. Opposing this theory is that of the renewal of time that is symbolized in well established rituals that are given special place by the more ancient nations, who through these rituals ensure for themselves and for their fellow nationals a constant renewal process thus endowing themselves with a heritage of an established past that has a promising and continuous future, proving the eternal existence of this nation. Looked at from the perspective of the internal society[93] this focus helps those nations who are specifically interested in exposing their history, to reinforce in their people a feeling for their ancient origins. The meaning to all this - if indeed we are an ancient People who has a rich history-is proving both our resilience and the fact that we will carry on surviving despite the hardships along the way. Myths help achieve various objectives, *inter alia* reproduction, the attainment of wisdom, and the curing of disease. Eliade models this statement on the Polynesian experience.[94] Rituals and ceremonies deal with problems relating to death, helping to overcome

[92] *Ibid.*, at pp. 46 -67.
[93] *Ibid.*, at pp. 70- 71.
[94] *Ibid.*, at p. 76.
[94] *Ibid.*, at p. 76.

the fear of death, which is dealt with by instilling the belief in the resurrection of the dead.[95]

Eliade explains that the removal of a historical dimension from so many religious ceremonies and rituals gives over the message to the believers that it within their power to overcome hardship and disaster if they turn to religion, since these selfsame events from which the historical timeframe was erased are events that continue to be as relevant in the present as they were in the past. [96]

Religious philosophy also helps religion, via its rituals, strengthening the believers who are faced with the suffering that continues to plague them. An example of this can be seen in the topic of the karma in India, which explains suffering by using the framework of reincarnation of the soul, and provides the notion of suffering with a positive dimension, where suffering comes to remove the imbalance caused by debts accrued in a past incarnation, so that the karma will positively help the reincarnated souls especially at the time when man must depart from this world.[97]

Even though in no other pace in the archaic world will you find such a clear version of the karma that deals with the "normality" of suffering there is a general tendency to attribute to the feeling of pain and to historical incidents "a normal meaning." Nearly everywhere there is this archaic understanding (quite dominant amongst primitives) which says that suffering is the unchallengeable will of God, whether God directly intervened in order to cause the suffering or whether He allowed other forces, Divine or satanic, to cause such harm. Destruction of the harvest, draught, the invasion of the enemy into the city, loss of freedom or of life, and any great calamity (a plague, an earthquake etc.) will always be readily explained by these believers as being justified in one way or another , being as they are the expression of a Divine transcendental reckoning. The explanation can be that the god of the conquered city was weaker than the victorious army, or that the stricken community was itself guilty of a ritual evil, or that the evil, that was performed, caused the harmed family to reach the level of Divinity (and to strike back), or was the result of magic, demons, neglectfulness, or curses. For any private or communal suffering there is always going to be an explanation. Because of this people tolerate suffering because it is tolerable.

Moreover: in the Mesopotamian region in its very early stages of history man's suffering was associated, by its populace, with that of God's. They therefore allied themselves with an archetype, which at the same time provided them with a sense

---

[95] *Ibid.*, at 79- 81.

[96] *Ibid.*, at p. 85.

[97] *Ibid.* at pp. 88 -89.

of realism and normalcy. The myth that would most often be repeated was that of the suffering, death and resurrection of Tammuz which myth took on various forms in nearly all of the Ancient East, and remnants of the script of this story were preserved amongst the post-Christian genus. The torments and the resurrection of Tammuz provided a model of the torments of other gods (Murdoch for example) and there is no doubt that every year the king tried to mimic this suffering. The popular lamentations and expressions of joy that marked the suffering, death, and resurrection of Tammuz or of any other Cosmic- Agricultural Divinity influenced the whole consciousness of the Ancient East. These rituals did not merely conjure up a sense that they could resurrect a man after his death; more than that they allowed each individual to feel that he was the comforter of Tammuz's suffering. Therefore it is possible to withstand any pain on condition that we remember the drama underwent by Tammuz[98]

As to the idea of the negation of history and of the eternal return, it was Greek philosophy that used this notion to "determine" the future and to eliminate the irreversibility of time. All the moments that pass and the events that happen in the universe repeat themselves indefinitely. All moments and all situations are frozen in their place and are merited by acquiring the ontological status of archetype In this context the myth of the world ending in fire, from which only the good (people) will be saved is then of a very ironic origin. Christian literature turned this myth into the basis for its belief in the apocalypse. In some odd way this myth is comforting, since the fire has the power to renew the world through which a new world habitation will come into being where old age, death, crumbling and rotting processes will cease to exist and the world will live and continue to expand forever. The dead will rise and the living will become immortal beings. Those who are good have no reason whatsoever to fear. The final catastrophe that will spell the end of history will enwrap man in eternity and in happiness. Everyone will be held accountable for their actions in the "history" that will have officially ended. Only the innocent will know happiness and eternal life. Calculations as to the time remaining until the end of history, or the existence as we know it of the world are found in the Will of Abraham according to the *Sefer Chinuch* (a Jewish religious book, whose authorship is unknown, the literal translation of the title is *The Book of Instruction*) citing Jewish tradition. Nevertheless the Jewish sages discouraged determining a time for the end of days that was mathematically calculated, and preferred to base the end of days on a series of cosmic and historical catastrophes which together will usher in the end of the world. Both in the Iranian and Judeo-Christian traditions, "history" which has to do with the universe must

---

[98] *Ibid. at pp. 89- 90.*

expire, and the end of the world will take place at the same time as all sinners are destroyed.[99]

To summarize, religion and its myths and rituals helps man bear history's load, taking into account both the social and individual dimensions. Modern man, who accepts the lessons of history or at least pretends to accept them, says Eliade, can argue against archaic man, whose mind is captive to the mythical constructs of the archetype and to the claim of "[eternal] return" that encourages a helpless attitude towards the creation and an inability to take any risks that are inevitably linked with any act of creation. From the modern man's perspective man cannot create anything that will not have a history. Modern man chose to make history, and in such a way creates his own image. It is possible to counterclaim, however that the freedom to create history, which freedom is a source of comfort to man is nothing but an illusion for the decisive majority of human race. Therefore, this counterclaim argues, modern man's freedom is essentially confined to choosing between two options: (a) to fight against a history that is created, for all practical purposes by a minority that determines the course of history (by finding refuge in a sub- human existence or by escaping). Accordingly, Marxism and fascism offer two types of living through history: either as a leader (one individual, who is truly free) or plodding through as a follower. The leader- follower relationship is not the archetypical kind, but rather a situation, where authority to prescribe what is or what is not permitted is of temporary validity.

Thus from the perspective of traditional man, says Eliade, modern man does not represent a free creature, he is not someone who is able to create history. Quite the contrary: the archaically cultured man can be proud of his existence, an existence that allows him to be both free and creative. He is free to be better than the man of the past, free to eliminate his personal history by eliminating the cycle of time and renewing the collective [history]. The person who wants to be "historical" will never be able to claim that freedom that says that his "history" actually belongs to him. The history of modern man is not only irreversible but also is determinant of the actual existence of humankind. Traditional and archaic societies received the freedom to begin every year with a truly new existence, "pure", virginal. One should not view this as imitating nature which also renews itself according to a set seasonal cycle, "starting anew" every spring; replenishing its powers every spring. In practice, however nature merely returns unto itself, and every spring renews that same eternal spring (going back to original creation); archaic man on the other hand, after he has abandoned the cycle of time and has undergone a "purification" process, and after he has returned to find that all his qualities are now complete, as

[99] *Ibid.*, at pp. 108- 113.

they were in times gone by, is now able at the beginning of all his "new lives," to exist on an eternal platform. It is therefore vital for him that he completely does away with secular notions of time. Archaic man then finds himself once again in a situation where it is possible to move away from the constraints of time. In the event that he commits a sin, he is forced to stumble and fall into "historical" existence, bound by time, and missing out that year on the possibility of surpassing time, yet he still reserves the possibility and the freedom to annul his mistakes, to try the next year to finally exit himself from time and to leave behind him the crops of "history".

Through viewing it in a certain way, the way that Eliade puts forward, archaic man can rightly see himself more of a creator than modern man. Every year archaic man returns to cosmogony which is after all the prototypical act of creation.[100]

Robert Hinde

-a biologist who published a book on the subject of religion in 1999,[101] deals with the question why it is that despite so many people (in the West and especially the Anglo- Saxon world, amongst whom he works) denying the truth as per the religious version, religion continues to be entrenched within us. Why has it not lost its grip upon us? He presents data that show that, over the course of the twentieth century amongst British Christians, excluding children below the age of 15, churchgoing has witnessed a sharp decline from 25% to 14%, and in America those who define themselves as being religiously inclined and believing in life after death fluctuates between 84% amongst Protestants, 76% amongst Catholics and, 30% amongst Jews, and 48% amongst those who define themselves as non-affiliated to any specific religion. This percentage did not significantly change from 1973 until 1991. He enumerates four reasons for why there is no foundation for pointing at the incongruence of the religious narrative with scientific findings, and they are: (a) Religion comforts and encourages a vast amount of people. (b) Such a claim is old and hackneyed, and has been around from at least the time of the enlightenment, and therefore the argument has lost its focus. This is especially so since many people distinguish between real religious belief and a general attitude that accepts that there is a greater reality, that there is a world that exits beyond the rigid reality. (c) Some of the religions do not only speak of a connection to the Divine but include much more complex issues, for instance Judaism which puts a much greater stress on historical narrative rather than on

[100] And indeed the traditional Jew and the religious Jew undergo this experience every year, during "The Days of Awe".

[101] See Robert A. Hinde, *Why Gods Persist- A scientific Approach to Religion* (London: Routledge, 1999).

pure ideas of belief, or Hinduism that emphasizes behavioral patterns: the Hindu practitioner emphasizes [Divine] service, meditation and imparting knowledge, Buddhism emphasizes values and experience, and there are some sects in Buddhism who do not accept the existence of any kind of superhuman beings. Early Buddhism laid stress on submission, self- discipline and devoted service. Faith only entered this religion during the period of the *Sutra* of the Lotus, and such beliefs were only put onto paper centuries after Buddha had died, even if what was written appears to be the Will of Buddha. (d) A deliberately targeted and vicious approach is not scientific. The impact of religion upon all forms of human behavior requires research into the nature of human behavior and not an attitude that dismisses the religious tendency as if it was some kind of deviation from human evolutionary development, as some have tried to claim.[102]

Hinde asks three questions: (a) is it possible to explain the spread of religions as owing to their suitability to the human soul? (b)Which aspects of religion can throw light on its being so entrenched? (c) Is it possible to completely dismiss religion because of its intolerable influence, or perhaps, it has a constructive influence, and if that is the true situation, what are the components of religion that bode well for people and is it then possible to preserve those elements without actually accepting the religion per se?

Hinde reveals what motivated his writing a book on religion[103] and it appears that what motivated him was not the question whether it is necessary to curb the influence of religion, but (given that it is necessary) how to go about doing so. In order to discover the most efficient way of curbing religious influence he relates to the fact that the majority of the globe's inhabitants do hold some kind of religious belief or think that they have undergone some kind of religious experience. This fact, he says, could stem from one of the following two reasons. (a) By it being the truth, that indeed there does exist a transcendental world with which humans can have contact. (b) By reason of a mentally related problem which comes about the moment man experiences contact with the society amongst which he lives or with the outside world that surrounds him. Hinde admits that science is not suitably equipped to totally refute option (a), and therefore it would be easier to deal with option (b). His approach is that of someone who sees the situation in the same way as scientists dealing with man and his problems, and asking how can they cure man from his impediments. In this instance the impediment is religion. This is similar to a researcher whose field of expertise is biology (and Hinde is in fact a biologist, as he explains) and who seeks to find a cure for a disease. This is not

---

[102] *Ibid.*, at pp. 5-6.

[103] *Ibid.*

about a cure for a physical disease, however it is, assuming that option (a) (a link to a transcendental world) is not the reason for the phenomenon of the existence of religions, at least a mental problem, or a mental disease. This therefore is a valid field for biological and scientific research. He explains that the background for his decision to deal with the topic of religion was the competition that exists between biologists and social scientists, where both these groups seek to investigate human behavior, the former (the biologists) are more interested in the brain and the human consciousness, and the latter (the social scientists) are more interested in the differences between cultures, and the differences within one culture that changed over the course of time, as well as the social status of the individuals and similar topics. He suggests that each group has their own aim, and therefore anyone who claims that there is an argument between them is foundationally flawed. Since there is some kind of overlap between these two trends of research, their meeting points ensure a mutual influence on both sides, and his intention is to research the subject of religion using this conception of a meeting point. Hinde also explains that his research will mainly deal with Christian society, since he claims that this field is very wide and varied.

These explanations of Hinde reveal the pattern of his writing, which show him be like someone who says: These (theistic) religions are very stubborn, it goes against any kind of logic for anyone to be intimately involved with any kind of society generally, and it especially makes no sense when it is Christian society. The fact that it exists is proof that it is a stubborn and undesirable phenomenon. Indeed we cannot successfully dismiss the truth in religion, but let us take the view that the reason for religion`s prominence has to do with a human mental problem, and we should therefore deal with this mental problem the way scientists deal with other human problems. Indeed we also see that religion has positive influences on man and society, but we should make an effort at trying to see if we can attain the same commendable results without having to contend with religion and thereby render the need for the latter redundant[104]. This approach is fully commensurate with the trend of civil religion as starkly witnessed in the United States, as was described in Part 4 of this book. In this regard, Hinde represents the spirit of civil religion as it developed in the West, like the call for separating religion and state and the attempt to generally curb the influence of religions.

As a man of science who seeks to discern things using scientific-rational tools, Hinde is nonplussed when trying to understand the religious person, the believer. An example of this happens when[105] he cannot understand how Isaiah the prophet

---

[104] *Ibid.*, at pp. 1- 8.
[105] *Ibid.*, at p. 36.

can on the one hand state[106] "to whom then will you liken God? Or what likeness will you compare to him?" and on the other hand he compares Him to a shepherd who feeds his flock. He expresses wonderment at the fact that religious people believe both these things at one and the same time. He is asking in other words how it can be that someone who is so abstract that he cannot be compared to any known or recognizable object can at the same time actually be feeding sheep.[107] It is difficult for Hinde to accept the elevation of the soul that allows the believer to accept both these visions, and to view the internal side of both of them and understand that they both express the same idea, but since it exists beyond human imagination, and because man struggles to grasp it, he requires that parables and speeches are delivered that do not reflect actual reality. One has to say to Hinde that if he really wants to be the healer of religious peoples` souls, he should try at times to elevate himself together with the latter to the worlds where they attain a certain state of mind If he is indeed a professional psychologists which role he claims to play in this scenario, it is vital that he does take to heart this suggestion. But Hinde viewing himself as elevated above his subjects refuses to stoop to their level. This is in evidence when in one of his descriptions[108] he asks, surprised, how it is that religious people have perfect faith in God, seemingly there is no reason to blindly have faith in something that has not been proven?! Obviously Hinde does not raise the issue that many people believe sometimes with more than a bit of confidence in what is written in the newspapers even if the truth of the newspapers is oftentimes suspect. He also does not ask himself how it is that so many people believe in Einstein's theory of relativity without having actually studied it, and sometimes without even knowing what the theory says, and without this theory having been thoroughly tested. Later on Hinde explains that with many religious believers, their faith is merely allegorical, so that their faith is not in the details of the religious story, but rather in the hidden ideas that exist beyond the storyline. By this he turns the whole story of religious belief into something more palatable for the western rational man. In this way too he can more readily understand the subject of his research, religious man. Yet by doing so he uncovers a further stumbling block to his research, in that he focuses his main observations on modern- western- Christian man without looking at other periods in history. For the purposes of his research into the debate on how it is possible to get rid of religion from the modern western world he does make some logical points, but for the purposes of the discussion in the part that asks "why religion?"- more specifically the discussion on the question "how did religion come about and how

[106] Isaiah. 40: 18. *The Holy Scriptures, supra note* 50 at p. 514.
[107] See the approach to exactly this topic in the review on Ephraim Urbach's writings, which appears at note 162 and note 163 *infra*.
[108] In his book in note 102, *supra, Why Gods Persist,* at p. 37.

does one relate to religion?" – the extent to which Hinde's discussion actually touches upon theistic religion is not really very useful, even if there is something in it which helps us understand how civil religion, these days has spread to so many countries, a religion which Hinde would like to see promoted.

Viktor E. Frankl[109]

-was a Jewish psychiatrist and survivor of the holocaust who expanded upon the theory of Sigmund Freud: Freud spoke of the creative unconscious, and Frankl added to it the spiritual unconscious.[110]He claims that the core spirit of man is unconscious whereas man's spiritual existence is his authentic essence that can never be fully contemplated and the mechanism that decides, with regard to man, whether an experience will form part of his consciousness or whether it will remain unconscious, is itself unconscious.[111] He also claims that man's conscience is irrational. This conscience gains access to the perplexities of the unconscious and is based on intuition. One of the tasks of the conscience is to reveal to man the one thing that is demanded of him. No law that has general application- the "imperative category"-as propounded by the Kantian system- has any application to him personally.[112] Man has links with a world that is beyond that to which he is exposed - when a person is the object of someone's love- there are dormant potentials that live within a beloved person- potentials that need to be realized[113]. Only love allows the lover to grasp the uniqueness of his beloved. Therefore whether it is a situation of someone falling in love or whether it is a time when the irrational intuition of man's conscience is at play, the connections that are formed as a result thereof are similar to the inspiration that an artist receives. The laws of morality and of aesthetics are both based and founded upon an unconscious spiritualism.[114]Dreams too are expressions of the unconscious, and through them a warning is delivered to the dreamer, as Frankl, in his capacity of spiritual healer, has demonstrated in his professional work.[115]

It is at this point that Frankl turns his attention to religion, and says that the intimate quality that is so characteristic of love is no less present in religion. True

---

[109] See [the Hebrew edition of] Viktor E. Frankl, *The Unconscious God. Psychotherapy and Theology,* translated into Hebrew by Shimon Levy, (Jerusalem: Dvir, 1985)
[110] *Ibid.,* at p. 19.
[111] *Ibid.,* at pp. 26- 28.
[112] *Ibid.,* at pp. 30- 32.
[113] *Ibid.,* at p. 32.
[114] *Ibid.,* at pp. 34- 35.
[115] *Ibid.,* at pp. 39- 40.

religiosity is hidden from the public for the sake of guarding its authenticity. As a result thereof- says Frankl speaking from his professional experience- religious patients on many occasions do not want to relay their intimate experiences to those people who perhaps lack an understanding in the subject and are bound to interpret the matters not as they were experienced. These people are bound to fear that the psychiatrist will tear away the "mask" of their religiosity as if it were "merely" a manifestation of an unconscious psycho- dynamic complex of one kind or other. Obviously they are bound to suspect that the therapists will interpret their religiosity in an improper way. Frankl provides practical and professional examples of this, and in some way provides a preemptive reply to Hinde- who authored his book roughly a half a century later.

Frankl speaks of irreligious people who had dreamt explicitly religious dreams. He explains this phenomenon by saying that those people had repressed their spiritual religious frontiers- in exactly the same way as Freud mentions the repression of the unconscious creative frontiers that took place in his practice. In this, as has been said, Frankl - basing himself on his own very practical medical- scientific experience- expanded the frontiers of man's unconscious to include not only the creative sphere, but also the religious sphere.

Frankl speaks in detail about the transcendental quality of the conscience-on which topic he gained insight by virtue of having been an inmate in a concentration and death camp, which is described in his book *Man's Search for Meaning*. He explains that the task of man's ego is to repress and to refine his urges and his instincts, which are not really part of him but exist externally to him. Although this task is indeed the responsibility of the ego, the ego is not responsible to guard against itself since a being can be held responsible only for someone else not for what it itself does. The ego cannot be its own legislator. It can never then receive authority from anywhere else but from the transcendental. Just as freedom has no meaning if it cannot objectively be determined "what" one can do with that "freedom", so too the act of taking responsibility is never complete if it has not been spelled out "what it is" that we are taking responsibility for. Superior man does not stand behind man's superior ego; rather it is "you O! God," that is standing behind his conscience[116].

In light of all of this Frankl claims that there is a phenomenon of unconscious religiosity, which is the hidden relationship that man has toward the transcendental, that is buried within man. If this relationship is aimed at the thing called God, then it ceases to be unconscious which would only be true if man was unaware of any God or of any relationship towards God. It therefore must be a

[116] *Ibid.* at pp. 59- 60.

hidden connection of man to a God who is Himself hidden.[117] Frankl identifies the religiosity of man with something personal to that man, and not a collective practice. The religious images that man encounters do not come from an impersonal storehouse of images common to all of mankind. This type of revelation occurs between this individual man and the unconscious thing to which is ascribed the title "God", but not actually God Himself. Notwithstanding this, there are behavior patterns and cultural formations which have always been around, and which are thus impersonal, yet each individual uses these elements to cast his own personal religiosity. These general forms include prayers, church and synagogue ceremonies, the words of the prophets, and the stories of pious and holy individuals. Culture offers multi-varied traditional vessels into which man can pour into his own brand of living religion- man does not need to invent God. Nevertheless, man does not transport God with him as if He were naturally implanted in him from his birth.[118]

Frankl says that religiosity becomes genuine the moment man is not shoved into it one way or another, but feels himself obligated towards it, which obligation is arrived at by the unfettered choice of man who using his free will opts for religion. The aim of religion is to attain spiritual salvation, not an insurance policy that guarantees a smooth life, free from all conflict. Religion can provide man with much more than can his local shrink, but on the other hand religion can also be more demanding. It is at this point that a link can be seen between morality and religion.

In further developing this idea and insight, Frankl says that just as a monkey is unable to appreciate and to grasp the much broader world of man so too it would seem man is unable to comprehend a world that exits beyond his reality, even if this world is able to provide man with meaning. And indeed man has always aspired to achieve meaning in his life. This has nothing to do with established religion, which has its own separate interests. The demands that the church imposes upon its people to believe is ridiculous and reminiscent of a father demanding his son to love him. As to the tie that bond the churches to the believing masses, Frankl comments that there are as many different religions as there are different languages and both are faced with the option of either lying or of telling the truth. The most important thing for man is that he paves his own way to the Lord- the one and only God.

Frankl acknowledges that are three alternative ways that lead man to uncover meaning[119]- by being creative, by experiencing love, and by contending with bleak

---

[117] *Ibid.* at pp. 62- 63.

[118] *Ibid.*, at pp. 68- 69.

[119] *Ibid.*, at p. 102

situations. In the last-mentioned man has the ability to turn suffering into an achievement. In this context he relays the story of one of his female patients who he helped achieve happiness through her suffering. This he did by causing her to view her state of suffering, as her own personal achievement, which no one else can take away from her. The status that she had attained was hers alone[120]. It is possible to say the same thing about Frankl who spent a long period in concentration camps and in the death camps, but there more to him than his albeit profound suffering, not least of which was his attribute of love.

Robert Ranolph Marett[121]

-was an anthropologist whose collections of articles that were published between 1900 and 1908 were turned into a book. He delved into the spiritual development of the "savages" from Australia and from other regions, and for all his efforts was harshly criticized for viewing the "savage" traditions of the taboo and of witchcraft as something spiritual that approximates a religion, even if their spirituality was of a murky nature. He criticized Taylor, who had used a rational approach when dealing with religion and who had insisted that religion had to follow a clear and ordered system in its relation to spirituality. Marett sought to study, through his analysis of anthropological evidence, general evidence of man's soul. He explained that he prefers to study a society that is far removed from British society, amongst whom he had lived, since he thought that researching a society to which he had no connection would yield more refined results from a scientific perspective. He claimed that the most consistent forms of human behavior have their source in human emotions rather than in logic[122]. He claimed that most anthropologists would agree with him that spirituality is not a sufficient enough definition for religion, and added that witchcraft also has a religious value, not merely as means of establishing a religious framework, but also in and of itself[123]. He spoke about the fact that all human activity, and included in this is religious activity, is based upon three components- thought, emotion, and desire[124].

According to evidence that was garnered from anthropological studies, Marett found that religion for the savages- which he calls pre- spiritual religion, because this was the accepted term- though he himself did find some spiritual elements

---

[120] *Ibid.*, at pp. 109- 111.

[121] See R. R. Marettt *The Threshold of Religion,* second edition, revised and enlarged (London, Methuen & Co., 1914 reprinted in 1979 in the USA as an AMS edition)

[122] *ibid.*, at p. X. ,see also Part 2 of this book , the section that deals with emotions and the mind.

[123] *Ibid.*, at p. XXII.

[124] *Ibid.*, at p. XXIX

amongst them- is connected to power or fear, but is not particularly connected to the spirit of man or even the spirit of an animal. He mentions in this context that there were objects which were attributed with having special powers like strangely shaped stones, and the rituals that involved animals celebrated the groan of an ox. He mentions as part of the religious experience the practice of witchcraft, and this proves his assertion that spirituality is not the only definitional element of religion[125]. Nevertheless he raises the question whether ancient savage man's religious experience did not make its appearance before the onset of spirituality or at least at a disconnected pace away from it, whether such an experience was attained through the thought process, or whether it was through physical sensation or alternately a combination of both these elements. Added to this rebuttal of most of the researchers is his assertion that religious feeling stems from an inner sensation, stimulated by fear, appreciation and wonderment when relating to the supernatural. The controversial question, to his mind, is – what drives man, his intellect or his emotions. Marett is of the opinion that the average man senses that the natural objects are no match against those things that instill within him a tremendous fear, and therefore in such a situation he turns to the supernatural thing and anthropomorphizes it, which in turn makes it less harmful so that he is able to join onto it and to appease it. In this way human emotion and human intellect work in tandem, and this scenario could occur before man adopted the idea of spirituality. Marett adds to this analysis the worldview of the Malagasy tribes as studied by Ellis, a worldview that says that anything that is great but unexplainable, anything that is new and helpful is Godly; this includes rice, money, thunder, lightning, earthquake, early ancestors, and even books which they read from. Even the Massai, who were developmentally considered to be on a lower level than the Malagasyans- according to the testimony of the researcher Joseph Thomson- called Thomson's research, his lamp and everything they considered odd, God.

Marett says that demons and spirits are most definitely [supernatural] forces; even if that does not mean that every [supernatural] force is considered either a spirit or a demon.[126]Marett mentions the Fijians, who do not kill geese, since they believe that if they did then rain, snow, wind, and storm would befall them, courtesy of a hermit who lives in the forest, and who is endowed with the powers necessary to deliver such calamities. To the question whether this can be defined as spirituality, Marett answers with a resounding "no".[127] [Though one can argue with him and

---

[125] *Ibid.*, at pp. 1-2.

[126] *ibid.* at pp. 10- 13.

[127] *Ibid.*, at p. 15. See in this regard the different perspective that I offered in chapter 2 of Part 1 of this book. Indeed Marett provides no grounds for why man would turn to strange

say that the imagined image of a mysterious man who no one can see, living in the forest, and endowed with supernatural gifts, is the anthropomorphosis of supernatural force.]

Marett explains that the development from spells, magic, and witchcraft to prayer is a development that takes place on the same matrix; they are all different forms of religious expression, and he criticizes those anthropologists who hold otherwise, like Fraser for instance. He explains that emotions that lead to violence -as one finds especially in times of anger or in times of love- is just a matter of their misapplication, which can as a result thereof lead to the blind acceptance of basic witchcraft. It is at this point that spells are cast, which marks a dubious entry into the supernatural world. The "manna", which is closely related to the idea of "obligation", of subjecting man to the whims of witchcraft, helps in transforming the symbolic will of the supernatural into something concrete[128]. The transition from here to prayer is a wholly natural one. Marett explains that a spell is relatable to witchcraft in the same way as prayer is relatable to witchcraft, yet the question remains whether witchcraft leads one to religion. Witchcraft is a mysterious matter and from this perspective it does enter religion. Therefore his conclusion is that witchcraft is religion's genesis.

Marett also argues with Fraser on the whole subject of the taboo. Fraser saw the taboo as a negative phenomenon and refused to incorporate as part of religion. Marett counters that the taboo was an amalgamation of supernatural forces that placed a sanction on things that were obviously impermissible, even harmful to society, but without the taboo as an institution the sanctions would have been toothless in the face of a transgression of the prohibition. It is therefore a positive institution, and in the context of its super naturalness, also a religious institution.[129] Marett explains that the taboo is a prohibition on having contact with those things that society has requested that no contact be established. Examples are contact with women, who are thought to be witches, and with strangers because of their undesirability> similarly one could not touch the tribal chief, since he possessed the "manna", which is the non- elicited force of a superior man. In this

stones and ask them for help during troubled times. How does this jell with man's experience of reality, which told him that when he was a baby or young child he could rely on his father for protection- is it not more natural, then, to suppose that he will seek the help of his father to protect him as he did when he was a helpless little thing, and why did the natural renewal of the seasons not instill in man the belief that his father would have a renewed fanade just like in the case of nature.

[128] *Ibid.*, at pp. 29- 30.

[129] *Ibid.*, at p. 73.

last-mentioned aspect the taboo itself is a negative "manna".[130] When it comes to discussing the taboo and its accompanying sanctions, Marett argues with Jevenus who sees the taboo in a negative light. Instead he claims it should be looked at from a philosophical point of view- like Kant did- and we should look at the essence of morality, and we should realize that there is no point on imposing a moral code if there are no sanctions backing it up, and that is precisely what the taboo provides.[131] Marett explains that the concept "manna," which was widespread amongst the savages in their various locales, even though they were situated far away from one another, included all expressions of mysticism, which were supernatural, occult forces as well as any force that had any connection with religion. Therefore the "manna" also includes things like the joy and contentment over a miracle that occurred. The taboo, in contradistinction is a negative force that only contains prohibitions. Marett poses the question whether it really would be incorrect to say that the combination of manna and taboo forms a kind of spirituality, which is the minimum requirement for defining religion. He replies to this question in the negative by saying that this combination of forces serves as a guide for man directing him how to behave in a reality that is enveloped in spirits and demons- but it cannot be said to independently contain spiritualism.[132]

Marett probes pre-historic findings from caves in France that show that in the pre-historical period rituals were conducted in sacred places, or quasi- temples, in order to ensure that there would be good prey. The rites of the totem were also conducted there since they too had a concept that was similar to that of the manna.[133]

Marett's approach to man's soul is similar to that of Hinde's, the only difference being that Marett did not attempt to confirm the superiority of modern man over

[130] *Ibid.*, at p. 74. However we may explain the prohibition on contact with women and with the head of the tribe as a social norm that could not be tampered with.

[131] *Ibid.*, at p. 78. We can include, in connection to what has been said here, the Jewish experience as personified by Rabbi Levy Yitzhak Berdichev, who asked a simple Jew if he can procure for him the choicest merchandise, and to which the Jew replied in the affirmative. This story occurred during Passover and so the next question that he asked this same Jew was whether he can procure leavened bread, to which the Jew replied- God forbid. When recalling this story the saintly rabbi said "Master of the universe, witness how the Tsar of Russia has so many policemen, and yet his ordinances are not kept, whereas your ordinances are meticulously observed though you have no law enforcement officers whatsoever." The discussion on the taboo relates to this story, since there was a prohibition without any police force and yet it remained rigidly in force, so that it was more powerful than any statute of modern day countries.

[132] See *ibid.*, at pp. 99- 100.

[133] *Ibid.*, at pp. 203- 204.

his primitive counterpart, neither did he see it his aim to prove the inferiority of belief in the Divinity or in the supernatural when measured up against rationalism prevalent in the cultured West. Because of these differences he received heaps of criticism in the West. The attitude of feeling superior to "savages" and of seeing anthropological research as a way of being entertained by the strange inferior and primitive "savages" characterized the anthropological research that was around the time of people like Evans Pritchard, Turner, Doogles, and Apia as has been shown in Part 1 of this book under the title "Why religion?", *Ibid.* in chapter 2 under the paragraph titles that bear their names. In practice, and for the purposes of our present overview, I suggest that we view these five anthropologists together with Marett as one bloc. These six researchers saw in witchcraft and in other African cultural elements a religious experience that suited the needs of black African society, before Western culture reached that continent.

Ernst Gellner[134]

-dealt with the subject of nationalism, and through discussing nationalism he related also to the issue of religion from two angles:

A. Nationalism is an abstract thing, which has nothing to do with reality, being as it is an abstract ideational concept. People direct their deeds and behavior according to the obligations that this ideology imposes upon them, each according to his belief. In accordance with the broadest definitions of religion, as was seen in Part 1 of this book, nationalism itself qualifies as a religion. It may not be a theistic religion, but it is a religion nonetheless.

B. One of the factors that are operative in the founding and preservation of nationalism is the religious factor (as in theistic religion). As transpired in part 3 of this book- "Jewish Nationalism and Arab Nationalism", and as explained there, in chapter 2 –"The End of Nationalism" -in the first section- "The Status of Ethnicity and Religion", as well as in Part 6 of this book, that deals with black Africa, *ibid.* at chapter 2 in the sections that deal with the influence of religion on the class relations, and the role of the religious struggle upon the growing ethnic nationalism in India.

Religion in its broadest sense includes non-theistic religion, which in turn embraces those ideologies advanced by Francis Fukayama, Stephen Hawking and Robert Hinde; all of whom sought to promote their common religion, the non-theistic civil religion- and indeed an overview of each of these personalities is provided above. This is not to say that Ernst Gellner sought to advance a

---

134 See Ernst Gellner, *Nations and Nationalism,* [Hebrew edition] translated from the English by Dan Daor (Tel Aviv: Open University, 1994).

non-theistic denomination, neither can it be said that he aimed to advance any denominations. Nonetheless Gellner, like the very many- or at the very least, a majority- of western philosophers who had researched the subject of nationalism in the contemporary era, failed to see any fundamental links between nationalism and any and all forms of theistic religion. This short sightedness suited the interests of the Western regimes which base themselves on a civic society composed of the citizens of their respective countries- without any essential connections to the ethnicity or to the religion of their population. As explained in Part 7 of this book; this is representative of the main currents of thought prevalent in the West. From this perspective, Gellner- in this overview- represents this central current, being one of its leaders and central pillars.

After investigating the matter, Gellner determines that man has undergone three fundamental stages in his history: pre-agrarian, agrarian, and industrial. While in the first period there were no political organizations, during the second period political organization was possible, and in the third it was mandatory. The problem of nationalism was non-existent until states came about. Belonging to a state is not one of the intrinsic qualities of man, even though nowadays for all intents and purposes it has become so. Gellner provides two alternative temporary definitions to the concept of nation:[135]
A. Objective-cultural definition: Two persons can be said to be from the same nation only if they share the same culture. Culture is interpreted as a set of concepts, symbols, associations, and modes of behavior, and of communication.

B. Subjective –voluntary definition: Two persons can be said to be from the same nation, if and only if they identify each other as affiliated to the same nation. In other words- nationalities are the creations of man. Nation is a product of the beliefs of human beings, their loyalties and their camaraderie. The condition is that each of the group's members recognizes that they have the same mutual obligations and rights.

In the agrarian society, according to Gellner, there was a minority government, and few knew how to read or write. There was also a class of scribes/ priests, who in certain societies were very devout, and generally speaking others did not interfere with these classes. In Islam the priests/ scribes had the missionary role of attracting people to the religion so that there was a possibility that others would eventually join this class, especially since the studying of religion was open to all

[135] *Ibid.*, at pp. 203- 204.

the other classes. In practice, however relatively few newcomers joined this class.[136]

When relating to the industrial society, Gellner mentions Weber's opinion on the link between Protestantism and Capitalism, but does not agree with it. He accepts that rationalism is an important ingredient in this type of society, as per Weber's theory, but adds that orderliness and utilitarianism which lead to that rationalism are also important components. The said society is built upon productivity and frequent changes in the division of labor. Professions are not passed down, like they were in the agrarian period, from father to son, but rather it is economic movements that determine the various occupations. Since society is based on egalitarian ideals, education is accessible to all. Owing to this free education the members of this society have turned into priests/ scribes, and the accurate and frequent communication between strangers ensures that leading trends in culture solidify and become the heritage of the masses. Culture and the state join together, and a common identity surrounds this axle, so that one nation is created for all the state's citizens[137]. The industrial state can only operate if its population is mobile, it knows how to read and write, and has a standardized culture. The state arranges that all its different ethnic groups are united under it. In this way nationalities are born. Religious people only worry about preserving the rituals, without caring about uniting the society. (Theistic) religion has thus lost its status. It is no longer possible to view a community through the prism of God. Nonetheless, this new nationalism is also riddled with disease: Society has become anonymous and its members are exploited by it as if they were a clogged up convertible mass. In such a situation it is possible that a certain ethnic group A will be shoved aside into the periphery, while at the same time ethnic group B holds on to the reins of power keeping for itself all the important state jobs. When such a scenario takes place, feelings of ethnicity are aroused, which before then did not play any important role, and members of ethnic group A become a nation seeking to secede and form their own independent state.[138]

Moving away from the industrial setting and going over to discuss cultural development, Gellner says that the higher cultured classes are the instigators for forming a new nationalism. This is what occurred in Algeria, where before nationalism became popular it was religion that was the dividing factor between those who had very restricted rights and those who enjoyed the full protection of the law. The Algerian nation, Gellner claims, would not have come into being

[136] *Ibid.*, at pp. 31- 37.

[137] *Ibid.*, at pp. 38- 61.

[138] *Ibid.*, at pp. 79- 90.

were it not for the general nationalist feeling that has been pervasive in the past century. Before then they were a community of believers in Islam alongside other smaller denominational communities, yet there was no group entity that one would have identified as an independent class of Algerian Muslims. This was also the case when it came to the Palestinian's self-identification in relation to the Land of Israel (Palestine) - only in that scenario it was not religion that was decisive but rather language, culture, and history that acted as adhesives towards the formation of a new nationalism. With regard to (theistic) religion Gellner adds that the Islamic culture during the agrarian period is a striking example of his thesis, which argues that agrarian societies did not view culture as important in establishing an independent political entity and hence they had no proclivity for nationalism. The loosely formed guild of the *Ulma*- made up of sages, legal scholars and theologians- which set the tone for the traditional Muslim world and which ruled over society in the traditional sense, transcended the political and ethnic boundaries, and had no connection whatever with any type of political state.[139]

When looking at the impact of the modern era on the status of the entrenched religions, Gellner focuses on how three of theses religions developed in their own and different ways. His focus was on Islam, the laws of Confucius, and Western Christianity. In addition to these three he also traced developments in the rather unique situation of sub-Saharan (black) Africa.

Christianity in the West was forced to retreat from its positions of power, since within the Christian world a transition had taken place from the agrarian period to the industrial, which necessitated a common united language being spoken across relatively wide sovereign territories. This phenomenon raised the cultural level of the populace which resulted in their secularization. Apart from Franco's Spain which was exceptional for it being under the influence of Catholicism which was the state religion [Gellner does not say this explicitly, we can read between the lines though, that what he intended top say was that that the economic-capitalist-governmental interests created a united secular state, by means of creating a civil religion for the said state]. Gellner says that the Reformation in North Western Europe at first changed the whole society to the class of priests/ scribes by instituting that the colloquial language be used for performing religious rites. After this development it was the enlightenment that ensured the secularization of this universal priest/ scribe class converting the spoken language into a united national language. Speaking in very general terms, he says that the industrial period drew its sustenance from economic growth. It also modeled itself on the increasingly popular notion, reaffirmed by philosophers such as Descartes,

---

[139] See *Ibid.*, at pp. 105- 106.

that any reputable claim with regard to the world's origins or workings can never be absolute, and that all determinations with regard thereto must be able to withstand rigorous testing by objective criteria, which are completely detached from any and every belief system. This approach is diametrically opposed to the absolutists feature that characterized the theistic religions, being an approach that asked questions and cast doubts on all and sundry, as is typical of secularism. And indeed subjectivism and skepticism have become the trademarks of modern western secularism, which has replaced the trust and faith that typified the era when religion had dominated humanity's consciousness[140].

The Muslim world, according to Gellner, was saved from western skepticism and subjectivity, since Islam, in contradistinction to Christianity, had always displayed a greater amount of internal flexibility. Islam has always revealed two faПades, one of which has been directed at the urban intellectuals, who are meticulous in their observance and who have a greater tendency towards individualism; whereas the other has been molded to suit the needs of the masses who are more group oriented and whose communities are more diverse from a religious cultural perspective. It is for this reason that Islam has never been uprooted and has never been downgraded as an important element in the lifestyle of the cultured Muslim. This is the reason too that Islam has been so entrenched within the Islamic states' nationalism.[141]

Far Eastern culture which used to be influenced by the Confucian hierarchical society was unable to withstand the egalitarianism mandated by modernity. The Confucian lifestyle was more appropriate for the agrarian period and was an utter failure when it came to be applied to modern life[142].

Sub- Saharan (black) Africa never adopted the Western style nationalism; in terms of which each country's civil religion determined its features. Even the fact that the universal religions had impacted African life had no effect. Sub Saharan Africa was never witness to the consolidation of its various traditional cultures, so that a local culture of a section of the population could never have been adapted and subsequently adopted as the general culture of all the citizens of the state. In Gellner's eyes Sub- Saharan Africa remains an unsolved mystery.[143]

---

[140] See *Ibid.*, at p. 108.
[141] *Ibid.*, at p. 110.
[142] *Ibid.*, at p. 111.
[143] See *ibid.*, at pp. 112- 113. However I would recommend that one studies Part 6 of this book, on Sub- Saharan (black) Africa where the clout of ancient African tribalism is reviewed. The African man consolidates his identity around this tribalism and within this

Baruch Spinoza[144]
-was a Jewish philosopher who was active in the first half of the seventeenth century. Owing to his nonconformist opinions in regard to religious ideas, he was excommunicated by his local Jewish community. Because his philosophy covered many prominent fields of study he was recognized and thought of as one of the leading lights in Western thought. Out of the many different writings attributed to him, I will only focus on one of his books.

Spinoza opines that the Holy Scriptures are the province of every Jew for every generation. These scriptures were penned by different writes over different periods to ensure that they are written in a language that speaks to the contemporary Jew's heart, thus enabling him to voluntarily obey the word of the Lord. He lays a greater stress on emotion than on intellect in the role that religion plays in guiding Jewish actions. The Holy scriptures were meant for the masses to be understood directly by them, without these scriptures being filtered through by the interpretations of the select elite of the wise and sagacious. The Holy Scripture's most sacred principles operate within the domains of emotion and of love- indeed the whole Torah is based on the one thing: loving one's neighbor. Anyone who loves his friend is considered born from God. God is love. Moses did not try and use wisdom to prove religion to the nation (again the basis of religion is emotion, not intellect) but rather imposed upon them obligations by covenant, by oath, and through loving kindness. He threatened them with a punishment for transgressing any statute while promising reward for their observance (again: the religious gospel is transferred through emotion). Good deeds are reflective of a person's religiosity rather than the understanding of theoretical concepts, since it is deeds that reflect a true and genuine religious understanding.[145]

As regards to the prophets who revealed- according to the revelations that they experienced-the word of God: God appeared to each prophet in the unique way that that prophet was familiar with, consequently the revelations differed. When it came to Moses God spoke to him in His own voice, which was also heard at the foot of Mount Sinai. Samuel on the other hand experienced God through a simulated voice, as did Avimelech. Christ also experienced God though this was a more surreal spiritual experience. Many other prophets experienced God through

---

framework; support and mutual aid are provided. This is symbolic of the inner strength of the African society.

[144] See Baruch Spinoza *Essay on Political theology* [in Hebrew], (Jerusalem: Magnes, 1989).

[145] *Ibid.,* at pp. 147- 149.

visions. There were some revelations that were received by the giving of signs, as is illustrated in the story of Gideon. The certainty of the signs were not measured in any mathematical sense (in other words that they were certain as to the concept that they comprehended or envisioned), but rather in absolute moral terms, and the signs were only of persuasive value. At times a prophet will require, in order that he is able to prophesy, the playing of a musical instrument, as seen in the example of Eliza. Yet there were revelations that required no intervening means, such as the case with Moses, Ezekiel and Jeremiah. Isaiah saw God adorned in garments and sitting on his throne, whereas Ezekiel saw him as a ball of fire. There is no doubt that each prophet visualized God according to his own powers of imagination. At times those who were under the spell of a revelation did not comprehend what was really happening. Joshua could not really fathom the unusually long span of sunshine, and he and all the masses that had accompanied him and who had thought that the sun had orbited the earth daily, believed that that day the movement of the sun had been suspended for a certain time. This, they reasoned was why the sun continued to shine for an unusually long period. They did not understand that that because there was a lot of ice in the vicinity it refracted the rays making their reach seem much longer even in the waning hours of the day so that it looked like it was still broad daylight. This same type of misunderstanding explains the actions of Noah and of Adam. Noah experienced a revelation in terms of which he believed that God had wiped mankind from off the face of the earth. Yet, this was only because Noah's limited understanding led him to believe that there was no habitation outside the boundaries of the Land of Israel. Adam, the first human to have experienced Divine Revelation, did not understand that God was the Omnipresent and the Omniscient; he therefore first tried to hide away from God and after being unsuccessful squeezed out of his mouth an apology for sinning against Him as if He, God was his human equal. That is why God in fact was revealed to Adam in a way that suited his limited comprehension of the Divinity so that it seemed to Adam that God could not be at all places simultaneously and did not really know where Adam was or what sin he had performed. Did Adam not hear, or did it not appear to Adam that he was listening to the sound of God wandering through the garden and calling out and asking where he is. Afterwards, because it was embarrassing for Adam, God actually asked him if he had eaten from the tree that was forbidden to him. We see from here that Adam was unaware of any of God's designated attributes save for the fact that He was the Creator of everything. The same can be said of Kane. He too experienced God's presence only to the extent that he comprehended what that meant. He thought that God was unaware of man's business. In any event for the purposes of showing true remorse over his actions, Kane did not require a greater comprehension of the Divine. The revelation experienced by Laban was that of the God of Abraham, since Laban believed that each nation had its unique God. Even in the case of Abraham, he did not know that is God is Omnipresent as well as prescient, and therefore when he was informed of the decree against the Sodomite People he prayed to God not to carry it out until it had been proven that indeed all the city's inhabitants were worthy of such a fate. Moses too did not sufficiently comprehend the idea of God's Omniscience and that all of man's future actions are completely dependent on what God decides. The Israelites knew next to nothing about their God, even though He was revealed to them. This we see all too clearly, when after a very short period they started honoring and worshipping a calf believing it to be the lord who had raised them out of Egypt. Samuel believed that God never relents after pronouncing His decree.[146]

Therefore, Spinoza opines that the relationship man has with God even the performance of the Divine commandments are all based on emotional encounters. It is this idea that reinforces what was said earlier on in this book in Part 3, "Jewish Nationalism and Arab Nationalism in a Jewish State", and more specifically in chapter 4, in the section dealing with the two types of ethical systems that find expression within the different types of nationalisms- Western (nationalism) –intellectual , and traditional- emotional. The claim made there is that the relationship with the Divinity is one based on emotion, and the actual fulfillment of the ethical and Divine precepts, which God is believed to have commanded, is instigated by the emotions. Such a claim then elucidates the difference between Divine morality and secular morality in that the former is rooted in emotions while having no claim to be based on human reason.

Peter Winch[147]

He was a philosopher, who while carrying out anthropological research sought to distinguish between the intersecting cultures with which the researcher is familiar, from those cultures that characterize the subject of the research. He criticizes the initial approach that was adopted by a researcher who had spent some time in Western Africa on the border of the Sudan, amongst the Santee tribe, E. E. Evans Pritchard- an approach which Evans Pritchard himself hastily modified to comply with that suggested by Winch. At first Evans Pritchard related to his subjects by measuring them against Western modes of thought and understanding, in terms of which the witchcraft practiced by the Santee tribe is incomprehensible. Looking at them from his pedestal he viewed their practices as wayward especially when tested by Western scientific measures. It almost goes without saying that this type

---

146 *Ibid.*, at pp. 9- 32.

147 See Peter Winch, "Understanding a Primitive Society," in *Rationality*, edited by Bryan R. Wilson (Oxford, G. Britain: Basil Blackwell, 1970). The paper was first published in the *American Philosophical Quarterly*, 1, 1964, pp. 307- 324.

of approach viewed the Santee as stuck in superstition and as deluding themselves into thinking that their healing methods, magic tricks, rituals, and myths actually helped them. Nevertheless, Evans Pritchard, as befitting a methodical Western scientist of his stature, presented to his Western reader an accurate and detailed portrait of the primitive philosophy on life, after having spent a prolonged period with the Santee tribe. Owing to their philosophy the Santee enjoyed a harmonious, serene and secure lifestyle, especially if compared to the modern Western lifestyle, where man failed to scale the same heights of serenity and social harmony. It was these findings of Evans Pritchard that earned him many admirers and at the same time aroused much interest in the subject of his research.
Winch asked whether there was any justification for a Western bred anthropologist to judge the primitive man according to Western yardsticks. It might very well be true that according to Western reasoning there is no logic to the Santee way of life. A western educated individual, who believes that rainfall is dependent on meteorological reasons, only believes this because that has been the accepted belief for generations before him. Similarly a member of the Santee tribe believes that rainfall is dependent upon the application of witchcraft because he too received this generations- old tradition. Someone trained in scientific norms will accept any facts as they appear to be superficially, whereas those who are trained in the methods of witchcraft will not trust that that which appears to be is in fact the case. Someone trained in the scientific method will not entertain the thought that anything unscientific be introduced into the logical equation; whereas God told Job not to think that he (Job) knows or is even capable of knowing everything, neither should he imagine that it is within his own powers to find all the solutions- there are things that exist exclusively within the province of God's knowledge, and no amount of human reason will transfer this knowledge to the province of man. It is only through entering the world of religion that man is able to achieve Divine knowledge. We have to understand that it is not an objective reality that determines our terms of reference, rather the opposite is the case, what is real and what is unreal, and what can be described as reality- are all determined by the terms of reference that we employ. Science has its own language, and only an expert in scientific terms is able properly to conduct scientific experiments. Is a society that has become used to the language of witchcraft- and for those who appreciate witchcraft there is a whole language that within its own framework uses terms that are specific to it- able to conduct a debate as to the utility of witchcraft and able to test to what extent it contains elements of truth?

Winch says that there is no similarity between western conceptions of witchcraft, which are associated with that which frightened our forefathers in the ancient period, and between the witchcraft as it is conceived by the Santee. 'For a member of the Santee tribe witchcraft is a routine and daily matter and he will be amazed if indeed one day goes by where he does not encounter something that has the hand of witchcraft written all over it. If a westerner, within the framework of his religious activities comes face to face with the phenomenon or incident of something resembling witchcraft, he would be compelled to test that encounter according to the rules of the religious system. After all this witchcraft incident claims to be an inseparable component of the religious framework, and so it is up to the religious framework to decide whether to accept or reject this claim. If there is a phenomenon or incident that appears to be parasitical to framework X, it would only be correct to view the phenomenon through the prism of framework X. It follows then that if witchcraft is active within the cultural and lifestyle framework of the Santee people, we have to assess it using Santee tools of analysis. In the eyes of the Santee, and according to Santee cultural concepts, any truth that becomes defective requires that the witchcraft that caused the defect be located. To do this we need to refer to the experts in these things who can locate the witch that is responsible for the defect. It is also possible that two experts will point to two different sources, or that one expert will find that there are two diametrically opposed forces that are responsible. In both these two cases, the fact that the two findings contradict one another does not disqualify the witchcraft theory, all it means is that there will be a need- in accordance with the Santee system – to investigate whether one of the contradictory findings only came about as a result of the fact that a spell had been cast that deliberately caused an error in locating the occult source. Therefore there is no basis, at least from the point of view of a Santee tribesman, for investigating whether the Santee system is correct, only whether its guiding principles have been adhered to in the correct manner. Members of the Santee tribe are captivated by their network of associations which all make perfect sense within the world of the occult in the same way as Europeans are captivated by the network of scientific ideas. It is illogical then to test the Santee lifestyle according the European scientific network. Therefore, Evans Pritchard was guilty of an error when he determined (without perhaps expressing it in such a crude manner) that the Santee people were in the wrong and the Europeans were in the right. This last- mentioned approach cannot be accepted.

Connected to this discussion is Wittenstein's theory, which although at first suggested that any determination- as a rule- if it is commensurate with reality must be correct, later on corrected itself and according to the amended version proposed that there are no one absolute truths, and just as one's terms of reference are variable and multifaceted so too are the resultant scientific determinations. He laid down the principle that "the limits of my world are the limits of my language" and therefore I cannot negate a possibility other than that which I have determined according to my terms of reference. This is because the possibility in question lies outside those boundaries with which I am unfamiliar. And indeed, Evans

Pritchard- later on in life- like Wittenstein- reached a different conclusion to the same facts on a matter of principle. Nonetheless, Evans Pritchard's concrete determination with regard to the Santee remained the same, viz. that the Santee had been misled when it came to their attitude to witchcraft.[148]
Winch adds to this and says- as an aside to his main discussion- that the Santee had no interest doubting the witchcraft system. In his opinion, this fact pulls the rug out from under Evans Pritchard's criticism of the Santee witchcraft system, since it makes it quite clear that that the Santee race takes no notice of arguments that are grounded in logic, when it comes to their theory on witchcraft.[149]
Winch explains that Alasdair Macintyre, who also criticizes Evans Pritchard, actually expresses an opinion that is contradictory to Winch's even if they are both critical of Evans Pritchard. This might seem absurd, but the mystery is solved, if one considers that Macintyre actually criticizes Evans Pritchard's amended approach, which can be seen in a second anthropological study, this time on the Nuer tribe. This time the research accepted in principle the amended approach of Wittenstein that directs one to assess the components of an examined culture according to the concepts, lifestyle, mores, and language of that examined culture, and not by using the researcher's own westernized concepts. Evans Pritchard's new approach suits Winch's. In contradistinction Winch's criticism of Evans Pritchard was on the latter's attitude towards the Santee.[150] In this way the mist is cleared and the contradiction is solved.

Winch and Macintyre fiercely debated the correct way of analyzing the "illogical" rituals and customs of the "savages". Macintyre, as mentioned, investigates "savage" customs according to the logic of a modern Western bred individual, whose logic is purely utilitarian. The "savages" organize certain rituals that are specially designated, so it would appear, to ensure a good agricultural yield, yet MacIntyre asserts that such rituals cannot possibly be responsible for producing anything. Neither does the practice, common to these savages, of carrying an object that symbolizes one's life and worrying that when that object gets lost the bearer of it has reached the end of his days, make any sense. For MacIntyre trying to explain this odd behavior is equivalent to proverbially "knocking his head against a brick wall," as he is unable to make any leeway into improving his

---

[148] See *Ibid.*, at pp. 79- 92.

[149] See, *Ibid.*, at pp. 93- 94. This claim can be linked to, and reinforce the claim made in this book in Part 1 – "Why Religion?" at chapter 2- "Primitive Man and the Utility of Religion".

[150] *Ibid.*, at pp. 94- 95. MacIntyre argued that criticism is based on logical grounds, and a researcher only has one type of logic, which is the logic of the culture in which he was bred. He has no other logic at his disposal.

understanding of the matter. Winch however believes that Macintyre's whole attitude is typical of the blindness common to the modern man, cut off, as he is, from his environment. This type of man is devoid of any true values, unlike the denigrated savage. Indeed we could do worse than learn from these "savages." We ought to alter our whole outlook towards life, specifically in three important areas:

(i) Which is the most correct lifestyle that we ought to lead?
(ii) What is the most important thing in life?
(iii) Does life itself have intrinsic value, and if so- what is that value?

It is incumbent upon us (representing the modern western culture, where everyone is concerned for his own welfare) to realize that life is entrusted to us so that we can make active use of it either for good or for bad. Therefore when death comes about it does not mean merely that our life has terminated but that our ability to choose between good or bad has also ended.

In the same way the agricultural crop is not produced merely to be consumed. It contains a deeper inner meaning for the farmer. Therefore the rituals that relate to the agricultural produce are not performed merely to increase its yield. Rather these rituals have their own inner meaning that affects the quality and substance of life and because of this; they also have social value within the community or village.

Similarly if I carry with me an object that symbolizes my life, it is just to remind me of what I am able to do in life, whether for good, or for bad. It gives purpose to my life.

Therefore the "progressive" western educated anthropological researcher who analyses the "savage" customs of the "primitives" by employing "western- logic" ought to relate to his subjects as his equals rather than as his "inferiors". He should rather use this opportunity to truly learn something.

In this context Winch refers to those "moral" western men who seem to have forgotten for whom morality was created. For all their erudition and refinement they still seem to prefer- in the extreme case- dealing with the length of the hair of their subjects rather than the relations between the sexes, as exemplified in the Biblical story of Samson and Delilah.[151]

Winch's piercing criticism, also for those who are uncomfortable with the point he makes about Samson, epitomizes for us the amount of humility that is required of the modern cultured classes who are faced with dealing with the primeval way of life of humans who live under conditions not dissimilar to those that existed at the time of the world' creation. They need to realize that as products of the modern

---

[151] *Ibid.*, at pp. 106- 110.

culture they have lost the mental perceptiveness primeval man possessed. Likewise they know nothing of the emotional, delicate, but effervescent way of living that existed amongst the prehistoric peoples, who did not know how to read or write and who therefore failed to leave behind them any signs of "culture". The primordial theistic religious values that were characteristic of the ancient period, and the role of society within those religious values are forever lost.

Martin Hollis[152]
- is an anthropologist, who has studied the natives of Australia, and with regard thereto claims that the explanations put forward by the natives for their behavior are untrue, and there is no escape from seeking out the real explanation. He mentions that the natives consider the sun to be a solid mass, and this has something to do with their ritual beliefs which rely on metaphoric images .In this context he introduces Susan Langer, whose 1963 study claimed that man is an imaginative creature. Man applies his imagination through one of these two models: A. Practical imagery that he conjures up in order to acquire benefit, and this man does through using verbal reasoning. B. Expressive symbolism, as found in music and religion- the aims in this case are self- serving, not for fostering ulterior goals. It is this latter type of symbolism that is perfect in the sense that it is has no constituent parts that in the ordinary course of events would not be connected to it. In accordance with the assertion in B- language is an excellent example of the exact opposite, of practical symbolism, in light of the fact that language is used as a tool of analysis serving goals that are external to it. As opposed to language, music is a good example of expressive symbolism. It has a perfect structure and is completely self- serving. Susan Langer studied the Yoruba tribe and within this framework she wrote that the Yoruba declarations could not be verbally expressed since they were not clear cut but were hinted at. In this sense they employed a similar medium to Beethoven who would have found it impossible to convey absolute belief in anything, exclusively through his music. It may very well be easier to express something through unambiguous words, yet the Yoruba tribe wanted their expressions to have exclusive meaning above and beyond that that was expressed. Therefore the reason why ritual declarations are not understandable outside their context is because they have no meaning when detached from their context. Langer goes on to quote Carnap who said that every metaphoric presentation like lyrical or emotion laden sentence uses tolls that represent something other than its superficial meaning. A metaphoric presentation, according to Carnap, is neither true nor false since it does not make any concrete claims. It is similar to laughter, an emotional song / poem, or expressive music- it

---

152 See Martin Hollis, "Reason and Ritual" in *Rationality*, edited by Bryan R. Wilson (Oxford, G. Britain: Basil Blackwell, 1970).

does not express any concrete and explicit thing, rather it conveys a general emotional trend.
Langer concludes her thesis with a critical comment on Carnap's outlook on symbolism saying that, methodologically, one may make the analogy between ritual and music, but this type of approach will inevitably lead to a gross misunderstanding of what ritual is all about. Therefore we should completely dismiss any explanations anthropologists come up with when commenting on rituals. Langer poses the question whether her recommendation leaves us with no option other than confining our research into rituals by looking only at its very broad meaning to society. If the Santee ritual (the very same that was the subject of Evans Pritchard's research) opens up for us a new channel in understanding the Santee communal lifestyle, does that really mean that an objective channel has been opened for us when we try and decipher the meaning of ritual. She argues that the Santee tribesman would explain that he was harmed by a spell which has nothing to do with the social fabric but was because he was a victim of the meddling of supernatural forces. As in the case of the Santee tribesman, so too with a Catholic believer, notwithstanding his beliefs, it could be argued that he conducts his life as a reaction to social events that have occurred during the course of history. This Catholic will not necessarily admit that it is simply a matter of social causes. If however he does admit that, it would be denying the fact that the source for any unusual occurrences is found outside the realms of nature. Hollis queries what Langer says in this connection and asks whether the beliefs of the Santee and of the Catholics who believe in things occurring beyond the plane of reality and which have their origin in the supernatural, whether these beliefs are mere fictions that have been passed down by society. Hollis is not prepared to offer any definite answer and he leaves the question hanging, explaining that it does not belong to his field of research. Langer argues that there are certain rituals that men believe in and the problem that we have is in identifying their purpose. Merely saying that it has to do with the society of the believers is not a satisfactory explanation for the institution of rituals.

Relating to what Langer has said Hollis argues that belief-rituals are indeed identifiable since they conform to the laws set by our concept of inevitability. Hollis admits that this kind of approach is, on the face of it, insular and limited, yet he asserts that when one undertakes an anthropological study one has to make use of certain tools of the trade and one does not have the luxury of neglecting this avenue of research. One of these tools is the concept of anthropological reasoning.

Hollis mentions in this regard Whorf's presumption, which states that man's ability to comprehend ideas is a function of his language skills. In other words man differentiates observed phenomena by allotting to them different linguistic categories according to his field of expertise. This presumption is based on empirical evidence that cannot be refuted by a philosopher. Yet this still does not mean that it is inevitable that two different individuals or even two different societies will observe things in a totally different light; there still exists the possibility that to a certain degree they will share the same perceptions, which possibility can only be dismissed after every single society and every single human being has been thoroughly studied. In any event, what is important from Hollis's perspective, when deliberating the matter, is the fact that the accuracy of Whorf's presumption cannot, for all intents and purposes, be conclusively asserted.

Hollis's exploration into the role language plays in the anthropologist's line of work and the into the other difficulties of anthropological interpretation coincides with Peter Winch's treatises and illustrates the difficulties one is faced with when one is trying to decipher ancient religions that exited before reading and writing was invented.

Robert Bellah[153]

Bellah says that trying to understand the modern idea of progress belongs to the category of trying to resolve questions that are important but are unsolvable. This category includes questions that deal with ancient myths that were believed by the primitive societies as well as those that deal with the philosophical beliefs of progressive society. Man has always tried to deal with questions that relate to human nature, since man is a rationally aware individual who measures the importance of his existence by his ability to add value and influence to his actions which on their own hold little prospect for him, in order that these potentially unfulfilling activities become fated to outlast the importance of man himself. Karl Popper, according to Bellah viewed the doctrine of inevitable progress as the source of many of the ills affecting the modern world.

Popper said that religion may be considered a set of symbols that are prone to institutionalization so that they either turn into social norms or become engrained in the individual man. Religious symbols are distinguished from all others in that they describe nature and reality in the broadest of terms. Religion offers an answer to the following questions: What is to the source of order or of disorder in the universe? What is behind the authority that is exercised over man? And what is the correct path man should follow in his conduct?

[153] See Robert N. Bellah "Epilogue: Religion and Progress in Modern Asia" in *Religion and Progress in Modern Asia*, edited by Robert N. Bellah (London: Collier- Macmillan, New York: The Free Press, 1965).

Society, according to Bellah, feels compelled to follow a set of religious precepts that have been accepted by the majority of its members. It is quite possible that religion's chief function is its being the axis around which the culture of a specific society rotates. Being this central axis it supplies rigid definitions of the world, so that its constituent individuals and societies will face this planet's transience and its crises from a balanced perspective. Religions are known for their proclivity to deal with life's crises and transitions [the mythical meaning of transitions is herein intended], which includes life and marriage -for the individual- hunger, war, change in the personnel of the regime, the crowning of a new premier, and the changing of seasons- for society.

Submitting to, and expressing respect for the sacred helps provide a dimension of orderliness, which sets up in its wake a framework for human activity. As Eliade explains religion provides positive attitudes towards the dimensions of time and space, which in turn provides man with a basis for his identity. Judaism, Christianity and Islam instructed men to think about the concept of time as one current that has a beginning, a purpose for being and an end which is all controlled by God and which is all run according to Divine Plan, as was stated by Father ("the spiritual shepherd") de la Costa. The modern idea of progress is merely a secularist adaptation of the Christian conception of history, of a positive progression from the past to the future. Modern times have however transformed religious motifs such as the Jewish "Zion" or the Islamic "Mecca" into symbolizing America as the Kingdom of God, valuing its patriotism and its progress. The durability of [theistic] religion projected itself, in a positive way, upon the durability of modern man as well as the durability of modernity and progress. Even the alterations made to religion did not annul this durability- in the sense that Jesus and Mohammed did not really do away with their predecessors. Even communism presented itself as an extension of religion, and even claimed that the (communistic) idea of constant revolution had always existed in religion.

The primitive religions that originated in the Bronze Age, like the Egyptian, Mesopotamian and ancient Chinese, all dealt with very specific problems having nothing to do with the precipice of time. Their fields of expertise were evil, suffering, frustration, confusion, and hunger; each phenomenon having its separate remedy. In contradistinction, the historical religions have all concentrated their efforts on one Supreme Being. The holy sites were transferred and instead of being spread out amongst various concrete and separate focal points and pertaining to the very realistic flow of life, everything was now concentrated on a world that existed outside the bounds of reality, in another world, i.e. the Lord's sanctuary. The historical religions intended that their members develop their study skills in order that they are able to fulfill the goals that they had striven for viz. the salvation of their souls. A perhaps unintended consequence was that these religious practitioners were able to use their study skills for the more mundane goals of advancing technology and of promoting economic modernity. So began the transition from the historical religions to today's age of progress. This progress receives its nourishment from the tensions between, and separation of religious and state institutions, since during the medieval period it was religion which had supported the political regime. At times the political regimes exploited religion for selfish purposes as can be witnessed in China where the Chin dynasty employed the Confucian system in all districts under its jurisdiction and thus turned all its jurisdictional territory into one solid and united bloc that were vulnerable to their governance. The religions themselves developed their own political institutions as well as universities, but, in the main, after the latter became strong enough they showed their gratitude by removing their religious patron from their affairs. Nonetheless the gradual decline during the medieval period of (theistic) religious influence upon other institutions- political or scientific- enabled the latter to develop so that they strengthened themselves to an extent that they were able to relegate the prime status enjoyed by (historical – theistic) religion. All of the historical religions speak about the spiritual summits that they had scaled at the time of their genesis, their disappointing troughs that they underwent at a later period, and the future historical- religious plan that would bring with it final salvation. Characteristic of all historical religions is the stratification of the members into a class of believers and a class of non-believers, and even within the former group this is further divided into those strongly affiliated and those more loosely tied to (theistic) religion.

Bellah describes the religious developments, especially those that occurred within the Protestant community, but also that which occurred in a less pronounced way amongst Catholics, where extra stress was put on the material world. This brought about a transition all the way from asceticism to an active interest in economics, politics, and science. This interest was justified by the claim that the Divine light could also shine through these things, and was not confined to dwelling exclusively within the realms of theology. Bellah defines modernity as the ability of man to decide for himself which goals he will pursue. The problem arises, so Bellah says, when man's ability to reach certain targets is greater than his ability to define for himself what these targets actually are. In such a situation the results can be quite devastating. He adds to this and says that defining man's goals is something that religion is particularly interested in and is something that it has no choice but to be interested in. Moreover: modernity, especially after the advances made in the fields of science and technology, inevitably trespasses on traditional religious domains. Religion unquestionably also had an influence on modernity as was amply demonstrated in the Puritan revolution that took place in 17th century

England, where according to Hans Kohn[154] ,it brought a sense of freedom to all and not only to those in the upper classes. People were now endowed with a newfound pride. They were not simply individuals but part of a nation. Instead of being passive subjects of history they were now its creators. God had chosen each one of them to play a role in the events- and this is exactly what creates the atmosphere around modern nationalism, which has religious, political, and social elements that act upon it simultaneously. At this point in time it still cannot be referred to as secular nationalism, which only came about at the end of the 18th century, yet it has already progressed from the patriotic statism that that typified the Renaissance period and before that, the monarchies. A nation had at this stage arisen, and had tasted the ingredients of freedom.

The English Puritan Revolution did not only leave in its trail elements of modern nationalism, but in addition thereto it was responsible for promoting the modern idea of *progress*, where humankind is viewed as essentially good. Milton[155] in this context states that the primary change effected by the Reformist movement was its appreciation of the good that is found in every individual.

In regard to Asia (the eastern and south- eastern parts) – modernity and with it Protestantism only reached that region one hundred years ago. These two ideologies arrived in Asia packaged in both their moderate and radical forms. The radical forms were those that were developed in the West and were a response to, and an immediate result of the advent of modernity, whereas the more moderate forms were those that developed (also) in the West (mainly France and England) simultaneous with the development of modernity. [Compared to the last example, in Asia there was no gradual development rather there both Christianity and modernity were accepted at the same time- Y. C.] Therefore it is easy to understand why in Asia there was a greater tendency to adopt the more radical forms, even if as mentioned that was not the only trend that typified that region. The moderate English nationalism (that took hold the same time as the Industrial Revolution) did not sever itself from religion, and even the French system of democracy and politics developed a restrained version of itself. In contrast to these two moderate models, there developed- also in the West- two radical forms, the first being primordial nationalism which sanctified blood ties, land, language, or religion, and the second being Radical Marxist Socialism, which speaks in terms of a world revolution.[156]

---

[154] *Ibid.*, at p. 197.
[155] *Ibid.*, at p. 198.
[156] *Ibid.* at pp. 199- 200.

I will not at this juncture, enter into the numerous details, as Bellah does, of the various developments that occurred in a long list of Eastern and Southern Asian countries; details that show how it came to be that these last-mentioned countries embraced western- style modernity, religion, and nationalism. What is important is that once matters of religious import are introduced they are inseparable from their cultural milieu which inevitably affects the preexisting culture. Ideologies, like religions and nationalism, are then transported to the adopting countries either because of an economic interest to embrace modernity or because of external pressures placed upon these countries by the western conqueror.

Saul Shaked[157]

He inferred from ancient manuscripts found in India that Hinduism started off in the period between 1900 and 1500 B. C. E. [158]as a polytheistic religion with the main deity being Indri, the god of war, and the second in command being Verona, who is involved with world order. Already at this early stage there existed the Brahman, which was the force implanted in every worldly thing, and which force was ruled over by incantations and oaths and whoever knew them could then control these forces. The Brahman is a type of worldly spirit that can be thought of as the world's soul which contains within it the soul of every individual in the world. These ancient manuscripts also contain in them the idea that the sacrificial offering, out of whose corpse a spiritual world that communicates with man is created, is of man himself. Man is identified, or actually identifies himself with the God to whom he offers his sacrifice. Looked at from this perspective man is in fact offering himself to himself. The world appears like a very human reality, a reality that is the outgrowth of the body of ancient man, and therefore this fact is accompanied by the feeling the only possibility of welcoming a new reality into the world is by natural means- by the death and resurrection of the human sacrifice. The only genuine sacrifice is when man offers up himself, even if it is acknowledged that offering an acquisition of man's is as if that man offered himself, since the thing offered is considered inseparable from man by virtue of man owning it. The ideal sacrifice then is when man feels himself at one with the god to whom he is offering the sacrifice. The reincarnation of the souls was an idea that made its appearance long after this, around the years 1000 to 500 B.C.E. Hinduism, which was the progenitor of the other far eastern religions, from its very beginnings, unifies the general transcendental idea with the doctrine of

[157] *See Saul Shaked "Hinduism" in *Anthology of Religions*[in Hebrew], edited by Joseph Bentwitch (Tel Aviv: Joshua Chechik Publication, 1964)

[158] This was between the period of the patriarchs and the period of resettlement by the Israelites.

specialized spirits (like the god of war and the god who determines by which laws the world is administered), and already then recommended that man choose the path of identification with and a relationship to the abstract spirit and to the forces that control nature and man's world. This whole amalgamation becomes one indistinguishable totality. In contrast to Judaism- everything that exists now has existed forever. There is no such thing as creation *ex nihilo.*

Ephraim Urbach[159]

Urbach deduces that it was from the Bible that our sages received their worldview with regard to the supernatural super- mythological Divinity. God is spirit and is not flesh.[160] God stands apart from the world, being above and beyond it, yet at the same time involved with it in the sense that he personally watches over it and is very close to it. God is transcendental, but man is still able to experience a feeling of closeness to Him.[161] In order to reconcile the contradiction between the remoteness on the one hand and the closeness on the other that typifies the relationship between God and his creatures, he relays, *inter alia,* the following story:[162]

> A Samaritan once asked Rabbi Meir: Is it possible that the same being of whom it is said "Do I not fill the heaven and earth?" would also speak to Moses through the two poles of the Ark (of the covenant)[163]. Rabbi Meir then said back to him: "Bring me large mirrors." And so the Samaritan did as he was told. Rabbi Meir continued "Can you see your reflection in the mirror. Look how big it looks. Now bring me small mirrors." The Samaritan then did as he was bidden. Rabbi Meir continued "Can you see your reflection now, look how small it is" He then turned and said to him "If you, a flesh and blood human being can change your image into whatever you want, then He 'who said and [then] there was a world' (i.e. God who created the world through His speech) , how much more so, if he desires to He can appear as one who ' fills the heaven and earth' and if he desires otherwise he can appear as one who 'speaks to Moses through the two poles of the Ark (of the covenant)'

[159] See Ephraim E. Urbach. *The Sages : their concepts and beliefs,* (Jerusalem: Magnes. 1978)

[160] *Ibid.* at p. 29.

[161] *Ibid.*, at p. 30.

[162] *Ibid.*, at p. 38.

[163] He is implying that to claim that a transcendental being reveals Himself to humans is a contradiction in terms- from the perspective of having a very concrete vision (of God).

One of the fundamental principles of Judaism is God's omnipresence, from which is derived the idea of the Almighty and Omnipotent Divinity, and which according to Urbach- is an idea that exists in all religions starting with the most primitive ones. The idea of omnipotence is not meant to stir fear, but rather to increase the feelings of closeness making the believer who senses this intimacy feel even more secure.[164]

Judaism, which is the subject of Urbach's analysis, is one of the two original monotheistic religions, the other being Hinduism. The latter entered the fray slightly after Judaism and is more ambiguous towards God's transcendentalism and the fundamental principle of God's oneness. All other religions that promote monotheistic belief are the offspring of either of these two religions. The Hindu stream- as mentioned -is not one of those that promotes an absolute belief in transcendental Divinity, but rather views everything over and above its spiritual representation, as a world of reality. The dichotomy of Judaism, in contrast to Hinduism, is not viewing God as possessing a dual essence; rather it is the dichotomous relationship towards God and the conception of the Divine, where the practitioner on the one hand undergoes a direct, personal and emotional encounter with the Divinity and on the other, conceives Him indirectly through intellectual processing.[165]

Edwin Arthur Burtt, Thomas Kohn, and Czerniwski [166]

The above three analyze the sociological aspect of the development of the natural sciences in the west which coincided with the receding influence of the Christian religion and the implementation of scientific theories which came to fill in the gaps left by the retreating religion. It turns out from their scholarly works that the so- called scientific theories were often speculative, with no clear cut evidence to support them. The reasons for the ready acceptance of scientific theory can be traced to a large extent to sociological events that took place within the scientific community. In this scenario theory B was considered to have superceded theory A

---

[164] In Urbach's book, note 159 *supra* at p. 69.

[165] See, regarding this the difference between nominism and the presumption of Divinity, Haim Judah (Leon) Roth, *Religion and the Value of Man* [in Hebrew] (Jerusalem: Magnes, 1973), at pp. 10- 14.

[166] See Edwin Arthur Burtt, *The Metaphysical Foundations of Modern Physical Science, A Historical and Critical Essay* (London, Routledge and Kegan Paul, 1924). See also Thomas S. Kohn *The structure of Scientific Revolution*, Hebrew edition translated from English by Judah Meltzer (Tel Universities projects, 1977, from English publication printed in 1962) and also A. Czerniwski, *Between Science and Religion* [in Hebrew] (Tel Aviv: Yehoshua Chechik).

when most scientists and philosophers had transferred their support to theory B. The transference of support, or the non- transference of support is due to many and varied reasons including- convenience, simplicity, the question whether this new theory challenges the whole set of conventions or just part of that set, the question as to the prominence of the person presenting the new theories and similar types of reasons -all of which are related to sociological factors and matters of convenience. According to the conclusions reached by Burtt and confirmed by Czerniwski (who wrote his book when he was already professor emeritus at the Haifa Technion), philosophers and scientists were predisposed to viewing science as something that appealed to them, since its simplicity and aesthetics were signs that the theory it embraced was correct, more so, at least, than those theories which were complex, and lacking in internal aesthetics. Czerniwski broadens this idea claiming that the tendency of these scientists to prefer simple scientific theories has a very restrictive influence over human intellectual inquiry. According to Burtt's conclusions part of the reason why Copernicus's theory was accepted had to do with the fact that it reflected mathematical thinking using geometric applications and not arithmetic, the former of which was more popular at the time. On the other hand the result yielded by the theory did not play out in its favor since it was a little too revolutionary in its general conception of the universe. Kepler- who continued along the same path as Copernicus- was convinced that God created the world using the principle of whole numbers and of internal harmony, and rallied behind the position taken by Plato, which -as he interpreted it- says that God created the world with numerical harmony and formed the human brain in such a way that it can only grasp matters that are of numerical relevance.

With regard to the transition from the religious, to the secular period- even if he does not express it in quite the same way- Burtt says that the main current of thought that was predominant during the medieval period saw man at the center of the universe and of nature, and to whom all the activities (obviously those which naturally occur) of the universe are directed. However with the onset of the secular period, science replaced man with nature and the universe, placing them at center stage. Under these conditions, scientists, at the beginning of this secular period, were forced to back up the conventional interpretation, in terms of which man was much less important than nature or than the universe. Man, in this situation was a product of nature, and his fate was likewise, dependent upon nature.[167] It is patently obvious that the philosophers, who supported this idea, including Burtt, were still captive to the idea formulated during the religious period, that God guided everything. They continued believing that there must be an all- powerful and key factor to which man is subject; all they did was change the name of that

---

[167] In Burtt's book, at p. 11.

factor. Instead of God playing the key role they substituted Him with nature. >From this perspective this man who had rebelled against God and who had tried to crown himself king found himself instead, even if for a very brief period of time, once more changing kings and in a position where he was subject to the whims of a superior force. And indeed historically this intermittent period did pass in a flash, since according to Burtt man invented two solutions for eventually placing himself at the centre, after having safely removed God from the all-controlling position that He had previously occupied. One solution mentioned by Burtt was to change the "terminology" as Burtt himself puts it.[168] Instead of speaking about nature in terms of its essential features, its haphazardness and causality, things which man had no hope to control, scientists and thinkers began to talk about those things that could harness nature so that one could ride upon nature's back, in the same way as one trains a galloping horse to bow to its master's will, and in the same way as a *golem* is subject to the whims of its creator, in that all its (i.e. nature's) forces and movements, all its laws and the whole list of its transformations in space and time are recorded. Another type of solution was to emphasize the greatness of the philosophers and scientists who managed to acquire great fame and admiration from an adoring world, which became their devotees for the reason of their high reputation and stature and not because they appreciated their detailed opinions. A good example of this phenomenon is the case of Newton. Only after his death, was there anyone who dared challenge, in any comprehensive manner, the truthfulness or otherwise of his theory, as did Leibniz. In both these scenarios it was man, whose mental and technical abilities, were accepted as empowering enough to rule the world. It is possible to summarize Burtt's thesis- even if not exactly the same way as he put it, but reflective of his conclusions- that so long as the dominant image was that of God, there was no possibility that man could occupy a truly central position- he was totally subject to God and God's centrality in the universe stemmed from God's desire to take such a position. At the moment that God was replaced by science, man was empowered to deny the superiority of science by turning this giant- the laws of nature- upside down and turning it into a giant that is controlled by man.

[168] *Ibid.*, at p. 13.

Chapter B:
Leading insights and developments: A broad and summary review on religion and its offshoots

It is not within my abilities neither is it within my knowledge to judge between the various opinions that have been conveyed. I am even unable to accurately summarize the opinions of others. All I can to do is raise myself up and distance myself sufficiently so that I am able to enjoy a bird eye's view, an outlook that is somewhat removed from the discussions that took place, both in regard to the previous chapter and in regard to this whole book. I am able then to absorb the main ideas and to a certain extent the relevant argumentation as it relates to the topic of the discussion in this part. I am also able through this very general and unelaborated overview, to present the views without arguing from the perspective of any one of those involved in the debate, but rather from the vantage point of one who has done a thorough reading of the subject, and to offer an opposing view to the leading opinions that have been transcribed here. After sifting through the elements and extracting those relevant parts that relate to the subject of the discussion here, I have come up with an opinion for which I take full responsibility, and which opinion links together all the parts of the book and which therefore forms the summary for the whole book, even if the summary is in some ways inconclusive.

Religions, as used in this book, are systems of faith, which, as a consequence of their central tenets, lay down rules mandating the actions of their followers. Humankind, for all of time and under every circumstance, believed in at least one religion. There has not been a human being in all of existence who has not been religious, and likewise there has not been a society that has sought to exist without at least one religion. Man is the product of his society, but also the product of his religion.

This book deals- in essence- with religion and the various branches that spring from it. The most loaded and most striking of its branches are morality and nationalism. And indeed this book deals with religion, morality and nationalism, and because of the particular interest of the author, the spotlight is focused- from the perspective of all these above three-more particularly on Israel and Judaism.
In the previous chapter, as can be noticed in the length and breadth of this book, there is essentially one key dispute- between those who conduct their social behavior according to the laws that stem from theistic religions and between those who conduct their social behavior according to laws whose underlying ideas are in

no way related to the Divinity having no connection with anything Divine. Another argument takes place within the "community of theistic religions" on the subject of how one bonds with God, and the two radically opposed positions are occupied at one polar end of the debate by those who believe in the "experiential-emotional" (connection) and at the other polar end by those who believe in the "intellectual" (connection). These are the two ways to attain intimacy with, and comprehension of the Divinity. Theistic religiosity itself- and perhaps the Divinity -can be divided into either idolatry- which includes witchcraft, spirits, demons, spells and pagan healing- or, the belief in one God- which itself is divided into two branches, the Jewish branch and the Hindi branch. Each of these original branches became a minority- in terms of the number of believers who still observe these religions- as compared to the buds that sprang from them, and which became intertwined and which developed into a great multitude. [These two parent -religions can be differentiated from their offspring in that they both relate to a particular nationalism, even if their God is supposed to be universal- they also require, each from their specific nation, that it feels doubly bound to its religion, in the private sphere- ethical behavior is a prerequisite of each of the members of the nation, and in the public sphere- their behavior has to follow a unique path that entails collective responsibility for all the members of the nation, in that each person is mutually and internally responsible for his fellow practitioner.[169]]

All of the theistic religions are in some way connected to emotion, while the non-theistic religions are the product of intellectual thought and of interests. This is so, even if it is true that many of those associated with this latter religion are emotional people, and even if the practitioners who derive their strength from their non- theistic beliefs attained their faith by journeying on the emotional path. Thus, for instance: Marxist socialists certainly feel that their system helps society's weaker elements, the liberals also want with all their (emotional) might to create a society within which the human spirit will be cultivated, and even the nationalists, who hold on to their nationalism can be likened to those who seek a[n] (emotional) way of holding on to their ethnic roots. There are many other examples in this vein. Nonetheless the basic difference between emotion and intellect when it comes to the formation of religions (as opposed to the conception of God within theistic religion) between the theistic and the ideological (non- theistic) religions amounts to the difference between those who believe in the revelation which is an emotional experience, and without which there would be no semblance of a theistic religion and those who put their trust in ideology which is the defining

---

[169] See Eva Hellman "Dynamic Hinduism: Towards a New Hindu nation," in *Questioning the Secular State- The Worldwide Resurgence of Religion in Politics*, edited by David Westerlund (London, Hurst & Company), p. 242.

element of the ideological (non-theistic) religions. The non- theistic ideology, much more so than the intimate encounters with the Divinity, is transmitted mainly via written and electronic communication, whereas the theistic religious experience is on the main transmitted through ritualistic means, even if more recently, in the modern state, civil religion is also transmitted – with the help of the state- through symbols that are ritualistic by nature. This may be seen in state ceremonies associated with independence and remembrance days, that include military parades, as well as the public display of the activities of the nation's representatives and its leaders, and similar events that are connected with state activity. Both of these- theistic religions and non- theistic religions may be equally regarded as religions that rely upon leaders and institutions, and on this point it bears mention that human nature not only craves religion but also seeks out leaders.

The lone individual will always follow the leader who leads him the path to religion, and who transmits to him an element of the spiritual (even if adjoined to this revelation is a practical plan that must be carried out). The shepherd- leaders who feel that the gospel, waiting to be released from their mouths, will be welcomed by a community of believers, will ask of their disciples to follow them like sheep after their shepherd. Just like sheep require a shepherd so too does man require an ideology and a leader who will set him on his way. Man needs religion. It is vital for man to believe in something. The tendency of man to form a society of likeminded individuals is not merely an organizational need. It is also a deeply spiritual need.

There is the phenomenon however that sometimes occurs, of a man who has lost his *joie de vivre*. Such a person is destined to resort to desperate acts, which generally speaking take on a very self- destructive nature. Physical self-destruction is usually less serious than spiritual self- destruction. Man is an existential creature and as such craves to continue existing- his inclination then for physical existence is the strongest of all inclinations, as is the case, in fact, with all living creatures. What is unique in man, and that which proves his superiority over all other creatures, is his need for spiritual existence alongside his physical existence.

The man who excels in establishing his spiritual roots is stronger and more able to withstand the tests of time than one who has excelled in, and scaled the heights of intellectual attainments. It is precisely this issue that causes the conflict between fundamentalist Islam and the modern west to stand out so prominently. From a materialist, physical perspective the West is much stronger than fundamentalist Islam, but for this same West, if it was to rely merely on its physical attainments

and did not try to muster its spiritual forces that are embedded within it- it would find itself in a difficult predicament. In the end, the one who outlasts his enemy in conflict is the one who is spiritually stronger, and indeed it is a truism: spiritual strength emanates from the feeling that there is an inner justice to the cause. In any event, Divine morality carries with it tremendous strength since it is linked so tightly with the emotions. On the other hand the one who confines himself exclusively to the path of non- theistic morality, i.e. intellectual morality, will be unable to ward off the aggressor especially if that intellectual morality is disconnected with the burning sensation that what is being done has an inner justice to it, that sensation so ably described by Viktor Frankl, whose views were reviewed in the previous chapter. Typical of this kind of belief was President George W. Bush's decision on the anniversary of September 11, 2001, to organize a ceremony for refortifying the American People, in the fields of Pennsylvania. This marked the site where a year prior to then, one of the planes crashed and where- it appears- the hijacked American plane passengers wrestled with their Islamic fundamentalist captors in a battle that forced- so it has been reported- the plane to come crashing down on that exact place. The ceremony was conducted as if it was a theistic religious service, accompanied as it was by the singing voices of a Protestant Christian choir. This is then a typical example of the stature of theistic religion, for no matter how far they try to proscribe its influence from the political stage, in times of real suffering and pain it receives and gives over support to those who tried to suppress it (the political elements) and strengthens the spirit of those battling it out in the political field. Theistic religion suffers from all the knocks administered to it but never begrudges those who try and knock it down. Like a loyal mother it is always ready to listen, to comfort, and to strengthen the spirit of those who try to approach it- even if they only return to it for a very short while.

One may possibly ask why it is that emotion will always overcome intellect. In order to deal with this matter one has to deal with the issue of human "programming." To understand this we need to travel all the way back to Imperial China and then move on from there to investigate the feminist struggle, the phenomenon of slavery, and the Israeli- Palestinian struggle, and only then will we discover that the thread holding together all these various incidents is the phenomenon of "human programming", a phenomenon that can be used to explain the superiority of emotion over intellect and which elucidates the phenomenon of the Islamic suicide martyrs who killed themselves and the airline passengers traveling with them, when they deliberately crashed the planes into the twin towers in New York City, and the Pentagon in Washington D. C. Connecting all these things together under one heading gives us a better understanding of our own souls helping to clarify the fact that our emotions are superior to our intellects and that

therefore the force of religion is by definition stronger than any other forces applied to man.

During the medieval period China was far more advanced than Europe in many areas. China's land mass and physical population as well as its technological capabilities including its novel inventions (such as gunpowder) put China above Europe in every respect. China was populated by human life for a period of two million years, but it was only from the ninth millennium B. C. E that organized settlement was started. Agriculture was introduced three millennia later in 6000 B. C. E. In the third century B. C. E. a legal system was set up that relied upon a written criminal code. China was thereafter united under one ruler during the Han Dynasty (beginning in the year 206 B. C. E.). The legal Code was then redrafted during the T'ang Dynasty, but it based itself on former legal codes that had always been in force in China. Although undergoing minor changes throughout its history, it remained binding up until the year 1911 C. E. At this time the Imperialist era came to a halt and was replaced by the Republican era. The whole of Imperial China was ruled over by a uniform yet decentralized administration.[170] What is important for our discussion is the fact that China based itself on a religion that was not patronized by the state, and which had very negligible influence over the establishment. The Buddhism of the northern region originated from India passing through Tibet on its way to its final destination. Like the Protestant religion Buddhism also preached a direct link between the believer and his God. It was a religion which integrated well with the other ancient and primitive religions of the surrounding area. It supported the imperial ruler and never became a focus of opposition to the leadership. Its primary message, dictating the behavioral norms of its adherents in respect of their ethical conduct, was derived from the philosophical system set up by Confucius. The Confucian system also backed the imperial leadership and was therefore supported by the latter, so that it was able to spread its influence throughout the whole of Imperial China in parallel with the broadening influence of the regime. This all occurred

---

[170] For all that has been said thus far see: Cho- yun Hsu, *Han Agriculture*, (Seattle and London: University of Washington Press); Cinai L. Barnes, *China, Korea, and Japan- The Rise of Civilization in East Asia* (London: Thames and Hudson, 1993); John King Fairbank, *China- A New History* (London, England and Cambridge, Massachusetts, 1992) ; *The T'ang Code*, Volume 1, General Principles, translated with an introduction by Wallace Johnson (Princeton, New Jersey, 1979); Endymion Wilkinson, *Chinese History- A Manual- Revised and Enlarged* (Cambridge, Massachusetts & London : Harvard University Press, 2000), pp. 538- 592; *T'ang Leang- Li*, Foreword by Dr. Tsai Yuan- Pei, Chancellor of the National University of Peking, late Minister of Education, and preface by the Hon. Bertrand Russell (London: Noel Douglas, reprint edition published in 1976 by University Publications of America, Arlington, Virginia), pp. 19- 37.

during the Han Dynastical Period. The Confucian system, which was incorporated into the criminal law code that was administered by the regime, had a connection with patriarchal rituals whose history preceded that of Confucius. According to the system, in every large sized family, the important members were the male adults headed by the *pater familias*, and therefore the rituals were used to communicate with the most ancient *pater familias* to whom the particular family could claim blood ties. The youth were ordered to be subservient and humble and to stay away from introducing new and independent initiatives. Linked to the whole subject of its industrial development and achievements is the Chinese attitude to work, which just as any other human endeavor, is considered to be an integral part of the Lord's holy deeds, since such work contains elements of the Divinity- as is found in the Hindi approach which was the progenitor of Buddhism- by virtue of the direct link between that that exists beyond reality- the transcendental thing- with the spiritual elements that exist down below within the reality, which spiritual elements inhere in every single thing that exists in the world of reality (similar to the dharma in the Hindu religion).[171]

Man and his deeds become attached to each other forming the third side in triangle which merges together with its two holy constituent parts (i.e. man being the first and his deeds being the second) , and thus from this perspective man's labor becomes sanctified.[172] In this way one can differentiate the Chinese person from other Europeans in his attitude towards work. In traditional European culture, physical labor was never considered holy. There was never in China a mental block against working and therefore despite the fact that new inventions were created there, it was not feted for being the place where the Industrial Revolution took place.

This is how the Chinese man was "programmed," he was part of a whole system, a whole worldview, which the Chinese Imperial ruler had no interest in dismantling into its constituent parts, since doing so would in effect endanger the whole institution of emperor.

The fact that spiritual reins are in fact much more powerful stimuli than are prohibitions, even when they are accompanied by sanctions for their infringement,

---

[171] See Eva Hellman, "Dynamic Hinduism- towards a New Hindu Nation" in *Questioning the Secular State- the Worldwide Resurgence of Religion in Politics*, edited by David Westerlund (London: Hurt & Company) p. 240.

[172] See *China in Revolt* at note 167, *supra* at p. 36.

can be illustrated from stories that exemplify Chinese culture.[173] There is a story told of a family where the oldest brother was fortunate to achieve respect and a prestigious position and wanted to find a way to ensure that his younger brothers also become respected, but without their achievements detrimentally affecting his own honour and stature. So what did he do? He convened a meeting with all his brothers and according to a joint plan they announced that the family property would be divided up, property which according to the law and according to tradition remains indivisible until one of the parties demands its division. Following the partition the eldest brother took for himself the choicest land leaving the second-rate parts to his younger brothers. The partition was however performed by written agreement of all of the affected parties. The immediate result of the partition was that the younger brothers achieved fame for relinquishing their rights in favor of their eldest and most respectable (owing to his senior age) brother, and were therefore recommended for the top and most respectable government positions which they eventually got. At the same time however the eldest brother's honor was not so well preserved. Everyone admonished him for his attitude towards his younger brothers. Time passed and the oldest brother announced that the portion that he had received in the partition was three times the size of everyone else, and he sincerely regrets his behavior towards his younger brothers. He therefore relinquishes that part of his share which is greater than the others. Immediately the respect for the eldest brother went up, without in any way lessening the respect for the younger siblings, so that their positions that they had previously attained remained intact. Without a doubt, the brothers had "programmed" the community and the regime, and the eldest brother managed, even if in a roundabout manner, to obtain honorable positions and some modicum of respect for his younger brothers, without at the end of the day doing any lasting harm to his position. Another story on the "programmed" influence of the spirit, within the framework of a family, is the story that is related about an eldest brother who lived together with his younger brothers in the home that fell within their joint inheritance. In this case they decided against dividing the property, yet this decision was to have problematic consequences. Within these crowded conditions it was probably no surprise that the wives of the brothers began to quarrel amongst themselves, and inevitably the youngest brothers were dragged by their wives into the fracas. What did the eldest brother do? One day he locked the front door of the house while all the inhabitants were stuck inside and he began to cry and to slap and rebuke himself that he did not dutifully fulfill his obligations as the oldest brother by failing to prevent these family feuds and by failing to stop the brothers and their wives as well as his own wife from getting entangled in petty squabbles,

---

[173] The following examples are mentioned in Tung- tsu Chu *Han Social Structure* (Seattle and London: University of Washington Press, 1972), pp. 299, 303.

until everyone caught the "hint" and from then onwards family life appreciably improved. The third story that concerns "programming," but this time on a much larger scale- a story which is indirectly related to the Imperial Chinese literature-tells how the emperors themselves "programmed"- without resorting to the coercive means that were at their disposal- all the Chinese and made them accept the criminal code that was drafted by the emperors themselves, a code that ensured that discrimination between the various Chinese classes would be written into law, and which also further entrenched the position of the heads of households, ensuring that the mantle of leadership be retained by them in each and every family- all these factors promoted the interests, of the Imperial leader, especially since his regime was based on the loyalty of members of the upper class and on the heads of households . The latter two in turn relied for their positions on the Code and by extension on their Imperial leader and therefore clung to their leader and strengthened his position. This method of "programming" was carried through into Chinese philosophy, which the Imperial leaders took pains to strengthen, and which as a result thereof they ensured that each Chinese subject would be educated to implicitly trust this philosophy. According to this philosophy's set of guidelines and commensurate with the Hindi Dharma idea that was imported into China via Buddhism, nature and man form one holistic unity and are so interrelated that the deeds of man are able to manipulate the flow of nature, and this aspect of man is thus able to cause natural disasters. The one in control of the chain that joins nature and man is the emperor whose duty is to preserve the balance, which he can only do if he is able to punish offenders. Therefore it is the emperor who determines the minute details of the law, in order that he is able to properly preserve the balance. Even if these laws discriminate between the classes and are not the most just they still need to be observed, because it is only the emperor who really knows how things should be balanced. If he has established a certain norm, that it is a sign that it is so important that if his words should, heaven forbid, not be complied with, terrible calamities would befall the populace. Therefore, it is quite apparent that rebelling against the emperor is a grievous sin, since it is liable to be the cause of the worst kind of disaster- the loss of the single responsible body empowered to balance nature and who is able to fend off any and every disaster.[174]

---

[174] See note 167 *supra* the book entitled *The T'ang Code*, at p. 10. And see there the analogy that is used of regarding the king's status as having been conferred upon him by the Divine. Therefore one who rebels against God's messiah (literally God's anointed one) is as if one has rebelled against God Himself. See also the oath that is recited while holding onto the Holy Scriptures, which oath is said by presidents and holders of key state positions. This oath adds a Divine element to their tenure and strengthens the regime by "programming" the masses. Even the President of the United States, a country that has gone out of its way, as we saw, more than any other country, to distance any semblance of

The unique setting created by feminist literature gave rise to the idea[175]that quite possibly the oppression of women has primarily to do with the state of consciousness of the women concerned. The subjugation of women by men was accepted by the latter, since they were convinced that they were inferior to and not "equals' of men when it came both to character and to capability. Therefore feminists have suggested that the path to liberation is paved with the acquisition of knowledge and with study. The moment women recognize that there is no truth in any inherent differences between men and women is the moment that they will be the true equal of man. And indeed the feminist movement's history of success owes a great deal to education and to the acquisition of knowledge. The urban family nurtured their boys and girls together and provided the female head of the family with a key position which was exclusive to her, and which commanded respect.

The whole topic of male and female slaves was viewed as something that had to do with the inner consciousness of the slave that allowed the institution of slavery to be sanctioned. In those regimes where slaves were found in abundance- besides it being the results of coercion, it was also the slaves' consciousness that sealed their fate. There were very few reported cases of slave rebellions, so that the phenomenon of rural estates in the South being populated by hundreds of slaves and only a handful of slave masters is attributable not only to the heavy hand of the local police, the national guard, and the internal institution of the local government, but had a lot also to do with the consciousness of servitude ingrained in the slaves.

Exactly the same phenomenon is observable in the Israeli-Palestinian conflict and the continuing *Intifada*. In the latter case the Israeli Jewish populace, almost to a man, reproves the prevalence of suicide bombers who blow themselves up amidst a civilian population, as well as the increasing shooting incidences that are the result of members of Palestinian organizations funded by the Palestinian Authority, aiming their firepower at civilian vehicles that are conveying women and children along the Judean and Samarian highways. They fully understand the actions taken by the IDF soldiers who open fire against those identified as shooting at Jerusalem's Jewish neighborhoods or against those who are preparing bombs or who are transporting suicide bombers whose missions are outlined

---

God from the government, even its leader swears in the name of God before taking charge of his new role

[175] See *Feminist Theorists-Three Centuries of Key Women Thinkers*, edited by Dale Spender (New York: Pantheon Books, 1983), p. xi.

immediately above- and they thus fully justify whatever course of action the Israel Defence Forces deem necessary. The Palestinians in contradistinction view the IDF soldiers and their activities, described above, as terrorist and portray the activities of the Palestinians, as described above, as merely retaliatory. These opposing views of the same events are the direct result of "programming". There will be those who say that it is only one side that has in fact been "programmed", yet, it is possible that even those who hold that both sides have been "programmed" and who thus claim to be able to view the situation taking into account both versions, will still not be free of the fundamental flaws that are created by their personal "programming".

When turning to the whole episode of the planes exploding into the twin towers and the Pentagon on September 11, 2001, we have to understand that the hijackers were convinced that they were defending truth and honor and thus fully believed in those things that led them to commit suicide with such explosive effect. There will be those who say that it was the fundamentalism of the Islamic religion which directed their actions, while others will venture that not all those on this suicide mission were religious and in this instance there were other motives that created this devastating inner conviction. Yet it is a fact that religion in this case was revealed to be the stronger motive, especially in its capacity to persuade its followers to perceive reality in a radically different light than do the majority of all other inhabitants of the world. In this way the power of religion is so plainly exposed, and since religion is so intimately connected with emotion, the ability of emotion to "program" logic[176] is so potently revealed. This personal programming can also be used to explain the tribal behavior that each African ethnic group displays even after they have migrated to the city, as well as the mutual help societies that operates on ethnic lines in the United States today.

Since man is a creature of religion, religion will always be triumphant. The only question is: What kind of religion?

****

---

[176] Yet it still needs to be pointed out that even a non- theistic religion, since it is connected with emotion, is able and indeed does "program" the minds of the masses who put their trust in it. This is quite striking in the example of the British soldiers, the majority of whom were denominationally Protestant, and who were raised with the internal feeling that the English were God's "chosen people", and that God had imposed upon them a special mission, and while fighting in a Protestant army had their spirits uplifted - for the purposes of the discussion here- through the songs, *God Save the King* or *Rule, Britannia* – This merely reflects how programmed they were in believing in British nationalism, which today we would call –"British Civil Religion."

By way of an epilogue which is more like an informed assumption, it would appear to me that the nurturing religion is a much stronger than the religion that places itself on the receiving end, in the exact same proportion as the difference between males and females of the human race. Women, so to speak, are weaker than men. In most societies they undergo heavy discrimination; in all societies they undergo pregnancies and births that exhaust their strength. Despite all this, their life expectancy is longer than men's. The objective and relevant distinguishing factor marking the woman as different from the man is her intimate relationship with her child and its rearing, where she undergoes a process of giving. This process- so I would suggest- is responsible for supplying the woman with her life-force.

When making the comparison between the historical theistic religions and the non-theistic religions (Communism, Liberalism), it appears *prima facie,* quite inexplicable that rules of morality that emanate from the historical theistic religions should have such staying power, while at the same time the rules of human behavior that are so closely associated with non- theistic ideas should undergo so many crises. The quantity and force of morality is quite an important yardstick-and it appears to me that measuring with such a yardstick, the emotional-morality associated with the Divinity is far stronger than the intellectual morality associated with man. One theistic religion can never be removed from this world even if it does have the power to create other theistic religions. It would be a stretch to say that Kant's system of morality has any surviving residues or that it gave rise to another morality system that is linked with it. The same can be said of Hobbes' social contract, of utilitarianism, or of the Marxist- Communist system, and even the post- modernist theory which was only invented a short while ago and already displays signs of aging. The very fact that one system has been so rapidly superceded by another in the course of the 18th, 19th and 20th centuries proves that these systems are unable to claim any semblance of stability. The overview in this book, especially Parts 2 and 5, illustrated that the force of morality associated with the Divinity is far greater than that associated with man.

The differences between Oriental pagan religions and religions that rally behind the belief in One God, the Creator of the Heavens and the earth, has been illustrated in Parts 6 and 7 of this book, and the power of the God who created the world, a matter elucidated in part 7, becomes even stronger when it is being rebelled against. The power of the Oriental gods who had never been able to grab the reins of government and who are not active in trying to attain political rule but rather prefer to win influence within the social setting is also well illustrated in Part 7. Also with regard to nationalism, which has been surveyed in part 3 and 4 of this book, it has of late displayed cracks and difficulties that bear no relation to religion.

The future of nation foundation and the problem of artificial nations has created a western culture that has been well illustrated in Part 8, where a forecast is made upon the viability of the formation of a super or united nation that will include previous non stable political nations. Such a united nation might possibly arise upon the ruins of artificial nations that were constructed by the countries of Europe and America.

The problem civil religion faces when it goes, head to head, with theistic religion has been surveyed in Part 3 of this book. It has become abundantly clear that nationalism has a strong impact on civil society, which has not been formed into a nation, but that theistic religion is stronger than political nationals.

Each and every of the religions, nation formation and moral theories are integrated networks, which contain in them elements of suckling and nurturing. This is especially so when the weaker tenets within this integrated system feed off the more established ones. From this standpoint, theistic religion is the more nourishing and stronger of religions, with ethnic religion being forced to occupy second place to it.

There is no reason to fear religion. Religion is something that enhances the world, something that man has always been in dire need of, that he has never in the past renounced, and for which it is most unlikely that he will ever renounce at any given time in the future.

Bibliography

Anderson, Benedict, **Conceptual Models of Societies: Reflections on the Roots and Spread of Nationalism**, Translated from the English by Dan Daor (Tel Aviv: Open University, 2000).

Anderson, Benedict, **Illusory Republics** (Tel Aviv: Open University Publications, 2000, trans. To Hebrew: Dan Daor, the original was published in English in 1983).

Anderson, Benedict, **Imagined Communities** [Hebrew Edition] (Tel Aviv: Haifa University Publishing House, 2000)

Appiah, K.A., **In My Father's House: Africa in the Philosophy of Culture** (Oxford: Oxford University Press, 1992)

Aston, W. G., **Nihongi, Chronicles of Japan from the Earliest Times to A. D. 697**, (Tokyo: Charles E. Tuttle Co., 1972)

Aviram R. "Secularisation as an Introduction to the Growth of the Last Man: Modern Criticism of Friedrich Nietzsche." In D. Stetman and A. Sagi (eds.), **Between Religion and Morality** (Ramat Gan: Bar-Ilan University Press, 1996)

Aviram, Roni, "The secularist as the forerunner to the last man: a critique of Friedrich Nietzsche's modernity" in **Bein Dat Lemussar,** edited by Daniel Stateman and Avi Shagya (Ramat Gan: Bar Ilan University, 1996).

Avritzer, Leonardo, "The Generation of Public Spares in Brazil: The Role of Abolitionism," in **Globality and Multiple Modernities – Comparative North American and Latin American Perspectives**, Luis Roniger and Carlos H. Waisman (ed.), (Brighton, Portland: Sussex Academic Press, 2002).

Baia LR, "Rethinking Transnationalism: Reconstructing National Identities Among Peruvian Catholics in New Jersey," in **Journal of Inter-American Studies and World Affairs 41 (4), 93, Winter 1999.**

Barak, Aaron, "The Constitutional Revolution: Human Rights Protected" (in Hebrew) in **Law and Administration vol. 1 1992,** p. 230

Baron, Salo Wittmayer, **Modern Nationalism and Religion** (New York and London: Harper & Brothers, 1947)

Barshack, Lior, "The court and civil religion," in **Hamishhpat Law Journal,** College of Administration (Rishon Le'tzion: ed. College of Administration Law School, 2000)

Barshack, Lior, "The Totemic Authority of the court," in **Law and Critique**, 11:301-328, (Kluwer Academic Publishers, Printed in the Netherlands, 2000).

Bates, Robert H., "Modernization, Ethnic Competition and Rationality of Politics in Contemporary Africa", in **State Versus Ethnic Claims,** pp. 152-171

Beck, Lewis White, **Six secular Philosophies, Religious Themes in the Thought of Spinoza, Hume, Kant, Nietzsche, Williams James and Santayana** (Thoemmes Press, 1960, 1997).

Bellah, R. N., "Civil Religion in America" in **Beyond Belief** (New York, Harper and Row 1970), Ch. 9.

Bentham, J., **An Introduction to the Principles of Morals and Legislation** (London: Athlone Press, 1970), ed. by J.M. Burns and H.L.A Hart.

Berghe van den, Pierre L, "Race and Ethnicity: A Sociobiological Perspective", **Ethnic and Racial Studies**, vol. 1, no. 4 (October 1978) pp. 401-411.

Bergson, Henri, **The Two Sources of Morality and Religion**, translated by R. Ashley Audra and Claudesley Brereton with assistance of W. Horsfall Carter (Garden City, N.Y.: Doubleday & Company, 1935).

Berlin, Isaiah, in his book **Four Essays on Religion,** translated into Hebrew by Reshafim Press in 1971

Biagioli, Mario, "Galileo's System of Patronage", in **History of Science, XXVIII (1990)** pp. 1-62.

Black, **Human Instincts and the Evolution of Cooperation** (NY: Penguin, 1996)

Bodde, Derk, **Chinese Thought, Society, and Science – The Intellectual and Social Background of Science and Technology in Pre-modern China** (Honolulu: University of Hawaii Press, 1991)

Boehm, C., "Conflict and the Evolution of Social Conflict," **Journal of Consciousness Studies 7:1/2 (2000)**, 79-102

Brass, Paul R., **Language Religion and Politics in North India** (Cambridge: Cambridge University Press, 1974).

Brill, **The Basic Writings of Sigmund Freud** (NY: Modern Library, 1938)

Bronovsky, Yaakov, **Sources of Knowledge and Imagination – Witchcraft, Science and Culture – Two Series of Lectures**, Translated from English by Sarah Yertzki-Kahanski (Tel Aviv: Am Oved, Ofakim Library, 1983, Published in English in 1978).

Bultmann, Rudolf, **Jesus Christ and Mythology**.(Englewood Cliffs, New Jersey: Prentice Hall, A Simon and Shuster Company, 1958)

Burtt, Edwin Arthur, **The Metaphysical Foundations of Modern Physical Science, a Historical and Critical Essay** (London: Routledge and Kegan Paul, 1924);

Casirer, Ernest, **Measure of Man: Prelude to the Human culture** (Am Oved, Tel Aviv, 1956)

Chang, K. C., **Art, Myth, and Ritual – The Path to Political Authority in Ancient China** (Cambridge, Massachusetts and London: Harvard University Press)

Charlton, D.G., **Secular religions in France 1815-1870,** (Oxford University Press, 1963).

Clark, J. C. D., **The Language of Liberty 1660-1832**, **Political discourse and social dynamics in the Anglo-American world** (Cambridge: Cambridge University Press, 1994)

Cohen, Hermann, **Religion of Reason from Jewish Sources** (Mossad Bialik Press and the Leo Beck Institute, 1971)

Cohen, Yehuda, **Who Fears a Jewish State?: An Ideological and Legal Perspective** (Tel Aviv: Legal Association Press, 2001) Chapter VI.

Colley, L., **Britons – Forging the Nation 1707-1837** (London: Yale University Press, 1992)

Colley, Linda, **Forging Protestantism and the Nation 1707-1837**, T. Claydon et al, eds. (New Haven, 1992)

Coloca, Eliora and Efrat Ben Zeev, "Ethnic Groups in Venezuela," Term Paper submitted to Dr. Luis Roniger of The Hebrew University in Jerusalem, Included in **Roniger's Anthology in the Library of Sociology and Humanities in Jerusalem.**

Dale, Peter N., **The Myth of Japanese Uniqueness**, (Beckenham, Australia: Croom Helm Ltd., 1986)

Denis, "Merchant Trade and Government in Late T'ang," in **Asia Major, 14 (1968)**

Dewey, John, **Reconstruction in Philosophy** (New York, N.Y.: Mentor Book, The New American Library, 1950)

Douglas, M., **Purity and Danger: An Analysis of Concepts of Pollution and Taboo** (London: Routledge and Kegan Paul, 1966)

Duhem, Pierre, **To Save the Phenomena, An Essay on the Idea of Physical Theory from Plato to Galileo** (Chicago and London: The University of Chicago Press, 1969, translated from French into English by Dolan and Maschler, the French original version written in 1908);

Dunbar Moodie, T., **The Rise of Afrikanerdom: Power, Apartheid, and the Afrikaner Civil Religion** (Los Angeles: University of California Press, 1975)

Durkheim, E., **The Elementary Forms of the Religious Life** (London: George Allen and Unwin, 1976)

Durkheim, Emile, **on the Division of Power in Society** (Translated by George Simpson), (The Macmillan Company, 1933);

Dvorkin, Ronald, "Liberal Community", **California Law Review, Vol. 77 [1989]**, 479

Edited By Delmer M. Brown, **The Cambridge History of Japan**, vol. 1, (Cambridge: Cambridge University Press, 1993).

Edited by Joseph Bentowitz **A Collection of Religions**, (Tel Aviv: Joshua Chichik Publishing, 1963).

Edited by Meir Shahar and Robert P. Weller, **Unruly Gods – Divinity and Society in China**, (Honolulu: University of Hawaii Press: 1996)

Edited by R. Joseph Hoffman and Gerald A. Laure, **Biblical V. Secular Ethics: The Conflict** (Promtheus Books, 1988).

Edited by Shlomo Avineri and Avner De-Shalit, **Communitarianism and Individualism** (Oxford University Press)

Edited by Theodore de Bary, **Sources of Japanese Tradition**, (New York: Columbia University Press, 1958)

Edited Elwyn A. Smith, **The Religion of the Republic**, (Philadelphia: Portress Press, 1971).

Edwards, David, "Toleration and Mill's Liberty of Thought and Discussion", in Susan Mendus ed., **Justifying Toleration** (Cambridge University Press, 1988)

Eisenstadt, S.N. "The First Multiple Modernities: Collective Identities, Public Spheres, and Political Order in the Americas," Chapter II in **Globality and Multiple Modernities – Comparative North American and Latin American Perspectives**, Luis Roniger and Carlos H. Waisman (ed.), (Brighton, Portland: Sussex: Academic Press, 2002).

Eisenstein, Elizabeth L., **The Printing Revolution in Early Modern Europe** (Cambridge, UK: Cambridge University Press, 1983)

Eliada, Mircha, **The Myth of the Eternal Old Age** – Archetypes and Review, Translated from French: Yotam Reuveni, Editing, notes: Ronit Nilolski (Jerusalem: Carmel, 2000)

Eliade, Mircea, **Le mythe de l'eternel retour: arch'types et r'p'tition** , translated from the French into Hebrew by Yotam Reuveni, with scientific editing and notes by Ronit Nikolsky, (Jerusalem: Carmel, 2000.)

Emerson, Rupert, **State and Sovereignty in Modern Germany** (New Haven: Yale University Press, 1928),

Enloe, Cynthia, "Religion and Ethnicity", in **Ethnicity**, edited by John Hutchinson & Anthony D. Smith (Oxford, New York: Oxford University Press, 1996)

Evans-Pritchard, E.E, **Witchcraft, Oracles, and Magic Among the Azande** (Oxford: Clarendon Press, 1976)

Evans-Pritchard, E.E. **Nuer Religion** (Oxford: Clarendon Press, 1956)

Farmer, Edward L., **Zhu Yuanzhang and Early Ming Legislation, The Reordering of Chinese Society Following the Era of Mongolian Rule** (Leiden, New York, Ko'ln: Brill, 1995).

Federbush, Shimon, **Morality and Law in Israel** (Mossad Harav Kook)

Fortes, F.B.A. Meyer, **Rules and the Emergence of Society** (Royal Anthropological Institute of Great Britain and Ireland, Occational Paper, No. 39).

Frankl, Viktor E., [the Hebrew edition of], **The Unconscious God. Psychotherapy and Theology**, translated into Hebrew by Shimon Levy, (Jerusalem: Dvir, 1985)

Freud, S., **Culture and Religion** (Merchavia, Doar Afula: Kibbutz Haartzi Publication, Ha-Shomer Hatzair 1943)

Freud, S., **Culture Without Satisfaction – and Other Essays** (Tel Aviv: Dvir, 1988)

Freud, S., **The Basic Writings of Sigmund Freud** (Translated and edited with introduction by Dr. A. A. Brill, The Modern Library, 1938)

Freud, S., **The Future of An Illusion** (The Kibbutz Ha-Artzi HaShomer HaTza'ir: 1943, trans. into Hebrew from the original title **Culture and Religion)**

Freud, S., **Totem and Taboo – and Other Essays**, translated by Haim Isaac, appears in the original – *Writings of Sigmund Freud* – part 3, (Tel Aviv: Dvir, 1988)

Geertz, C., **The Interpretation of Cultures**, trans. By Yoash Meisler (Jerusalem: Keter, 1973)

Gelner, Ernest, **Nations and Nationalism** translated to Hebrew by Dan Daor (Tel-Aviv: Open University, 1994, originally printed in 1983)

Gluck, Carol, **Japan's Modern Myths - Ideology in the Late Meiji Period** (Princeton, New Jersey: Princeton University Press, 1985)

Greenfeld, Liah, **Nationalism - Five Roads to Modernity** (London: Harvard University Press, 1992)

Gross, J.J., "Why Do We have an Obligation to Obey G-d's Commandments" in **Between Religion and Morality** (Ramat Gan: Bar-Ilan University Press, 1994)

Haas, Ernst B., **Nationalism, Liberalism, and Progress** (Ithaca, NY and London: Cornell University Press, 1997).

Habermas, Jurgen, **The Structural Transformation of the Public Sphere – An Inquiry into a Category of Burgeois Society**, translated by Thomas Burger with the assistance of Frederick Lawrence (Cambridge, Massachusetts: The MIT Press)

Hall, Robert King, **Shushin: The Ethics of a Defeated Nation** (New York: Bureau of Publications, Teachers College, Columbia University, 1949)

Han, Tung-tsu Ch'u,, **Social Structure** (Seattle and London: University of Washington Press, 1972)

Hart, H. L. A, **The Concept of Law,** Second Edition, Edited by Peter Cane, Tony Honor'e and Jane Stepleton (Oxford, England: Clarendon Press, 1961. 1994, 1997)

Harz, Louis, "United States History in a New Perspective," in **The Founding of New Societies – Studies in the History of the United States, Latin America, South Africa, Canada and Australia**, by Louis Hattz et. Al (New York: Harcourt & World, 1964)

Hawking, Stephen W., *A brief history of time: from the big bang to black holes*. Hebrew edition is translated from the English by Emanuel Lutes; scientific editor is Yakhin Una (Tel Aviv: Ma'ariv Library, 1989).

Hechter, Michael, **Internal Colonialism - The Celtic Fringe in British National Development, 1536-1966** (Berkeley and Los Angeles: University of California Press)

Heinz, Wolfgang S., and Hugo Fru'hling, **Determinants of Gross Human Rights Violations by State and State-Sponsored Actors in Brazil, Uruguay, Chile, and Argentina 1960-1990**

Hellman, Eva, "Dynamic Hinduism – Towards a New Hindu Nation", in **Questioning the Secular State – The Worldwide Resurgence of Religion in Politics**, edited by David Westerlund (London: Hurst & Company)

Hinde, Robert A., **Why Gods Persist – A Scientific Approach to Religion** (New York, Routledge, 1999)

Horio, Teruhisa, **Educational Thought and Ideology in Modern Japan, State Authority's and Intellectual Freedom**, edited and translated by Steven Platzer, (Tokyo: University of Tokyo Press, 1988)

Horowitz, Donald L., **Ethnic Groups in Conflict** (Berkeley, Los Angekes, London: University of California Press)

Horton, R. "Tradition and Modernity Revisited," in Robin Horton, **Patterns of Thought in Africa and the West, Essays on magic, religion and science** (Cambridge, Massachusetts: Cambridge University Press, 1993)

Horton, Robin, "African Traditional Thought and Western Science" in **Rationality** edited by Bryan R. Wilson (Oxford, England: Basil Blackwell, 1970), pp. 131-171.

Hsu, Cho-Yun, **Ancient China in Transition – An Analysis of Social Mobility, 722-222 B.C.** (Stanford, California: Stanford University Press, 1968, original printing 1965)

Hudson, Meadwell,, "Ethnic Nationalism and Collective Choice Theory," in **Comparative Political Studies (1989)** p. 54.

James, W., **Religious and Other Experiences – A Study of the Nature of Man** (Jerusalem: Bialik Institute, 1968)

James, W., **The Variety of Religious Experience** (NY: Modern Library, 1929)

Johnson K.R., "Melting Pot or 'Ring of Fire'? Assimilation and the Mexican-American Experience," in **California Law Review 85 (5): October 1997,1259-1313.**

Kant, I. **A Premise of Metaphysics,** Magnes Press.

Kaufman, E, **History of the Israelite Religion – From its Beginning until the End of the Second Temple Period** (Jerusalem, Tel Aviv: Bialik Institute, Dvir, 1948)

Kleinburger, Aviad, **Christianity from its Genesis until the Reformation** [in Hebrew] (Tel Aviv: A publication of the Israel Foreign Ministry, 1995)

Koenker, Ernest B, **Secular salvation, The Rites and Symbols of Political Religions** (Fortress Press, 1965)

Kone, Thomas S., **The Structure of Scientific Revolutions** (Tel Aviv: Israel Institute of Poetry and Semitics, University of Tel Aviv, 1977) translated from the English by Yehuda Meltzer.

Kübler-Ross, E., **On Death and Dying** (London: Macmillan, 1969)

Leang-Li, T'ang, **China in Revolt – How a Civilization Became a Nation** (London: Noel Douglas, reprint edition (Arlington, Virginia: University Publications of America Inc., 1976)

Leibowitz, Yeshayahu, **Five Books of Faith** (Jerusalem: Keter, 1995)

Levitt P., "Local-level Global Religion: The Case of US-Dominican Migration," in **Journal For the Scientific Study of Religion 37 (1): March 1998**, pp. 74-88.

Liebman, C., and E. Don-Iyechiya, **Civil Religion in Israel: Traditional Judaism and Political Culture in the Jewish State** (Los Angeles: University of California Press, 1983)

Lind, Michael, **The Next American Nation: The New Nationalusm and the Fourth American Revolution** (The Free Press, 1995)

Linz, Juan J., and Alfred Stepan, **Problems of Democratic Transition and Consolidation, Southern Europe, South American and Post Communist Europe** (Baltimore, Maryland: The John Hopkins University Press, 1996)

Lipset, Seymour Martin ,"The 'Newness' of the New Nation," in C. Vann Woodward (ed.) **The Comparative Approach to American History** (NY: Basic Books, 1968)

Lipset, Seymour Martin, **Continental Divide – The Values and Institutions of the United States and Canada** (New York: Routledge, 1990)

Lusky, Lois, **By What Right? A Commentary on the Supreme Court's Power to Revise the Constitution** (1975)

Macintyre, Alasdair, **After Virtue A Study of Moral Theory**, second edition (Note Dame, Indiana: University of Notre Dame Press, 1984)

Malloy, James M., "Authoritarianism and Corporatism in Latin America: The Modal Pattern," in James M. Malloy (ed.) **Authoritarianism and Corporatism in Latin America** (Pittsburgh: University of Pittsburgh Press, 1977) p. 3.

Marett, R.R., **The Threshold of Religion** (London: Methuen & Co. Ltd, 1979)

Margalit, A. **The Decent Society** (Cambridge, Massachusetts: Harvard University Press, 1996)

Maruyama, Masao, (ed. By Ivan Morris) **Thought and Behviour in Modern Japanese Politics** (London: Oxford University Press, 1963)

Michaelson, Robert, "Is the Public School Religious or Secular," in **The Religion of the Republic** (ed. Elwyn. A. Smith, Fortress Press Philadelphia, 1971),

Moodie, T. Dunbar, **The Rise of Afrikanerdom, Power Apartheid and the Afrikaner Civil Religion** (Los Angeles: University of California Press, 1975).

Needham, Joseph, **Science and Civilization in China** (Cambridge: Cambridge University Press).

Newberd, Andrew, M.D., Eugene D'Aquili, M.D., Ph.D., and Vince Rause, **Why God Won't Go Away** (New York: Ballantine Books, 2001).

Nimni, Ephraim, "Marx, Engels, and the National Question", in Will Kymlicka ed., **The Rights of Minority Cultures** (Oxford: Oxford University Press, 1995)

Otto, Rudolf, **The idea of the holy: an inquiry into the non-rational factor in the idea of the Divine and its relation to the rational**. Translated from German into Hebrew by Miriam Ron, (Jerusalem: Carmel, 1999)

Palmer, Robert, "The 'Newness' of the New Nation," in C. Vann Woodward, ed. **The Comparative Approach to American History** (N.Y: Basic Books: 1968)

Pfister J., and N. Schnog, **Inventing the Psychological: Towards a Cultural History of Emotional Life** (New Haven: Yale University Press, 1997)

Pines, Yuri, " 'The one that pervades the all' in ancient Chinese political thought: The origins of the great unity' paradigm" in **Toung Pao LXXXVI**

Pocock, John, "England" ' chapter IV, in **National Consciousness, History, and Political Culture in Early-Modern Europe**, editted by Orest Ranum (Baltimore, Maryland: The John Hopkins University Press, 1975)

Ponton, Ardila A., "The Future of Neuropsychology with Hispanic Populations in the United States," in **Archives of Clinical Neuropsychology 14 (7): October 1999**, pp. 565-580.

Rambam, **Introduction to Commentary on the Mishnah**, ed. and explained by Mordechai Dov Rabinovitch (Jerusalem: Mossad Harav Kook Publications, 1961)

Ramon, N., **The Birth and Death of God: Man and Death in Primitive Religion and Existentialism**, (Thesis presented to the Department of Comparative Religion at the Hebrew University in fulfilment of the requirements for the MA, 1983)

Rawls, J., **A Theory of Justice** (Oxford, New York: Oxford University Press, 1972).

Raz, Jacob, **Japanese Mythology** [Hebrew], (Tel Aviv: Sifri, 2000)

Rehnquist, William H., **All the Laws but One – Civil Liberties in Wartime** (New York: Random House, 1998).

Rodo, Enrico, Manuel Ugarte, and Jose Vasconcelos, "Has it Really Been 500 Years Since the Discovery of America? Historosophy and the Struggle over the Shaping of Latin American Consciousness," Printed in **Roniger's anthology** located in the Library of Sociology and Humanities in Hebrew University Library in Jerusalem.

Rogowski, Ronald, "Causes and Varieties of Nationalism: A Rational Account," in **New Nationalisms of the Developed West: Toward Explanation** (Boston: Allen & Unwin, 1985)

Roniger, Luis, "The Fragmentation of the Spanish Empire and Collective Identity Construction in Latin America", in S.N. Eisenstadt et al (ed.) **Van-Leer Public Forum no. 4** [in Hebrew]. (Jerusalem: Van Leer, 1999)

Roniger, Luis, and Mario Sznajder, **The Legacy of Human-Rights Violations in the Southern Cone – Argentina, Chile, and Uruguay** (Oxford, New York: Oxford University Press, 1999)

Roniger, Luis, **Hierarchy and Trust in Modern Mexico and Brazil** (New York: Praeger, 1990).

Roniger, Luis, **Variations of Patronage Patterns in Mexico and Brazil** (Doctoral dissertation in Philosophy, submitted to the Hebrew University in

Jerusalem in June 1984)

Rousseau, Jean Jacques, **On the Social Contract** (Magnes Press, 1996),

Rubie S. Watson, "The Creation of a Chinese Lineage: The Teng of Ha Tsuen, 1669-1751", in **Modern Asian Studies, 16, I (1982)** (Great Britain: Cambridge University Press) pp. 69-100.

Sandel, Michael, "The Procedural Republic and Unencumbered Self", in **Communitarianism and Individualism** (Oxford: Oxford University Press, 1992), Avineri and A. De-Shalit ed., Political Theory 12, pp. 81-96

Santoro WA, "Conventional Politics Takes Center Stage: The Latino Struggle Against English-Only Laws," in **Social Forces 77 (3): March 1999**, pp. 887-909.

Schleirmacher, Fredrich, **On Religion – Speeches to Its Cultured Despisers,** Introduction, translation and notes by Richard Crouter, Carleton College (New York: Cambridge University Press, 1988).

Sefer HaChinuch, 7th edition (Mossad Harav Kook Publications, 1966), authored by an anonymous Jew from Barcelona in approximately 1407 who due to his humility wrote under the assumed name of R. Aharon Zalhahan. First published in Venice in 1523.

Sefer Hakuzari in five articles with the two well-known commentaries of Kol Yehuda and Otzar Nechmad. First printing by R. Yitzchak Golman , Warsaw. Reprinted by Hadran Pub. In Israel, 1959. Attributed to the Sage R. Yitzchak HaSangari. Second article

Seymour, Michae,l **Rethinking Nationalism**. (Calgary, Alberta, Canada: Canadian journal of Philosophy, University of Calgary Press)

Shafir, Gershon, "Land, Labor and Population in Zionistic Colonization: General and Specific Aspects", from **Israeli Society – Critical Aspects**, edited by Uri Ram (Tel Aviv, Breirot Press, 1993).

Shapin, Steven & Simon Schaffer, **Leviathan and the Air-Pump – Hobbes, Boyle, and the Experimental Life** (Princeton, New Jersey: Princeton University Press, 1985).

Sharet, Moshe, "Examinations of the Problem of the Gathering of Exiles", from **Immigrants in Israel – A Study**, edited by Moshe Lisk and others (Jerusalem, Academon Press)

Shelach, Ilana, **Effects of Secular Religion on Israel,** shortened version of thesis submitted for the degree of M.A, Hebrew University Library Faculty of Arts and Social Studies, Mount Scopus, Jerusalem

Shiloni, Ben- Ami, **Modern Japan-Culture and History** (Tel Aviv: Schocken, 1997)

Sieder, Rachel, "War, Peace, and Memory Politics in Central America," in **The Politics of Memory – Transitional Justice in Democratizing Societies**, Alexandra Barahona de Brito, Carmen Gonzalez Enriquez and Paloma Aguilar (ed.) (Oxford: Oxford University Press, 2001) pp. 171, 176, 178.

Sieyes, Emanuel Joseph, **What is the Third Estate?** Translated by M. Blondel and edited with historical notes by S.E. Finer (Pall Mall Press, 1963)

Smith, A., "The Voluntary Establishment of Religion." In E. Smith (ed.), **The Religion of the Republic** (Philadelphia: Fortress Press, 1971)

Smith, Elwyn A, "Introduction," **The Religion of the Republic** (ed. Elwyn A. Smith,) (Philadelphia: Fortress Press, 1971)

Smith, Peter H., **Talons of the Eagle – Dynamics of US Latin American Relations** (New York, Oxford: Oxford University Press, 2000).

Smolen L.A, Oriz-Castro V, "Dissolving Borders and Broadening Perspectives Through Latino Traditional Literature," in **The Reading Teacher, 53 (7) 566-578, April 2000.**

Sober E. and D. Wilson, "Summary of: 'Unto Others, the Evolution and Psychology of 'Unselfish Behavior'", **Journal of Consciousness Studies 7 (2000)**

Sonobe, Itsuo, "Comparative Administrative Law: Trends and Features in Administrative Law Studies" *(Japan)* **Administrative Law: Trends and Features, Volume 19:40, 1986**

Spielberg, Chaim, **India-Beliefs and Opinions**, [Hebrew], (Israel: Hadar, 1990)

Spinoza, Baruch, *Essay on Political theology* [in Hebrew], (Jerusalem: Magnes, 1989).

Sznajder, Mario, and Luis Roniger, **Politics, Social Ethos, and Identity in Contemporary Cuba** (Jerusalem: The Hebrew University of Jerusalem: The Harry S. Truman Research Institute for the Advancement of Peace, 2001, a publication no. 15 of Gitelson Peace Peace Publication, January 2001)

Talmon, Jacob, **The Beginning of Totalitarian Democracy** (Tel Aviv: Dvir, 1956)

The T'ang Code, translated with an Introduction by Wallace Johnson (Princeton, New Jersey: Princeton University Press, 1979)

Turner, V., "Witchcraft and Sorcery: Taxonomy versus Dynamics" in **The Forest of symbols : aspects of Ndembu ritual** (Ithaca, N.Y. : Cornell University Press, 1967)

Varshney, Ashutosh, "Contested Meanings: India's national Identity, Hindu nationalism and the Politics of Anxiety", in **Daedalus (Summer 1993**

Vile, M.J.C, **Constitutionalism and the Separation of Powers** (Oxford: Clarendon Press)

Waisman, Carlos H. **Reversal of Development in Argentina – Postwar Counterrevolutionary Policies and Their Structural Consequences** (Princeton, New Jersey: Princeton University Press, 1987).

Wallas, Graham, **Human Nature In Politics - with a foreword by A. L. Rowse** (London: Caonstable and Company, 1948, first edition 1908)

Walzer, M., **What it Means to be an American** (New Delhi: Affiliated East-West Press, 1994)

Warnuk, Jeffrey G., **Modern-day Moral Philosophy,** Translated by Shaul Chanani, Ed. David Had, (Magnes Press: 1987, 1992)

Weber, M., **The Sociology of Religion** (Boston: Beach Press, 1963)

Weber, Max, "The Origins of Ethnic Groups", in **Ethnicity,** edited by John Hutchinson & Anthony D. Smith (Oxford, New York: Oxford University Press, 1996)

Weber, Max, **On Charisma and Institution Building** [in Hebrew] (Jerusalem: Magnes, 1979).

Weber, Max, **On Charisma and Institution Building, Selected Papers**, Edited and with an Introduction by S. N. Eisenstadt (Chicago and London: The University of Chicago Press 1968).

Weber, Max, **The Protestant Ethic and the Capitalist Spirit**, translated from German by Baruch Moren (Tel Aviv: Am Oved, 1984), original published in 1920.

Weisman, Carlox H., **Reversal of Development in Argentina, Postwar Counterrevolutionary Policies and Their Structural Consequences** (Princeton, New Jersey: Princeton University Press, 1987),

Westfall, Richard S., "Science and Patronage, Galileo and the Telescope" in **Isis, 1985, pp. 11-30;**

Winch, Peter, "Understanding a Primitive Society," in *Rationality*, edited by Bryan R. Wilson (Oxford, G. Britain: Basil Blackwell, 1970). The paper was first published in the *American Philosophical Quarterly*, 1, 1964, pp. 307-324.

Yaku, Masao, **The Kojiki in the Life of Japan**, (Tokyo: The Centre for East Asian Cultural Studies, 1969, reprinted 1972)

Yashar, Deborah J., "Indigenous Politics and Democracy: Contesting Citizenship in Latin America," Prepared for delivery at the **1996 Annual Meeting of the American Political Science Association**, The San Francisco Hilton and Towers, August 29 –September 1, 1996.

Zakai, A., "Religion and Revolution: The Contribution of Puritan Rhetoric to American Democracy." In **Democracy in America** (Tel Aviv: Zemora-Beitan Modan, 2001)

Zakai, Avihu, "Reformation, History, and Eschatology in English Protestantism", in **History And Theory**, Vol. XXVI, No. 3, 1987, pp. 300-318

Zohar on Torah (Jerusalem: Yosef Lugassi, 1959)

Index

(n) = footnotes